The Implementation and Enforcement of International Humanitarian Law

The Library of Essays in International Humanitarian Law
Series Editors: Michael N. Schmitt and Wolff Heintschel von Heinegg

Titles in the Series:

The Development and Principles of International Humanitarian Law
Michael N. Schmitt and Wolff Heintschel von Heinegg

The Scope and Applicability of International Humanitarian Law
Michael N. Schmitt and Wolff Heintschel von Heinegg

The Conduct of Hostilities in International Humanitarian Law, Volume I
Michael N. Schmitt and Wolff Heintschel von Heinegg

The Conduct of Hostilities in International Humanitarian Law, Volume II
Michael N. Schmitt and Wolff Heintschel von Heinegg

Detention and Occupation in International Humanitarian Law
Michael N. Schmitt and Wolff Heintschel von Heinegg

The Implementation and Enforcement of International Humanitarian Law
Michael N. Schmitt and Wolff Heintschel von Heinegg

The Implementation and Enforcement of International Humanitarian Law

Edited by

Michael N. Schmitt

US Naval War College, USA

Wolff Heintschel von Heinegg

Europa-Universitat Viadrina, Germany

Routledge
Taylor & Francis Group
LONDON AND NEW YORK

First published 2012 by Ashgate Publishing

2 Park Square, Milton Park, Abingdon, Oxfordshire OX14 4RN
711 Third Avenue, New York, NY 10017

Routledge is an imprint of the Taylor & Francis Group, an informa business

First issued in paperback 2018

British Library Cataloguing in Publication Data
The implementation and enforcement of international
humanitarian law. – (The library of essays in
international humanitarian law)
1. Humanitarian law. 2. War (International law) 3. War
crimes. 4. War crime trials.
I. Series II. Schmitt, Michael N. III. Heintschel von
Heinegg, Wolff.
341.6'7–dc23

Library of Congress Control Number: 2011946113

ISBN 978-0-7546-2938-2 (hbk)
ISBN 978-1-138-37865-0 (pbk)

Contents

Acknowledgements

The editors and publishers wish to thank the following for permission to use copyright material.

Cambridge University Press for the essays: F. Kalshoven (1990), 'Belligerent Reprisals Revisited', *Netherlands Yearbook of International Law*, **21**, pp. 43–80. Copyright © 1990 TMR Asser Press, The Hague and the contributor; Jelena Pejic (2002), 'Accountability for International Crimes: From Conjecture to Reality', *International Review of the Red Cross*, **84**, pp. 13–32. Copyright © 2002 International Committee of the Red Cross; Frits Kalshoven (1991), 'State Responsibility for Warlike Acts of the Armed Forces: From Article 3 of Hague Convention IV to Article 91 of Additional Protocol I of 1977 and Beyond', *International and Comparative Law Quarterly*, **40**, pp. 827–58. Copyright © 1991 British Institute of International and Comparative Law.

Charles J. Dunlap Jr (2001), 'Law and Military Interventions: Preserving Humanitarian Values in 21st Conflicts', *Carr Center for Human Rights Policy*, http://duke.edu/~pfeaver/dunlap.pdf. Copyright © 2001 Charles J. Dunlap.

Copyright Clearance Center for the essays: G.I.A.D. Draper (1979), 'The Implementation of the Geneva Conventions of 1949 and the Additional Protocols of 1978', *Recueil des Cours*, **164**, pp. 9–54. Copyright © 1978 Brill Academic Publishers; Edwin M. Borchard (1915), 'Private Pecuniary Claims Arising Out of War, *American Journal of International Law*, **9**, pp. 113–46. Copyright © 1915 American Society of International Law; Leslie C. Green (1977), 'The Role of Legal Advisers in the Armed Forces', *Israel Yearbook on Human Rights*, **7**, pp. 154–65. Copyright © 1977 Brill Academic Publishers; A.R. Albrecht (1953), 'War Reprisals in the War Crimes Trials and in the Geneva Conventions of 1949', *American Journal of International Law*, **47**, pp. 590–614. Copyright © 1953 American Society of International Law.

L.C. Green (1981), 'The Man in the Field and the Maxim of Ignorantia Iuris non Excusat', *Archiv des Volkerrechts*, **19**, pp. 169–87. Copyright © 1981 L.C. Green.

Naval War College for the essay: Yoram Dinstein (1998), 'The Universality Principle and War Crimes', in M.N. Schmitt and L.C. Green (eds), *The Law of Armed Conflict: Into the Next Millennium*, Newport, RI: US Naval War College, pp. 17–37.

Oxford University Press for the essay: Yves Sandoz (2009), 'The History of the Grave Breaches Regime', *Journal of International Criminal Justice*, **7**, pp. 657–82. Copyright © 2009 Oxford University Press.

Public domain: William H. Parks (1973), 'Command Responsibility for War Crimes', *Military Law Review*, **62**, pp.1–104.

Royal Institute of International Affairs for the essays: H. Lauterpacht (1944), 'The Law of Nations and the Punishment of War Crimes', *British Year Book of International Law*, **21**, pp. 58–95; Richard R. Baxter (1951), 'The Municipal and International Law Basis of Jurisdiction over War Crimes', *British Year Book of International Law*, **28**, pp. 382–93.

UBS Press for the essay: L.C. Green (1970), 'Superior Orders and the Reasonable Man', *Canadian Yearbook of International Law*, **8**, pp. 61–103.

Every effort has been made to trace all the copyright holders, but if any have been inadvertently overlooked the publishers will be pleased to make the necessary arrangement at the first opportunity.

Series Preface

Over half a century ago, Sir Hersch Lauterpacht, then Whewell Professor of International Law at the University of Cambridge, observed that 'if international law is the vanishing point of law, the law of war is at the vanishing point of international law'. He was wrong. While it is true that the law of war, or international humanitarian law as it has become known, is particularly vulnerable to the vagaries of political, social and economic influences, it has nevertheless proven itself a robust normative regime that positively shapes man's most destructive undertaking – warfare. No other body of law can be credited with saving more lives or alleviating as much suffering.

These six volumes comprise a collection of particularly significant works on humanitarian law. They are intended for use by scholars, practitioners and students who seek to better understand the topics addressed herein, together with their lineage. Just as importantly, they allow users to begin to separate the wheat from the chaff. The proliferation of publications in the field, in part a sad reflection of the fact that armed conflict remains so horribly pervasive, as well as the digitization that facilitates access to journals that would not otherwise be readily available, often results in information overload. A Ministry of Defence legal adviser looking for background material to address a situation involving belligerent occupation will, for instance, uncover scores of articles. The student writing a dissertation on the law of targeting or a scholar penning an article on detention will find him- or herself buried in material. Unfortunately, some of what they unearth will prove misguided, out of context or simply wrong. This collection will not break down these obstacles in their entirety. But it does afford a useful starting-point by offering topically arranged humanitarian law journal essays that have been thoroughly vetted by many of the top experts in the field.

In this regard, a few words on the process used to choose the essays are helpful. It began with the selection of those subjects that we believed comprised the *sine qua non* of international humanitarian law – development, principles, scope, application, conduct of hostilities, detention, occupation, and implementation and enforcement. We then contacted over 60 recognized humanitarian law experts, both academics and seasoned legal advisers. They were provided the topics and asked in a very open-ended fashion to identify pieces they considered 'classics', believed to be 'essential' in a compilation of this nature, have found to be especially influential, used regularly in their work or deserved greater attention on the basis of their quality and insights. The experts were asked to pay particular attention to those essays that may have been 'forgotten' over time, but merited 'rediscovery'. Many of them responded in depth. We also benefited from the work of a five-member team from Emory Law School's International Humanitarian Law Clinic which conducted an exhaustive literature review to locate essays relied on regularly by writers – the 'usual suspects', if you will. Finally, as editors we took the liberty of adding a few pieces to the pool *sua sponte*.

Armed with a daunting inventory of candidates for inclusion, we began the difficult task of whittling it down. Many essays proved to be consensus choices among the experts; often the Emory team had also identified them. These provided the skeleton for the project. We then fleshed out the collection based on two key factors: quality assessments by the experts and topic coverage. The latter criterion proved particularly central to the process, for our objective was to produce a collection that not only contained thoughtful and influential works, but also addressed most key humanitarian law topics.

Beyond esteem factors and topical relevance, some essays were selected on account of their temporal significance, that is, having been written at key junctures in the development of international humanitarian law. As an example, the collection includes pieces written in the immediate aftermath of the First and Second World Wars and the attacks of 11 September 2001. Others were published soon after adoption of the 1949 Geneva Conventions or the 1977 Additional Protocols. We hope they both afford insight into the perspectives at play as humanitarian law was evolving and provide a context for understanding the genesis of contemporary norms.

In the end, we were unable to include many insightful and influential works. Exclusion was frequently a mere matter of being cursed with too many good choices on a particular topic. Although no reader is likely to be entirely satisfied with the essays included, or comfortable with the omission of others, we hope the rigorous selection process has resulted in a collection that is both useful and enlightening.

This project would not have been possible without the help of many supporters. We are, of course, deeply indebted to the many international experts who took time from their busy schedules to offer recommendations and comments over the course of the three-year effort. Although we cannot possibly name them all, particular appreciation is due to Ken Anderson, Yutaka Arai, Louise Arimatsu, Laurie Blank, Gabriella Blum, Bill Boothby, Ove Bring, Claude Bruderlein, Knut Dörmann, Alison Duxbury, William Fenrick, Dieter Fleck, Steven Haines, Agnieszka Jachec-Neale, Dick Jackson, Marie Jacobsson, Claus Kress, William Lietzau, Noam Lubell, Lindsay Moir, John Murphy, Sean Murphy, Mary Ellen O'Connell, Bruce Oswald, Hays Parks, Stephen Pomper, Jean-Francois Queguiner, Noelle Quenivet, Adam Roberts, A.P.V. Rogers, Peter Rowe, Joseph Rutigliano, Robert Sloane, Dale Stephens, Ken Watkin and Sean Watts.

We are equally indebted to the brilliant group of young scholars at Emory Law School, whom we dubbed our 'IHL Detectives' – Flora Manship, Carmel Mushin, Jeannine Privat, Nandini Rao and, in particular, Benjamin Farley. Their ability to identify and locate 'lost treasures' of humanitarian law was awe-inspiring. All have since graduated, and we wish them the very best in their professional careers.

Three people deserve special mention and gratitude. Laurie Blank, Director of the Emory's International Humanitarian Law Clinic, ably and tirelessly supervised her team. Beyond supervision, she also devoted an enormous amount of her own time to the substance and administration of the project. At European University Viadrina, Kaya Kowalski took on the task of collating materials and later working with us as we made the final selections for the collection. She was unflappable in the face of our long and sometimes contentious deliberations and always exceptionally good-natured and professional. Finally, we thank our editor at Ashgate, Valerie Saunders, who showed the patience of Job throughout.

We hope this collection proves valuable in the years to come. For our part, it was a fascinating endeavour.

MICHAEL N. SCHMITT
Newport, Rhode Island, USA

and

WOLFF HEINTSCHEL VON HEINEGG
Frankfurt (Oder), Germany

Introduction

Reciprocity is often characterized as the seminal incentive for belligerents to respect international humanitarian law. Sadly, it appears that this is so primarily with regard to stereotypical international armed conflicts. Many contemporary conflicts, whatever their nature, are replete with deliberate violations of the law – committed sometimes by weaker parties and sometimes by those professing noble aims. Nevertheless, a grasp of the principle of reciprocity and the related concept of belligerent reprisals remains essential to a full understanding of the dynamics of international humanitarian law. For instance, although reprisals are widely prohibited today, they were traditionally viewed as inadmissible only when disproportionate to the prior violation of the law by the other side. Thus, the contemporary prohibition is very much the result of belligerent practices during the two world wars that caused unimaginable suffering.

The subject of implementation and enforcement of international humanitarian encompasses a wide range of issues, including the role of legal advisers and compensation claims by individuals or the enemy state. In view of Article 3 of the 1907 Hague Convention IV and of Article 91 of the 1977 Additional Protocol I, academic examination of the topic used to focus on state responsibility for violations. In contemporary practice, the provisions play only a minor role in supporting the effectiveness of humanitarian law. Today, scholars and international courts tend to turn to human rights law when considering compensation for individuals suffering injuries and damage during armed conflict. Unfortunately, the rules of international humanitarian law that regulate individual claims seem to have been forgotten.

Compliance with international humanitarian law can be fostered through the education and training of the armed forces (and of the general public) and by the implementation of internal disciplinary and penal systems. Indeed, until the end of the Second World War, violations of the law, including war crimes *strictu sensu*, were dealt with via the mechanism of the respective belligerents' domestic law. That approach had two shortcomings. First, certain war crimes escaped regulation. Second, relevant domestic legal provisions often fell short of the gravity of the crimes. In response, the 1949 Geneva Conventions provisions on grave breaches obliged states parties to 'to enact any legislation necessary to provide effective penal sanctions for persons committing, or ordering to be committed, any of the grave breaches of the present Convention(s)'. Moreover, they introduced the universality principle for grave breaches. Thus, contemporary international humanitarian law benefits from a well-elaborated legal system which guarantees that those who have committed a grave breach (or are responsible for such a breach) will not go unpunished.

The two problems have not been entirely solved because the prosecution of grave breaches was left to the respective domestic legal systems. Indeed, for decades the Nuremberg and Tokyo war crimes tribunals were considered historical anomalies. Yet, their statutes and jurisprudence laid the foundation for what is today commonly recognized as criminal international law. The essays reprinted in this volume highlight the criticality of rules of public international law in providing for the individual criminal responsibility of those who have seriously violated international humanitarian law. Moreover, they address some of the most serious obstacles to bringing war criminals to justice, especially the plea of superior orders, the contested issue of command responsibility, the immunity of government officials and the lack of political will on the part of governments to comply with their obligations under the Geneva Conventions and the Additional Protocols.

A related issue is the role of international humanitarian law in public perception. Practical experience demonstrates that allegations of violations negatively impact military operations by diminishing public support. In view of this 'CNN effect', armed forces and governments have become increasingly sensitive to reports of (alleged) violations. To an extent, this is a positive development because, with news transmitted in near real time, it is difficult for governments to hide abuses. But there is a negative aspect to this phenomenon. Such transparency can be misused by the enemy to distribute false information about purported international humanitarian law violations in what has been labelled 'lawfare'.

'War Reprisals in the War Crimes Trials and in the Geneva Conventions of 1949', by A.R. Albrecht (Chapter 1), offers an interesting analysis of reprisal practice against the background of the post–Second World War war crimes trials and the prohibitions of reprisals in the four 1949 Geneva Conventions. Reprisals are:

> ... otherwise illegitimate acts of warfare which under certain conditions may legally be used by a belligerent against the enemy in order to deter the enemy from a repetition of his prior illegal acts and thus to enforce compliance with the generally recognized rules of war. (p. 1)

The war crimes trials 'transformed the previously sketchy rules on reprisals into a more comprehensive and elaborate system of control' (p. 1). Accordingly, reprisals must satisfy both preliminary and operative conditions. As to the former, reprisals are only lawful in response to an illegal act by the enemy. In this context, Albrecht rejects the notion of a distinction between legal and illegal wars as 'lead[ing] to the breakdown, or at least the serious impairment, of the laws of war' (p. 5). Illegal acts giving rise to a reprisal include those of a state, its organs and even civilians.

A violation of international humanitarian law justifies reprisals only when previous attempts to punish the guilty and resort to other means of redress have proven futile; reprisal is an option of last resort. Moreover, a judicial hearing is essential in the case of reprisals taken against individuals. This preliminary condition requires not an inquiry into the guilt of the person subjected to reprisals, but rather a fair trial before a judicial body in order to assess whether the legal prerequisites for reprisals have been fulfilled. Albrecht concedes that such proceedings may fall prey to abuse, but emphasizes that 'the very need for it may help to increase in some degree the realization of the gravity of exercising reprisals and add to the protection of potential victims' (p. 9).

With regard to the operational conditions that must be fulfilled, Albrecht addresses the unresolved issue of the authority entitled to decide upon reprisals, emphasizes that reprisal measures need not be in kind, examines the prohibition of reprisals against prisoners of war and considers the issue of reprisals against hostages. As to the last subject, his examination of the war crimes trials leads to the conclusion that the prohibition on taking hostages must be distinguished from the matter of reprisals. Accordingly, 'reprisal law ... must take precedence over hostage law' (p. 14). Additional operational conditions include a geographical relationship between the reprisal's victim and the initial illegal act and proportionality – that is, that the reprisal not be excessive in relation to the prior illegal act. A fixed ratio for the general application of automatic reprisals will typically violate this requirement. Finally, reprisals must be publicized because of their purpose of enforcing compliance with international humanitarian law.

Albrecht concludes that the law of reprisals, as identified by the war crimes tribunals, constitutes a workable basis for enforcing compliance with humanitarian law. However, he expresses ambivalence regarding the value of the reprisal provisions in the 1949 Geneva Conventions. He lauds the prohibitions on reprisals against prisoners of war, the wounded, sick and shipwrecked, especially the fact that they are subject to no exceptions. Yet, he considers certain reprisals, including those against civilians, to perform 'an extremely valuable function' (p. 23) and warns that a comprehensive ban of reprisals could weaken the efficacy of the law. Accordingly, any prohibition should be based on a determination that '(1) the reprisal is unlikely to have any deterrent effect ...' or '(2) regardless of the efficacy of the reprisal, it can be dispensed with because other reprisals may be relied upon to produce the requisite deterrent effect' (p. 24).

Frits Kalshoven's 'Belligerent Reprisals Revisited' (Chapter 2) is a follow-up to his famous book on the subject, the second edition of which has recently been published.[1] He takes a rather critical position vis-à-vis belligerent reprisals, considering them a generally ineffective means for enforcing compliance with international humanitarian law – one that risks escalation of atrocities.

Reviewing the relevant provisions of the 1949 Geneva Conventions and the Additional Protocol, Kalshoven concludes that those in the latter instrument cannot 'be regarded as anything but rules of treaty law' (p. 37). He rejects the criticism that the prohibitions are unacceptable from a military point of view. In his opinion, the respective provisions, despite being 'essentially humanitarian in nature' (p. 42), have been 'so phrased that military considerations are heeded to the maximum' (p. 56). Recalling that the 1974–1977 Geneva Conference struggled with whether to agree upon specific prohibitions or ban belligerent reprisals altogether, Kalshoven suggests that those asserting the former position took a 'rather over-optimistic view of what reprisals ... can achieve, combined with an underestimation of the adverse effects inherent in such measures' (pp. 44–45). He reminds us that Article 90 of Additional Protocol I provides for an International Fact-Finding Commission as an appropriate means of ensuring compliance with international humanitarian law and warns states against issuing reservation to reprisal provisions in treaties.

Moving from the general to the specific, Kalshoven addresses areas with regard to which no formal prohibition of reprisals appears – methods and means of warfare, the 1925 Geneva Gas Protocol and internal armed conflict. He rejects the argument that indiscriminate attack under Article 51 of Additional Protocol I may be responded to by reprisal in kind, taking the position that the prohibition on reprisals therein encompasses the article in its entirety. As to other provisions on the conduct of hostilities, he highlights their humanitarian character and

1 *Belligerent Reprisals* (2nd edn), Leiden: Martinus Nijhoff Publishers (2005). First published 1971.

points to the 1969 Vienna Convention on the Law of Treaties to 'demonstrate that application of the central idea in Article 60, paragraph 5 ... may lead to the conclusion that such reprisals are morally wrong' (p. 57). With regard to the 1925 Geneva Protocol, Kalshoven, while acknowledging that a considerable number of states parties have set forth reservations to it, argues that even in the case of a serious and systematic violation of the Protocol there is 'little utility in the initiation of all-out gas war in reaction' (p. 58). Finally, he cannot but concede that the law of non-international armed conflict contains no treaty rule prohibiting resort to reprisals. States either reject application of the concept in relation to non-state actors or are simply unprepared to abandon that means of enforcing compliance. Tempering this finding is his assertion (one equally embraced by the ICRC) that the relevant provisions on humane treatment are of such a fundamentally humanitarian nature that they must be considered absolute in character, allowing for no exceptions. And, from a practical perspective, he argues that reprisals would, in most cases, prove futile and risk escalation.

Ultimately, Kalshoven sees no way of advancing beyond Additional Protocol I with regard to the prohibition of reprisals in international armed conflicts. However, he stresses the necessity of ratification without reservations and the need to strengthen the Article 90 Fact-Finding Commission. As to non-international armed conflicts, he advocates the exploration of 'other ways' to improve the situation, especially by mobilizing public opinion through reference to international human rights law (p. 64).

'The Implementation of the Geneva Conventions of 1949 and of the two Additional Protocols of 1978' is the written version of G.I.A.D. Draper's 1979 Hague Academy lecture (the contemporaneous nature of the lecture explains the error in the date attributed to the Protocols in the titles). Draper defines 'implementation' as 'those devices, institutions and rules designed to monitor and ensure its observance' and 'enforcement' as the 'collection of mechanisms and rules available to the law of war to secure the restoration of observance when that law has been violated' (p. 65).

The essay begins by addressing the following issues: (1) the protecting power system; (2) dissemination and instruction; (3) legal advisers in armed forces; (4) the use of qualified persons; and (5) implementation of the law of non-international armed conflicts. As regards the protecting power system, Draper is unconvinced that Additional Protocol I abolished the deficiencies that had previously characterized the system because its success depends on consent. Moreover, in view of the unresolved issue of the relationship between the Conventions and the Protocol, it might be that 'any advance made by the conventions in common Articles 10/10/10/11, paragraph 3, is negated by Article 5(4) of the protocol, controlling the role of the ICRC as a substitute' (p. 74). Nevertheless, Article 5, paragraphs 5 and 6, are considered 'gains'.

Draper is equally unimpressed by the provisions on dissemination and instruction, although he concedes that, if carried out in good faith, they will limit the number of individuals who can claim ignorance of international humanitarian law. In that context, Draper reminds us that the 1907 Hague Convention IV already requires the issuance of instructions to the armed forces that conform to international humanitarian law. Moreover, doing so is a consequence of the general obligation to carry out treaty obligations in good faith. The obligation under Additional Protocol I to introduce 'the legal adviser to an advisory role affecting combat operations' (p. 80) fosters compliance.

With regard to non-international armed conflicts, Draper notes that, under common Article 3 of the 1949 Geneva Conventions, '[m]onitoring implementation has rarely proved possible' (p. 83) and that Additional Protocol II 'does little to reinforce or contribute modes for implementation' (p. 84). He rejects the assertion that the implementation machinery of the Geneva Conventions is applicable to such conflicts qua customary international law. In sum, he concludes that the 'mechanisms to ensure implementation of the modern law of war are weak' and that '[a]t the present time it is probable that the developments in the humanitarian law of armed conflicts have outrun its capacity to supervise its own observance' (p. 86).

Draper next explores the philosophical and practical considerations that have contributed to the emergence of international humanitarian law over the past centuries (pp. 87ff.). He reminds us that since the seventeenth century three principal means of enforcement of the law of war by self-help have emerged: (1) reprisals, (2) hostages and (3) punishment of war criminals who have fallen into enemy hands. In his estimation, the Geneva Conventions and Additional Protocol I have added little to enforcement. The taking of hostages has been forbidden and reprisals have been widely eliminated; thus, '[t]he main burden of enforcement of the modern law of war has been imposed upon the penal repression of "grave breaches"'. The obligation to pay compensation, laid down in the 1907 Hague Convention IV and reaffirmed in Additional Protocol I, forms part of the law, but is 'rarely applied' (p. 89). Hence, the Fact-Finding Commission under Article 90 of Additional Protocol I is the only new 'ancillary method of enforcement' (p. 89).

Draper's conclusions as to the effectiveness of the implementation and enforcement mechanisms contained in the respective treaties are less than glowing. It must be borne in mind, however, that they are based on an early assessment of the Additional Protocols and that in the meantime some of the deficiencies have proven less significant than feared. This does not diminish the value of Draper's essay because it brilliantly sets forth the underlying rationale of the respective rules and their historical context.

'The Role of Legal Advisers in the Armed Forces' by Leslie C. Green (Chapter 4), examines an aspect of implementation that Draper deals with only cursorily. It is one of the first analyses of Additional Protocol I's Article 82, its historical context and the practical problems surrounding its implementation.

According to Green, Article 82 is 'merely a recognition of practical necessity and the purpose that it aims to achieve is not quite so innovative as might appear', but, he admits, 'a treaty requirement to this effect is undoubtedly a new element' (p. 111). Nevertheless, the proper implementation of the obligation faces a variety of problems, especially in light of the widening scope of international humanitarian law and of the varying interpretations of its rules. Moreover, the hierarchic relationship between the commander and the legal adviser may prove problematic. Therefore, the parties to the Protocol must 'instil into their armed forces an entirely new approach to the law' (p. 119). Commanders must be aware that 'their legal advisers have a special role to play and that their advice must be heeded, regardless of rank' (ibid.).

It is also necessary to agree upon the exact meaning of the term 'at the appropriate level'. In order to prevent confusion, 'some further international agreement laying down the level of command at which the appointment of advisers is necessary' should be considered (p. 120). Finally, Green regrets that Additional Protocol I contains 'no indication of the type of training that the legal advisers should be given or the type of person who should be selected' (p. 121). In this regard, he suggests either another international agreement, which he considers an 'idealistic solution' (p. 121), or the creation of training manuals and training courses by the ICRC and the International Institute of Humanitarian Law.

Green concludes by stressing that those who support international humanitarian law should be specialists in the field. In particular, the courses that they teach must be carefully prepared: 'After all, the legal advisers who are the products of their training will be responsible for ensuring that commanders to whom they are attached observe the provisions of the Conventions and the Protocol' (p. 122).

'The Man in the Field and the Maxim Ignorantia Juris Non Excusat', also by Leslie Green (Chapter 5), is a compelling plea for improvement in the knowledge of international humanitarian law applicable in both international and non-international armed conflicts. Green rightly observes that the grasp of humanitarian law by soldiers accused of having committed war crimes has been afforded insufficient attention, 'even though the inevitable defence of superior orders and the reaction to it of the tribunal concerned to a very extent are based on this factor' (p. 123). The maxim of *ignorantia juris non excusat* rather easily applies in a domestic context, but not with regard to international law, especially international humanitarian law, which is a highly sophisticated, and somewhat controversial, system.

Green thoroughly analyses the various binding and non-binding international instruments that have contained a dissemination obligation – a collection reaching back to the 1880 Oxford Manual. Seemingly, that obligation was considered necessary only in the context of purely humanitarian rules ('Geneva Law') and not of the law governing the conduct of hostilities ('Hague Law'). The 1949 Geneva Conventions have contributed to an improvement in this situation, as has the 1954 Convention on Cultural Property, although the latter lacks the necessary specificity. In addition, the conflicts in Korea and Vietnam had a positive impact insofar as the United States, *inter alia*, began to grasp the importance of teaching international humanitarian law to its armed forces.

Green welcomes the provisions of Articles 82 and 83 of the 1977 Additional Protocol I, but deplores the fact that no such obligations exist with regard to non-international armed conflicts. This situation reflects the reluctance of governments to educate their civilian population in matters bearing on civil war. Still, he concludes, if governments began to approach their dissemination obligations seriously, 'we would see the dawn of an era in which it will be true of the man in the field during combat, as it is for the civilian charged with a criminal offence, that *ignorantia juris non excusat*'.

Edwin M. Borchard's 'Private Pecuniary Claims Arising Out of War' (Chapter 6) is a thorough analysis of the law on compensation for losses of private property as of 1915. In view of the 1856 Paris Declaration and of the 1907 Hague Conventions, Borchard observes that 'private [property] rights during war have gained greater and greater recognition' (p. 143). Although Borchard only briefly refers to Article 3 of the 1907 Hague Convention IV, he is prepared to apply that provision to 'all violations of the laws of war besides those included in the Hague Regulations' (p. 145). In doing so, he distinguishes between authorized and unauthorized acts by members of the armed forces. The focus of his essay is on those rules of the *jus in bello* whose applicability depends on the existence of a state of war and which provide for private property loss compensation.

At the outset, Borchard emphasizes that the *jus in bello* applies to all property situated in enemy territory without distinction as to the nationality of the respective owner. While this is generally recognized for land warfare, there is no consensus on the criteria for determining the enemy character of private property at sea. The continental practice is to look to the owner's nationality; the Anglo-American rule is based on the test of (commercial) domicile. Of course, the enemy character of a ship is determined by the flag it legitimately flies. In that context, Borchard reminds us that neutral vessels acquire enemy character if they engage in certain acts, such as breach of blockade, non-neutral service or resistance to visit and search.

As regards war on land, private property is unprotected when damage is a direct result of belligerent acts, at least provided that such acts were in accordance with international humanitarian law. It is important to note that, according to Borchard, there is a legal presumption 'in favor of the regularity and necessity of governmental acts' (p. 155). Moreover, a state is exempted from liability for 'incidental and consequential results of a state of war' (p. 156) and for '[u]nauthorized pillage by uncontrollable soldiery' or 'wanton destruction of private property by unofficered soldiers', unless it can be proven that the offence was committed 'by authority of commanding officers' (p. 157).

The section on appropriation of private property deals with Articles 46, 49, 51, 52, 53 and 54 of the 1907 Hague Regulations. In principle, Borchard welcomes those provisions as improving the protection of private property, but criticizes their rather vague wording. In view of the 1856 Paris Declaration, the 1907 Hague Conventions and the (unratified) 1909 Declaration of London, Borchard devotes a separate section to war at sea. He reminds us of the belligerent right to interfere with enemy trade and – in the cases of contraband, blockade and non-neutral service – neutral trade. As regards the latter, Borchard provides valuable references to the decisions of prize courts and arbitral tribunals that have awarded indemnities for unlawful seizure, capture and destruction of neutral vessels and cargo.

Borchard's analysis is based on the *jus in bello* as codified in the respective treaties and as applied by arbitral commissions. It is not only a snapshot of the state of the law in 1915, but also an excellent examination of the customary rules on the legal status of private property in land and naval warfare.

In 'State Responsibility for Warlike Acts of the Armed Forces', Frits Kalshoven examines Article 3 of the 1907 Hague Convention IV and Article 91 of the 1977 Additional Protocol I. His interpretation of Article 3 of Hague Convention IV can be summarized as follows: (1) enemy and neutral civilians, not their respective states or combatants, are the 'sole intended beneficiaries of Article 3' (p. 183); (2) Article 3 is 'designed to cover fairly small-scale events', as distinguished from 'impersonal, large-scale, military operations such as long-distance bombardment' (p. 184); and (3) it only applies to acts of armed forces which are effectively subject to the government's instructions, thus excluding acts of a *levée en masse* or militia and volunteer corps. Kalshoven bases these conclusions on the article's drafting history, as well as a systematic interpretation of Article 3 in the light of those provisions of the 1907 Hague Regulations that provide for private pecuniary claims. Despite the absence of actual application of Article 3, a comparison with the general rules on state responsibility reveals that any act, including those that are not performed by someone acting in his capacity as a state organ, result in the liability of the respective state.

Given the drafting history of Article 91, Kalshoven characterizes the provision as inter-state; but that finding has no bearing upon Article 3's scope of applicability. Moreover, Article 91 applies to the conduct of all armed forces of a state, 'whether regular or irregular' (p. 198), and to all violations of international humanitarian law.

Kalshoven concludes with a short analysis of the *Nicaragua* judgment, especially the concept of 'effective control', and UN Security Council practice in the aftermath of the 1991 Iraq–Kuwait War, paying particular attention to Resolutions 687 and 692. Although some would hold that Iraq's obligation to compensate those suffering damage from the illegal war is an exclusive matter of the *jus ad bellum*, Kalshoven considers the practice to be a 'remarkable step forward'.

'The History of the Grave Breaches Regime' by Yves Sandoz (Chapter 8) is a *tour de force* not only of the development of the grave breaches regime, but also of the broader international law of war crimes. Sandoz begins by reminding readers that despite the Lieber Code's emphasis on military necessity, the Code set absolute limits and provides for penal sanctions. While some of the sanctions bore on the maintenance of internal discipline, others were based on 'fundamental principles of human dignity, honour and chivalry' (p. 214). During the second half of the nineteenth century, views on penal sanctions for violations of the law of war were divided. Proposals for international penal sanctions and even an international criminal court went unheeded. The same held true for coordinating and standardizing national legislation, as suggested during the 1874 Brussels Conference. Nevertheless, Sandoz describes these proposals as 'a first step in the direction of a common definition of grave breaches' (p. 215).

Sandoz then turns to the aftermath of the First World War and the subsequent Treaty of Versailles, especially to the work of the 'Commission on the Responsibility of the Authors of the War and on Enforcement of Penalties". One of the Commission's products was a non-exhaustive list of 32 crimes, about which Sandoz is unenthusiastic because 'it cannot be viewed as the result of a serious and systematic work of scholarship carried out to show established doctrine or state practice' (pp. 220–21). For instance, with regard to the criminal responsibility of heads of state, he concludes that it 'is ad hoc and arguably too limited in scope to constitute an important precedent for the notion that immunities do not apply to a head of state' (p. 222). Nevertheless, he characterizes Articles 228 to 230 of the Treaty of Versailles as a 'major historical event' (p. 223), for '... the idea of an international criminal court and code ... continued to exercise an influence in the quest for means to curb international violence' (p. 223).[2]

As to the grave breaches regime, Sandoz emphasizes that the 1949 Geneva Conventions 'impose punishments for the identified grave breaches and this is specified as being of international concern' (p. 226). It must be borne in mind that, under the Geneva Conventions, grave breaches could not be equated with war crimes. Rather, the regime 'maintain[ed] a separate approach' (p. 227). Because the Geneva Conventions were not designed to 'work out international penal law' (ibid.), the conditions for prosecution and punishment of grave breaches were left to the national courts.

The distinction between grave breaches and war crimes became obsolete with the adoption of the 1977 Additional Protocol I. All grave breaches under the Conventions and the Protocol

---

2 Citing J.E. Willis, *Prologue to Nuremburg: The Politics and Diplomacy of Punishing War Criminals of the First World War*, Westport, CT and London: Greenwood, 1982, p. 113.

constitute war crimes. In that context, Sandoz regrets the fact that it proved impossible to agree upon a grave breaches regime for non-international armed conflict. Yet, in light of the establishment of the ICTY, the ICTR and the ICC, he suggests that in 1995 'the notion that serious violations of international humanitarian law constitute war crimes, whether committed during international or non-international armed conflict, was finally accepted' (p. 229). Sandoz closes by pointing out that despite the merger of the grave breaches regime and the concept of war crimes, important differences between Additional Protocol I and the ICC Statute remain.

In 'The Universality Principle and War Crimes' (Chapter 9), Yoram Dinstein analyses the principle of universality which he characterizes as an 'exceptional measure granting the State special extraterritorial power' that is 'limited to specific offenses defined by international law'. Accordingly, it must 'be exercised strictly in accordance with limitations imposed by that law' (p. 237).

Dinstein offers convincing evidence of the customary character of the universality principle in the context of war crimes, but also stresses that those technical violations of international humanitarian law that do not constitute such crimes *strictu sensu* are not covered by the principle. He distinguishes the universality from the protective principle; the latter protects the single state, whereas the former 'lends its aegis to the collectivity of States'. Consequently, there is no 'genuine overlap' between them (p. 240).

The *aut dedere aut judicare* formula and the practical challenges surrounding its implementation are examined, as is the closely related issue of whether certain states enjoy priority in exercising jurisdiction over other states under the universality principle. Dinstein maintains that customary international law is silent on the matter, but believes it is worth taking certain international conventions into consideration in that regard, even though they are not directly germane to war crimes. He suggests that the 'nonbinding preference scheme may be looked upon with favor in that setting too' (p. 244).

For Dinstein, concurrent jurisdiction under the universality principle can be exercised jointly – that is, on a multinational level. Hence, the establishment of the ICTY could be characterized as a joint exercise of universal jurisdiction by means of a UN Security Council resolution. If an international tribunal enjoys jurisdiction, it will regularly be endowed with primacy over national courts. The problem of double jeopardy in situations of national and international jurisdiction, although not settled in customary international law, can be solved by applying the principle of *non bis in idem*, provided that the respective act has not been tried as an ordinary crime and the national court proceedings were effective, impartial and independent. Finally, Dinstein analyses the jurisdiction to prescribe, the jurisdiction to adjudicate and the jurisdiction to enforce in light of the universality principle.

Hersch Lauterpacht's 'The Law of Nations and the Punishment of War Crimes', published in 1944 and reproduced here as Chapter 10, is a modified version of a memorandum the author submitted in 1942 to the Committee on Crimes against International Public Order set up by the International Commission for Penal Reconstruction and Development. It is a compelling call for punishment of persons guilty of war crimes within the framework of a legal process. He believes that '[in] the existing state of international law it is probably unavoidable that the right of punishing war criminals should be unilaterally assumed by the victor' (p. 258). Consequently, Lauterpacht begins by scrutinizing the legal basis of the demand for surrender of war criminals. He first proves the existence of a rule of international law according to which a belligerent is entitled to punish for war crimes those members of the enemy armed forces who have fallen into its hands. In doing so, he demonstrates that such punishment is not a matter of 'victor's justice'. Dissatisfied with merely citing Vitoria, Grotius, Wolff, Moser and the Institute of International Law, he locates a right to punish war crimes in the territorial principle, which includes violations in territory or national airspace under military occupation and criminal acts committed on the high seas against vessels flying the belligerent's flag. Further considerations include the rights to punish those who have committed acts against safety or the belligerent's nationals.

Lauterpacht emphasizes the importance of enforcing international, rather than municipal, law. In that context, he convincingly argues that the laws of war 'are binding not upon impersonal entities, but upon human beings' (p. 263) and that '[t]he immediate subjection of individuals to the rules of warfare entails, in the very nature of things, a responsibility of a criminal character' (p. 264). Moreover, their force flows from the fact that they are 'dictated by generally recognized principles of humanity' (ibid.).

On this basis, the right to punish enemy war criminals for violations of the laws of war is justified, as is any argument that an exercise of such criminal jurisdiction amounts to vindictive (and procedural) retroactivity. The right to demand their surrender from the defeated state follows from the normative fact that 'international law permits the punishment of war criminals ... regardless of the manner in which they happen to fall into his power' (p. 266). The source of that right lies in the exercise of military authority over foreign territory – that is, the law of belligerent occupation.

Having established these rights, Lauterpacht examines their international law limitations – the plea of superior orders, international humanitarian law's uncertainties and reprisals. As to superior orders, he stresses that the law 'does not reduce the soldier to the status of a mere mechanism' and 'adds the substantial qualification to the effect that obedience is due only to lawful orders' (p. 270). However, his analysis of municipal legal orders reveals no consensus on the issue, and there is no international judicial authority on the subject. Accordingly, Lauterpacht considers it necessary 'to approach the subject of superior orders on the basis of general principles of criminal law, namely, as an element in ascertaining the existence of *mens rea* as a condition of accountability' (p. 272).

With regard to the uncertainties, he concludes that 'there may be lacking ... that degree of *mens rea* which ... constitutes an essential condition of criminality' (p. 273). Pointing to the difficult issue of aerial bombardment, he doubts whether criminal tribunals are 'the proper agency for solving controversial and difficult problems of the law of war' (p. 274). Such uncertainties have a direct bearing on the issue of superior orders.

As to reprisals, Lauterpacht maintains that 'as a rule, an act committed in pursuance of reprisals, as limited by international law, cannot properly be treated as a war crime' (p. 275). Moreover, '[t]he element of reprisals may have a significant and perplexing bearing upon the plea of superior orders' (ibid.). However, this does not necessarily mean that reliance on a superior order justified as a reprisal will result in impunity because 'it does not seriously affect the most potent source of war crimes which originates in the lawlessness and the brutality of the occupying State' (p. 276).

For Lauterpacht, a belligerent must make it clear that 'his claim to inflict punishment on war criminals is in accordance with established rules and principles of the law of nations and … does not represent a vindictive measure of the victor resolved to apply retroactively to the defeated enemy the rigours of a newly created rule' (p. 279). Therefore, such actions must be 'accompanied by the provision of safeguards of impartiality and by a measure of equality in the application of the law' (ibid.). While not advocating absolute equality, he sees three ways of achieving impartiality: (1) establishment of an international criminal court; (2) modification of municipal court organization; or (3) creation of quasi-international courts. These solutions have recently regained the attention of the international community.

Finally, the essay deals with the obligation of neutral states to surrender war criminals to the victorious belligerent. Here, Lauterpacht stresses that that obligation is subject to the safeguards of impartiality and fair trial. This being so, neutral states 'are entitled to ask for an assurance that the intended prosecution of war crimes will not be used as an instrument of revenge' (p. 294).

In 'The Municipal and International Law Basis of Jurisdiction over War Crimes' (Chapter 11), Richard R. Baxter examines the divergent legal bases applied by states and military tribunals in the prosecution of war crimes. Not surprisingly, he advocates application of the law of war rather than application of municipal law. Baxter briefly mentions the deliberations over the 1949 Geneva Conventions and the reluctance of states to accept 'grave breaches' as war crimes proper. In view of the practice at Nuremberg and elsewhere, 'a forthright stand on the primacy of international law was thus lost' (p. 300).

Baxter's arguments against the application of municipal law may be summarized as follows: (1) the alleged advantage of a 'secure' legal basis decreases due to the necessary reliance on either the territoriality or passive personality principles; (2) deprivation of immunity under international law may not be sufficiently based on municipal law; (3) application of various domestic legal orders will lead to sometimes contradictory decisions; (4) municipal law is not designed to capture the specific nature of war crimes; (5) '[a]ny theory which relies on the law of nations as a defence for belligerent acts … fails to accord with the true *raison d'être* of the law of war' (p. 301); and (6) '[w]hether or not to punish war crimes is not left to the unfettered discretion of the state' (ibid.) because the punishment of war crimes under international law is in the interest of the international community, not in that of a single state.

Prosecuting war crimes on the basis of international law implies 'the direct application of a uniform law of a specialized nature to acts which are distinguished from common law crimes by reason of their occurrence in time of war' (p. 303). For Baxter, mere application of the universality principle would fall 'considerably short of that goal as long as the jurisdiction is exercised by a belligerent only over persons associated with its enemies' (p. 305).

In 'Superior Orders and the Reasonable Man' (Chapter 12), Leslie C. Green offers a rich survey of sources – including domestic law, civil jurisprudence and decisions of international military tribunals – bearing upon the issue of superior orders. On the basis of these sources, Green concludes that obedience to a superior order neither excuses a violation of the law nor acts to mitigate punishment 'unless the order is *so palpably unlawful that a reasonable man in the position of the person obeying it would perceive its unlawful quality*' (pp. 314–15, emphasis in original). Although the plea of superior orders has not always been dealt with uniformly, the post-Second World War authorities relied on by Green remain unchallenged. Thus, his assertion correctly reflects the law as it presently stands.

It follows that the yardstick for determination of whether an order is 'palpably illegal' is that of the 'reasonable man', the '*man of ordinary sense and understanding*' (p. 321, emphasis in original). For Green, the standard is operable with regard to offences that are not based on considerations of military necessity or are committed against prisoners of war. He cautions that

> ... there are offences which are of such a kind and occur in circumstances so closely connected with operations that it is probably unfair to measure them by any standard other than that of a 'reasonable soldier,' and it may even be unfair to judge them by persons other than those possessed of military experience. (p. 347)

Moreover:

> ... justice may well demand that consideration be paid to the general conditions in which the accused found himself, the length of time he had been in action, the nature of the hostilities, the type of enemy confronting him and the methods of warfare employed against him. (p. 348)

Finally, Green stresses the necessity of entrusting only those 'who are themselves likely to be aware of how the reasonable soldier thinks, reacts and does' with deciding war crimes cases (p. 349).

William H. Parks's 'Command Responsibility for War Crimes' (Chapter 13) is, as the author humbly states, '[a]n historical and comparative analysis of war crimes trials involving command responsibility' (p. 351). In fact, Parks's determination of 'the standards of conduct required of a military commander in combat with regard to the prevention, investigation, reporting, and prosecution of war crimes' (ibid.) is of continuing validity, and this comprehensive and sober legal analysis of the concept of command responsibility thus serves as a touchstone for those faced with command responsibility issues, whether in the context of general military affairs or war crimes.

On the basis of his assessment of national military law rules and court decisions holding military commanders responsible for their subordinates' conduct, Parks concludes that although command responsibility always existed, in the past 'there was not sufficient warrant or authorization to interfere in what was essentially an area of "state action"' (p. 369). This changed with the development of criminal international law before, during and after the Second World War. The result is that today a commander is held responsible for his subordinates' offences if:

> (a) he personally ordered the illegal act charged, or (b) with knowledge that such actions were taking place, he failed in his duty as a commander to prevent such offenses, either intentionally ... or through neglect ... (p. 370)

Parks examines the key post-Second World War war crimes trials (for example, General Yamashita, Admiral Toyoda, the Tokyo Trials, the 'High Command' case and the 'Hostage' case) as a basis for identifying the relevant standards in establishing command responsibility. He outlines them as (1) incitement, (2) acquiescence, (3) command and control, (4) knowledge and (5) 'subjective factors'. Subjective factors that influence whether the commander either should have known or must have known of his subordinates' offence include the rank of the accused, experience of the commander, duties of the commander by virtue of the command held, mobility of the commander, isolation of the commander, the 'sliding probability ratio' of unit/incident/command, size of the staff of the commander, comprehensiveness of the duties of the staff, communications abilities, training/age/experience of the subordinates, composition of forces within the command and the combat situation (pp. 440–45).

'Accountability for International Crimes: From Conjecture to Reality' by Jelena Pejic (Chapter 14) appraises recent efforts, especially on the international level, to combat impunity for war crimes and crimes against humanity. Pejic welcomes the establishment of the ad hoc tribunals for the former Yugoslavia and Rwanda as a 'breakthrough' and endorses the jurisprudence of the ICTY in the *Tadic* case. However, she is less than satisfied with the degree and quality of states' cooperation with the tribunal and demands that steps be taken with a view to establish 'international accountability mechanisms' with enforcement powers (p. 459).

Pejic also positively assesses the so-called 'hybrid courts' in Cambodia, Sierra Leone and East Timor, as well as the International Criminal Court. With regard to the ICC, she reminds us that the 'Court's creation is based on the recognition that national authorities have far too often proven unable or unwilling to deal with the perpetrators of serious crimes under international law' (p. 463). In her view, the recognition of the concept of war crimes in non-international armed conflict and the provisions on the protection of victims are two of the key achievements of the ICC Statute.

Despite her doubts as to the effectiveness and efficiency of national proceedings on war crimes, Pejic forcefully advocates an increased exercise of universal jurisdiction by third states. She recalls the respective obligations of states under the Geneva Conventions, Additional Protocol I and the Convention against Torture that very few have implemented in their domestic legislation.

Pejic opposes grants of amnesty to suspected perpetrators of war crimes and crimes against humanity because they violate 'the duty of States, under treaty-based and customary law, to bring to justice and punish suspected offenders' (p. 470). In that context, she emphasizes that Article 6(5) of the 1977 Additional Protocol II must not be misinterpreted 'as supporting amnesties for war crimes or other international offences committed in internal armed conflict' (p. 472). Finally, she deplores the lack of political will by national authorities to 'tackle current or past offences' (p. 473) and stresses that the rights of the accused to a fair trial are to be respected and safeguarded if efforts against impunity are to prove successful.

Charles J. Dunlap, in 'Law and Military Interventions: Preserving Humanitarian Values in 21st Conflicts' (Chapter 15), addresses the impact of international humanitarian law on contemporary military operations. He highlights two factors that have contributed to the increased importance of international law in military interventions: (1) globalization and the related growing influence of NGOs on military affairs, including international humanitarian law; and (2) the 'Information Revolution' and its impact on public perceptions.

Closely linked to the second factor is the phenomenon of 'lawfare'. The term 'describes a method of warfare where law is used as a means of realizing a military objective' (p. 478). Its most striking feature is 'a cynical manipulation of the rule of law and the humanitarian values it represents' (ibid.). Indeed, recent events have demonstrated how public support of an ongoing military operation can be shattered by creating the impression that the armed forces are conducting operations in violation of humanitarian law. In that context, Dunlap refers to lawful incidents during the 1991 Gulf War that were reported as unlawful. He also points to the deliberate positioning of lawful military objectives in the vicinity of protected persons and objects and the use of human shields.

The role of military legal advisers is essential in this regard. They face a complex battle environment. For instance, practical and legal problems abound when conducting attacks on dual-use or 'psychological or message' targets – that is, strikes against lawful military objectives 'whose intended effect is primarily psychological' (p. 482) – or when engaging in 'time critical targeting' (p. 483). But he is sceptical about endeavours to prohibit certain methods and means of warfare, such as anti-personnel landmines and cluster munitions. In his estimation, the recent bans on certain conventional weapons, although allegedly based on genuinely humanitarian considerations, can result in attacks that are less humanitarian in character than they would have been if conducted by the banned weapons.

It must be emphasized that Dunlap does not argue against international humanitarian law; on the contrary, he is a committed supporter. However, he harbours concerns that, under the guise of humanitarian or other pretences, the armed forces (which are, after all, entrusted with enforcing the will of their political masters) will be deprived of effective means to achieve their aims. While not everyone may agree with Dunlap's conclusions, nobody can deny the legitimacy of widening the dialogue on such matters.

WOLFF HEINTSCHEL VON HEINEGG

[1]

WAR REPRISALS IN THE WAR CRIMES TRIALS AND IN THE GENEVA CONVENTIONS OF 1949

By A. R. Albrecht

Of the District of Columbia Bar

The war crimes trials following the second World War and the Geneva Conventions of 1949 have posed a question about war reprisals which is likely to be important in any future war and which has immediate practical significance in the current wars in Asia. On the one hand, the trials have transformed the previously sketchy rules on reprisals into a more comprehensive and elaborate system of control. On the other hand, the Geneva Conventions have provided for almost the complete abolition of reprisals in the very area for which the rules of control were formulated. Moreover, the conventions remain unratified by many of the major Powers,[1] of which at least one has already demonstrated its inability to observe the abolition of reprisals.[2] The core of the problem concerns reprisals against civilian persons in occupied territories, for this was by far the most significant point in the trials on reprisals and was the subject of the most outstanding innovation introduced by the Geneva Conventions. Nevertheless, the issues raised by the contradiction between the trials and the conventions cannot properly be discussed without reference to the general theory of war reprisals.

War reprisals may be defined as otherwise illegitimate acts of warfare which under certain conditions may legally be used by a belligerent against the enemy in order to deter the enemy from a repetition of his prior illegal acts and thus to enforce compliance with the generally recognized rules of war.[3] The practice of some form of reprisals in war dates

1 Thus far twenty-four states have ratified the Geneva Convention of 1949: Austria, Belgium, Chile, Czechoslovakia, Denmark, Egypt, El Salvador, France, Guatemala, Holy See, India, Israel, Italy, Lebanon, Liechtenstein, Luxembourg, Mexico, Monaco, Norway, Pakistan, The Philippines, Spain, Switzerland, and Yugoslavia. Japan, Jordan, San Marino and South Africa have adhered to the conventions.

2 See footnote 108 below.

3 Oppenheim, International Law (7th ed., 1952), Vol. II, pp. 561 ff. Substantially similar definitions may be found in the American Rules of Land Warfare (1940), p. 89, par. 358, and the British Manual of Military Law (1929), p. 85, *cf.* Amendments of 1936, par. 452. The term has a special meaning in French domestic law; see Trial of Jean-Pierre Lex, War Crimes Reports, Vol. 7 (1948), pp. 74–75; Trial of Hans Szabados, War Crimes Reports, Vol. 9 (1949), p. 60; and Trial of Carl Bauer, War Crimes Reports, Vol. 8 (1949), pp. 19–20. For the distinctions among French writers between "représailles," "rétorsions," "réparations," and "sanctions," see De La Brière, *Recueil des Cours de l'Académie de Droit International,* Vol. 11 (1928), p. 240. Compare

back at least as far as Alexander the Great[4] and seems to have enjoyed universal acceptance until modern times, when humanitarian sentiments, which were shocked by their cruelty, brought about a movement for their limitation.[5] This movement led to the prohibition of reprisals against prisoners of war in the Geneva Convention of 1929.[6] The excesses of the second World War, particularly under the changed conditions of warfare, demonstrated the inadequacy of the existing limitations and gave new impetus to the movement for reform, not only for general humanitarian reasons, but also to prevent the disintegration of the whole body of the laws of war, which were seriously threatened by the new and wide use of reprisals or the pretext of reprisals.[7] It was in response to this new impetus that the divergent developments in the war crimes trials and the Geneva Conventions of 1949 took place.

The function of the law of war reprisals is to provide a sanction for the rules of war, particularly to specify the conditions under which reprisals may legally be exercised. There are two basic assumptions underlying the attempt to regulate the conduct of war in this manner. The first is that it is possible within reasonable limits to establish and apply legal rules which will regulate the use of reprisals so that proper reprisals may be

other definitions: Jessup and Deák, Encyclopedia of the Social Sciences, Vol. XIII (1934), p. 315; Politis, *Revue Générale du Droit International Public*, Vol. XXXI (1924), p. 7; Hyde, International Law (1945), Vol. II, p. 1662; Clark, this JOURNAL, Vol. 27 (1933), p. 694; McNair, Transactions of the Grotius Society, Vol. 11 (1926), p. 35; and Maccoby, Cambridge Law Journal, Vol. 2 (1924), p. 70.

[4] See Wilkinson, Law Magazine and Review, Vol. XL (1914–1915), p. 294. See also Dareste, *Revue des Etudes Grecques* (1870), p. 316; Spiegel, this JOURNAL, Vol. 32 (1938), p. 64; Clark, *loc. cit.*, p. 694; and Latrie, *Du Droit de Marque ou Droit de Représailles au Moyen Age* (1875).

[5] See Westlake, International Law, Vol. II (1913), p. 123; Spaight, War Rights on Land (1911), p. 463, and Bordwell, Law of War (1908) p. 109.

[6] Art. 2, Sec. 3, of the Geneva Convention of July 22, 1929, relative to the Treatment of Prisoners of War, provided: "Measures of reprisals against them are forbidden." Art. 50 of the Hague Convention of 1899 respecting the Laws and Customs of War on Land provided: "No collective penalty, pecuniary or otherwise, shall be inflicted upon the population on account of the acts of individuals for which it cannot be regarded as collectively responsible," but this was without prejudice to the question of reprisals. The exclusion of reprisals from the scope of Article 50 was not stated in the convention itself but in the Rolin Report thereon. See Reports of the Hague Conferences of 1899 and 1907 (1917), p. 152; Trial of General von Mackensen, War Crimes Reports, Vol. 8 (1949), p. 4, and Trial of Wilhelm List and Others, *ibid.*, p. 78. See also British Manual of Military Law (1929), p. 85 of Amendments of 1936, par. 452 and footnote 2, and American Rules of Land Warfare (1940), p. 86, par. 344.

[7] "Among other factors which may limit, or until recently have limited, the effectiveness of the rules of war may be mentioned: (a) the institution of reprisals which, though designed to ensure the observance of rules of war, have systematically been used as a convenient cloak for disregarding the laws of war. . . ." History of the United Nations War Crimes Commission and the Development of the Laws of War (1948), p. 29.

distinguished from mere pretexts for violation of the laws of war. As experience has shown, this is a task of extraordinary difficulty.[8] The difficulty lies both in the formulation of principles which can be readily applied in changing conditions of war and also in the ascertainment of the relevant facts to which such principles must be applied. Recent improvements in the techniques of war have exacerbated the problem by casting doubts upon many of the rules of war, on which the doctrine of reprisals is completely dependent. At the same time, however, they have so conspicuously broadened the scope of warfare that, short of the unlikely solution of total abolition of war, the possibility of a workable law of reprisals to enforce the international rules of war has become a matter of importance.

The second basic assumption underlying the attempt to regulate the conduct of war through reprisals is that once a clear and readily applicable doctrine has been established and there is some machinery for the ascertainment of facts, then the legal threat or use of reprisals will have the desired effect, that is, to provide restitution for the damage done by the enemy or to produce a change in his conduct or, preferably, both. Neither the second World War nor any earlier wars can provide the basis for a reliable estimate of the extent to which the institution of reprisals has succeeded in its function of enforcing compliance with the rules of war. Not only are there no adequate reports of the success and failure of the proper use of reprisals or the reasons for such success or failure, but the extent to which the mere threat of reprisals has prevented infractions of the rules of war which might otherwise have occurred must always remain an imponderable factor. Nevertheless, the practice or the threat of reprisals, insofar as either may work, is the only protection against an unscrupulous enemy in war.[9]

The two different lines of development in the doctrine of war reprisals which are exemplified respectively in the war crimes trials and the Geneva Conventions of 1949 reflect a fundamental difference of approach which may be stated in terms of the above-mentioned assumptions. The movement for the improvement of the rules controlling the practice of war reprisals is based upon the view that there must be a sanction of reprisals to enforce the rules of war and that rules of reprisal can be adequately

[8] See Trial of Hans Rauter, War Crimes Reports, Vol. 14 (1949), p. 123; Trial of Franz Holstein and Others, *ibid.*, Vol. 8 (1949), p. 27; and Lord Wright's Foreword to the History of the United Nations War Crimes Commission and the Development of the Laws of War (1948), p. vi.

[9] The American Rules of Land Warfare, *op. cit.*, p. 89, par. 358(b), states: ". . . commanding officers must assume responsibility for retaliative measures when an unscrupulous enemy leaves no other recourse against the repetition of barbarous outrages." The British Manual of Military Law, *op. cit.*, p. 85, par. 452, states: ". . . They [reprisals] are by custom admissible as an indispensable means of securing legitimate warfare."

formulated and properly applied which are reasonably likely to have the desired effect. The movement for the abolition of reprisals is based upon the view that, on the whole, reprisals are more a threat to the laws of war than a sanction for their protection because such rules cannot be adequately formulated or properly applied, and in any case are not likely to produce the desired results.

It is now proposed to examine in their turn both the war crimes trials and the Geneva Conventions of 1949 for their bearing on this issue.[10]

THE WAR CRIMES TRIALS

The rules on reprisals which were developed in the course of the war crimes trials fall into two general groups: (1) the rules governing the preliminary conditions which must be satisfied before there can be any resort to reprisals; and (2) the rules governing the operative conditions which must be satisfied in the exercise of reprisals.

I. PRELIMINARY CONDITIONS

1. *Illegal Act Giving Rise to Reprisals*

Reprisals are legal only if they are justified, in the first instance, as a counter-measure to some prior illegal act of the enemy. Does the initiation of a war of aggression constitute such an act? In the *Trial of Hans Rauter*,[11] the defendant was accused of war crimes against the inhabitants of The Netherlands during the German occupation. His main defense was that his actions were justified as reprisals for violations of the rules of war committed by the Dutch. The Netherlands Special Court of Cassation rejected this defense on the theory that since the original wrong lay with Germany as the initiator of an unprovoked war of aggression against The Netherlands, The Netherlands was entitled to resort to reprisals against Germany, but that Germany had no right to take counter-reprisals against The Netherlands.[12]

There is no question that if an act is a proper reprisal, then it is a legal measure and it cannot lawfully be the excuse for counter-reprisals.[13]

[10] In discussing the war crimes trials reference will also be made to the American and British war manuals, which were relied upon by the tribunals. See also Oppenheim, International Law (7th ed., 1952), Vol. II, p. 561.

[11] *Op. cit.*

[12] Trial of Hans Rauter, *op. cit.*, pp. 134–135.

[13] Nevertheless, during the second World War Hitler ordered the reprisal execution of Allied airmen who bombed non-military targets in reprisal for German use of the V–1. See Major War Criminals Tribunal, Pt. 6 (1946), p. 128, and Pt. 11 (1947), p. 102. The V-weapons were themselves supposed to be weapons of retaliation, the "V" signifying "Vergeltungswaffen," which means "retaliation weapon." Germany's Lieutenant-General Dittmar described them as "true weapons of retaliation." See Spaight, Air Power and War Rights (1947), p. 53.

Nevertheless, the rule that unprovoked aggression may constitute the ground for reprisals by the victim cannot be regarded as a desirable one. It means that the "victim" may take almost unlimited reprisals, chiefly because there is no hope of any reasonable measure of reprisals against the illegal act of unleashing war, while the aggressor, on the other hand, is not entitled to have any recourse to reprisals against the acts of the "victim," since the latter are theoretically legal. In practice this rule would lead to the breakdown, or at least the serious impairment, of the laws of war by making their very applicability a point of dispute between the belligerents. This problem has been recognized in the view, generally adopted by writers, that for the purposes of the application of the rules of warfare, there should be no distinction between legal and illegal wars.[14] The United States Military Tribunal at Nuremberg agreed with this position in the *Trial of Wilhelm List*,[15] deciding upon the basis of the rules in the American and British military manuals,[16] that, regardless of the legal responsibility for the origin of the war, reprisals may be taken against the inhabitants of an occupied state to ensure that the latter will do their duty under international law.[17]

There was another and perhaps sounder basis for the decision in the *Rauter* case that the Germans had no right to take reprisals. The Court of Cassation mentioned that Germany lost the right to take reprisals because of her violations of the laws of war incident to the aggression.[18] It is difficult to deny the cogency of this view. The rule of law requiring obedience by the inhabitants of occupied territory towards the occupying Power is conditional: such obedience is due only in return for observance of the rules by the occupant himself. This means that Germany could not

14 See Oppenheim, *op. cit.*, p. 217.

15 Trial of Wilhelm List, *op. cit.*, p. 59. See British Manual of Military Law (1929), p. 72 of Amendments of 1936, par. 384, and American Rules of Land Warfare (1940), p. 78, par. 301.

16 See the American Rules of Land Warfare (1940), p. 86, par. 344, and the British Manual of Military Law (1929), p. 72 of Amendments of 1936, par. 386.

17 Trial of Wilhelm List, *op. cit.*, p. 65. Compare Trial of Hans Rauter, *op. cit.*, pp. 127, 129–130. For the treatment of the special argument of the defense based on the alleged violation of the terms of surrender to the Nazi forces, see pp. 124–125. The view has been advanced that the duty owed by the inhabitants of occupied territory towards the occupying Power should not be regarded as an obligation imposed directly by international law, but rather as an obligation imposed by the occupant which international law will recognize as long as it is reasonable. See Baxter, in British Year Book of International Law, Vol. 27 (1950), p. 235. The significance of this distinction, however, is not entirely clear where reprisals are concerned. It would seem that violation of a duty imposed by the occupant and recognized by international law would just as much constitute the type of offense which justifies a reprisal as would a violation of international law. If the theory means that there is no duty towards the occupying Power whose violation can justify reprisals, then it is open to the same objections as other theories which prevent the use of reprisals in occupied lands. See *infra*, p. 595.

18 Trial of Hans Rauter, *op. cit.*, pp. 127 and 137.

legally take reprisals for the disobedience of her subjugated populations when her own disregard for her duties towards them had already released them from their obligations towards her.[19]

2. *Perpetrator of the Illegal Act*

The illegal act which forms the basis of reprisals must be an offense by the enemy—but precisely whose offense must it be? The American *Rules of Land Warfare* say: "Illegal acts of warfare justifying reprisals may be committed by a government, by its military commanders, or by a community or individuals thereof, whom it is impossible to apprehend, try, and punish."[20] There is no reason to believe that in general the theory or the practice has been different. In the *Rauter* case the view of the Dutch court was that the illegal act justifying reprisals could only be an act of state, represented by its organs, and not one of individual members of the population.[21]

So far as is known, the *Rauter* case is the only authority for this proposition, which seems to run counter to the general theory of reprisals.[22] The intolerable situation into which an occupant would be placed by the "act of state" theory can be illustrated by the facts of the very case in which the principle was enunciated. During the German occupation of The Netherlands there existed a widespread resistance movement among the population which frequently resulted in acts of violence against the Germans and their installations. Although it was in exile, the Netherlands Government in London kept up a constant and successful campaign of incitement against the German authorities both by means of the wireless and by sending weapons. It may be, as the Netherlands Special Court said, that "the Netherlands Government was justified in inciting to resistance . . . and it cannot be reproached for having had arms dropped for this purpose on occupied Netherlands territory from aeroplanes,"[23] but it may be impossible, in the face of such facts, for the occupying forces to observe their duties to the inhabitants and exercise no reprisals.[24]

3. *Requirement of Previous Attempt to Punish the Guilty*

Once the requisite illegal offense has occurred, a reprisal is not automatically justified, for there must first be an attempt to find, try, and

[19] The question whether guerrilla activities constitute a basis for reprisals was touched upon in the Trial of Carl Bauer, *op. cit.*, p. 17, and the Trial of Gerhard Flesch, War Crimes Reports, Vol. 6 (1948), p. 115. The question whether resistance activities justify reprisals was involved in the Trial of Franz Holstein, *ibid.*, Vol. 8 (1949), p. 29.

[20] *Op. cit.*, p. 89, par. 358(c). See also the British Manual, *op. cit.*, p. 85, par. 453.

[21] Trial of Hans Rauter, *op. cit.*, p. 132.

[22] See the American Rules of Land Warfare, *op. cit.*, p. 89, par. 358(d), and the British Manual of Military Law, *op. cit.*, p. 85, par. 458.

[23] Trial of Hans Rauter, *op. cit.*, p. 125.

[24] The problem is more vividly presented in the *List* case, *op. cit.*, pp. 38, 56.

punish the guilty, which will usually require some investigation into the facts. Punishment of the guilty is in all cases preferable to reprisal action and removes the excuse for reprisals. The American *Rules* state: "The rule requiring careful inquiry into the real occurrence will always be followed unless the safety of the troops requires immediate drastic action and the persons who actually committed the offense cannot be ascertained." [25] How far the investigation and search for the guilty must proceed before reprisals can be exercised must always be a relative matter depending on the circumstances of each case. The most relevant criteria for determining the answer to this question would be, as the American *Rules* suggest, the urgency of the need for retaliation and the chances of identifying and then securing the guilty parties for trial and punishment. The inquiry should always proceed far enough, however, to make sure that the illegal offense has in fact been committed by the enemy, for it would never be proper, no matter how urgent the circumstances, to exercise reprisals for an occurrence not clearly due to enemy action.[26]

It would seem to be in the interest of the occupying authority as well as in the interest of justice that every effort be made to apprehend the actual perpetrator of the offense before resorting to reprisals,[27] but it is difficult to formulate this principle in terms of a general rule. The best that can be done is to require that there be a thorough examination of every source which is reasonably likely to lead to information about the guilty party except to the extent that the safety of the troops or some other emergency makes immediate action imperative.

4. *The Duty to Resort to Protest and Other Means of Redress*

Even after it has been determined that the perpetrators of the illegal offense are unascertainable or unavailable for trial and punishment, the right to resort to reprisals does not follow as a matter of course. There is a duty to exhaust every other means of redress short of reprisals. Like the requirement of an attempt to punish the guilty party, this is a rule of reasonableness, which must depend upon the circumstances of the par-

25 American Rules of Land Warfare, *op. cit.*, p. 90, par. 358(f). See also the British Manual of Military Law, *op. cit.*, p. 85, par. 456.

26 See Trial of Wilhelm List and Others, *op. cit.*, pp. 44, 78; also the Trial of General von Mackensen and General Maelzer, *op. cit.*, p. 5.

27 Hitler himself is alleged to have expressed the view that punishment of the guilty was more important than reprisal measures. See Major War Criminals Tribunals, Pt. 11 (1947), p. 170. The statement is reported in the testimony of Dr. H. H. Lemmers, Chief of the Reich Chancellery, in the Trial of Field Marshal Keitel. General von Falkenhorst was even more emphatic on this point and requested that more time be devoted to searching for the guilty. See Major War Criminals Tribunal, Pt. 5 (1946), p. 132. So did General Wuehlisch, the German Chief of Staff in Holland, whose opposition to the indiscriminate reprisals of General Rauter caused the latter to complain to Himmler. See Trial of Hans Rauter, *op. cit.*, pp. 103–104.

ticular case. But the flexibility of the rule does not constitute a license to interpret it to suit any purpose, for it imposes a positive compulsion to use every method other than reprisals which might reasonably be expected to obtain redress, or else to justify departure from this rule by proving necessity. In the words of the American *Rules,* reprisals are "adopted . . . only as an unavoidable last resort . . . "[28]

What are some of the "other means" which a belligerent may be expected to use before resorting to reprisals? One of the most important is a protest to the offending Power.[29] Where redress has been obtained through protest, the right to reprisals ceases forthwith.[30] The public warning is similar to the protest, with which it may be combined, but it has a special use in the administration of occupied territories. Here there is frequently no state organization to represent the population whose members are guilty of the illegal acts, or, if a state organization exists, it is either in exile and not recognized by the occupant or else completely subservient to him. The normal protest is then impossible or useless. There must be a protest or warning to the people, followed by retaliatory measures if the warning is not heeded. Of course, if the warning is heeded, and satisfaction given, then there can be no legal reprisals.[31]

The chief form of reprisal in the administration of occupied territories is the use of hostages.[32] A public warning to the population is a prerequisite to the exercise of reprisals against hostages who are taken to ensure the good conduct of the population. According to the United States Military Tribunal at Nuremberg in the *List* case,

> It is essential to a lawful taking of hostages under customary law that proclamation be made, giving the names and addresses of hostages

[28] *Op. cit.*, p. 89, par. 358(b). See also the British Manual, *op. cit.*, p. 85, par. 454.

[29] See American Rules of Land Warfare, *op. cit.*, p. 86, par. 346(b), and British Manual of Military Law, *op. cit.*, p. 85, par. 456. See also Trial of General von Mackensen, *op. cit.*, p. 5.

[30] It is so seldom that a belligerent state will admit to its enemy that it was guilty of a violation of the laws of war and offer redress, that there is little authority on what constitutes sufficient redress to end the right to reprisals. A belligerent which violates the Regulations Respecting the Laws and Customs of War on Land, annexed to the Hague Convention (IV) of 1907, may be liable under Art. 3 of that convention to pay compensation for the wrong. Art. 3 reads: "A belligerent party which violates the provisions of the said Regulations shall, if the case demands, be liable to pay compensation. It shall be responsible for all acts committed by persons forming part of its armed forces."

[31] See British Manual, *op. cit.*, p. 86, par. 460. An instance is recorded of how a wounded German officer had been taken prisoner by the Dutch resistance. The Germans declared that if the officer were released within 24 hours there would be no reprisals. The officer was released, having received medical care from the Dutch soldiers who had captured him. In spite of their pledge, however, the Germans exercised reprisals on the village of Putten. See Major War Criminals Tribunal, Pt. 5 (1946), p. 322.

[32] See discussion *infra*, at pp. 602 ff.

taken, notifying the population that upon the recurrence of stated acts of war treason that the hostages will be shot.[33]

Various other types of measures may be employed in occupied lands in connection with public warnings before reprisals are used.[34] Which and how many of these measures must be taken before there can be a legitimate resort to reprisals will vary from one situation to another, but a good case for reprisals will not be made out unless there is proof of a compelling reason why these or similarly mild measures could not have been employed before reprisals were used.[35]

5. *Requirement of Judicial Hearing*

Several of the war crimes cases refer adversely to the absence of judicial hearings before reprisals,[36] but it was only in the *Trial of Wilhelm List and Others* that this matter was given more than perfunctory attention. Although counsel had not mentioned the matter in argument,[37] the Tribunal stated that a court-martial proceeding was essential for the execution of hostages and reprisal prisoners.[38]

Except for its reference to "a fair trial before a judicial body," the Tribunal did not specify any minimum standards for the judicial hearing or state what rights the hearing should afford to the potential victims. A fair trial in the sense of an impartial inquiry into the guilt of the accused would be out of the question for the reason that a judicial hearing on reprisals would not be concerned with the guilt of the potential victim but solely with the problem whether the legal prerequisites of legitimate reprisals had been fulfilled. It is unlikely that the potential victim of the reprisal action would have sufficient information at his disposal to challenge the allegations that these prerequisites have been fulfilled. Consequently he would probably need to rely heavily on the fairness of the deliberative body in accepting proof of facts. Admittedly the entire proceeding is subject to grave abuses, but the very need for it may help to increase in some degree the realization of the gravity of exercising reprisals and add to the protection of potential victims.[39]

33 Trial of Wilhelm List and Others, *op. cit.*, pp. 44, 61, 62, 64, 78, 79, 85. See also Waltzog, *Recht der Landkriegsführung* (1941) p. 83, in Trial of Albert Kesselring, War Crimes Reports, Vol. 8 (1949), p. 12.

34 In the Trial of Wilhelm List the United States Military Tribunal suggested numerous procedures before resorting to reprisals against hostages. See Trial of Wilhelm List and Others, *op. cit.*, pp. 61–62.

35 See British Manual, *op. cit.*, p. 85, par. 457.

36 See, for example, the Trial of Gerhard Flesch, *op. cit.*, p. 119, where it is pointed out that the executions of Norwegian citizens without previous trial could not be justified as reprisals.

37 Trial of Wilhelm List and Others, *op. cit.*, p. 85.

38 See *ibid.*, pp. 62, 64–66.

39 Judicial hearings prior to reprisals were appreciated by Hitler for their propaganda value. A document from Hitler's headquarters dated Jan. 9, 1944, points out the im-

II. Operational Conditions

1. *Authority and Responsibility*

One of the propositions in the *Rauter* case, and fundamentally a sound one, although the authorities are on the whole only in tacit agreement, is that the authority to take legal reprisals is peculiar to the state.[40] It would seem to follow that the responsibility for reprisals should lie, at least in the first instance, in exactly the same place. This does not mean, however, that individuals will be absolved of ultimate responsibility for such acts, since it is clear that "rules of warfare, like any other rules of international law, are binding not upon impersonal entities, but upon human beings."[41]

Granted that the legal authority to exercise reprisals and consequently the responsibility for them both lie with the state acting through its representatives, who are the particular representatives of the state who are endowed with this power and responsibility? The American *Rules of Land Warfare* state:

> They [reprisals] should never be employed by individual soldiers except by direct orders of a commander, and the latter should give such orders only after careful inquiry into the alleged offense. The highest accessible military authority should be consulted unless immediate action is demanded as a matter of military necessity, but in the latter event a subordinate commander may order appropriate reprisals upon his own initiative. Hasty or ill-considered action may subsequently be found to have been wholly unjustified, subject the responsible officer himself to punishment as for a violation of the laws of war, and seriously damage his cause. On the other hand, commanding officers must assume responsibility for retaliative measures where an unscrupulous enemy leaves no other recourse against the repetition of barbarous outrages.[42]

In the *Trial of Wilhelm List and Others* it seems to have been argued that reprisals could not be ordered by a commander lower than a division commander, but this argument was opposed by the defense, which pointed out that the American manual permits reprisals, when necessary, by "a

portance of "show trials"; see Major War Criminals Tribunal, Pt. 4 (1946), p. 117. This document also quotes Field Marshall Keitel as saying "I am against legal procedure. It does not work out." In another document it is suggested that commandos against whom Hitler had issued his retaliatory Commando Order should be executed and posthumously tried and sentenced.

[40] Trial of Hans Rauter, *op. cit.*, pp. 132–133.

[41] Lauterpacht, British Year Book of International Law, Vol. 21 (1944), p. 64. See also Trial of Wilhelm List and Others, *op. cit.*, p. 73.

[42] American Rules of Land Warfare, *op. cit.*, p. 89, par. 358(b). The British Manual says briefly: "Although there is no rule of International Law respecting the matter, reprisals should never be resorted to by the individual soldier, but only by order of a commander." See British Manual, *op. cit.*, p. 85, par. 455.

subordinate commander." [43] The language of the American *Rules* refers also to "officers" but does not specify whether this means only commissioned officers or non-commissioned ones as well.[44] A "subordinate commander" or "the highest accessible military authority" in the words of the American *Rules* might be of almost any military rank depending on the circumstances.[45] The point was not clarified in the war crimes trials.[46]

2. *Means of Reprisals*

What instruments may be used to carry out reprisals and at what or at whom may they be directed? The American *Rules of Land Warfare* say: "The acts resorted to by way of reprisal need not conform to those complained of by the injured party. . . . " [47] There is in fact no limit in international law on the choice of instruments of reprisals, and almost every known instrument has been used.[48] The view that reprisals need not conform to the offenses complained of may be said to apply to the objects of reprisals as well as to the instruments used in carrying them out.[49]

The objects of reprisals may be categorized broadly as property and

[43] Trial of Wilhelm List and Others, *op. cit.*, p. 85.

[44] In *In re Kooymans,* cited in the Annual Digest of Public International Law Cases (1946), p. 398, the Dutch Special Court of Cassation mentioned as one of the factors establishing the illegality of a German reprisal measure, that it was authorized only by a non-commissioned officer.

[45] The rejected Russian draft on reprisals which was submitted to the Brussels Conference in 1874 provided quite unmistakably that reprisals should be ordered only by the highest authority: "Reprisals shall be allowed only on the authority of the commander-in-chief, who shall likewise determine the degree of their severity and duration." Sec. 71 of the Russian draft in Westlake, International Law (1913), Vol. II, pp. 123–124.

[46] Under the Barbarossa Jurisdiction Order the Germans were more specific than the Americans and the British about which ranks had the power to order reprisals, but less discretion was left in the hands of the officers. See Trial of the German High Command, War Crimes Reports, Vol. 12 (1949), p. 30. See also Major War Criminals Tribunal, Pt. 11 (1947), p. 20, Pt. 5 (1946), p. 321, and Pt. 6 (1946), p. 141. The order, which provided for collective coercive measures on the order of an officer of the rank of at least battalion commander, also provided, however, that offenses against enemy civilians by members of the Wehrmacht or its auxiliaries should be prosecuted only if the maintenance of discipline or security should so require. See Trial of the German High Command, *op. cit.*, pp. 30–31. Illegal reprisal action by an unauthorized person against an enemy civilian might therefore have gone unpunished.

[47] American Rules of Land Warfare, *op. cit.*, p. 90, par. 358(e). The British Manual says: "What kinds of acts should be resorted to as reprisals is a matter for the consideration of the injured party." See British Manual of Military Law, *op. cit.*, p. 86, par. 459.

[48] In the opinion of one expert the air arm is the most suitable. See Spaight, Air Power and War Rights (1947), p. 49. Although the most inhuman weapons, such as bacteriological warfare, may be banned from general use as reprisals, they may be approved as reprisals in kind. See Oppenheim, *op. cit.*, p. 275.

[49] Trial of Hans Rauter, *op. cit.*, pp. 133–134.

person. Reprisals against property may be destructive [50] or confiscatory.[51] Reprisals directed against the person may range from temporary detention [52] to physical torture [53] and death. The restrictions on reprisals against persons, however, have usually been expressed in terms of the status of the potential object of the reprisals rather than as general prohibitions against the deprivations employed. We shall turn now to a brief examination of these restrictions, which deal chiefly with prisoners of war and hostages.

The most firmly established prohibition against reprisals in international law is the prohibition of reprisals against prisoners of war, which was first enacted in the Geneva Convention of 1929 on Prisoners of War.[54] In the *Dostler* case [55] it was decided that this rule admits of no exception. General Dostler, who was accused of the summary execution of fifteen United States Army personnel captured by his forces, pleaded that the execution was a legitimate reprisal. His argument rested on the decision of the German Supreme Court in the *Dover Castle* case [56] in which it was held that the accused, who pleaded guilty to torpedoing a British hospital ship, was entitled to rely on information supplied by his superiors that the sinking was a legitimate reprisal against illegal enemy attacks on hospital ships in violation of Hague Convention X. The United States Military Commission

50 See Trial of General von Mackensen and General Maelzer, *op. cit.*, p. 5. The destruction of property, often of whole villages, was not an unusual measure of reprisal by the Germans in the second World War. See, for example, the German High Command Trial, *op. cit.*, p. 20, and the Trial of Wilhelm List and Others, *op. cit.*, p. 38. Furthermore, the Germans engaged in a special type of reprisal against property which became known as the "Baedeker Raids." The "Baedeker Raids" were air attacks upon landmarks, palaces, cathedrals, museums, and other places of cultural, historical, or artistic importance. For authority opposed to the destruction of property as reprisals, see Trial of Hans Szabados, *op. cit.*, p. 61, and the Trial of Franz Holstein and Others, *op. cit.*, p. 30.

51 According to the American Rules, "Collective punishments may be inflicted either in the form of fines or otherwise." See American Rules of Land Warfare, *op. cit.*, p. 90, par. 358(e). As a result of a general order by Hitler, a decree was issued by Göring on Aug. 14, 1943, which provided that in retaliation for Allied raids on Germany, enemy property in occupied areas would be seized to replace the house furnishings of Germans which were destroyed in the raids. Trial of Hans Rauter, *op. cit.*, p. 99; also *ibid.*, p. 101.

52 See Trial of Hans Rauter, *op. cit.*, pp. 91–92; also p. 103.

53 See Trial of Richard Bruns, War Crimes Reports, Vol. 3 (1948), p. 15.

54 Art. 2, Sec. 3, of the convention says: "Measures of reprisals against them are forbidden." The Geneva Convention of 1949 on Prisoners of War contains a similar provision. Art. 13, Sec. 3, thereof says: "Measures of reprisal against prisoners of war are prohibited." The above discussion will not treat the Geneva Conventions of 1949, since they are discussed separately, *infra*, at pp. 607 ff.

55 The Dostler Case, War Crimes Reports, Vol. 1 (1947), p. 22.

56 Annual Digest of Public International Law Cases (1922–24), Case No. 231.

in Rome overruled this argument on the ground that the Geneva Convention of 1929 made all reprisals against prisoners of war illegitimate.[57]

The protection of prisoners of war from reprisals extends to prohibition of torturing,[58] making them hostages,[59] harming their families,[60] or of taking any other measure of reprisal against them. It has been stated that quarter may be denied to enemy troops as reprisal for refusal of quarter by the other side, and this raises the difficult question of when troops who seek to surrender are to be considered prisoners of war.[61] There is no doubt that refusal of quarter, like any other reprisal, would be illegal after the troops can be said to have become prisoners of war. It is submitted that this category should be extended as far as possible to include surrendering troops in order to prevent the reprisal slaughter of helpless soldiers on the ground that they are not protected by the Convention on Prisoners of War.[62]

As contrasted with the status of prisoners of war, the status of hostages in connection with reprisals is unclear. Both the American and British military rules recognize that hostages may be taken and held to insure against illegal acts by the enemy.[63] The American *Rules of Land Warfare* also provide that hostages must be treated like prisoners of war, which would ban reprisals against them.[64] On the other hand the American *Rules* state that

> [h]ostages taken and held for the declared purpose of insuring against unlawful acts by the enemy forces or people may be punished or put to death if the unlawful acts are nevertheless committed.[65]

The confusion about hostages is by no means restricted to the American *Rules*. "Putting hostages to death" was the second item on the list of war crimes drawn up by the Commission on Responsibilities at the Paris Conference following the first World War for the purpose of the future classification of the laws of war.[66] At the end of the second World War

57 The Dostler Case, *op. cit.*, p. 31. See also the Trial of Gerhard Flesch, *op. cit.*, and *infra*, p. 607.

58 Trial of Richard Bruns, *op. cit.*, p. 22.

59 Major War Criminals Tribunal, Pt. 5 (1946), p. 128.

60 *Ibid.*, pp. 145 ff., 316–317.

61 See Trial of Generaloberst Nicholaus von Falkenhorst, War Crimes Reports, Vol. 11 (1949), p. 30.

62 For a discussion of the legal status, as regards reprisals, of prisoners other than prisoners of war who are protected by the Geneva Convention, see Trial of Karl Buck, War Crimes Reports, Vol. 5 (1948), p. 42, and Trial of Carl Bauer, *op. cit.*

63 See American Rules of Land Warfare, *op. cit.*, p. 89, par. 358(d), and British Manual of Military Law, *op. cit.*, pp. 86–87, pars. 461–464.

64 American Rules of Land Warfare, *op. cit.*, p. 90, par. 359, and p. 18, par. 76(h). Compare the British Manual of Military Law, *op. cit.*, p. 86, par. 461. See also Trial of Wilhelm List and Others, *op. cit.*, p. 82.

65 American Rules of Land Warfare, pp. 89–90, par. 358(d).

66 History of the United Nations War Crimes Commission, *op. cit.*, p. 34.

the killing of hostages was officially condemned as a war crime by Article 6(b) of the Charter of the International Military Tribunal at Nuremberg, Article 5(b) of the Charter of the International Military Tribunal for the Far East, and Article II(b) of Control Council (for Germany) Law No. 10. At the same time the practice was still recognized as legally valid in war manuals and by expert opinion.[67]

The defense in the *List* case tried to explain the provision against killing hostages in the Charter of the Tribunal and Control Council Law No. 10 by maintaining that it was directed only at certain kinds of hostages, that is, hostages in the old sense of prisoners held as a guarantee for the observance of treaties or other agreements or as security for requisitions, but not hostages taken in occupied territory to ensure the observance of good order in such territory.[68] The prosecution replied with considerable force "that it was inconceivable that, since thousands of hostages were executed in reprisals for hostile acts during the last two wars, this was not precisely the practice which the Charter and the Control Council Law condemned." [69]

It is submitted that the most plausible view under the circumstances would be to regard the effect of the provisions in the Charter and the Control Council Law as expressing a general rule of warfare, which, like other rules of warfare, is without prejudice to the question of reprisals.[70] The prohibition against killing hostages has nothing to do with reprisals; it simply means that persons taken as hostages may not summarily be killed. If reprisals enter the picture, then, provided all the prerequisites are satisfied, the hostages may be subject to reprisals. Here it is reprisal law which must take precedence over hostage law.[71] The decisions of the war

[67] Oppenheim, International Law, Vol. II (6th ed., 1940), pp. 449–450, 461, and Hammer and Salvin, this JOURNAL, Vol. 38 (1944), p. 33. Compare Wright, British Year Book of International Law, Vol. 25 (1948), p. 298, and Oppenheim, International Law, Vol. II (7th ed., 1952), pp. 564–565 589 ff.

[68] Trial of Wilhelm List and Others, *op. cit.*, p. 83. As applied to the American Rules, the argument of the defense was that the requirement that hostages be treated as prisoners of war applied only to the type of hostages mentioned in par. 359 of the Rules, where that requirement is stated, but not to the practice of taking hostages in occupied lands to force the inhabitants to abide by international law.

[69] Trial of Wilhelm List, *op. cit.*, p. 83.

[70] As applied to the American Rules, this theory is that the requirement that a hostage be treated as a prisoner of war must be applied to all types of hostages, but only as a standard of general treatment without prejudice to reprisals. When the right to reprisals arises, the hostages may then be subjected to them by virtue of the specific provision of par. 358(d).

[71] This result is supported by the wording of the provisions in the Charter of the International Military Tribunal, and in Control Council Law No. 10. These define war crimes as follows: "War Crimes: namely, violations of the laws or customs of war. Such violations shall include, but not be limited to, murder, ill-treatment or deportation to slave labor or for any other purpose of civilian populations of or in occupied territory, murder or ill-treatment of prisoners of war, or persons on the seas, killing of hostages, plunder of public or private property, wanton destruction of cities, towns, or

crimes trials on the question of hostages may be fitted into this rationale, although they do not advance it.[72]

3. *Requirement of a Connection between the Victim of the Reprisal and the Illegal Act*

There is a general principle that there should, wherever possible, be some connection between the victims of reprisals and the illegal act which has given rise to the reprisals. A connection, however, cannot arbitrarily be assumed to exist.[73] For the purpose of reprisals against the inhabitants of occupied territories, one relationship which has been stressed is that the victims of the reprisals should be selected from the same geographical area where the illegal act occurred. Without such a connection, it has been argued, reprisals would lose their deterrent effect on the community where the offense was committed.[74] This argument assumes that the perpetrators of the illegal act come from the area where the act was committed, which may often be the case. On the other hand, in cases where the perpetrators of the illegal act do not come from the area where the act occurred, that argument would be inapplicable.[75] Nevertheless the area where the illegal

villages, or devastation not justified by military necessity.'' See Art. 6(b) of the Charter and Art. II(b) of Control Council Law No. 10. It will be noted that except for the reference to prisoners of war, all the above-listed crimes are ordinary war crimes which are subject to the exception of reprisals. There seems to be no good legal reason for making the prohibition of a crime equivalent to prohibition of the universally recognized exception of reprisals. This is not done in the case of other war crimes. Why should it be done in the case of killing hostages.

72 The decisions in the trials clearly do not adopt the prohibition against killing hostages. See Trial of Wilhelm List and Others, *op. cit.*, p. 61. Further on the Tribunal specified the conditions under which hostages may be taken and the pre-conditions for their legal execution. See *ibid.*, pp. 61, 62. The tribunal also distinguished between reprisal prisoners and hostages. See *ibid.*, pp. 61, 79. Some doubt about the List decision may be implied from the decision in the Trial of the German High Command. See Trial of the German High Command, *op. cit.*, pp. 84–85. Note also the cautious statement of the Judge Advocate in the Trial of Albert Kesserling, *op. cit.*, pp. 12, 13. A different view on hostages may be found in the Rauter case based upon the theories of that case which have already been discussed. See Trial of Hans Rauter, *op. cit.*, pp. 137–138. Compare the Trial of Hans Szabados, *op. cit.*, p. 60, and the Trial of Franz Holstein, *op. cit.*, p. 22.

73 See Trial of Wilhelm List and Others, *op. cit.*, p. 46. For other examples of arbitrary assumptions about the connection between the alleged act and the victims, see Trial of Hans Rauter, *op. cit.*, pp. 101–102, and the Trial of General von Mackensen and General Maelzer, *op. cit.*, p. 2.

74 Trial of Wilhelm List and Others, *op. cit.*, pp. 64, 66, 48. See the Barbarossa Jurisdiction Order, Art. 1, Sec. 4, in the Trial of the German High Command, *op. cit.*, p. 30. This provides for collective measures ''against localities from which troops have been attacked in a treacherous or deceitful manner.''

75 See the submission by Professor Bonfils in the Trial of Wilhelm List and Others, *op. cit.*, p. 84.

act occurred may be the only link which can be established between the act and the reprisal victims.[76]

4. *Requirement of Proportionality in Reprisals*

There must be quantitative as well as qualitative limits on reprisals, but what are they? Both the American *Rules of Land Warfare* and the British *Manual of Military Law* provide that reprisals must not be excessive or exceed the degree of violation committed by the enemy.[77] There is a clear decision on what constitutes excessive reprisals in the *Trial of Wilhelm List and Others.* On September 16, 1941, Field Marshal Keitel, Chief of the High Command of the Armed Forces, issued an order containing the following directive:

> In such a case [opposition to the German authorities in occupied countries] the death penalty for 50 to 100 communists must be in general deemed appropriate as retaliation for the life of a German soldier.[78]

The judgment in the *List* case condemned the reprisals taken under the authority of the Keitel order as "clearly excessive."[79] Nevertheless, the wording of the judgment in the *List* case seems to be open to the view that certain circumstances might justify reprisals exceeding the damage inflicted by the original offense.[80] The Tribunal declared, however, that

[76] The problem of establishing a connection between the victim of reprisals and the illegal act giving rise to the reprisals has sometimes been discussed by reference to Art. 50 of the Hague Regulations despite the fact that Art. 50 was intended to be inapplicable to reprisals (*supra,* note 6). See the Einsatzgruppen Case, Trial of War Criminals, Vol. 4 (1949), pp. 493–494. Thus American and British military rules confirm that Art. 50 was intended to have no application to reprisals. See the American Rules of Land Warfare, *op. cit.,* p. 86, par. 344, and the British Manual of Military Law, *op. cit.,* p. 85, note 2. Note the discussion of this point in the "Notes" to the Trial of Wilhelm List, *op. cit.,* p. 88.

[77] See American Rules of Land Warfare, *op. cit.,* p. 90, par. 358(e), and British Manual of Military Law, *op. cit.,* p. 86, par. 459.

[78] Trial of Wilhelm List and Others, *op. cit.,* p. 39. General Keitel's testimony in the German High Command Trial indicated that when the above orders were first drawn up the ratios were 5–10 to one, but that Hitler changed the numbers from 5–10 to 50–100. Trial of the German High Command, *op. cit.,* p. 39. See also the orders of General Boehme, *ibid.,* of General Kuntze, *ibid.,* p. 41, and of General Rendulic, *ibid.,* p. 44.

[79] Trial of Wilhelm List and Others, *op. cit.,* p. 65.

[80] See Trial of Wilhelm List and Others, *op. cit.,* p. 65. In the Trial of Hans Rauter, according to the "Notes on the Case," the Netherlands Special Court "found that by killing several hostages at a time for the death of one member of the German authorities, he [General Rauter] had committed excessive reprisals in violation of the rule requiring due proportion." Trial of Hans Rauter, *op. cit.,* p. 131. See also *ibid.,* p. 103. This finding, which seems to be based upon the requirement of a numerical equivalency between the reprisal and the offense, was not adopted by the Netherlands Special Court of Cassation in its review of the case, since the latter court concluded

any fixed ratio for the general application of automatic reprisals was unlawful:

> An order to take reprisals at an arbitrarily fixed ratio under any and all circumstances constitutes a violation of International Law.[81]

It is difficult to draw a satisfactory rule from these authorities on how to fix the quantitative limits of reprisals. The difficulty is increased where the reprisals cannot be measured in the same terms as the offense. No rules have been suggested for quantitative limits on reprisals against property for offenses against the person or for limits on reprisals against the person for offenses against property. An example of the former is the reprisal system described in the *Trial of Franz Holstein,* according to which the Germans would burn down three farms for every German soldier who was killed and one farm for every German soldier wounded.[82] An example of the latter is the reprisal order of General Lanz in Greece:

> On account of the repeated cable sabotage in the area of Arta: 30 distinguished citizens (Greeks) from Arta, 10 distinguished citizens (Greeks) from Filipias, are to be arrested and kept as hostages. The population is to be notified that for every further cable sabotage 10 of these 40 hostages will be shot to death.[83]

Perhaps at least the following rule should be adopted: When an offense has been committed against property and no injury to life or limb can be traced directly to such offense, then reprisals should be limited to property and not take the form of bodily harm.

5. *Requirements of Publication of the Execution of Reprisals*

The fact that one of the main objects of reprisals is deterrence from the repetition of illegal acts makes it essential that the reprisals be publicized if they are to be regarded as legitimate. So it was held in the *Trial of Richard Bruns:*

> Reprisals were generally understood to aim at changing the adversary's conduct and forcing him to keep to the generally accepted rules of

that the reprisals were illegal on different grounds. In the Trial of General von Mackensen and General Maelzer and the Trial of Albert Kesselring the question was presented whether it was excessive to execute ten Italians for every German who was killed in the Rosella Street explosion. The defense argued that this ratio "was not excessive in view of the extremely dangerous situation, as Rome was only a few miles from the front line." (Trial of General von Mackensen and General Maelzer, *op. cit.*, p. 6.) Although von Mackensen, Maelzer, and Kesselring were convicted, it is not certain whether the courts reached their conclusion on the ground that the reprisal ratio was excessive. *Ibid.*, p. 7.

81 See Trial of Wilhelm List and Others, p. 47.

82 Trial of Franz Holstein, *op. cit.*, p. 23.

83 Trial of Wilhelm List and Others, *op. cit.*, p. 48.

> lawful warfare. If this aim were to be achieved, the reprisals must be made public and announced as such.[84]

In the *Trial of Hans Rauter* the two Netherlands courts which expressed opinions in the case both pointed out, in answer to the argument of the accused that his actions were justified as reprisals for violations of the Netherlands capitulation agreement, that the Germans had never made the agreement public or publicly sought to justify their actions by it, and so could not now be heard to say that they were relying upon it.[85] It was also held that public announcements on reprisals must be truthful.[86]

THE GENEVA CONVENTIONS OF 1949

On August 12, 1949, four conventions were signed at Geneva which introduced significant changes in the law of war reprisals.[87] The four conventions are: Convention relative to the Treatment of Prisoners of War, Convention for the Amelioration of the Condition of the Wounded and Sick in Armed Forces in the Field, Convention for the Amelioration of the Condition of the Wounded, Sick and Shipwrecked Members of Armed Forces at Sea, and Convention relative to the Protection of Civilian Persons in Time of War.

I. THE GENEVA CONVENTION OF 1949 ON THE TREATMENT OF PRISONERS OF WAR

The Geneva Convention of 1949 on the Treatment of Prisoners of War,[88] is a revision of the 1929 convention of the same name,[89] and its provision on reprisals is practically identical to the one in the earlier agreement.[90] At the Conference of Government Experts for the Study of the Conventions for the Protection of War Victims, which took place at Geneva in 1947, it was urged that this provision of the Convention of 1929 should be retained. The report said:

> The Commission recommended that this Section should be kept in its present form.

[84] Trial of Richard Bruns, *op. cit.*, p. 22; see also p. 19. The Norwegian Lagmannsrett expressed the same opinion in the Trial of Gerhard Flesch. See Trial of Gerhard Flesch, *op. cit.*, p. 115.

[85] *Op. cit.*, p. 125. [86] *Ibid.*, p. 104.

[87] For a general discussion of the conventions, see Gutteridge, British Year Book of International Law, Vol. 26 (1949), p. 294; De La Pradelle, *Les Nouvelles Conventions de Genève* (1951); Pictet, this JOURNAL, Vol. 45 (1951), p. 462; Yingling and Ginnane, *ibid.*, Vol. 46 (1952), p. 393. See footnote 1 above.

[88] Cmd. 8033; Dept. of State Publication 3938, p. 84; Supplement to this JOURNAL, p. 119.

[89] U. S. Treaty Series, No. 846; Cmd. 3941; this JOURNAL, Supp., Vol. 27 (1933), p. 59.

[90] Art. 2, Sec. 3 of the Convention of 1929 provided: "Measures of reprisal against them are forbidden." Pt. II, Art. 13, Sec. 3 of the Convention of 1949 provides: "Measures of reprisal against prisoners of war are prohibited."

> When this principle was inserted in 1929, it was argued that in case of illegal acts connected with treatment of PW, reprisals or threats of reprisal were one of the only means of returning to normal state of affairs. This argument was finally rejected, in view of the impossibility of admitting that unoffending and defenceless men should be held indirectly responsible for acts committed by their home Governments.
>
> The Commission shared this view, some delegations even recognized, on the grounds of their experience, that reprisals were useless in relation with PW treatment. The proposal made to list in this section certain forms of reprisal, such as handcuffing, holding up of mail, and so forth was not entertained, the present wording appearing adequate to prevent any kind of reprisals on any sort of pretext.[91]

It should be noted that although the Convention of 1949 contains substantially the same provision as the 1929 Convention, the 1949 Convention has the effect of prohibiting reprisals against a larger group because of its extension of the definition of "prisoners of war."[92]

II. THE GENEVA CONVENTION OF 1949 FOR THE AMELIORATION OF THE CONDITION OF THE WOUNDED AND SICK IN ARMED FORCES IN THE FIELD

The Geneva Convention of 1949 for the Amelioration of the Condition of the Wounded and Sick in Armed Forces in the Field[93] is a revision of the Geneva Convention of 1929 for the Relief of the Wounded and Sick of Armies in the Field.[94] The 1929 Convention contained no provision on reprisals. In 1947 the Conference of Government Experts at Geneva recommended that a prohibition of reprisals be included in the revision of the convention, a suggestion which had been made by an earlier conference in 1937.[95] As a result Chapter VIII, Article 46, of the convention provided:

> Reprisals against the wounded, sick, personnel, buildings or equipment, protected by the Convention are prohibited.

Under Article 13 of the convention the protected persons are defined as wounded and sick who belong to substantially the same categories specified

91 Report on the Work of the Conference of Government Experts for the Study of the Conventions for the Protection of War Victims (1947), p. 118.

92 For the definition in the 1929 Convention, see Art. I thereof, which refers to the three articles of the Hague Convention of 1907. The definition in the 1949 Convention is in Art. 4 thereof.

93 Cmd. 8033; Dept. of State Publication 3938, p. 25.

94 U. S. Treaty Series, No. 847; Cmd. 3940; this JOURNAL, Supp., Vol. 27 (1933), p. 43.

95 See Report on the Work of the Conference of Government Experts for the Study of the Conventions for the Protection of War Victims (1947), p. 59, and Report on the Work of the Preliminary Conference of National Red Cross Societies for the Study of the Conventions (1947), pp. 51–52. See also "Projets de Conventions Revisées ou Nouvelles Protégeant les Victimes de la Guerre," 17th International Conference of the Red Cross (1948), p. 24.

in Article 4A of the 1949 Convention on the Treatment of Prisoners of War.[96]

III. THE GENEVA CONVENTION OF 1949 FOR THE AMELIORATION OF THE CONDITION OF THE WOUNDED, SICK AND SHIPWRECKED MEMBERS OF ARMED FORCES AT SEA

The Geneva Convention of 1949 for the Amelioration of the Condition of the Wounded, Sick and Shipwrecked Members of Armed Forces at Sea[97] is a revision of the Tenth Hague Convention for the Adaptation to Maritime Warfare of the Principles of the Geneva Convention of 1906.[98] Neither the Tenth Hague Convention nor the Geneva Convention of 1906 had any provisions on reprisals. A provision on reprisals was suggested at the 17th International Conference of the Red Cross in 1948.[99] Chapter VII, Article 47, of the 1949 Convention now provides:

> Reprisals against the wounded, sick and shipwrecked persons, the personnel, the vessels or the equipment protected by the Convention are prohibited.

Article 13, where the protected persons are defined, like Article 13 of the Convention for the Amelioration of the Condition of the Wounded and Sick in Armed Forces in the Field, covers substantially the same categories of persons specified in Article 4A of the 1949 Convention on the Treatment of Prisoners of War.

IV. THE GENEVA CONVENTION OF 1949 RELATIVE TO THE PROTECTION OF CIVILIAN PERSONS IN TIME OF WAR

The fourth convention dealing with the law of war reprisals is the Geneva Convention of 1949 relative to the Protection of Civilian Persons in Time of War.[100] As early as 1934 the International Committee of the Red Cross in its Tokyo Draft had begun to suggest limitations on the right to exercise reprisals and take hostages.[101] In 1946 the Preliminary Conference of National Red Cross Societies meeting in Geneva reviewed the Tokyo Draft and endorsed the prohibition of all reprisals and collective punishments against civilian persons in occupied territory.[102] In 1947

96 See Final Record of the Diplomatic Conference of Geneva of 1949, Vol. II, p. 199.

97 Cmd. 8033; Dept. of State Publication 3938, p. 55.

98 Tenth Hague Convention, Cmd. 4175, this JOURNAL, Supp., Vol. 2 (1908), p. 153; Convention of 1906, Cmd. 3502, this JOURNAL, Supp., Vol. 1 (1907), p. 201.

99 See "Projets de Conventions Revisées ou Nouvelles Protégeant les Victimes de la Guerre," 17th International Conference of the Red Cross (1948), pp. 46–47.

100 Cmd. 8033; Dept. of State Publication 3938, p. 163.

101 Report of the Conference of Government Experts for the Study of Conventions for the Protection of War Victims, Vol. III (1947), p. 9.

102 Report on the Work of the Preliminary Conference of National Red Cross Societies for the Study of the Conventions and Various Problems Relative to the Red Cross, Geneva, July 26–August 3, 1946 (1947), p. 96.

the Conference of Government Experts in dealing with the problem of the protection of civilians in time of war agreed with the recommendations of the International Committee of the Red Cross that measures of reprisal and the taking of hostages should be prohibited.[103] The next step was the 17th International Conference of the Red Cross in Stockholm, where a Draft Convention for the Protection of Civilian Persons in Time of War was drawn up embodying these proposals.

The final product of this series of international conferences, stretching over many years, was the Geneva Convention of 1949 relative to the Protection of Civilian Persons in Time of War, which provides in Part III, Section I, entitled "Provisions Common to the Territories of the Parties to the Conflict and to Occupied Territories," that:

> Article 33:
>
> No protected person may be punished for an offence he or she has not personally committed. Collective penalties and likewise all measures of intimidation or of terrorism are prohibited.
>
> Pillage is prohibited.
>
> Reprisals against protected persons and their property are prohibited.
>
> Article 34:
>
> The taking of hostages is prohibited.[104]

V. THE SCOPE OF THE CONVENTIONS

These four conventions constitute a significant step in the development of the law of war reprisals, for not only do they extend legal protection against reprisals, but what is perhaps even more important, they represent the first attempt in two decades to continue from the small beginning made in the Convention on the Treatment of Prisoners of War in 1929 to clarify the law on war reprisals through international agreement, and by means of outlawing rather than attempting to regulate the practice. The conventions thus raise two chief questions: first, regarding their scope, and second, regarding the precise effect of their attempt to abolish reprisals insofar as they are applicable.

It cannot be said that the three conventions on prisoners of war and the wounded, sick and shipwrecked members of the armed forces mark

103 Report on the Work of the Conference of Government Experts for the Study of the Conventions for the Protection of War Victims (1947), pp. 275–276. See also Annex D on Regulations relative to Civilian War Internees (CWI), Art. 2.

104 "Protected persons" are defined in Art. 4. Art. 13 of Pt. II provides: "The provisions of Part II cover the whole of the populations of the countries in conflict, without any adverse distinction based, in particular, on race, nationality, religion or political opinion, and are intended to alleviate the sufferings caused by war."

any far-reaching extension of the prohibition of reprisals. The Convention of 1949 on the Treatment of Prisoners of War merely repeats the provision on reprisals in the Convention of 1929 and enlarges the definition of prisoners of war. The Conventions of 1949 for the Amelioration of the Condition of the Wounded and Sick in Armed Forces in the Field and of the Wounded, Sick and Shipwrecked Members of Armed Forces at Sea broaden this prohibition of reprisals to include members of the armed forces, who, although they are not prisoners of war, are, like them, helpless and exposed to the enemy.

On the other hand, the effect of the Convention on the Protection of Civilian Persons in Time of War is to outlaw some of the most important forms of reprisals which have been used up to this time, including those forms of reprisals for which rules of control were so laboriously formulated in the war crimes trials. With the exception of the population of non-adhering states and of neutral and co-belligerent states maintaining diplomatic representation with the state in control of the potential victim, every person in territories of the parties to the conflict or in occupied territories who, in case of conflict or occupation, finds himself in the hands of a Power other than his own, is legally immunized from reprisals both as to his person and his property.

By no means, however, does the convention abolish all forms of reprisals against civilian persons. First, it applies only to "Territories of the Parties to the Conflict and to Occupied Territories" but not to the open sea. The possession of the nationality of the Power in control of the potential victim deprives the latter of his status as a "protected person." Furthermore, the limitation of the exemption to those who are "in the hands of" a Power not his own, however broadly interpreted, leaves wide scope for the variety of reprisals which are not dependent on physical control over the potential victim, but can be carried out from great distances through all the devices of modern technological warfare.[105]

VI. THE EFFECT OF THE CONVENTIONS

The next question is the effect of their prohibition of reprisals within the area which they cover. It is to be noted that the language of all four provisions on reprisals is practically identical. They say that "reprisals" or "measures of reprisal" are "prohibited." What is the precise meaning of this proscription? Is it merely another rule in the international

[105] An additional point about the applicability of the Convention on Civilian Persons arose at the Geneva Conference in connection with state property. The Soviet delegate felt that state property should be protected against reprisals, but the American delegate believed that this would open the way to abuses. See Art. 30 of the Draft Convention for the Protection of Civilian Persons in Time of War as Amended and Approved by the 17th International Red Cross Conference, and Final Record of the Diplomatic Conference of Geneva of 1949, Vol. II (1949), pp. 648–651.

law of warfare which is itself open to exception by way of reprisals or does it ban reprisals altogether insofar as it applies? It is clear that the former interpretation renders the provision completely futile and cannot have been intended. To say that a rule prohibiting reprisals is open to exception by way of reprisals is simply to repeat the existing law, a result which was obviously not what the drafters of the conventions had in mind.

It might be argued that the prohibition of reprisals applies only to the use of the specified types of reprisals against general violations of the laws of war, but that when another Power violates the prohibition itself by doing the specifically forbidden acts, then this justifies reprisals in kind. It is submitted that this view is also untenable. Not only does a literal reading of the prohibitions leave no room for exceptions, but the history of the provisions also shows that their object was to prevent reprisals against the enumerated categories of persons and property under all conditions.[106] Furthermore, it was held in the *Dostler* case that the Geneva Convention of 1929 made all reprisals against prisoners of war illegitimate, even when they were alleged to be reprisals in kind.[107] The slight difference in the wording of the Convention of 1929, which stated that reprisals were "forbidden" rather than "prohibited," would not afford any basis for distinction between it and the Convention of 1949. Consequently the Conventions of 1949 must be held to admit of no exception by way of reprisals.

CONCLUSION

The development of the law of war reprisals in the war crimes trials illustrates the very great difficulty involved in attempting to formulate and apply rules which will permit the successful use, but not the abuse, of reprisals in warfare. Even apart from the few rules which may not be entirely sound, the general body of law on war reprisals evolved from the trials provides no more than a rough check against the obvious excesses perpetrated in the name of reprisals. Furthermore, it seems that this must necessarily be so, due to the flexible manner in which most of the rules must be stated in order that they may be applicable in widely varying and unforeseeable types of situations. The resulting uncertainty is far from beneficial to the object of maintaining minimum standards of conduct in war.

It cannot be immediately concluded, however, that the complete prohibition of reprisals is the logical solution to the problem. Despite the fact that they are subject to abuse, war reprisals may perform an extremely valuable function. How successfully they do so on the whole, it is un-

106 See *supra*, footnote 91 and text concerning the Convention of 1949 on the Treatment of Prisoners of War. Note the similar wording of the other 1949 conventions.

107 See *supra*, p. 601.

fortunately impossible to say. Nevertheless, the basic hypothesis of the theory that war reprisals should be completely outlawed, namely, that in general they are more a threat than a protection to the laws of war, cannot be maintained with certainty. Indeed, it is questionable whether would-be violators of the laws of war are likely to be deterred by the removal of the legal justification for their acts which the doctrine of reprisals may seem heretofore to have supplied. The greatest abuses in connection with reprisals have been caused by deliberate disregard for the law rather than by legitimate doubts about what the law would permit and what it would forbid. Thus it may fairly be asked whether the prohibition of reprisals, rather than their use, does not to some extent weaken the efficacy of the laws of war by relieving potential war criminals from the fear of reprisals, although in no way diminishing the likelihood that they themselves will commit violations of the laws of war.

It is true that if reprisals were prohibited, the prospect of eventual retribution by trial and punishment might deter some who would otherwise seek to use the law of reprisals as a legal excuse for their misdeeds. Only in this measure, and it is speculative, would the prohibition of reprisals serve as a real deterrent to violation of the laws of war. But the rules regulating reprisals also provide a deterrent, not only through trial and punishment of war criminals, but by prompt retaliation during the course of conflict, when retaliation or the threat of retaliation is likely to be more effective, since it can be almost immediate and is not dependent upon the many contingencies involved in the trial and punishment of war criminals. In short, while the law would be clearer if reprisals were prohibited, there is good reason to believe that it would also be much less effective in fulfilling its function of providing minimum standards of conduct in war.

On the other hand, it cannot be concluded that there should be no prohibitions on the use of reprisals. By banning certain kinds of reprisals and yet allowing others, it is possible to establish clear and inviolable standards of protection for selected categories of war victims without taking the risky step of abandoning the protection afforded by reprisals. It would seem to be a desirable policy to prohibit reprisals in as many cases as feasible without endangering the effective use of reprisals as a sanction against violations of the rules of war.

The major question is how to decide which reprisals to prohibit and which to allow. To prohibit a particular kind of reprisal is to renounce the sanction of such an act against violations of the laws of war. Thus prohibition of a particular form of reprisal should be based on the decision that (1) the reprisal is unlikely to have any deterrent effect upon the enemy and so may be dispensed with, or (2) regardless of the efficacy of the reprisal, it can be dispensed with because other reprisals may be relied upon to produce the requisite deterrent effect, especially when the reprisal in question is particularly offensive to humane principles. It should be noted that, however inhuman they may seem, certain forms of reprisals may have to be reserved to meet the threat of various kinds of violations of the laws of war against which other reprisals are inadequate.

It is by these standards that the prohibitions of reprisals in the Geneva Conventions of 1949 should be judged. The prohibitions of reprisals against prisoners of war and wounded, sick, and shipwrecked members of armed forces are desirable because they afford increased legal protection to these classes of war victims without interfering with the general function of war reprisals. Experience has demonstrated that reprisals against prisoners of war are by no means indispensable and there is no reason to believe that the case is different for wounded, sick, and shipwrecked members of armed forces. The prohibition of reprisals against "protected persons" in the Convention on Civilian Persons, however, is of more doubtful merit. In prohibiting almost all reprisals against civilian persons in occupied areas, it could create grave difficulties for an occupying Power. Under circumstances of widespread and active resistance, an occupant may find the prohibition almost impossible to observe, for reprisals or the threat of reprisals against the local civilian population may be a vital measure in maintaining order among a hostile civilian population. The resort to reprisals against civilians by the British forces during the current war in Malaya,[108] despite Great Britain's signature of the Geneva Convention, affords powerful evidence of the compelling need to use such reprisals at least to a limited degree in certain types of situations. For this reason it is suggested that the blanket abolition of reprisals in the Geneva Convention on Civilian Persons may need to be reconsidered and that the rules which were developed in the war crimes trials may be useful in establishing a sounder basis for the regulation of war reprisals against civilians.

108 See Parliamentary Debates (Hansard), Vol. 499 (1951–1952), pp. 1453–1455; Vol. 501 (1951–1952), pp. 1345–1347. Concerning collective punishments in Kenya, see *ibid.*, Vol. 501, pp. 1340–1341; Vol. 508 (1952–1953), pp. 1554, 53–54 (written answers).

[2]

BELLIGERENT REPRISALS REVISITED

F. Kalshoven**

1. INTRODUCTION

The international law of armed conflict aims to regulate the conduct of hostilities by belligerent parties and their armed forces and to protect certain especially vulnerable categories of people, such as prisoners of war and the inhabitants of occupied territories. How effective can it be in this pretension, and what mechanisms are available to promote compliance?

In common with most other branches of public international law, the law of armed conflict lacks community institutions of the type normally found in

** Professor of International Humanitarian Law (ret.). The author wishes to thank Professor George H. Aldrich for reading and commenting on an earlier version of the present paper.

systems of municipal law to ensure respect of the law. Yet it has never been devoid of all means to promote compliance either: e.g., State responsibility as well as individual liability for war crimes, supervision by outside powers, and obviously, dissemination of knowledge of the law.

This paper examines one classic device, available to the parties to the conflict themselves and recognized since time immemorial as an institution of customary international law. It is the belligerent reprisal, i.e., an act in breach of a rule of the law of armed conflict, directed by one belligerent party against the other with a view to inducing the latter party to stop violating that or another rule of this branch of international law (reprisal in kind or not in kind, respectively).[1]

While belligerent reprisals were never entirely free of controversy, the very idea of recourse to such draconian measures over time became exposed to ever louder criticism. The main grounds for such criticism were that they were rarely effective, apt to affect persons who could not be held accountable for the other party's violation of the law, and tended to set in motion a spiral of reciprocal reactions resulting in an escalation of violence in complete disregard of the law.

The criticism was not shared in all quarters. Yet it was sufficiently strong to lead to the introduction in an ever growing number of treaties on the law of armed conflict, of provisions outlawing reprisals against specified categories of persons or objects protected by those treaties. The parties to an armed conflict governed by these treaties thus saw themselves deprived of the means of enforcement that the reprisal in breach of the specific rules embodied in the treaties (and more often than not in response to a violation of the same rules) purported to be. At the same time, other mechanisms were introduced, such as outside supervision, and it was hoped that these could take over the role of the banned reprisal.

Not all belligerent reprisals were so prohibited. And apart from this, the debate continued unabated: were belligerent reprisals really as bad as they were depicted, and were they not perhaps indispensable after all? In the 1970s, when along with other major parts of the law of armed conflict, the rules for the protection of the civilian population against the effects of hostilities were brought up for revision, the debate gained fresh impetus.[2]

1. This is a mere working definition. For a fuller discussion of the concept and a definition of reprisal, see F. Kalshoven, *Belligerent Reprisals* (1971) Chapter I (pp. 1-44).

2. See the articles by the present author in this *Yearbook*: 2 (1971) pp. 68-90, 3 (1972) pp. 18-61, 5 (1974) pp. 3-34, 8 (1977) pp. 107-135, 9 (1978) pp. 107-171.

In 1971, at a time when the process of 'reaffirmation and development' of the law of armed conflict was in its initial stages, this author happened to publish a book on 'Belligerent Reprisals'[3] that may have exerted some influence on subsequent events. In view of the continuing topicality of the subject he now ventures to return to it, in an attempt to clarify the present state of affairs and the prospects of reprisals as a means of enforcement in the international law of armed conflict.[4]

Chapter 2 provides a short history of the existing conventional prohibitions on recourse to reprisals in international armed conflicts. Chapter 3 enters into the debate around those prohibitions specifically designed to protect the civilian population in non-occupied territory. Chapter 4 explores some areas where reprisals at first sight have remained permissible. Chapter 5 discusses some specific problems attending the notion of reprisals in internal armed conflicts. Finally, and by way of conclusion, the author sets forth his views on possible trends in development. One thing he hopes will become clear, and that is that the question of belligerent reprisals has always been, and still is, less simple than it may seem.

2. SHORT HISTORY OF PROHIBITIONS IN FORCE

The first conventional prohibition on a specific case of recourse to reprisals dates back to 1929. In that year, a Diplomatic Conference[5] met in Geneva to draft two conventions, one being a revision of the 1906 Wounded and Sick Convention[6] and the other a new Prisoners of War Convention.[7] The Conference inserted in Article 2 of the latter Convention a paragraph laying down that 'Measures of reprisal against them [i.e., prisoners of war] are prohibited.'[8]

3. Op. cit. n. 1.

4. An earlier version of the present paper appeared in German in 2 *Humanitäres Völkerrecht, Informationsschriften* 4 (October 1989) pp. 4-17. This periodical is a joint publication of the German Red Cross in the Federal Republic of Germany and the *Institut für Friedenssicherungsrecht und Humanitäres Völkerrecht of the Ruhr University, Bochum.*

5. Final Act, D. Schindler and J. Toman, *The Laws of Armed Conflicts*, 3rd edn. (1988) p. 321.

6. Text of the 1906 Convention in Schindler and Toman, op. cit. n. 5, p. 301. The full title of the revised Convention is Convention for the Amelioration of the Condition of the Wounded and Sick in Armies in the Field, signed at Geneva, 27 July 1929; Schindler and Toman, ibid. p. 325.

7. Convention Relative to the Treatment of Prisoners of War, signed at Geneva, 27 July 1929; Schindler and Toman, op. cit. n. 5, p. 339.

8. The Diplomatic Conference of 1929 saw no need to introduce a similar provision in its

The introduction of this first prohibition of reprisals had not gone unchallenged. In 1921, in the aftermath of World War One, the International Committee of the Red Cross (or ICRC) put forward the suggestion to place a ban on reprisals against prisoners of war.[9] That same year, opposition to this idea came to light when the International Law Association examined a draft code for the treatment of prisoners of war. The crux of the argument contra was that, no matter how abhorrent the practice of reprisals against prisoners of war, the prohibition of such measures could never be relied on as effective, as no army 'could reasonably be expected to renounce in war so effective and powerful a weapon for the redress or cessation of supposed intolerable wrong upon its own nationals at the hand of the enemy as immediate or threatened reprisal on enemy units in its own hands'.[10]

When the proposal for a categorical ban on reprisals against prisoners of war was formally introduced in the Diplomatic Conference of 1929, the British representative raised the same objection. Instead of a total ban, he argued, the Conference should accept a provision morally condemning recourse to reprisals against prisoners of war. This moral condemnation might then be followed by a set of rules designed to limit such recourse to cases where the adversary was himself guilty of unlawful acts against prisoners of war (i.e., reprisals 'in kind') and even then requiring that the execution of a planned measure of reprisal be preceded by a series of formal steps aimed at removing the causes of, and thus the need for, the measure. However, the British proposal failed to muster any support, and the proposed prohibition was unanimously accepted (i.e., including the British vote!).[11]

Once this first hurdle had been taken, the next steps were surprisingly easy. After World War Two, the Diplomatic Conference of 1949[12] did not hesitate

other product, the revised Wounded and Sick Convention (Schindler and Toman, op. cit. n. 5, p. 325). As explained by P. des Gouttes, *La Convention de Genève du 27 juillet 1929, Commentaire* (1930) pp. 22-24, the two Conventions of 1929 should be read together and the Conference consciously limited the sphere of application of the Wounded and Sick Convention to the armies on the battlefield, relegating to the Prisoners of War Convention all matters connected with the treatment of wounded or sick combatants evacuated as prisoners of war to the rear.

9. The suggestion was made in a report to the Xth International Conference of the Red Cross; see Kalshoven, op. cit. n. 1, pp. 71-72.

10. Ibid. at p. 74.

11. Ibid. pp. 79-80. It should be noted that the Conference also introduced in Arts. 86-88 of the 1929 Prisoners of War Convention, a set of rules defining the functions and powers of Protecting Powers in their role as outside supervisors and mediators, and expressing support for the ICRC in its humanitarian activities.

12. Final Act, Schindler and Toman, op. cit. n. 5, p. 367.

long before including categorical bans on reprisals against protected persons and goods in all four Geneva Conventions of that year for the protection of victims of war.[13] And in 1954, the Hague Intergovernmental Conference on the Protection of Cultural Property in the Event of Armed Conflict, convened by UNESCO,[14] needed equally little time to agree on a ban on reprisals against cultural property protected under the Convention it adopted.[15]

While important categories of persons and objects were thus protected from reprisals, one particularly vexing problem remained, i.e., whether the civilian population and civilian objects in enemy, non-occupied territory could and should be afforded similar protection. It remained for the Diplomatic Conference on the Reaffirmation and Development of International Humanitarian Law Applicable in Armed Conflicts, Geneva, 1974-1977,[16] to wrestle with this problem.

The draft for a Protocol I on the protection of victims of international armed conflicts which the ICRC submitted to the Conference, contained in the part on general protection of the civilian population against the effects of hostilities, a prohibition on attacks by way of reprisal against the civilian population and individual civilians but not against civilian objects.[17] The ICRC had thought it wise to so limit its proposal because '[to] forbid reprisals against civilian objects in general would exclude the possibility of carrying out reprisals under the laws of war', and it feared that 'there might be strong opposition to the inclusion of such a strict prohibition'.[18] The important thing was to prevent the parties from directing their reprisals against the enemy

13. I. Geneva Convention for the Amelioration of the Condition of the Wounded and Sick in Armies in the Field, Art. 46; II. Geneva Convention for the Amelioration of the Condition of Wounded, Sick and Shipwrecked Members of Armed Forces at Sea, Art. 47; III. Geneva Convention relative to the Treatment of Prisoners of War, Art. 13, para. 3; and IV. Geneva Convention relative to the Protection of Civilian Persons in Time of War, Art. 33; Schindler and Toman, op. cit. n. 5, p. 367 et seq.

14. Final Act, Schindler and Toman, op. cit. n. 5, p. 741.

15. Art. 4, para. 4, of the Convention for the Protection of Cultural Property in the Event of Armed Conflict, signed at The Hague, 14 May 1954; Schindler and Toman, op. cit. n. 5, pp. 745-768, at p. 748.

16. Final Act, Schindler and Toman, op. cit. n. 5, p. 605.

17. ICRC, Draft Protocol Additional to the Geneva Conventions of August 12, 1949, and Relating to the Protection of Victims of International Armed Conflicts, Art. 46, para. 4; 1 *Official Records of the Diplomatic Conference on the Reaffirmation and Development of International Humanitarian Law Applicable in Armed Conflicts, Geneva (1974-1977)* (hereinafter O.R.) Part Three, at p. 16.

18. 14 O.R. p. 109: CDDH/III/SR.14, para. 5. Mrs. Bindschedler-Robert, introducing the draft article on behalf of the ICRC, added that 'There was of course nothing to prevent the Committee from introducing the concept of prohibition of reprisals into article 47, should it so desire.'

civilian population. Civilian objects, on the other hand, could be regarded as comparatively expendable.[19]

At the Conference, a strong majority manifested itself against this distinction. One argument contra was that in practice it would prove extremely difficult if not simply impracticable to maintain the distinction and attack only objects while sparing the people.[20] On these and other grounds, and notwithstanding staunch opposition from several quarters, the Conference decided to supplement the prohibition proposed by the ICRC with a prohibition on reprisals against civilian objects.[21] Once this step had been taken, the fences were down and similar prohibitions were adopted in rapid succession on reprisals against a series of specially protected objects. For some of those who had been prepared to go along with the insertion of a general ban on reprisals against civilian objects (such as Australia) this was going too far, and they registered their opposition to the ensuing avalanche of prohibitions.

For other delegations, notably those of France, Great Britain and the United States, the very principle behind the whole set of rules was and remained unacceptable. To the last, the French delegates in particular did their utmost to convince the Conference of the unwisdom of its set course. At various stages of the proceedings they submitted proposals designed to substitute for the categorical prohibition of reprisals against the civilian population, rules that would place recourse to such measures under legal constraints, more or less along the lines already suggested in 1929 by the British delegate to the

19. On the drafting history of the prohibitions at issue, see S.E. Nahlik, 'Belligerent Reprisals as Seen in the Light of the Diplomatic Conference on Humanitarian Law, Geneva, 1974-1977', 42 *Law and Contemporary Problems* (1978) no. 2, pp. 36-66; also in French, 'Le problème des représailles à la lumière des travaux de la conférence diplomatique sur le droit humanitaire', in 82 RGDIP (1978) no. 1, pp. 130-169; F. Kalshoven, 'Reprisals in the CDDH', in R.J. Akkerman et al., eds., *Declarations on Principles: A Quest for Universal Peace – Liber Amicorum Discipulorumque Prof. Dr. Bert V.A. Röling* (1977) pp. 195-216, at p. 197; id., 'The Belligerent Reprisals in the Light of the 1977 Geneva Protocols', in *European Seminar on Humanitarian Law (Jagellonian University, Krakow, 1979)* (1980) pp. 31-46; R. Bierzanek, 'Reprisals as a Means of Enforcing the Laws of Warfare: The Old and the New Law', in A. Cassese, ed., *The New Humanitarian Law of Armed Conflict* (1979) pp. 232-257; see also W.A. Solf in M. Bothe, K.J. Partsch and W.A. Solf, *New Rules for Victims of Armed Conflicts* (1982) pp. 312-315.

20. Introducing in 1975 an amendment to this effect in Commission III, the present author emphasized that acceptance of the proposed ban on reprisals against civilians and civilian objects alike 'would make it an urgent task for the Conference to continue its search for other mechanisms that could effectively contribute to enforcing the rules on protection of the civilian population.' 14 O.R. p. 114: CDDH/III/SR.14, para. 26.

21. The vote in Commission III was 58 in favour, 3 against, with 9 abstentions; 14 O.R. p. 219: CDDH/III/SR.24, para. 16.

Diplomatic Conference of that year.[22] The main thrust of their proposals was to preserve at least the right to threaten such reprisals: they repeatedly expressed the hope that acceptance of their plans would effectively remove the need for the actual taking of such measures. But their efforts were in vain, and the majority was not to be budged. Their last formal proposal was ultimately withdrawn simultaneously with a Polish counter-proposal to insert in Protocol I a prohibition on all reprisals without exception against persons and objects protected under the Protocol.[23]

In the end, the whole list of specific prohibitions was accepted without change. As embodied in Part IV of Protocol I of 1977,[24] it contains the following items:

— Article 51, paragraph 6: 'Attacks against the civilian population or civilians by way of reprisals are prohibited.'[25]

22. 3 O.R. p. 323: CDDH/1/221, 19 February 1975: proposal for a new Art. 74 *bis*; ibid. p. 324: CDDH/I/221/Rev.1, 22 April 1976, revised version of the proposal.

23. Polish proposal for a new Art. 70 *bis*: 3 O.R. p. 313: CDDH/III/103, 1 October 1974; simultaneous withdrawal of French and Polish proposals: 9 O.R. p. 417: CDDH/I/SR.72, paras. 1-4. See also, for a fuller discussion of the negotiating history of these proposals, Bierzanek, loc. cit. n. 19, in particular pp. 249-250.

24. Protocol Additional to the Geneva Conventions of 12 August 1949, and Relating to the Protection of Victims of International Armed Conflicts (Protocol I), adopted on 8 June 1977; 1 O.R. pp. 115-183; Schindler and Toman, op. cit. n. 5, p. 621. The Conference also adopted a Protocol II on internal armed conflict: Protocol Additional to the Geneva Conventions of 12 August 1949, and Relating to the Protection of Victims of Non-international Armed Conflicts (Protocol II); 1 O.R. pp. 185-198; Schindler and Toman, ibid. p. 689.

25. Art. 51 reads as follows:

1. The civilian population and individual civilians shall enjoy general protection against dangers arising from military operations. To give effect to this protection, the following rules, which are additional to other applicable rules of international law, shall be observed in all circumstances.

2. The civilian population as such, as well as individual civilians, shall not be the object of attack. Acts or threats of violence the primary purpose of which is to spread terror among the civilian population are prohibited.

3. Civilians shall enjoy the protection afforded by this Section, unless and for such time as they take a direct part in hostilities.

4. Indiscriminate attacks are prohibited. Indiscriminate attacks are:

(a) those which are not directed at a specific military objective;

(b) those which employ a method or means of combat which cannot be directed at a specific military objective;

(c) those which employ a method or means of combat the effects of which cannot be limited as required by this Protocol;

and consequently, in each such case, are of a nature to strike military objectives and civilian objects without distinction.

5. Among others, the following types of attacks are to be considered as indiscriminate:

(a) an attack by bombardment by any methods or means which treats as a single military objective

— Article 52, paragraph 1: 'Civilian objects shall not be the object of attack or of reprisals.'[26]

— Article 53 prohibits, without prejudice to the provisions of the Hague Convention of 1954, making 'historic monuments, works of art or places of worship which constitute the cultural or spiritual heritage of peoples' the 'object of reprisals.'[27]

— Article 54, paragraph 4: 'These objects [i.e., objects indispensable to the survival of the civilian population] shall not be made the object of reprisals.'[28]

---

a number of clearly separated and distinct military objectives located in a city, town, village or other area containing a similar concentration of civilians or civilian objects; and
(b) an attack which may be expected to cause incidental loss of civilian life, injury to civilians, damage to civilian objects, or a combination thereof, which would be excessive in relation to the concrete and direct military advantage anticipated.
6. Attacks against the civilian population or civilian objects by way of reprisals are prohibited.
7. The presence or movements of the civilian population or individual civilians shall not be used to render certain points or areas immune from military operations, in particular in attempts to shield military objectives from attacks or to shield, favour or impede military operations. The Parties to the conflict shall not direct the movement of the civilian population or individual civilians to attempt to shield military objectives from attacks or to shield military operations.
8. Any violation of these prohibitions shall not release the Parties to the conflict from their legal obligations with respect to the civilian population and civilians, including the obligation to take the precautionary measures provided for in Article 57.

26. Art. 52 continues as follows:
1. . . . Civilian objects are all objects which are not military objectives as defined in paragraph 2.
2. Attacks shall be limited strictly to military objectives. In so far as objects are concerned, military objectives are limited to those objects which by their nature, location, purpose or use make an effective contribution to military action and whose total or partial destruction, capture or neutralization, in the circumstances ruling at the time, offers a definite military advantage.
3. In case of doubt whether an object which is normally dedicated to civilian purposes, such as a place of worship, a house or other dwelling or a school, is being used to make an effective contribution to military action, it shall be presumed to be not so used.

27. Art. 53 reads as follows:
Without prejudice to the provisions of the Hague Convention for the Protection of Cultural Property in the Event of Armed Conflict of 14 May 1954, and of other relevant international instruments, it is prohibited:
(a) to commit any acts of hostility directed against the historic monuments, works of art or places of worship which constitute the cultural or spiritual heritage of peoples;
(b) to use such objects in support of the military effort;
(c) to make such objects the object of reprisals.

28. Art. 54 reads as follows:
1. Starvation of civilians as a method of warfare is prohibited.
2. It is prohibited to attack, destroy, remove or render useless objects indispensable to the survival of the civilian population, such as foodstuffs, agricultural areas for the production of foodstuffs, crops, livestock, drinking water installations and supplies and irrigation works, for the specific purpose of denying them for their sustenance value to the civilian population or to the adverse Party, whatever the motive, whether in order to starve out civilians, to cause them to move away, or for any other motive.

— Article 55, paragraph 2: 'Attacks against the natural environment by way of reprisals are prohibited.'[29]
— Article 56, paragraph 4, prohibits 'to make any of the works, installations or military objectives mentioned in paragraph 1 [i.e., works or installations containing dangerous forces, namely dams, dykes and nuclear electrical generating stations . . . even where these objects are military objectives] the object of reprisals.'[30]

---

3. The prohibitions in para. 2 shall not apply to such of the objects covered by it as are used by an adverse Party:
(a) as sustenance solely for the members of its armed forces; or
(b) if not as sustenance, then in direct support of military action, provided, however, that in no event shall actions against these objects be taken which may be expected to leave the civilian population with such inadequate food or water as to cause its starvation or force its movement.
4. These objects shall not be made the object of reprisals.
5. In recognition of the vital requirements of any Party to the conflict in the defence of its national territory against invasion, derogation from the prohibitions contained in paragraph 2 may be made by a Party to the conflict within such territory under its own control where required by imperative military necessity.

29. Para. 1 of Art. 55 provides that:
Care shall be taken in warfare to protect the natural environment against widespread, long-term and severe damage. This protection includes a prohibition of the use of methods or means of warfare which are intended or may be expected to cause such damage to the natural environment and thereby to prejudice the health or survival of the civilian population.

30. Art. 56 reads as follows:
1. Works or installations containing dangerous forces, namely dams, dykes and nuclear electrical generating stations, shall not be made the object of attack, even where these objects are military objectives, if such attack may cause the release of dangerous forces and consequent severe losses among the civilian population. Other military objectives located at or in the vicinity of these works or installations shall not be made the object of attack if such attack may cause the release of dangerous forces from the works or installations and consequent severe losses among the civilian population.
2. The special protection against attack provided by paragraph 1 shall cease:
(a) for a dam or dyke only if it is used for other than its normal function and in regular, significant and direct support of military operations and if such attack is the only feasible way to terminate such support;
(b) for a nuclear electrical generating station only if it provides electric power in regular, significant and direct support of military operations and if such attack is the only feasible way to terminate such support;
(c) for other military objectives located at or in the vicinity of these works or installations only if they are used in regular, significant and direct support of military operations and if such attack is the only feasible way to terminate such support.
3. In all cases, the civilian population and civilians shall remain entitled to all the protection accorded them by international law, including the protection of the precautionary measures provided for in Article 57. If the protection ceases and any of the works, installations or military objectives mentioned in paragraph 1 is attacked, all practical precautions shall be taken to avoid the release of the dangerous forces.

Besides these prohibitions in Part IV (Civilian Population), Part II (Wounded, Sick and Shipwrecked) contains an entirely non-controversial prohibition of reprisals 'against the persons and objects protected by this Part'.[31]

Shortly after these events, a conference met in Geneva under the auspices of the United Nations (1979-1980) to examine possible prohibitions or limitations on the use of specified conventional weapons. Among the texts it finally adopted[32] one finds just one reference to reprisals. It is in Article 3, paragraph 2, of the Mines Protocol,[33] prohibiting the setting of mines, booby-traps and other similar devices 'either in offence, defence or by way of reprisals, against the civilian population as such or against individual civilians.' This amounts to a reaffirmation of the prohibition found in Article 51, paragraph 6, of Protocol I of 1977.

---

4. It is prohibited to make any of the works, installations or military objectives mentioned in paragraph 1 the object of reprisals.
5. The Parties to the conflict shall endeavour to avoid locating any military objectives in the vicinity of the works or installations mentioned in paragraph 1. Nevertheless, installations erected for the sole purpose of defending the protected works or installations from attack are permissible and shall not themselves be made the object of attack, provided that they are not used in hostilities except for defensive actions necessary to respond to attacks against the protected works or installations and that their armament is limited to weapons capable only of repelling hostile action against the protected works or installations.
6. The High Contracting Parties and the Parties to the conflict are urged to conclude further agreements among themselves to provide additional protection for objects containing dangerous forces.
7. In order to facilitate the identification of the objects protected by this Article, the Parties to the conflict may mark them with a special sign consisting of a group of three bright orange circles placed on the same axis, as specified in Article 16 of Annex I to this Protocol. The absence of such marking in no way relieves any Party to the conflict of its obligations under this Article.

31. Art. 20; the 'persons and objects protected by this Part' are, in the main, the wounded, sick and shipwrecked, whether military or civilian; medical and religious personnel; and medical units and transport; all of this as defined in Art. 9. The ban on reprisals in Art. 20 is, so to say, a natural prolongation of the earlier prohibitions in Conventions I, II and IV of 1949.

32. Convention on Prohibitions or Restrictions on the Use of Certain Conventional Weapons Which May be Deemed to Be Excessively Injurious or to Have Indiscriminate Effects, with annexed Protocols, of 10 October 1980; Schindler and Toman, op. cit. n. 5, p. 179.

33. Protocol on Prohibitions or Restrictions on the Use of Mines, Booby-Traps and Other Devices (Protocol II).

3. A CLOSER LOOK AT THE LEGAL STATE OF AFFAIRS, WITH SPECIAL ATTENTION TO PROTOCOL I

The main features of the above survey of existing prohibitions on belligerent reprisals may be summarized as follows:

The Geneva Conventions of 1949 categorically prohibit reprisals against protected persons and objects in situations of international armed conflict. As the Conventions have been ratified or acceded to by nearly all States, old and new, the prohibitions on reprisals laid down in these instruments may safely be stated to be in force worldwide.

The Hague Convention of 1954 equally categorically bans reprisals against protected objects in international armed conflicts. As this Convention has less parties,[34] the ban is in force as treaty law between the parties. This leaves open whether in relations with or among non-parties, reprisals against cultural property are still permissible. Article 53 of Protocol I, with its prohibition of reprisals, provides a partial answer to this question. The answer is partial on two counts: Article 53 applies only to the narrower group of objects defined in that Article, and Protocol I has not so far been ratified or acceded to by a number of States. On the other hand, reprisals against cultural property in practice have never represented a particularly serious issue.

The situation is different when it comes to the set of prohibitions in Part IV of Protocol I (and the single prohibition in the 1980 Mines Protocol). The state of customary international law with regard to reprisals against the civilian population and civilian objects continues to be a matter of considerable controversy.[35] Moreover, at the Diplomatic Conference of 1974-1977 the proposals for their prohibition met with strong opposition. Even after their adoption the battle has continued virtually unabated. Due to their controversial nature, they cannot for the time being be regarded as anything but rules of treaty law, binding the parties to the Protocol but no one else.

Their controversial character is demonstrated, first of all, by subsequent State practice. In the recent armed conflict between Iran and Iraq (whose representatives at the Diplomatic Conference of 1974-1977 had been among the majority condemning all reprisals against the civilian population and civilian objects) both sides openly and frequently resorted to reprisal bombardments

34. The list in Schindler and Toman, op. cit. n. 5, pp. 769-773, based on a communication from UNESCO dated 28 July 1986, contains 74 ratifications and accessions.

35. On this, see Kalshoven, op. cit. n. 1.

directed against the enemy civilian population. And while the United Nations and others repeatedly condemned this practice, the belligerent parties apparently saw no reason to regard their acts as something particularly reprehensible. Admittedly, neither Iran nor Iraq had become a party to Protocol I. In all events, the most the two belligerents were from time to time prepared to agree to was a temporary cease-fire (or, perhaps more accurately, a 'cease-bombing'), each time renewing bombardments as soon as they saw fit.

It may be noted in passing that their activities clearly failed to bring about a change in the other party's behaviour: at no time did either party budge an inch under the impact of the bombs. Nor was this the first time for belligerents to gain this experience of the futility of so-called reprisal bombardments against the enemy civilian population: an earlier, well-known example is provided by the long series of such bombardments, carried out by belligerent parties during the course of the Second World War.[36]

Apart from these rather unfortunate events in the war between Iran and Iraq, the prohibitions on reprisals in Part IV of Protocol I have ever since their adoption been the target of more or less vicious attacks in scholarly writings. It is here the place to enter into some of these arguments.

3.1 Are the prohibitions on reprisals in Protocol I, Part IV, militarily acceptable?

The most far-reaching criticism appears to be that the prohibitions at issue here are unacceptable from a military point of view. It may already be read in the brief comment by G.I.A.D. Draper that 'At the same time [i.e., when these prohibitions were enacted] the content of the humanitarian law of war has been extended, with some precision, to battle conduct. This places a heavy strain upon the residual methods of law enforcement'.[37]

The criticism has been voiced more explicitly in the United States of America. The official position of the Joint Chiefs of Staff appears to be that the 'total elimination of the right of reprisal' is among the factors rendering Protocol I 'unacceptable from the point of view of military operations' as it 'would hamper the ability of the United States to respond to an enemy's intentional disregard of the limitations established in the Geneva Conventions of

36. Ibid. p. 358.

37. G.I.A.D. Draper, 'The Implementation and Enforcement of the Geneva Conventions of 1949 and of the Two Additional Protocols of 1978', 164 Hague Recueil (1979-II) pp. 9-53, at p. 35.

1949 or Protocol I, for the purpose of deterring such disregard.'[38] In the same vein, Guy Roberts argues 'that Protocol I goes beyond a simple prohibition on reprisals against civilians to protect a number of objects of economic and military value as well [i.e., the objects protected under Articles 53-56]. Attacks and threatened attacks on such resources might well influence even the most callous enemy to refrain from further attacks on friendly civilians and their property.'[39]

While these views appear to regard the military utility of reprisals against the enemy civilian population or civilian objects as an element in the general framework of military operations, the British author, Christopher Greenwood, going one step further, undertakes to demonstrate the military indispensability of such reprisals.[40] Taking as his point of departure that Part IV of Protocol I represents a mixture of Geneva law and Hague law, he argues that observance of some of the rules in Articles 51-56 'will restrict the options open to an army engaged in hostilities and will, in many cases, require such an army to sustain greater casualties than it would otherwise do in order to minimise the loss of civilian life.' This leads him to conclude that:

> 'a State which disregards its obligations under Part IV of Protocol I may derive a considerable military advantage from doing so. For example, attacks on dams, dykes or nuclear electrical generating stations, which in most circumstances are prohibited by Article 56, may seriously damage the victim State's capacity to wage war. . . . In such a case, the need to respond and to prevent future violations becomes more than simply a matter of law enforcement, it may be essential if the victim is to avoid defeat.'

The present author believes, with Greenwood, that Part IV of Protocol I provides a mixture of Geneva-law and Hague-law impulses, in that it seeks to protect the civilian population by means of rules regulating certain features of the conduct of military operations. He is less convinced by the rest of the argu-

38. A.D. Sofaer, 'The Rationale for the United States Decision Not to Ratify', 82 AJIL (1988) pp. 784-787, at p. 785.

39. G. B. Roberts, 'The New Rules for Waging War: The Case Against Ratification of Additional Protocol I', 26 Virg. JIL (1985) pp. 109-170, at p. 143-144. G.H. Aldrich, in his response to Roberts' attack on Protocol I, concedes that 'the Protocol may have gone too far in prohibiting reprisals': 'Progressive Development of the Laws of War: A Reply to Criticisms of the 1977 Geneva Protocol', ibid. pp. 693-720, at p. 710.

40. C.J. Greenwood, 'The Twilight of the Law of Belligerent Reprisals', 20 NYIL (1989) pp. 35-69. An earlier version of this essay was given as a paper to the British Institute of International and Comparative Law and published in M.A. Meyer, ed., *Armed Conflict and the New Law* (1989) pp. 227-250.

ment with its implied criticism that the prohibition of reprisals against the objects specified in Articles 53-56 must be qualified as unreasonable.[41]

For one thing, the argument appears rather far-fetched as regards the provisions in Articles 53-55 for the protection of cultural objects, objects indispensable to the survival of the civilian population and the natural environment. These provisions, which have with some justification been characterized as belonging to Geneva law,[42] either add little to existing general obligations or have been so phrased that military considerations are heeded to the maximum.

The only provision where the argument might be felt to cut some ice is the one Greenwood advances as his single example, on the protection of works or installations containing dangerous forces enumerated in Article 56. After all, this Article prohibits attacks on such objects even when they constitute military objectives; i.e., according to the definition in Article 52, paragraph 2, when they 'make an effective contribution to military action' and their 'total or partial destruction . . . in the circumstances ruling at the time, offers a definite military advantage.'[43]

Obviously, an attack on a work or installation protected by Article 56, can only yield a military advantage if the chosen object actually constitutes a military objective. A simple perusal of the Article reveals that in such a case, the prohibition to attack applies solely if the attack 'may cause . . . severe losses among the civilian population'. In view of the forces involved, this requirement may in many instances be little more exacting than the general obligation in Article 57, paragraph 2(a)(iii), to refrain from attacking any military objective if the attack may be expected to cause civilian losses 'excessive in relation to the concrete and direct military advantage anticipated.' Moreover, the special protection ceases and attack becomes permissible, generally speaking, if the object is used 'in regular, significant and direct support of military operations and if such attack is the only feasible way to terminate such support.'

41. The interpretation Greenwood places on some of these provisions reminds the reader of objections raised by certain military circles after the adoption of the Protocol. Their objections may stem not so much from a genuine concern that faithful application of the provisions in question would expose their armed forces to an increased risk of casualties, as from a certain reluctance to accept a set of rules not of their own making and, where necessary, adjust their operations plans to the precise terms of these rules.

42. H. Meyrowitz, 'Die Repressalienverbote des I. Zusatzprotokolls zu den Genfer Abkommen vom 12. August 1949 und das Reziprozitätsprinzip', 5 *Neue Zeitschrift für Wehrrecht* (1986) pp. 177-193, at p. 182.

43. For the text of Art. 56, see *supra* n. 30.

Thus, while Article 56 incontestably lays down Hague law-type rules relating to the conduct of military operations, and while compliance with these rules may at times require some modest adjustment of military planning, it appears somewhat exaggerated, to put it mildly, to maintain that such compliance would as it were by definition entail major military disadvantage as well as the risk of greatly increased casualties among a party's armed forces.

But let us suppose for the sake of argument that an attack in flagrant disregard of Article 56 on a 'dam, dyke or nuclear electrical generating station' actually brings the enemy the feared significant military advantage: will this necessitate a reprisal in kind (i.e., in disregard of Article 56, paragraph 4) to restore the military balance? Obviously, everything depends here on the situation, and one cannot discard off-hand, as entirely implausible, that in a given case such recourse to reprisals would make military sense. It should be emphasized, however, that this would require a rather unusual confluence of circumstances:

(1) there must be reason to fear a recurrence of the original occasion, in the shape of an attack on another 'work or installation containing dangerous forces' in the territory of the victim of the first attack: if no such risk exists, there is no ground for any measure aimed at preventing a recurrence;

(2) there must be a comparable object, belonging to the same class of 'dams, dykes and nuclear electrical generating stations' and situated in the territory of the enemy;

(3) an attack on that object must be feasible and, in the circumstances at the time, yield at least equivalent military advantage;

(4) the attack must be expected to entail civilian losses in the same order of severity as those caused by the initial breach of the law.

Only if all these conditions are fulfilled can the reprisal attack in breach of Article 56, paragraph 4, be said to constitute a genuine reprisal as well as an effective military operation against an object of significant military value. It will probably be conceded that the likelihood of such a concurrence of favourable circumstances is at best slight. More often than not, the territory of the enemy will, e.g., provide no dam, dyke or nuclear power station worth attacking from a military point of view (so that the military balance cannot be restored); or the object in question can be attacked without exposing the civilian population to severe losses (so that the attack is simply legitimate so long as the chosen object constitutes a military objective); or, the other way round, the object can only be attacked at the risk of civilian losses far graver than those caused by the initial attack in violation of Article 56 (so that the requirement of proportionality, inherent in the notion of reprisal, cannot be respected).

With that, the argument of the indispensability, from a military point of view, of the capacity to resort to reprisals in response to a violation of Article 56, for all practical purposes loses its cogency. To put it differently: recourse to reprisals in a hypothetical situation such as the one described above is just that: a reprisal against the enemy civilian population, serving at best (i.e., unless it is an act of pure retaliation) to bring the message home that attacks against objects protected under Article 56 shall not be tolerated. Thus, although the main provisions in the Article may aim at accommodating conflicting military and humanitarian considerations, the prohibition of reprisals in this as in the other named Articles (53-55) should be regarded as a measure purely for the protection of the civilian population and, hence, as one essentially humanitarian in nature.

3.2 Are the prohibitions on reprisals in Part IV of Protocol I desirable?

Another, somewhat milder criticism questions the desirability of the prohibitions on reprisals against the civilian population. It was heard shortly after the adoption of Protocol I, at an international symposium organized by the Netherlands Red Cross Society and held in September 1978 in The Hague. Sir David Hughes-Morgan, a British military lawyer who had been a prominent member of the British delegation to the Diplomatic Conference of 1974-1977 and who in that capacity had cooperated closely with the French delegation in their attempts at finding rules limiting rather than banning recourse to reprisals against the civilian population, stated in his introduction that in his opinion:

> 'It may be that the Geneva Diplomatic Conference did not appreciate the clear distinction between retaliation, which is always unlawful, and reprisals which in law are governed by strict conditions. If there are serious and long term attacks upon the civilian population of a country at war, in breach of the provisions of the Protocol, it is likely that public opinion would demand that similar action be taken against the enemy and there is an argument for suggesting that this latter action should be controlled by legal norms rather than become uncontrolled and unlawful retaliation.'[44]

44. *The New Humanitarian Law in War and Conflict,* report of an international symposium held on 25 and 26 September 1978, under the auspices of the Netherlands Red Cross Society, at the Peace Palace in The Hague, p. 11.

In the discussion, he added that he 'felt that reprisals or the threat of reprisals has been a factor in the enforcement of law.'

Responding to this argument, the present author conceded that a difference exists between reprisals carried out and reprisals merely threatened, as well as the fact that the threat of such measures against the civilian population has occasionally proved effective. He maintained, however, that their execution has never demonstrably been so. Sir David thereupon gave expression to his sense of bewilderment at the whole matter when he said that:

> 'It is a very, very difficult problem indeed, because who wants to be in a position to say "we are making law" but allows you to attack the civilian population, even to stop the breach; nobody does. It is purely a question as to whether it is going to be an effective means of control. And frankly, what one is doing here is tossing a coin in the air, and depending on which side it comes down you either do this or do that. You are not going to know in either case what its effect is going to be.'[45]

More recently, views very similar to those of Sir David Hughes-Morgan were voiced in an essay by another British lawyer, Françoise Hampson. After a careful analysis of the legal situation and the negotiating record of the Diplomatic Conference she writes that:

> 'It is regrettable that States should require such a deterrent or such a violent reminder of their obligations. In suggesting, however, that "the threat of reciprocal treatment would always be real to those who violated the rules of humanitarian law . . . but that a formal legalisation of reprisals would be an invitation to misuse and abuse", the Swedish delegate to the Diplomatic Conference and those who supported his point of view did nothing for the protection of victims of armed conflicts. On the contrary, in refusing to set practicable limits to reprisals whilst recognising that they will in fact happen, they condemned those victims to arbitrary, unpredictable breaches of humanitarian law which might not otherwise have taken place. The Diplomatic Conference missed an opportunity to make humanitarian law "a living reality rather than a series of hopeful aspirations" and, in so doing, did a disservice both to the rule of law and to humanity itself.'[46]

The present author has much sympathy for Ms. Hampson's sense of frustration at what she evidently, and with some right, considers a less than perfect solution to an awfully difficult problem. Yet he believes she is rather

45. Ibid. pp. 32-34.

46. F.J. Hampson, 'Belligerent Reprisals and the 1977 Protocols to the Geneva Conventions of 1949', 37 ICLQ (1988) pp. 818-843, at p. 843; footnotes omitted.

too harsh in her judgment of some of those who, like the Swedish delegate at the Diplomatic Conference, were instrumental in bringing the solution about.

For one thing, she may be insufficiently aware of the sheer force of events that led to the result she rejects. In actual fact, the choice was never between prohibition or regulation of reprisals against the civilian population and civilian objects. It was, rather, between accepting (or acquiescing in) an expansion of the list of prohibited reprisals with these specific items or having to face a categorical ban on all belligerent reprisals without exception.[47] In these circumstances, the choice was not really a difficult one. There was, for one thing, the incontestably dubious efficacy of reprisals against the civilian population and civilian objects. For another thing, the Conference also introduced, in Article 90 of Protocol I, fact-finding machinery that, even though optional, one may hope in the end would prove to be a somewhat more effective, and at all events non-destructive, means of preventing the recurrence of gross violations of the rules for the protection of the civilian population.[48]

Apart from this argument of conference diplomacy, the present author sees a ground for a more fundamental objection to Ms. Hampson's conclusion. When she expresses regret at the fact 'that States should require such a deterrent or such a violent reminder of their obligations', she apparently presupposes that States, when so reminded, will in effect mend their ways. Unfortunately, experience shows that they seldom if ever do so react, especially if it is not a matter of a 'deterrent' (a threat of reprisal) but of a 'violent reminder' (the reprisal carried into effect). In the situation at issue, the outcome will be an ever increasing number of victims among the civilian population on both sides. And no matter what one may say about its changed role in present-day armed conflict,[49] it appears certain that in many (perhaps most) countries the population is an instrument in the hands of those in power, rather than the other way round. Ms. Hampson's view, in short, appears to be based on a rather over-optimistic view of what reprisals as a means of law enforcement can achieve, combined with an underestimation of the adverse effects inherent

47. See the history of the French and Polish proposals for new articles aiming, respectively, to restore and regulate the right of reprisal, or to ban all reprisals; *supra*, text at nn. 22, 23.

48. Interestingly, the Polish delegate made the withdrawal of his proposal for a ban on all reprisals 'conditional on the agreement by other delegations, that the proposed fact-finding commission should be optional'; *supra* n. 23, para. 4. The Polish view at the time was, of course, that such a commission of individuals empowered to investigate violations of the law of armed conflict was totally unacceptable.

49. See the fascinating discussion by G. Best, 'Civilians in Contemporary Wars: A Problem in Ethics, Law, and Fact', 35 *Air University Review* (1984) no. 3, pp. 29-40.

in such measures. The present author therefore remains firmly committed to the view that the prohibition of reprisals against the civilian population and civilian objects, even though not an entirely satisfactory solution to a well-nigh intractable problem, is at least to be preferred to the previous lack of legal clarity.

There is, furthermore, a possible misunderstanding of the precise meaning of the statement made by the Swedish delegate. His words[50] seem to reflect no more than the simple truism that 'those who violate the rules of humanitarian law' always have to consider the risk of negative 'reciprocal treatment', and this, as he said, 'irrespective of any legal rules', i.e., even if recourse to reprisals is formally outlawed – or regulated, for that matter. And, one may add, whether such 'reciprocal treatment' is actually threatened or not.

It may also be noted that the effect of this awareness on the actions of a potential violator will depend on many factors: Is he, so to speak, a first offender or a hardened criminal? Is he at all inclined to heed the law? How does he calculate the cost effectiveness of the contemplated violation in the light of the threat of a negative reaction? Is he under any particular pressure to go ahead regardless? In a word, it is by no means certain that a threat of reprisals will actually ward off the violation, or the recurrence of violations. And if it fails to bring about the desired effect, the chances that actual execution of the reprisal will do so are at best slim. For, once again, there is precious little evidence that actual recourse to reprisals against the enemy civilian population has ever led to such a positive outcome.[51]

50. It may be useful to quote the relevant paragraph from Mr. O. Bring's statement in full: 'In the Working Group his delegation had opposed the proposed article regulating the permissibility of reprisals. Several delegations had sought to explain such opposition by the emotional revulsion generated by the very word "reprisals". His delegation had pointed out that its stand was based not on an emotional reflex but on the knowledge that in practice counter-measures never led to observance of the law. It had attempted to show that the threat of reciprocal treatment would always be real to those who violated the rules of humanitarian law – irrespective of any legal rules – but that a formal legalisation of reprisals would be an invitation to misuse and abuse. Sweden had attempted to weigh up the pros and cons of the idea of reprisals and had found that the balance was against it. It was therefore with a sense of satisfaction that his delegation noted that the results achieved by the Conference aimed at a further limitation of the institute of reprisals in customary law': 6 O.R. p. 210: CDDH/SR.42, para. 35.

51. The present author suggested earlier (at the 1978 Hague symposium, *supra* n. 44) that the prohibitions of recourse to reprisals in Arts. 51-56 do not exclude the power of belligerents to threaten such reprisals. W. A. Solf has objected that the argument is fallacious because 'a threatened reprisal will be regarded as a bluff if made by a Party which usually complies with the law of armed conflict. The credibility of such a threat is enhanced only if there is a general cynical attitude about the effectiveness of conventional restraints on the use of force': Solf, op. cit. n. 19,

It may be objected that in the past, such measures were never genuine reprisals in the legal sense of the term: i.e., measures preceded, whenever possible, by a formal warning and carried out with due respect for the requirements of the law, notably the condition of proportionality. Put differently, bombardments such as the ones carried out in World War Two and the armed conflict between Iran and Iraq may have been reprisals in name but in fact were wilful attacks on the enemy civilian population as such, carried out as part of a strategy to break the enemy's backbone and with the reprisal argument merely serving as a flimsy excuse.

The objection is probably correct; in effect, the present author has earlier come to precisely that assessment with respect to the events of the Second World War.[52] But it cannot support the conclusion that rather than being prohibited outright, recourse to reprisals against the enemy civilian population ought to have been made the subject of legal regulation. After all, even at the time of that war (when, in apparent contrast with the armed conflict between Iran and Iraq, the law of armed conflict played a distinct role) there existed 'the clear distinction between retaliation, which is always unlawful, and reprisals which in law are governed by strict conditions' (to quote Sir David Hughes-Morgan's words). Yet, although the belligerents frequently sought to justify their acts as measures of reprisal against the enemy civilian population, none of these so-called reprisals appear to have been genuinely 'governed' by the existing 'strict conditions'. This rather corroborates the conclusion that the chances for any such formal regulation to exert any significant influence on the behaviour of belligerents are minimal at best.

In these circumstances, this author cannot subscribe to Ms. Hampson's conclusion that 'The Diplomatic Conference . . . did a disservice both to the rule of law and to humanity itself'. On the contrary, for the Conference to have regulated and thereby formally condoned reprisals against the civilian population and civilian objects would have risked creating a dangerous illusion of 'rule of law' where law, unless supported by strong enforcement machinery, cannot be expected to reign.

Paradoxically, once such effective enforcement machinery is in force, it is likely that it will not serve in the first place to make belligerent parties respect

---

p. 315. The criticism is repeated by Roberts, loc. cit. n. 39, p. 142. While this once again amounts to a matter of 'tossing a coin in the air', this author is not convinced by the criticism. In his view, the potential effect of a threat of reprisal depends at least as much on the circumstances on the side of the 'threatee' as on that of the 'threator'.

52. See Kalshoven, op. cit. n. 1, pp. 177-178, 358.

the strict conditions governing recourse to reprisals. On the contrary, its main effect will probably lie in the removal of the very need to take reprisals. This points, once again, to the urgent necessity of bringing to life the International Fact-Finding Commission of Article 90, Protocol I, and of having its competence accepted by ever more States party to the Protocol. In this respect, it is a fortunate circumstance that the establishment of the Commission no longer appears to be a matter of some distant future.

3.3 Are the provisions outlawing reprisals against the civilian population reservable?

Academic arguments like the above in support of the rules in Protocol I prohibiting recourse to reprisals against the civilian population and civilian objects, are not in all circumstances sufficient to withhold governmental circles from considering whether to make a reservation to the rules at issue. The Protocol is silent on the matter of reservations: it neither limits nor permits them. In these circumstances, the question arises whether such a reservation would be permissible, in particular in the light of Article 19 sub (c) of the Vienna Convention on the Law of Treaties, that declares inadmissible reservations 'incompatible with the object and purpose of the treaty'.[53]

In this respect, Roberts notes that 'Several delegates at the Diplomatic Conference declared that the prohibitions banning recourse to reprisals must be non-reservable', and he concludes that were the United States to accompany its eventual ratification of Protocol I with such reservations 'it can be expected that several states will reject the reservations and possibly preclude the entry into force of the Protocol between the United States and the objecting state'.[54] Aldrich does not share the same concern: although rejection of treaty relations 'is, of course, conceivable' he doubts that it would happen.[55]

To this author, there is no straightforward answer to the above question. Especially as regards the rules in Protocol I on general protection of the

53. Art. 19 reads as follows:
A State may, when signing, ratifying, accepting, approving or acceding to a treaty, formulate a reservation unless:
(a) the reservation is prohibited by the treaty;
(b) the treaty provides that only specified reservations, which do not include the reservation in question, may be made; or
(c) in cases not falling under sub-paragraphs (a) and (b), the reservation is incompatible with the object and purpose of the treaty.

54. Loc. cit. n. 39, p. 145. In the same sense: Bierzanek, loc. cit. n. 19, p. 255.

55. Loc. cit. n. 39.

civilian population, it is difficult to go any further than the obvious statement that such general protection is the 'object and purpose' of this section and, indeed, a major 'object and purpose' of the whole Protocol. Opinions may differ, though, as to whether the prohibitions on reprisals are indispensable tools to achieve this lofty objective.

On this score, one might conceive the following argument. Starting out from the proposition that the general protection of the civilian population against the effects of hostilities indubitably represents one of the basic objectives of Protocol I, it is probably fair to say that the prohibitions on reprisals were added to promote that objective. Yet, even while fully accepting the wisdom of the primary rules for the protection of the civilian population as well as the good faith of those States who were responsible for the bans on reprisals added to those rules, a State may be convinced in equally good faith that these additions were ill-conceived. It may, in effect, be unshakable in its belief that to better realize the basic objective it must retain the power, when its civilian population is made the victim of attacks in gross violation of the rules of the Protocol, to subject the enemy to the same treatment (i.e., take reprisals in kind). In reserving the right to do so it might make it explicit that any such recourse to reprisals shall remain subject to the rules of customary international law, namely, subsidiarity, proportionality and discontinuance as soon as the purpose has been achieved.[56]

This would then bring up the question of acceptance of such a reservation by other States party to the Protocol. To accept or object to a reservation is a matter left to the discretion of States. In the present instance, acceptance would constitute the reserving State a party to the Protocol in relation to the accepting State and would give both States the right, in the event of an armed conflict between them, to take reprisals against the other's civilian population.

Objection, on the other hand, may or may not preclude the entry into force of the Protocol as between the reserving and the objecting State, dependent on the expressed intention of the latter party. If it would limit the scope of its objection to the reservation itself while for the rest accepting that in the event of an armed conflict the Protocol will apply in its relations with the reserving State, the consequence would be, in the terms of Article 21, paragraph 3, of the Vienna Convention on the Law of Treaties, that 'the provisions to which the reservation relates do not apply as between the two States to the extent of the reservation.'[57]

56. Kalshoven, 'The Belligerent Reprisals . . .', loc. cit. n. 19, pp. 40-42.

57. While the matter of acceptance and objection to reservations is not without controversy, the above text simply relies on Arts. 19-21 of the Vienna Convention on the Law of Treaties.

At its most restrictive, the quoted phrase would simply leave the provisions banning reprisals inapplicable in an armed conflict between the two parties. Given this reading, the effect of objection would be indistinguishable from that of acceptance. There is another conceivable interpretation, though. For the objecting State, the prohibitions on reprisals may be so inextricably linked to the other rules for the protection of the civilian population and civilian objects that in its relations with the reserving State, it is not prepared to consider itself bound by the entire section of the Protocol on that subject. This would imply that as between these two States, the whole matter of protection of the civilian population, including recourse to reprisals, is left to customary law.[58]

Pierre-Henri Imbert, writing on the theory and practice of reservations to multilateral treaties, has suggested yet another distinction between acceptance and the 'soft' variety of objection without refusal of treaty relations. In his submission, the latter reaction provides a starting-point for consultations between the two States concerned, with a view to establishing how the reserved provisions should be applied (in case of a reservation to part of a provision) or by what rules they should be substituted. In contrast with plain acceptance, the 'soft' objection could thus set in motion a negotiating process that in the most favourable case might even result in a withdrawal of the reservation.[59]

Needless to say, for one who like the present author is a confirmed supporter of the prohibitions on reprisals in Protocol I, this would be a particularly desirable outcome, especially in view of the conceivable alternative of a total non-application of the conventional rules in the Protocol on the protection of the civilian population.

This author has earlier had occasion to raise another point in the discussion about the acceptability and desirability of reservations to the bans on reprisals in Protocol I. After having argued along the lines indicated above, that a State could in good faith consider itself entitled to make such a reservation, he added that:

> 'a State which has not itself accepted the competence of the international fact-finding commission of Article 90, Protocol I, and which thus has failed to contribute to realizing the one single alternative to reprisals against the civilian population which Protocol I provides, will by that fact alone be in a singularly weak position to object to the reservation, no matter how undesirable, which another State might formulate with respect to (part of) the prohibitions on those reprisals.'[60]

58. For such a line of argument, see P.-H. Imbert, *Les réserves aux traités multilatéraux* (1979) p. 265.

59. Ibid. at p. 266 et seq.

60. Art. 90 provides, in the main, that an International Fact-Finding Commission consisting

At the time, his remark was aimed in particular at the communist States (as they then were). At the Diplomatic Conference of 1974-1977, these States had: (1) strongly upheld the sovereign right of States to make reservations; (2) repeatedly declared that reservations to the provisions prohibiting reprisals would be unacceptable, and (3) been utterly opposed to the inclusion of Article 90. It is therefore gratifying to learn that the Soviet Union has accompanied its recent, most welcome, ratification of Protocol I with a declaration accepting the competence of the International Fact-Finding Commission of Article 90 – and, fortunately, has made no reservation to the reprisals provisions.[61]

In effect, no State has so far made such a formal reservation. Italy, however, has declared on ratification that it:

> 'will react to serious and systematic violations by an enemy of the obligations imposed by Additional Protocol I and in particular its Articles 51 and 52 with all means admissible under international law in order to prevent further violations.'[62]

Although not in terms a formal reservation to the prohibitions in these Articles on reprisals against the civilian population and civilian objects, the declaration is sufficiently vague to admit of more than one interpretation. Under the most benignant reading, it does no more than state the obvious, as after all, States by definition have the right to 'react to serious and systematic violations by an enemy . . . with all means admissible under international law in order to prevent further violations.'

Even given this interpretation it is ambiguous in that it appears at least to hint at the concept of reprisals. These undeniably belong to the 'means admissible under international law' – admissible, that is, unless they are prohibited. Articles 51 and 52 of Protocol I do just that, and the Italian declaration does not explicitly exclude the operation of these prohibitions. In law, it cannot therefore reinstate that particular right of reprisal. Is it, then, meant as a reminder of the possibility of a threat of reprisal? But for that purpose, no special declaration is required, as the provisions in question do not, strictly

---

of fifteen members of high moral standing and acknowledged impartiality shall be established once not less than twenty High Contracting Parties have agreed to accept its competence as defined in the Article, and that those elected as members shall serve in their personal capacity; according to para. 2(c), the Commission shall be competent to: (i) enquire into any facts alleged to be a grave breach as defined in the Conventions and the Protocol or other serious violation of these instruments; (ii) facilitate, through its good offices, the restoration of an attitude of respect for the Conventions and the Protocol.

61. 29 Int. Rev. of the Red Cross (1989) p. 591.

62. 26 Int. Rev. of the Red Cross (1986) p. 114.

speaking, prohibit such threats. So, this interpretation leaves one wondering what made Italy go to all the trouble.

Even on this reading, one element in the declaration is of particular interest: it concerns the specific reference to 'serious and systematic violations by an enemy'. This phrase echoes the terms of reference of certain human rights bodies. In the present instance, it may have been chosen to indicate that the dire consequences, darkly hinted at in the declaration, will materialize only when the situation has assumed the characteristics of a major 'material breach' of Protocol I by the adverse party . . . as opposed, perhaps, to a mere incidental violation by an enemy field commander.

One way of determining whether an act in breach of the rules for the protection of the civilian population signifies a 'serious and systematic violation' will be to protest against the act, to demand the immediate termination of such acts, to threaten counter-measures . . . in short, to take all those steps which in law must precede actual recourse to reprisals, and which the French delegates to the Diplomatic Conference of 1974-1977 would have wished to see incorporated in a regulation of reprisals in Protocol I. This goes to show, once again, how close the Italian declaration comes – not necessarily to a blunt all-out reservation to the prohibitions on reprisals in Articles 51 and 52, but to the indication of an intention to set those prohibitions aside when the situation turns really serious: a 'worst-case reservation', so to speak.

This already alludes to the other possible interpretation of the Italian declaration. The phrase 'all means admissible under international law' may in effect be read as referring to means admissible under general international law. This might be intended to exclude and thus overrule special treaty provisions such as the ones in Articles 51 and 52. Given this interpretation, the declaration would indeed amount to an outright reservation to the prohibitions of reprisals in those Articles.[63]

In this light it may be of interest to note that to the present day, no State has objected to the Italian declaration. If anything, this is evidence of the care with which it has been phrased.

63. Meyrowitz regards the Italian declaration as an outright reservation of the right of reprisal; loc. cit. n. 42, p. 192.

4. AREAS WHERE REPRISALS HAVE NOT BEEN FORMALLY PROHIBITED

There remain some areas of the law of armed conflict where recourse to belligerent reprisals may still appear permissible. One author raises a somewhat dubious argument about a claimed lacuna in Part IV of Protocol I on the protection of the civilian population. Not open to doubt is that Part III on 'Methods and Means of Warfare' (Articles 35-42) does not contain a single reference to reprisals, whether in the form of a prohibition or otherwise. The same holds true (with the one exception mentioned previously) about the 1980 Conventional Weapons Convention with its annexed Protocols, as it does for a much older instrument like the Geneva Protocol for the Prohibition of the Use in War of Asphyxiating, Poisonous or Other Gases and of Bacteriological Methods of Warfare, of 17 June 1925[64] (the 1925 Gas Protocol for short). And unfortunately, similar silence reigns in the law relating to internal armed conflicts. It now remains for us to examine to what extent silence in these instances implies a continued right of reprisal.

4.1 A loophole in Part IV of Protocol I?

The French author, Henri Meyrowitz,[65] has raised the following curious point about an alleged loophole in the provisions in Part IV of Protocol I that aim to protect the civilian population against attacks by way of reprisal. Suppose one party is the victim of indiscriminate attacks as prohibited specifically by Article 51, paragraphs 4 and 5, of Protocol I: is it not the case that under the terms of those provisions a reprisal in kind has remained permissible? His ingenious argument appears to be that rather than taking the civilian population as its object, such a reprisal attack would after all be directed, no matter how loosely, against one or more military objectives in enemy territory. He is not very firm in his conclusion, though: while stating that according to general rules of interpretation the question seems to warrant a positive answer, he hastens to add that such a reprisal in kind may easily and in good faith be taken for an attempt to circumvent the prohibitions in Article 51, paragraph 6, and Article 52, paragraph 1.

64. Schindler and Toman, op. cit. n. 5, p. 115.
65. Meyrowitz, loc. cit. n. 42, p. 185.

To the present author, the argument must be rejected, not just on account of the difficulty signalled by Meyrowitz but because the argument itself is rather too ingenious. The ground rule on treaty interpretation, as laid down in Article 31 of the Vienna Convention on the Law of Treaties,[66] is that 'a treaty shall be interpreted in good faith in accordance with the ordinary meaning to be given to the terms of the treaty in their context and in the light of its object and purpose'. Meyrowitz' argument rests exclusively on a literal reading of the provisions prohibiting reprisals in Articles 51 and 52 and appears to disregard entirely their context and the 'object and purpose' of Part IV of Protocol I. Taking these factors into account there is no doubt in my mind that the prohibitions on reprisals embedded in these Articles cover the Articles in their entirety and not merely those provisions specifically addressing attacks that take the civilian population or civilian objects as their object.[67]

4.2 Means and methods of warfare

In discussing the question of the permissibility of reprisals in respect of the rules in Part III of Protocol I on means and methods of warfare, certain rules may be discarded straight away. This applies, for instance, to the rule in Article 35, paragraph 1, that the right of belligerent parties 'to choose methods or means of warfare is not unlimited'. It is difficult to envisage how this general principle could be susceptible to the right of reprisal – or to gross violation, for that matter. A similar comment may be made about the rule in Article 36 requiring a State to determine whether the employment of a new weapon would bring it into conflict with the law:[68] a failure to fulfil such an obligation of implementation cannot seriously be regarded as a major breach of the Protocol.

Other rules may be discarded for different reasons. This applies, first, to provisions found in the means-and-methods part of Protocol I but that are specifically designed to protect specified categories of persons, such as the wounded and sick or medical personnel, against whom reprisals are forbidden.

66. The Convention was adopted by the United Nations Conference on the Law of Treaties on 22 May 1969 and opened for signature on 23 May 1969; text in A/CONF. 39/27.

67. In the same sense: Bierzanek, loc. cit. n. 19, p. 252.

68. Art. 36 provides that 'In the study, development, acquisition or adoption of a new weapon, means or method of warfare' a State party 'is under an obligation to determine whether its employment would, in some or all circumstances, be prohibited . . .'

A case in point is the prohibition in Article 38, paragraph 1, against making 'improper use' of the red cross or red crescent emblem: without doubt, this rule must be regarded as covered by the prohibitions of reprisals in the First, Second and Fourth Geneva Conventions of 1949 as, indeed, by Article 20 of Protocol I.

Another instance is provided by rules which, although not included in a section of the law specifically designed to protect the civilian population, may in effect be seen to serve that purpose. Provisions of this type are found, *inter alia,* in the Mines and Incendiary Weapons Protocols annexed to the Conventional Weapons Convention of 1980.[69] Examples are: the restriction in Article 4, paragraph 2, of the Mines Protocol on the use of certain mines in areas containing a concentration of civilians,[70] and the prohibition in Article 2, paragraph 1, of the Incendiary Weapons Protocol against attacking the civilian population with incendiary weapons.[71] In such cases, for a State party to Protocol I of 1977 the prohibition of reprisals against the civilian population governs these provisions as well.

With regard to the remaining general problem it may be recalled, first, that at the Diplomatic Conference of 1974-1977, a Polish proposal to insert into Protocol I a prohibition on all reprisals against persons and objects protected under the Protocol, was withdrawn simultaneously with the opposite, French, proposal to reintroduce and regulate recourse to reprisals.[72] If anything, this implies that the Conference has left the matter to the development of customary law. It may be asked, therefore, in what direction customary law is developing and, perhaps, should develop. Specifically: can it not be argued that recourse to reprisals may sometimes be deemed unacceptable even where it is not formally prohibited?

It is submitted that at least by way of analogy, Article 60 of the Vienna Convention on the Law of Treaties, on the consequences of a material breach, is of relevance here.[73] Paragraph 2(b) provides that 'A material breach of a

69. On this, see F. Kalshoven, 'Arms, Armaments and International Law', 191 Hague Recueil (1985-II) p. 251 et seq.

70. Art. 4, para. 2, of the Mines Protocol prohibits the use of mines that are not remotely delivered and certain other devices 'in any city, town, village or other area containing a similar concentration of civilians in which combat between ground forces is not taking place or does not appear to be imminent, unless . . . measures are taken to protect civilians from their effects.'

71. The Article prohibits 'in all circumstances to make the civilian population as such, individual civilians or civilian objects the object of attack by incendiary weapons.'

72. *Supra,* text at n. 23.

73. This author has advanced the argument developed in the text above on an earlier occasion: loc. cit. n. 19: 'The Belligerent Reprisals in the Light of the 1977 Geneva Protocols'. The present

multilateral treaty by one of the parties entitles . . . a party specially affected by the breach to invoke it as a ground for suspending the operation of the treaty in whole or in part in the relations between itself and the defaulting State.' According to paragraph 5, this general rule '[does] not apply to provisions relating to the protection of the human person contained in treaties of a humanitarian character . . .'[74]

While the general rule in paragraph 2(b) appears to be a codification of customary international law, the exception in paragraph 5 may more properly be regarded as a case of progressive development or, in other words, new conventional law. As such, it binds the parties to the Convention, and it can acquire general binding force only if it is in turn incorporated into customary law. While it seems open to serious doubt that this has actually happened, it is simply assumed here for the sake of argument, and without further investigation, that the rule in paragraph 5 is generally accepted as law.

Suspension of the operation of (part of) a multilateral treaty (i.e., the application of strict negative reciprocity) goes further than a mere reprisal in that, for the duration of the suspension, it effectively frees the 'party specially affected' from all its obligations connected with the suspended (part of the) treaty. In contrast, recourse to reprisals under customary international law remains subject to a series of legal restraints. Legally, if in a specific case the party concerned is denied the customary right to suspend, this leaves its equally customary but minor right of reprisal unaffected.[75] Yet it may be argued that the moral ground underlying the prohibition of suspension renders recourse to reprisals equally undesirable.

The question then is whether the instruments at issue here are 'treaties of a humanitarian character'. It seems safe to state that Protocol I has this character, and so probably has the Conventional Weapons Convention (or, rather, the Protocols annexed to it). Actually, even the 1925 Gas Protocol may be deemed to qualify as such. But this is not enough: the next point to examine is whether the provisions in these instruments that have *prima facie* remained

---

further development and, it is hoped, clarification of the argument is in response to some critical comments by Prof. George Aldrich.

74. The text adds: 'in particular to provisions prohibiting any form of reprisals against persons protected by such treaties'. In the context of the present argument this phrase is irrelevant, as the question at issue is precisely whether reprisals are permissible where they have not been prohibited.

75. Meyrowitz rightly points out that the reprisal itself does not imply a suspension of the rule: a reprisal, whether or not in kind, serves precisely to uphold the rule or rules involved: loc. cit. n. 42, p. 178.

susceptible to reprisals are perhaps, in the sense of Article 60, paragraph 5, of the Vienna Convention, 'provisions relating to the protection of the human person'.

For the time being, and in the absence of relevant State practice, the answer to this question is bound to remain a matter for individual appreciation. Even so, there is little room for doubt that a rule like the one in Article 41, paragraph 1, of the 1977 Protocol 'relates to the protection of the human person': it provides that an adversary 'who is recognized or who, in the circumstances, should be recognized to be *hors de combat* shall not be made the object of attack.' The same would seem to apply to the rule in Article 42, paragraph 1, that 'No person parachuting from an aircraft in distress shall be made the object of attack during his descent.' Yet, the two rules are not entirely similar in all respects.

The enemy *hors de combat,* as defined in paragraph 2 of Article 41, is a person who, either, is in the power of the enemy or, if he is not, 'clearly expresses an intention to surrender' or is unconscious or 'otherwise incapacitated by wounds or sickness, and therefore is incapable of defending himself'; provided always that he 'abstains from any hostile act and does not attempt to escape'. In contrast, the 'person parachuting from an aircraft in distress' may be full of fighting spirit and, indeed, be heading for territory controlled by his party, where a fresh plane is awaiting him. Put differently, the rule protecting the latter person in these circumstances also protects the military interests of the enemy. Conceivably, therefore, the part of the rule protecting even the airman who may be expected to reach the ground in territory controlled by his party might be held susceptible to encroachment by way of reprisal.

Again, some rules, e.g., on the prohibition or limitation of use of specified weapons, on the face of it seem to have been written solely for the protection of combatants. At the same time, there may be a military interest involved as well. When this is the case, the enemy may gain a considerable military advantage by using the weapon in violation of the rule. Depending on the situation, a reaction by way of reprisal in kind may then be indispensable to restore the military balance.[76]

In contrast, the (complicated) rules on the prohibition of perfidy and the permissibility of ruses of war, in Article 37, may provide yet another example of rules 'relating to the protection of the human person' whose violation by way of reprisal would serve no conceivable interest.

76. Meyrowitz suggests that with respect to such rules, a state ratifying Protocol I might reserve the right to apply the customary principle of reciprocity: loc. cit. n. 42, p. 192.

It should be reiterated that the above reasoning does not aim to establish that by virtue of positive international law, reprisals in violation of this or the other rule of the law of armed conflict are unlawful even though the treaties do not explicitly say so. Its purpose is, rather, to demonstrate that application of the central idea in Article 60, paragraph 5, of the Vienna Convention may lead to the conclusion that such reprisals are morally wrong . . . against Grotian moral justice, as it were, and therefore had better be avoided.[77]

4.3 The special case of the 1925 Gas Protocol

The 1925 Gas Protocol is a case apart. Its special situation arises from the fact that a number of States have accompanied their ratification or accession with a sweeping reservation to the effect that the Protocol ceases to be binding on the State in regard to any enemy State whose armed forces or whose allies fail to respect the prohibitions laid down in the Protocol. Most of these reservations were made long ago by the original signatories.[78] In quite a few instances, the reservations were later simply 'inherited' by newly independent States confirming their participation in the Protocol which (and hence, apparently, as it) had been made applicable to them by the former colonial power. In one case (Fiji) the reservation was expressly reiterated, in another (Barbados) it was withdrawn. Also Ireland, a reserving State since 1930, withdrew its reservation in 1972.

Again, some newcomers also made the reservation, in some cases with interesting additions. Thus, Israel specified in 1969 that its reservation would take effect also in the event of use of chemical means of warfare by 'the regular or irregular forces or the groups or individuals operating from' the territory of an enemy State. Jordan, in 1977, simply stated that 'it undertakes no commitment toward States whose regular or irregular armed forces do not observe the provisions of the Protocol'. The United States, one of the original signatories but ratifying only in 1975, attached the classical reservation without embellishments of the Israeli type.[79]

77. H. Grotius, *De Jure Belli Ac Pacis*, III, X, 1.1; and see F. Kalshoven, 'Grotius' Jus in Bello with Special Reference to Ruses of War and Perfidy', in A. Dufour, P. Haggenmacher and J. Toman, eds., *Grotius et l'Ordre juridique international* (1985) pp. 89-100.

78. For the facts mentioned in the text and for further detailed information, see the list of signatures, ratifications, accessions and notifications of continuity in Schindler and Toman, op. cit. n. 5, p. 117.

79. It did, on the other hand, accompany its ratification with a long statement reserving to the President the right to resort to the use of tear-gases in certain well-defined situations; 40 US

The result of this network of reservations is that in many cases the Protocol will apply as treaty law merely on the basis of plain reciprocity, and this not between reserving States alone but, on grounds of general treaty law, even if only one of the parties to an international armed conflict has made or maintained the reservation.[80] A case in point is the recent war between Iran and Iraq. Both are parties to the Protocol (since 1929 and 1931, respectively). Iran did not make the reservation but Iraq did, and this entitled Iran to avail itself of Iraq's reservation in the event of non-respect of the Protocol on the part of the latter State.

Obviously, a State need not avail itself of its full rights under the reservation. In particular, it may prefer to reserve its reactions, in terms of the Italian declaration attached to its ratification of Protocol I, to events amounting to 'serious and systematic violations by an enemy': cases, in other words, where the employment of chemical weapons by the enemy has assumed large dimensions and threatens significantly to affect the military balance. There is, after all, little utility in the initiation of all-out gas war in reaction, say, to a mere whiff of tear-gas from the other side.

Besides the absence of utility, there would be an evident lack of proportion in such an unrestrained reaction. This brings us to a second set of restraints a victim State might apply in its reaction to 'serious and systematic violations' of the Protocol. Even though, according to their terms, the effect of the reservations in force would be entirely to free it of its obligations under the Protocol for the duration of the armed conflict, it may confine itself to a proportionate reaction, using chemical agents no more harmful and against targets no less acceptable than the enemy has done, and terminating its reaction as soon as it becomes evident that the enemy has done the same. The victim State could, in other words, instead of giving the reservation its fullest effect, limit itself to a reprisal in kind. This might well prove to be the more commendable course of action, in terms of economy of force, harm done and result achieved. Even better, of course, would be altogether to desist from action in reprisal, unless urgent military reasons so require.

Federal Register, No. 70 (1975) p. 16187; reprinted in 14 ILM (1975) p. 794; see also Kalshoven, loc. cit. n. 69, pp. 269-270.

80. Vienna Convention on the Law of Treaties, Art. 21, para. 1(b).

5. INTERNAL ARMED CONFLICT

When it comes to the matter of reprisals in situations of internal armed conflict, the treaties in force are simply silent. This includes the texts specifically relating to such conflicts, viz., Article 3 common to the Geneva Conventions of 1949, Article 19 of the Hague Convention of 1954, and Protocol II of 1977. Needless to say, it would be too rash to conclude from this general silence that in such situations, reprisals are still widely regarded as an entirely acceptable mode of reacting to an adversary's unlawful methods of waging war. Rather, the negotiating parties in the conferences of 1949, 1954 and 1974-1977 simply neglected, or expressly refused, to address the question of international legal restrictions on their freedom of action in this respect.[81]

Here the debate at the Diplomatic Conference of 1974-1977 is illuminating. One striking feature was the flat denial by some delegates that in a situation of internal armed conflict the notion of reprisal could apply at all.[82] A working party set up to consider the question eventually emerged with a compromise solution, to the effect that certain provisions of Protocol II 'shall not, in any circumstances or for any reason whatsoever, be violated, even in response to a violation of the provisions of the Protocol'.[83] Even this proposal ultimately failed to muster sufficient support: in the plenary session of the Conference it was rejected by 41 votes to 20, with 22 abstentions.[84]

81. The neglect applies to the conferences of 1949 and 1954, the refusal to that of 1974-1977.

82. As noted in the ICRC's *Commentary on the Additional Protocols of 8 June 1977 to the Geneva Conventions of 12 August 1949* (1987) p. 1372 note 18, 'Several delegations argued that rules on reprisals concerned only relations between States, as subjects of international law possessing *facultas bellandi*'.

83. 10 O.R. pp. 181-296, at pp. 234-235: CDDH/405/Rev.l: Report of Committee 1, Annex II: Report of Working Group B, Addendum: Report of Sub-Group on Reprisals in Draft Protocol II; pp. 217-219: consideration of proposals in Working Group B.

84. 7 O.R. p. 109: CDDH/SR.51, para. 16. On the occasion of the vote, the representative of the United States of America, Aldrich, 'said he hoped that if put to the vote, [the proposed article] would be rejected, since the whole concept of reprisals had no place in Protocol II'; ibid. p. 108: para. 7. In this, he was immediately supported by Dixit, the representative of India; ibid. para. 8. While Aldrich may have had a legal argument in mind, Dixit definitely was only considering the political aspect of the matter.

I. Detter de Lupis suggests that the failure to incorporate reprisals in Protocol II may be a result of 'the confused notion of belligerent reprisals as being undefined and mistaken for having similar characteristics and legal effects as State reprisals': to her, 'belligerent reprisals are of a completely different type: they are not used to retaliate against a State for what that State has done in violation of international law. In a large majority of cases it is individuals who have committed an act of hostility, perhaps in violation of the laws of war by using civilian status, or by abusing the pro-

How little consensus there had been even before this ultimate failure, may be gathered from the report of the working party. It notes that while some participants had suggested the deletion of the phrase 'even in response to a violation of the provisions of the Protocol' (thus depriving the proposed text of its most salient part), others had wanted to see it replaced by the phrase 'even for the purpose of inducing the adverse party to comply with its obligations' (which would for all practical purposes have modified it into a direct prohibition of reprisals).[85]

In this uncertain state of affairs, the ICRC takes a firm stand. Commenting on the character of the rules on humane treatment in Article 4, paragraph 2, of Protocol II,[86] it argues forcefully that these 'are explicit and do not allow for any exception . . . They are absolute obligations.'[87] This 'also means that no derogation is allowed . . .'[88] Indeed, 'there is in fact no room left at all for carrying out "reprisals" against protected persons.' Reminding the reader that it already put forward this interpretation in its commentary on Article 3 common to the Geneva Conventions of 1949, the Committee finds it now confirmed by the 'strengthening of fundamental guarantees of humane treatment in Protocol II and, in particular, the inclusion of a prohibition on collective

---

tective status of an open town, and the reprisals are taken against other innocent individuals, usually against civilians.' *The Law of* War (1987) pp. 254-255, 258. Needless to say, the present author does not endorse her redefinition of belligerent reprisals.

85. *Supra* n. 83. See also Bothe, Partsch and Solf, op. cit. n. 19, pp. 636-637.

86. Art. 4 is headed 'Fundamental guarantees'. Paras. 1 and 2 read as follows:

1. All persons who do not take a direct part or who have ceased to take part in hostilities, whether or not their liberty has been restricted, are entitled to respect for their person, honour and convictions and religious practices. They shall in all circumstances be treated humanely, without any adverse distinction. It is prohibited to order that there shall be no survivors.

2. Without prejudice to the generality of the foregoing, the following acts against the persons referred to in paragraph 1 are and shall remain prohibited at any time and in any place whatsoever:

(a) violence to the life, health and physical or mental well-being of persons, in particular murder as well as cruel treatment such as torture, mutilation or any form of corporal punishment;
(b) collective punishments;
(c) taking of hostages;
(d) acts of terrorism;
(e) outrages upon personal dignity, in particular humiliating and degrading treatment, rape, enforced prostitution and any form of indecent assault;
(f) slavery and the slave trade in all their forms;
(g) pillage;
(h) threats to commit any of the foregoing acts.

87. Op. cit. n. 82, p. 1372: para. 4528.

88. *Supra* n. 17.

punishments . . .'[89] With respect to this prohibition in particular, it notes that it:

> 'was included in the article relating to fundamental guarantees by consensus. That decision was important because it is based on the intention to give the rule the widest possible scope, and to avoid any risk of a restrictive interpretation. In fact, to include the prohibition on collective punishments amongst the acts unconditionally prohibited by Article 4 is virtually equivalent to prohibiting "reprisals" against protected persons.'[90]

Having said all this, the Committee takes care to stipulate that its interpretation does not '[call] into question the refusal of the negotiators to introduce the legal concept of reprisals in the context of non-international armed conflict.'[91]

A nice job, one is inclined to comment. The Committee makes the most of its strong beliefs while reducing the 'refusal of the negotiators' to a legal qualm. This may be something of an oversimplification, though. To be sure, there were those among the negotiators who held on legal grounds that reprisal is a mechanism that can operate only between sovereign States (as well as, apparently, between a State and a liberation movement, witness the inclusion in Protocol I of Article 1, paragraph 4, which includes the so-called wars of national liberation among international armed conflicts).[92] For quite a few others, however, the refusal to admit any specific reference to 'reprisal' in Protocol II may have been not so much a matter of legal nicety as of stark reality, based on their conviction that in an internal armed conflict, harsh countermeasures may be indispensable and the law had therefore better stay silent on this point.

The actions of parties to several recent internal armed conflicts regrettably serve to reinforce the impression that more than one government interprets the vacuum in the treaty law in force as an indication that in such a situation, whether of the Article 3 or Protocol II variety, their right to take reprisal-type measures (although of course not so named) continues unabated.

89. Op. cit. n. 82, pp. 1372-1373: paras. 4530-4531.

90. Ibid. p. 1374: para. 4536.

91. Ibid. p. 1373: para. 4531.

92. Art. 1, para. 4, provides that the situations to which it applies 'include armed conflicts in which peoples are fighting against colonial domination and alien occupation and against racist régimes in the exercise of their right of self-determination, as enshrined in the Charter of the United Nations and the Declaration on Principles of International Law concerning Friendly Relations and Co-operation among States in accordance with the Charter of the United Nations.'

In this situation and as far as substance goes, the present author finds himself unreservedly on the side of the ICRC. Yet in his view, the most convincing argument against such measures of reprisal does not lie in their alleged resemblance to measures of collective punishment: reprisals by definition are measures not of punishment but of enforcement. It is and remains, rather, their general futility and escalating effect. This argument applies with equal force in internal armed conflicts as in international ones.

For the rest, and in addition to the arguments adduced by the Committee, a reasoning by analogy may be of some help. Thus, when Part III of Protocol II explicitly extends protection to the wounded, sick and shipwrecked as well as to medical and religious personnel, this is a faithful translation of the comparable rules applicable in international armed conflict. As part of those rules, the prohibition of reprisals has become almost a matter of course. Therefore, it seems permissible to regard it as implied in the rules for internal armed conflict as well.

When it comes to measures of reprisal against persons captured in the course of an internal armed conflict while taking part in hostilities, this line of reasoning faces an additional obstacle. In international armed conflict, captured combatants have the status of prisoners of war, and the prohibition of reprisals is specifically designed to protect them in that capacity. In internal armed conflict, the legal notions of combatant and prisoner of war do not obtain, and captured opponents fall under the protection of Part II of Protocol II (of which Article 4 forms part). A simple copying of the rule prohibiting reprisals against prisoners of war may therefore not seem permissible. As against this, it may be advanced that on the whole, the rules in Part II, and notably those in Articles 5 and 6, reflect the main principles governing the treatment of prisoners of war, so that the situation is really as sufficiently similar to that of the wounded and sick that the same principle should apply.

Part IV of Protocol II lays down rules for the protection of the civilian population. Needless to say, this is the area of greatest concern. At the Diplomatic Conference, many members of the majority that imposed its will when it was a matter of prohibiting reprisals against the civilian population in case of international armed conflict, were equally firmly opposed to introducing the concept of reprisal in Protocol II. And it seems not at all unlikely that the reasons for their opposition were just about the same as the reasons why the minority was opposed to the prohibitions of reprisals in Part IV of Protocol I: simply stated, the fear that they might one day come to need the measures at issue.

In these circumstances, and taking into account the relative novelty and controversial character of the prohibitions of reprisals against the civilian population and civilian objects in Part IV of Protocol I, this author would not venture to argue by way of analogy that as a matter of law, measures resembling reprisals against the civilian population are prohibited in internal armed conflict as well. Of course, this leaves the other practical and moral arguments against recourse to reprisals entirely intact: their dubious effectivity, their escalating effect, the harm they do both to the people chosen as targets and to one's own standard of civilization – in one word, their general undesirability.

6. PERSPECTIVE

Where do we go from here? It seems safe to state that the time is not ripe for further efforts at legislation of the reprisal issue in the specific context of international humanitarian law. As far as international armed conflicts are concerned, the written law may have gone as far as it can, or, as some would say, even farther. The Geneva Conventions of 1949 bind virtually all States; and, while fewer States have consented to be bound by the Hague Convention of 1954, Protocol I of 1977 and the Conventional Weapons Convention of 1980, their numbers are impressive and, certainly in the case of the latter instruments, still rising. In no case – with the possible exception of Italy – has a State reserved its right to take reprisals in derogation of the provisions in these treaties expressly banning such recourse.

Yet, ratification without reservation is not enough: what is needed now is the realization in practice of what was agreed on paper. More than anything, this requires a constant concern for, and propaganda in favour of, the faithful implementation of the law. Especially where the prohibitions on reprisals against the civilian population and civilian objects are concerned, this will require a great effort; but then, this is true of the entire set of rules for the protection of the civilian population.[93] In this regard, special importance attaches to the speedy establishment and activation of the International Fact-Finding Commission provided in Article 90 of Protocol I.

Always in the sphere of international armed conflict, there is the problem of the permissibility or otherwise of reprisals consisting in the non-observance

93. As this author wrote earlier, 'after the participants to the Conterence, it will be the turn of the participants in actual hostilities to demonstrate their willingness to take, in terms of Article 57, paragraph 1 [of Protocol I], "constant care . . . to spare the civilian population, civilians and civilian objects".': 9 NYIL (1978) pp. 107-171, at p. 146.

of prohibitions or restrictions on the use of means and methods of warfare. This will probably remain a dark area for a long time to come: for one thing, because of the conflicting interests at stake, and for another in view of the (fortunate) rarity of situations where the conduct of belligerent parties could contribute to the development of practice. Meanwhile, the point should be emphasized that an absence of prohibitions does not necessarily mean permissibility, let alone advisability.

As regards the retaliatory use of chemical weapons, the chances seem slim indeed that many States party to the 1925 Gas Protocol will soon follow the Irish example and give up their reserved right to suspend the operation of the Protocol as against any enemy whose armed forces, or whose allies, fail to respect its terms. More may perhaps be expected here, as in the case of bacteriological means of warfare, of the current attempts at banning these weapons altogether. Once such a ban would be effective, the need for retaliatory action in the event of breach would no longer exist.

There remains the most vexing problem of all, and that is the complete silence on the reprisal question in the treaty law applicable in situations of internal armed conflict. The problem is all the more acute in view of the frequency of such conflicts and the recurrence of modes of conduct that in a situation of international armed conflict would amount to prohibited reprisals.

As it is unlikely that the lacuna in Article 3 of the Geneva Conventions of 1949 and Protocol II of 1977 will soon be filled, other ways must be explored to improve the situation. One possibility, discussed above, is to use the argument by analogy as an instrument of moral persuasion against the current negative tendencies. Another element of hope lies in the great interest of public opinion in human rights issues. Given the close connections, especially where fundamental norms are concerned, between the international humanitarian law of armed conflict and international human rights law, there is an urgent need for a mobilization of public opinion and, indeed, of the various official and unofficial bodies established to ensure respect for human rights, in defence of those fundamental values reflected, for the event of international armed conflict, in the prohibitions on reprisals.

[3]

THE IMPLEMENTATION OF THE GENEVA CONVENTIONS OF 1949 AND THE ADDITIONAL PROTOCOLS OF 1978

G.I.A.D. Draper

A. Introduction

The distinguished jurist and judge of the International Court of Justice, the late Sir Hersch Lauterpacht, who gave much attention to the law of war, saw fit to say [1]: "if international law is . . . the vanishing point of law, the law of war is even more conspicuously the vanishing point of international law [2]". In his concern to establish the reality of the science of international law he found it necessary to meet certain criticisms directed at the law of war :

> ". . . it is in particular with regard to the law of war that the charge of a mischievous propensity of unreality has been levelled against the science of international law. The very idea of the legal regulation of a condition of mere force has appeared to many incongruous to the point of absurdity."

It follows that in treating of the devices provided by the law of war for its own implementation and enforcement we are dealing with matters central to the claim to reality of the science of international law. Recent developments in the law of war under the title of the "Re-affirmation and Development of the Humanitarian Law of Armed Conflict" have in no way lessened the charges of unreality and artificiality that are likely to be directed against the contemporary law of war, conceived as a body of rules which seek to restrain and to govern conduct in warfare. For these reasons alone it may be worthwhile to examine and assess that part of this law designed to secure its implementation and enforcement.

By implementation in this context is meant those devices, institutions and rules designed to monitor and ensure its observance. By enforcement of the law of war, the topic for the following course, is meant the collection of mechanisms and rules available to the law of war to secure the restoration of observance when that law has been violated. International law, and no less the law of war, relies heavily upon meta-legal forces for its implementation. Part of those forces resides in the nature of man and his awareness of his place in the universe. At first sight, it seems paradoxical that warfare, born of irrational conduct and aggravated by the lust for killing and destruction, can be subjected to law, a product of the human reason. Had not St. Thomas Aquinas, the great ornament of mediaeval scholasticism, defined law as "an ordinance of reason for the common good made by him who has the care of the community, and promulgated". Had not the Greek philosophers pointed out that law is the answer of man's reason to the question of order in the universe, part of the perennial human endeavour to accommodate the well-being of man in society with the upholding of order without which no well-being is possible ? Can the law of war fall within these ideas ? In the specific context of international law, Grotius had pointed out that the welfare of the individual human being is the primary object of all law, including international law. He saw the primary purpose of the law of war, in his famous appendix devoted to the *temperamenta belli* [3], as the mitigation of human suffering in war and the reduction of its brutalities. It would seem to follow that whatever approach we make to the fundamental nature of law, it is not easy to exclude the law of war from the meaning of law. The question of the difficulty of its enforcement is another and different matter. Municipal law has in the course of a long history experienced and, with difficulty, partly resolved that difficulty in its own way. International law, of which the law of war forms part, has evolved its own and different mechanisms of enforcement. They are defective and often fail, but that does not destroy their existence. Moreover, it is part of the singular moral strength of international law, that not only is it proximate to the tenets of morality, but that much of its observance in daily life is secured in the absence of those coercive sanctions regularly available to most civilized and mature systems of municipal law. Such a contrast cannot afford evidence of the weakness of international law.

The dichotomy between the purposes of the law of war and the nature of warfare is probably the most acute point of tension between law and life. The primary object of the law of war today is to achieve the maximum humanitarian restraint in warfare compatible with the nature of war. We have been reminded that [4] "international lawyers have a duty to contribute, though without sanguine hope and without much enthusiasm, to the achievement of that humanitarian object". That is one of the reasons why the International Committee of the Red Cross, of Geneva, with a degree of realism that is not always appreciated, have styled the contemporary Law of War "The

Humanitarian Law of Armed Conflict". It is this ascendancy of the humanitarian principles in the development of the contemporary law of war, difficult though they may be to accommodate with the nature of modern warfare, that refutes the criticism that the law of war, comprising a body of rules of restraint in war conduct, makes war more, and not less, acceptable to mankind.

This humanitarian element also answers a further perennial moral difficulty, namely whether the law of war applies to all belligerents alike. Is the aggressor belligerent to enjoy the full benefit of the law, with its collection of rights, powers and privileges, and shall the victim belligerent lie under the full burden of the duties thereunder? This was a moral and legal question which became acute in the post-United Nations Charter era. Probably the most important provision in that paramount legal instrument is Article 2 (4):

> "All Members shall refrain in their international relations from the threat or use of force against the territorial integrity or political independence of any State, or in any other manner inconsistent with the purposes of the United Nations."

Did not this provision preclude the equal application of the law of war to aggressor belligerents and their victims? Here again, Grotius, over 300 years ago, had found a resolution of this question in terms of humanity.

> "The justice or injustice of the war [he said], is irrelevant for the purpose of observing the rules of warfare as between the belligerents. Any other rule would add to the inherent evils of war the horrors of unrestrained licence accentuated by what must often be an unverified *ex parte* claim to wage a just war [5]".

Although the implementation of the law of war, and its enforcement, are perhaps the supreme challenge to the idea of law, the law of war has had a long and elaborate history. At the outset it is necessary to dispel the myth that "in wars the laws are silent", sometimes inscribed on war memorials. The law of war is complex and its extent is considerable. Until comparatively recently, its study, let alone the study of its history, has not been a noticeable feature of academic or professional studies. In point of time the law of war was the first pact of international law to receive extensive codification, in a series of multilateral conventions concluded at the turn of the nineteenth century. It was part of the positivist ascendancy with its preference for written law, and the movement in favour of a secular humanitarianism, which marked the second half of that century. This codification was achieved in large part through the initiatives of Imperial Russia, under Tsar Nicholas II, and was inspired by Professor Fedor de Martens, a legal adviser of the Imperial Foreign Ministry and the holder of the chair of international law at the University of St. Petersburg. At the First and Second Hague Peace Conferences of 1899 and 1907, respectively, some 13 conventions were eventually concluded. Seven dealt with the law of sea warfare, three with resort to war, two with neutrality in sea warfare, and one, the most famous, No. IV, with the Laws and Customs of War on Land. This precocious codification was achieved at a certain price in that by the middle of the twentieth century, if not earlier, the law of war had become a major anachronism, particularly that part of it which sought to govern the conduct of hostilities on land.

Since 1945, as a result of the gross excesses in the Second World War, a substantial amount of new law was established, primarily humanitarian in content, and directed mainly at the protection of war victims, i.e., those who find themselves defenceless in the hands of the enemy. This law is to be found mainly in the four Geneva Conventions of 1949 now binding 146 States. The first relates to the protection of the sick and wounded in the armed forces, the second to the sick, wounded and shipwrecked members of armed forces at sea, the third, to prisoners of war, and the fourth exclusively to civilians, whether in the territory of the adversary belligerent or in occupied territory. Generally, these four conventions did not touch the conduct of hostilities except in vestigial areas. This formidable body of humanitarian law comprises 417 articles in all and is complicated in nature. They reflect the experiences suffered by prisoners of war and civilian detainees in the Second World War and particularly the exterminations and cruelties practised in German concentration camps and in Japanese prisoners of war camps. A defect of these instruments is their backwards looking posture and, possibly, their euro-centric preoccupations. They paid insufficient attention to internal armed conflicts, to irregular fighting, to the effects of modern weaponry, to international commands and to United Nations peacekeeping forces. Yet these instruments mark a substantial humanitarian gain and are a dignified response to the challenge of horror in war by law.

The two Additional Protocols of 1978 [6] seek to modernise and give greater precision to those parts of the Hague Convention No. IV of 1907 dealing with the conduct of hostilities and to expand and develop the Geneva Conventions of 1949 [7]. Both are designed primarily for the protection of civilians. Protocol I deals with international armed conflicts, as did the four Geneva Conventions of 1949 save and except the common Article 3, limited to internal armed conflicts. Protocol I, by Article 1 (4), includes within its ambit "armed conflicts in which peoples are fighting against colonial domination and alien occupation and against racist régimes in the exercise of their right of self determination", now styled "national liberation movements". Protocol II is devoted exclusively to internal conflicts, without superseding common Article 3 of the Conventions of 1949. Its ambit is defined, with some particularity, to include only those internal conflicts of a certain level of intensity, and accompanied by a measure of organisation and territorial control by the parties to such conflicts. The redactors of both Protocols experienced formidable difficulties in introducing methods of securing their implementation, albeit for different reasons.

Protocol I limits means and methods of attacks and lawful targetry, but opens up the range of lawful combatancy by reducing the requirements of "openness" required of irregular fighters. In some ways these two tendencies clash. The sparing, as much as possible, of civilian and civilian objects from the effects of modern weaponry, is counterbalanced by the extended class of lawful combatants. These now include guerrilla fighters upon whom the requirements of "openness" is limited strictly to the display of arms for the duration of military engagements. In effect, Protocol I has sought, obliquely, to limit the use of certain categories of conventional weaponry distinguished by their capacity for indiscriminate destruction and the superfluous sufferings they cause. Such important and far reaching changes in the law of war call for the monitoring and supervising of implementation, over and above the traditional mode of auto-implementation reinforced by the innate force of reciprocity. These modalities and their efficacy demand our attention.

B. The Protecting Power System

The modern Protecting Power system consists of a neutral State designated by one belligerent to safeguard the interests of its nationals in the hands of the opposing belligerent. Such a system is not old. It was introduced in the Franco-Prussian War of 1870-1871, as a result of the belligerents expelling the adversary's consuls and resorting to severe restrictions imposed upon enemy aliens in their respective territories. This system evolved by belligerent practice and custom and was not embodied in treaties. Gradually, extended functions were undertaken by the delegates of the Protectiong Power. The Geneva Conventions of 1949 fall to be "applied under the co-operation and the scrutiny of the Protecting Powers whose duty it is to safeguard the interests of the Powers in conflict . . . The Parties to the conflict shall facilitate to the greatest extent possible the tasks of the representatives or delegates of the Protecting Powers . . .": Articles 8/8/8/9.

A close scrutiny of the provisions of the Geneva Conventions shows that the supervised implementation of a large part of a large number of their humanitarian provisions, devolves upon the Protecting Power. Without it, the monitoring system for implementation is largely threadbare and implementation is left to the good faith of the belligerent and the force of reciprocity. The conventions are not reciprocal in their operation. The obligations imposed by them do not depend upon the observance of such obligations by the adversary. Reprisals against the classes of individuals protected by each convention are expressly prohibited.

Two factors in particular have weakened the Protecting Power system in our time. First, in a world divided by conflicting ideologies neutrality is neither widespread nor appreciated. The number of neutral States willing to act as Protecting Powers and which are acceptable to one or other belligerent is limited. Thus Switzerland and Sweden bore the burden of the role of Protecting Powers in the Second World War. Second, the functioning of the system requires a threefold consensuality by the three States concerned, each of which can bring its sovereignty to prevent the system from being effective. Thereby the supervision of the implementation of a large part of the conventions is impeded. The Designating Power may refuse to appoint a Protecting Power. The Protecting Power may decline so to act. The Detaining Power can decline to accept the Protecting Power proposed by the adversary, the Designating Power. Any one of these discretionary acts of sovereignty will negate the role of the Protecting Power. There is no treaty obligation to designate or to accept or to act as a Protecting Power. Sovereignty allows an unfettered discretion to the three States concerned. Hague Convention No. IV of 1907 made no reference to Protecting Powers.

In the First World War the system matured. In spite of some restrictive practices by Germany and the USA, belligerents designated a substitute neutral State if the original Protecting Power ceased to function or became a belligerent. Bilateral arrangements were made during the war setting out in some detail the agreed activities of the

Protecting Power. Article 86 of the Geneva (prisoners of war) Convention of 1929 reflects some of this progress made by belligerent practice and gave it permanent form. However, nothing in that provision or elsewhere made the appointment or the acceptance of a Protecting Power mandatory.

The Second World War exposed this embryonic system to strains, fissures and defects that largely frustrated its operation. It was hardly operative in 1945, at the close of six years of war. The matter was aggravated in that neither the USSR nor Japan was a Party to the Geneva (prisoners of war) Convention of 1929. Article 86 of that Convention of 1929 had been a modest affair :

> "The . . . Parties recognize that a guarantee of the regular application of the present Convention will be found in the possibility of collaboration between the Protecting Powers charged with the protection of the interest of the belligerents."

Sovereignty is untouched by this provision. It is an example of one of the many and diverse types of norms known to international law which lie in that wide area between the obligatory and the hortatory. States were willing to accept the humanitarian obligations contained in the (prisoners of war) conventions of 1929, but were not willing to accept, as a legal obligation, the presence of a neutral State to supervise their implementation of those obligations. There is little advantage to a State in being designated a Protecting Power, except in the tribute to its neutrality. Financial recoupment is often delayed long after the end of the war. On occasions there is a real risk of impairing its relations with both belligerents.

In the light of the sufferings of prisoners of war and civilian detainees both in Europe and the Far East in the Second World War, the like of which the world had never previously had the misfortune to know, a determined effort was made by the framers of the Geneva Conventions of 1949 to amplify and extend the functions of the Protecting Power and to reduce to a minimum the likelihood of there being no Protecting Power available for belligerents at any stage of a war. Moreover, the humanitarian provisions of those conventions were deprived of much of their value unless some body or agency was present to supervise implementation, and to warn of, or report or head off, impending violations. There is some uncertainty whether the Conventions of 1949 imposed a legal obligation upon belligerents Parties thereto to designate, and to accept the services of a Protecting Power. On balance, it is thought that no legal obligation was imposed.

The moral obligation clearly existed. The failure to impose any such legal obligation is generally seen as a defect, but understandable. Sovereignty requires agreement before new obligations are imposed by a convention. The common Articles 8/8/8/9 of the Conventions of 1949, mentioned above, impose a number of legal obligations upon Protecting Powers, but not upon belligerents to designate or to accept such a Power. This was the more regrettable in that the Conventions of 1949 placed considerable reliance for their implementation upon the guarantee afforded by the Protecting Power system. Thus, the conventions provided for access for the delegates of the Protecting Power to all places where prisoners of war or civilian detainees were held by the Detaining Power, and for their presence at trials of such persons to ensure that the obligatory judicial safeguards were being implemented. The functioning of a Protecting Power is manifestly crucial.

A default system was therefore established by the common Articles 10/10/10/11 of the Conventions:

> "When protected persons do not benefit or cease to benefit, no matter for what reason, by the activities of a Protecting Power or of an organisation (international, impartial and efficacious), the Detaining Power shall request a neutral State, or such an organisation, to undertake the functions performed under the present Convention by a Protecting Power designated by the Parties to a conflict.
>
> If protection cannot be arranged accordingly, the Detaining Power shall request or accept . . . the offers of the services of a humanitarian organisation, such as the International Committee of the Red Cross, to assume the humanitarian functions assumed by Protecting Powers under the present Convention."

This is not a foolproof system. Apart from disputes between belligerents as to whether the conventions apply between them, e.g., because of non-recognition of the adversary government or State, the international situation since 1945 has not added to the number of neutral States available to act as Protecting Powers. Moreover, the International Committee of the Red Cross of Geneva is not willing to indicate in advance that it will accept every request, or make an offer on all occasions, to act as a substitute organisation, although it will normally do so if it sees the remotest chance of being accepted by the belligerents. It will, also, seek to exercise its normal humanitarian functions, but this exercise has to be "subject to the consent of the parties to the conflict" (Article 9/9/9/10). The common Articles 10/

10/10/11, cited above, came sufficiently close to imposing an obligation upon State Parties to the Conventions of 1949 for the USSR and its associated States to make a reservation to it. Likewise, the resolution adopted by the Diplomatic Conference of 1949 for the proposed establishment of an international body to act as Protecting Power was negatived by a declaration of the USSR to the effect that it saw no necessity so to do in that the provisions in the conventions on that matter were adequate. This was an unedifying example of the diplomatic frustration of implementation of a humanitarian law instrument, but it lay well within the limits of State sovereignty.

The experience of armed conflicts in the post-1950 period has not shown the Protecting Power system working well, although it has had some success. On one pretext or another, Protecting Powers have not been appointed. Sometimes the conflicts are "mixed", i.e., neither international nor internal. Sometimes recognition difficulties have proved decisive. At others a belligerent has claimed that diplomatic relations were not severed at the opening of the conflict. On that basis a Detaining Power has claimed that there was no need to appoint or to accept a Protecting Power. Again, many of the armed conflicts, including some fought with little regard to humanitarian restraint, have been internal, where the Protecting Power system, by definition, does not operate, as yet. For these and other reasons the Diplomatic Conference of 1974-1977, which framed the two Additional Protocols of 1978, applied itself to try to remove or diminish this major *lacuna* in the implementation system in these new instruments of the international humanitarian law of armed conflict. An effort was made to make the Protecting Power system both mandatory and default proof. This entailed a serious inroad upon State sovereignty. The outcome can now be seen in Protocol I, Article 5, which may be called "the triumph of sovereignty". The need was the greater in this instrument. Detailed and explicit rules about battle conduct, combatancy, and targetry were established in Parts III and IV of Protocol I. These rules were designed to secure the maximum protection for the civilian and the whole civilian habitat, including the environment, from the effects of modern weaponry. The new humanitarian law is now reaching beyond the protection of war victims in the hands of the enemy and limited restrictions for the benefit of combatants. The need for effectively supervised implementation became urgent and more difficult to ensure. Moreover, now that national liberation "struggles" were within the protocol the difficulties in ensuring implemention were likely to be greater.

The redaction of Article 5 is a story of initial success and ultimate failure. The opening words of paragraph 1 display the former:

> "It is the duty of the Parties to a conflict from the beginning of that conflict to secure the supervision and implementation of the Conventions and of this Protocol by the application of the system of Protecting Powers including, *inter alia*, the designation and acceptance of those Powers in accordance with the following paragraphs. Protecting Powers shall have the duty of safeguarding the interests of the Parties to the conflict."

The crucial words "in accordance with the following paragraphs" display the latter. In the other paragraphs of the article we find words showing the need for the consent of both of the belligerents and, in paragraph 3, of the proposed Protecting Power. In a case where the ICRC may make an offer to act, as a substitute, in the absence of a Protecting Power, it must be accepted without delay by the Parties to the conflict. By paragraph 4, "the functioning of such a substitute is subject to the consent of the parties to the conflict". Moreover, the ICRC made it clear during the conference that it could not give an undertaking in advance that it would always be in a position to make such an offer. The United Nations for its part made it no less clear that it would not be willing to act as an international standing Protecting Power. The question remains as to the effect of Article 5 upon the existing provisions as to Protecting Powers in the Conventions of 1949. For States Parties to the protocol and the conventions, the former "supplements" the latter. Only States Parties to the conventions may become Parties to the protocol. To the extent that States are Parties to both it would seem that the protocol varies the conventions to the extent of any inconsistency between them because the conventions apply as supplemented by the protocol. The effect may be that in relation to the role of the ICRC as a substitute for a Protecting Power, any advance made by the conventions in common Articles 10/10/10/11, paragraph 3, is negatived by Article 5 (4) of the protocol, controlling the role of the ICRC as a substitute. It is one of the less successful achievements of Protocol I that its precise impact upon the conventions, which are, for some purposes, welded together by the terms of the protocol, is far from clear. In the event of a conflict between a State Party to both instruments and a State Party to the conventions only, the protocol will operate reciprocally and not unilaterally.

Two gains are achieved by Article 5 of Protocol I. The first is made in paragraph 5, whereby "the designation and acceptance of Protecting Powers for the purpose of applying the conventions and this protocol shall not affect the legal status of the Parties to the conflict, or of any territory, including occupied territory". The other is in paragraph 6 :

> "The maintenance of diplomatic relations between Parties to the conflict . . . is no obstacle to the designation of Protecting Powers for the purpose of applying the conventions and this protocol."

Although the protocol extends to armed struggles by national liberation movements against a State Party, the former are not Parties to the protocol. They become bound by, and entitled to, the benefit of it if they make a unilateral declaration under Article 96 (3). The effect of such a declaration, so far as the provisions relating to Protecting Powers and substitutes are concerned, is far from clear and was not considered at the conference. The matter may be resolved by a neutral State being designated by the "authority representing" the liberation movement, and if accepted by the adversary State, could function as such. Any Protecting Power or substitute designated by the adversary State may find the tasks imposed on it by the conventions of the protocol virtually impossible to discharge. Covert fighting conducted by clandestine fighters from bases in third States not engaged in the conflict does not lend itself to supervision. In certain of such struggles prisoners are not taken. In the absence of an international and permanent Protecting Power, it is probably inevitable that States will reserve the right to make an *ad hoc* decision whether to accept a neutral State as a Protecting Power or a substitute body such as the ICRC in any specific conflict in which it may currently be engaged. As long as wars form a part of international relations it is probably premature to expect that States will limit their sovereignty to the extent required to accept a mandatory system of Protecting Powers to monitor the implementations of the law governing such wars, however humanitarian in content such law may be.

C. Dissemination and Instruction

Unlike enforcement, implementation is concerned with action taken under the obligation in point. Enforcement action is brought to bear when compliance with the obligation has been supplanted by violation of it, whether by acts of commission or of omission. Implementation may take many forms, such as domestic legislation, subordinate orders and instructions, publicity, training, communications with other States or the depositary, according to the nature of the obligation to be implemented. Pervading all treaty obligations is the obligation imposed by customary international law that all treaties must be performed by the parties in good faith. Here law and morality merge. This principle is now made explicit in Article 26 of the Vienna Convention on the Law of Treaties, 1960 : "Every treaty in force is binding upon the parties to it and must be performed by them in good faith." The Geneva Conventions of 1949 bind 146 States. Protocols I and II are binding upon five States to date. These States are required to carry out a number of activities if such instruments are to be implemented in good faith. Some are required in time of peace.

Thus legislation will be required under the Constitutions of some States to make the "grave breaches" specified in Articles 11 and 85 of Protocol I criminal offences and to provide the penalties under municipal law. Some States do not ratify until such legislation is enacted. On the occasion of the ratification of the Geneva Conventions of 1949 the United Kingdom Parliament had already enacted the Geneva Conventions Act 1957, as its constitution requires, in respect of the "grave breaches" of those instruments listed in Articles 49/50/129/146.

In spite of the obligation to issue instructions to armed forces in accordance with the Hague Regulations of 1907, war crimes trials in Europe and the Far East at the conclusion of the Second World War, in the years 1945-1950, disclosed that the governments of certain belligerent States had done little to bring to the attention of their armed forces, police and ancillary services, the existence of the law of war, let alone its content. The general ignorance on this subject, not excluding that of lawyers, contributed to the widespread and gross war criminality committed by members of armed, para-military and police forces. Where there is a prevailing ignorance about the legal restraints operative in the conduct of war, the system of discipline imposed by orders from superiors to subordinates meets no obstacles to compliance, however criminal the nature of the order. The government of a State which has, as a matter of policy, decided to ignore the obligations of the law of war for reasons of its own ideology, can ensure compliance with its criminal orders by the use of the hierarchy of command and orders to subordinates. German and Japanese military commanders of seniority, as well as Ministers, disregarded the existence of the law of war, and were aware that their subordinates had received no instruction in it. The omission is not accidental or to be excused. They were aware that the very system under which their ideologies were enabled to be given reality presupposes a system of strict military discipline based upon undeviating obedience to orders of whatever nature, reinforced by ideological propaganda. The idea that military law instruction, part of the necessary education of all military officers, should be accompanied by some knowledge of the international law of war was not beyond their perception. Their ideology gave no place to the restraints of the law of war, except possibly contempt, and a central place to military law and obedience to the orders of a superior. Thus was the stage set for the mass atrocities from 1939-1945. In 1945, Ministers and military commanders, when charged in war crimes trials with "the commission of crimes on a scale larger and more shocking than the world has ever had the misfortune to know [8]" pleaded that they were military commanders obeying orders, or that they did not know that the orders were criminal, or that they disobeyed such orders. In most cases the evidence established beyond peradventure the exact opposite. At the lower levels in the armed forces and para-military organisations it was manifest that the personnel had received no sort of instruction in the law of war. Neither was this omission limited to the armed forces of the Axis Powers. In the light of this experience the ICRC caused to be included in the draft texts that came before the Geneva Diplomatic Conference in 1949 what are now the common Articles 47/48/127/144 of the four Geneva Conventions of that year :

> "The . . . Parties undertake, in time of peace as in time of war, to disseminate the text of the present Convention as widely as possible in their respective countries, and, in particular, to include the study thereof in their programmes of military, and, if possible, civil instruction, so that the principles thereof may become known to the entire population."

Bearing in mind the provisions of the common Article 1 of the Conventions of 1949, that the Parties agree to "respect and to ensure respect" for the conventions, the dissemination and instruction provision recited is a valuable and necessary part of the implementation process. If carried out in good faith by the governments of 146 States, it would limit the number of military commanders and subordinates who would be in a position to claim with any conviction that they did not know the order they issued or received was criminal, or that they were bound to obey such an order. In other words, the standard plea of "superior orders" by accused taxed with war criminality would have a substantially reduced area of validity and credibility. It follows as a corollary that law observance is seriously impeded if the existence and content of the law is not brought to the attention of those required to observe it in armed conflicts.

A defect in the Conventions of 1949 is that no monitoring device was inserted to ensure implementation, i.e., that the required instruction is being given, adequately, to those for whom it is required. Governments know that if their armed forces do not receive the instruction, they expose them to some risk if they are held and accused by an enemy using war crimes trials as an instrument of oppression and not of justice. At the same time, they know that if proper instruction is given to their armed forces, a certain psychological resistance to criminal orders is built up in the individual subordinate which might cause trouble in time of armed conflict. At a less malevolent level, States do not welcome the querying of the validity of orders given to military subordinates. A further defect is the weakness in the provision of the convention so far as instruction of the civil population is concerned. The words "if possible" were included in 1949 to meet the federal situation in those States in which education is not a function of the federal government. However, even in "unitary" States, the government may not have the existing legal power to control the curricula in schools and places of further or professional education. Instruction of the civil population has a direct relevance to the implementation of the common Article 3 governing internal armed conflicts taking place within the territory of the State Party. If instruction were given to the bulk of the adult population, as well as to the armed forces, if follows that the parties to any future internal conflict would be compromised.

The system of discipline and training in the armed forces of States makes the giving of the instruction required by the Geneva Conventions of 1949 relatively simple to implement, and the excuse for failure to do so less easy to justify. The giving of this instruction thus becomes a matter of good faith in carrying out the obligations under a treaty, a matter of legal obligation in itself. Instruction is not limited to subordinates. Ministers and senior commanders also need such instruction. Neither is the availability of books and films, "if requested", a form of implementation in good faith of the provision in question. Neither is dissemination the same as instruction. Both are required. Moreover, it is doubtful whether the requirement of dissemination is met by enacting an Act of Parliament to which the texts of the Geneva Conventions are scheduled, as in the United Kingdom Geneva Conventions Act, 1957.

Some of these defects received attention at the diplomatic conference which established the two Additional Protocols of 1978. However, the ultimate text of Protocol I, Article 85, substantially repeats, but was not able to improve upon, the instruction provision in the Conventions of 1949. Some strengthening of the instruction requirement was achieved in Article 87 (2) of Protocol I :

> "In order to prevent and suppress breaches, High Contracting Parties and Parties to the conflict shall require that, commensurate with their level of responsibility, commanders ensure that members of the armed forces under their command are aware of their obligations under the Conventions and this Protocol."

This provision places obligations upon States Parties and "authorities representing" liberation movements, and is a modality both of implementation and enforcement. Nothing in these instruction provisions supersedes the original requirement in Article 1 of the Hague Convention No. IV of 1907 :

> "The Contracting Powers shall issue instructions to their armed forces which shall be in conformity with the Regulations respecting the Laws and Customs of War on Land annexed to the present Convention."

This provision launched the official government manuals issued for the armed forces which are a necessity adjunct to the instruction requirements of the Geneva Conventions and of Protocol I, and may be considered today as an obligation of the customary law of war. The system is amplified in Article 84 of Protocol I, whereby :

> "The . . . Parties shall communicate to one another as soon as possible, through the depositary and, as appropriate, through the Protecting Power, their official translations of this Protocol, as well as the laws and regulations which they may adopt to ensure its application."

Thus, communication of legislative texts and directives has been made obligatory. This is a necessary and valuable provision to complete the implementation mechanisms. It echoes the like provision in Articles 48/49/128/145 of the Conventions of 1949.

D. Legal Advisers in Armed Forces

An important and novel device for ensuring implementation has been introduced in Article 82 of Protocol I, whereby :

> "The High Contracting Parties at all times, and the Parties to the conflict in time of armed conflict, shall ensure that legal advisers are available, when necessary to advise military commanders at the appropriate level on the application of the Conventions and of this Protocol and on the appropriate instruction to be given to the armed forces on this subject."

The implications of this novel requirement are far reaching and have not yet been assessed. Legal advisers in disciplinary matters and for advising commanders on court-martial proceedings and the conduct of grave or complex prosecutions are part of the accepted staff organisation of modern armed forces. This is a requirement that goes far wider. The legal advisers, under this article, are to advise commanders on the application of the conventions and of the protocol. The latter includes, in Parts III and IV, a number of wide restraints upon battle conduct, e.g., as to lawful targetry, means and methods of combat and precautions in attacks. This introduces the legal adviser to an advisory role affecting combat operations, strategical planning and operational directives. The commander is awkwardly placed if advice is requested and ignored. To meet the difficulties of certain States, the Article does not require such advisers to be qualified lawyers. Nor are they required at all levels of command. A number of practical difficulties may arise in ensuring that such legal advice is sought by commanders and in placing such advisory services within the hierarchy and structures of command. Many details have yet to be worked out in order that this important mode of supervising implementation can be made effective. A mature system of legal advice to commanders probably calls for a high level "directive". The provision of legal advisers to commanders, together with the corollary requirement of instruction to be given in the forces under command, could and should provide a powerful means of implementation of the law of armed conflict. In general, it may be said that governments would do well to carry out these two interlocking modes of implementation with a generous measure of good faith. Failure in this area may expose commanders, staffs and troops to a serious risk of war crimes proceedings wherein the defence of superior orders for the latter and ignorance of the law for the former, will have only a minimal validity. It will be noticed that the requirement of advice, unlike that of instruction, can extend to national liberation movements and the authorities which represent them.

E. The Use of Qualified Persons

Protocol I, in Article 6, introduces a mode of implementation designed to be ancillary to the role of the Protecting Power. Thereunder, in time of peace, State Parties "shall endeavour, with the assistance of the National Red Cross Societies . . . to train qualified personnel to facilitate the application of the Conventions and of this Protocol, and, in particular, the activities of the Protecting Power". However, by paragraph 4 "the conditions governing the employment of such personnel outside the national territory shall, in each case, be the subject of special agreements between the Parties concerned". As the system of Protecting Powers is consensual, in deference to State sovereignty, it follows that the employment of such qualified personnel is in like case. This means that nationals of one neutral State, if so qualified, may with the consent of the Parties concerned, which includes the belligerents, be employed to work with and for another neutral State functioning as a Protecting Power, or may facilitate the application of the conventions and the protocols, in the absence of such a Protecting Power. Whether such an augmentation of personnel would aid or render more difficult the activities of an existing Protecting Power is uncertain, but there is value in trained neutral nationals being accepted and employed as delegates of an existing Protecting Power not being the State upon which such qualified personnel depend.

If the qualified personnel are nationals of a belligerent Party, their role can be of undoubted value. If they are nationals of a Protecting Power, it will enable that Power to discharge its functions with less burden and more effectively and, political objections on one side, may make that Power more acceptable – for that reason – to the Parties in conflict. The provision is of particular importance to the ICRC when acting as a "substitute for a Protecting Power" which is frequently the case. By Article 5 (7) of Protocol I "Any . . . mention in this Protocol of a Protecting Power includes also a substitute".

F. Implementation of the Law Governing Internal Armed Conflicts

So far we have considered implementation of international armed conflicts which today include struggles for self-determination as defined in Article 1 (4) of Protocol I. What can be said of the implementation of internal armed conflicts which have been a dominant feature of the post-1945 era? Apart from recognised belligerency in civil wars to which the customary law of war applies, as well as the common Article 3 of the four Conventions of 1949, and, in due course, Protocol II, the law governing internal armed conflicts presents a somewhat confused picture. Such conflicts can range from low-level sporadic exchanges of armed violence between dissident elements and governments, to a full-scale armed confrontation such as the Spanish Civil War, 1936-1939, in which upwards of a million men and women were killed. Before 1949, in the absence of recognised belligerency accorded to the elements opposed to the government of a State, the law of war, i.e., *jus in bello*, had no application to internal armed conflicts. By international law an armed rebellion was not a violation of it. International law had little or nothing to say as to how the armed rebellion was crushed by the government concerned, for such matters fell within the domestic jurisdiction of States. Such conflicts were often waged with great lack of restraint and cruelty. Such conduct was a domestic matter. The "humanitarian intervention" by Western European Powers at the close of the nineteenth century was of dubious legality. The customary law of war did not apply to the conduct of government and dissident parties in internal armed conflicts if the dissidents were not accorded recognition as belligerents. The common Article 3 of the Geneva Conventions, which proved the most difficult of the 417 Articles to secure acceptance by States, applied to armed conflicts within the territory of a State Party "not being international in character". No definition of such internal conflicts was inserted in the conventions. The extent to which the municipal law of the State applied was uncertain, but it probably applied, subject to the application of common Article 3.

Article 3 was a pioneer endeavour to impose some basic and minimal humanitarian legal restraints upon both parties to an internal conflict conducted within the territory of a State Party to those conventions. Such restraints were a "microcosm" of those applicable to international armed conflicts. Governments do not welcome legal restraints in the handling of armed violence directed against them for the express purpose of secession or at securing a change in the government of the State. There was some consensus among jurists that Article 3 did not apply to demonstrations or to sporadic displays of violence, but it was uncertain whether it applied to full scale civil war, together with the customary law of war. Many of the internal conflicts of the post-1945 era were armed struggles against colonialism or ideological cleavages within an existing State. Article 3 of the Conventions derived an added impetus with the acceptances of international régimes of Human Rights, from about 1968. Basic humanitarian rules restraining excesses in internal armed conflicts were manifestly required, but any implementation by international devices encountered *instanter* the full force of State sovereignty. The Protecting Power system would normally be precluded. Dissemination and instruction might be achieved if one assumed that these requirements in the conventions extended to Article 3. Such could be contended, but the point is doubtful. The main burden of supervising implementation, apart from outside world opinion as reflected in the United Nations, often devolved upon the ICRC. By Article 3 (2):

> "An impartial humanitarian body, such as the ICRC, may offer its service to the Parties to the conflict. The Parties should further endeavour to bring into force, by means of special agreements, all or parts of the other provisions of the present Convention."

The first provision is permissive and requires the consent of the Parties engaged in conflict, but is not confined to humanitarian services. The second is hortatory and consensual. It reflects the reality that the scale of internal conflicts may be so various and changeable in any one internal conflict that it may assume the scale of an international armed conflict when the mechanisms of implementation applicable to such conflicts might be brought to bear. However, in most internal conflicts the common Article 3 is dependent upon auto-implementation by the Parties to the conflict.

Article 3 has not proved a success although the standards it demands are valuable. Monitoring implementation has rarely proved possible. Sovereignty renders the implementation of international armed conflicts difficult; *a fortiori*, is this the case with internal conflicts. Matters have not been helped by the phenomenon of "mixed armed conflicts" in which the armed forces of third States support the Parties to an otherwise internal conflict. This situation was not met by the Conventions of 1949 or the two Protocols of 1978. To date such "mixed conflicts" have not been subjected to the "agreements" envisaged in common Article 3. The experience of internal conflicts led to a major effort to establish an instrument of international law dealing exclusively with internal armed conflicts and designed to be as close as possible to the régime of Protocol I. This was an ambitious project and it did not succeed. Protocol II, as it emerged from the

Diplomatic Conference in 1977, is a markedly debilitated instrument. Sovereignty and the fragility of many new States cast a blight over this embryonic development in humanitarian law in an area where it was particularly needed. Protocol II, in its final text, consists of 28 Articles. It is now in force between four States and signed by about 45. Its scope (Article 1) has been carefully defined to extend only to conflicts of an intensity and scale which are tantamount to classical civil wars. It has left common Article 3 of the Conventions of 1949 intact within its own ambit which still remains undefined. Protocol II expands and develops the humanitarian prohibitions in Article 3, but does little to reinforce or contribute modes of implementation. Article 3 of Protocol II is an attempt to accommodate the sovereignty of the State concerned with the humanitarian restraints imposed by the instrument:

> "Nothing in this Protocol shall be invoked for the purpose of affecting the sovereignty of a State or the responsibility of the Government, by all legitimate means, to maintain or re-establish law and order in the State or to defend the national unity and territorial integrity of the State."

The precise significance of that provision may be debatable. It would seem that the question of observing the legal restraints in it has ceased to be a domestic matter. All else that is "domestic" remains such. It would also seem that implementation defects remain, as they do under common Article 3 of the Conventions of 1949. The latter provision does not cease to apply to the types of conflict controlled by Protocol II. However, by Article 19, the Protocol is to be "disseminated as widely as possible". Thus, although the humanitarian content of the Protocol goes well beyond that of Article 3 of the conventions, its implementation machinery advances no further. The contention that the Geneva Conventions of 1949 now form part of the customary law of war, and that their implementation machinery is applicable to internal conflicts of the scale of Protocol II requirements, is a difficult argument to sustain. In such matters as the functioning of Protecting Powers, a better route for implementation may be the use of special agreements to that end, under the terms of common Article 3 above mentioned. The law of internal armed conflicts remains substantially deficient in its own means of ensuring implementation in the absence of consensual arrangements to that end.

G. Conclusions

The main burden of supervising the implementation of the Geneva Conventions of 1949 and of Protocol I will continue to devolve upon the system of the Protecting Power for some time to come. Those instruments have been framed on the basis that the Protecting Power is the key device in this area of law. It is no less clear that that system can work only by agreements between belligerents and the Protecting Power on the outbreak of conflicts. No permanent or international body exists to perform that role. Neither, in the present climate of international relations, is such a body likely to be established. In so far as the monitored implementation of the new and substantial body of the humanitarian law of war is concerned, sovereignty is still in the ascendant ; neither is it surprising that that should be the case. That in itself is not evidence of a lack of reality in this new and humanitarian law of war. Adequate machinery for detailed supervision of this law exists if the belligerents wish to use it. If they decline, other methods known to the classical law remain, such as good offices, mediation, and complaints to neutral States, reinforced by complaints to all other States which are Parties to the Geneva Conventions of 1949.

The obligations of State Parties to give instruction to their armed forces in the conventions and Protocol I can inculcate standards of conduct required in armed conflict, including battle conduct, as part of their professional military training, as is considered essential for the care and use of weapons. The idea of law applicable to armed forces is not novel. The very cohesion by which armed forces exist and carry out their wartime roles is based upon the military law of States. Alongside that law, officers and soldiers are now required to be taught the international law restraints binding upon them and the consequences of departure from such law. The presence of legal advisers with commanders, even in its attenuated form as seen in Protocol I, is a mode of supervising implementation of the law of war, both for military operations and generally, of considerable importance. The training of qualified personnel by States supplements and strengthens both the Protecting Power system and the giving of instruction to the armed forces and the civilian population.

In the case of internal conflicts the monitoring of implementation is rarely feasible, but to the extent that international norms of restraint are now applicable to such conflicts, their implementation is now a matter of international concern and no longer domestic. This enables complaints to be made to all the other State Parties to the Geneva

Conventions, some 146 in all, and violations to be ventilated, debated, and condemned by resolutions of the United Nations organs. If internal conflicts attain the scale required for the application of Protocol II, there would seem to be some possibility that the Geneva Conventions and Protocol I provisions for Protecting Powers can be brought to bear if special agreements are concluded between the Parties to the conflict, to that end. To the extent that the difference between Protocol I and Protocol II conflicts may be reduced in practice, it may become easier to apply the implementation devices applicable to international armed conflicts to internal armed conflicts.

At the end of the day systematic instruction to members of the armed forces, and gradually to the adult population, in the principles of the humanitarian law of armed conflicts, as is now required by the Geneva Conventions and Protocol I, may do more to ensure observance of those instruments than the trial and punishment of those who have violated them. Instruction works at a time ahead of violation. Punishment operates when implementation has failed. In the case of death penalties, which may be imposed for all "grave breaches", it is the irremovable seal upon the failure to implement.

The mechanisms to ensure implementation of the modern law of war are weak. Yet it is one of the unique features of international law which dispels the charge of its unreality that a large part of it operates by auto-implementation, without the devices available to municipal law. International law, including the law of war, makes considerable use of municipal law for its implementation, in legislation, administrative instructions and the system of military discipline and orders in the armed forces. At the present time it is probable that the developments in the humanitarian law of armed conflicts have outrun its capacity to supervise its own observance. Only time will tell whether this margin can be reduced. There are devices to enable this to be done. Whether they are used is a question of good faith, which ultimately is a question for the men and women who comprise the governments of the international community of States.

CHAPTER II

THE ENFORCEMENT OF THE GENEVA CONVENTIONS OF 1949 AND THE ADDITIONAL PROTOCOLS OF 1978

A. History and Theory

By the enforcement of the law of war we mean the responses known to the law when observance has failed and violation has occurred. The greater sophistication of municipal law in dealing with such situations and the wider range of devices open to that law to restore observance have led critics of international law either to deny the obligatory nature of the law of war, or to point out its mischievous propensity to artificiality. Warfare subjects the idea of law to maximum strain and the enforcement of the law of war to demands that are frequently beyond its resources. To some critics war and law stand in contradiction and cannot be accommodated one with the other. History contradicts these assertions. For many centuries there has existed a body of rules, rough hewn and embryonic in nature, designed to secure some minimal legal order in time of war. The reasons for this phenomenon lie at the centre of man's nature and yield to no ready explanation. It is possible that even in war man declines to abandon or deny his rational and social nature. Perhaps the discovery of the nexus between the system of ordering and discipline for effective military operations by fighting men, and the rise of a professional military class, may have meant an association of military order and effectiveness in battle.

Some restraints enter the law of war early in its history. Prisoners slaughtered cannot work for their captors and, in a later time, cannot yield ransom. Thus, in the Middle Ages, the system of ransom, closely controlled by the law of arms, demanded the sparing of the life of the prisoner and some modicum of decent treatment[9]. Hence those prisoners who could not provide ransoms were least likely to be spared, at least if not members of the fighting classes. There is a point at which indiscriminate atrocities dissipate discipline on the battlefield and thereby impair or impede the operations. The early *jus militare* was based upon a firm conception of knightly honour which excluded treachery, a form of bad faith, and some idea of mutual respect between military adversaries, i.e., those engaged in the same calling, considered to be honourable. The influence of the Christian Church through canon law and penance and, to a limited extent, the war practices of Moslems enjoined by the Koran, also introduced some element of restraint in warfare, e.g., the prohibition of the use of poison, the sparing or immunity from hostilities of certain classes of civilians, e.g., clerks, pilgrims and cultivators of the soil.

Could this early law of war be enforced in the sense that offenders could be punished and others deterred thereby, or the opposing belligerent induced to refrain from further illegitimate warfare? Under the post-Grotian classical law of war three main means of enforcement of the law of war by self-help had come to be accepted: first, the system of resorting to reprisals, a form of self-help of considerable antiquity; second, the system of taking hostages for the good behaviour of the adversary, a device of general use in enforcing treaties from very early times; and third, the punishment of war criminals when they fell into the hands of the enemy.

Over and above the means of self-help there was the system of complaints to, and intervention by, neutral States, as well as the use of good offices and mediation by such States. Finally, there was the system of compensation payable by belligerents as embodied in Article 3 of the Hague Convention No. IV of 1907. Thereby, a belligerent is responsible for all acts committed by members of its forces and is also liable to pay compensation, if the case demands, for violations of the Hague Regulations appended to that Convention. This provision is still extant, and is repeated and made applicable to the Geneva Conventions of 1949 and Protocol I of 1978, by Article 91 of the latter instrument.

In the main, little progress has been made in the development of new means of enforcement of the law of war. In our time there has emerged the humanitarian law of armed conflict which is substantially coterminous with the law of war on land. This new humanitarian law is built upon the Hague Convention No. IV of 1907, an early codification of the law of land warfare, and comprises the four Geneva Conventions of 1949 and the two Additional Protocols of 1978 [10]. Not much was added to the modes of enforcement by these latter instruments. Conversely, taking hostages was forbidden and the legitimate recourse to reprisals has been reduced to vestigial proportions, if not eliminated. The main burden of enforcement of the modern law of war has been imposed upon the penal repression of "grave breaches" of the Conventions of 1949 and of Protocol I.

"Grave beaches" of those instruments are war crimes of gravity, but do not exhaust that concept. The payment of compensation by a belligerent for violation of those instruments committed by its armed forces is a part of the law rarely applied. Finally, an ancillary method of enforcement of the law of war has been introduced by the international fact-finding commission to be established under Article 90 of Protocol I. These modes of enforcement are now examined.

B. Hostages

The taking of hostages in advance of any breach of the law of war is strictly a method of securing implementation of that law. The taking of hostages after a breach of the law was a mode of enforcement in stages. If further breaches occurred, the hostages might be killed. A third method was to seize so-called hostages after illegal acts by the adversary and to kill them on that account, sometimes in a particular ratio for those wounded or killed by the initial illegality by the adversary.

This last "hostage" taking and killing is more properly considered to be a form of reprisals action, i.e., an orthodox mode of enforcement of the law. The experiences of the Franco-Prussian war in 1870, of the Boer War of 1900, and of the two World Wars, 1914-1918 and 1939-1945, led to a widespread condemnation of the practice of taking and of killing hostages. In the Second World War the German Reich took and killed "hostages" on a large scale for acts of resistance in occupied territory. Sometimes, the ratio of killings was as much as 100 : 1. The required number of persons, on that ratio, were often arrested on the streets, irrespective of age or sex, and summarily executed. Sometimes announcements were made in advance that for certain types of activity this would be done. Strictly, these acts were illegal resorts to reprisals. The killing of "hostages" formed part of the Indictment before the International Military Tribunal at Nuremberg and in the *Hostages Case (list and others)*[11] tried before a US Military Tribunal at Nuremberg in 1949. The general opinion of jurists at that time was that the killing of hostages was an illegal act. The four Geneva Conventions of 1949 were framed mainly in the light of the excesses committed by the Axis Powers in the Second World War. The Fourth (Civilians) Convention, Article 34, prohibited "the taking of hostages". This prohibition is applicable to civilians in the territory of the belligerents and in occupied territory. By Article 33 of the same Convention: "No protected person" as defined in Article 4, "may be punished for an offence he or she has not personally committed. Collective penalties and, likewise, all measures of intimidation or terrorism are prohibited". The general opinion of jurists today is that the taking of hostages in any circumstances is unlawful. This is now reflected in Article 147 of the Geneva (Fourth) Convention whereby "taking of hostages" from "protected persons" is expressly made a "grave breach" which States Parties have a legal obligation to repress by penal proceedings in their courts. This prohibition is repeated in Article 75 (2) of Protocol I. Thus it can be said that the taking of hostages has ceased to be a mode of enforcement of the law of war and has become, instead, a serious breach of it to be enforced by penal proceedings. The passage of time transforms a mode of law enforcement into an act of war criminality.

C. *Reprisals*

Reprisals have a long history and are a classical means of enforcement of the law of war. Reprisals in war are not to be confused with reprisals in peace. In the mediaeval law of arms reprisals took the form of letters of *marque* [12] issued by the Prince to enable acts of war to be taken in time of truce in response to hostile acts committed against his subjects during a truce. It was the response of the Prince to his subjects claim "to do them right". The canon law difficulty was that such acts of reprisal operated against the innocent and thus were unjust. In the later development of the customary law of war in the eighteenth and nineteenth centuries reprisals came to be seen as a means whereby a belligerent enforced observance of the law of war after it had been violated by the adversary. A reprisal came to be an act directed against the enemy, otherwise illegal, in order to compel the enemy to return to legality. A number of rules evolved to limit resort to reprisals. They could be taken only by the authority of a government. They could be taken only after a failure to induce the enemy to return to legality. They might be used only after a warning. They had to cease if the enemy desisted from its illegalities for whatever reason. In theory, reprisals were not to be excessive to their purpose, i.e., to procure the return of the adversary to lawful conduct. It was controversial whether reprisals were required to be acts of the like kind to that of the initial illegality. In practice, reprisals frequently were disproportionate and led to mounting excesses. The development of the law of sea warfare has been marked by the transition from reprisals to accepted and lawful practice. Thus, actions taken as reprisals in one epoch become the accepted lawful practices of a later epoch, e.g., the device of the "long range" or "paper blockades" used in the First and Second World Wars. Reprisals of excessive severity were resorted to by the German Reich in occupied territory in the Second World War and were the subject of a number of war crimes trials [13].

The first express prohibition of resort to reprisals occurred in the Geneva (prisoners of war) Convention of 1929, Article 2 (3). This was the logical and necessary derivative from the positive obligation to treat prisoners of war humanely. Each of the four Geneva Conventions of 1949 expressly prohibited reprisals against the classes of persons protected thereunder, i.e., (i) sick and wounded in the armed forces, (ii) sick, wounded and shipwrecked members of the armed forces at sea, (iii) prisoners of war and (iv) civilians in enemy hands or in occupied territory. Thus the taking of reprisals against persons defenceless in the hands of the enemy was expressly made an unlawful act. By Protocol I of 1978, reprisal attacks against civilians, civilian objects, cultural objects and buildings, the environment and installations containing dangerous forces, were expressly prohibited. International humanitarian law finds it difficult to accommodate reprisals within its régime. The question now arises whether reprisals have any vestigial place within the modern law of war on land. Possibly, they may be taken by resorting to otherwise illegal methods of combat, e.g., the use of unlawful weapons directed against combatants. Thus, it is now an open question whether poison gas might be used, contrary to the Geneva Gas Protocol of 1925, against an enemy that has systematically starved prisoners of war or attacked civilians. Thus it may be that reprisals, unlike the taking of hostages, may still retain vestigial legality in strictly limited circumstances. As a general proposition of the contemporary law of war, reprisals are no longer a lawful method of law enforcement, but are themselves violations of that law. Thus two of the oldest means of law enforcement have been removed. At the same time, the content of the humanitarian law of war has been extended, with some precision, to battle conduct. This places a heavy strain upon the residual methods of law enforcement.

D. The Trial of War Criminals

By the classical law war crimes are those acts by enemy personnel, soldiers or civilians, which may be tried by the enemy on capture of the offender. Such trials have a long history. Unlike piracy, war crimes expose the perpetrators to the direct impact of international law. Under the law of war there is individual responsibility for violating that law. It is not a matter of each State conceding to other States criminal jurisdiction over its own nationals, as in the case of piracy. The experiences of the trials of war criminals, at the close of the First World War, by the German Supreme Court at Leipzig [14], did not inspire confidence in the penal process when the accused were nationals of the State exercising jurisdiction. The experiences of the Second World War, culminating in the "unconditional surrender" of the German Reich and the complete occupation of all its territory, led to the International Military Tribunal at Nuremberg, established by the London Four-Power Agreement of 8 August 1945, and a great number of war crimes trials conducted by a variety of national jurisdictions of the individual victor Powers. Most war crimes trials took place after the close of hostilities, both in Europe and the Far East. The USSR conducted the *Kharkov Trial* in 1944, but such war-time trials were exceptional. War crimes, as defined in the Charter to the London Agreement of 8 August 1945, fell into three classes: (i) crimes against peace; (ii) war crimes *stricto sensu*, i.e., violations of the law of war; and (iii) crimes against humanity. Crimes against peace were a novelty in international penal law, although they emerged as a logical legal concept. Crimes against humanity were also a new concept and were designed to embrace acts of killing and gross maltreatment before or during the war, directed against any population including a State's own nationals.

At no other time in history have such a large number of enemy personnel been brought to trial and punishment for acts of war criminality. Of these accused a considerable number were sentenced to death and executed. The convicted ranged from government ministers to private soldiers and policemen. In every case the jurisdiction exercised was that of a victor State or States. No defeated belligerent or neutral State national was a member of any of these war crimes tribunals. A considerable amount of case law was developed by the decisions of these courts [15] and has augmented the content of international substantive penal law.

No permanent international criminal court yet exists. The International Court of Justice has jurisdiction, as between States, in respect of disputes concerning the application or interpretation of the Genocide Convention of 1948 and the responsibility of a State for acts of genocide as therein defined. Thereunder, the sole courts entrusted with penal jurisdiction over individuals for acts of genocide are, by Article 6, the courts of the State in which those acts have been committed or an international criminal court. The result is that no individual is likely to be brought to trial for genocide. This form of war criminality is normally beyond the resources of the private individual and tends to be a State ordered activity. A State which pursues a policy of genocide is not likely to prosecute its own officials and nationals for carrying out its orders. The enforcement mechanisms under the Genocide Convention, in relation to individuals, are virtually non-existent and expose the conventions to a justifiable criticism of artificiality.

The trial of individuals for war crimes has been largely superseded by the modern system of the penal repression of "grave breaches" established in the Geneva Conventions of 1949 and extended in Protocol I. Hitherto the trial of war criminals had been seen as an exercise of the right of self-help enjoyed by States as part of their sovereignty. Under the Geneva Conventions of 1949 a new system was introduced whereby the trial of perpetrators of "grave breaches" has been made quasi-mandatory. In point of time the Genocide Convention of 1948, Article 6, had already made the trial of an offender for any of the acts therein defined as genocide mandatory. The Geneva Conventions, in the common Articles 49/50/129/146, impose legal obligations upon State Parties to : (i) enact any legislation necessary to provide effective penal sanctions for any person committing or ordering to be committed, any of the "grave breaches" of each of the conventions defined in the following Article ; and (ii) to search for such persons and to bring them to trial, irrespective of their nationality, before "its own courts". The State Party may also, if it so prefers, "under its own legislation, hand such persons over to another State Party which has made out a *prima facie* case. Upon examination most of the acts listed as "grave breaches" are already serious war crimes. Crimes against peace and crimes against humanity are not included within "grave breaches" and therefore stand outside the Geneva Conventions system of penal jurisdiction and repression. Thus the Detaining Power lies under no obligation to bring persons accused of those two categories of war criminality to trial. As to war criminals *stricto sensu*, they must be tried, or handed over if its law permits.

The system of penal repression of "grave breaches" was adopted in its entirety in Protocol I and has now been made applicable to the new "grave breaches" of the Protocol. These include the serious battle crimes specified in Article 85 (3). In States such as the United Kingdom this will entail legislation before ratification. Certain States at the Diplomatic Conference, 1974-1977, showed a marked enthusiasm for the extensive resort to this method of enforcement of the modern humanitarian law of war. Other States were less enthusiastic and saw this as a possible method of oppression by a Detaining Power. Article 85 marks the *via media*, attained with some difficulty. Some of the acts listed as "grave breaches" in that Article reflect contemporary racial issues, e.g., "practices of *apartheid*". In the anxiety of a group of States to secure the quickest repatriation of prisoners of war, no reference was made to the large scale compulsory repatriation, in 1945 and 1946, by belligerents to an allied belligerent, prisoners of war, nationals of the latter, captured by the former when serving in the enemy's armed forces.

The international penal law system is still in a rudimentary stage. The modern system of penal repression of "grave breaches" has reduced the competent jurisdiction exclusively to the courts of the Detaining Power. Thereby multi-power courts such as the International Military Tribunal at Nuremburg and at Tokyo have today no competence in respect of "grave breaches" of the Geneva Conventions and of Protocol I. "Grave breaches" include most of the existing war crimes except crimes against peace and the majority of crimes against humanity. It would appear that all forms of "special" war crimes courts and occupation courts are also excluded. Courts-martial are competent to entertain war crimes charged against prisoners of war if so competent under the law of the Detaining Power.

The trial of war criminals engages three distinct areas of law, not all of which are to be found within contemporary international penal law. First, there is the substantive law of war criminality. To the extent that war crimes are violations of the law of war, customary or conventional, international law is the sole source and basis of war criminality. Many of the principles of individual penal responsibility have not yet been worked out in international law. The possible defences to war criminality of duress, necessity, claim of right, mental disease, alcoholism and drug addiction, as well as the contested effect of "superior orders" or ignorance of the law, may still depend in part upon the municipal penal law of the State exercising the war crimes jurisdiction. From the point of view of the accused, probably faced with a death sentence, the jurisdiction exercised over him and part of the penal law applied to him turns upon the identity of the Detaining Power, an accident of capture in or after a war.

Second, there is the jurisdictional law. One hundred and forty-six

States are now Parties to the Geneva Conventions of 1949. The ordinary penal courts of the Detaining Power have exclusive and mandatory jurisdiction for all acts of war criminality which are "grave breaches" or non-grave breaches of the conventions or of Protocol I, except in cases where the accused is handed over for trial by another State Party. For crimes against peace and crimes against humanity there may be a wider range of jurisdiction for all accused other than prisoners of war. The latter must be tried by the same courts and under the same procedures as members of the armed forces of the Detaining Power ; Articles 85 and 102 of the Geneva (Third) Convention. A prisoner of war handed over for trial to a neutral State for "grave breaches" or any war crime ceases to be a prisoner of war in the hands of the neutral State.

Third, there is the law of evidence and procedure. In the main, these topics are governed by the municipal law of the Detaining Power, subject to the judicial safeguards and procedural requirements imposed by the Geneva Conventions of 1949 or Protocol I. International penal law is a developing body of rules, but it still relies substantially upon municipal law for the penalties and for many of the rules of evidence and procedure applicable in a war crimes trial.

Although no resort to the Geneva Conventions system of repression of "grave breaches" is known since the conventions came into force in 1950, there has been no dearth of acts that amounted to "grave breaches". Also, the perpetrators and the evidence against them have been available to the Detaining Power. The situation which prevailed in Europe and the Far East at the end of the Second World War was unique. That war concluded with the total defeat of the enemy States and the occupation of the whole of their territories. Although the crimes were gross and committed on a huge scale, the war crimes trials held between 1945-1950 led to considerable criticism and dissatisfaction not entirely explained by the novelty of the penal enforcement of the law of war. The Geneva Conventions of 1949 and Protocol I of 1978 attempted to remove some of these criticisms. Nevertheless, in spite of the fact that no person has, in the 30 years since the Geneva Conventions came into force, been brought to trial for a "grave breach" of those conventions, Protocol I continued and expanded the system of penal repression of "grave breaches". Article 85 extended the list of "grave breaches" to include battle crimes. The Protocol, in Article 75, improved the evidentiary and procedural safeguards in penal proceedings.

No attempt was made to introduce any new mode of enforcement of the law except the international fact finding commission (Article 90). The rejection of the system of hostages and, in substantial measure, the resort to reprisals, has weakened the modalities of enforcement. Penal processes could not be jettisoned without expanding the new humanitarian law to the criticism of artificiality. The reason why there had been no resort to trials for "grave breaches" of the Geneva Conventions was that most of the post-1945 armed conflicts to which the conventions have been applicable concluded with a general armistice and without the total surrender of either Party. A belligerent with members of its armed forces held as prisoners of war by the enemy is reluctant to embark upon war crimes trials against enemy personnel even if evidence of gross criminality be available. Reciprocity may be a factor inducing implementation of the law of war, but it may also be a factor dissuasive of enforcement of that law by the penal process. A further impediment to the penal enforcement of the law of war is the difficulty in securing the surrender of a suspected war criminal to the State where the crimes were committed or which holds the evidence against the suspect. This evidence cannot in many cases be made available to the State in which the suspect is found. Some jurists have contended that all States, including neutral States, are under a legal obligation to surrender a wanted war criminal to the requesting State upon proof of a *prima facie* case against him. They contend that even if there be no such obligation known to international law the failure to surrender war criminals in such circumstances is an abuse of sovereignty. On the other hand, many States consider that war crimes are political offences for which extradition is excluded and asylum may be given at discretion. In practice, a number of States have declined to surrender persons accused of war criminality and against whom clear evidence is presented. Sometimes these States plead that their extradition law does not enable such a surrender. Sometimes there is a plea that the suspect demanded is a national of the requested State and that the Constitution of that State precludes any surrender of a national. The result has been that war criminals seek the territory of a State which they know will not surrender them. This occurred at the conclusion of the Second World War. Certain of the worst of the war criminals, persons against whom overwhelming evidence exists, e.g., SS doctors and camp staff who selected prisoners for the gas chambers of such camps as Auschwitz and Birkenau in Poland. have by this method managed to survive to this day.

The law of extradition varies considerably from State to State. As yet, the only international law governing the surrender of war criminals is the provision of the common Articles of the Geneva Conventions of 1949 above referred to and Article 7 of the Genocide Convention of 1948. These conventions do not apply to acts committed in the Second World War. In cases where they do apply, the obligation to surrender the accused, if not brought to trial by the Detaining Power, is qualified by the words "in accordance with the provisions of its own legislation". This means that international law is not controlling in this context. It was found impossible to secure agreement on any provision for the mandatory surrender of war criminals in the Diplomatic Conference, 1974-1977, which established Protocol I. The ceiling of achievement can be seen in Article 88 of that Protocol :

> "32. Subject to . . . (the obligations in the Conventions and the Protocol) and when circumstances permit, the High Contracting Parties shall co-operate in the matter of extradition. They shall give due consideration to the request of the State in whose territory the alleged offence has occurred.
>
> 3. The law of the High Contracting Party requested shall apply in all cases . . ."

Thereby any new rule of international law is precluded in favour of the existing extradition law of States. War criminals are well advised to make themselves acquainted with the comparative law of extradition and act accordingly. Thus, one major defect in the enforcement of the international law of war criminality remains substantially unremedied.

In terms of justice to the accused war criminal, the Detaining Power is often faced with a dilemma. If the accused is placed in custody during the war, a trial before its conclusion will normally debar the accused from access to important evidence, e.g., superior orders, which if not going to his defence, will normally go to mitigation of his sentence. Also, the climate of opinion in the belligerent State during the war may not be consistent with the doing of impartial justice at his trial. If the trial be delayed until the conclusion of hostilities, there may have been a long period of pre-trial custody. Delayed justice is normally not justice. If the delay be sufficiently lengthy, there may be a prescription law applicable. Moreover, experience has shown that the severity of the sentences imposed tends to be conditioned, in large part, by the proximity of the trial to the time of the act of criminality of which the accused is convicted.

Protocol I has retained the jurisdictional system of the Geneva

Conventions of 1949 for the trial of persons accused of "grave breaches"; Article 85 of the Protocol. Accordingly, it has excluded international jurisdictions of whatever nature, for "grave" and other breaches, including such Tribunals as the Four-Power and Fifteen-Power International Military Tribunals of Nuremberg and Tokyo, respectively. It has also excluded special war crimes courts for the trial of enemy nationals charged with such breaches. The trial of a State's own nationals for war crimes is rare. The German Federal Republic and the Netherlands have held such trials in respect of war crimes committed during the Second World War.

What is needed today is an international instrument governing the trial of war criminals and which deals comprehensively with the substantive law, evidence and procedure, and inter-State surrenders of accused. That calls for a high measure of international agreement which probably does not exist at the present time. Although an international criminal court has been under consideration for a number of years, as yet no result has been achieved. The use of neutral judges as members of the ordinary courts of the Detaining Power is not practicable. They would not normally be familiar with the municipal law applicable to the conduct of the trial and the governments of neutral States may not be desirous of providing members of the judiciary to participate in the trial of war criminals by the belligerents. No attempt seems to have been made, at the conclusion of the Second World War, to have procured the services of neutral judges either at Nuremberg or at Tokyo. State policies seem to have been firmly inclined to trials by judges of the victor belligerents. Likewise, a system of neutral war crimes jurisdictions may, in theory, be possible, but is not likely to be asserted in practice. The existing law precludes any exclusive neutral jurisdiction over war criminals.

The imperfections of the enforcement of the law of war by penal processes remain substantial. Nevertheless, certain States place great emphasis upon this mode of enforcement. When used imperfectly, this mode can cause grave injustice to the individual accused. When used in bad faith, it can constitute a major engine of oppression.

E. Compensation

This is not a means of enforcement of the law which has received much attention in State practice during the current century. Certain war crimes, such as mass extermination, are so gross that compensation is not adequate, and can hardly be calculated. As a method of enforcement against the individual war criminal compensation has only a marginal relevance. At the conclusion of a war compensation is more likely to be demanded against the defeated belligerent as a form of reparation payment. Such matters are normally dealt with in a treaty of peace, a phenomenon which is rare in current international transactions. It is arguable that a treaty of peace which failed to make express provision for the payment of compensation for the commission of war crimes committed by the personnel of the defeated belligerent, would preclude subsequent demands for such compensation.

By Article 3 of the Hague Convention No. IV of 1907 :

> "A belligerent party which violates the provisions of the (annexed) Regulations, shall if the case demands, be liable to pay compensation. It shall be responsible for all acts committed by persons forming part of its armed forces."

Of these two rules the second is not novel, but is merely a particular example of vicarious State responsibility. The first rule, however, is novel and is not considered to be limited to violations of the Hague Regulations of 1907. It therefore has far reaching effects if it extends to all violations of the law of war.

Article 91 of Protocol I of 1978 has brought forward the two rules and made them applicable to violations of the provisions of the Geneva Conventions or of the Protocol, in these terms :

> "A Party to the conflict which violates the provisions of Conventions or of this Protocol shall, if the case demands, be liable to pay compensation. It shall be responsible for all acts committed by persons forming part of its armed forces."

Article 90 would thus be applicable to self-determination conflicts as defined in Article 1 (4) to which the conventions and the protocol have been made applicable by the system of unilateral declaration deposited under the terms of Article 90 (3). It remains to be seen whether the liability to pay compensation for breaches of the conventions or of Protocol I will be used as a mode of enforcement of those instruments. So far, resort to the earlier provision in the Hague Regulations of 1907 has not been a feature of belligerent practice.

F. The International Fact-Finding Commission

Part of the difficulty in enforcing the law of war is that allegations of war crimes committed by the enemy have now come to form part of the accepted pattern of war propaganda and psychological warfare. There has not existed to date any standing machinery to investigate allegations of war criminality except the limited competence of the International Court of Justice under Article 9 of the Genocide Convention 1948, to which the Soviet States made a reservation.

The Geneva Conventions of 1949 provided no satisfactory machinery for ascertaining whether the violations alleged had been committed. Unless the facts can be ascertained the enforcement of the law is considerably weakened. The common Articles 52/53/132/146 of the Geneva Conventions of 1949 provide that a Party to a conflict may request an enquiry, in a manner to be agreed between the Parties, into "any alleged violation of the Convention". If the manner of proceedings cannot be agreed, then it is to be decided by an umpire, to be agreed. Nothing is said as to action in default of such latter agreement. In other words, this article provides what can be done by the Parties, without any provision in the conventions. Experiences such as those in the Korean conflict of 1950 when the Chinese Volunteer Army authorities alleged that the US airforce spread bacteriological contamination, showed the sterility of any enquiry procedures without an agreed procedure. The USA offered, through the ICRC, to participate in such an enquiry, but the Peoples Republic of China, having made the initial allegation, failed to respond to the ICRC's proposals for an enquiry.

In Protocol I of 1978, a major attempt was made to remedy this defect. By Article 90 "an international fact-finding commission" is to be established upon the initiative of not less than 20 States Parties to the Protocol who accept the competence of the Commission under paragraph 2 of the Article. Detailed provisions in paragraph 1 specify who may be the members, 15 in number and how they are to be elected. By paragraph 2 *(c)* of the Article the competence of the commission is declared to be :

> "(i) (to) enquire into any facts alleged to be a grave breach as defined in the Conventions and this Protocol or other serious violations of (those instruments) ;
> (ii) (to) facilitate, through its good offices, the restoration of an attitude of respect for the Conventions and this Protocol."

By paragraph 2 *(a)* it is open to each State Party to declare that it recognises *ipso facto* and without special agreement in relation to any other such Party accepting the same obligation, the competence of the commission to enquire into allegations by such other Party as authorised in the article. It is possible that this article will introduce those complexities that have attended the operation of the "optional clause" (Article 36 (2)) of the Statute of the International Court of Justice. This means that declarations with reservations can be made, with reciprocal effect, limiting the competence of the commission according to the wishes of States making such declarations. The degree of co-operation and good faith required of the parties to an armed conflict to enable the fact-finding commission to operate according to the terms of the protocol is considerable. The elaborate nature of this fact-finding machinery will prolong its proceedings. It is not likely to be able to function in time of armed conflict.

G. *Enforcement in Struggles by National Liberation Movements*

Struggles by peoples in exercise of their right of self-determination have been brought within the scope of Protocol I ; Article 1 (4). This is one of the outstanding features of the instrument. The juridical coherence of its exclusion was overborne by the political demand for its inclusion. It may be said that no single division of opinion during the diplomatic conference that established the protocol reached such a pitch of intensity as that displayed in the debates upon this topic. Under the existing law of war struggles by peoples against racial, colonial or foreign domination are a class of internal armed conflicts taking place within the territory of a State Party to the conventions and the protocol. Such armed struggles fall within the terms of common Article 3 of the conventions. Whether or not they would fall properly within the scope of Protocol II did not arise. At the stage of the diplomatic conference at which the debates for the inclusion of such struggles within Protocol I took place, the scope of Protocol II had not been debated or determined. The result was that Protocol II, Article 1, expressly included such struggles.

The voting in favour of the inclusion of self-determination struggles showed a substantial, but not overwhelming, majority for inclusion. The outcome is now to be seen in Article 1 (4) of Protocol I. This provision is of considerable importance as long as there remain governments from a racial and foreign minority. Article 1 (4) provides :

> "The situations referred to in the preceding paragraph (the common Article 2 of the Geneva Conventions of 1949) include armed conflicts in which peoples are fighting against colonial

domination and alien occupation and against racist régimes in the exercise of their right of self-determination as enshrined in the Charter of the United Nations and the Declaration on Principles of International Law concerning Friendly Relations and Co-operation among States in accordance with the Charter of the United Nations."

This provision was aimed primarily at Israel, South Africa and Portugal, at the time it was framed. Subsequently, during the conference, Portugal dissolved the colonial nexus with its African dependent territories. Two new States, Mozambique and Angola, emerged in their stead. Such "peoples" are not, and cannot be, State Parties to the protocol, or to the Geneva Conventions. It was therefore requisite that some device be introduced into the protocol whereby such "peoples" might assume the benefit and the burdens of the conventions and the protocol. This was achieved by Article 96 (3) of the protocol. Thereby :

> "The authority representing a people engaged against a High Contracting Party in an armed conflict of the type referred to in Article 1 (4) may undertake to apply the Conventions and this Protocol in relation to that conflict by means of a unilateral declaration addressed to the depositary (Switzerland). Such declaration shall, upon its receipt by the depositary, have in relation to that conflict the following effects :
>
> *(a)* the Conventions and this Protocol are brought into force for the said authority as a Party to the conflict with immediate effect ;
> *(b)* the said authority assumes the same rights and obligations as those which have been assumed by a High Contracting Party to the Conventions and this Protocol ; and
> *(c)* the Conventions and this Protocol are equally binding upon all Parties to the conflict."

Questions of enforcement of the conventions and the protocol by a "people" so engaged in armed conflict against a High Contracting Party will arise. No special provisions are made in the protocol to meet enforcement difficulties. The term "authority representing a people" does little to resolve such questions. Does Article 96 (3) imply that a unilateral declaration can be made only when the authority is able and willing to apply the provisions of the conventions and the protocol ? It would seem that Article 90 (3) assumes capacity. "Liberation movements" were not prepared to admit any lack of such capacity. The modalities of enforcement were not debated at the conference. Under Article 1 (4) the depositary Power is not called upon to make a determination of the capacity of such a movement, or its "authority", to observe the conventions or the protocol. Does this mean that such "authority" representing such a "people" can make its own determination of its capacity to observe those instruments ?

It was in the light of such consideration that the United Kingdom saw fit to make explicit its understanding of the operation of Article 1 (4) in an interpretative statement made at the time of signature of the protocol at Berne on 12 December 1977, originally made on signing the final act of the protocol on 10 June 1977. Therein the United Kingdom declared its understanding of Article 1 (4) as follows :

> ". . . in relation to Article 1 . . . the term 'armed conflict' of itself and its context implies a certain level of intensity of military operations which must be present before the Conventions or the Protocol are to apply to any given situation, and this level of intensity cannot be less than that required for the application of Protocol II, by virtue of Article 1 of that Protocol, to internal conflicts".

This declaration has been exposed to the criticism that it seeks to undermine, if not change, the proper meaning of the text of Protocol I, in that no such level of intensity is to be found expressed in any part of Protocol I. A more valid comment might be that although the protocol is silent on the level of intensity of the conflict in the case of "liberation struggle", the effective functioning of the instrument demands that minimal level of intensity in Article 1 (4), if the protocol is to be effective. Under the interpretative statement of the United Kingdom we are required to consider the terms of Protocol II, Article 1, the scope provision. Had it not been for the insertion of Article 1 (4) in Protocol I, struggles for self-determination, as therein specified, would, under the Geneva Conventions of 1949, to which the protocols are "additional", have found their proper classification as internal armed conflicts within Common Article 3. Protocol II, Article 1, provides :

> "This Protocol . . . shall apply to all armed conflicts which are not covered by Article 1 of (Protocol I) and which take place in the territory of a High Contracting Party between its armed forces and dissident armed forces or other organised armed groups which, under responsible command, exercise such control over a

part of its territory as to enable them to carry out sustained and concerted military operations and to implement this Protocol."

Some such provision might have been included in Protocol I, probably as part of Article 96 (3), in order to make the instrument effective, although the terms of paragraph 3 *(c)* probably carry that interpretation by necessary implication. Nevertheless, even in the light of the United Kingdom interpretative understanding of "armed conflicts" in Protocol I, difficulties in applying the enforcement mechanism will arise. How, for example, are the complex requirements of penal enforcement of the conventions and the protocol, in relation to "grave breaches", to be met by the "authority" representing a people in a self-determination struggle ? Where is the penal law system, the judicial apparatus, the substantive and procedural law to govern the trial of a person in the hands of such an "authority" charged with a "grave breach" of the conventions or of Protocol I ? Where is to be found the law governing the extradition of such person to a third State for trial ? How can the provisions of the Geneva (Fourth) Convention relating to occupied territory be enforced ? Who are "protected persons" for the purposes of that convention ? From the nature of the situation, the "people" are of the same nationality as those of the adversary Party, i.e., the High Contracting Party concerned. How is the requirement of Article 84 (rules of application) to be met by a liberation movement ? Are they required to have a legal system from the inception of the armed struggle ? These and many other difficulties will fall for determination if the protocol is to be "equally binding upon all Parties to the conflict" (Article 96 (3) *(c)*).

Any contention that the obligation imposed upon a "people" is limited to the extent of its degree of organisation is negatived by the wording of Article 96 (3) *(b)* and *(c)* of Protocol I. What may have happened here is that the difficulties already attending the enforcement of the common Article 3 of the Conventions of 1949 have, in this context, been carried over to Protocol I designed to govern the conduct of State belligerents in international armed conflicts. The inclusion of struggles for self-determination within Protocol I, as international armed conflicts, is no more than a political flourish with unfortunate and uncertain juridical results. It weakens the humanitarian law which has been invoked to regulate such struggles. The juridical commingling of international and internal armed conflicts, as advocated by certain States, is here exemplified in its true delineaments. It has aggravated the existing difficulties of effective enforcement of the law of war and thereby lowered that respect for it which the Conventions of 1949 and the additional protocols thereto were designed to enhance.

H. Enforcement and Internal Armed Conflicts

Article 3, common to the Geneva Conventions of 1949, posed major juridical difficulties in its enforcement. Armed rebellion of itself is not a violation of international law, but is a clear and most serious offence under the penal law of the State concerned. The dissident armed forces would appear to lack juridical personality in which the rights and obligations flowing from Article 3 may inhere. It has been suggested that the dissident Party to the conflict has that measure of legal personality conferred upon it by international law to enable it to meet its obligations under Article 3, e.g., to conduct a trial "by a regularly constituted court affording all the judicial guarantees which are recognised as indispensable by civilised peoples". Under the terms of Protocol II, Article 1, which are almost coterminous with a full scale civil war, the enforcement of the protocol by penal processes may not be feasible unless there are two *de facto* régimes operating under their own legal systems in the territory under their control. Much of the content of Protocol II assumes that such will be the situation. Such a "legal system" may be that of the State concerned or one established by the dissident authority.

Reprisals do not appear to have been excluded from the modalities for the enforcement of Article 3 common to the Geneva Conventions, or from Protocol II. "Collective punishments" are, however, expressly forbidden by Article 2 *(b)*. Certain obligations must be observed "in all circumstances", e.g., Article 13 (1) relating to the protection of the civilian population from military attacks. Such provisions do not, it is thought, exclude reprisals. To that extent Protocol II enjoys a modality of enforcement not available to Protocol I. The internal penal law of the State in which the internal conflict is waged continues to apply, subject to Article 3 common to the conventions and to Protocol II, if applicable. The provision contained in Article 6 (5) of Protocol II as to amnesty at the conclusion of the internal conflict is hortatory in nature although it applies to whichever Party to the conflict attains political power. The means of enforcement under the Geneva Conventions and Protocol I for international conflicts are not available to such internal conflicts, but this penal law of the State is, by Article 3 (1) of Protocol II, available for that purpose. Protocol II has probably cured few of the defects of Article 3 of the conventions in relation to the enforcements of the obligations, but has added considerably to the volume of obligations to be enforced. For the future, the enforcement of the law governing internal armed conflicts will have to continue to rely upon meta-legal forces such as reciprocity, external opinion of the community of States and the desire to obtain the support of the bulk of the population of the State in which the conflict has arisen.

I. Conclusions

The Geneva Conventions of 1949 and the two Additional Protocols of 1978 sought to augment and strengthen the humanitarian content of the law of war in the light of the inhumanity experienced in the Second World War and the armed conflicts, both international and internal, that have occurred since the conclusion of that War. The Geneva Conventions were primarily concerned with the protection of service personnel, i.e., the sick, wounded, shipwrecked and Prisoners of War, with one (the Fourth) Convention devoted exclusively to the protection of civilian war victims who found themselves in enemy territory or in territory occupied by the enemy. As it was in occupied territory that the civilians were subjected to the grossest enormities, including extermination, in the Second World War, particular emphasis was laid upon ensuring proper protection of civilians in such areas. The humanitarian endeavour behind the Geneva Conventions could allow no place to the device of hostage taking or reprisals, for their enforcement. Those conventions relied for their enforcement mainly upon the penal repression of defined "grave breaches" directed against the various classes of war victims, together with the activities of the Protecting Power in monitoring implementation and enforcement.

Post-Second World War experience showed two gaping *lacunae* in the humanitarian law of war as established by the Geneva Conventions of 1949, first, the anachronistic and fragmentary nature of much of the Hague Convention No. IV of 1907 governing the conduct of hostilities on land, and, second, the inadequacy of the law governing internal armed conflicts. The first was met by Protocol I and the second, less satisfactorily, by Protocol II. After considerable debate, as to enforcement of the law, Protocol I substantially excluded the resort to reprisals from the law governing hostilities on land as inconsistent with the humanitarian endeavour and ineffective in practice. Protocol II, following Article 3 of the conventions, dealt with reprisals by not referring to them. Thus they may have survived as a legal device for the enforcement of the law governing internal conflicts.

Protocol I adopted, virtually as established in the conventions, the system of penal repression of "grave breaches". It augmented the categories of such "grave breaches" by including the more serious violations of the prohibitions restraining battle conduct, primarily that which was directed against civilians. It did little to augment the content of international penal law which still remains in embryonic form. It sought to establish a viable international fact-finding machinery operative during conflict, but made it so complex that effective functioning is uncertain. Thus, once again we have a position not unknown in the development of the law of war. We are confronted by a refinement and amplification of the rules governing conduct in warfare, but with little addition to, or improvement of, the enforcement mechanisms. In the humanitarian content of the law of war there has been much advance. In the methods available for its enforcement there has been little progress or originality. To date we can discern next to no use of the method of penal repression of "grave breaches" established by the Geneva Conventions of 1949. There has been no dearth of "grave breaches" committed in the post-1950 conflicts. This does not spell out much success in the implementing machinery, e.g., the requirement of instruction in the armed forces. The subjection of unlawful battle conduct to the system of penal repression of "grave breaches" may have placed the enforcement mechanisms available under the modern humanitarian law of armed conflict to a degree of strain that may reintroduce that artificiality of the law of war that has been its traditional misfortune. The nature of modern conventional weaponry, the width of the humanitarian prohibitions in battle conduct, and the unsatisfactory nature of certain aspects of penal enforcement, do not augur well for the future enforcement of the modern law of war.

The burden placed upon meta-legal forces for observance of the law will remain a heavy one. There is a certain inherent dichotomy between the establishment of humanitarian norms of conduct in war and their enforcement. Reprisals can no longer be accommodated as means of enforcement of humanitarian law. It is too soon to assess the effectiveness of the presence of legal advisers with commanders in time of armed conflict, as a method of implementation. Implementation operates ahead of and negates violation. Penal proceedings function in response to violations. The methods of monitoring implementation have progressed. The same cannot be said of means of enforcement of the law of war. The Geneva Conventions of 1949 and the two Additional Protocols of 1978 represent the high-water mark of humanitarian achievement in the law of war to date. We can no longer allow the law of war to be considered "as the vanishing point of international law" [16]. The failure to secure the implementation and enforcement of the modern humanitarian law of war will do little to maintain the faith of man in man.

53

NOTES

1. H. Lauterpacht, "The Revision of the Law of War", *The British Year Book of International Law*, Vol. 29 (1952), pp. 381-382.
2. H. Lauterpacht, *International Law, Collected Papers*, Vol. 2, Cambridge, 1975, p. 37.
3. *Ibid.*, p. 319.
4. See note 1, *supra.*
5. H. Grotius, *De Jure Belli ac Pacis* (1925), Book iii, Ch. IV, para. iv.
6. *International Review of the Red Cross*, Geneva, September 1977, No. 197-198.
7. *UN Treaty Series*, Vol. 75 (1950), I, Nos. 970-3.
8. Judgment of the International Military Tribunal (Nuremberg), 1946, p. 83.
9. M. E. Keen, *The Laws of War in the Late Middle Ages*, London, 1963, pp. 136-185.
10. See notes 6 and 7, *supra.*
11. *Annual Digest* (1948), Case No. 215, p. 632.
12. Keen, *op. cit.*, pp. 218-238.
13. See note 11, *supra.*
14. *History of the UN War Crimes Commission*, 1968, pp. 32-52.
15. *Ibid.*, pp. 454-474.
16. See note 1, *supra.*

54

SELECT BIBLIOGRAPHY

A. General Works

Oppenheim, L., *International Law*, Vol. 2, "Disputes, War and Neutrality", 7th ed., London, 1952.

The Law of War on Land, being Part III of the *Manual of Military Law*, HMSO, London, 1958.

Stone, J., *Legal Controls of International Conflict*, Sydney, 1959.

Pictect, J., *Commentary on the Geneva Conventions of 1949*, 4 vols., 1952-1960, Geneva (International Committee of the Red Cross).

The Law of Land Warfare, Department of the Army Field Manual FM 27-10, USA, 1956.

Draper, G., *The Red Cross Conventions*, London, 1958.

Levie, A. S., *Prisoners of War in International Armed Conflict, International Law Studies*, US Naval War College, Vol. 59, 1977.

Verzijl, J., *International Law in Historical Perspective*, Vol. IX, A, *The Laws of War*, Sijthoff, 1978.

The New Humanitarian Law of Armed Conflict, Cassese, Naples, 1979.

B. Articles in Periodicals

Pilloud, C., "The Penal Protection of International Humanitarian Conventions", *International Review of the Red Cross*, Geneva, 1952.

Baxter, R., "The Duty of Obedience to the Belligerent Occupant", *British Year Book of International Law*, 1950.

Draper, G., "The Geneva Conventions of 1949", *Recueil des cours*, 1965-I.

Draper, G., "The Implementation of International Law in Armed Conflicts", *International Affairs*, Vol. 48, 1972.

Draper, G., "The Modern Pattern of War Criminality", *Israel Year Book of Human Rights*, Vol. 6, 1976.

[4]

THE ROLE OF LEGAL ADVISERS IN THE ARMED FORCES *

By Leslie C. Green **

Article 82 of Protocol I Additional to the Geneva Conventions of 12 August 1949, and relating to the protection of victims of international armed conflicts,[1] provides that

> The High Contracting Parties at all times, and the parties to the conflict in time of armed conflict, shall ensure that legal advisers are available, when necessary, to advise military commanders at the appropriate level on the application of the Conventions [2] and this Protocol and on the appropriate instruction to be given to the armed forces on this subject.

This is a new departure in that it lays an obligation upon States to take proper steps to ensure that at least the commanders of their own forces may apprise themselves of the legality of the actions which they contemplate undertaking. At the same time, the commander is obligated to make certain that the men under his command are aware of the law of Geneva, so that they, too, may assess the legality of the actions in which they are required to participate. If one looks at the history of the law of war and of its enforcement, which may to some extent be regarded as an extension of national criminal law into the international sphere, this provision is merely a recognition of practical necessity and the purpose that it aims to achieve is not quite so innovative as might appear, although a treaty requirement to this effect is undoubtedly a new development.

As early as the fifteenth century, at the trial of Peter von Hagenbach [3] at Breisach, it was made clear that commanders are presumed to know the law. Two centuries later, at the trial of the regicides, Cooke,[4] the former Chief Justice of Ireland who presented the indictment against Charles I, was held to be obviously liable for treason in that, as Chief Justice, he was certainly

* Paper prepared for delivery to IVth Roundtable of the International Institute of Humanitarian Law, San Remo, September 1977.

** LL.B., LL.D., University Professor, University of Alberta (Canada).

1. International Committee of the Red Cross, Final Act, June 1977.

2. 74 *U.N.T.S.* 31, 85, 135, 287.

3. (1474), Schwarzenberger, 2 *The Law of Armed Conflict* ch. 39 (1968); Green, *Superior Orders in National and International Law* 263 (1976).

4. (1660), 5 *St. Tr.* 1077; Green, *supra* note 3, at 24.

aware of what constituted a proper court and the limits of that court's jurisdiction. In so far as the law of war is concerned, the trial of Sawada[5] by a United States Military Commission sitting in Shanghai illustrates the somewhat more severe line adopted towards an accused who is legally qualified as compared with one who is not.

On the other hand, it must be borne in mind that the majority of members of the armed forces not only are not legally qualified, but frequently know little or nothing of the law of war, whether this relates to their own rights or to the rights of others and the duties that they owe to such others. Thus, in *Re Buck*[6] the Judge Advocate at a British war crimes trial asked

> What did each of these accused know about the rights of a prisoner of war? . . . The Court may well think that the men are not lawyers: they may not have heard either of the Hague Convention or the Geneva Convention; they may not have seen any book of military law upon the subject; but the Court has to consider whether men who are serving either as soldiers or in proximity to soldiers know as a matter of the general facts of military life whether a prisoner of war has certain rights . . . .

Nevertheless one must not overlook the fact that nowadays we have abandoned the principle of unquestioning obedience on the part of the most common soldier, who is no longer to be considered

> an automaton but a reasoning agent who is under the duty to exercise judgment in obeying the orders of a superior officer to the extent that, where such orders are manifestly beyond the scope of the issuing officer's authority and are so palpably illegal on their face that a man of ordinary sense and understanding would know them to be illegal, then the fact of obedience to the order of a superior officer will not protect a soldier for acts pursuant to such illegal orders.[7]

This is not the place to consider how to assess the duties or the understanding of the ordinary soldier,[8] nor is it necessary to examine the law concerning compliance with superior orders, provided, of course, that such orders are lawful.[9] The problem lies in the fact that so much of international law, and particularly of the law of war, is controversial with varying writers asserting conflicting arguments and not all countries accepting the same view of its

5. (1946), 5 *War Crimes Reports* 1; Green, *supra* note 3, at 315.

6. (1946), 13 *Annual Digest* 292; Green, *supra* note 3, at 286.

7. U.S. v. Kinder (1954), 14 *C.M.R.* 742, 776; Green, *supra* note 3, at 132. *See, also,* In re Ohlendorf (Einsatzgruppen Trial) (1948), 15 *Ann. Dig.* 656, 665; Green, *supra* note 3, at 312.

8. *See, e.g.,* Green, "Superior Orders and the Reasonable Man," 8 *Can. Y.B. Int'l L.* 61 (1970).

9. For a full discussion of this problem, *see* Green, *supra* note 3.

scope. Thus, it was not until 1975 the the United States, by its ratification of the Geneva gas protocol,[10] accepted that, save in certain very limited and carefully defined circumstances, the use of gas and other deleterious materials was contrary to law. Furthermore, when operating in the field the serviceman, officer and private soldier alike, is more concerned with the need to defeat his enemy than with the niceties of the law, particularly as in such circumstances he has no means of ascertaining what that law is, for it is most unlikely that a qualified international lawyer will be available for consultations, while the necessities of the service will frequently mean that there is no time for such consultations in any case.

Too frequently, the ordinary soldier has argued that, since he is bound to obey, since his superiors have greater knowledge of the situation than he has, and since he has been trained to assume that his superiors will only issue orders that are in accord with the law,[11] it goes without comment that he cannot be held liable for acts which he commits that are contrary to the law of war and, if they are, then, he has contended, he is protected by the concept of superior orders. As has already been seen, in so far as an order involves an act that is so "palpably illegal . . . that a man of ordinary sense and understanding would know [it] to be illegal," this defence will not lie. As to officers, there is a wealth of jurisprudence concerning war crimes to illustrate that they, too, will frequently contend that compliance with superior orders suffices to excuse all actions, especially when it is clear, to them at least, that such actions are justifiable on the basis of military necessity. Here, too, the decisions of war crimes tribunals amply illustrate the futility of such contentions. In addition, it is easy to argue that, while the ordinary person is aware that in so far as his national criminal law is concerned *ignorantia juris quod quisque tenetur scire, neminem excusat*,[12] this cannot be true of the international law of war, for those who live within a national system of law may be presumed to accept the national ethic and to be aware of the nature and basic principles of their country's criminal code, or at least know where to find them, while international law is a highly sophisticated system, much of which is controversial and, from the point of view of the layman, shrouded in mystery.

To some extent, even before the adoption of Article 82, attempts had been made to ensure that members of the armed forces would be made aware of the contents of the treaty rules of war by imposing obligations with regard to

10. (1925), 94 *L.N.T.S.* 65; Hudson, 3 *Int'l Legislation* 1670.

11. *See, e.g.*, U.S. Army "Lesson Plan" on teaching "The Geneva Conventions of 1949 and Hague Convention IV of 1907," Dept. of the Army, ASubjScd 27-1 (8 Oct., 1970).

12. *See* Selden, *Table Talk*, "Law" (1689); Blackstone, 4 *Commentaries on the Laws of England* ch. 2, s. 5 (1769).

their dissemination.[13] A number of States have issued manuals of military law outlining the obligations imposed by the laws of war upon their respective armed forces. However, such manuals are only intended

> for the guidance of military and naval forces ... [and] may, of course, be altered by the government which issues them, except in so far as the obligatory character of their rules is established by international law.[14]

On a more official level, the *United States Army Field Manual—Law of Land Warfare*[15] expressly states

> those provisions of the *Manual* which are neither statutes nor the text of treaties to which the United States is a party should not be considered binding upon courts and tribunals applying the law of war.

Perhaps the true status of such manuals is best seen in the comments of the United States military tribunal in *Re List (The Hostages Trial)*:[16]

> The fact that the British and American armies may have adopted [Oppenheim's views on the validity of superior orders as a defence to a war crimes charge] for the regulation of their own armies as a matter of policy does not have the effect of enthroning it as a rule of International Law .... Army regulations are not a competent source of International Law. They are neither legislative nor judicial pronouncements. They are not competent for any purpose in determining whether a fundamental principle of justice has been accepted by civilized nations generally. It is possible, however, that such regulations, as they bear upon a question of custom and practice in the conduct of war, might have evidentiary value, particularly if the applicable portions had been put into general practice .... Determination, whether a custom or practice exists, is a question of fact. Whether a fundamental principle of justice has been accepted is a question of judicial or legislative declaration. In determining the former, military regulations may play an important role but, in the latter, they do not constitute an authoritative precedent.

Some armed forces have attempted to go further in assisting those of their personnel who may feel that they have received an order which involves conduct contrary to the laws of war. Among these, perhaps the most important is the United States. While recognizing that it "takes courage" to question a superior as to the legality of the order that has been given, a soldier who considers that he has received an illegal order is advised to report this fact:[17]

13. *See, e.g.*, Green, "Humanitarian Law and the Man in the Field," 14 *Can. Y.B. Int'l L.* 96 (1976).

14. Garner, 1 *International Law and the World War* 12 (1920).

15. FM 27-10, para. 1.

16. (1948), 8 *War Crimes Reports* 34; Green, *supra* note 3, at 308.

17. *Supra* note 11; Green, "Aftermath of Vietnam: War Law and the Soldier," in Falk, 4 *The Vietnam War and International Law* 147 (1976) [reproduced in Green, *Law and Society* 397, 424 (1975)].

> Usually, the soldier will report any known or suspected violations of the law of war through his chain of command. . . . Most commanders have established reporting procedures by local regulations and directives which require prompt, initial reports through the chain of command. Failure to comply with these regulations and directives may subject you to prosecution under the Uniform Code of Military Justice.
>
> While a soldier should normally report through his chain of command, you may hesitate to do so if someone in the chain above you was involved in the alleged crime, or if for some other reason you feel that such channels should not be effective. At such times, there are other officers to whom you can report or with whom you may properly discuss any possible violations of the laws of war . . . .
>
> . . . You may also discuss the problem with a Judge Advocate, a military lawyer who knows the law of war and how it applies. Many soldiers prefer to discuss problems with the Chaplain, and this is an accepted way to report violations of the law of war.

This directive deals with the dilemma of the soldier after receiving an order to commit an illegal act. While its purpose and aim may be highly laudable, it is submitted that its content is somewhat unrealistic. As it points out, it takes a great deal of courage to question and report a senior officer alleged to have given an illegal order. Further, it is highly questionable whether many of the members of the Judge Advocate's Department of any army are really acquainted with the rules of international law or are able to say whether a particular order is likely to result in a breach of the law of war. This is even more true of members of the chaplaincy. Finally, it is extremely doubtful whether such a legally qualified officer will be present in the field when the ordinary soldier receives an order which places him in such a dilemma. Moreover, the role of the Judge Advocate, at least in those forces organized in a fashion similar to those of the United Kingdom, tends to be somewhat restricted. His role is more related to the organisation and supervision of military discipline by way of courts martial, although he is also regarded as legal adviser to the forces and, at lower echelons, frequently serves the ordinary serviceman as would a solicitor in civil life. While it is true that some members of the Judge Advocate General's staff may have some knowledge of international law of war, it probably goes too far to describe Judge Advocates as such as "military lawyers who know the law of war and how it applies."

The Protocol has made the problem even more urgent than it ever was. The scope of legal regulation has been greatly widened, affecting both the law of The Hague and of Geneva. In so far as the former is concerned, a wealth of new regulations has been introduced concerning means and methods of warfare, declaring certain objects, which might in the past have been regarded as legitimate military objectives, as no longer within the realm of attack. At the same time, on the level of Hague humanitarian law, efforts have been made to clarify and extend the rights of medical personnel, and to define more precisely their units and transports which are now rendered immune from attack. Equally, special provision has been made with regard to chaplains and civil defence personnel. Again, vastly extending the scope of the Fourth Geneva Convention, the Protocol has enlarged the protection and respect to which civilians and civilian objects are now legally entitled. On all these issues, the commander in the field, as well as the commandant of a prisoner of war camp, will require to be far more acquainted with the rules of law than might have been considered necessary before 1977. Throughout the Protocol there is to be found a desire to increase the scope of humanitarian law in armed conflict. The draftsmen were, however, aware of the pressures and doubts of the military mind, and realised that it would always be necessary to seek to harmonise these humanitarian ideals with the realities of military necessity. The commander in the field is far too prone to be aware of the latter and may not necessarily agree that humanitarianism is something with which he need be too concerned. He might also feel that a critic's view of humanitarian law is somewhat partisan or subjective and the result of a lack of knowledge of military realities. The presence of a legal adviser, properly trained and knowledgeable, is likely to help to reduce the imbalance between humanitarian law and *raison de guerre*.

The decision to require legal advisers to be made available to advise military commanders on the application of the law of Geneva could in practice remove some of the difficulties that have been outlined above, while it is clear that their purpose would differ from that normally fulfilled by Judge Advocates at the present time. Moreover, it is hardly likely that the type of official envisaged in Article 82 would be able to fulfil the tasks outlined in the United States "Lesson Plan," nor perhaps should he.

Much could be made of the language in which Article 82 has been expressed, but it is not the purpose here to consider whether this is compulsive or hortatory. In accordance with the normal assumptions of treaty law, it is being presumed that the parties will act on the basis of good faith,[18] so that any State ratifying the Protocol will, in fact, proceed with the appointment of the adviser in question. Similarly, it is not considered necessary to enter into any discussion of problems which may be faced by those States in which there

18. *See, e.g.*, Cheng, *General Principles of Law* 105–60 (1953); Herczegh, *General Principles of International Law and the International Legal Order* 30, 34–39 (1969); Kelsen, *Principles of International Law* 447 (Tucker ed., 1966); Lauterpacht, "The Definition and Nature of International Law," 1 *Collected Papers* 5, 47 (1970); "Règles générales du droit de la paix," 62 *Hague Recueil* 99 (1937); Schwarzenberger, "The Fundamental Principles of International Law," 87 *Hague Recueil* 195, 290–326 (1955); Tunkin, *Theory of International Law* 86, 218–24 (1974).

is an armed forces ombudsman, or where some of the personnel may be organised in trade unions. Nor is it considered necessary, for the purposes of this paper, to examine the situation that exists when there is a recognised procedure for protest whereby the individual receiving an order which he deems to be illegal may seek some form of protection when the superior issuing the order persists in maintaining it despite the subordinate's protest.[19]

Before considering the practical implications of Article 82, it may be as well to point out that, while showing a sense of realism, the Article reflects the non-reciprocity which has almost become a feature of Protocol I.[20] The Protocol has redefined international armed conflict to include wars of national liberation.[21] However, since national liberation movements are not States, they cannot become High Contracting Parties, although by Article 96(3) they are able to make declaration whereby they assume the same rights and obligations as High Contracting Parties. Since this will only occur when they are recognised as national liberation movements engaged in an armed conflict seeking self-determination, it is only as a party to the conflict that they are required to appoint the requisite legal advisers. Nothing is said in the Protocol as to where these are to be found, how they are to be trained or what their status is to be. Is it to be assumed that lawyers—military lawyers trained in the international law of armed conflict—will always be found in the ranks of a national liberation movement? What if none is available? Is the military commander of a national liberation movement to be in a better position than that of a State force because he does not have available to him the legal advice which may temper his conduct and save him from breaches of the law?

Let it be assumed for the sake of argument that States have carried out their obligations under Article 82 and legal advisers have in fact been appointed. Does this necessarily mean that the number of breaches of the laws of war will decrease? In the first place, since the military officer considers that his first task is to overcome the enemy and achieve his immediate objective with minimum losses, there is little doubt that a determined military commander will almost invariably place the needs of his operation before all else, and it may well be that some commander will treat the views of his adviser in the same cavalier fashion as Keitel did those of Canaris relating to the ill-treatment of Soviet prisoners of war.[22] Canaris stated:

> The Geneva Convention for the treatment of prisoners of war [of 1929] is not binding in the relationship between Germany and the U.S.S.R.

19. *See, e.g., re* U.S.A. and Imperial Ethiopia, Green, *supra* note 3, at 253–54, 209.

20. *See* Green, "The New Law of Armed Conflict," 15 *Can. Y.B. Int'l L.* (1977).

21. Art. 1, *see* discussion *supra* note 20.

22. H.M.S.O., *Trial of German Major War Criminals* (1956), Part 22, Judgment, 452.

> Therefore only the principles of General International Law on the treatment of prisoners of war apply. Since the eighteenth century, these have gradually been established along the lines that war captivity is neither revenge nor punishment, but solely protective custody, the only purpose of which is to prevent the prisoners of war from further participation in the war. This principle was developed in accordance with the view held by all armies that it is contrary to military tradition to kill or injure helpless people .... The decrees for the treatment of Soviet prisoners of war enclosed are based on a fundamentally different viewpoint.

Although Keitel testified that he "really agreed" with Canaris,[23] he nevertheless made a note on the memorandum:

> The objections arise from the military concept of chivalrous warfare. This is the destruction of an ideology. Therefore I approve and back the measure.[24]

Clearly if, in future, a commander were so to disregard the advice given him by his legal adviser, advice which, in the words of the Nuremberg judgment, "correctly stated the legal position," it would merely mean that such a commander would have absolutely no basis on which to rest his defence when faced with a charge alleging war crimes or grave breaches of the Convention or Protocol. The legal adviser, on the other hand, would have recourse to any protest procedure that may be available.

Moreover, it has to be remembered that controversy rages as to the exact scope of the rules of war, particularly in so far as they have not been embodied in treaties but are claimed to be part of general or customary international law. This divergence is well illustrated by examination of the comments on superior orders to be found in the various editions of Oppenheim's *International Law* and in the British and American *Manuals* based thereon,[25] or in the comments on chemical weapons to be found in Hyde's *International Law chiefly as Interpreted and Applied by the United States*[26] as compared with the views of Major-General Cramer, United States Judge Advocate General in 1945,[27] and of the General Counsel of the Department of Defence during the 1971 hearings of the Senate Committee on Foreign Relations concerning ratification of the Geneva Protocol[28] and the subsequent statement issued concomitant with ratification.[29] What will be the position, therefore, if the legal adviser gives advice which is in accordance with his own country's views of the

23. *Ibid.*, 492.
24. *Ibid.*, 453.
25. *See* Green, *supra* note 3, at 265–75.
26. Vol. 3, 1818–22 (1947).
27. Reprinted in 10 *Int'l Legal Materials* 1304 (1971).
28. *Ibid.*, 1300.
29. 69 *Am. Int'l L.* 403–5 (1975); *U.S. Digest* 857–60 (1975).

customary law of war but does not coincide with the view of the enemy in whose hands the commander who has acted in accordance with that advice might find himself? Would the commander be able to plead that he has acted in accordance with that advice, honestly though mistakenly believing it to be correct? Would the legal adviser in question be liable to stand trial in accordance with the *ignorantia juris* maxim or the principle that he who holds himself out as an expert must show the expertise of an expert, bearing in mind that the legally qualified accused in *Sawada* [30] was more severely punished than his non-qualified co-accused?

Another problem that may arise relates to the hierarchic relationship as between the commander and his legal adviser. Difficulties may well be encountered when the latter is junior to the commander and seeks to advise him that the action which he proposes taking is contrary to the law and, if pursued, will render the commander liable to criminal charges which, if the action amounts to a grave breach, should be instituted by the legal adviser himself. Clearly, it will be necessary for the parties to the Protocol to instil into their armed forces an entirely new approach to the law. This, of course, is incumbent upon them anyway in accordance with Article 83 relating to dissemination:

> The High Contracting Parties undertake, in times of peace as in time of armed conflict, to disseminate the Conventions and this Protocol as widely as possible . . . ,, and to include the study thereof in their programmes of military instruction . . . , so that these instruments may become known to the armed forces . . . .

In fact, Article 82 must remain a somewhat empty obligation if Article 83 is not obeyed. It might even be possible to argue that the responsibility for supervising the study of the Conventions and Protocol should rest upon the legal adviser. This, of course, will depend on the structure of particular armies and is probably only feasible in time of peace, for in time of war any legal adviser attached to a serving unit would probably be fully employed in watching the acts of the commanding officer on a day-to-day basis—that is to say, if such advisers were actually deployed in the field. It would be necessary not only to instil into the forces a new respect for the law, but also to emphasise to commanders that their legal advisers have a special role to play and that their advice must be heeded, regardless of rank. To ignore such advice will entail criminal liability, and the legal adviser must be protected from any possible victimisation or disciplinary or other proceedings arising from the unpopular nature of his advice or the determination with which he seeks to press it.

30. *See* note 5 *supra*.

Article 82 merely requires legal advisers to be made available to military commanders "at the appropriate level." It is apparently open to each party to the Protocol to decide for itself at what level they shall be made available. This is particularly so in view of the fact that the Protocol makes no attempt to define commander and in accordance with military hierarchy it may be contended that even the lowest non-commissioned officer is a commander *vis-à-vis* the men below him. There can be no doubt, of course, that, for the purpose of Article 82, a commander is, normally at least, an officer in the field or one capable of giving orders which lead to military operations. This means that at some stage or other determination must be made of the level of the command at which it becomes necessary to accredit legal advisers. To leave this to individual States is likely to result in great confusion, and in the possibility that when and if trials take place the accused commander will be provided with a legitimate defence on the basis that the illegality of the act in question was by no means clear; that he honestly thought that it was legal, and his high command did not consider it necessary for a legal adviser to be allocated to him. To prevent this possibility, consideration will have to be given to some further international agreement laying down the level of command at which the appointment of advisers is necessary. In so far as an alliance like NATO is concerned, this may be relatively simple. If, however, hostilities involving rival ideologies and interpretations of the law were to take place, the matter could become serious.

Some countries, the Federal German Republic, for example, have had legal advisers of the kind envisaged here for some time. In West Germany they are specially selected and trained lawyers who retain their civilian status and are attached to military commands in peace-time and accompany the commander to whom they are attached on field exercises. In this way hierarchic difficulties are avoided, and it is hoped that a special relationship of trust is created between the commander and his adviser, with the latter regarded by his commander as an administrative specialist to whom he must pay proper attention, while remaining personally responsible for all military decisions which may be made. In the event of hostilities, the status of the adviser changes. He will then be put into uniform and given a rank so that he receives combatant and, if necessary, prisoner of war status. While problems of rank may inevitably arise, it is hoped that prior training and the relationship already created will mitigate any difficulties and prevent the commander looking upon his adviser as an interloping civilian in uniform. In The Netherlands, on the other hand, the practice is to take serving field officers of at least ten years standing and send them to the university to pursue courses in war law, after which they are posted to commands as military legal advisers.

In contrast to this, in armed forces which would be instituting a relatively new concept and in which, traditionally, the legal officer is a member of the armed forces, it might suffice, in view of the different and specialist type of work involved, to create a new division in the Judge Advocate's Department where military lawyers, either those already serving or specially recruited, could be trained in the law of war, bearing in mind in their training, also, that they require, if their advice is to receive due attention in operations, more than basic military training. These officers could then be posted to fulfil the tasks of legal advisers as provided for in Article 82. If properly trained, and if separated from their colleagues in the Judge Advocate's Department, they should also be able to satisfy the teaching demands of Article 83, especially as they are not likely, in peace-time, to be fully employed in their advisory work. In so far as their training is concerned, some of the courses organised at present for this purpose by the International Institute of Humanitarian Law might well be useful.[31]

Not only is the Protocol silent as to the level of command involved, but there is no indication of the type of training that the legal advisers should be given or the type of person who should be selected.

While it may be relatively easy for United Nations forces or those of allied nations, particularly, perhaps, those belonging to regional organisations, to coordinate on this matter, the problem is more complex when there is no common training or service as between the armed forces of various nations. This may be met, in the case of NATO, the United Nations or regional alliances by instituting common programmes. However, it must not be ignored that States are jealous of their sovereignty and regard the training of their armed forces as a matter of domestic jurisdiction, concerning which they are not likely to be open to interference. Once again, therefore, confusion is likely to ensue owing to varying conceptions of what the law is, different interpretations of what the recognised law means, dissimilar methods of training and unequal levels of education. Clearly, the most useful solution to these problems would be the adoption of an international agreement laying down standards of training and perhaps involving the drafting of an acceptable manual. This, however, is probably an idealistic solution unlikely of achievement at the present time. Failing this, it might be helpful if, for example, the International Committee of the Red Cross or the San Remo International Institute of Humanitarian Law were to issue such training manuals in the hope that they might be acceptable by the parties to the Protocol, at least as guides to help in preparing their own courses. Even more useful would be the organization of training courses by either of these bodies open to members of the legal branches of the armed forces of parties to the Protocol,

31. *See* "1er Cours International sur le Droit de la Guerre pour Officiers, Sanremo (16–23 Juin 1976)," 16 *Revue de Droit Pénal Militaire et de Droit de la Guerre* (special issue, 1977).

enrolment being limited on the basis of minimal qualification and perhaps minimum rank. This, however, would mean that the instructors would have to be chosen with extreme care, perhaps solely from neutral countries, while the programmes that they use and the commentaries on which they base themselves might have to be approved by the authorities of the services from which the students are enrolled.

Perhaps more practical at the present moment, and recognising the prejudices and reservations of States, is to express the hope that the parties to the Protocol will themselves institute proper training programmes making full use of the resources at their disposal. This means that they should be prepared to support the introduction of courses in war law at universities and law schools, and the authorities running such institutions should not be averse to accepting advice and assistance from such sources without putting forward specious arguments relating to academic independence. The authorities must also be prepared to resist the complaints that will inevitably be made by idealistic pacifists and their bemused followers of every age-group. On the other hand, it cannot be regarded as sufficient basis for helping in the running of such courses that a person is a member of a national Red Cross society who may have read the Conventions and the Protocol.

War law is a highly technical subject, whether in its offensive or its humanitarian aspect. Those who support to deal with it must themselves be specialists in the field. The courses that they teach must be carefully prepared. After all, the legal advisers who are the products of their training will be responsible for ensuring that the commanders to whom they are attached observe the provisions of the Conventions and the Protocol. While they may not be able to prevent wars, they are required to seek maintenance of the rule of law when war takes place. On their advice depend the prestige and honour of their country together, often, with the freedom and very life of the commanders whom they have been posted to advise.

[5]

The Man in the Field and the Maxim Ignorantia Juris non excusat

L. C. GREEN
LLB., LLD., F.R.S.C.
Professor of International Law
University of Alberta, Edmonton/Canada

War crimes trials, whether conducted by tribunals established under international agreement, like that at Nuremberg[1], or under municipal law, like that which rendered the decision regarding the Llandovery Castle[2], as well as trials under national military law, like that of Lieutenant Calley[3] inevitably raise a multitude of legal problems. Among the most important of these is the knowledge of the accused. Too often, insufficient attention is paid to this, even though the inevitable defence of superior orders and the reaction to it of the tribunal concerned[4] to a very extent are based on this factor, since success or otherwise of the plea depends on whether or not the act ordered was palpably or manifestly illegal, which obviously depends on the accused's knowledge of what is in fact lawful. If the writer's experience on joining the British Army during the Second World War is anything to go by, the extent of the knowledge of the law of the ordinary soldier stems rather from his own resources thant those of the military establishment. While he was told that, as a prisoner of war, the Geneva Convention of 1929[5] merely required him to give his name, number and rank, he was never given any instruction as to the rights of enemy person-

---

1 The London Charter, 8. Aug. 1945, 82 UNTS 280 (*Schindler & Toman*, The Laws of Armed Conflicts, 1973, 689).

2 (1921) HMSO Cmd. 450 (Cameron, The Peleus Trial, 1948, App. IX).

3 U.S. v. Calley (1973) 46 C.M.R. 1131, 48 C.M.R. 19; Calley v. Callaway 1974 382 F Supp 650, (1975) 519 Fed. Rep. (2 d) 184 (*Goldstein* and others, The My Lai Massacre and its Cover-Up; Beyond the Reach of Law? (1976), 475—573).

4 See, e. g., *Dinstein,* The Defence of 'Obedience to Superior Orders' in International Law (1965); *Green,* Superior Orders in National and International Law (1976); *Keijzer,* Military Obedience (1978).

5 Art. 5, 118 LNTS 343 (*Schindler/Toman*, 261).

nel, his duties towards them or the nature of illegal weapons or acts of war. Moreover, it would appear that in some armies the situation has probably not changed too radically. Thus, in one of the courts martial arising out of the operations of United States personnel during the Vietnam War it was held that even though the acts perpetrated by the accused were in keeping with the training received during basic training, this would not provide a defence if the order concerned was palpably illegal on its face[6].

It is difficult to expect the ordinary soldier to know what orders he is permitted and required to obey, or the officer what orders he is allowed to give, without in either case running the risk of trial for breach of the law of war, if he does not know what that law is. While it may be true that most systems of criminal law postulate the maxim ignorantia juris quod quisque tenetur scire, neminem excusat[7], it must not be forgotten that those who live within a national system of law may be presumed to accept the national ethic and to be aware of the nature and basic principles of their country's criminal code, or at least know where to find them. This is hardly the case in so far as international law is concerned. This is a hirgly sophisticated system parts of which are controversial, and this is particularly true of that part of it which relates to the law of war. After all, the soldier nderstands that his task is to kill his enemy, that the aim of his country is to subdue that enemy, and it may seem somewhat strange to him that while his act and the purpose for which it is done are both lawful, nevertheless he is only allowed to carry out this act in a particular way and in accordance with certain rules, which rules are often abstruse, complex in form and certainly difficult to find. However, if Protocol I Additional to the Geneva Conventions of 12 August 1949, and relating to the Protection of Victims of International Armed Conflicts, 1977[8], receives general acceptance both the man and the officer may be a little better off from this point of view in any future war. By Article 82 legal advisers are supposed to be attached to service units[9], while Article 83 imposes duties of teaching and dissemination upon the Contracting Parties, and this service is supposed to extend to the civilian population as well as the armed forces.

In the meantime, it is important to examine the extent to which states are already obliged to inform their armed forces of the law of war and to refer, if possible, to the steps and methods which have been or ought to be taken to this end.

---

[6] U.S. v. Keenan (1969) 39 C.M.R. 108.

[7] „Ignorance of the law, which every man is bound to know, excuses no man" (see *Selden,* Table Talk (1689), „Law", 4 *Blackstone,* Commentaries on the Laws of England, ch. 2, s. V (10th ed., 1787, 27).

[8] 16 Int Legal Materials (1977), 1391.

[9] See *Green,* The Role of Legal Advisers in the Armed Forces, 7 Israel Yearbook on Human Rights 1977, 154.

In looking at this problem it must be borne in mind that international law is made up of treaties, customary law and, nowadays to an increasing extent, judicial decisions. Also, unlike municipal law, international law is, in theory at least, universally applicable and the law of one country's courts in this field has as much validity as that of any other country. As it was so aptly put by *Vattel*[10]: „Since men are by nature equal, and their individual rights and obligations the same, as coming equally from nature, Nations, which are composed of men and may be regarded as so many free persons living together in a state of nature, are by nature equal and hold from nature the same obligations and the same rights. Strength or weakness, in this case, counts for nothing. A dwarf is as much a man as a giant is; a small Republic is no less a sovereign State than the most powerful Kingdom."

It becomes necessary, therefore, to examine where this equally applicable law is to be found and the extent to which it imposes an obligation upon its subjects to ensure that it is made known to their nationals. With treaties the situation is relatively straightforward. All that is required is to determine which are the relevant documents and then to examine the terms of those treaties. Frequently, to a very great extent these treaties are simply codifications of customary law and, in so far as they are not themselves law-creative, the only obligation that rests upon non-parties ist to be derived from that customary law. To the extent that this is so it may be argued that even states which are not parties to any particular treaty will, nevertheless, be bound perhaps even by its very terminology in so far as that treaty is merely a codification of customary law. The members of a non-party's armed forces would be bound by this customary law[11], and it is in their interest that they be informed as to its content.

For the most part, it has been generally said that the law of war is to be found in the Hague Conventions of 1907 as amended by the various Red Cross Geneva Conventions of 1929 and 1949[12]. However, even the Hague Conventions themselves refer to 'the laws and customs of war' and at times do not spell out in excessive detail what even the treaty law entails. Thus, all that Hague Convention IV[13] with respect to the laws and customs of war on land says about penalties for violations of the Regulations attached thereto is to be found in Article 3: „A belligerent party which violates the provisions of the said Regulations shall, if the case demands, be liable to

---

10 Le Droit des Gens ou Principes de la Loi Naturelle (1758), Bk. I, Intro., s. 18 (Carnegie tr., 1916, vol. 3, p. 7.

11 See, e. g., in relation to the law of maritime warfare comments by Sir Samuel Evans in The Möwe [1915] P. 1, 12; see, also, The Blonde [1922] 1 A. C. 313; and more generally, the Nuremberg Judgment (1946) Cmd. 6964, p. 65 (41 Am. J. Int'l Law (1947), 172, 246—9).

12 See *Schindler/Toman*, op. cit.

13 Ibid., 57.

pay compensation. It shall be responsible for all acts committed by persons forming part of its armed forces." There is no provision for personal liability or for punshment of the soldier who actually commits the violation. The only basis on which such individuals can therefore be tried is either their own municipal law which would not, of course, extend to any enemy, or customary international law, just as nonmilitary personnel who indulge in warlike acts are similarly liable as war criminals under the same customary law. In the first edition of his International Law[14] *Oppenheim* says „according to a generally recognised customary rule of International Law hostile acts on the part of private individuals are not acts of legitimate warfare, and the offenders can be treated and punished as war criminals. Even those writers who object to the term „criminals" do not deny that such hostile acts by private individuals, in contradistinction to hostile acts by members of the armed forces, may be severely punished. The controversy whether or not such acts may be styled „crimes" is again only one of terminology; materially the rule is not at all controverted". Although, in this passage *Oppenheim* apparently excludes from his concept of war crimes „hostile acts by members of the armed forces", he points out that „belligerents have not an unlimited right as to the means they adopt for injuring the enemy"[15], and comments[16] that „the roots of the present Laws of War are to be traced back to practices of belligerents which arose and grew gradually during the latter part of the Middle Ages. The unsparing cruelty of the war practices during the greater part of the Middle Ages began gradually to be modified through the influence of Christianity and chivalry".

At this juncture it might be useful to draw attention to the 1474 trial of Peter Hagenbach at Breisach[17]. As Governor for the Duke of Burgundy Hagenbach established a „regime of arbitrariness and terror [which] extended to murder, rape, illegal taxation and wanton confiscation of private property, and the victims of his depradations included inhabitants of neighbouring territories as well as Swiss merchants on their way to and from the Frankfurt fair". After Hagenbach's capture, the Archduke of Austria, as sovereign of Breisach, set up a tribunal of 28 judges from the Allied towns, and at his trial the accused pleaded that everything that he had done had been on the orders of his master, but the prosecution alleged that he had „trampled under foot the laws of God and man". The tribunal was of opinion that to accept such a defence would be contrary to the laws of God and, since the crimes were established beyond doubt, sentenced Hagenbach

14 Vol. 2 (1906), 63.

15 Ibid., 114 (citing Art. 22 of Hague Regulations of 1899, *Schindler/Toman*, 76).

16 Ibid., 74.

17 *Schwarzenberger*, International Law, vol. 2, The Law of Armed Conflict (1968) ch. 39.

to death. In many ways the charge with its reference to the laws of God and of man seems like a predecessor of the provision of the Treaty of Versailles aimed at bringing the Kaiser to trial[18]: „The Allied and Associated Powers publicly arraign William II of Hohenzollern, formerly German Emperor, for a supreme offence against international morality and the sanctity of treaties . . . In its decision the tribunal will be guided by the highest motives of international policy, with a view to vindicating the solemn obligations of international undertakings and the validity of international morality".

When the Treaty called for the establishment of a specially established international tribunal, it did not specify the law which this tribunal would apply and by which the offences were to be judged. A somewhat similar hiatus is apparent in the Treaty provision[19] concerning the trial by military tribunals of „persons accused of having committed acts in violation of the laws and customs of war", who if found guilty are to „be sentenced to punishments laid down by law". While the Treaty does not indicate what law it has in mind, the Reichsgericht which delivered the Llandovery Castle judgment[20] was clearly aware that it was operating in accordance with international law: „The firing on the boats was an offence against the law of nations. . . . Any violation of the law of nations in warfare is . . . a punishable offence, so far as, in general, a penalty is attached to the deed. The killing of enemies in war is in accordance with the law of the State that makes war . . ., only in so far as such killing is in accordance with the conditions and limitations imposed by the Law of Nations. The fact that his deed is a violation of International Law must be well known to the doer, apart from acts of carelessness, in which careless ignorance is a sufficient excuse. In examining the existence of this knowledge, the ambiguity of many of the rules of International Law, as well as the actual circumstances of the case, must be borne in mind, because in wartime decisions of great importance have frequently to be made on very insufficient material. This consideration, however, cannot be applied to the case at present before the Court. The rule of International Law, which is here involved [regarding the sinking of the hospital ship and the firing on the boats of the survivors], is simple and universally known. No possible doubt can exist with regard to the question of its applicability. The Court must in this instance affirm [the commander's] guilt of killing contrary to International Law . . .".

Perhaps the earliest codification of the law of war was that prepared by Professor *Lieber* of Columbia University, during the American Civil War

---

18 (1919) Art. 227 (112 B.F.S.P. 1; 13 Am. J. Int. Law (1919), Supp.).

19 Art. 228.

20 Loc. cit., n. 2 above.

and promulgated by President Lincoln in 1863[21]. This reflects what was generally understood by the European states as constituting the law at the time and clearly provides for the trial and punishment of a variety of specified offences committed by troops against the inhabitants of invaded territory, but it makes no reference to the need to ensure that members of the United States armed forces are made aware of what they may and what they may not do, although by and large the offences listed are those which would be found in any national penal code. The first call for recognition of the need to inform the armed forces of the rules of war is to be found in the Oxford Manual prepared by the Institute of International Law at its Oxford meeting in 1880[22]. In the Preface the Institute states why it has drawn up its statement of the laws of war on land: „By so doing, it believes it is rendering a service to military men themselves. In fact so long as the demands of opinion remain indeterminate, belligerents are exposed to painful uncertainty and endless accusations. A positive set of rules, on the contrary, if they are judicious, serves the interests of belligerents and is far from hindering them, since by preventing the unchaining of passion and savage instincts — which battle always awakens, as much as it awakens courage and manly virtues — it strengthens the discipline which is the strength of armies; it also ennobles their patriotic mission in the eyes of the soldiers by keeping them within the limits of respect due to the rights of humanity. But in order to attain this end it is not sufficient for sovereigns to promulgate new laws. It is essential, too, that they make these laws known among all people, so that when a war is declared, the men called upon to take up arms to defend the causes of the belligerent States, may be thoroughly impregnated with the special rights and duties attached to the execution of such a command. The Institute, with a view to assisting the authorities in accomplishing this part of their task, has given its work a popular form, attaching thereto statements of the reasons therefor, from which the text of a law may be easily secured when desired".

While the text of the Oxford Manual seems to satisfy the expressed desire of achieving a 'popular form', it must not be overlooked that the ordinary person, civilian or military, was unlikely to seek this document out. Furthermore, while the Institute might have been composed of the most eminent international lawyers of the day, it must be borne in mind that it was, as it is now, an unofficial learned society whose proposals possessed no binding force and could only aim at providing suggestions which, if

---

[21] U. S. Adjutant General's Office, General Orders No. 100 (*Schindler/Toman*, 3).

[22] Institut de Droit International, Tableau général des résolutions, 1873—1956, (1957), 180; *Scott*, Resolutions of the Institute of International Law (1916) 26; *Schindler/Toman*, 35.

acceptable to governments, would be enacted into law, either by way of statute or by treaty. It would appear that, despite the expressed desire of the Institute, little was done to make the contents of the Manual known to the members of the armed forces. Even when countries started issuing Manuals of Military Law with sections devoted to the law of war, these manuals were not issued to the troops or even all officers, and in many cases non-officers were actively discouraged from seeking access to them.

To some extent the voeu of the Institute did have an effect. In Hague Convention II of 1899[23] it was clearly provided in Article 1 that „The High Contracting Parties shall issue instructions to their armed land forces which shall be in conformity with the 'Regulations respecting the laws and customs of war on land' annexed to the present Convention" and the same provision was repeated in the IVth Convention of 1907[24], respecting the law of warfare on land.

The only other Hague Convention to deal with dissemination is No. X of 1907[25] for the Adaptation to Maritime Warfare of the Principles of the Geneva Convention of 1864[26] which related to the amelioration of conditions of the wounded and sick of armies in the field. In its form, however, it differed from the wording in Convention IV and appeared to lay more emphasis on the knowledge of those who were to be protected than of those whose conduct was restricted: „The Signatory Powers shall take the necessary measures for bringing the provisions of the present Convention to the knowledge of their naval forces, and especially of the members entitled thereunder to immunity, and for making them known to the public".
Although other Conventions agreed at the Hague dealt with such issues as the rights of neutrals and naval bombardment, the signatories apparently did not consider it necessary to include a provision seeking to ensure that the rules and prohibitions were made known to the personnel who were most directly affected and upon whose conduct it was necessary to rely to ensure compliance.

Perhaps even more surprising is the silence in this matter of the Rules regarding Air Warfare[27] drafted by the Commission of Jurists called for by the 1922 Conference of Washington. While it is true that these Rules were never adopted and so have no legal significance as such, they cannot be cavalierly ignored, for, „to a great extent, they correspond to the customary rules and general principles underlying the conventions on the law of war

---

[23] *Scott*, The Hague Conventions and Declarations of 1899 and 1907 (1918), 100 (Schindler/Toman, 57).

[24] Ibid.

[25] Art. 20, *Scott*, op. cit., 163 (*Schindler/Toman*, 235).

[26] 1 Am. J. Int Law (1907), Supp. 90 (*Schindler/Toman*, 203).

[27] 1923, 17 Am. J. Int'l Law (1923), Supp. 245 (*Schindler/Toman*, 139).

on land and at sea"[28]. While the Rules go into great detail as to what may not be done in aerial warfare, the members of the Commission apparently did not consider it necessary for the states which might adopt these Rules to undertake any commitment to make them known to their respective air forces. Equally strange is the silence of the Draft Convention for the Protection of Civilians against New Engines of War drawn up by the International Law Association at Amsterdam in 1938[29].

In what has now come to be described as humanitarian law in armed conflict, the International Committee of the Red Cross has consistently endeavoured to ensure that treaties relating to the wounded and sick or prisoners of war contain provisions obligating the parties to inform their personnel of the commitments involved. Article 27 of the 1929 Convention on the Amelioration of the Condition of the Wounded and Sick in Armies in the Field[30] is reminiscent of Hague Convention X. This reads „The High Contracting Parties shall take the necessary steps to instruct their troops, and in particular the personnel protected, in the provisions of the present Convention, and to bring them to the notice of the civil population". A somewhat similar concern with the interest of those protected is to be found in the 1929 Prisoners of War Convention[31], for by Article 84 the text of this Convention is to be posted, „whenever possible, in the native language of the prisoners of war, in places where it may be consulted by all the prisoners". It even has to be communicated, when so requested, to prisoners „who are unable to inform themselves of the text posted". Presumably, it is anticipated that those responsible for the prisoners of war will be sufficiently acquainted with the terms of the Convention by such posting — that is, if they can read the language of the prisoners — for there is no obligation on the parties to make the terms known to their own personnel.

A somewhat new departure is to be found in the revised texts of the Geneva Conventions of 1949 which resulted from the desire of the International Committee of the Red Cross to bring the 1929 texts up to date, taking into consideration the experiences learned during the Second World War. Article 47 of the Convention on Wounded and Sick in the Field[32], and Article 48 of that on Wounded, Sick and Shipwrecked Members of Armed Forces at Sea[33] are much wider than their precursors, reflecting recognition of the fact that modern armies are frequently conscript in character and their personnel should, to the extent that is possible, be aware of their obli-

[28] Ibid., 139; see, also, 2 *Oppenheim*, International Law (7th ed., 1952), 519, *Spaight*, Air Power and War Rights (1947) 42—3.

[29] I.L.A., Report of 40th Conference, 40 (*Schindler/Toman*, 155).

[30] 5 *Hudson*, International Legislation (1936), 1 (*Schindler/Toman*, 247).

[31] 5 ibid., 20 (*Schindler/Toman*, 261).

[32] 75 UNTS 31 (*Schindler/Toman*, 295).

[33] Ibid., 85 (323).

gations before enlistment, and certainly before the outbreak of hostilities: „The High Contracting Parties undertake, in time of peace as in time of war, to disseminate the text of the present Convention as widely as possible in their respective countries, and, in particular, to include the study thereof in their programmes of military and, if possible, civil instruction, so that the principles thereof may become known to the entire population, in particular to the armed fighting forces, the medical personnel and the chaplains."

The 1949 Conventions on Prisoners of War[34] and the Treatment of Civilian Persons in Time of War[35] take due account of their specialist character: Art. 127, Prisoners of War Convention „The High Contracting Parties undertake, in time of peace as in time of war, to disseminate the text of the present Convention as widely as possible in their respective countries, and, in particular, to include the study thereof in their programmes of military and, is possible, civil instruction, so that the principles thereof may become known to all their armed forces and to the entire population. Any military or other authorities, who in time of war assume responsibilities in respect of prisoners of war, must possess the text of the Convention and be specially instructed as to its provisions."

The High Contracting Parties are bound to enact any legislation necessary to give penal effect to the Convention and, by Article 128, „shall communicate to one another through the Swiss Federal Council and, during hostilities, through the Protecting Powers, the official translations of the present Convention, as well as the laws and regulations which they may adopt to ensure the application thereof." The 1929 provision with regard to the posting of the Convention has been extended so that all regulations and orders must be in a language that the prisoners can understand.

The first paragraph of Article 144 of the Civilians Convention is in the same terms as Article 127 of the Prisoners of War Convention, but it proceeds „Any civilian, military, police or other authorities, who in time of war assume responsibilities in respect of protected persons, must posses the text of the Convention and be specially instructed as to its provisions", and the same requirement respecting intercommunication of legislation appears in Article 145.

At the present time there has been some widening of the concept of non-military objectives and a treaty now exists for the Protection of Cultural Property in the Event of Armed Conflict[36]. It cannot be denied that in the past the military have not been over-scrupulous in respecting cultural property and at times occupying forces have not hesitated to destroy

---

[34] Ibid., 135 (345).

[35] Ibid., 287 (417).

[36] 1954, 249 UNTS 240 (*Schindler/Toman*, 525); see, also, *Williams*, The International and National Protection of Movable Cultural Property (1978), 15—51; and Protocol I, Art. 53.

monuments in the territory of their enemy. Moreover, even in peacetime states have on occasion considered that modernisation is perhaps more important than the preservation of those national cultural monuments which might constitute part of „the cultural heritage of every people". Cultural property is defined as „a) movable or immovable property of great importance to the cultural heritage of every people, such as monuments of architecture, art or history, whether religious or secular; archeological sites; groups of buildings which, as a whole, are of historical or artistic interest; works of art; manuscripts; books and other objects of artistic, historical or archeological interest; as well as scientific collections and important collections of books or archives or of reproductions of the property defined above; b) buildings whose main and effective purpose is to preserve or exhibit the movable cultural property defined in sub-paragraph (a) such as museums, large libraries and depositaries of archives, and refuges intended to shelter, in the event of armed conflict, the movable cultural property defined in sub-paragraph (a); c) centres containing a large amount of cultural property as defined in sub-paragraphs (a) and (b) to be known as 'centres containing monuments'."

This definition is so comprehensive and yet so vague that it is clear some measures of dissemination to inform the military and others concerned will be absolutely vital if the Convention is to have any meaning, especially as troops engaged in actual operations are unlikly to view as protected an article regarded by the enemy or a neutral as having significant cultural significance and enjoying immunity, if respect for such an object or group of them might interfere with the success of the operation or involve its cancellation. The draftsmen seem to have been aware of this danger and of the need to inform troops of their obligations. There are two provisions relating to the dissemination which to some extent are repetitive: Art. 7 — „The High Contracting Parties undertake to introduce in time of peace into their military regulations or instructions such provisions as may ensure observance of the present Convention, and to foster in the members of their armed forces a spirit for the culture and cultural property of all peoples. The High Contracting Parties undertake to plan or establish in peacetime, within their armed forces, services or specialist personnel whose purpose will be to secure respect for cultural property and to cooperate with civilian authorities responsible for safeguarding it." Art. 25 — „The High Contacting Parties undertake, in time of peace as in time of armed conflict, to disseminate the text of the present Convention and the Regulations for its execution as widely as possible in their respective countries. They undertake, in particular, to include the study thereof in their programmes of military and, if possible, civilian training, so that its principles are made known to the whole population, especially the armed forces and personnel engaged in the protection of cultural property."

It is obvious that the only way such 'property of great importance to the cultural heritage of every people' can be protected without the items becoming so numerous and trivial as to be ridiculous — for every person's idea of what constitutes such property from the point of view of, for example, art is likely to be higly subjective — will be by the compilation of agreed lists that will be available to the armies in the field. Such lists are envisaged, but later experience suggests that these may perhaps not be available by the time armed conflict begins and, as became clear during debate at the 1976 session of the Diplomatic Conference on Humanitarian Law in Armed Conflict, it can easily happen that one belligerent is so determined not to recognise its adversary, that it will not even agree to the compilation of such lists if it means that co-operation is in any way necessary with what is now known as the 'adverse party' rather than the 'enemy'. Nevertheless, Article 53 of Protocol I prohibits the commission of „any acts of hostility directed against the historic monuments, works of art or places of worship which constitute the cultural or spiritual heritage of peoples," but it gives no hint as to how the man in the field is to be informed of their identity. Since the Article is prefaced by the statement that it is adopted „without prejudice to the provisions of the [1954] Hague Convention for the Protection of Cultural Property in the Event of Armed Conflict", it must be presumed that the draftsmen of the Protocol were satisfied with the identification process embodied in that Convention. Article 6 of the Convention requires cultural property to „bear a distinctive emblem so as to facilitate its recognition", and by Article 16 „the distinctive emblem ... shall take the form of a shield, pointed below, per saltire blue and white (a shield consisting of a royal-blue square, one of the angles of which forms the point of the shield, and of a royal-blue triangle above the square, the space on either side being taken up by a white triangle). The emblem shall be used alone, or repeated three times in a triangular formation (one shield below) ..."

Clearly, military personnel will have to receive instruction as to the nature of this emblem, as well as all other emblems now recognised as conferring protection, but neither the Convention nor the Protocol indicates how they are to be made aware of these emblems. Presumably, the general provision for dissemination embodied in the Protocol is regarded as sufficient. Cynics might be excused if they regard such provisions as somewhat idealist and completely out of tune with the realities of active warfare. Their cynicism will not be reduced by the further provision in Article 17 of the Convention that „the distinctive emblem may not be placed on any immovable cultural property unless at the same time there is displayed an authorization duly dated and signed by the competent authority of the High Contracting Party." This will necessitate further instruction to the man in the field as to who the 'competent authority' of the enemy for this purpose is — and is it to be expected that operations are to cease while some member of an attacking force excamines the immovable cultural object to ascertain whether it has the correct certificate affixed?

In the years since the Second World War most of the armed conflicts which have occurred have been non-international, so that generally speaking there have been no rules of international law, with the possible exception of the minimal rules of humanity as outlined in common Article 3 of the 1949 Geneva Conventions, applicable, for states have traditionally relied upon the argument that civil wars and the like are matters of domestic jurisdiction with which the rest of the world has no concern. And this principle is confirmed by Article 2(7) of the Charter of the United Nations unless there is a threat to international peace[37]. However, an early effort at bringing civil war situations within the purview of international law is to be found in the Nyon Agreement of 1937[38] aimed at suppressing unlawful submarine attacks upon merchant ships trading with ports under the control of, primarily, the Spanish Government. By Article 1 „The participating Powers will instruct their naval forces to take the action indicated in paragraphs II and III below with a view to the protection of all merchant ships not belonging to either of the conflicting Spanish parties." While it may be argued by the purist that this is not really directed at imparting rules of humanitarian behaviour to the citizens or military personnel of any contracting party, in the sense that they may need to know the law in order to defend themselves, it is nevertheless an instance of an international obligation that requires states parties to the agreement to inform their personnel of the new law that has been created and which they would be required to observe and carry through".

It became clear during the operations in Korea and Vietnam that the law of war as it had been drawn up at the Hague and Geneva was now, to some extent at least, out of date. For one thing, there was no provision with regard, for example to the rights, if any, of combatants who did not identify themselves in accordance with the rules in Hague Convention IV, with the result that when the International Committee of the Red Cross drew up its draft proposals for amendments to the 1949 law to be presented to a diplomatic conference on humanitarian law in armed conflict, it decided to take the opportunity, in so far as it could, to bring the traditional law up to date, as well as to attempt to extend at least the basic prin-

---

[37] „Nothing contained in the present Charter shall authorize the United Nations to intervene in matters which are essentially within the domestic jurisdiction of any state or shall require the Members to submit such matters to settlement under the present Charter, but this provision shall not prejudice the application of enforcement measures under Chapter VII [with respect to threats to the peace, breaches of the peace and acts of aggression]".

[38] 181 LNTS 137 (*Schindler/Toman*, 667).

ciples of humanitarian law to non-international conflicts too. This is not the place to discuss the proposals embodied in the two Protocols intended to be additions to the Geneva Conventions and aimed at achieving this end[39]. We are concerned solely with the problem of dissemination and enlightenment of those likely to be called upon to give effect to the new rules, whether they be described as part of the law of war or as rules of humanitarian law. Before looking at the provisions of the Protocols it should be pointed out that it matters little what conventions say or require, if the states which are parties to them do not ensure that their military personnel are in fact sufficiently aware of their provisions and understand what is required of them as not to be likely to breach their provisions.

The operations in Korea and Vietnam and the United States courts martial arising therefrom[40] demonstrate that there was something gravely lacking in the education being given to United States armed forces, and perhaps indicate that not enough emphasis was being imparted to officers to show that the United States accepted the view expressed in Article 22 of the Hague Regulations that „the right of belligerents to adopt means of injuring the enemy is not unlimited", even though this article is reprinted in the United States Department of the Army Field Manual on the Law of Land Warfare[41], accompanied by the comment „The means employed [in injuring the enemy] are definitely restricted by international declarations and conventions and by the laws and usages of war." It is perhaps because of what happened in these two theatres that the United States military authorities thereafter issued a variety of pamphlets on the teaching of the law of war to the armed forces[42]. However inadequate these might be[43], they show a determination to make some effort to ensure that American troops have at least some knowledge of what they may and may not do during armed conflict. As a result, where they are concerned there may now be some validity in upholding the validity of the ignorantia juris maxim.

---

39 See, e. g., *Green,* The New Law of Armed Conflict, 15 Canadian Y.B. of Int'l Law (1977), 3.

40 See, e. g., *Green,* Superior Orders and the Reasonable Man, 8 Can. Y.B. Int'l Law (1970), 61, 96 et seqq.; Superior Orders in National and International Law (1976), 126 et seqq.; 'Aftermath of Vietnam: War Law and the Soldier', in 4 *Falk,* The Vietnam War and International Law (1976), 147 et seqq.

41 Dept. of the Army, FM 27—10 (1956), para. 33.

42 Dept. of the Army, 27—200, 'The Law of Land Warfare — A Self-Instructional Text' (1972), ASubjScd 27—1 (1970), 'The Geneva Conventions of 1949 and Hague Convention No. IV of 1907' (2-hour lecture course).

43 For criticisms see *Green,* Aftermath of Vietnam: War Law and the Soldier, 4 *Falk,* The Vietnam War and International Law — The Concluding Phase (1976), 147, 168 et seqq.)

44. Art. 79.

Among the new departures in Protocol I is a provision concerning the protection of journalists[44]. This aims at giving journalists who are not accredited war correspondents some protection by means of an identity card to ensure that when captured they are treated as civilians. Obviously, members of the armed forces will have to be aware of the nature of this card and know that any attempt by them to use such an identity certificate would amount to a breach of the law of war. In fact the British Government has now ceased the practice in Northern Ireland of having soldiers in civilian clothing passing themselves off as regular journalists, thus indulging in a form of 'perfidy', while at the same time endangering true journalists entitled to such cards and the civilian status concomitant therewith[45].

Similar measures of instruction will be necessary in view of the new provisions concerning the protection of civil defence personnel[46], who are now protected by a distinctive emblem comprising a blue equilateral triangle on an orange background. Moreover civilian defence personnel, like journalists, and medical and religious personnel, are required to carry a distinctive identity card. The truly educated soldier anxious not to deny immunity to any protected person or object will have to carry a booklet of his own listing all the distinctive emblems and reproducing the relevant identity cards. Failure to do this may well lead to a charge of breaches of the law of war, to which it will now be impossible for him to plead ignorance of the law. While the national authorities may have carried out their obligations to teach the new law, it can hardly be expected that the ordinary man in the field will be able to remember the shape and colour of every distinctive emblem, or the particulars which he would find on a properly issued identity card.

Protocol I imposes an obligation to disseminate the Geneva law as amended. By Article 83: „the High Contracting Parties undertake, in time of peace as in time of armed conflict, to disseminate the Conventions and the Protocol as widely as possible in their respective countries and, in particular, to include the study thereof in their programmes of military instruction and to encourage the study thereof by the civilian population, so that those instruments may become known to the armed forces and to the civilian population. Any military or civilian authorities who, in time of armed conflict, assume responsibilities in respect of the application of the Conventions and this Protocol shall be fully acquainted with the text thereof".

Since it may well happen that this has been inadequately done, or since issues may arise which lead the troops to question whether particular orders or activities comply with the Geneva law, and as in time of total war there

---

45 See *Green,* letter on 'Journalists in Battle Areas', The Times (London) 1 Mar. 1976.

46 Ch. VI.

may be insufficient time to impart such instruction before conscripts are sent into action, Article 82 attempts to fill this potential hiatus: „The High Contracting Parties at all times, and the Parties to the conflict in time of armed conflict, shall ensure that legal advisers are available, when necessary, to advise military commanders at the appropriate level on the application of the Conventions and this Protocol and on the appropriate instruction to be given to the armed forces on this subject".

A number of points arise in connection with these proposals. In the first place, Article 82 implies that some of the officers attached to the judge advocate division of a military force should be knowledgable in at least that part of the law of war that may be described as humanitarian law. Such a requirement would almost certainly necessitate a revision of the training afforded by the relevant military services and pehaps also the placing of a greater emphasis on the international law of war with particular reference to the principles of humanitarian law in armed conflict. The reason that states are only required to 'encourage' civilian study of these principles is to be found in the constitutional difficulties confronting some federal states where education is not within the central government's cómpetence, and also to preserve the position in those countries where independence is demanded by such educational authorities as universities in so far as their curricula and teaching programmes are concerned. There can be little doubt that, even if these provisions are conscientiously carried out, military commandes will have to recognise that, while their function may be to conduct hostilities with a view to the early defeat of the enemy, regulation of the conduct of the men in their command so as to ensure compliance with the law and its restrictions is a fundamental obligation, as well as a policy matter of importance to national dignity. If this occurs, there are likely to be less transgressions of the law and certainly fewer opportunities for those accused of breaches to plead ignorance in their defence. However, there is inherent in the provisions the assumption that proper educational programmes, at least of the military, conducted by properly qualified persons will be instituted. This draws attention to activities already commenced in cooperation with the International Committee of the Red Cross by the Institut Henri Dunant in Geneva. Under the direction of Professor Pictet, who is also Vice-President of the International Committee of the Red Cross, the Institut has introduced a number of courses in humanitarian law in armed conflict which have already been attended by members of the armed forces from various countries, as well as by graduate students. In addition, the Institut is anxious to organise seminars for interested parties and on a regional basis, and is receiving encouragement and cooperation particularly from some of the developing countries. Where developed countries are concerned difficulties are encountered in view of historical backgrounds and a desire to follow their own tradition. The International Institute of Humanitarian Law at San Remo also runs such courses. It is to be hoped that in both cases care is taken that idealism and belief in the principles of humanitarian law does not prejudice the awareness of the instructors as to the realities of war. If they ignore these and elevate the principles of Geneva to too high a level, rather than achieving their object of instruction to ensure respect for the law, they may induce an attitude of disbelief and cynicism. In addition, some constries have instituted courses on the law of war for ther armed forces, or elaborated those that already existed.

Problems of a somewhat different kind arise concerning Protocol II[47] which deals with non-international armed conflicts. In so far as the regular armed forces are concerned, their position is already governed by the provisions in Protocol I just referred to, although it could easily be argued that since Protocol I only deals with international conflicts, any education in relation thereto is completely irrelevant for non-international conflicts. Specific steps must therefore be taken to ensure that no such escape from the obligation to observe humanitarian law is possible. In the event of a non-international conflict, however, one of the contestants is likely to be recruited primarily from civilians, as well as dissident members of the armed forces. If the Protocol is to have any meaning and come into operation immediately upon the conflict becoming sufficiently serious to be considered an armed conflict rather than a riot or a minor insurrection, it will be necessary for the civilian population to be educated in the basic principles of humanitarian law as part of the country's ordinary educational programme and regardless of the likelihood of any conflict arising. However, any attempt to postulate an international obligation requiring states to educate their subjects as to their rights and duties in time of civil war or other non-international armed conflict may easily be construed as an attempt to interfere in the domestic jurisdiction of a state. Further, it smacks of encouragement to dissidents to resort to armed conflict, secure in the knowledge that the government is subject to restrictions on its freedom in restoring order and re-establishing its authority, having already taught those who are now opposed to the government exactly what rights they will be entitled to, and which might limit the normal operation of the criminal law, should they decide to resort to armed force. In fact, at Geneva this proposal met with opposition from some Latin American countries, where it might be thought that their past history suggests a real likelihood of non-international conflict breaking out with the resultant creation of a Protocol II situation. A further objection was raised by the Soviet Union which contended that any obligation to educate its civilian population along such lines would be contrary to the prohibition contained in

[47] 16 Int Legal Materials (1977), 1442.

the Law on the Defence of Peace[48] which forbids war propaganda in whatever form it is carried out, arguing further that such education would also be contrary to the Soviet commitment to enducate for peaceful purposes. In view of these reservations, it is perhaps not surprising that although instruction of the civilian population as to the law regulating civil conflict is of prime importance, all that appears in Protocol II is the simple statement „The Protocol shall be disseminated as widely as possible"[49] leaving it to each state to decide on the identification of those to whom the dissemination should be directed and the manner in which this should be done.

As originally drafted, and in fact accepted in Committee, the commitments for dissemination were somewhat more effective, and included an obligation[50] „to disseminate the present Protocol as widely as possible in time of peace, so that it may become known to the armed forces and to the civilian population. In time of armed conflict, the Parties to the conflict shall take appropriate measures to bring the provisions of the present Protocol to the knowledge of their military and civilian agents and persons subject to their control."

While one may sympathise with a government which finds it objectionable to accept an obligation to educate its people as to their rights against the government should they decide to resort to armed force to overthrow that government, this unaccepted provision appears reasonable. The anti-government forces will not be a party to the Protocol which is only open for signature or accession by parties to the Geneva Conventions, and is thus only avaiblabe to states. It would seem, therefore, that unless this anti-government contestant makes a statement accepting the obligations of the Protocol, there would have been imposed upon the government a unilateral obligation as to its operations for re-establishing its authority and, moreover, a requirement to inform the military and the civilians supporting it of their duties to observe the provisions of the Protocol, even though their opponents were not so doing. On the other hand, it might be argued that by becoming a party a state accepts the obligations for all its citizens, so that during a non-international conflict even its opponents would be, in law at least, still bound by the state's international undertakings. This one-sidedness of burdens might have proved in practice, therefore, more apparent than real. What is perhaps of more significance than the rather narrow obligation that the Protocol imposes upon parties is the absence of any provision like that in Protocol I relating to the teaching of Protocol II in military curricula. The reason for this lacuna lies in the fact that some countries were unwilling, in relation to a non-international conflict, to

48 21 Mar. 1951, c. *Tunkin,* Theory of International Law (1974), 85—6.

49 Art. 19.

50 I.C.R.C. Doc., D/1388/1 b (1976).

accept directions as to the precise method by which their armed forces were to be informed of their obligations under Protocol II, especially as this Protocol is intended to limit the freedom of action of the contestants in such a conflict, including the rights normally accruing to state forces in upholding state authority during an armed confrontation.

There can be little doubt that if the states parties to the Geneva Conventions and the two amending Protocols, particularly Protocol I, take their obligations regarding dissemination seriously, and in fact introduce proper educational programmes, there would be more realisation by both the armed forces and the civilian population that there is in fact a real law of war carrying as much risk of punishment in the event of its breach, as is the case with national criminal law. At the same time, no member of the field forces would be able to contend, if charged with a breach of the law, that not only was he unaware of the existence of any particular rule, but that no attempt had ever been made to enlighten him. Moreover, military commanders would have to rethink their attitudes to the whole conspectus of the law of war and give it its due and proper place in military training. In so far as the civilian population is concerned, if the obligations are to be fully carried out, both as regards Protocol I and in any real sense for Protocol II, there would be a need for governments to rethink the nature of their educational programmes, despite the possibility that schools and pacifists among the teaching staffs might offer real objections. In fact, in spite of tradition, there would have to be some measure of cooperation between civilian education authorities and the military. Since this would almost certainly be rejected in many countries, use might have to be made of the personnel of the national Red Cross Society. But this too would often mean a rethinking of the entire approach and philosophy of such Society. For the main part, in most conntries the members of the national Society are concerned with internal medical auxiliary aid programmes and the offer of assistance in the event of national and sometimes international catastrophes, but they are hardly concerned with problems of armed conflict or the law relating thereto. Perhaps, if they were able to enlist qualified persons, and this again raises the problem of cooperation with the military or at least of the legal branch, this would be reasonable. Otherwise, it must be remembered that the international law of peace and war, as well as the principles of humanitarian law, is highly technical and the terms of treaties are often ambiguous if not actually obtuse. For unqualified persons to attempt to educate others as to their meaning may be just as dangerous as the absence of any education at all.

While in the past it might have been possible for any state to argue that while common sense dictated that it should educate its troops in the law of war, the legal obligation so to do was somewhat nebulous and rather in the nature of a pious hope, although they probably did to some extent provide some information to their own troops as to their rights as prisoners of war. If they failed to do so, prisoners were entitled to have access to the Prisoners of War Convention which was to be available to them in the prison camp. Now, however, the obligation is clearly laid down and states are obliged to educate their troops as to their duties towards the enemy. What may still be necessary is the establishment of some observation centre or clearing house which might be able to oversee and advise whether this is being carried into effect in a reasonable manner such that ordinary soldiers may understand, while a bare minimum may be presumed as equally accepted by all services regardless of arm or nationality. To some extent this is being attempted by the Henri Dunant Institut, while the International Committee of the Red Cross may be expected to continue to issue pamphlets outlining the basic minima of obligations in the field of humanitarian law — a practice which has been introduced by some national authorities too. These educational activities, combined with the obligation in the Conventions to report to the International Committee which, presumably, is entitled to comment on such reports, may be the beginning of a new era of education of both the military and the civilian populations in that part of international criminal law which is concerned with breaches of the principles of international humanitarian law in time of armed conflict. Should this be the case, we would see the dawn of an era in which it will be true of the man in the field during combat, as it is for the civilian charged with a criminal offence, that ignorantia juris non excusat.

[6]

PRIVATE PECUNIARY CLAIMS ARISING OUT OF WAR *

Edwin M. Borchard

Any attempt to discuss the international responsibility of the State for injuries sustained by private individuals in time of war immediately encounters the difficulty of establishing any definite rules in the practice of awarding indemnities or compensation for private losses arising out of war. Nevertheless, an examination of the subject in the light of precedent and principle may not be without some useful results.

In a general way, this responsibility of the State may be measured by the State's obligation as a belligerent or a neutral to observe the rules of international law and of war. As it is obviously, however, beyond present possibilities to undertake a detailed review of these rules—which indeed have been ably treated in numerous works on the subject—the discussion here will be confined to the more important classes of cases in which pecuniary claims have been or are likely to be brought for injuries sustained by individuals or private property in time of war.[1]

At the outset it may be observed that in the progress of time private rights during war have gained greater and greater recognition, coincident with the narrowing of the sphere of belligerent rights, the imposition of more stringent rules for the conduct of war, and the enlargement (until very recently) of the rights of neutral commerce. It is in the matter of injuries sustained by private persons during war that Rousseau's somewhat inexact doctrine that war is a relation of State to State and not of man to man has found perhaps its greatest field for application, for both in international and municipal law there has been a marked and growing tendency to relieve individuals and their property from the losses incident to war and to cast the burden upon the State. While this modern principle of State indemnity is to a large extent a matter of municipal

* This article constitutes in substance a chapter from the author's forthcoming book, *The Diplomatic Protection of Citizens Abroad*, to be published by the Banks Law Publishing Co., New York, with whose permission the article is printed, and by whom all rights are reserved.

[1] The awards of arbitral commissions and the practice of the United States have been used as principal sources.

law and national policy and equity only, international law has endeavored in many directions to preserve the immunity of private rights from the destructive effects of war. Nevertheless, while the conduct of warfare has in increasing degree been brought within definite rules, private property rights in war necessarily can not be safeguarded so minutely or be affected with the fine distinctions incident to civil affairs. A margin of uncertainty is hardly separable from a sphere of rights in which so much depends on military necessity.

THEORY OF COMPENSATION FOR WAR LOSSES

Before discussing the particular phases of war claims, it seems desirable to take up briefly the general question of compensation for individual war losses. In former times, no rules existed for pecuniary indemnity to individuals for war damages. In the matter of the State's duty to indemnify its own subjects, Vattel appears to have been the first to draw a distinction between the different kinds of war losses. He distinguished, first, those caused by the enemy, for which no indemnity was due; and, secondly, those caused by the State itself. The latter he sub-divided into two classes: first, losses caused by the voluntary and deliberate action of the army by way of precaution or strategy; and, secondly, inevitable accidents of war caused either by stress of circumstances or without premeditation. For losses coming within the last subdivision, the State incurred no strict obligation, although, if its finances allowed, it was equitably proper to compensate individuals. For losses within the first subdivision, it was bound to give indemnities at the close of the war.[2] This distinction between acts done voluntarily in preparation for war, and injuries inevitable or inflicted only by imperious military necessity has been followed by France and the French courts[3] from the period beginning with the French Revolution, and the principle of State indemnity has thus found its way into modern practice. Attention will

[2] Vattel, Chitty-Ingraham ed., sec. 232, p. 402; Bentwich, N., Private Property in War, London, 1907, 41–42; H. Rep. 386, 22nd Cong., 1st sess., pp. 9–10; Lawrence's Report on Claims against Governments, H. Rep. 134, 43rd Cong., 2nd sess., 126; Nys (1912 ed.), III, ch. XI, 450–462.

[3] Brémond in article "Actes de gouvernement," 5 *Rev. Dr. Pub.* (1896), 69, 227. As to Italian law to the same effect see H. Rep. 134, 43rd Cong., 2nd sess., 129, 135–191.

be called hereafter to a number of special occasions on which large voluntary indemnities have been granted by various States to inhabitants sustaining war losses.

The matter of exacting pecuniary indemnity on behalf of injured private individuals from belligerent or neutral States violating the laws of war is of comparatively recent origin. The rule of indemnity was developed by international commissions and domestic boards as the only practical sanction for a violation of those private rights which international and municipal law have expressly sought to safeguard. At the Second Hague Conference, it was for the first time definitely provided (Art. 3 of Convention IV): first, that a belligerent in land warfare who violates the provisions of the Hague Regulations, shall, if the case demand, be liable to make compensation; and secondly, that he shall be responsible for all acts committed by persons forming part of his armed forces.[4] It is probable that the first rule extends to all violations of the laws of war besides those included in the Hague Regulations. Whether the second rule will serve hereafter to make the State liable for the wanton or unauthorized acts of unofficered soldiers, for which, under an almost uniform practice, the State has heretofore been held not to be responsible, is a grave question.

A STATE OF WAR

The measure of private rights in war and the extent to which they are subject to belligerent rights depends on the existence of a state of war, and not on a declaration of war or a recognition of belligerency. The indicia of a state of war may be said to be an armed contest between two States or parts of the same State conducted by regularly organized military bodies and having an avowed political object in view. War may exist where no battle has been or is being fought,[5] as well as when war

[4] Oppenheim, 2nd ed., II, 319–321, 300. One of the best discussions of Art. 3 of Convention IV is to be found in a small work by Cuno Hofer, *Der Schadenersatz im Landkriegsrecht*, Tübingen, 1913. 91 p.

The Institute of International Law at its Oxford meeting of 1913, proposed to extend the principle of indemnity to naval warfare. Additional Article to Rules adopted, 15 *Rev. Dr. Int.* (1913), 677.

[5] Ex parte Milligan, 4 Wall. 127, 140. Upon the question whether war exists, the courts must follow the political departments of the Government. Gray *v.* U. S., 21

has not been declared nor belligerency recognized.[6] War, then, is a fact, and the rights and duties of individuals, as well as the exercise of belligerent rights by enemy governments or by parties to a civil war result from the *fact* of belligerency alone.[7] Thus, while the Cuban insurgents were never granted belligerent rights, the Spanish Treaty Claims Commission nevertheless held that war existed in a material, if not in an international, sense, thereby granting to Spain and to the insurgents the right to exercise belligerent rights and immunity for such injuries to private persons and property as the laws of war permit.[8] The determination that no legal state of war existed between the United States and France between 1798 and 1800 was vital to the decision of the Court of Claims in the French Spoliation claims.[9]

It is equally necessary to determine when belligerent rights end. This is usually, though not always, fixed at the date of a treaty of peace, but in fact a treaty is not in effect until ratified and proclaimed, and belligerent rights have often been exercised (1) between the date of signing and ratification, and (2) in the case of military forces in distant colonies, after the date of ratification. If the armistice which is usually provided for in the first case is broken, or if in the second case belligerent rights are exercised after knowledge of the cessation of the war by the military commanders, liability would seem to attach to the offending government.[10]

Ct. Cl. 340; Cushing *v.* U. S., 22 Ct. Cl. 1. See also G. G. Phillimore in V. 4 U. S. Journ. of the Soc. of Comp. Leg. (1902), 128–134.

[6] The Prize Cases, 2 Black, 636, 670; Teresa Jeorg *v.* U. S., Spanish Treaty Cl. Com., Briefs, V. 2, pp. 80, 81.

[7] Hall, 31 and note. Prats (Mexico) *v.* U. S., July 4, 1868, Moore's Arb. 2886, 2888.

[8] Span. Treaty Cl. Com. Special Rep. of W. E. Fuller, 1907, 22. Sen. Doc. 308, 59th Cong., 1st sess. 26.

[9] Gray *v.* U. S., 21 Ct. Cl. 340; Cushing *v.* U. S., 22 Ct. Cl. 1. The French Spoliation Claims, by Geo. A. King, Sen. Doc. 964, 62nd Cong., 3rd sess., 9.

[10] Oppenheim, 329. Hall, 6th ed., 555. The decisions of arbitral and other courts, however, leave this question in much uncertainty. *John* (U. S.) *v.* Gt. Brit., Feb. 8, 1853, Moore's Arb. 3793 (Government held liable for capture made after signing of treaty of peace, on ground of failure to notify the cessation of hostilities promptly). See also the *John*, 2 Dodson, 336 and the *Mentor*, 1 Rob. 183. The Japanese Government ordered the release of "all ships and their cargoes captured after Sept. 5, 1905" (the date of the treaty of peace with Russia). Imperial Ordinance No. 228, November, 1905. But see case of the *Swineherd*, captured by a French privateer after knowledge (though not official notification) of cessation of war. She

It is often important to determine, on the military occupation of a town or larger area, when belligerent rights merge into the more limited rights of a military occupant.[11]

In the case of maritime capture the question has occasionally been raised whether neutral vessels captured before the treaty of peace, can be tried or condemned in a prize court after the conclusion of peace. Inasmuch as title in the captured vessel or cargo does not pass until actual condemnation, there is some ground for the view that a prize, captured but not yet condemned when peace is concluded, must be released. While the matter must still be regarded as a moot question, the weight of authority, supported by the celebrated *Doelwyk* decision of the Italian Prize Commission,[12] favors the view that the neutral prize may be tried after peace is concluded.[13] Whether the prize may be condemned and confiscated is more doubtful. While some eminent authorities maintain that condemnation after peace is lawful, inasmuch as it is a punishment for an unlawful act committed before the peace,[14] the Italian court in the *Doelwyk* case decreed the restoration of the vessel on the ground that condemnation and confiscation after peace is unlawful.

POSITION OF ALIENS IN HOSTILE TERRITORY

Without entering into a discussion of the general position of aliens in time of war, it is necessary to examine the principal burdens which individuals in hostile territory must bear. A long course of practice and The Hague Regulations have given some authority to certain rules for the treatment of alien enemies in the country of the territorial sovereign. But even a departure from these rules, which has occurred in several

was condemned by a French prize court. Hall, 556 criticizes the decision. See also Phillimore III, sec. 521. See also cases of Torres (Mexico) *v.* U. S., July 4, 1868, Moore's Arb. 3798; Ayama, *ibid.* 3804; Serrano, *ibid.* 3805 (where a claim was allowed); and Revilla, *ibid.* 3805.

11 Meng (France) *v.* U. S., Jan. 15, 1880, Moore's Arb. 3689. Gumbes *v.* An award of the commissioners for liquidating the claims of British subjects on France (1834), 2 Knapp P. C. Rep. 369.

12 Martens, *Recueil*, 2nd series, V. 28, 66–90.

13 Oppenheim, II, sec. 436.

14 *Ibid.*; Liszt, 5th ed., 374; Gareis, 2nd ed., 258; Brusa in 4 *R. G. D. I. P.* (1897), 157–175, criticizing the *Doelwyk* decision; decision of Japanese Prize Court in *Antiope* case, MS. Dept. of State.

instances during the present European War, can hardly give rise to individual pecuniary claims in law. The alien enemy's individual grievances are settled by the treaty of peace, and if his country should happen to lose in the war, he is without redress. If his country should be the conqueror, indemnities may be demanded from the defeated nation, but his pecuniary remedy then depends on the bounty of his own state. In either case, he apparently has no legally protected rights, so that as between nations and alien enemies, the rules of war have only a moral and not a legal sanction. If the transgressor of the rules should be victor in the conflict, no legal means exists for compelling him to accord redress to injured alien enemies. While he may be held more accountable to neutral aliens, either as victor or vanquished, for certain transgressions of the rules of war, there are many respects in which neutral aliens domiciled in enemy territory share the burdens of war equally with alien enemies.

Neutral aliens domiciled in an enemy state, with their property there situated, are exposed to the consequences of actual belligerent operations to the same extent as subjects of the enemy.[15] This rule applies not only to aliens who permanently reside in a country, but to those who come with knowledge of the existence of the war, and particularly to those who came before the war and continued to reside for a period longer than necessary for convenient departure. Both with respect to his property and his capacity to sue such an alien is deemed an enemy.[16] Foreign offices and municipal and international courts have frequently laid down the rule that neutral property permanently situated in enemy territory, or property of neutrals who voluntarily enter or continue to reside in belligerent territory assumes the risks of injury incident to war.[17]

[15] Hall, 740; Bentwich, 29. The rule that war makes subjects of one belligerent the enemies of the government and subjects of the other is admitted. It applies equally to civil and international war. See also U. S. *v.* Cooke (*The Venice*), 2 Wall. 258, 274; Mrs. Alexander's Cotton, 2 Wall. 419; Jecker *v.* Montgomery, 18 How. 110; White *v.* Burnley, 20 How. 235, 249.

[16] Whiting's War Powers under the Constitution, 43rd ed., Boston, 1871, p. 341. Society *v.* Wheeler, 2 Gallison, 105. The rule that aliens entering or continuing to reside in enemy territory may be treated as enemies is found in Grotius, III, 4, secs. 6, 7.

[17] Palmerston's opinion in Greytown, Copenhagen and Uleaborg bombardments. Hansard's Debates, 3rd series, V. 146, pp. 37, 49; Granville to Lord Lyons, Jan. 11,

In strict law, even the property of loyal citizens situated in enemy territory is subject to the casualties of war as enemy property.[18] The particular liabilities to which such property is thus ordinarily exposed will be examined presently. It is here merely to be noted that on land, the fate of property located in belligerent territory depends not on the nationality or loyalty of the owner, but on the location of the property.[19] The only important qualification of this rule relates to neutral property *temporarily* in the belligerent country. If this is used or destroyed for recognized belligerent reasons, the owner is entitled to compensation, which is not the case with property permanently so situated. The right to use such neutral property, subject to payment of compensation, is known as the right of angary quite analogous to the right of eminent domain.[20]

1871 and Granville to Sackville West, March 1, 1871, Hale's Rep., Appendix, For. Rel. 1873, V. 3, 368–370, 65 St. Pap. 458.

Mr. Cass, Sec'y of State, to Mr. Burns, April 26, 1858, Moore's Dig. VI, 885; Mr. Seward to Mr. Wydenbruck, Nov. 16, 1885, *ibid.* 885; Mr. Fish, Sec'y of State, to Mr. Washburn, April 28, 1871, For. Rel. 1871, 335; Mr. Fish to Mr. Thornton, May 16, 1873, Moore's Dig. VI, 890; Mr. Fish to Mr. Gibson, Dec. 30, 1875, *ibid.* 891; Mr. Bayard to Mr. O'Connor, Oct. 29, 1885, *ibid.* 891; Whiting's War Powers, 352; 12 Op. Atty. Gen. 21; 22 Op. Atty. Gen. 315. See also Wharton's Dig. III, secs. 352, 353.

Gallego, Mesa, *et al. v.* U. S., 43 Ct. Cl. 444; Herrera *v.* U. S., 222 U. S. 558.

Cooke (U. S.) *v.* Mexico, Act of March 3, 1849, Moore's Arb. 2659, 2661; Haggerty, *ibid.* 2665; Thompson, *ibid.* 2669; Castel (U. S.) *v.* Venezuela, Dec. 5, 1885, *ibid.* 3710; Foster (U. S.) *v.* Mexico, July 4, 1868, *ibid.* 3349; Costa (U. S.) *v.* Mexico, *ibid.* 3724; Brook (Gt. Brit.) *v.* U. S., May 8, 1871, *ibid.* 3738. (Rule admitted, but award here made for property taken for military use, because loyal citizens had been granted compensation in similar cases. 16 Stat. L. 524.) Same rule in Henderson (Gt. Brit.) *v.* U. S., *ibid.* 3727, Frazer dissenting in both cases, Hale's Rep. 43, 44; Laurent (Gt. Brit.) *v.* U. S., Feb. 8, 1853, *ibid.* 2671; Uhde, *ibid.*, 2691; Bacigalupi (U. S.) *v.* Chile, May 24, 1897, Report, 1901, p. 151; Volkmar (U. S.) *v.* Venezuela, Feb. 17, 1903, Ralston, 258, 259; Upton (U. S.) *v.* Venezuela, Feb. 17, 1903, Ralston, 72; Orr and Laubenheimer (U. S.) *v.* Nicaragua, For. Rel. 1900, 826; Tongue (Gt. Brit.) *v.* U. S., May 8, 1871, Moore's Arb. 3675.

[18] Jaragua Iron Co. *v.* U. S., 212 U. S. 297, 306; Page *v.* U. S., 11 Wall. 268; Prize Cases, 2 Black, 635; *The William Bagaley*, 5 Wall. 377; Green *v.* U. S., 10 Ct. Cl. 466; *Gooch* v. *U. S.*, 15 Ct. Cl. 281; Brandon *v.* U. S., 46 Ct. Cl. 559.

[19] 11 Op. Atty. Gen. 405; 12 *ibid.* 486, 488; Lawrence's Wheaton, 565. In practice indemnities are often paid for such loyal citizen's property as may have been used or destroyed by the citizen's own State. See Southern Claims Commission, Act of March 3, 1871, 16 Stat. L. 524.

[20] Hall, 741; Bentwich, 27; Oppenheim, secs. 364–367.

ENEMY CHARACTER

The belligerents are entitled to exercise certain measures against enemy persons and property from which neutrals are free; but while the rule as to private property on land is comparatively simple, its location constituting the test of enemy character, private property at sea is tested by other criteria to determine whether or not it is vested with enemy character. According to the Continental practice,[21] nationality is the test of enemy character, so that the subjects of the belligerents and their property bear enemy character, whereas the subjects of neutrals and their property do not. But under the Anglo-American rule, in which domicil is the test, regardless of nationality, as well as under prescribed exceptional circumstances, subjects of the enemy state do not necessarily bear enemy character, whereas neutrals may by their domicil or their acts be properly considered as enemies. Neither the Second Hague Conference nor the London Naval Conference of 1908 was able to reconcile these conflicting views concerning nationality or domicil as the controlling factors in determining the neutral or enemy character of individuals and their goods.[21a]

Under the Anglo-American rule, the political character of private property at sea depends on the commercial domicil of its owner.[22] This differs from civil domicil, inasmuch as it does not require long-continued residence with an intention not to return, but only such a residence for the purposes of trading as makes a person's trade or business "contribute to or form part of the resources of such country, and renders it therefore reasonable that his hostile, friendly or neutral character should be determined by reference to the character of such country." [23] Such commercial domicil may differ from the actual civil domicil of the owner. For example, in Anglo-American law, his house of trade (commercial

[21] Fiore, III, sec. 1432 *et seq.;* Calvo, IV, sec. 1932 *et seq.;* Bonfils, sec. 1343 *et seq.*

[21a] The recent British Aliens Restriction (Consolidation) Order, 1914, § 31, and Trading with the Enemy Proclamation, No. 2, clauses 3 and 6 modify the general rules as to enemy character. See Schuster, E. J. Effect of War * * * on commercial transactions. 2nd ed. London, 1914, p. 3 *et seq.*

[22] Bentwich, 142; Westlake, II, 140; Oppenheim, II, secs. 88, 90; Laurent (Gt. Brit.) *v.* U. S., Feb. 8, 1853, Moore's Arb. 2671; *The Pizarro,* 2 Wheaton, 246. Japan appears to have adhered to the principle of domicil in these matters.

[23] Dicey, Conflict of Laws, 737.

domicil) may be in neutral territory and the property at sea emanating from that house of trade escape belligerent capture, notwithstanding his civil domicil in enemy territory.[24] The obverse rule has equal force. So an owner may have several houses of trade, some in neutral, some in enemy territory, according to which his property may be judged. The rule as to commercial domicil is applied even to friendly subjects. It may be added that all goods on enemy vessels are presumed to be enemy goods unless the contrary is proved.

The enemy character of a ship is determined by its flag, regardless of the nationality or domicil of the owner, provided she is sailing under it legitimately according to the municipal law of the State of the flag.[25] However, a vessel under a neutral flag may acquire enemy character or at least forfeit its neutral protection by taking part in the hostilities, by rendering unneutral service, by carrying contraband in excess of the permitted proportions, by the use of fraudulent means to evade just capture, by breaking or attempting to break a lawfully established blockade, or by forcibly resisting visit and search.[26] Individuals may also lose their neutral character by rendering unneutral service to either belligerent.[27] The questions involved in the transfer of enemy vessels and goods to a neutral flag in contemplation of or during war have found a generally accepted solution in the rules formulated by the London Naval Conference of 1908.[28] But the fact that a neutral individual

[24] Attention may be called to the peculiar rule of American prize law, according to which a partner's residence in the enemy's country will condemn his share in a house of trade established in neutral territory. *The Antonia Johanna*, 1 Wheat. 159.

[25] Oppenheim, II, sec. 89; Westlake, II, 147. A reservation might, however, be made to the effect that the municipal law conferring the right to fly the national flag must not conflict with the rules of international law as to transfer of flag in time of war.

[26] Westlake, II, 153; Oppenheim, II, sec. 89, sec. 406.

[27] See Art. 17 of Convention V of the Second Hague Conference, and Oppenheim, II, sec. 88. *The Industrie* (German) and *The Quang-nam*, condemned by Japanese prize courts in Russo-Japanese war. Takahashi, S., International Law applied to the Russo-Japanese War, New York, 1908, pp. 732–738.

[28] Articles 55, 56 and 60 of the Declaration of London; Oppenheim, II, secs. 91, 92. The former conflicting rules are discussed by Westlake, II, 148 *et seq.* See the *Sophia Rickmers*, 61 St. Pap. 1091. For the opinion of the State Department rendered during the present European War concerning the transfer of merchant ships during war, see Sen. Doc. 563, 63rd Cong., 2nd sess.

furnishes supplies or makes loans to either belligerent from neutral territory does not affect his neutral character.[29]

WAR ON LAND

The effects of war upon private property on land may now be considered. It has already been observed that neutral and enemy property in hostile territory are in general subject to the same treatment. Where such property is seized or destroyed for strategic reasons directly incident to belligerent action, the private owners need not be compensated for their losses.[30] This rule is based on military necessity, and the difficulty of its application, as will be seen presently, arises in determining whether a particular seizure or destruction was prompted by imperious military necessity or constituted a deliberate appropriation of private property for public use, although perhaps indirectly connected with belligerent purposes. It has been noted that under certain circumstances neutral property merely temporarily in hostile territory, such as ships, may only be seized on payment of compensation, under the belligerent right of angary.[31]

Injuries sustained by private property as a direct result of belligerent acts—battle, siege, bombardment—or incidental thereto are not the subject of indemnification. The conduct of the belligerent, however, must conform to the laws of war, both in justification and execution. Private losses thus sustained in war are considered as due to necessity and *force majeure*. Vattel first stated what has since been accepted as the correct grounds for the non-liability of the State for these war losses—"the public finances would soon be exhausted" and "these indemnifications would be liable to a thousand abuses." [32] Yet as an act of grace, as has been remarked, a State may, after peace, consent to compensate its subjects and even domiciled aliens for their losses, thus distributing the individual loss equitably over the whole nation. As be-

[29] Art. 18 (a) of Convention V. See Dept. of State circular Aug. 15, 1914, "Neutrality—contraband—seizure of ships and cargo."

[30] Bentwich, 27.

[31] Westlake, II, 119; Oppenheim, II, secs. 364, 365. Neutral cargo, even conditional contraband, not destined to enemy forces, has at times been requisitioned under payment of compensation.

[32] Vattel, Bk. III, ch. XV, sec. 232, p. 402.

tween the belligerents and enemy subjects, the treaty of peace usually constitutes a final settlement of grievances, even of those arising out of a violation of the laws of war to the injury of enemy persons and property. Neutrals, however, even with respect to property in hostile territory, retain the right to make diplomatic claims against the offending belligerent for violations of the laws of war.

While the general rule as to war claims is that no compensation is due to private individuals, on account of injuries to their persons or property, resulting from legitimate acts of war, it is not always easy to determine what is a legitimate act of war. The Hague Regulations, and instructions issued by nations to their own armies, have established a set or code of rules according to which warfare shall be conducted. An examination of numerous claims brought before municipal and international courts, will, in connection with the Hague Regulations, furnish an approximate guide to the general rules governing compensation for injuries sustained in war.

Compensation is not due for damages sustained during actual military operations, whether caused by one belligerent or the other. Thus injuries sustained during hostilities—in battle or siege,[33] in the track of war,[34] during bombardment,[35] or attacks on towns,[36] and in similar cir-

[33] Wilson (U. S.) *v.* Spain, Feb. 12, 1871, Moore's Arb. 3674; Blumenkron (U. S.) *v.* Mexico, July 4, 1868, *ibid.* 3669; Riggs (U. S.) *v.* Mexico, *ibid.* 3668; Castel (U. S.) *v.* Venezuela, Dec. 5, 1885, *ibid.* 3710; Padron (Spain) *v.* Venezuela, Feb. 13, 1903, Ralston, 923; Petrocelli (Italy) *v.* Venezuela, Feb. 13, 1903, *ibid.* 762; Bembelista (Netherlands) *v.* Venezuela, Feb. 28, 1903, *ibid.* 900; Rule 1 of the Mixed Claims Commission of Nicaragua, 1911, Managua, 1912. See also Amer. St. Pap. Claims, 199, Feb. 15, 1797.

[34] Vattel, Bk. III, ch. 15, sec. 232; Oppenheim, II, sec. 151; U. S. *v.* Pacific R. R., 120 U. S. 233; Puerto Cabello Ry. (Gt. Brit.) *v.* Venezuela, Feb. 13, 1903, Ralston, 458; Bembelista (Neth.) *v.* Venezuela, *ibid.* 900; Rule 8 of Spanish Treaty Claims Commission, Final Report, May 2, 1910, pp. 4–5.

[35] Dutch bombardment of Antwerp 1830, 30 St. Pap. 212 *et seq.* Numerous cases of bombardment, in which compensation by the bombarding belligerent was uniformly denied, are set out in Moore's Dig. VI, secs. 1168–1170. See also Dutrieux (France) *v.* U. S., Jan. 15, 1880, Moore's Arb. 3702; Cleworth (Gt. Brit.) *v.* U. S., May 8, 1871, *ibid.* 3675; Tongue, *ibid.* 3675; Meng (France) *v.* U. S., Jan. 15, 1880,

[36] Schultz (Mex.) *v.* U. S., July 4, 1868, Moore's Arb. 2973; Wyman (U. S.) *v.* Mexico, *ibid.* 2978; Cleworth (Gt. Brit.) *v.* U. S., May 8, 1871, *ibid.* 3675; Volkmar (U. S.) *v.* Venezuela, Feb. 17, 1903, Ralston, 258.

cumstances connected with the immediate necessities of armed conflict and subserving some proper military end [37] are not subject to indemnity,

ibid. 3689, 3697; Perkins (Gt. Brit.) *v.* Chile, Trib. Anglo-Chileno, 1891, I, 34; Strobel's report, Moore's Arb. 4930–36, parag. 1 and 18, For. Rel. 1896, 35; Amer. Elec. L. and P. Co. (U. S.) *v.* Venezuela, Feb. 17, 1903, Ralston, 36; Bembelista (Neth.) *v.* Venezuela, Feb. 28, 1903, *ibid.* 901; Guerrieri (Italy) *v.* Venezuela, *ibid.* 753. See, however, the Colin case, Germany *v.* France, 1888, 15 Clunet, 241. For limitations of the rule, see notes 38 and 39, *infra.*

[37] All destruction and damage to enemy property for purpose of offense and defense is considered necessary and hence lawful. Oppenheim, II, sec. 150.

Soldiers passing over land in belligerent area and injuring crops. Shattuck (U. S.) *v.* Mexico, July 4, 1868, Moore's Arb. 3668; Cole (U. S.) *v.* Mexico, *ibid.* 3670; Sterling (Gt. Brit.) *v.* U. S., May 8, 1871, *ibid.* 3686.

Cutting of timber to clear away obstructions, erection of fortifications, etc., in the enemy's country. Barclay and other cases (Gt. Brit.) *v.* U. S., May 8, 1871, Hale's Rep. 50, Moore's Arb. 3678.

Seizure or destruction of property for the public welfare. Heflebower *v.* U. S., 21 Ct. Cl. 229, 237. See also Sen. Doc. 318, 57th Cong., 1st sess., pp. 19, 36, 37; *e. g.*, destruction of buildings as sanitary measure, Jaragua Iron Co. *v.* U. S., 212 U. S. 297, 306, and Hardman (Gt. Brit.) *v.* U. S., Aug. 18, 1910, 7 A. J. I. L. 879. (The arbitral court suggested that voluntary payment might be made by U. S.)

Seizure and detention of private enemy vessel after occupation of enemy port, for use of army—the doctrine of immunity of private property not followed. Herrera *v.* U. S., 222 U. S. 558, 572; Diaz *v.* U. S., 222 U. S. 574; Costa (U. S.) *v.* Mexico, July 4, 1868, Moore's Arb. 3724.

Destruction of property useful to the enemy for military purposes. Cox (Gt. Brit.) and Smythe (Gt. Brit.) *v.* U. S., May 8, 1871, Moore's Arb. 3678. See also Oppenheim, II, sec. 152; 11 Op. Atty. Gen. 378; U. S. *v.* Pacific R. R., 120 U. S. 227; Magoon's Rep. 345 and 615; Cotton Claims (Gt. Brit.) *v.* U. S., Moore's Arb. 3679–82. See also Sen. Doc. 2, 42nd Cong., spec. sess.; Giles (U. S.) *v.* France, Jan. 15, 1880, Moore's Arb. 3703 (dictum).

The owner of property seized and destroyed to prevent its falling into the hands of the enemy is not entitled to compensation if the danger was immediate and impending, and its capture by the enemy be reasonably certain. Sparhawk *v.* Respublica, 1 Dallas, 362; 1 Op. Atty. Gen. 255; Final Report of Spanish Treaty Cl. Com. May 2, 1910, p. 12; Cotton Claims (Gt. Brit.) *v.* U. S., Moore's Arb. 3679. See H. Rep. 262; 43rd Cong., 1st sess., pp. 44 *et seq.* Cotton was seized in the Southern states during the Civil War by the Union troops, as constituting resources of the enemy, and liability denied. Moore's Dig., VI, 895 and cases cited at p. 901. But where the danger does not appear immediate, the destruction is regarded merely as the appropriation of private property for public use for which an indemnity is due. *Infra,* note 50. The State may and often does waive its exemption from liability.

Seizure of money belonging to enemies on deposit in occupied territory in 1863 (probably unlawful to-day, except as legal contributions). New Orleans *v.* S. S. Co., 20 Wall. 394.

Other acts of military necessity. Killing of animals, opinion of Dec. 22, 1905 of the necessary condition being that such act shall have been in accordance with the rules of war.

For example, in the matter of bombardment, definite regulations have been established which limit the principle of non-liability. If the bombardment is directed against an unfortified and undefended part of the town, or if it may be regarded as a wanton or unnecessary act liability is incurred.[38] The legal presumption, however, is in favor of the regularity and necessity of governmental acts. The Hague Regulations and Convention IV of the Second Hague Conference have established important limitations on the justification, legitimacy, and conduct of bombardment.[39] Among other limitations, the bombardment of undefended towns is prohibited; the commander must endeavor to notify his intention to bombard; hospitals, churches, schools, etc., must so far as possible be spared; and bombardment for non-payment of contributions by coast towns is prohibited. In like manner, submarine mines should be laid according to certain rules.[40]

Judge Advocate Gen. of the Army. Howland's Digest, 250. See also *ibid.* 251, 253, 254 and paragraph 15, Gen. Orders 100. Burning of cane by Spanish forces in Cuba, Casanova (No. 33), Spanish Tr. Cl. Com. *Ibid.*, burning of buildings when a legitimate war measure, Sen. Ex. Doc. 85, 42nd Cong., 2nd sess.; Bacigalupi (U. S.) *v.* Chile, No. 42, May 24, 1897, Rep. of Commission, 1901, 151.

Property destroyed in preparation for attack or defense. Jardel (France) *v.* U. S., Jan. 15, 1880, Moore's Arb. 3199; opinion of Judge Adv. Gen. May 1, 1906, Howland, 252; Parham *v.* Justices, 9 Georgia, 341.

[38] Barletta (Italy) *v.* Venezuela, Feb. 13, 1903, Ralston, 754; Cuneo (Italy) *v.* Chile, Jan. 4, 1883, Moore's Arb. 4929. See also *obiter* remarks in De Lemos (Gt. Brit.) *v.* Venezuela, Ralston, 304, 314 (counsel), 319, and in Guerrieri, *ibid.* 753 and Bembelista, *ibid.* 901; Perrin *v.* U. S., 12 Wall. 315, 4 Ct. Cl. 543; Hall, 532; Samoan claims arising out of unlawful bombardment of Apia by Great Britain and United States, H. Doc. 1257, 62nd Cong., 3rd sess.

[39] These rules are set out in Oppenheim, II, secs. 158, 212, 213. See also Rules of the Institute of International Law, adopted at Oxford, 1913, Arts. 25 and 27, 15 *R. D. I.* n. s. (1913), 677.

[40] Failure of Turkey properly to notify neutral shipping of the laying of certain contact mines in the harbor of Smyrna is the principal ground of claim in the case of the *Nevada* (U. S.) and *Senegal* (France) *v.* Turkey. Most of the Powers have not yet agreed upon rules for the laying of submarine mines. It is reported that Austria has consented to compensate certain Italian subjects whose vessels were blown up recently by floating mines in the Adriatic. Neutral vessels injured by floating mines probably have just claims against powers which may be proved to have sowed mines in the open sea.

The same principle which exempts the State from liability for injuries to private property caused by military necessity, extends to the incidental and consequential results of a state of war. Thus, interference with business, prohibitions of trade between enemy subjects and the limitations upon the trade of neutrals with belligerents in the matter of contraband, etc., the accidental destruction of innocent property by misdirected shots, arrests and detentions on suspicion, and similar injuries incidental to a state of war must be borne by the individuals sustaining the loss without a right to compensation.[41]

[41] On war claims arising out of direct and indirect injuries to private property, see Lawrence's Report on War Claims, etc., H. Rep. 262, 43rd Cong., 1st sess., and Feraud-Giraud, *Recours à raison des dommages causés par la guerre*, Paris, 1881, 85 p. Reprinted from *La France Judiciaire*, Pamphlets, Dept. of State, V. I; Rule 2 of Nicaraguan Mixed Claims Commission, 1911, MS. Dept. of State. Thus the following claims were disallowed as being accidents due to a state of war: burning of buildings as a ruse to deceive the enemy (Opin. of Judge Adv.-Gen., H. Rep. 262, *supra*, p. 57); private liens destroyed by capture of public movables Barrett (Gt. Brit.) *v.* U. S., May 8, 1871, Howard's Rep. 60, Moore's Arb. 2900; firing guns across private land (Peabody *v.* U. S., 43 Ct. Cl. 5); accidental destruction of innocent property involved in the destruction of public stores and works of the enemy. Various claims (Gt. Brit.) *v.* U. S., May 8, 1871, Moore's Arb. 3677; claims before Anglo-Chilean Tribunal, 1893, Duncan, Recl. pres. al. Trib. Anglo-Chileno I, 536; Hübner, *ibid.* III, 20; Club Inglés, *ibid.* III, 47; Dawson, *ibid.* III, 55; Cesarino (Italy) *v.* Venezuela, Feb. 13, 1903, Ralston, 770.

Arrests and detentions on suspicion. Hannum (U. S.) *v.* Mexico, July 4, 1868, Moore's Arb. 3243; Cramer (U. S.) *v.* Mexico, *ibid.* 3250; Forwood (Gt. Brit.) *v.* U. S., May 8, 1871, Hale's Rep. 84; Gatter (U. S.) *v.* Mexico, Moore's Arb. 3267; Jarman *et al.* (Gt. Brit.) *v.* U. S., May 8, 1871, *ibid.* 3308. Thus a state may temporarily restrain the departure of merchant vessels, to insure the secrecy of naval operations. But see Bailey (*The Labuan*), Gt. Brit. *v.* U. S., May 8, 1871, Hale's Rep. 171, Moore's Arb. 3791. Where the military detention is unnecessarily long or harsh, awards have been made. Berron (U. S.) *v.* Mexico, July 4, 1868, Moore's Arb. 3960; Story (U. S.) *v.* Spain, Feb. 12, 1871, *ibid.* 3269; Bigland (Gt. Brit.) *v.* U. S., May 8, 1871, Hale's Rep. 161.

Interference with business gives no right to compensation. Grant (Gt. Brit.) *v.* U. S., May 8, 1871, Hale's Rep. 162; Kerford and Jenkins (Gt. Brit.) *v.* U. S., Feb. 8, 1853, Moore's Arb. 3788; Money (Gt. Brit.) *v.* U. S., May 8, 1871, Hale's Rep. 168; Heny (U. S.) *v.* Venezuela, Feb. 17, 1903, Ralston 14, 25; Dix (U. S.) *v.* Venezuela, *ibid.* 7; Genovese (U. S.) *v.* Venezuela, *ibid.* 174; Martini (Italy) *v.* Venezuela, Feb. 13, 1903, *ibid.* 819. Workmen of claimants compelled to serve in national guard. Siempre Viva (U. S.) *v.* Mexico, July 4, 1868, Moore's Arb. 3784; Cole (U. S.) *v.* Mexico, *ibid.* 3785, and similar awards there cited. Government may order suspension of traffic on railroad in war area. Great Venezuelan R. R. (Germany) *v.* Venezuela, Feb. 13,

Unauthorized pillage by uncontrollable soldiery has been almost uniformly considered to be a hazard of war and to relieve the government from liability.[42] A similar principle governs the wanton destruction of private property by unofficered soldiers.[43] The claimant has the burden of proving that the injury was committed by authority of commanding officers.[44]

Pillage is now formally prohibited by Article 47 of the Hague Regulations,[45] and under a broad interpretation of Article 3 of Convention IV of the Second Hague Conference, it is not improbable that pillage by unofficered soldiers of a regular army may be held to cast responsibility upon the State. Even property of enemies found on the battlefield may no longer be indiscriminately confiscated as booty.[46] Only military papers, arms, horses, carts, etc., may be appropriated as booty, although experience has shown that it is difficult to hold soldiers in check and carry out this regulation to the letter.

While the belligerent necessity for a particular destruction of private property is usually within the discretion of the commanding officer, international commissions may pass upon the legitimacy of war measures in a given case.[47] Thus awards have been made on numerous occasions for wanton and manifestly unnecessary acts of destruction and pillage by the military forces of the government.[48] The destruction of private

1903, Ralston, 640. And prohibit traffic of certain residents with towns in insurrection. Longstroth (U. S.) *v.* Mexico, July 4, 1868, Moore's Arb. 3784.

[42] Antrey (U. S.) *v.* Mexico, July 4, 1868, Moore's Arb. 3672; Dresch (U. S.) *v.* Mexico, *ibid.* 3669; Weil, *ibid.* 3671; Schlinger, *ibid.* 3671; Buentello (Mexico) *v.* U. S., *ibid.* 3670; Cole (U. S.) *v.* Mexico, *ibid.* 3670; Claims of Great Britain *v.* Chile, Sept. 26, 1893, La Fontaine, 455. Sen. Rep. 544, 55th Cong., 2nd sess. 6.

[43] Rule 3 of Nicaraguan Mixed Claims Com. 1911; Barclay (Gt. Brit.) *v.* U. S., May 8, 1871, Moore's Arb. 3678; burning of Columbia (Gt. Brit.) *v.* U. S., *ibid.* 3675.

[44] Weil (U. S.) *v.* Mexico, Moore's Arb. 3671; Michel, *ibid.* 3670.

[45] Oppenheim, II, sec. 143, sec. 213. See also Art. 7 of Convention IX of Second Hague Conference.

[46] See Art. 14 of Hague Regulations and Oppenheim, II, sec. 181.

[47] Rule 6 of Spanish Treaty Claims Commission. In Rules 7 and 8 the Commission prescribed definite limitations to concentration and devastation as legitimate war measures. Final Rep., p. 4. Award of the Commission in Tuinicú *v.* U. S., No. 240.

The opinion of the military authorities as to the necessity of a destruction is not ordinarily justiciable by the regular courts. Ex parte Marais (1902), A. C. 109. See also Wentworth *v.* U. S., 5 Ct. Cl. 309.

[48] Usually with respect to neutral's property. Quotations from publicists and state

property in war where no military end is served is illegitimate. This rule gained universal recognition during the nineteenth century, and it is now expressly provided by Article 23 (g) of the Hague Regulations that "to destroy * * * enemy's property, unless such destruction * * * be imperatively demanded by the necessities of war, is prohibited."

One of the most important results of this codification of the rules of war has been the enlargement of the sphere of immunity of private property on land from the injurious consequences of the war. Vattel, as already observed, was the first to draw a clear distinction between the injuries to property due to imperious and immediate military necessity, for which compensation is not generally due, and the more deliberate use of or injury to private property for some public belligerent purpose, analogous to eminent domain, for which the State owes compensation to the individual.[49] It has not always been easy to draw the line between imperious unavoidable necessity and a deliberate act of use, occupation or destruction involving an element of choice. Yet in a general way, international commissions have endeavored to maintain the distinction by making awards for various kinds and degrees of appropriation of private property for public belligerent purposes, and municipal legislation and courts have also recognized the distinction.

papers in Moore's Dig. VI, sec. 1037; Chourreau (France) *v.* U. S., Jan. 15, 1880, Moore's Arb. 3705; Du Bois (U. S.) *v.* Chile, Aug. 7, 1892, *ibid.* 3712; Moss (U. S.) *v.* Chile, May 24, 1897 (extending 1892 commission) Report, 1901, No. 25; Rule 5 of Span. Tr. Cl. Com.; S. B. Crandall in 4 A. J. I. L. 820; Award of King Oscar on Samoan claims of Germany against Great Britain and United States, Convention Nov. 7, 1899, La Fontaine, 613, for unwarranted military action; Strobel's Report, item V on British claims against Chile, For. Rel. 1896, 35 *et seq.*, Moore's Arb. 4930; Shrigley (U. S.) *v.* Chile, Aug. 7, 1892, Moore's Arb. 3711–12; Peruvian Indemnity, Mar. 17, 1841, Moore's Arb. 4591; Willet (U. S.) *v.* Venezuela, Dec. 5, 1885, *ibid.* 3743; Brooks (U. S.) *v.* Mexico, July 4, 1868, *ibid.* 3672; Johnston, *ibid.* 3673 (defendant government held to have burden of proving damage necessary); Jeannotat, *ibid.* 3673; H. Rep. 386, 22nd Cong., 1st sess. 14; *Indus* (U. S.) *v.* Mexico, Moore's Arb. 3718 (violation of rules of war by selling captured vessel without determination of prize courts). For extracts dealing with liability for violations of rules of civilized warfare, see Wharton's Digest, II, sec. 225. See Rule 18 of the Rules of the Institute of International Law on Naval Warfare adopted at Oxford, 1913.

[49] Vattel, Bk. III, ch. XV, sec. 232.

APPROPRIATION OF PRIVATE PROPERTY

A long line of decisions has established the principle that the appropriation of private property for military purposes involves the responsibility of the State.[50] That such a use justifies the taking is uniformly admitted. The rules relating to requisitions and contributions adopted at recent Hague Conferences, which will be examined presently, endeavor to give precision to the practice of appropriation of private property in belligerent territory. Under the present Hague Regulations private

[50] Mason *v.* U. S., 14 Ct. Cl. 59; Waters *v.* U. S., 4 Ct. Cl. 299; Kimball *v.* U. S., 5 *ibid.* 252; Heflebower *v.* U. S., 21 *ibid.* 228, 237; Grant *v.* U. S., 1 *ibid.* 41, 43–44 (a leading case). Sen. Rep. 544, 55th Cong., 2nd sess. 6. The Court of Claims has proceeded on the theory of implied contract and intention to pay. The U. S. Supreme Court leans more toward a direct theory of eminent domain. Mitchell *v.* Harmony, 13 Howard, 113, 134; U. S. *v.* Russell, 13 Wall. 36.

Saulnier (U. S.) *v.* Mexico, March 3, 1849, Moore's Arb. 3715; Hollenbeck (U. S.) *v.* Costa Rica, July 2, 1860, *ibid.* 3717 (building burned down in operations for defending town); Baker (U. S.) *v.* Mexico, July 4, 1868, *ibid.* 3668 (cattle and horses taken by Mexican army); Marks (U. S.) *v.* Mexico, *ibid.* 3722; Hall, *ibid.* 3722; Elliott, *ibid.* 3720; Bartlett, *ibid.* 3721; Cole, *ibid.* 3721; *The Macedonian* (U. S.) *v.* Chile, Nov. 10, 1858, *ibid.* 1465; cases cited in Hale's Rep. 44, Moore's Arb. 3688, Commission of May 8, 1871, and Henderson (Gt. Brit.) *v.* U. S., May 8, 1871, Moore's Arb. 3728, Wilkinson, *ibid.* 3736; Braithwaite, *ibid.* 3737; Adlam, *ibid.* 2552. Means (France) *v.* U. S., Jan. 15, 1880, Moore's Arb. 3706 (property destroyed in friendly territory to give better range to guns); Labrat (France) *v.* U. S., *ibid.* 3706; Shrigley (U. S.) *v.* Chile, Aug. 7, 1892, *ibid.* 3712; Dix (U. S.) *v.* Venezuela, Feb. 17, 1903, Ralston, 7; Kunhardt (U. S.) *v.* Venezuela, *ibid.* 63, 69; Spanish Treaty Cl. Com. Final Rep., May 2, 1910, p. 12 (allowances for property used by Spanish authorities, regardless of the purpose); Reyes, No. 153; Del Valle, No. 222, No. 278; Izuaga, No. 279; Constancia, No. 196.

See Act of April 9, 1816, sec. 5 (3 Stat. L. 261); Act of July 4, 1864 (13 Stat. L. 381). The Act of Mar. 3, 1871 (16 Stat. L. 524) establishing Southern Claims Commission provided that "stores and supplies furnished by or taken from loyal citizens in the insurrectionary states should be paid for." Conventions of July 4, 1868 with Mexico, May 8, 1871 with Great Britain, and Jan. 15, 1880 with France permitted of similar payments to subjects of those countries. But where the person or property was tainted with unneutral character no recovery was allowed. Davidson, No. 66, Hale's Rep. 43. See House Doc. 460, 56th Cong., 1st sess. 9; order of Sec'y of War, June 22, 1862, Moore's Arb. 1036; proclamation of the President, July 13, 1898; Sen. Doc. 318, 57th Cong., 1st sess., 19. See Abandoned or Captured Property Act, March 12, 1863 (12 Stat. L. 820), Moore's Dig. VI, 901 and Moore's Arb. 3745.

See also Lawrence's Rep. *supra;* Whiting's War Powers under the Constitution, p. 340; article by Wm. King, War Claims for Property, 20 Amer. Law Reg. (1881) 227, 233. See also a few pertinent extracts in Moore's Dig. VI, sec. 1034.

enemy real property can not be appropriated. Private movables which may serve as war material may be appropriated, but they must be restored at the conclusion of peace and indemnities paid (Article 53). They must be acknowledged by receipt, and as between the belligerents, the treaty of peace determines upon whom shall fall the duty of making compensation. Personal property other than war material may not as a rule be appropriated. Article 46 provides that "private property may not be confiscated." But under exceptional circumstances of necessity, where there is no time for ordinary requisitions of food, etc., or where the property has been abandoned by its owner, the belligerent may properly seize it.[51] It has already been noted that private enemy property found in belligerent territory at the outbreak of war or brought into it during the war may not be confiscated.

When the invading belligerent becomes a military occupant he is under still greater restrictions with respect to private property, which is subject to appropriation only under the rules governing requisitions and contributions.[52]

The use and occupation of buildings or real property in more than a temporary way and when not impelled by overruling military necessity has been held to involve the responsibility of the State,[53] and especially where the territory had come into the permanent possession of the occupying belligerent.[54] Loyal citizens in the Southern states during the Civil War were given the right, under the Abandoned or Captured Property Acts, to sue for the rents of their abandoned property covered into the Treasury. It has been held lawful to quarter troops on and occupy the property of active enemy subjects.[55] Under imperious mili-

[51] Oppenheim, II, p. 179 *et seq.* See the Bulgarian decree of Feb. 25, 1913 to the effect that private real property abandoned by its Mussulman owners would become the property of Bulgaria. This is contrary to Art. 46. 40 Clunet (1913), 1043.

[52] The military occupant's relation to public property is discussed by Oppenheim, II, sec. 134 *et seq.*

[53] H. Ex. Doc. 124, 43rd Cong., 1st sess.; U. S. *v.* Speed, 8 Wall. 83; Armendariz (Mexico) *v.* U. S., July 4, 1868, Moore's Arb. 3722; Willet (U. S.) *v.* Venezuela, Dec. 5, 1885, *ibid.* 3743.

[54] Crutchett (Gt. Brit.) *v.* U. S., May 8, 1871, Hale's Rep. 46, Moore's Arb. 3734. Other similar cases cited in Moore's Arb. 3735.

[55] German practice in Franco-Prussian War, Bentwich, 33. See also Gonzales (Mexico) *v.* U. S., July 4, 1868, Moore's Arb. 2824; Opin. of Judge Adv.-Gen., How-

tary necessity, a belligerent may without indemnification use both public and private buildings and convert them into hospitals, barracks, stables and fortifications, as occasion requires.[56]

The government has been held liable on numerous occasions for such a use and occupation of private neutral property as to expose it specially to the fire of and destruction by the enemy.[57] This rule extends only to property occupied in advance of actual fighting, rather than such as is occupied during an attack or retreat. It is the seizure of private property for the public use and its loss and destruction while so employed, that warrants an indemnity to the owner.

It has been noted that when military necessity in the presence of the enemy demands the immediate destruction of property to prevent its falling into the enemy's hands no liability is incurred by the belligerent. The line between overruling necessity in the face of immediate danger and deliberate destruction for the ultimate end of preventing its capture by the enemy is often exceedingly vague, so that courts and commissions in numerous cases have considered such destruction under the latter head as an appropriation of private property for the public use and have awarded indemnities to the owner.[58] To justify its destruction without title to indemnity, the danger of its capture by the enemy must be immediate and impending.

The cutting of privately-owned cables connecting occupied territory with neutral territory, when a military necessity, was considered, before

land, 250 and 253. (In Civil War, residents in insurrectionary states had to prove their loyalty; in Philippines, government had to prove native's disloyalty.)

[56] Oppenheim, II, secs. 136, 140.

[57] Putegnat's Heirs (U. S.) *v.* Mexico, July 4, 1868, Moore's Arb. 3718, 3720,—other cases cited p. 3720; Bowen (U. S.) *v.* Mexico, *ibid.* 3731; Willet (U. S.) *v.* Venezuela, Dec. 5, 1885, *ibid.* 3743; Amer. Elec. and Mfg. Co. (U. S.) *v.* Venezuela, Feb. 13, 1903, Ralston, 35; Petrocelli (Italy) *v.* Venezuela, Feb. 13, 1903, *ibid.* 762; Matamoras Fire Claims (Gt. Brit.) *v.* Mexico, 52 St. Pap. 281; H. Rep. 386, 22nd Cong., 1st sess. 3, 9, 12; 3 Stat. L. 263, sec. 9; 3 Stat. L. 397, sec. 1. See opinion of Judge Adv.-Gen. Sept. 4, 1902, *contra*, Howland, 253.

[58] Grant *v.* U. S., 1 Ct. Cl. 41; Wiggins *v.* U. S., 3 Ct. Cl. 412; Mitchell *v.* Harmony, 13 Howard, 115; Turner (Gt. Brit.) *v.* U. S., May 8, 1871, Moore's Arb. 3684; Anderson and Thompson (U. S.) *v.* Mexico, July 4, 1868, *ibid.* 2479; Barrington (U. S.) *v.* Mexico, July 4, 1868, *ibid.* 3674; Bertrand (France) *v.* U. S., Jan. 15, 1880, *ibid.* 3705; *The Phare* (France) *v.* Nicaragua, Award of French court of cassation, *ibid.* 4870 at 4873.

the First Hague Conference, as not to afford a legal ground for a claim to indemnity.[59] The view of the United States was that such cables were exposed to the risks of war, as was other neutral property, in which view it was confirmed by Article XV of the Convention of March 14, 1884 for the protection of submarine cables, which left the belligerents freedom of action.[60] But in considering the claims for neutral cables cut by United States forces in Cuba and the Philippines during the Spanish-American War, the President recommended their payment by Congress as a matter of equity, and several claims were accordingly paid.[61] Article 54 of the Hague Regulations provides that cables connecting occupied enemy territory with neutral territory shall not be seized or destroyed, except in case of absolute necessity, in which event the cables must be restored at the conclusion of peace and indemnities paid.[62]

Embargo, or the detention of private property, meant originally only the detention of vessels in port. The term has been used in several senses: (1) as a form of reprisal by which enemy merchantmen in belligerent ports were formerly confiscated, (2) the detention of vessels to prevent the spread of important military information, and (3) the right, better known as angary, to use and if necessary, destroy neutral vessels temporarily in a belligerent port. The United States in its treaty of 1795 with Spain stipulated that "Citizens * * * shall not be liable to any embargo or detention * * * for any military expedition, or other public or private purpose whatever." [63] This inhibition of embargo has been held to extend to property on land as well as to vessels and their cargoes.[64] In former times, it was a common practice for

[59] Atty. Gen. Griggs, 22 Op. Atty. Gen. 654.

[60] See also Art. 5 of the U. S. Naval War Code.

[61] See quotations and citations in Moore's Dig. VI, 924–926 and H. Rep. 8, 57th Cong., 1st sess., pp. 1, 2, 5, 8 and S. Doc. 16, 58th Cong., 2nd sess., pp. 6, 10, 22, 23.

[62] Oppenheim, II, sec. 214. See Rule 54 of the Rules of the Institute of International Law on naval warfare adopted at Oxford, 1913.

[63] A somewhat similar clause is contained in Art. 7 of the treaty of 1828 with Brazil.

[64] Macias (U. S.) *v.* Spain, Feb. 12, 1871, Moore's Arb. 3775; Thompson, *ibid.* 3779; Rivas, *ibid.* 3780. The cases of embargo under the decree of 1869 in Cuba are discussed in Moore's Arb. 3754 *et seq.* Indemnities for similar embargoes were provided for in the unratified Strobel-Figuera agreement of May 3, 1887. For the embargoes under decree of 1896 and the embargo claims arising out of the 1895–1898

belligerents to lay an embargo on enemy merchantmen in their ports at the outbreak of war. Article 1 of Convention VI of the Second Hague Conference provides that it is *desirable* that an enemy merchantman in port be allowed freely to depart, and it is probable that only for grave reasons will a belligerent now detain an enemy merchantman. Such vessels as are detained may not be confiscated, but must either be returned, without indemnity, at the end of the war or may be requisitioned on payment of compensation (Article 2). The same rule applies to vessels which left their last port before the outbreak of war, and while ignorant of the war, are met at sea by a belligerent war vessel (Article 3).[65] As in modern days vessels rarely remain ignorant of war for any length of time, this apparent exemption from capture is likely to be illusory.

The right of belligerents in case of necessity, for belligerent purposes, to detain, use, or even destroy neutral property not vested with enemy character is known as the right of angary, a modern development of the former *jus angariæ*.[66] The payment of indemnity is a necessary condition of such use of neutral property. The application of this rule has generally arisen through the detention, use or destruction of neutral vessels temporarily in the ports of a belligerent.[67]

Requisitions and contributions are a modern survival of the old usage of spoliation and confiscation. They are levies of supplies and money

Cuban insurrection, see Moore's Dig. VI, 908–914 and cases of Hernsheim, No. 297, Bauriedel, No. 239, and Gato, No. 171, before the Spanish Treaty Cl. Com. See also Rule 10 of that commission.

[65] Oppenheim, II, secs. 40, 102a. See full discussion in Scott, Hague Conferences, 556–568. The United States is not a signatory of this convention. Contrary to the general practice, Turkey, which has not ratified Convention VI, seized some Italian vessels in Turkish ports at the outbreak of the Turko-Italian war of 1911. 15 *R. D. I.* (1913) 577.

[66] Oppenheim, II, sec. 364; Westlake, II, 119; Hall, 741; U. S. Naval War Code, Art. 6.

[67] *Labuan* (Gt. Brit.) *v.* U. S., May 8, 1871, Moore's Arb. 3791; *Ophir* (U. S.) *v.* Mexico, April 11, 1839, *ibid.* 3045; Brig *Splendid* (U. S.) *v.* Mexico, *ibid.* 3714; Kidder (U. S.) *v.* Mexico, March 3, 1849, Opin. 519 (not in Moore); Orr and Laubenheimer (U. S.) *v.* Nicaragua, March 22, 1900, For. Rel. 1900, 824, 829; The *Moshona* and the *Beatrice* (U. S.) *v.* Great Britain, For. Rel. 1900, 529–618; The *Tabasqueno v.* U. S., For. Rel. 1907, 614 (neutral cargo is in the same position as the neutral vessel); U. S. *v.* Russell, 13 Wall. 623 (implied contract in municipal law). See the celebrated case of the sinking by German troops of British vessels in the Seine, 1870, in which indemnity was paid. 61 St. Pap. 575, 600, 611 and Moore's Dig. VI, 904.

made by a belligerent on the theory that he may make his enemy pay for the continuation of the war. They are imposed usually in territory under military occupation, although requisitions may also be levied by an army on the march. By municipal law, States often levy requisitions upon their own subjects, but this is generally conditioned upon payment of proper indemnities. While the property of neutral aliens useful for military purposes, such as horses or automobiles, is subject to requisition, the national governments of these aliens may properly insist upon payment in cash, or else acknowledgment by receipt with a view to future payment. It is also proper to insist that there be no discriminatory treatment of the subjects of any one foreign nation.

When exercised by a belligerent upon enemy territory, the unrestricted right of requisitions and contributions is too apt to become an indirect means of spoliation, and the Regulations adopted at the Hague Conferences are intended, first, to limit the right to immediate military necessities, and secondly, to prevent the burden falling upon the individual alone, but rather to distribute it equally over the population as a whole. Article 52 of the Hague Regulations provides that "neither requisitions in kind, nor services, can be demanded from localities or inhabitants except for the needs of the army of occupation. They must be in proportion to the resources of the country. * * * Supplies in kind shall as far as possible be paid for on the spot; if not, the fact that they have been taken shall be established by receipts." [68] In addition only the local commander, and not individual officers or soldiers, may order requisitions. Quartering is a special kind of requisition, which comes under the general rule.

The great weakness of these Regulations is that no definite limitation is imposed upon a military commander, and the owner of private property is only in a little less precarious condition than heretofore. There is no guide to what may be considered "the needs of the army of occupation," and because of the fact that payment need be made only "as far as possible," the right of indemnity is problematical. It is true that receipts evidence the exaction of goods, but no promise to pay is implied, either by the occupant or the occupied country. The treaty of peace

[68] Bentwich, 34; Albrecht, *Requisitionen von neutralem Privateigentum*, Breslau, 1912, p. 1 *et seq.;* Oppenheim, II, sec. 146 *et seq.;* Westlake, II, 96 *et seq.*

may settle the question of payment, but if left open, the owner is dependent on the bounty of his government, unless as in France the law provides that the individual shall have an action against the commune for reimbursement of requisitions.[69]

Contributions are a further menace to private property. They consist in the levy of money upon the inhabitants of occupied territory, in excess of the produce of regular taxes. The Hague Regulations (Articles 49–51) have endeavored to prevent extortionate demands amounting to spoliation, by systematizing and limiting the right to levy contributions. They may be levied for the needs of the army only or of the administration of the occupied territory. This is to operate as a check upon pillage. Again, the contributions must be levied on the written order and on the responsibility of a commander-in-chief, and not merely of a local commander. They must not be imposed indiscriminately, but must follow the assessment rolls, and receipts must be given.[70] These limitations upon the levy of contributions do not prevent a belligerent from imposing fines upon inhabitants who commit acts of hostility against him, or disobey his commands. Under such circumstances, private property may even be confiscated. This is forfeiture, rather than appropriation. The belligerent may no longer properly, however, "inflict a general penalty, pecuniary or otherwise, on the population on account of violent acts for which it can not be regarded as collectively responsible." [71]

A belligerent government often levies forced loans upon its own subjects immediately before or during the war, and resident neutrals are equally liable to such payment. The United States in 1868 in a case in Italy admitted that its citizens resident abroad are subject to these exactions, on the condition that they be levied on all the inhabitants impartially and in just proportions.[72] On the other hand, the United States

[69] Dalloz, Supplement XV, 1895, p. 459; 21 *Journ. du Dr. Administratif* (1873), 171–187; 37 Clunet (1910), 255, case in Chile. A French law of July, 1909, makes automobiles the subject of requisition, regardless of the nationality of the owners. See proceedings against John Morris, a British subject, noted in Jan. 1914, *Journ. of the Soc. of Comp. Leg.*, p. 283.

[70] Bentwich, 36; Oppenheim, II, sec. 148.

[71] Hague Regulations, Art. 50; Bentwich, 37.

[72] Moore's Dig. VI, 916. Although British subjects were protected by treaty

has protested against the usage on several occasions, or at least insisted upon repayment.[73] Well-ordered countries do not levy forced loans. Mexico has resorted to the practice on several occasions, and numerous claims of this kind have come before arbitral commissions between the United States and Mexico. The commissions of 1839, 1849 (domestic), and 1868 (until Thornton became umpire), considered forced loans illegal, and made awards in favor of the claimants.[74] When Thornton succeeded Dr. Lieber as umpire of the 1868 commission, he held forced loans to be legal, and that if equally distributed amongst all the inhabitants, without discrimination in the exaction or the reimbursement between native and foreigner, even if neither are repaid, there is no ground of complaint.[75] Transient aliens are not subject to forced loans.[76] Umpire Thornton also expressed the opinion that treaties exempting the citizens of certain countries from forced loans merely prevented a discriminatory exaction against those citizens, but that they are subject to such loans equally with other inhabitants.[77] The United States, in numerous treaties with foreign countries, has stipulated for the exemption of its citizens from forced loans.

against forced loans, it seems Mr. Seward would have regarded their exemption as a discrimination against U. S. citizens who enjoyed no such treaty exemption. See also McManus (U. S.) *v.* Mexico, July 4, 1868, Moore's Arb. 3411, 3415 and Rose (U. S.) *v.* Mexico, *ibid.* 3417, 3421.

[73] Mr. Bayard, Sec'y of State, to Mr. Buck, Min. to Peru, May 20, 1886, Moore's Dig. VI, 918; Mr. Fish, Sec'y of State, to Mr. Foster, Min. to Mexico, Aug. 15, 1873, *ibid.* 917.

[74] Ducoing (U. S.) *v.* Mexico, April 11, 1839, Moore's Arb. 3409; Homan (U. S.) *v.* Mexico, March 3, 1849, *ibid.* 3409; Robinson (U. S.) *v.* Mexico, *ibid.* 3410, and other cases cited on p. 3410; Moke (U. S.) *v.* Mexico, July 4, 1868, *ibid.* 3411 (opinion by Wadsworth, Amer. commissioner). See also Beckman (Germany) *v.* Venezuela, Feb. 13, 1903, Ralston, 599 and De Caro (Italy) *v.* Venezuela, Feb. 13, 1903, *ibid.* 818.

[75] McManus (U. S.) *v.* Mexico, July 4, 1868, Moore's Arb. 3411, 3415; Rose (U. S.) *v.* Mexico, *ibid.* 3417, 3421; Cole, *ibid.* 3422 and cases cited p. 3423. But he awarded indemnities when the exaction of the loan was enforced by arrest and imprisonment, as he believed there must have been means of enforcing payment by judicial proceedings.

[76] Weil (U. S.) *v.* Mexico, July 4, 1868, Moore's Arb. 3424, Thornton, Umpire.

[77] Moore's Arb. 3416.

WAR AT SEA

With respect to war at sea, only a few rules have thus far been formulated at The Hague.[78] As contrasted with land warfare, one of the most important phenomena of maritime war is the difference between private enemy and neutral property. Notwithstanding the efforts of the United States, enemy merchantmen and enemy cargo in such vessels are still subject to seizure.[79] Neutral property, however, since the Declaration of Paris, enjoys a considerable range of immunity from seizure, which extends, in the case of vessels, to enemy goods on board, with the exception of contraband, and in the case of goods, exempts them from seizure, if not contraband, even under the enemy flag. Convention VIII of the Second Hague Conference provides for certain methods of legitimate attack upon and capture of enemy merchantmen. Any violation of these rules on the part of ratifying Powers would involve the responsibility of the State, and in the case of neutral property injured thereby, would give rise to international reclamation. Certain kinds of enemy vessels, however, are immune from seizure, *e. g.*, those engaged in scientific discovery, and fishing boats and small vessels engaged in local trade.[80] Merchantmen bound for enemy ports in ignorance of the outbreak of the war may not be confiscated if still ignorant at the time of capture, but they may be detained on condition that they be restored at the end of the war or indemnity paid if used or destroyed. There is no general rule as to the exemption of mail-boats, this matter being usually agreed upon in special treaties, but enemy mail bags are immune from seizure.[81]

Although neutral property enjoys a considerable measure of immunity from seizure it is still in many respects subject to molestation in war, by virtue of the belligerent's right of self-preservation. The belligerent's

[78] The Institute of International Law, at its Oxford meeting in 1913, adopted a code of naval warfare. 15 *R. D. I.* n. s. (1913), 677 *et seq.*

[79] The history of private property at sea is discussed by Oppenheim, II, sec. 176 and by Bentwich, ch. VII. See also Loreburn, R., Capture at Sea, London, 1913.

[80] It seems that Turkey did not observe these rules in her recent war with Italy, 15 *R. D. I.* (1913), 577–578. Turkey has not ratified the Hague Convention.

[81] Oppenheim, II, sec. 186. It is obviously beyond the scope of this article to enter into the details of the conduct of maritime warfare and its related questions, including neutrality. These matters are fully discussed in the more important works on international law and in special treatises.

right of interference with neutral commerce falls under the three heads of contraband, blockade and unneutral service. Under the first, he may under certain conditions, confiscate neutral property which may aid his enemy or interfere with his military operations; [82] under the second, he may forbid neutrals to have any communication with such part of his enemy's maritime frontier as he can effectually watch, confiscation being the penalty for an attempt to run a legitimately established blockade; [83] and under the third, he may forbid neutral vessels from rendering certain services which may directly assist his enemy.[84] To give effect to these rights, the belligerent's cruisers may visit and search, and detain any suspected neutral vessel, and his sanction is the power to confiscate the offending vessel or cargo after it has been condemned in the belligerent's prize court.[85] By resistance to the belligerent's right of visit and search, the neutral constructively assumes enemy character and becomes subject to capture and confiscation. If a suspected vessel is found innocent by a prize court, she is only entitled to compensation if there was no probable cause for her detention.[86]

The belligerent may, subject to the limitations established by acknowledged principles of international law, fix upon the articles which he will regard as contraband, and compel neutrals to respect his decision, under penalty of confiscation. There are certain international rules which have been adopted and have received general sanction at recent Conferences, particularly the London Naval Conference of 1908, and certain well-established principles of prize law, which belligerents can disregard only at the risk of international reclamation. For example, the seizure of conditional contraband such as foodstuffs, without evidence of its destination for hostile military use, under a presumption that its consignment to enemy commercial ports is proof of its intended military use, is an

[82] The intricate rules governing contraband carriage, which have been much simplified by the Declaration of London, will be found discussed in Oppenheim, II, sec. 391 and in the special works cited by him at the head of Chapter IV.

[83] Oppenheim, II, secs. 368–390.

[84] *Ibid.*, II, secs. 407–413.

[85] Bentwich, 108.

[86] Bentwich, 109 and cases cited. See also the *Eastry* (Gt. Brit.) *v.* Japan, Takahashi, S., International Law Applied to the Russo-Japanese War, New York, 1908, pp. 358, 739.

abuse of belligerent and a violation of neutral rights and has afforded ground for diplomatic claims.[87] Vessels violating the belligerent's contraband regulations or his interpretation, on facts or law, of his right of capture, are tried in his municipal prize courts; but as the decisions of these courts are not necessarily binding on neutral nations, the latter have often successfully brought international claims against erroneous condemnations by municipal prize courts.[88]

[87] See *e. g.*, *Arabia* (U. S.) *v.* Russia, For. Rel. 1904 and 1905 and MS. Dept. of State, 1911; and *Antiope* (U. S.) *v.* Japan, MS. Dept. of State, 1911–1913. Belligerents have frequently violated the rule that a presumption of innocent use attaches to conditional contraband not consigned to a military base or destination and that the burden lies upon the captor to prove, and not upon the cargo owner to disprove, its intended hostile military use. Legal presumptions and the burden of proof play an exceedingly important part in claims arising out of captures on account of contraband. The designation of provisions as absolute contraband evoked earnest protests from neutrals during the Russo-Japanese war. Bon, Louis, *La guerre Russo-Japonaise et la neutralité*, Montpelier, 1909, p. 227.

[88] See, *e. g.*, the recent award of the Hague court, May 6, 1913, in the case of the *Carthage* (France) *v.* Italy, Jan. 26 and Mar. 6, 1912, 7 A. J. I. L. 623, in which Italy was held liable in damages for the capture and detention of a neutral vessel and the confiscation of an aeroplane on board, the seizure having been made without sufficient grounds to assert the hostile destination of the aeroplane. Hostile destination being a condition of contraband, the most important difference between absolute and conditional contraband lies in the presumptions of hostile use arising out of its consignment. Thus absolute contraband consigned to enemy territory is presumed to be destined for hostile military use, and the doctrine of continuous voyage applies. Conditional contraband, on the other hand, is presumed to have a non-hostile destination unless consigned to the military arm of the government, directly or indirectly, and the captor has the burden of overcoming the presumption. Oppenheim, II, § 395; Hirschmann, Otto, *Das internationale Prisenrecht*, München, 1912, § 38. The generally accepted rule now is that the doctrine of continuous voyage does not apply to conditional contraband. Again, goods found in an enemy's ship are presumed to be enemy's property. The neutral must prove its neutral ownership, the evidence required depending upon the nature of the case. The matter of ownership is often a determining issue in prize cases. In the case of the *Manouba* (France) *v.* Italy, Jan. 26 and Mar. 6, 1912, Hague Court of Arbitration, indemnity was awarded for the capture and detention of a vessel having on board certain suspected enemy soldiers, the ground of award being that no demand for their surrender had been made. See also cases reported in Moore's Arb. 3843–3885.

The impartial student of international law must have greeted with astonishment Great Britain's recent radical departure from the accepted principles of maritime law in war, a course grievously subversive of the rights of neutrals. It seems inconceivable that Great Britain could have expected neutral nations to consent to the

Since the Declaration of Paris of 1856 a blockade to be binding must be effective, which means, according to the Anglo-American practice, that the force maintaining the blockade must be sufficient to make it dangerous for neutrals to enter. Thus the interference with neutral commerce by the establishment of a paper blockade of ports in the hands of insurgents has in numerous cases been held to involve the responsibility of the State.[89] Similarly, erroneous notice of the blockade of a port causing an abandonment of the voyage was held to justify an award.[90] The rules relating to notice must be strictly followed, except in the case

practical abrogation of the distinction between absolute and conditional contraband in the matter of hostile and innocent destination, and of the presumptions thereto attaching, as well as the remarkable enlargement of the contraband lists. The Order in Council of October 29, 1914 provides that notwithstanding the provisions of Art. 35 of the Declaration of London, which renders conditional contraband liable to capture only if destined "for the use of the armed forces or of a government department of the enemy state," conditional contraband "shall be liable to capture on board a vessel bound for a neutral port if the goods are consigned 'to order,' or if the ship's papers do not show who is the consignee of the goods or if they show a consignee of the goods in territory belonging to or occupied by the enemy." Moreover, "the owner of the goods" must "prove that their destination was innocent." Not only has the immunity of conditional contraband from the application of the doctrine of continuous voyages been practically set aside, but conditional contraband bound for *any* neutral port, if consigned "to order" is confiscable. Moreover, the established rule that the captor has the burden of proving the hostile destination of conditional contraband, a rule which Great Britain earnestly supported during and after the Russo-Japanese War, has been completely reversed by the Order. It is interesting to compare Sir Edward Grey's contention in the *Oldhamia* case against Russia, Jan. 4 and Aug. 22, 1910. Misc. No. 1, 1912, Cd. 6011, pp. 15–17. Great Britain has left very little on the non-contraband list. In addition, if a neutral vessel has proceeded to an enemy port with false papers, she is liable to capture and condemnation "if she is encountered before the end of her *next* voyage." Unless neutral governments have acquiesced in these Napoleonic restrictions upon neutral commerce, and thereby estopped themselves from supporting diplomatic claims of their citizens sustaining injury by these violations of international law, it would seem that Great Britain is laying the ground for a large number of just pecuniary claims by neutral nations on behalf of their citizens.

[89] Comp. Gen. des Asphaltes (Gt. Brit.) *v.* Venezuela, Feb. 13, 1903, Ralston, 331, 336; Orinoco Asphalt Co. (Germany) *v.* Venezuela, *ibid.* 586; De Caro (Italy) *v.* Venezuela, *ibid.* 810; Martini, *ibid.* 819, and cases before the Anglo-Chilean Tribunal of 1893; Williamson, Balfour (Gt. Brit.) *v.* Chile, Recl. pres. al Trib. Anglo-Chileno, III, 335; *St. Mary's Bay, ibid.* 557.

[90] *Bayne, Monmouth* and *Hilja* (Gt. Brit.) *v.* U. S., May 8, 1871, Moore's Arb. 3923–3928.

of a vessel having an intention to run a blockade.[91] The penalty for violation of the blockade is confiscation of vessel and cargo, for knowledge of the owner of the cargo is presumed. Numerous international claims have been brought against the decisions of prize courts having condemned and confiscated vessels for violation of a blockade.[92]

Prize courts are established in the interests of neutrals and belligerents. The belligerents wish to be protected by a decision of these municipal courts, instituted by themselves, against the claims of neutrals based on alleged unjustifiable captures. Numerous claims have been paid on account of unlawful seizures of neutral vessels or cargo, when the prize court held the seizure to have been illegal and without probable cause.[93] As prize courts are municipal courts interpreting international law, their judgments are not necessarily internationally binding.[94] Indemnities have frequently been awarded by arbitral courts or have been arranged through diplomatic settlements on claims arising out of wrongful condemnations by national prize courts.[95] By Convention XII of the Second Hague Conference, as yet unratified, an international prize court to serve as a court of appeal from decisions of national prize courts was provided for.[96]

[91] Hale's Rep. 127. See Portendic claims in which France was held liable for failure to properly notify a blockade. 30 St. Pap. 581; 34 *ibid.* 1036; 42 *ibid.* 1377; Moore's Arb. 4937, and note in Lapradelle's *Recueil*, p. 538.

[92] Moore's Arb. 3885–3923.

[93] See, *e. g.*, cases of the British schooners *E. R. Nickerson* and *Wary*, illegally seized during war with Spain, Sen. Doc. 396, 57th Cong., 1st sess., 32 Stat. L. 552; *The Eastry* (Gt. Brit.) *v.* Japan, Takahashi, *op. cit.* 739, 358; *Manouba* (France) *v.* Italy, *supra*, 7 A. J. I. L. 629. Certain cases reported in Moore's Arb., ch. LXVI, p. 3815 *et seq.*

[94] As between private parties, the decree of a prize court is a judgment in a proceeding *in rem*, and hence is conclusive against all the world as to matters within its jurisdiction. Cushing *v.* Laird, 107 U. S. 69.

[95] Certain cases in Moore's Arb., ch. LXVI, p. 3815 *et seq.* and cases in Russo-Japanese War, Takahashi, *op. cit.*

See also treaties between United States and Venezuela, May 1, 1852, Malloy, II, 1842; United States and Two Sicilies, Oct. 14, 1832, 20 St. Pap. 277; France and Brazil, Aug. 21, 1828, 15 St. Pap. 1242; United States and Portugal, Jan. 19, 1832, 19 St. Pap. 1379; Great Britain and Brazil, May 5, 1829, 18 St. Pap. 689; France and United States, July 4, 1831, Moore's Arb. 4447–4485.

[96] Oppenheim, sec. 192; Scott, J. B., The Hague Peace Conferences, ch. X, pp. 465–511.

A captured merchant vessel may not as a rule be destroyed instead of being conducted to a port of a prize court, since the transfer of title only becomes final after adjudication by a prize court. The few exceptions to this rule are based upon necessity, each country having its own regulations. A frequent justification for destruction is the unseaworthy condition of the prize which prevents sending her in for adjudication, or the inability of the captor to spare a prize crew.[97] If the capture is subsequently held by a prize court to have been lawful, the neutral owner of goods on the destroyed vessel has no claim to indemnity.[98]

The seizure by a belligerent of an enemy or neutral vessel or cargo within the territorial waters of a neutral Power has given rise to numerous cases before prize courts. It is clear that such violation of neutral territory renders the belligerent liable to the neutral, and the latter may rightfully demand the restitution of the captured vessel.[99] Lord Stowell and Justice Story in several prize cases decided in the early part of the nineteenth century, held that the claim for restitution could be made by the neutral government only,[100] and not by the captured vessel, for as between the belligerents the capture was rightful.[101] However, the British-American Mixed Commission of 1871, in passing upon the claim of the *Sir William Peel,* which was decided adversely to the vessel by the

[97] See Oppenheim, sec. 194, in which numerous grounds are stated which have justified destruction. Under the Oxford rules of the Institute of International Law (1913), destruction is only permitted if the safety of the captor ship or the success of actual present military operations requires it (Art. 104). In Arts. 107, 113 and 114 indemnities are provided for in case the capture, seizure or destruction is held unwarranted.

[98] Oppenheim, sec. 194. But see probable effect of Art. 3 of Convention XII, Scott, 485.

[99] Art. 3 of Convention XIII of the Second Hague Conference makes it obligatory upon such neutral Power to "employ the means at its disposal to release the prize with its officers and crew." Oppenheim, II, sec. 360; Scott, I, 620, *et seq.* See *The Florida,* 101 U. S. 37, a Confederate cruiser seized by United States in territorial waters of Brazil. On the reparation made to Brazil, see Moore's Dig. VII, 1090. See also *The Chesapeake,* Moore's Dig. VII, 937, and cases mentioned in same volume, § 1334.

[100] The *Diligentia,* 1 Dodson, 412; *Eliza Anne,* 1 Dodson, 244 (dictum); The *Anna,* 5 Rob. 373; The *Sir William Peel,* 5 Wall. 517; The *Anne,* 3 Wheat. 447. See also Dana's Wheaton, sec. 430 and note; the *Twee Gebroeders,* 3 Rob. 162, and Oppenheim, II, sec. 362.

[101] The *Anne,* 3 Wheat. 447; The *Sir William Peel,* 5 Wall. 517.

United States Supreme Court, held that a neutral vessel could institute a claim for capture in neutral waters, regardless of any protest by the territorial neutral.[102] Affirmative duties are now incumbent upon a neutral to prevent any violation of his neutrality by a belligerent seizure in his territorial waters, for a breach of which his own responsibility may properly be invoked.[103] In land warfare, injuries inflicted by belligerents in permitting bullets to fall into neutral territory, constitute a violation of the territorial sovereignty of the neutral and justify international reclamation against the wrongdoing belligerents. Violations of a nation's neutrality by a belligerent entails international responsibility.

NEUTRAL OBLIGATIONS

The state of war casts upon neutrals numerous duties incident to the maintenance of neutrality, for a violation of which duties liability is incurred either toward the belligerent or toward neutrals who sustain injury thereby.[104] A neutral must prevent a belligerent from setting up prize courts on his neutral territory. This practice was not considered illegitimate in the eighteenth century, but after the United States in 1793 had refused permission to France to set up prize courts in United States territory, it became the recognized rule that such a use of neutral territory by belligerents is a violation of neutrality and entails responsibility on the part of the neutral.[105] This rule is confirmed by Article 4 of Convention XIII of the Second Hague Conference.[106]

[102] The *Sir William Peel* (Gt. Brit.) *v.* U. S., May 8, 1871, Moore's Arb. 3948; Lawrence's Wheaton, 2nd ed., 716.

[103] Oppenheim, II, secs. 360–363. See Commodore Stewart's case, 1 Ct. Cl. 113.

[104] It will not be possible to refer to these duties in any detail. These obligations of neutrals are now largely codified in Convention V of the Second Hague Conference respecting the rights and duties of neutral powers and persons in war on land and in Convention XIII concerning the rights and duties of neutral powers in maritime war. See Scott, Hague Peace Conferences, I, 541, *et seq.*, 620, *et seq.*; Oppenheim, II, sec. 313, *et seq.*; Westlake, II, 117–119, 284–287, 321–331; Dupuis, *Le Droit de la guerre maritime*, Paris, 1912, ch. 12. On Convention V, see A. S. de Bustamente in 2 A. J. I. L. (1908), 95–120. Einicke, P., *Rechte und Pflichten der neutralen Mächte im Seekrieg*. Tübingen, 1912.

[105] Wheaton, as representative of the United States, obtained heavy indemnities from Denmark for such breaches of neutrality during the Napoleonic Wars. Treaty

[106] Oppenheim, II, sec. 327.

As far as lies in his power, a neutral must prevent a belligerent man-of-war from cruising within his territorial waters for the purpose of capturing enemy vessels leaving his ports. It has already been observed that a neutral must use diligence to prevent hostilities being carried on in his territorial waters, and that an enemy attacked may invoke this neutral protection, for a failure to extend which the neutral is liable.[107]

One of the most important duties which the obligation of impartiality makes incumbent upon neutrals is the use of "due diligence"—in Articles 8 and 25 of Convention XIII, it reads "the means at [their] disposal"—to prevent their subjects from building and fitting out vessels within their jurisdiction or the departure of vessels intended for warlike purposes, and to prevent either belligerent from making use of neutral ports as a base of naval operations.[108]

While a neutral Power incurs no responsibility from the fact that individuals leave its territory to enlist in the service of a belligerent, it is responsible if it permits enlistment on its territory by either of the belligerents.[109] It is also bound to use due diligence to prevent hostile expeditions from being organized in its territory to operate against either belligerent.[110] A neutral Power, however, is not bound to prevent the export or transit of arms or anything which may be of use to an army or fleet.[111] Such trade is merely subject to the belligerent rights of cap-

of March 28, 1830, Moore's Arb. 4549–4573. Spain was similarly held liable under the Florida treaty of Feb. 22, 1819, Moore's Arb. 4487, 4513. The United States assumed heavy liabilities under Art. 7 of the Jay treaty of Nov. 19, 1794, for such use of its territory by France. Moore's Arb. 3967, *et seq.*, 3981.

[107] But where the claimant vessel began the hostilities upon her captor, she forfeits neutral protection. The *Anne*, 3 Wheat. 435. The claim of the *Brig Armstrong* (U. S.) *v.* Portugal, attacked by a British vessel in Fayal, was dismissed because the brig had failed to notify the Portuguese authorities of the necessity of protection and that they were not physically in a position to protect. Moore's Arb. 1071–1132. The decision has been severely criticized. Lapradelle and Politis, *Recueil*, I, 650, *et seq.*

[108] These obligations had their origin in the Three Rules of Washington, applied in the Geneva Arbitration. Moore's Arb. 4057–4178. See Convention XIII, 2nd Hague Conference, Arts. 6, *et seq.*; Hershey, ch. XXXI.

[109] Arts. 4 and 6 of Convention V. The United States and British neutrality laws which prohibit citizens and subjects from enlisting within the jurisdiction (or by British law, even without his Majesty's Dominions) exceed the requirements of international law.

[110] But its negligence must be clearly proved. See cases in Moore's Arb. 4027–4056.

[111] Art. 7 of Convention V.

ture as contraband, the neutral State incurring no responsibility in the matter.

STATE INDEMNITY

It remains merely to note that it is becoming a growing practice for nations to alleviate the individual losses sustained during war, for which no legal liability is incurred, by making voluntary awards of indemnity as a matter of grace and favor, in order to distribute the loss equally over the whole nation. This beneficent practice was begun by France in 1792 and other states have from time to time followed this worthy example.[112] The statute making the appropriation may limit the classes of the beneficiaries as the State deems best, so that occasionally foreigners have not been included among those indemnified. By treaty, diplomatic arrangement or arbitral convention the Latin-American States and certain others among the weaker countries have at times been compelled by the nations of Europe to assume a heavy liability, beyond that required by the strict rules of law, for injuries sustained by aliens during war.[113]

[112] France, law of Aug. 11, 1792, Feb. 27, 1793, Nys, III, 456, 458; Law of Sept. 6, 1871, July 28, 1874 and Aug. 16, 1876, 65 St. Pap. 71 and 621; For. Rel. 1884, 357. Bentwich, pp. 42–43, cites various cases of voluntary indemnities in France, Germany, Italy and Great Britain. Germany in 1871 extended the indemnity to Germans and to subjects of such neutral States only as promised reciprocal treatment in a similar case. Moore's Dig. VI, 905. Bentwich cites England's generous conduct after the South-African War (p. 44). Great Britain also made compensation to deported neutrals. 26 Law Mag. and Rev. 486; For. Rel. 1903, 479–480; 28 Clunet (1901), 189. See also U. S. Act of April 9, 1816, *supra*, and Abandoned or Captured Property Act; Briggs *v.* U. S., 143 U. S. 346. Latin-American States often establish claims commissions after a civil war for deciding claims arising out of war injuries. See treaty between United States and Switzerland, Nov. 25, 1850, Art. 2, Malloy II, 1765, providing for equality with natives with respect to war indemnities.

[113] Many European countries pressed claims against Chile arising out of her war of 1879–1883 with Bolivia and Peru. Large indemnities were paid. Moore's Arb. 4916 (Germany). Some were submitted to arbitration. Seijas, V, 544–551; 73 St. Pap. 1211; 79 *ibid.* 670 (Italy); Martens, *Nouv. rec. gén.*, 2e ser., 11, 638 (Belgium) 74 St. Pap. 128, 131, and 79 *ibid.* 671 (France); 77 St. Pap. 826 (Switzerland); 82 St. Pap. 1292 (Portugal); 76 St. Pap. 98; Martens, *Nouv. rec. gén.*, 2e ser., 12, pp. 507–509 (Austria-Hungary). See also For. Rel. 1883, 97 and For. Rel. 1896, 42. See also claims conventions between Italy and Uruguay, Apr. 5, 1873, 63 St. Pap. 1322; Sardinia and Argentine, August 31, 1858, 49 St. Pap. 477, 480; Great Britain–France and Uruguay, June 28, 1862, 63 St. Pap. 1063; France and New Granada, Ecuador

The war indemnities which are often exacted from the conquered nation by the victor at the end of a war frequently have been used in part to compensate subjects who have sustained injury during the war.[114]

The growing tendency to impose upon belligerents and neutrals a strict compliance with the rules of war in the interests of private property, under penalty of pecuniary liability, and to regard war as a national disaster, the burdens of which shall be distributed equally over the whole nation, should not be permitted to be interrupted or impaired.

EDWIN M. BORCHARD.

and Venezuela, 49 St. Pap. 1301; Great Britain and Nicaragua (seizures of neutral property and personal injuries) For. Rel. 1894, App. I, 234–363; Moore's Arb. 4966; Great Britain and China, 1899 (*Kowshing* case), Parl. Pap. (Cd. 93) China, No. 1, 1900.

[114] *E. g.*, France *v.* China, treaty of Oct. 25, 1860, Art. V, Hertslet's China Treaties, 3rd ed., London, 1908, I, 289; France and Madagascar, French domestic commission, March 18, 1886, 77 St. Pap. 801, 78 St. Pap. 708; Great Britain and South African Republic, Aug. 3, 1881, 72 St. Pap. 900; Brazil and Paraguay, Jan. 9, 1872, La Fontaine, 167–170; Chile and Peru, Oct. 20, 1883, Art. 12, La Fontaine, 592, 593.

[7]

STATE RESPONSIBILITY FOR WARLIKE ACTS OF THE ARMED FORCES

From Article 3 of Hague Convention IV of 1907 to Article 91 of Additional Protocol I of 1977 and Beyond

FRITS KALSHOVEN*

I. INTRODUCTION

EVERY State is responsible for its internationally wrongful acts,[1] i.e. for conduct attributable to it under international law and which constitutes a breach of an international obligation of the State.[2] Among the various forms of conduct attributable to the State, conduct of its organs holds pride of place.[3]

The armed forces furnish a striking example of an organ whose acts may be so attributable and hence engage the responsibility of the State. They—or, rather, the innumerable individuals who compose their ranks—are called upon to do their duty whenever their country gets involved in an international or internal armed conflict or other situations of lesser violence.[4] To that end they are equipped with a broad range of weapons the use of which may be expected, and is in fact calculated, to bring grave if not fatal harm to human beings and things alike. And significantly, their acts are not beyond the grasp of the law: the applicable rules of international law, no matter how tolerant in principle of basic considerations of military necessity, effectively set limits to the ways and means by which the armed forces may wish to perform their functions.

In consequence, a State may have to bear international responsibility for the comportment of its armed forces whenever they actively participate in an armed conflict. Numerous such occasions have arisen in the recent past or persist to this day. While the greater part were internal or

* Professor of international humanitarian law, Leiden University (rtd). A version of this article was given as an address to the Discussion Group on the Laws of Armed Conflict, held at the British Institute of International and Comparative Law on 5 November 1990.

1. International Law Commission (ILC), Draft Articles on State Responsibility, Part I (The origin of international responsibility), Arts.1, 2; text of Part I in UN Doc.A/35/10, Report of the ILC on the work of its 35th session (1980), p.59.

2. Draft Art.3.

3. Draft Art.5.

4. Armed forces are also frequently deployed in situations of lesser disturbance not amounting to an armed conflict in the proper sense of the term. We shall not enter into this aspect of the matter.

mixed[5] armed conflicts, the war[6] between Iran and Iraq, 1980–1988, provides an example of a major international armed conflict, and one noticeable for the frequency of serious violations of basic precepts of the law, including maltreatment of prisoners of war, use of chemical weapons, and attacks wilfully directed against the civilian population. The United Nations repeatedly raised its voice against such practices.[7]

While all this could already serve to remind us of the responsibility of States for the warlike conduct of their armed forces, the topicality of the subject was highlighted once again by the Iraqi invasion and occupation of Kuwait on 2 August 1990, with the tumultuous events that followed. This time, the Security Council formally reminded Iraq more than once of its liability in respect of the losses, damage and injury arising as a result of the acts committed by its armed forces in occupied Kuwait, and it is taking steps to ensure that these formal reminders will lead to practical results.[8]

The question of responsibility of States for the conduct of their armed forces can be considered from various angles. There are, first of all, the aspects of breach of the peace and act of aggression on the one hand and, on the other, the right of self-defence (*ius ad bellum*). Then, even if one simply takes instances of recourse to armed force as a fact (as will be done in this article) and thus restricts the discussion to the conduct of armed forces actively engaged in such acts, issues that come to mind include the nature and scope of responsibility of the State in respect of war crimes (matters of prevention, discipline and punishment) and, in that connection, questions of responsibility *erga omnes* or, as an even more futuristic development, international criminal responsibility of the

5. The rules of international law applicable in armed conflicts do not recognise a separate category of "mixed" armed conflicts, i.e. conflicts within the territory of one State but with outside intervention on one or both sides. Yet in practice, such situations present sufficient special features to warrant separate attention. See e.g. Martin Hess, *Die Anwendbarkeit des humanitären Völkerrechts, insbesondere in gemischten Konflikten* (The applicability of international humanitarian law, in particular in mixed conflicts) (1985); the author examines in particular the conflicts in Afghanistan, Angola, Cambodia, Chad and the Lebanon.

6. The term "war" is used here in its non-technical sense as a synonym for armed conflict, i.e. as a factual notion not involving the legal consequences traditionally attached on the international level to a formal state of war between two or more States. On this see, generally, Yoram Dinstein, *War, Aggression and Self-Defence* (1988).

7. See Paul Tavernier, "La guerre du Golfe: Quelques aspects de l'application du droit des conflits armés et du droit humanitaire" (1984) 30 Annuaire français de dr. int. 43; Eric David, "La guerre du Golfe et le droit international" (1987–I) 23 Rev. belge de dr. int. 153. As regards the conduct of war on land, the Security Council itself (rather than the President on behalf of its members) for the first time expressed its concern at the civilian losses in both countries in S.C. Res.540, 31 Oct. 1983; it took the Council even longer, virtually until the end of the war, before it finally and rather cautiously deplored "the use of chemical weapons contrary to obligations under the 1925 Geneva Protocol"; S.C. Res.598, 20 July 1987.

8. Res.674, 29 Oct. 1990, 686, 2 Mar. 1991, 687, 3 Apr. 1991 and 692, 20 May 1991.

State; and, somewhat more down to earth, its responsibility for damage done to enemy or neutral individuals or States. An intriguing question in regard to each of these issues is how to define the armed forces that can so engage the responsibility of a State.

This article is confined to an examination of the rules of international law that govern the question of responsibility of the State for damage done by its armed forces engaged in armed conflict. The greatest attention will be paid to the rules that regulate the conduct of war and the behaviour of armed forces (*ius in bello*). Where appropriate, these will be set against the rules of general international law governing the international responsibility of the State.

The relevant rules of *ius in bello* are embodied in treaties on the law of armed conflict, notably the Hague Convention of 1907 on land warfare,[9] the four Geneva Conventions of 1949 for the protection of war victims,[10] and Additional Protocol I of 1977 for the protection of the victims of international armed conflicts.[11] The main focus will be on the provisions in the Hague Convention of 1907 and Protocol I of 1977: they both deal expressly with the responsibility of a State for all acts committed by members of its armed forces in the course of an armed conflict; however, while closely similar in language, they are not necessarily identical in meaning. The rules on responsibility in the Geneva Conventions of 1949 are of somewhat lesser import to our central theme and accordingly will be dealt with in a more cursory manner. In the Epilogue, attention is paid to two recent developments: first, certain phrases in the judgment of the World Court in the case of *Nicaragua* v. *The United States of America*, that have a bearing on the possible

9. Convention (IV) Respecting the Laws and Customs of War on Land, signed at The Hague, 18 Oct. 1907; authentic (French) text in Deuxième Conférence internationale de la Paix, La Haye 15 juin–18 octobre 1907, Actes et Documents (hereinafter *Actes*), Vol.1, p.626; English translation with further references in D. Schindler and J. Toman, *The Laws of Armed Conflicts* (3rd edn, 1988), p.69.

10. Convention (I) for the Amelioration of the Condition of the Wounded and Sick in Armed Forces in the Field; Convention (II) for the Amelioration of the Condition of Wounded, Sick and Shipwrecked Members of Armed Forces at Sea; Convention (III) Relative to the Treatment of Prisoners of War; Convention (IV) Relative to the Protection of Civilian Persons in Time of War; all four Conventions signed at Geneva, 12 Aug. 1949; authentic texts in Final Record of the Diplomatic Conference of Geneva of 1949 (hereinafter *Final Record*), Vol.1, pp.205, 225, 243, 297; texts also in Schindler and Toman, *idem*, pp.373, 401, 423, 493.

11. Protocol Additional to the Geneva Conventions of 12 August 1949, and Relating to the Protection of Victims of International Armed Conflicts (Protocol I), adopted at Geneva, 8 June 1977; Official Records of the Diplomatic Conference on the Reaffirmation and Development of International Humanitarian Law Applicable in Armed Conflicts, Geneva (1974–1977) (hereinafter *O.R.*), Vol.1, p.115; text also in Schindler and Toman, *idem*, p.621. It should be noted here that while some 100 States are now party to Protocol I, the remaining ones are not as a matter of treaty law bound by those of its provisions that lay down new law. Among the non-parties are the US, France and, at the time of writing, the UK.

responsibility of a State for the conduct of armed forces not its own;[12] and second, the measures, referred to above, taken by the Security Council to implement its decision that Iraq is liable for its wrongful deeds in Kuwait.

II. ARTICLE 3 OF HAGUE CONVENTION IV OF 1907

The treaty law governing armed conflict has long contained a special rule on the responsibility of States for the wartime conduct of their armed forces. Article 3 of the Hague Convention on land warfare 1907[13] reads as follows:

> A belligerent party which violates the provisions [of the Regulations on Land Warfare annexed to the Convention] shall, if the case demands, be liable to pay compensation. It shall be responsible for all acts committed by persons forming part of its armed forces.

What does this text really mean? The main point at issue concerns the type of responsibility the authors had in mind. A related point of interest, to be dealt with briefly, is the meaning of the term "armed forces".

A. *Responsibility* vis-à-vis *Individual Persons*

The records of the conference that adopted the text, i.e. the Second Hague Peace Conference 1907, provide convincing evidence that the delegates sought not so much to lay down a rule relating to the international responsibility of one State *vis-à-vis* another, as one relating to a State's liability to compensate the losses of individual persons incurred as a consequence of their direct (and harmful) contact with its armed forces.

The matter came up in the course of the revision of the original, 1899, Hague Convention on land warfare with annexed Regulations.[14] This is itself silent on the question of State responsibility. Yet Section III of the Regulations, on "Military Authority over Hostile Territory", refers in two places to the obligation of an occupying power to pay indemnities. Article 52 establishes such a duty in respect of requisitions in kind "demanded from communes or inhabitants . . . for the necessities of the army of occupation" (to be paid for, as far as possible, "in ready money; if not, their receipt shall be acknowledged"); and Article 53, especially for "railway plant, land telegraphs, telephones, steamers and other

12. *Case Concerning Military and Paramilitary Activities in and Against Nicaragua (Nicaragua* v. *United States)*, Merits, Judgment, I.C.J. Rep. 1986, 14.

13. *Supra* n.9.

14. Schindler and Toman, *loc. cit. supra* n.9.

ships" etc. (to be "restored at the conclusion of peace, and indemnities paid for them").

Note that neither of these provisions refers to unlawful conduct in particular: on the contrary, they appear to cover primarily cases where, under the rules in force, the requisitions were perfectly in order. Another point of interest is that the Articles clearly envisage the direct (and speedy) settlement of individual claims, by the armed forces: they represent, in effect, an early attempt to curb the tendency of land armies to "live off the land" without payment.

In the course of the 1907 Conference the Russian delegation submitted a proposal to amend Article 52 of the Regulations with a clause requesting the commanding officers of occupation forces to settle the payment of such receipts as soon as possible.[15] This modest suggestion was soon completely overshadowed, however, by a much broader German proposal to introduce two new articles.[16] One required a belligerent party to indemnify neutral persons as soon as possible for any detriment suffered as a consequence of violations of the Regulations; and it specified that such a party would be responsible for all acts committed by individual members of its armed forces. The other article provided that if the victims of the violation were persons belonging to the adverse party, the question of indemnification would be settled on the conclusion of peace.

The German delegate, Major-General Von Gündell, introduced the proposal in terms that made clear where it differed from the earlier provisions in Articles 52 and 53: it was narrower, he explained, in that it applied solely to cases of violation of the Regulations; and it was broader in that it was not confined to events occurring in occupied territory.[17] The Convention of 1899 contained just one general rule on implementation, and this concerned the duty of signatory powers to issue instructions to their armed land forces in conformity with the Regulations (Article 1). This, he said (with marked understatement), did not suffice to guarantee respect of the law in all cases, since not only governments but a great number of individuals were involved in the actual waging of the war.

There was thus a need to envisage the consequences of infractions. Since in his (optimistic) view, these would not usually be the result of

15. *Actes*, *op. cit. supra* n.9, Vol.3, at p.142: 2nd Commission, 1st sub-commission, 4th sess., 31 July 1907: Mr Tcharykow introduces proposal; text of amendment: *idem*, p.248. The proposal resulted in the addition of a clause at the end of Art.52, para.3, specifying that "the payment of the amount due shall be made as soon as possible"—unfortunately, the practical effect of the Art. was negligible and it remained virtually a dead letter.

16. *Idem*, p.144; text of amendment: *idem*, p.247.

17. *Idem*, p.144.

negligence on the part of the government, it was necessary to get away from the notion of subjective fault of the government as an element of liability: after all, it would be unacceptable for a victim to be able to claim damages only from the officer or soldier guilty of the infraction. Governments should therefore be held responsible for all unlawful acts, without exception, committed by members of their armed forces in violation of the Regulations. As for the fact that the amendment distinguished between enemy and neutral persons, the delegate confined himself to underscoring the practical need for such a distinction.

The principle underlying the German proposal was never a matter of controversy at the Conference. On the contrary, it found broad support among the delegates, as may be evident from the following passage in the report of the competent Commission:[18]

> As the rules of the Regulations on the laws and customs of war must be observed, not only by the commanding officers of belligerent armies but, generally, by all officers, non-commissioned officers and other ranks, the German delegation has considered it useful to propose that the Convention extend to the Law of Nations, for all cases of infraction of the Regulations, the principle of Private Law according to which the master is responsible for his subordinates or agents. The principle of the German proposal has not encountered any objection.

Such criticism as there was focused on the distinction made in the proposal between enemy and neutral persons. According to the critics this reflected a general doctrine of the German delegation, apparent elsewhere in the Conference, which purported to favour neutral persons over persons belonging to the adverse party.[19] In spite of Von Gündell's repeated assurances that the distinction was not a matter of principle but solely concerned the method and moment of payment, and in spite of the Swiss delegate's support for his position,[20] the Conference removed this element from the proposal and, combining the two draft articles into a single one, arrived at the text as ultimately adopted.[21]

B. Scope of Application of Article 3

In attempting to determine the scope of application of this Article, we may conveniently start out from the character of the Regulations annexed to the Hague Convention IV of 1907. In the perception of the

18. Report of the 2nd Commission (*idem*, Vol.1, p.103; my translation).
19. *Idem*, Vol.3, p.146: Mr Louis Renault (France); p.147: Lord Reay (UK).
20. *Idem*, p.147: Colonel Borel.
21. *Idem*, p.15: 2nd Commission, 2nd session (14 Aug. 1907) adopts text, with German support; *idem*, p.28: report of the 1st sub-commission; *idem*, Vol.1, p.87: 4th Plenary Session (17 Aug. 1907) votes text; *idem*, p.103: report of 2nd Commission to Conference.

draftsmen[22] these were primarily designed, as well as basically suited, to be implemented by the armies of the contracting States, it being left to each State to make such adjustments as might be necessitated by the national situation. Therefore, even though the Regulations form an integral part of the Convention and to that extent lay down rules of treaty law,[23] they were not so much conceived as a set of rules defining obligations of the contracting States but, rather, as model instructions directly addressed to their armed forces. The Regulations do in fact provide rules of conduct for the wide range of situations these forces could expect to come across in the course of their military operations, including contact with members of the enemy armed forces as well as (enemy or neutral) civilians and their property.

As regards Article 3 in particular, its drafting history and, indeed, its internal logic make clear that its two sentences must be read together as an indivisible whole. This is to say that it specifically addresses the liability of a State to indemnify enemy or neutral persons for damages incurred as a result of acts committed by members of its armed land forces in contravention of the Regulations.

1. Civilians as sole beneficiaries

It is suggested that even so, not all acts in contravention of the Regulations are meant to fall under the scope of the Article. Although none of the delegates made the point explicitly, it seems highly unlikely that they would have thought of the Article as designed, or even suitable, to cover combatants' complaints, say, of maltreatment while detained as prisoners of war,[24] or about wounds inflicted treacherously or with the aid of forbidden means of warfare.[25] Indeed, it appears entirely justified to regard enemy and neutral civilians as the sole intended beneficiaries of Article 3.

22. See the paragraph from the report, quoted *supra* n.18.

23. That the drafters were not entirely oblivious of the conventional character of the Regulations may be deduced e.g. from Art.2 of the Convention. This provides that "The provisions contained in the Regulations referred to in Article 1, as well as in the present Convention, do not apply except between Contracting Powers, and then only if all the belligerents are parties to the Convention."

24. Regulations, Art.4. The ICRC mentions this example in its commentary to Art.12 of the Third Convention of 1949, where it notes that damages may ensue e.g. from "the physical and mental injury suffered by prisoners who, despite the individual safeguards provided in the Convention, have been brutally treated while in captivity"; ICRC, *The Geneva Conventions of 12 August 1949, Commentary Published under the General Editorship of Jean S. Pictet: III Geneva Convention* (1960), p.130. The ICRC published commentaries to each of the four Conventions; the English versions were published as follows: Convention I: 1952; II: 1960; III: 1960; IV: 1958; they will be referred to hereinafter as ICRC *Commentary* I, II, III or IV.

25. Regulations, Art.23.

2. Small-scale events

A further restriction, once again implicit in the drafting history rather than openly expressed, appears to be that, always in the perception of the draftsmen, the Article would be designed to cover fairly small-scale events. The reader gains this impression from some of the words Von Gündell used in introducing the German proposal: it would be unacceptable, he said, if a victim could claim damages only from the officer or soldier guilty of the infraction. This suggests events involving direct, personal contact between offender and victim, rather than impersonal, large-scale, military operations such as a long-distance bombardment, where the victim does not get to know the identity of the offender.

3. Armed forces

While Article 3 refers to the "armed forces" of the State, Article 1 of the Regulations determines in some detail to whom the "laws, rights and duties of war" apply: these include, besides the regular armies, "militia and volunteer corps" that fulfil a set of four conditions.[26] In effect, even those involved in a *levée en masse* in unoccupied territory may under certain conditions be "regarded as belligerents".[27] Are all these categories of "belligerents" (or combatants, as we would say) covered by the notion "armed forces" in Article 3 of the Convention? And what of armed resistance in occupied territory?

The records of the Conference of 1907 provide no specific information as regards the intentions of the draftsmen. The single clue lies in the fact that the Article was included in the Convention (rather than, as originally proposed, in the Regulations). The phrase "armed forces" in Article 3 must therefore be deemed to have the same meaning here as in Article 1 of the Convention (which is identical to Article 1 in the Convention of 1899).[28] Unfortunately, the records of the Conference of

26. The conditions (in the version of 1907) are: 1. to be commanded by a person responsible for his subordinates; 2. to have a fixed distinctive emblem recognisable at a distance; 3. to carry arms openly; and 4. to conduct their operations in accordance with the laws and customs of war.

27. Regulations, Art.2; the conditions are that they "spontaneously take up arms to resist the invading troops without having had time to organise themselves in accordance with Article 1" and that they "carry arms openly" and "respect the laws and customs of war".

28. This impression is gained both from the introduction of the German proposal and from the inclusion of the Art. as ultimately adopted in the Convention (where it is a logical sequel to the obligation of Art.1) rather than in the Regulations. In the closing phase of the Conference Louis Renault, reporting on the work of the Drafting Committee of the Conference, explained that because the article based on the German proposal lays an obligation on governments it was incorporated in the Convention rather than in the Regulations, which contain instructions to the armed forces; *Actes, op. cit. supra* n.9, at p.581: 10th Plenary Session (17 Oct. 1907).

1899 are equally silent.[29] In these circumstances, the logical conclusion to be drawn from the text of Article 1 must be that the crucial element lies in whether a particular "armed force" has sufficiently close links with the government of a belligerent State to be effectively subject to its instructions. This construction doubtless includes its regular armed forces (the "armies" of Article 1 of the Regulations). It equally unmistakably excludes the *levée en masse* in unoccupied territory[30] and, *a fortiori*, armed resistance in occupied territory.[31] As for the "militia and volunteer corps", the conditions for "belligerency" specified in the Regulations do not in so many words require them to be effectively subject to the instructions emanating from the central political and military authorities; yet, this may be deemed to represent the decisive factor for the State to bear responsibility for their acts.[32]

4. Subsequent State practice

While it is submitted that the above accurately reflects the meaning and scope of application of Article 3 according to the intentions of its draftsmen, there remains the matter of its practical application. The draftsmen stopped far short of providing individual beneficiaries with precise rules for the presentation and settlement of their claims ("war damages refunded at this window"), let alone that they would have held out prospects of effective remedies against doubtful or even obviously unjust rejections. Yet, the Article is unmistakably designed to enable

29. The records of the Peace Conference of 1899 tell us no more than that Art.1, like the other articles of the Convention (as opposed to those of the Regulations) stems from the Drafting Committee. There is no report on the work of that Committee, and the Plenary Conference accepted their proposals for articles to be included in the Convention without a word in comment. *Conférence internationale de la Paix, La Haye 18 mai–29 juillet 1899*, records published by the Netherlands Ministry of Foreign Affairs (new edn, 1907), 1st part, p.152.

30. While the inhabitants of unoccupied territory who participate in such a spontaneous effort of armed resistance against an invading enemy force may under certain conditions, as Art.2 of the Regulations stipulates, be "regarded as belligerents", they do not belong to the class of organised armed forces a government may hope to reach with its instructions and whose conduct could therefore engage the direct responsibility of the State.

31. This had proved an insoluble problem to the Conference of 1899. On that occasion the discussions resulted in the so-called Martens clause in the preamble to the Convention, by which the contracting States declared "that, in cases not included in the Regulations adopted by them, the inhabitants and the belligerents remain under the protection and the rule of the principles of the law of nations, as they result from the usages established among civilised peoples, from the laws of humanity, and the dictates of the public conscience".

32. Obviously, their status as "armed forces" is beyond dispute when they are not just "commanded by a person responsible for his subordinates" (being the first, rather vague condition laid down in Art.1 of the Regulations) but actually "constitute the army, or form part of it"—in which case, as expressly (and somewhat redundantly) specified in para.2 of that Art., "they are included under the denomination 'army' ".

these people to present their bills directly to the State, i.e. to its competent (military or other) authorities, either during or after the war.

On this score, State practice has proved disappointing. The Hague Convention and Regulations of 1907 are generally held to have long since entered into the domain of customary international law, and there is no obvious reason to exclude Article 3 from this appreciation. At the same time, it should be recognised that, like Article 52 of the Regulations, Article 3 of the Convention has in important respects remained "law on the books". In particular as regards damage incurred by persons of enemy nationality, application of the Article, with its right of direct individual access to, and compensation by, the State, has largely been replaced by a practice of lump sum settlements concluded after the war by and between the one-time belligerent States.[33] The agreements usually lay an obligation on the vanquished State to pay a more or less random amount, determined more by its perceived financial capabilities than by any serious attempt to assess the damage caused by the unlawful acts of either party's armed forces; and the victor State may or may not distribute (part of) the money to individual claimants.

This development perhaps should not surprise too much. Even the original German proposal suggested that if the victims of a violation of the Regulations were persons belonging to the adverse party, the question of indemnification could be settled only on the conclusion of peace. And today, enemy persons will apparently find no effective remedy in the courts of England: as related by Colonel Rogers,[34] "where [in a situation of martial law such as arises during war] the armed forces of the Crown are engaged on active service abroad, acts done against an alien enemy cannot be the subject of proceedings in an English court as the defence of act of State is always open to the Crown in respect of them". On the face of it, this need not exclude direct settlement by other (administrative) authorities. Yet the evident futility of recourse to the courts in the event of their rejecting a claim might reduce to vanishing point any inclination they might otherwise have felt to hand out significant amounts of money to individual enemy claimants, either during or after the war. And it may safely be assumed that the English example is not unique.[35]

The lack of actual application of the Article, at least as far as persons of enemy nationality are concerned, has resulted in its original meaning

33. ICRC, *Commentary on the Additional Protocols of 8 June 1977 to the Geneva Conventions of 12 August 1949* (1987), p.1054, para.3647, with further references.

34. A. P. V. Rogers, "War Crimes Trials under the Royal Warrant: British Practice 1945–1949" (1990) 39 I.C.L.Q. 780, 796; the author relies on Heuston, *Essays in Constitutional Law* (1964), pp.150 *et seq*.

35. For the problems a private claimant may encounter in the US, see Jordan J. Paust, "Suing Saddam: Private Remedies for War Crimes and Hostage-Taking", (1991) 31 Va.J.I.L. 351–379.

and purpose receding into the background. Owing to the same lack of practice there is, however, insufficient ground to assume that it has acquired any other clear, specific, meaning instead (for instance, including damage to combatants or large-scale events, or claims by States). In this situation one cannot simply disregard the original meaning of the Article as this results from its drafting history, with as its core element the attribution to individual victims of a right to claim compensation for war damages directly from the responsible State.

C. Article 3 and the General Rules on State Responsibility

How does Article 3 compare with the general rules on State responsibility? To answer this question we shall rely on some of the non-controversial draft articles elaborated by the International Law Commission,[36] which may be deemed faithfully to render the traditional customary law on the subject.

For an act of a State organ to be considered as an act of that State under international law, the draft articles require that the organ "was acting in that capacity in the case in question", and this "even if, in the particular case, the organ exceeded its competence according to internal law or contravened instructions concerning its activity".[37] The sole condition appears to be, therefore, that the organ in question was acting "in that capacity".

Applying these rules to the armed forces, it follows that an internationally unlawful act, committed in the course of an armed conflict by a member of the armed forces, engages the responsibility of the State irrespective of whether the actor was competent to perform that particular act and whether in performing it he abided by the instructions issued to him (indeed, the instructions themselves may have been against the applicable rules of international law). He must, however, have been acting in his capacity as (a member of) an organ of the State.

In this regard, Article 3 is broader in that it encompasses all violations of the Regulations committed by persons belonging to the armed forces, irrespective of whether these were done in that capacity or otherwise. The point is relevant because members of an armed force at war stand a greater chance than do other State organs of becoming entangled in ambiguous situations where it may be unclear whether they were acting in their capacity as an organ of the State. What, for instance, of the incidents that allegedly happened in the course of the invasion and occupation of Kuwait: can all acts of wanton brutality or savagery done by members of the Iraqi army be regarded as committed in that capacity?

36. *Supra* n.1.
37. Draft Arts.5, 10.

This one example may suffice to illustrate that putting the acts of an armed force to the test whether they were committed "in that capacity" may set an uncertain and certainly undesirable limit on the responsibility of the State. In other words, the wider scope of Article 3 is definitely to be preferred.

For the rest, Article 3 in several respects is more restricted than are the draft articles. It is expressly limited to violations of the Regulations committed by members of the armed land forces. It is plausibly limited, according to the intentions of the draftsmen, to acts doing harm to enemy or neutral civilians, thus excluding enemy combatants. And it has probably been designed to cope especially, if not exclusively, with relatively small-scale events.

As a related point, the question of responsibility of one State *vis-à-vis* another apparently never entered the minds of the draftsmen. Accordingly, the possible relationship of the matter at issue with general rules on diplomatic protection simply did not arise in the debate.

Obviously, there is nothing to suggest that Article 3 could ever have been designed to exclude the applicability of any existing general rules on the responsibility of States for acts of war committed by their armed forces. It may be the case, though, that at the time of the Second Hague Peace Conference the general rules were of little practical import in relation to the problem the delegates sought to solve, so that in tackling it they were more or less oblivious of such general rules. At any rate, the rule they purported to lay down in Article 3, with its special characteristics adapted to the perceived needs of the situation, even today is entirely capable of coexisting with, and supplementing, the general rules on State responsibility.

III. INTERLUDE: THE GENEVA CONVENTIONS OF 1929 AND 1949

The treaties on humanitarian law concluded between the world wars contribute hardly anything of interest to the present subject. One notable exception is Article 28 of the Prisoners of War Convention of 1929.[38] Dealing with the situation where a prisoner of war is set to work for private individuals, i.e. outside the sphere of direct control of the detaining authorities, it provides that in such a situation, the detaining power "shall assume entire responsibility" for their maintenance, care and treatment and wages. This effectively removes any lingering doubt that a State could perhaps deny such responsibility on the argument that, after all, the conduct of private persons is none of its business. In the system of the International Law Commission's draft articles, the

38. Convention relative to the Treatment of Prisoners of War, signed at Geneva, 27 July 1929; Schindler and Toman, *op. cit. supra* n.9, at p.339.

case would seem to be covered by the provision that such conduct is attributable to the State if "it is established that [they were] in fact acting on behalf of that State"[39] (and in the case at issue, at its behest or at all events with its full consent).

More of interest is to be found in the four Conventions of 1949.[40] Here too, however, we shall be brief, as the additions brought by these instruments are somewhat marginal to the main line of argument of this article.

Article 57 of Convention III or the "Prisoners of War" Convention of 1949 reaffirms the rule in Article 28 of the 1929 Convention. Article 12 lays down the general rule that irrespective of any individual responsibilities, the detaining power is responsible for the treatment of prisoners of war from the moment of their capture. Article 29 of Convention IV or the "Civilians" Convention provides likewise that:

> The Party to the conflict in whose hands protected persons may be, is responsible for the treatment accorded to them by its agents, irrespective of any individual responsibility which may be incurred.

In its commentary on these Articles,[41] published shortly after the adoption of the Conventions, the International Committee of the Red Cross (ICRC) emphasised the distinction between the principles of individual liability for punishment for infractions of the Conventions, and of responsibility of the State; and it derived from the latter principle "an obligation on the Parties to the conflict to instruct their agents in their duties and their rights".[42] The principle also "demands that a State whose agent has been guilty of an act in violation of the Convention, should be required to make reparation". In this context the ICRC referred to Article 3 of the Hague Convention of 1907, thus going beyond the original meaning of that Article: for one thing, because the delegates never intended it to cover reparation to enemy combatants;[43] and for another, because it is expressly limited to damage done by members of the armed forces (and not other State agents, who would be likely to be involved in the treatment of interned civilians).[44] In other words, the ICRC appeared to read Article 3 as if it were, and had always been, the statement of a general principle rather than a specific rule.

39. ILC draft arts., Art.8.

40. *Supra* n.10.

41. ICRC *Commentary*, *op. cit. supra* n.24, III at pp.129–131, IV at pp.209–211.

42. The commentary refers in this connection to common Art.1, which binds the contracting States "to respect and ensure respect for the Conventions in all circumstances", and to the undertaking of the contracting States "to disseminate the text [of the Conventions] as widely as possible" (Convention III, Art.127, Convention IV, Art.144).

43. Text at *supra* n.23.

44. In Section IV we shall revert to the latter point.

This suggests that even at that stage, the experts of the ICRC had lost sight of the original meaning of the Article.

There remains an article common to the four Geneva Conventions of 1949, on "liability" of the contracting States in respect of grave breaches of the Conventions. The article (51 of Convention I, 52 of Convention II, 131 of Convention III and 148 of Convention IV) reads as follows:

> No High Contracting Party shall be allowed to absolve itself or any other High Contracting Party of any liability incurred by itself or by another High Contracting Party in respect of breaches referred to in the preceding Article.

The "preceding Article" defines the grave breaches of the Conventions which the contracting States are obliged to prevent or repress in accordance with the article preceding the "preceding Article", i.e. Article 49, 50, 129 or 146 respectively. The notion of grave breaches belongs to the sphere of individual criminal liability for war crimes, whereas prevention and repression, i.e. the enactment of any necessary legislation and the application of existing legislation to individual perpetrators of grave breaches, represent obligations of the State. So the question arises: what "liability" of the State is meant here? This is far from self-evident.[45] Neither do the records of the discussions lead to any unequivocal answer. Yet some attention should be given to the proceedings that eventually resulted in the adoption of the above text.

The Article stems from an Italian amendment, originally introduced as a rider to a provision on special agreements between contracting States[46] and which purported to preclude the conclusion of such an agreement "even should it take the form of a clause to a Treaty intended to regulate matters which have remained in suspense at the conclusion of an armed conflict" and the effect of which would be to "relieve any Party from the responsibilities it has incurred by its failure to observe" one of the Conventions. As explained by the Italian delegate, Mr Maresca, the amendment related in particular to the case of an agreement between victor and vanquished, with the former imposing on the latter "a renunciation of . . . claims to which it might be entitled owing to the non-observation of the Conventions in time of war, such as for instance the payment of an indemnity to prisoners who had been wounded while

45. A literal interpretation, to the effect that they would exclude the possibility for a State to absolve itself or other contracting States of any "liability" in respect of their legislative and other obligations, clearly makes no sense. The ICRC states without hesitation that the Arts. do "not, of course, affect the obligation to prosecute and punish the authors of infractions, since that obligation is absolute"; ICRC *Commentary*, *op. cit. supra* n.24, I, at p.373.

46. This ultimately became Art.6 common to Conventions I–III (Art.7 of Convention IV). Its crux lies in that no such special agreement is permitted to affect adversely the situation of persons protected by the Convention in question.

carrying out dangerous tasks such as were prohibited by the Convention".[47] When it met with strong opposition[48] it was withdrawn by its proponents, only to be reintroduced subsequently as a separate text with a slightly different wording[49] and dealt with in the entirely different context of the prevention and repression of breaches of the Conventions.[50] This led to another round of somewhat inconclusive debate, with Maresca intervening more than once in ways that, instead of contributing to greater clarity, led to increased confusion.[51] At any rate, the

47. *Final Record*, *op. cit. supra* n.10, Vol.IIB, at p.17: 3rd meeting of the Joint Committee, 29 Apr. 1949. When the proposal came up for discussion at the Special Committee of the Joint Committee, Maresca reiterated that: "The purpose of the amendment submitted by the Italian delegation was to prevent the victor from forcing the vanquished to renounce claims which a possible non-compliance with the Conventions would entitle him to make" *idem*, p.55: Special Committee of the Joint Committee, 10th meeting, 27 May 1949.

48. This came, first, from Miss Gutteridge (UK); in her assertion, "A peace treaty did not represent violence, but the acceptance by a defeated Power of terms which it found itself able to accept." Another sceptical delegate, M. Lamarle (France), held that "the Convention could not amend the clauses of a treaty which was already signed, nor give directives on the contents of a future treaty". (He probably overlooked the fact that the draft Article to which the Italian amendment was to be added, actually purported to "give directives on the contents" of future agreements: *idem*, pp.55, 56; see also the First Report drawn up by the Special Committee of the Joint Committee, 27 June 1949; *idem*, p.109).

49. The new text proposed that "No contracting Party shall be allowed to absolve itself or any other contracting Party of any liability incurred by itself or by another contracting Party as a result of a failure to observe the present Convention": *idem*, p.76: 23rd meeting of the Special Committee, 14 June 1949.

50. Although the proposal was introduced immediately after the adoption of the Article on special agreements, the records of the meeting specify that it would be examined later, in the entirely different context of the draft articles on breaches of the Conventions. On that later occasion the Chairman noted, probably by way of explanation of the shift, that "the Italian delegation had modified its proposal by replacing the words 'as a result of failure to observe the present Convention' by 'as a result of breaches provided for in the preceding Article' ": *idem*, p.91: 33rd meeting of the Special Committee, 29 June 1949. The Special Committee adopted the new text without discussion (and by a vote of four in favour and two against, with four abstentions) and with that forwarded it to the Joint Committee for further decision; *ibid*.

51. The Rapporteur of the Special Committee had written that: "The State remained responsible for breaches of the Convention and could not refuse to recognise its responsibility on the ground that the individuals concerned had been punished. There remained, for instance, the liability to pay compensation": *idem*, p.118: Fourth Report drawn up by the Special Committee, 12 July 1949. Maresca subsequently, and rather surprisingly, requested, and obtained, the deletion of the second sentence: *idem*, p.31: 10th meeting of the Joint Committee, 16 July 1949. This induced the French delegate to reverse his former position and express himself in agreement with the proposal precisely on the grounds that "recent peace treaties had provided for agreements between former adversaries in full settlement of debts between them": *ibid*. The Australian delegate, Colonel Hodgson, chose this moment to enquire "what was the meaning" of the Art. (*idem*, p.32) and thereby induced Maresca to state that: "The new concept contained in this Article was that prior to their own responsibility, the perpetrators of violations had involved the responsibility of their State, and that the latter stood liable, even after individual penalties had been inflicted on the offenders who had acted as agents of that State": *ibid*.

proposed text failed to gain consensus:[52] it was ultimately adopted in Committee by a majority vote that showed clearly how controversial the Article had remained to the very last.[53]

The final round came with the presentation of the Report of the Joint Committee to the Plenary Assembly. As the relevant paragraphs in the Report provide what seems to be the most generous and lucid presentation of the views expressed at various stages by Maresca and others, they deserve to be quoted at some length:[54]

> This is a new provision . . . intended to render null and void, in advance, any contractual exemption by which a victor State could prevail upon the conquered State to cease to hold the victor responsible for any violations of the Conventions committed by the organs of the latter; any clauses of this kind might render useless the prosecution of individual guilty persons, for where a State has obtained a promise that it shall not be held responsible, it would be extremely difficult to condemn an individual agent acting under its orders. This provision was the only means of ensuring that the compulsory character of the prosecution, as proclaimed in the preceding Article, should continue in force.
>
> The scope of this Article is comparatively restricted. It does not cover special financial arrangements under which a State can finally liquidate a claim to damages by an agreed lump sum payment or a settlement in compensation. . . . The minority criticised the Article as wanting in clearness.

Presented thus, the Article was adopted in Plenary without a further word:[55] an outcome that was probably as much the result of Italian insistence as of any intrinsic merits of the new provision. For there can be no doubt that the Article has remained "wanting in clearness" to the bitter end.

It may be commented, first, that in accordance with the explanations offered from the outset by the Italian delegate, the liability to which it refers cannot very well be understood as anything but the financial liability incurred during the war by a victor State in relation to the vanquished State or its nationals. Indeed, when one substitutes Italy for the vanquished party, the suggestion is strong that the idea behind the proposal was to exclude the possibility of the victors of the Second World

52. The UK delegate, Sir Robert Craigie, once again criticised the Art. for its attempt "to bind States . . . in particular, in their liberty to conclude a treaty of peace at the end of a war. Special agreements between States for financial settlements would be interfered with": *idem*, p.36: 12th meeting of the Joint Committee, 20 July 1949. And Colonel Hodgson, who at this stage, confused by the proceedings, introduced but rapidly withdrew an amendment of his own, did not hide the fact that the Australian delegation would prefer to see the Art. deleted: *idem*, p.35.

53. The vote in the Joint Committee was 18 in favour to 16 against, with three abstentations: *idem*, p.36.

54. *Idem*, p.133.

55. *Idem*, p.364: 22nd Plenary Meeting, 1 Aug. 1949.

War (such as the United Kingdom, which opposed the Italian amendment to the very last) contracting out of any obligations they might have incurred to pay compensation for wrongs suffered by Italy or its nationals at the hands of its former enemies.

Another point is that at no time in the course of the proceedings did the Italian delegate succeed in convincingly explaining the alleged link of the new proposal to the preceding Articles on grave breaches. The choice of that context may therefore have been no more than a fortuitous solution. And lastly, the statement in the final Report of the Joint Committee that the Article "does not cover special financial arrangements under which a State can finally liquidate a claim to damages by an agreed lump sum payment or a settlement in compensation" was in accordance with what the Italian delegate had said at a late stage of the proceedings and was not contradicted by anyone else; it may therefore be taken as an authentic interpretation of the limited scope of the Article.

The upshot of it all appears to be that a victor State cannot after the war openly contract out of any financial liability it might have incurred as a result of grave violations of the Conventions. Claims under this heading on the part of the vanquished State or its nationals may, on the other hand, be dealt with in the context of a post-war lump sum agreement between the two sides. In somewhat cynical terms, this outcome may in practice be difficult to distinguish from plain disregard of those claims.

The ICRC commentary, qualifying Article 51 of the First Convention as "an entirely new Article . . . the sense of which is not altogether clear", goes on to assert, rather surprisingly, that:[56]

> In this matter of material reparation for infractions of the Convention it is not possible, at any rate as the law at present stands, to imagine an injured party being able to bring an action individually against the State in whose service the author of the infraction was. Only a State can put forward such claims against another State.

In saying this, the ICRC appears to disregard the fact that Article 3 of the 1907 Hague Convention (to which the commentary specifically refers) undeniably accords such a capacity to individual injured parties, be they enemy or neutral persons. True, as far as persons of (former) enemy nationality are concerned, practice has moved away from Article 3, making it increasingly difficult to imagine such a person bringing his claim "individually against the State in whose service the author of the infraction was". Yet this development does not necessarily affect "the

56. ICRC *Commentary*, *op. cit. supra* n.24, I, at p.373.

law as it stands", unless it be shown that State practice has purposely set aside Article 3 in regard to enemy persons; a proposition for which this author has found no convincing evidence. At all events, Article 51 has no influence whatsoever on the capacity of neutral persons individually to claim damages incurred as a result of violations of the law of armed conflict, grave breaches of the Geneva Conventions of 1949 included.

IV. ARTICLE 91 OF PROTOCOL I

SEVENTY years after the introduction and adoption of Article 3, the matter of its reaffirmation was brought up in the course of the final (1977) session of the Diplomatic Conference on the Reaffirmation and Development of International Humanitarian Law Applicable in Armed Conflicts, 1974–1977. An amendment to that effect, proposed by Vietnam, with Algeria and Yugoslavia as co-sponsors,[57] resulted in the adoption of Article 91 of Additional Protocol I of 1977.[58] The new Article reads as follows:

> A Party to the conflict which violates the provisions of the Conventions or of this Protocol shall, if the case demands, be liable to pay compensation. It shall be responsible for all acts committed by persons forming part of its armed forces.

As may be seen, the wording of the new Article follows closely that of its predecessor. One minor difference (irrelevant in the present context) is that its opening words do not refer to a "belligerent party" but, in more contemporary language, to a "Party to the conflict". Greater importance attaches to another textual difference: whereas the first sentence of Article 3 confines its scope to violations of the Regulations, Article 91 speaks in much broader terms of violations of the 1949 Conventions and the 1977 Protocol. We shall come back to this point shortly. A first question to answer is whether the identical words in the two Articles are in effect intended to carry the same meaning.

A. *Responsibility* vis-à-vis *a State or a People*

The recorded drafting history of Article 91 contains little more than an introduction by the delegate of Vietnam.[59] As he explained, the amendment was designed, on the one hand, to restate the principle of reparation laid down in Article 3 of the Hague Convention and, on the

57. *O.R.*, *op. cit. supra* n.11, Vol.3, at p.347: CDDH/I/335 and Add.1 and 2, 15 Apr. 1977. For text of the proposal see *infra* n.60.

58. *Supra* n.11.

59. *O.R.*, *op. cit. supra* n.11, Vol.9, at p.355: CDDH/I/SR.67, paras.2–5, Mr Van Luu.

other, to reaffirm the principle of non-exoneration from responsibility as embodied in the 1949 Geneva Conventions.[60] The sponsors, he said, had taken their inspiration from "the destruction and ravages resulting from the wars of colonial and neo-colonial aggression inflicted on the home territory of weak and ill-armed people in Asian countries, as had happened in Viet Nam and in some African countries". These wars had unavoidably delayed their development. The speaker recalled that the UN General Assembly in 1974, and the Conference of Heads of State or Government of Non-Aligned Countries in 1976, had "called for reparations for the developing countries victims of foreign occupation, which had caused them serious losses in life and property while reducing and degrading the natural and other resources of such States, territories and peoples".

With that, the proposal was referred to a working group. From this it emerged a few days later in its present, considerably reduced form. The record merely shows that the working group had regarded inclusion of the second paragraph as superfluous since it "reproduced existing provisions in the Geneva Conventions". "In order to achieve a consensus, and in a spirit of conciliation", the sponsors had accepted this reduction of their proposal. They apparently had also accepted that the text no longer, as their original proposal had done, referred specifically to "grave breaches": at all events, the report places on record that "the text thus adopted" in the working group reads in conformity with the present Article 91.[61]

It may be noted in passing that the quoted phrase in the report of the working group may be deemed to settle a question that might otherwise have remained somewhat obscure: *viz.*, whether the "Italian" provisions in the Geneva Conventions on non-exoneration of a State's liability in respect of grave breaches[62] apply to the provisions on grave breaches in the Protocol as well. Article 85 of the Protocol provides that the provisions of the Conventions "relating to the repression of

60. The proposed text read as follows (*idem*, Vol.3, p.347: CDDH/I/335 and Add.1 and 2):
"1. A Party to the conflict which violates the provisions of the Conventions and of the present Protocol, and in particular commits grave breaches as defined in Articles 11 and 74 [85 in the final version] of the present Protocol, shall if the case demands, be liable to pay compensation. It shall be responsible for all acts committed by persons forming part of its armed forces.
2. No High Contracting Party shall be allowed to absolve itself or any other High Contracting Party of any liability incurred by itself or by another High Contracting Party in respect of the violations and breaches referred to in paragraph 1 of this Article."

61. *Idem*, Vol.10, p.215: CDDH/I/338/Rev.1/Add.1, Report on the work of Working Group A of Committee I. The Committee subsequently adopted the text by consensus without a word in comment; *idem*, Vol.9, p.397: CDDH/I/SR.70, paras.55, 56.

62. *Supra* Section IV.B.

breaches and grave breaches . . . shall apply to the repression of breaches and grave breaches of this Protocol". While the "Italian" articles in the Conventions follow immediately after the articles that directly dealt with grave breaches and other violations and were presented as linked to those articles, it was seen that this link was tenuous at best. However, in the eyes of the working group, the link was evidently sufficiently close to regard these articles as "relating to" the breaches provisions. The matter is not without importance, since Article 85 of the Protocol considerably extends the scope of the breaches and grave breaches system to encompass acts that in traditional terms belong to the law of The Hague rather than Geneva.[63]

At any rate, as far as Vietnam was concerned, the immediate political goal behind the proposal may have been to obtain an express reaffirmation of (its understanding of) the principles of 1907 and 1949 with a view to the war crimes allegedly committed by the American armed forces in the course of the Vietnam war. Not, of course, in the hope that the proposed article could become retroactively applicable as treaty law to the events of that armed conflict. Rather, because in future negotiations with the United States the official and solemn reaffirmation of the principle might serve to buttress Vietnamese claims of compensation for the damages caused by the American armed forces.

The main point to be distilled from the above remarkably brief drafting history of Article 91 is that Vietnam and its co-sponsors evidently were no longer thinking in the first place, as their predecessors in 1907 had done, of a State's duty to indemnify individual enemy or neutral victims of infractions of the law of war. Indeed, they may have been totally unaware of this earlier meaning of the text they sought to reaffirm, nor would they probably have greatly cared. As the introduction clearly shows, the object they had in mind was compensation due to a State (or the collectivity of "a people") for the "destruction and ravages" of war it had suffered, notably as a result of (alleged) criminal breaches of the law of armed conflict by a brutal invader or occupant. And the complete silence of other delegates may indicate that they too were no longer aware of the original significance of Article 3, or alternatively, considered it of insufficient interest to raise the point.

The Vietnamese intervention and the silence that followed could never by themselves deprive Article 3 of its original meaning. Yet in interpreting Article 91 the intention expressed by the delegate of Vietnam must obviously be taken into account. The result is that in the rela-

63. It is of interest to note that the ICRC Commentary (*op. cit. supra* n.33) refers neither in relation to the section of the Protocol on repression of breaches, nor to Art.85 in particular, to the "Italian" Articles on State liability: it does mention them, though, in its commentary on Art.91: p.1054, para.3648.

tions between the parties to the conflict, the old and the new articles may together be assumed to provide for compensation both to the State and to individual victims. And of course, all this leaves the rights of neutrals and neutral States entirely unaffected.

B. *"Armed Forces"*

The introductory statement by the Vietnamese delegate also makes clear that the sponsors were thinking of damage caused by the regular armed forces of a State party to the conflict, notably those of a colonial power engaged in a war of national liberation against a people struggling for its self-determination. But here they may have been overlooking two things. In the course of its first (1974) session the Diplomatic Conference had by a strong majority vote accepted the principle that wars of national liberation, as defined in Article 1, paragraph 4 of the Protocol, would be counted among the category of international armed conflicts.[64] And in the course of the 1976 session, always well before the introduction of the Vietnamese amendment, it had reached consensus on a completely new definition of "the armed forces of a Party to the conflict".[65]

By virtue of the first-mentioned decision, supported vigorously by Vietnam and its consorts, a liberation movement waging such a war would henceforth be regarded in all respects as a "Party to the conflict" in the sense of the Geneva Conventions of 1949 and the Protocol. One consequence is that such a liberation movement must be deemed to bear responsibility, in the terms of Article 91, "for all acts committed by persons forming part of its armed forces". Viewed from this angle, the principle expressed in the Article might even have backfired against Vietnam in its eventual negotiations with the United States.[66]

The plausible objection that liberation movements often have no "regular" armed force in the accepted sense of the term brings us to the second point the proponents of the amendment on responsibility may have been overlooking. The "armed forces", as now defined in Article 43 of Protocol I, "consist of all organised armed forces, groups and units

64. See e.g. Georges Abi-Saab, "Wars of National Liberation in the Geneva Conventions and Protocols" (1979–IV) 165 Hag. Rec. 353–446.

65. For an account and analysis of the drafting history of the definition, see e.g. by this author, "Reaffirmation and Development of International Humanitarian Law Applicable in Armed Conflicts: The Diplomatic Conference, Geneva, 1974–1977, Part I: Combatants and Civilians" (1977) 8 Neth Y.B.I.L. 107, 116.

66. More accurately, this consequence would arise as a matter of treaty law with the entry into force of the Protocol and as between ratifying States. In view of the attitude of Vietnam at the Conference, however, the US would doubtless be able to use the above argument as a political tool in negotiations with that State on reparations for war damages.

which are under a command responsible to that Party for the conduct of its subordinates".[67] This definition does not admit of any distinction between regular and irregular armed forces; and obviously so, since it was the declared purpose of the authors to do away with the traditional distinction between those two categories of armed forces.[68]

This brings us back to Article 91. The records provide no indication that Vietnam and consorts would have wished for the phrase "armed forces" to have a different connotation here from that it had acquired in Article 43. The latter Article had been brought about with their active co-operation, and they cannot be deemed to have been oblivious of its existence and significance just one year after its adoption. In the absence of any such indication, the sound principle of interpretation must apply that a term used more than once in a treaty has the same meaning everywhere. The principle applies *a fortiori* if the treaty makers have gone out of their way to provide an authentic definition of the term, as they did on this occasion with "armed forces".

Admittedly, it may not always be easy to submit irregular forces fighting on one's side to instructions similar to those a State normally issues to its regular armed forces. But this is a purely practical problem.[69]

There is, in short, nothing in the drafting history or the text of Protocol I to detract from the conclusion that the effect of Article 91, read in conjunction with Article 43, is to make a party to such an international armed conflict equally responsible for the conduct of all its armed forces, whether regular or irregular.

67. Art.43, para.1 reads as follows: "The armed forces of a Party to the conflict consist of all organised armed forces, groups and units which are under a command responsible to that Party for the conduct of its subordinates, even if that Party is represented by a government or an authority not recognised by an adverse Party. Such armed forces shall be subject to an internal disciplinary system which, *inter alia*, shall enforce compliance with the rules of international law applicable in armed conflict."

68. See, recently, George H. Aldrich, "Prospects for United States Ratification of Additional Protocol I to the 1949 Geneva Conventions" (1991) 85 A.J.I.L. 1, 8. The effect of the equality of regular and irregular armed forces extends to all international armed conflicts, including the case where such a force of a resistance movement conducts its operations in or outside occupied territory. Art.43 requires that it be under a command that is responsible to a party to the conflict for the conduct of its subordinates. It also specifies that the armed force "shall be subject to an internal disciplinary system which, *inter alia*, shall enforce compliance with the rules of international law applicable in armed conflict". Once these conditions are met (and they are not necessarily prohibitive), any armed force, no matter how irregular, must be regarded as an "armed force" in the sense of Art.43.

69. Moreover, Protocol I no longer maintains the close connection between the rule on responsibility and the duty to issue instructions. The latter obligation, embodied in Art.80(2) and providing that "The High Contracting Parties and the Parties to the conflict shall give orders and instructions to ensure observance of the Conventions and this Protocol, and shall supervise their execution", applies in time of peace as in time of war and is not restricted to the armed forces (but, rather, in abstract terms, requires the issue of instructions "to ensure observance of the Conventions and this Protocol").

C. Scope of Application of Article 91

There remains the marked textual difference, noted earlier, between Article 3 of 1907 and Article 91 of 1977: whilst the former speaks of violations of provisions of the Regulations, the latter refers to violations of "the provisions of the Conventions or of this Protocol". The question is what effect the difference in wording has on the scope of the new article.

As mentioned before, the Regulations were primarily designed to serve as model instructions for the armed forces. The same can no longer be maintained of the Geneva Conventions of 1949 and the Protocol of 1977. These instruments contain many provisions that are either designed to be implemented by other persons or institutions besides the armed forces,[70] or are even entirely unsuited, and were never intended, to provide rules for the conduct of military operations by armed forces.[71] Again, numerous provisions address the "Parties to the conflict" without further specification.[72] As practice shows, each and every one of these provisions is open to violation by the respective addressees. And in the event of individual damage, such violations may at least in theory give rise to claims for compensation.

This raises the question of the right interpretation of Article 91. Like its predecessor of 1907 it is composed of two sentences, with the first one positing the principle of liability to pay compensation and the second that of responsibility of the State for "all acts committed by persons forming part of its armed forces". The construction of Article 3 of the 1907 Convention meant that the first sentence was read not as serving to repeat a general principle of State responsibility, but as forming part and parcel of a special rule on the liability of a State to pay compensation first and foremost for damage incurred by individual persons as a result of infractions of the Regulations committed by members of the

70. This is true of the provisions relating to the wounded and sick, both in the Conventions and the Protocol, prescribing conduct not only to military medical personnel (which is properly regarded as part of the armed forces) but to civilian medical doctors and other personnel as well, including Red Cross or Red Crescent volunteers. E.g. Convention I, Art.26 (personnel of aid societies); Convention IV, Art.91 (medical attention to internees in the territory of a party to the conflict or in occupied territory); definition of medical personnel in Art.8(c) of the Protocol, which places military and civilian personnel on an equal footing.

71. This applies e.g. to the entire Section II of Part III ("Status and Treatment of Protected Persons") of the Fourth Convention, dealing with "Aliens in the Territory of a Party to the Conflict". Articles in this Section concern such matters as the right to leave the territory, means of existence, employment, and internment: Arts.35, 39, 40 and 41–46.

72. Thus, they are required to take measures for the protection of children under 15 who are orphaned or separated from their families as a result of the war (Convention IV, Art.24); and it is for each of them to establish and operate an official information bureau for prisoners of war and other protected persons in their power (Convention III, Art.122, Convention IV, Art.136). Then, the "High Contracting Parties" are obliged to facilitate the passage of relief consignments (Convention III, Arts.73–75, Convention IV, Art.23, Protocol I, Art.70).

State's armed forces. The drafters of Article 91 were no longer thinking in terms of claims of individuals; but must the two sentences of Article 91 nevertheless be read as a single construction or does the first sentence stand on its own?

If interpreted in the latter sense, the single feature distinguishing the sentence from a simple restatement of a general principle of State responsibility lies in its explicit restriction to the parties to the conflict, thus leaving out the generality of the contracting States. This interpretation might have the effect of restricting the sentence, and by inference the entire Article, to acts done by the organ in question, whether military or civilian, in its capacity as an organ of the State.

Another interpretation appears at least as plausible, however. It is that the restatement of the Article has left the meaning of the first sentence unaffected. This interpretation takes inspiration from the introduction by the Vietnamese delegate, who was evidently thinking only of the wrongful acts imputed to the American armed forces. In effect, the records provide no indication whatever of an intention to place a new and different interpretation on the sentence—or any interpretation at all, for that matter. In the light of this utter silence, this author sees good grounds to treat the sentence as unchanged in its meaning, and to continue to regard the two sentences that compose Article 91 as an indivisible whole in the same sense, and with the same consequences, as Article 3 of the 1907 Convention.

Even so, in certain other respects the significance of the Article may have perceptibly changed, at least as compared to the intentions of the draftsmen of 1907. For one thing, as argued above, the delegates at that earlier Conference plausibly had in mind comparatively small-scale events, where the victim of the damaging act could identify the culprit and only by way of last resort, as a safer method of recovering his damages, needed to be given an individual right of access to the competent authorities behind that guilty person. This mode of thinking was certainly very far from what the Vietnamese and other delegates in 1977 had in mind.

Not that small-scale, man-to-man actions no longer occur in the type of armed conflict they were familiar with; witness My Lai,[73] to give just the one example. The example makes starkly clear, however, that the

73. On 16 Mar. 1968, an attack by some 80 American infantrymen under the command of 1st Lt. William L. Calley, Jr. on the My Lai No.4 hamlet of Son My village in South Vietnam resulted in the slaughter of more than 400 Vietnamese civilians. On this massacre see, e.g., Telford Taylor, *Nuremberg and Vietnam: An American Tragedy* (1970); Richard A. Falk (Ed.), *The Vietnam War and International Law* Vol.3 (1972) p.327 *et seq.*; Peter D. Trooboff (Ed.), *Law and Responsibility in Warfare: The Vietnam Experience* (1975) *passim*; Leon Friedman, *The Law of War, A Documentary History* Vol.2 (1972) p.1703: instructions from the military judge to the court members in the trial of William L. Calley, Jr.; p.1729: *ibid.* in the trial of Ernest L. Medina.

notion of direct compensation for losses suffered at the hands of the enemy is very far from the reality of such situations. Furthermore, as hinted earlier, actions of an entirely different character have long since taken over the role of major damaging factor, in particular where damage to the civilian population is concerned. The oft-described main factor here was the development of the air arm, with its dual capability of stand-off air support to ground forces and independent long-distance operations against targets deep inside enemy-held territory. To this can now be added the increased sophistication of munitions and their guidance systems. In these circumstances, there can no longer be any question of a victim "claim[ing] damages from the officer or soldier guilty of the infraction"—if infraction there was, of course. Even if one accepts that Article 91 at least also envisages claims by individual persons of enemy nationality, such claims can at best be addressed to the State behind the actual but unknown offender. The probability that in such a case the State rather than the individual victim will be the actual claimant is all that much greater.

The virtual substitution of the individual enemy national by his State as principal claimant may entail yet another expansion of the scope of Article 91, as compared with its predecessor of 1907. There are no longer any good grounds to conclude, as we did in respect of Article 3 of 1907, that Article 91 does not cover damage suffered by combatants as a result of unlawful acts of their adversaries. To the extent that such damage falls under the scope of Article 91, practices such as the use against the enemy armed forces of forbidden weapons or methods of warfare (e.g. chemical weapons,[74] or a refusal of quarter[75]) may lead to claims for compensation on the part of the victim or, rather, his State. And the same would apply to claims arising out of maltreatment by members of the armed forces of enemy combatants detained as prisoners of war.

All this applies to damage suffered by persons of enemy nationality. Matters may be different when it comes to neutral persons: there is no valid reason why they should be cut off from the possibility (or indeed, where the requirement of exhaustion of local remedies obtains, the necessity) to submit their claims personally and directly to the proper authorities of the responsible State. In this regard, the ICRC asserts that "apart from exceptional cases, persons with a foreign nationality who have been wronged by the unlawful conduct of a Party to the conflict should address themselves to their own government, which will submit their complaints to the Party or Parties which committed the

74. Such use is prohibited under the Protocol for the Prohibition of the Use in War of Asphyxiating, Poisonous or Other Gases, and of Bacteriological Methods of Warfare, signed at Geneva, 17 June 1925; Schindler and Toman, *op. cit. supra* n.9, at p.115.

75. Protocol I, Art.40.

violation".[76] This author sees no good grounds for this assertion, even as a matter of general theory. And of course, it goes directly against the purport of Article 3 of the Hague Convention of 1907 which, as the ICRC itself notes,[77] is not abrogated by Article 91 "in any way, which means that it continues to be customary law for all nations".

D. *Article 91 and the General Rules on State Responsibility*

Compared to the International Law Commission's draft articles on State responsibility, one striking feature of Article 91 is that apart from States it can be construed to apply to liberation movements as well. This expands the notion of international responsibility for acts of war to cover entities other than States. In principle, there is nothing against this: as long as the movement's struggle for self-determination lasts, the situation is sufficiently similar to the one contemplated in the Commission's draft articles to justify applying the notion of international responsibility. A difficulty will arise, though, when the war is over and the liberation movement has lost: it then ceases to exist as a (temporary) international subject, and with that its capacity to be held liable for any damages unlawfully caused under its responsibility.

Another interesting feature of Article 91, though not one that sets it apart from the Commission's draft articles, is that its scope of application encompasses irregular armed forces besides the regular ones. The former will not normally have the status of organs of the State under its internal law and therefore cannot be brought under the scope of draft article 5 to make their conduct directly attributable to the State.[78] They may, on the other hand, be counted among the "groups of persons . . . in fact acting on behalf of the State" whose conduct, according to draft article 8, is equally "considered as an act of the State under international law". It may be repeated that in order to qualify as an armed force under Article 43 of Protocol I, they must be "under a command that is responsible [to the State] for the conduct of its subordinates"; moreover, their actions are generally seen to be for the benefit of the State.

76. ICRC Commentary, *op. cit. supra* n.33, pp.1053–1058, at p.1056. The argument in the text does not purport to deny that in certain circumstances neutral States may take the initiative in claiming damages, including those caused to their nationals. A (rather unusual) case in point concerns the Swiss claims lodged after the Second World War against Germany, for damages German bombs had caused on Swiss soil, in the neighbourhood of Schaffhausen; see Maurice Jacquard, "Über Neutralitätsverletzungsschäden in der Schweiz während des Zweiten Weltkrieges" (1951) 87 Zeitschrift des Bernischen Juristenverbandes 225–251.

77. ICRC, *idem*, p.1053.

78. This may be different in countries with an "all people's defence" system. This point will not be examined here.

For the rest, some of the comments made earlier with respect to Article 3 of the Hague Convention apply with equal force here. Most importantly, like Article 3, Article 91 as interpreted above is broader than the Commission's draft articles in that it makes the State responsible for "all acts committed by persons forming part of its armed forces", not just those performed by an organ "acting in that capacity in the case in question". This is no slight extension of the responsibility of the State, but once again, one entirely justified by the specificities of the situation. The State should bear responsibility, not merely for (unlawful) acts of war properly so called, but equally for those acts of wantonness or savagery committed by members of its armed forces outside the sphere of duty but in violation of the law of armed conflict. This applies to acts against civilians and enemy combatants alike. A (not entirely imaginary) instance of the latter category is that of the soldier who, in the aftermath of an engagement in which he lost many close comrades, out of sheer frustration and despair wilfully kills an enemy his unit had taken prisoner. No matter how far deviating from sound military practice and entirely outside the sphere of duty, such irrational conduct falls indubitably under the scope of the same rule on responsibility of the State as do acts of war in the proper sense.

V. EPILOGUE: STATE RESPONSIBILITY FOR ACTS OF ARMED FORCES, THE INTERNATIONAL COURT OF JUSTICE AND THE SECURITY COUNCIL

IN the case of *Nicaragua* v. *The United States of America* the International Court of Justice came up against the interesting question under what conditions, if any, a State can be held responsible for conduct of armed forces which cannot be regarded as "its" armed forces, not even in the sense of Article 43 of Protocol I.

In the perception of Nicaragua, the *contras* were no more than a mercenary army "conceived, created and organised" by the United States.[79] While the Court did not unreservedly accept this proposition, it recognised that the influence of the United States over the *contras* was generally strong; indeed, it held it established that the US authorities "largely financed, trained, equipped, armed and organised" the force.[80] It then posed itself the question, in terms taken straight from the International Law Commission's draft articles on State responsibility, "whether or not the relationship of the *contras* to the United States Government was so much one of dependence on the one side and control on the other that it would be right to equate the *contras*, for legal purposes, with an organ of the United States Government, or as acting on behalf of that

79. I.C.J. Rep. 1986, 43, para.93.
80. *Idem*, p.52, para.108.

Government". It rapidly concluded, implicitly, that they could not be equated to an organ of the United States, and in express terms, that "there is no clear evidence of the United States having actually exercised such a degree of control in all fields as to justify treating the *contras* as acting on its behalf".[81] Even so, the Court stressed once again "that a degree of control by the United States Government . . . is inherent in the position in which the *contra* force finds itself in relation to that Government".[82]

Was this "degree of control" sufficient to justify the Nicaraguan claim that the United States was responsible for activities of the *contras* to such an extent that it could be held itself "to have violated an obligation of international law not to kill, wound or kidnap citizens of Nicaragua"?[83] In this regard, the Court considered that "United States participation, even preponderant or decisive, in the financing, organising, training, supplying and equipping of the *contras*, the selection of its military or paramilitary targets, and the planning of the whole of its operation, is still insufficient in itself, on the basis of the evidence in the possession of the Court, for the purpose of attributing to the United States the acts committed by the *contras* in the course of their military or paramilitary operations in Nicaragua". And it continued:[84]

> All the forms of United States participation mentioned above, and even the general control by the respondent State over a force with a high degree of dependency on it, would not in themselves mean, without further evidence, that the United States directed or enforced the perpetration of acts contrary to human rights and humanitarian law alleged by the applicant State. Such acts could well be committed by members of the *contras* without the control of the United States. For this conduct to give rise to legal responsibility of the United States, it would in principle have to be proved that that State had effective control of the military or paramilitary operations in the course of which the alleged violations were committed.

This, the Court held, had not been the case:[85] "The Court does not consider that the assistance given by the United States to the *contras* warrants the conclusion that these forces are subject to the United States to such an extent that any acts they have committed are imputable to that State."

Two comments seem pertinent. First, the argument that acts contrary to the relevant law could "well be committed by members of the *contras* without the control of the United States" seems rather unfortunate: even members of the most regular of a State's armed forces are apt to

81. *Idem*, para.109.
82. *Idem*, p.53, para.111.
83. *Idem*, para.113.
84. *Idem*, p.64, para.115.
85. *Idem*, p.65, para.116.

commit such acts without the control of their State or, indeed, against pertinent instructions and direct orders. After all, Article 3 was introduced into the Hague Convention IV of 1907 precisely with an eye to that eventuality.

Second, and more importantly, although the Court in the case before it came to a negative conclusion, it did recognise the possibility in principle for a State to become directly responsible for conduct of a foreign armed force that cannot, under the terms of Article 43 of Protocol I, be regarded as part of its armed forces, or, for that matter, as an organ of the State in the sense of Articles 5 and 6 of the International Law Commission's draft articles, or even as a group of persons acting on its behalf in the sense of Article 8. For this direct responsibility to arise, the Court requires proof "that that State had effective control of the military or paramilitary operations in the course of which the alleged violations were committed".

There remains the question of which circumstances could warrant the conclusion that a State actually has such effective control. When one rereads the long list of factors the Court regarded as insufficient "for the purpose of attributing to the United States the acts committed by the *contras* in the course of their military or paramilitary operations in Nicaragua", because they "would not in themselves mean, without further evidence, that the United States directed or enforced the perpetration of acts contrary to human rights and humanitarian law alleged by the applicant State", one wonders how a State could ever achieve the required high level of control over a body of men operating in another country without actually incorporating it in its armed forces.

Be this as it may, it remains to be seen whether, and how, this view of the Court on the effect of "effective control" over armed forces is going to influence the doctrine of responsibility of States for breaches of the international humanitarian law of armed conflict.

Meanwhile, another recent development, of greater practical interest, ensued from the Iraqi invasion, occupation and purported annexation of Kuwait in August 1990. As mentioned in the Introduction, the Security Council has included in the impressive list of resolutions adopted in connection with that event measures to ensure that Iraq effectively compensates the damage caused by its unlawful actions. One aspect, *viz.*, the patent illegality of the aggression against Kuwait as a matter of *ius ad bellum*, need not be discussed here. On the other hand, of obvious interest in the present context is Iraq's liability for damage resulting from unlawful acts of war committed by members of its armed forces in the course of their operations: how to give effect to it?

It need hardly be emphasised that simple application of the principle embodied in Article 3 of the Hague Convention IV of 1907 could be of little avail here: the sheer number and size of potential individual claims against Iraq would overwhelm even the most diligent administration (and it may be doubted whether the present Iraqi administration falls in that category). The other traditional solution, conclusion of lump sum agreements between Iraq and other States, would be equally unsatisfactory in that it would fail to guarantee a just and effective settlement of individual claims.

To overcome these and other problems involved in the matter at issue, the Security Council has taken an entirely new departure. By its Resolutions 687 (1991) of 3 April 1991 and 692 (1991) of 20 May 1991,[86] and in accordance with the suggestions in the Secretary-General's report of 2 May 1991,[87] it has created a UN Compensation Fund, to be established by the Secretary-General as a special account of the United Nations. To administer the Fund, the UN Compensation Commission is established as a subsidiary organ of the Council and charged with the task of addressing the numerous issues connected with the settlement of claims. These issues can roughly be grouped under the following headings: how to get and evaluate the claims, and how to make Iraq pay money into the Fund.

As regards the filing of claims, the Secretary-General recommends "that the Commission should entertain, as a general rule, only consolidated claims filed by individual Governments on their own behalf or on behalf of their nationals or corporations". As he explains, "The filing of individual claims would entail tens of thousands of claims to be processed by the Commission, a task which could take a decade or more and could lead to inequalities in the filing of claims disadvantaging small claimants."[88]

If the Commission is to entertain only consolidated claims, it will be for each State to consolidate both its own claims and those of its nationals and corporations. The Secretary-General mentions the possibility of a categorisation: by type ("for example, claims for loss of life or personal injury and property damage, environmental damage or damage due to the depletion of natural resources"), by size (small, medium and large), and according to whether a loss has been incurred by the government or by a national or corporation. While recommending that a fixed period be established for the filing of all claims, he suggests by way of alternative that the Commission could set different limits for different types of claims "to ensure that priority is given to certain claims, for example, loss of life or personal injury". This leads him to give as his "opinion that there would be some merit in providing for a priority consideration of small claims relating to losses by individuals so

86. Para.18 of Res.687 (1991), para.3 of Res.692 (1991).
87. S/22559, Report pursuant to para.19 of Res.687 (1991).
88. *Idem*, para.21.

that these are disposed of before the consideration of claims relating to losses by foreign Governments and by corporations".[89]

The "priority consideration" referred to in this phrase cannot mean anything but consideration by the Commission. If this reading of the report is correct, it follows that although the Commission is to be confronted only with consolidated claims, it will nonetheless fall within its province to evaluate individual claims included in a consolidated claim. As the Secretary-General notes: "The processing of claims [by the Commission] will entail the verification of claims and evaluation of losses and the resolution of any disputed claims. The major part of this task is not of a judicial nature; the resolution of disputed claims would, however, be quasi-judicial." A preliminary point preceding the verification of claims will in his view be the determination whether the loss, damage or injury for which a claim is presented is, in terms of paragraph 19 of Resolution 687 (1991), "direct, . . . as a result of Iraq's unlawful invasion and occupation of Kuwait".[90]

When one compares this planned procedure with the two existing methods, namely, application of Article 3 and the practice of lump sum agreements, it seems evident that the Security Council and the Secretary-General are making a serious attempt to avoid the drawbacks of either of these methods. The filing by governments of consolidated claims relieves individual victims of the need to go and present their claims to the Iraqi authorities; the procedure also removes the implicit difference in the treatment of enemy and neutral individuals. While this amounts to the abandonment of a method that in the circumstances would be plainly impracticable, the rejection of the lump sum method implies the avoidance of the arbitrariness and risk of injustice inherent in the latter method.[91]

As mentioned above, the Secretary-General characterises the planned procedure as largely non-judicial and only partly quasi-judicial.

89. *Idem*, para.24. As a fixed time period for the filing of claims, the report suggests that "A period of two years from the adoption of the filing guidelines [by the Commission] would appear to be adequate."

90. *Idem*, para.25.

91. An example demonstrating these features of the lump sum method may be seen in the manner in which after the Second World War claims of Dutch ex-prisoners of war and ex-civilian internees against Japan were settled in two separate agreements between the governments of the Netherlands and Japan. For the ex-POWs, the Dutch authorities accepted in 1951 a sum that amounted to Dfl.264 each (Art.16 of the Peace Treaty concluded at San Francisco on 16 Sept. 1951). As a result of further negotiations, the two governments subsequently reached an agreement settling the matter of compensation for the ex-civilian internees; the sum paid by Japan amounted to Dfl.385 per person (Protocol of Tokyo, 13 Mar. 1956). In both instruments, the Netherlands government renounced for itself and its nationals all further claims for compensation. In recent years, the gross inadequacy of the sums paid in compensation for the hardships suffered has been argued, *inter alia*, in the Dutch Parliament, but to no avail, as the government has stuck to its position that the agreements of 1951 and 1956 have definitively settled the matter.

In effect, he recognises that the Commission will have no exclusive competence to deal with claims arising out of Iraq's recent ill-advised activities. He considers it "entirely possible, indeed probable, that individual claimants will proceed with claims against Iraq in their domestic legal systems".[92] Strictly speaking, such an occurrence will not amount to a reanimation of the principle of Article 3, since that would require the presentation of claims to the (military or other) authorities of the country to which the armed forces in question belong, *in casu*, Iraq.

In sum, the procedure as briefly summarised here seems a remarkable step forward. Obviously, to be effective, it requires an influx of money. It is not appropriate here to enter into the difficulties involved and the solutions suggested by the Secretary-General.[93] Suffice it to say that the success or failure of the operation depends entirely on these problems being solved.

For the purposes of this article, the main point of interest in this latest development lies in the apparent determination of the Secretary-General and, presumably, the Security Council to do justice to the claims of individual persons besides those of governments and corporations. I am fully aware that all the peculiarities of the present situation do not permit of any over-hasty generalisations. Even so, one may perhaps entertain some hope that in future, States that send their armed forces into war will have to count more seriously than ever before the possibility that they will be held effectively liable for any violations of the law of armed conflict committed by these forces in the course of their operations.

92. Report, *op. cit. supra* n.87, at para.22.
93. *Idem*, paras.13–19.

[8]

The History of the Grave Breaches Regime

Yves Sandoz*

Abstract

Criminal punishment for violations of the laws of war date to the earliest formal codifications. In particular, the Lieber Code of 1863 contained a large number of references to criminal punishment, which ultimately influenced a large number of the subsequent treaties. This said, initial codifications of the laws and customs of war after Lieber but before the Geneva Conventions of 1949 made only scant reference to individual criminal liability. Nonetheless, the grave breaches regime emerged in 1949 as an important response to the sufferings of Second World War. The idea behind the regime was that certain offences were sufficiently grave to warrant explicit codifications as war crimes. The development of grave breaches was then continued in 1977, first by the inclusion of further offences within Additional Protocol I, then by inclusion of the grave breaches regime within the Statute of the International Criminal Court. As a general rule, this development has nonetheless involved developing rules to deal with the horrors of the past. Potentially, history will serve as a helpful guide for countering the numerous challenges that face grave breaches in the future.

1. Introduction

Modern international humanitarian law starts in the middle of the nineteenth century,[1] when states decided to adopt conventions with the ambition not only of binding the participating states, but also of identifying and adopting principles and rules of universal value.[2] They first tried to attract as many states as possible to the process of negotiation, then left the treaties they had adopted open to signature or adhesion by any state, whether or not it had

* Member of the International Committee of the Red Cross (ICRC), Professor of International Humanitarian Law at the Geneva Academy of International Humanitarian Law and Human Rights and the University of Fribourg.

1 The 1856 Paris Declaration 'appears to have been the first open-ended multilateral treaty': A. Roberts and R. Guelff, *Documents on the Laws of War* (3rd edn., Oxford: Oxford University Press, 2000), at 5.

2 Even if we keep in mind that we were still in the heart of the colonial period and that a distinction was made between what were called the 'civilized States' and the rest of the world.

658 JICJ 7 (2009), 657–682

participated in the negotiation. The first of these treaties were very brief. The 1856 Paris Declaration,[3] the 1864 Geneva Convention[4] and the 1868 San-Petersburg Declaration[5] contained only a small number of articles, none of which addressed penal sanctions. In fact, the question of individual criminal liability was not discussed during the negotiation of those treaties. The state parties accepted obligations towards each other, but it was up to them, and to them alone, to see that they discharged those obligations. At the time, governments would not tolerate external interference in such matters.

These initial three treaties each dealt with a specific topic within warfare. The first systematic codification of the laws of war appeared in a domestic code rather than international treaty. The 'Instructions for the Government of Armies of the United States in the Field', prepared by Professor Francis Lieber[6] and promulgated by President Abraham Lincoln during the American Civil War had an appreciable influence on the development of war crimes. This article will commence by examining the Lieber Code as one of the initial predecessors to the grave breaches regime. Second, the article will examine the evolution of the notion of penal sanctions and of grave breaches since the promulgation of the Lieber Code until the adoption of the 1949 Geneva Conventions. The grave breaches regime in the Geneva Conventions, and its evolution afterwards, will form the third part of this article, before I conclude with some brief final remarks.

2. The Lieber Code

A. *Context and Preparatory Phase*

Francis Lieber is often thought of as an old professor, but he also lived an eventful and tumultuous life that had many dimensions.[7] Military problems fascinated the old scholar, and during the first confused months after the outbreak of the American Civil War he turned his intellect to clarifying one hazy legal question after another. The most significant of these concerned the treatment of the foe on the battlefield. The enemy in this case were Confederate rebels, and according to the reasoning of many, they should

3 Paris Declaration Respecting Maritime Law (1856). This text (along with those following) are found, inter alia, in D. Schindler and J. Toman, *The Laws of Armed Conflicts: A Collection of Conventions, Resolutions and other Documents* (4th rev. edn., Leiden: Martinus Nijhoff, 2004), at 1055–1058.

4 Geneva Convention for the Amelioration of the Condition of the Wounded in Armies in the Field (1864), in Schindler and Toman, *supra* note 3, at 365–368.

5 Saint-Petersburg Declaration Renouncing the Use, in Time of War, of Explosive Projectiles under 400 Grammes Weight (1868), in Schindler and Toman, *supra* note 3, at 91–93.

6 The 'Instructions for the Government of Armies of the United States in the Field' were promulgated as General Orders Number 100 by President Lincoln on 24 April 1863: Schindler and Toman, *supra* note 3, at 3–20.

7 F.B. Freidel, *Francis Lieber: Nineteenth-Century Liberal* (Baton Rouge: Louisiana State University Press, 1947), at vii.

simply have been prosecuted for treason. This would, of course, have resulted in the:

> unspeakable shambles of no-quarter war .... The skilful Lieber delved into treatises on international law and came up with a formula. For humanitarian reasons, even in times of rebellion, the customary rules of warfare and treatment of prisoners should continue. Precedents proved this did not involve either the recognition of the rebels nor a foregoing of the right to try rebels for treason after the rebellion was crushed .... Since the dictum was sound international law and backed by a general humanitarian sentiment, it became the official viewpoint.[8]

This success, and the fact that for the average officer the laws of war 'were no more than rhetorical expressions to justify one's own conduct and damn the enemy's', encouraged Lieber in his desire to write 'a little book on the Laws and Usages of War, affecting the Combatants, some 200 pages'.[9] Fortunately for this enterprise, General Henry Wager Halleck had been appointed by President Lincoln as Commander in Chief of the Western Armies. Halleck was himself the author of a treatise on international law of which more than two thirds was devoted to the laws of war.[10] Halleck and Lieber were also friends, which certainly encouraged Lieber in his efforts.

Lieber therefore set about drafting a comprehensive 'set of rules and definitions providing for the most urgent cases, occurring under the Laws and Usages of War, and on which our Articles of War are silent'. In terms of form, he was certain that 'the President ought to issue such rules'. Eventually, Lieber received the President's assent to prepare these rules in the framework of a military committee. He then 'quickly prepared a draft code during the first few weeks of 1863', drawing on various writings, including Heffter,[11] Grotius, Bijnkershoek, Pufendorf and of course Halleck as precedents.[12]

He submitted the draft and received suggestions from General Hallek and a handful of others. After amendments, the 'Instructions for the Government of Armies of the United States in the Field' were approved by the President who ordered that it 'be published for the information of all concerned'. It was not binding, but as General Halleck pointed out, it was 'a statement of general principles which apply only in the absence of a special agreement and which could be tempered at the discretion of the President, the War Department or commanders in the field .... In sum, General Order 100 was a logical outgrowth of the conflict, a guide for its conduct, and an interpretation of its meaning'.[13]

Lieber's code dealt with numerous problems that are still at the heart of present debates: guerrilla warfare, the status of rebels, the applicability of the laws of war to internal armed conflicts and, particularly important for the present purposes, the importance of penal sanctions. We also see that Lieber's sources

8 *Ibid.*, at 320.
9 *Ibid.*, at 323–324 and fn. 16
10 *Ibid.*, at 324.
11 A.W. Heffter, *Das Europäische Völkerrecht der Gegenwart* (3rd edn., Berlin: E.H. Schroeder, 1855).
12 Freidel, *supra* note 7, and letter from Lieber to Halleck, 3 October 1863, also quoted by Freidel.
13 *Ibid.*, at 335.

were still, apart from a few contemporary scholars, the well-known authors of the seventeenth and eighteenth centuries mentioned above. This demonstrates the influence of their writings, considered for the most part as an indication of the 'laws and usages of war' already mentioned in the 1806 Articles of War (which conclusively revised the military Code adopted first by the Continental Congress in 1775 and later amended in 1775 and 1786.) Those sources probably had a tangible influence on the conduct of armies, composition of courts-martial, and generally, the administration of military justice before the publication of the Lieber Code, leaving the influence of Lieber's seminal code difficult to assess. Nonetheless, there is little doubt that the content of the Code inspired subsequent legal developments, as the following sections show.

B. Content

Although a full analysis of the Lieber Code is beyond the scope of this article, a review of some specific characteristics is relevant. With respect to criminal jurisdiction, for example, the Lieber Code set out many details on the subject of martial law, which was 'simply military authority exercised in accordance with the laws and usages of war'. According to the terms of the Code, martial law required those in charge of administering it 'to be strictly guided by the principles of justice, honor, and humanity — virtues adorning a soldier even more than other men, for the very reason that he possesses the power of his arms against the unarmed' (Article 4). In occupied territory the foreign armed force could substitute their own penal and civil laws, but 'the commander of forces may proclaim that the administration of all civil and penal law shall continue either wholly or in part' (Article 3). In fact, the 'usual course' of local civil and penal law could only be interrupted by order of the occupying military power (Article 6).

The key principle of the Lieber Code is military necessity, which it described as 'measures which are indispensable for securing the ends of the war, and which are lawful according to the modern law and usages of war' (Article 14). The provisions protecting the civilian population in general were less well developed than they are today, with the idea that 'the citizen or native of a hostile country is thus an enemy, as one of the constituents of the hostile state or nation, and as such is subjected to the hardships of the war' (Article 21). Starvation is accepted as a legitimate mean of warfare (Article 17). Killing was accepted not only of all armed enemies, but of all other persons whose 'destruction is incidentally unavoidable' (Article 15). Prisoners of war 'are liable for the infliction of retaliatory measures' (Article 59). Hostages could even be taken (but only for a limited purpose, 'as a pledge for the fulfilment of an agreement concluded by governments during the war') (Article 54). Escape was not a war crime but 'conspiracy for a general escape ... may be vigorously punished' (Article 77). Though there was no right to declare that there would be no quarter, it was nevertheless permitted for a commander to deny quarter 'when his own salvation makes it impossible to cumber himself with prisoners' (Article 60). The general idea defended by Lieber was that 'the most vigorously wars are pursued, the better it is for humanity'. In other words, 'sharp wars are brief' (Article 29).

Lieber nevertheless set some absolute limits, some acts for which even military necessity could not serve as an excuse. There must be no 'cruelty (suffering for the sake of suffering or for revenge)', no 'maiming or wounding except in fight', no 'torture to extort confession', no 'use of poison in any way', no 'wanton devastation', and no 'acts of perfidy' (Article 16). On the question of torture, Lieber insisted further that 'the modern law of war permits no longer the use of any violence against prisoners in order to extort the desired information or to punish them for having given false information' (Article 80). Murder was prohibited, in the sense that 'the laws of war do not allow proclaiming either an individual belonging to the hostile army, or a citizen, or a subject of the hostile government, are outlaw .... It abhors such outrage ... made by whatever authority' (Article 148). In spite of the fact that he viewed the suffering of the entire enemy population as justified, Lieber recognized that 'the principle has been more and more acknowledged that the unarmed citizen is to be spared in person, property and honor as much as the exigencies of war admit' (Article 22). As for the direct contact with the population, there was a recognition of the 'sacredness of domestic relations, and that all wanton violence committed against persons in the invaded country, all destructions of property not commanded by the authorized officers, all robbery, all pillage or sacking, even after taking a place by main force, all rape wounding, maiming or killing of such inhabitants are strictly forbidden' (Article 44). Finally, Lieber also prohibited all 'crimes punishable by all penal codes' (Article 47).

The Lieber Code frequently punished violations of these rules with penal sanctions — the Code contains numerous references to the death penalty. The discipline of soldiers was perceived as being key to military success. But it was not only acts clearly contrary to the interest of an army (desertion, giving information to the enemy, refusal to obey legitimate superiors orders, etc.) which were severely criminally punished. Acts that might be perceived as committed in the short-term interests of an army (such as torturing prisoners to obtain information) were also criminal. Maintaining moral standards was deemed to be in the long-term interests of the army. In turn, this was perceived as a way to create a perception of integrity and legitimacy, which promoted chances that the defeated nation and population would accept conquest. As the Code emphasized, '[m]en who take up arms against one another in public war do not cease on this account to be moral beings, responsible to one another and to God' (Article 15 *in fine*).

The Lieber Code stated that behind severe penalties lay 'the principles of justice, honor and humanity' (Article 4). A soldier must behave in the manner expected from a normal citizen indeed even better than a normal citizen. He was judged as a normal citizen for penal law crimes, such as rape, or injuring, or killing civilians. He could be sentenced to 'the penalty of death or such other severe punishment as may seem adequate for the gravity of the offense' (Article 44) and criminal acts punishable by penal codes are 'not only punishable as at home, but in all cases in which death is not inflicted, the severe punishment shall be preferred' (Article 47).

But equally importantly, the very effectiveness of the army was at stake. Penalties were needed to maintain discipline in armies and their execution in some cases appears even more important than the demands of justice and strict rules of procedure. The military courts, for instance, were competent to give sentences of death in principle with the approval of the chief executive and of the chief commander 'provided the urgency of the case does not require a speedy execution' (Article 12). And a soldier who refused to obey a superior's order to refrain from acts of wanton violence like those mentioned above 'may be lawfully killed on the spot by such superior' (Article 44).

The treatment of spies is also interesting in this regard. Spies were not considered as criminal to the extent that they were not subject to criminal punishment for their espionage if they safely rejoined their army afterwards before being re-captured and recognized (Article 104). However, if captured in the course of spying, they had to be given a spectacular penalty to dissuade everyone from engaging in such activity. This was the only rule in the Code that prescribed 'death by hanging by the neck' (Article 88).

In short, the Lieber Code highlights the importance of punishment in armies. Violations of the laws of war and unlawful acts committed against the enemy, in particular civilians, are severely punished on the basis of fundamental principles of human dignity, honour and chivalry. At the same time, however, a significant portion of the criminal offences enumerated also sought to maintain discipline and to motivate the troops.

3. Further Evolution of International Penal Sanctions and of Grave Breaches

A. *From the Lieber Code to the First World War*

The Lieber Code presupposed that the values of justice, honour, and humanity were inherent to all 'civilized nations'. In this context, the risk that a commander might order, tolerate or cover up wrongful acts committed by his soldiers did not appear important. But the reality quickly proved quite different. The laws and customs of war were regularly flouted during the 1870–1871 Franco–Prussian War,[14] and this failure sparked two kinds of reaction. The law's detractors viewed it as confirming their conviction that it was ridiculous to try mitigating the suffering caused by war, which was cruel by nature and had to be without any restriction in order to be as brief as possible. On the

14 For a detailed description of the problem encountered in the application of the 1864 Geneva Convention during this war, see P. Boissier, *From Solferino to Tsushima: History of the International Committee of the Red Cross* (Geneva: Henry Dunant Institute, 1985).

contrary, the supporters of international humanitarian law drew the conclusion that it was important to strengthen the provisions of that law in order to increase its effectiveness. In response, Gustave Moynier, one of the founders of the International Committee of the Red Cross (ICRC) and its longest-serving president (1864–1910), proposed international penal sanctions. In 1872 he even made a formal proposal — alas, to no avail — for the creation of an international criminal court.[15] This, nonetheless, did not prevent a range of further important historical developments during the period.

1. *The Brussels Conference of 1874*

In 1874, Czar Alexander II of Russia convened an international conference held in Brussels in order to draft a comprehensive set of rules applicable in armed conflict on the model of the Lieber Code. The 15 European states invited to the event adopted an 'International Declaration concerning the Laws and Customs of War',[16] but this declaration never entered into force since not all participating governments were prepared to accept it as a binding convention.[17] The Declaration nevertheless remains a good instrument of reference if one is seeking some idea of the type of rules discussed at that time. In many respects, they were quite similar to those included in the Lieber Code. The idea of an international criminal court was not proposed, but a delegate to the conference named General Arnaudeau suggested that states be asked to coordinate their internal legislation so as to ensure equal punishment for those who violated the laws of war.

This suggestion reflected a concern not only for stronger measures to ensure better implementation of adopted laws, but also for justice that transcended national borders. The proposal that national legislations be standardized may be considered a first step in the direction of a common definition of grave breaches. Unhappily, this was not mentioned in the declaration and apparently led to no other concrete action.

2. *The Oxford Manuals of 1880 and 1913*

A few years after states failed to adopt the Brussels Declaration as a treaty, the members of the Institute of International Law judged it important to give new impetus to the idea of a comprehensive code of the laws of war on land again modelled on the Lieber Code. The question of penal sanctions was not forgotten, but there were no new proposals. The Oxford Manual on the Laws of

15 See J.S. Pictet, *Commmentary to the First 1949 Geneva Conventions* (Geneva: ICRC, 1952), especially Chapter IX.

16 Project of an International Declaration Concerning the Laws and Customs of War, in Schindler and Toman, *supra* note 3, at 21–28.

17 *Ibid.*, at 21.

War on Land[18] finally adopted by the Institute in 1880 proposed that those responsible for violating the laws of war be liable for punishment as provided for in criminal law. But no detail was provided elaborating on the nature of the offences or jurisdictions capable of trying these offences.[19] In other words, the Oxford Manual acknowledged that internal penal sanctions were necessary but without reference either to standardization or to an international jurisdiction. And in 1913, when the second Manual was drawn up on the Laws of Naval War Governing Relations between Belligerents,[20] no changes were made regarding these issues.

3. The Hague Conferences of 1899 and 1907

The numerous texts on the laws of war drawn up at the Hague Conferences of 1899 and 1907 make no further mention of criminal sanctions.[21] However, Article 3 of the 1907 Convention regarding the Laws and Customs of War on Land stipulates that 'a belligerent Party which violates the provisions of the said Regulations shall, if the case demands, be liable to pay compensation. It shall be responsible for all acts committed by persons forming part of its armed forces.'[22] This marks a return to the traditional view of relations between states as being confined to reparation for damages, and leaves to states the responsibility to stop and repress violations committed by members of their respective armed forces.

4. The 1906 Geneva Convention

Although the texts adopted in The Hague in 1899 and 1907 did not provide for penal sanctions, one year before the second conference two articles on repressing violations were introduced in the new Geneva Convention (6 July 1906),[23] which expanded on and replaced the 1864 Geneva Convention.

18 *Oxford Session of 1880, The Laws of War on Land* (Manual published by the Institute of International Law).

19 Art. 84 of the Manual.

20 *Oxford Session of 1913, The Laws of Naval War Governing the Relations between Belligerents* (Manual published by the Institute of International Law).

21 One school of thought holds, however, that the absence of penal provisions in the Hague Conventions is not the result of a political choice. For example, Louis Renault states with regard to penal sanctions: 'So they weren't thought of in 1899. In 1907 they could have been', as they had been mentioned in the 1906 Geneva Convention, but 'the matter of penal law, quite frankly, never came to mind'. See L. Renault, 'Dans quelle mesure le droit pénal peut-il s'appliquer, à des faits de guerre contraires aux droits de gens', *Revue pénitentiaire et de droit pénal* (1915), 416. However, this 'lack of attention' points to the fact that repression of violations for the sake of universal justice was not a concern at the time.

22 Convention Respecting the Laws and Customs of War on Land (Second Hague, IV), 18 October 1907, in Schindler and Toman, *supra* note 3, at 62.

23 Convention for the Amelioration of the Condition of the Wounded and Sick in Armies in the Field, 6 July 1906, in Schindler and Toman, *supra* note 3, at 385–395.

Those articles were, in fact, 'injunctions' to governments lacking the necessary legislation to take steps to prevent misuse of the Red Cross emblem in time of peace and war, and to repress in wartime those violations of the Convention considered to be most grave, i.e. individual acts of robbery, ill-treatment of the wounded and sick in armies in the field, and wrongful use of the Red Cross flag or armlet. Thus, the 'international community' had started to concern itself with the internal affairs of states in line with the proposal of General Arnaudeau at the 1873 Brussels Conference, albeit timidly and in the form of advice. It is also worth noting that this injunction was intended for the most grave violations of the Convention, thus paving the way for the distinction between breaches and grave breaches that would follow some years later.

B. The First World War and the 1919 Treaty of Versailles

The decisive steps towards international sanctions and eventual international jurisdiction were taken during and after the First World War. As with many aspects of international law, the development of new norms often follows major humanitarian upheaval. What was particularly challenging about the First World War was that the barbarous behaviour that constituted war crimes turned out to occur in 'civilized' states as well. The decline of what was considered to be shared values of those 'civilized' states, the flagrant violation of the law not only by soldiers but also by the most senior authorities, and the lack of internal repression in response to those violations, were all good reason to reconsider the need to reinforce those values at the international level, in particular by means of penal sanctions.

Indeed, large-scale atrocities were committed during the First World War, though this fact is nowadays somewhat obscured by the scale of barbarity reached during the Second World War. Rape, summary executions, indiscriminate bombing, sinking of civilian boats — the First World War grew into a total war, leaving 'almost no sanctuary of person safe from violent assault'.[24] New technologies emerged, such as the U-boat, the Zeppelin and poison gas, and they were used without humanitarian concern, sometimes as reprisals. In addition, grave violations were not only reported, but also exaggerated to spur the population's will to fight. On both sides, the war was presented as being waged between 'civilization and barbarism'. In France the German Kaiser was referred to as 'Guillaume le ravageur' and in Great Britain as the 'Butcher of Berlin'. All governments published reports of atrocities.[25]

Unsurprisingly, determination to punish war criminals gathered strength in the very first months of the war. As early as 2 December 1914, France set up a commission to investigate crimes committed by the enemy in violation of the

24 See J.F. Willis, *Prologue to Nuremberg: The Politics and Diplomacy of Punishing War Criminals of the First World War* (West Port and London: Greenwood Press, 1982), 15–16.

25 *Ibid.*, 13.

'law of nations'. Great Britain issued a similar proclamation in September 1914, when it declared that:

> We may be far still from the final abolition of war, but we should not be far from the end of atrocities in war if those responsible for them in whatever rank had the risk before their eyes that they might have to suffer just penalties as common felons.[26]

Some even suggested shooting prisoners of war without trial. While this idea was not implemented, there was nevertheless a great deal of similar discussions, in particular about punishing the Zeppelin crews.[27] There was a feeling that repression was needed, not only of massive violations of the law of war, but also of aggression itself.

But there was also reluctance to go too far and too quickly in the direction of international repression, for fear that each side would use prosecutions as a basis for reprisals. The trial of three German soldiers for pillage in October 1914, for instance, was followed by the incarceration in Spandau of six French officers including the son of the French foreign minister. A spiral of retaliation followed. And when in 1917 French parliamentarians urged the prosecution of Germans for war crimes in the occupied regions, René Viviani, the justice minister, dismissed the idea saying 'one must first conquer before speaking of justice'. The escalation of violence against civilians during First World War, especially the deliberate sinking of the famous ocean liner *Lusitania* that killed 1198 civilians, increased the determination of the general population to find a way to punish these sorts of atrocities. In particular, the United States was determined to pursue justice in response to atrocities.

Nevertheless, even repression after the war encountered some opposition. Professor Louis Renault, who had been a French delegate to the Hague Conferences of 1899 and 1907, 'warned that attempt to require surrender of offenders through a peace treaty might fail',[28] doubting 'that any government even if conquered, could consent to such a clause'. Others protested that 'war crimes trials hav[e] never been in the past part of a major peace settlement'.[29] Even a senior figure in the peace movement argued that 'trials having the appearance of victor's justice should be avoided'.[30]

There were also other reasons for foregoing the punishment of war crimes. The priority for US President Woodrow Wilson, as founder of the League of Nations, 'was the future organization of permanent peace, not the punishment of individuals for past transgressions'.[31] Wilson also had reservations about judging the crime of aggression. For him, aggression:

> was certainly a crime, but for which no sanction has been provided, because there is no legal precedent for it. We are founding today the regime of the League of Nations from

26 Reverend Arnold Page in The Times, 16 September 1914 (quoted by Willis, *supra* note 24), at 9.

27 Willis, *supra* note 24, at 16.

28 See 'De l'application du droit pénal aux faits de la guerre', 40 *Journal du droit international* (1915) 313–315 (quoted in Willis, *supra* note 24, at14).

29 Willis, *supra* note 24, at 4.

30 *Ibid.*, at 14.

31 *Ibid.*, at 37.

which will emerge the new rules and the new formulas of international law. But today, we are obliged to create the principle and the punishment.[32]

The question of prosecuting the Kaiser himself was also a matter of dispute. Napoleon was cited as a precedent but this was hardly convincing: 'The victorious European powers issued a Declaration at Vienna declaring Napoleon an international outlaw ... and he was displaced on the remote island of St. Helena ... but Napoleon was never tried'.[33]

Finally, the Allies established a 'Commission on the Responsibility of the Authors of the War and on Enforcement of Penalties' (hereafter the Commission) at the end of the war, which presented its final report to the preliminary peace conference on 29 March 1919.[34] The Commission was assigned various tasks, not all of which are of interest to us here, but a significant portion of the Commission's work focused on the prosecution of war crimes. The Commission's precise mandate in this regard, was to establish 'the facts as to breaches of the laws and customs of war committed by the forces of the German Empire and their Allies on land, on sea, and in the air, in the course of the recent war'.[35] It appears from the report that identifying the relevant offences was not the object of abstract theoretical discussion — the main objective was to list all the atrocities committed by the Germans and then to create a coherent catalogue of violations to the 'laws and customs of war'. For the Commission, the priority was to establish facts, considering 'a large number of documents' in the process. The Commission's report stated that the offences 'constitute the most striking list of crimes that has ever been drawn up to the eternal shame of those who committed them'.[36] For the Commission, whether a crime was international or not was not a question of great concern. The facts were so 'numerous and so vouched for that they admit no doubt and cry for justice'.[37]

The Commission thought that there were good grounds for setting up a special body 'to collect and classify all information for the purpose of preparing a complete list of charges'. The information already available enabled it to establish the following list of violations of the laws and customs of war that warranted criminal punishment:[38]

(1) Murders and massacres; systematic terrorism;
(2) Putting hostages to death;
(3) Torture of civilians;
(4) Deliberate starvation of civilians;

32 Proceedings of the Council of Four meeting, 1 April 1919.
33 M.R. Marrus, *The Nuremberg War Crimes Trial, 1945–46: A Documented History* (Boston-New-York: Bedford Books, 1997), at 2.
34 This report has been reproduced, together with the minority report drawn up by the US delegation, in 14 *American Journal of International Law* (*AJIL*) (1920) 95.
35 *Ibid.*, at 115.
36 *Ibid.*, at 114.
37 *Ibid.*
38 *Ibid.*, at 114–115.

(5) Rape;
(6) Abduction of girls and women for the purpose of enforced prostitution;
(7) Deportation of civilians;
(8) Internment of civilians under inhuman conditions;
(9) Forced labour of civilians in connection with the military operations of the enemy;
(10) Usurpation of sovereignty during military occupation;
(11) Compulsory enlistment of soldiers among the inhabitants;
(12) Attempt to denationalize the inhabitants of occupied territory;
(13) Pillage;
(14) Confiscation of property;
(15) Exaction of illegitimate or of exorbitant contributions and requisitions;
(16) Debasement of the currency, and issue of spurious currency;
(17) Imposition of collective penalties;
(18) Wanton devastation and destruction of property;
(19) Deliberate bombardment of undefended places;
(20) Wanton destruction of religious, charitable, educational and historic buildings and monuments;
(21) Destruction of merchant ship and passenger vessels without warning and without provision for the safety of passengers or crew;
(22) Destruction of fishing boats and of relief ships;
(23) Deliberate bombardment of hospitals;
(24) Attack on and destruction of hospital ships;
(25) Breach of other rules relating to the Red Cross;
(26) Use of deleterious and asphyxiating gases;
(27) Use of explosive or expanding bullets, and other inhuman appliances;
(28) Direction to give no quarters;
(29) Ill-treatment of wounded and prisoners of war;
(30) Employment of prisoners of war on unauthorized works;
(31) Misuse of flags of truce; and
(32) Poisoning of wells.

Importantly, the Commission drew attention to the fact that this list made no claim to be 'complete and exhaustive' and that 'such additions can from time to time be made as may seem necessary'.[39] It is curious to note, however, that there was no real discussion as to the classification of different acts as war crimes, and even the minority report of the US delegation does not view the simple drawing up of a list of war crimes as a problem, arguing that 'the laws and customs of war are a standard certain, to be found in books of authority and in the practice of nations'.[40] But as we have seen, the process of identifying war crimes was driven by facts first, after which legal labels were attributed to practices of specific concern. Consequently, although the list is somewhat interesting historically, it cannot be viewed as the result of a serious and

39 *Ibid.*, at 115.

40 'Memorandum of Reservations Presented by the Representatives of the United States to the Report of the Commission of Responsibilites', *AJIL* (1920), *supra* note 34, 127, at 134.

systematic work of scholarship carried out to show established doctrine or state practice.

Moreover, the partial nature of this report undermines its precedential value. The numerous crimes committed by the Allies were simply not taken into consideration. Regarding responsibility for the war itself, the Commission simply concluded that:

> The war was carried on by the Central Empire together with their allies, Turkey and Bulgaria, by barbarous or illegitimate methods in violation of the established laws and customs of war and the elementary laws of humanity.[41]

A further point, however, is of particular interest. The Commission was prepared to determine the degree of responsibility assigned to particular members of the enemy forces for war crimes, including members of the general staffs and other political figures, however highly placed. On this point the Commission's report is clear:

> In the hierarchy of persons in authority, there is no reason why rank, however exalted, should in any circumstances protect the holder of it from responsibility when that responsibility has been established before a properly constituted tribunal. This extends even to the ease of heads of states. An argument has been raised to the contrary based upon the alleged immunity, and in particular the alleged inviolability of a sovereign of state. But this privilege, where it is recognized, is one of practical expedience in municipal law, and is not fundamental. However, even if, in some countries, a sovereign is exempt from being prosecuted in a national court of his own country, the position from an international point of view is quite different.[42]

The Commission went on:

> If the immunity of a sovereign is claimed to extend beyond the limits above stated, it would involve laying down the principle that the greatest outrages against the laws and customs of war and the laws of humanity, if proved against him, could in no circumstances be punished. Such a conclusion would shock the conscience of civilized mankind .... There is little doubt that the ex-Kaiser and others in high authority were cognizant of and could at least have mitigated the barbarities committed during the course of war.

The Commission thus recognized what is sometimes called 'passive responsibility', the failure to prevent violations when one is in position to do so, especially in a hierarchical chain of command. The grounds for prosecuting the Kaiser are all the more compelling if, as some sources argue, he in fact directly participated in certain decisions to act in clear violation of fundamental principles of the law of war.[43]

The Commission's conclusions were therefore that '*all persons belonging to enemy countries, however high their position may have been, without distinction of rank, including Chiefs of States, who have been guilty of offences against the laws and customs of war or the laws of humanity, are liable to*

41 *Ibid.*

42 Report, *supra* note 34, at 116.

43 *Ibid.*, at 117.

670 JICJ 7 (2009), 657–682

criminal prosecution'.[44] This is naturally an important statement. However, it contains a word that greatly diminishes its impact — 'enemy' — since this implies a highly selective focus on only one side of the offending. Considering that assignment of responsibility for war crimes is possible only in the case of *enemy* heads of state, this statement is ad hoc and arguably too limited in scope to constitute an important precedent for the notion that immunities do not apply to a head of state. Some previous passages in the report take a more general stance, not limited to the particular case examined by the Commission, but these are in effect a type of *obiter dictum*.

It is also clear from this report that the Commission drew a distinction between the *jus ad bellum* and the *jus in bello* aspects of war, and experienced certain difficulties with the former. The acts which provoked the world war and accompanied its inception were, according to the Commission, 'not strictly war crimes'. Moreover, 'by the reason of the purely optional character of the institutions at the Hague for the maintenance of peace ... a war of aggression may not be considered as an act directly contrary to positive law'.[45] The Commission ultimately concluded on the subject of *jus ad bellum* that specific treaties recognizing the neutrality of Belgium and Luxemburg had been violated, not simply that there had been aggression, which in itself was not clearly outlawed at the time.

On the question of jurisdiction over these war crimes, the Commission proposed trying war criminals before national courts, with the exception of four categories which should be placed before an ad hoc high tribunal. The Commission's proposition was contested by the US delegation in a minority report.[46] The main points of divergence were subjects which are still today the object of controversy. The first issue was the concept of 'passive responsibility'. The US representatives contested the idea that there was such a thing as 'indirect responsibility for violations of the laws and customs of war committed after the outbreak of war and during its course'.[47] The second issue was the punishment of 'heads of enemy States, even though heads of states were not hitherto legally responsible for the atrocious acts committed by subordinate authorities'. For the authors of the minority report, 'the laws and principle of humanity vary with the individual, which, if for no other reason, should exclude them from consideration in a court of justice, especially one charged with the administration of criminal law'.[48] It is the country which is responsible for violations, the head of state having political responsibility only vis-à-vis his country. A third point of disagreement was the concept of 'crime against humanity'. The US representatives felt that this was no more than a moral notion and not sufficiently established in law to warrant penal sanctions.

44 *Ibid.* (italics in original).
45 *Ibid.*, at 118.
46 US Memorandum, *supra* note 40, 127.
47 *Ibid.*, at 128.
48 *Ibid.*, at 134.

A discussion took place on the basis of the two reports. In the end, Wilson himself drafted the three relevant articles of the treaty and he preserved 'the essence of the American legal position, excluding an international tribunal, the laws of humanity, and negative criminality'.[49] The provisions as drafted by Wilson were adopted without substantial amendment the next day and became Articles 228, 229 and 230 of the Versailles Treaty.

The provisions were a major historical event. 'For the first time a major international peace treaty had established the principle in international law that war crimes punishment was a proper conclusion of peace, that the termination of war did not bring a general amnesty as a matter of course'.[50] But the Treaty's weakness was that it amounted to victor's justice and the German delegates to the peace conference did not hesitate to point this out. Moreover, Articles 228, 229 and 230 of the Versailles Treaty were not seriously implemented. The Kaiser was not extradited by the Dutch government — he died in the Netherlands in 1941 — and the Germans, who were forced by the threat of a new military intervention to accept those Articles, did not respect them. The Allies did not even urge them to do so, fearing that their insistence might 'provoke civil war in Germany or a new war between Germany and the Allies'.[51] Very few war criminals were therefore tried, which the Times of London described as 'a scandalous failure of justice'.[52] Though this 'first major effort to bring criminals to justice failed ... the idea of an international criminal court and code ... continued to exercise an influence in the quest for means to curb international violence'.[53]

C. World War II and the Nuremberg Tribunal

The large-scale atrocities committed during the Second World War gave massive new impetus to the question of international repression of war crimes. Once again, different ideas were expressed. The first proposal, similar to that which arose after the First World War, was for summary executions. Some were of the opinion that there was no need for judicial procedure in response to such atrocities. In this context, Stalin made allusion to the possible massive killing of officers and technicians;[54] Churchill was also sympathetic to the advice of some of his legal advisers who favoured the shooting of top

49 Willis, *supra* note 24, at 80.

50 *Ibid.*, at 85–86.

51 *Ibid.*, at 113.

52 A demand was made to surrender 854 Germans but the right to try them was immediately conceded to the Germans (see Willis, *supra* note 24, at 113). Finally, the Germans agreed to try 45 and only 12 were brought to court. Six were convicted, one was immediately released and the others received very light sentences and several managed to escape from their prison (see Marrus, *supra* note 33, at 12).

53 Willis, *supra* note 24, at 113.

54 See Marrus, *supra* note 33, at 23.

Nazi, one of them declaring that 'the method by trial, conviction, and judicial sentence is quite inappropriate for notorious ringleaders as Hitler, Himmler, Göring, Goebbels and Ribbentrop'.[55] In addition, a Memorandum for President Roosevelt mentioned that after the establishment of a list, 'the persons identified shall be put to death forthwith by firing squads'.[56]

As was the case during the First World War, there were also statements by politicians on the importance of initiating prosecutions, but these were frequently accompanied by a degree of hesitation due to the fear of 'German vengeance in the event of a too aggressive policy against war criminals'. Moreover, Great Britain and United States were uneasy 'about working with the Soviets on this issue'.[57]

Nevertheless, the preference for judicial procedure prevailed. The Allies elected to create an international penal tribunal which was ultimately achieved by an institution they had created under the auspices of the League of Nations entitled the London International Assembly.[58] Having chosen this method of criminal accountability, the states were anxious to avoid the failure of war crimes repression after the First World War. Consequently, the United Nations War Crimes Commission was set up in 1943 especially to avoid the lack of previous agreement and preparation that was thought to have been the fundamental mistake of Allies during the First World War'.[59]

Once the War Crimes Commission was created, it established three Committees. The third committee was legally focused and therefore placed in charge of dealing with the concept of war crimes. We cannot explore in detail the long and difficult discussions that took place, especially since the Commission's report of December 1943 runs to 450 pages.[60] Key elements of its work nonetheless warrant emphasis. As we saw in previous sections, the list of war crimes established by the 'Commission of Responsibility' in 1919 was not the result of an in-depth scientific investigation. Nevertheless, the Commission's members adopted this list of crimes as the basis for their work.

Discussion on war crimes focused on other issues, in particular whether aggression amounted to a war crime; and if war crimes could be committed against citizens of an allied state, or even against ones' own citizens. Politicians realized that public opinion would not support moves to categorize the terrible crimes committed by the Germans as crimes perpetrated only against some specific categories of people, excluding Jews, Tziganes and homosexuals. This position again re-opened the debate on the issue of 'crimes

55 Declaration of Lord Chancellor Sir John Simon on War Cabinet in September 1944 in the Records of the Prime Minister's office on the treatment of major war criminals (PREM 4/100/10), National Archives at Kew, London. Also quoted in Marrus, *supra* note 33, at 23.

56 H. Morgenthau Jr., *Memorandum for President Roosevelt*, 5 September 1944. Also quoted by Marrus, *supra* note 33, at 23.

57 Marrus, *supra* note 33, at 20.

58 See *History of the United Nations War Crimes Commission and the Development of the Law of War* (compiled by the UN War Crimes Commission, 1948), 99 ff.

59 Willis, *supra* note 24, at 174.

60 *London International Assembly, Reports on the Punishment of War Criminals* (1963).

against humanity'. The US delegates were always reluctant to consider crimes against humanity as a basis for penal sanctions, but this new situation changed their minds. In response to the genocidal policy of the Nazi regime, the choice was either to broaden the notion of war crimes or to introduce crimes against humanity. This latter option ultimately prevailed, the final result of those discussions being Article 6 of the Statute of the Nuremberg Tribunal, which included Crimes Against Peace, War Crimes and Crimes Against Humanity.

The negative side of these developments were also numerous. Once again, the Nuremberg Tribunal was only an ad hoc tribunal, rather than a body that had universal jurisdiction. Likewise, the Tribunal's work remained a form of 'victor's justice', keeping in mind the great number of war crimes committed by the Allies through large-scale sexual violence or massive, indiscriminate bombings of cities. Substantively speaking, the war crimes in both situations were similar.

If a comparison is made between the list of war crimes established by the Responsibility Commission in 1919 and the list in Article 6, we see that the latter is more concise and less detailed than the former, even if we take into account the fact that some crimes specified in the 1919 list have been inserted in the new list of 'crimes against humanity'. In essence, however, there is no real substantial difference, highlighting a historical continuity in the development of war crimes that would also flow into the development of the grave breaches regime.

4. The Grave Breaches Regime in Positive International Law

A. The 1949 Geneva Conventions

In 1949, four years after the adoption of the United Nations (UN) Charter, states finally decided to engage in the negotiation of a total revision of the laws of war, or international humanitarian law. The renewed interest in the laws of war stemmed from doubt that the UN Charter's goal of preventing wars could be guaranteed in the absence of a central military force. The ICRC therefore prepared a draft of a new body of international humanitarian law, taking into account the experiences of the Second World War and consultations with experts. The resulting draft was submitted by the Swiss Government to a diplomatic conference, which adopted the four different Conventions after long discussion and several amendments. Several articles were common to these four conventions, some of which addressed penal sanctions.

The Geneva Conventions distinguish two categories of breaches of the Conventions. Some are qualified as 'grave breaches' and are exhaustively enumerated in each of the Conventions. The others are not qualified or precisely identified. While grave breaches had to be criminally punished, state parties are only under an obligation to ensure that non-grave breaches cease. Though repression is the natural way to ensure that non-grave breaches are brought to an end, it is not the only means.[61] By contrast, the Conventions impose punishments for the identified grave breaches and this is specified as being of international concern — any state party to the Conventions is obliged to exercise universal jurisdiction over those responsible for these violations. In fact, a state party is also compelled to 'search for persons alleged to have committed, or to have ordered to be committed, such grave breaches, and shall bring such persons, regardless of their nationality, before its own courts'. In addition, there is also the possibility to 'hand such persons over for trial to another High Contracting Party concerned provided such High Contracting Party has made out a *prima facie* case' (Articles 49, 50, 129 and 146 of the Geneva Conventions 1 through 4 respectively).

The idea of grave breaches is perfectly logical and, as we have mentioned above, is inherent to a system of war crimes. The fact that civilian internees cannot buy tobacco or soap in a canteen 'at prices not higher than local market prices' (Article 87 of the Fourth Geneva Convention), for example, does not justify accusing the person in charge of the canteen of a war crime or bringing the affair before a supranational jurisdiction. Therefore, some legal concept had to differentiate violations of the Geneva Conventions that warranted criminal punishment from those that a state was simply required to end by potentially other mechanisms. As a special committee convened to consider penal sanctions during the negotiation process concluded:

> In order to allow for reluctance to include all breaches even trifling ones in penal legislation, we limited the obligation to enact legislation to grave breaches which no legislator would object to having included in the penal code, and left the Contracting Parties free to take their own measures for the repression of breaches which don't come within the category defined as grave breaches.[62]

A further common article of the Geneva Conventions has important implications for criminal liability by providing that '[n]o High Contracting Party shall be allowed to absolve itself or any other High Contracting Party of any liability incurred by itself or by another High Contracting Party in respect of breaches referred to in the preceding article' (Articles 51, 52, 131 and 148). The provision clearly encompassed grave breaches, and emphasizes the universal nature of these offences.

61 It is indeed by repressing (and, therefore, by providing for penal sanctions in national criminal law) that, generally, states can fulfil their obligation to suppress such acts. See C. Pilloud, 'Les sanctions pénales dans la première Convention de Genève (blessés et malades) du 12 aout 1949', 400 *Revue internationale de la Croix-Rouge* (1952) 286–311.

62 *Final Record of the Diplomatic Conference of Geneva of 1949*, Vol. II (Bern: Federal Political Department, 1949; reprinted Buffalo: W.S. Hein, 2005) [Section B, Fourth report drawn up by the Special Committee of the Joint Committee (Report on penal sanctions in case of violations of the Conventions), 12 July 1949.]

The expression 'war crime' was proposed but refused, with the argument that it should be reserved for violations of the Hague Conventions. The rationale was apparently that the grave breaches regime should maintain a separate approach.[63] Judicial safeguards, notions of complicity, attempts, duress, self-defence or the plea of superior orders were not included, since it was felt that these issues should be left to judges 'who would apply the national laws'. The overriding philosophy was that the Diplomatic Conference was not there 'to work out international penal law'.[64] Nonetheless, it was clarified that universal jurisdiction applied for all parties to the Conventions 'in whose power the accused is' — and not only those engaged in an armed conflict.[65]

As the commentary to the Conventions mentions, the obligation to enact penal legislation implies a duty to 'fix the nature and duration of the punishment for each offence, on the principle of making the punishment fit the crime'.[66] The duty to enact legislation also implied that this legislation involved universal jurisdiction for the grave breaches of the Conventions. Superficially, the provision represented a decisive step towards international justice and the beginnings of a universal fight against impunity for war crimes. But the reality was disappointing. Many states did not fulfil their obligation to enact the 'legislation necessary to provide effective penal sanctions'[67] and the system of universal jurisdiction was never applied in practice.

One of the major innovations of the 1949 Geneva Conventions was the introduction of Article 3 common to the four Conventions on non-international armed conflicts. This innovation was congruent with the adoption of the 1948 Declaration of Human Rights and the recognition of the notion of crimes against humanity in the framework of the Nuremberg Tribunal. The 'taboo' of national sovereignty had been infringed. But states were still very cautious and fearful of ceding too much of their reserved domain. The obligation to punish grave breaches of the Conventions and their exposure to universal jurisdiction do not concern violations committed in internal armed conflict. The provision, in common Articles 50, 51, 130 and 147, that grave breaches have to be committed 'against persons or property protected by the Convention' has to be taken in the narrow sense of the notion of 'protected persons or property', which are those precisely defined by the Conventions as applicable to international armed conflicts.

63 *Ibid.*

64 *Ibid.*

65 *Ibid.*

66 J. de Preux, *Commentary on the Geneva Conventions of 12 August 1949*, Vol. III, ed. by J.S. Pictet (Geneva: ICRC, 1960), at 622.

67 See *Respect of the Geneva Conventions — Measures taken to repress violations*, ICRC Reports to the 20th and 21st International Conferences of the Red Cross (1965, 1969), based on a study undertaken by all National Red Cross Societies on the legislation in force in their countries.

676 JICJ 7 (2009), 657–682

B. Additional Protocol I of 1977

Additional Protocol I of 8 June 1977 compliments the Geneva Conventions by adding new grave breaches without undermining the pre-existing offences. In particular, Articles 11 and 85 of Additional Protocol I adds numerous grave breaches to the list contained in the Geneva Conventions themselves, criminalizing violations of 'Hague Law' provisions which had not been included in the Geneva Conventions. In so doing, the process confirmed violations of various provisions of the 1899 and 1907 'Regulations respecting the laws and customs of war on Land' as war crimes, many of which had been included in Article 6 of the Nuremberg Statute.

Additional Protocol I also clarifies the fact that grave breaches of the Conventions and Additional Protocol I are war crimes (specified in Article 85(5)). This clarification was included despite strong opposition, in line with the refusal to use the expression 'war crime' in the Geneva Conventions, from states that expressed the fear that it would create confusion between international humanitarian law and criminal law.[68] From this relationship established between grave breaches and war crimes one can also deduce, *a contrario*, that breaches not considered to be grave are not war crimes. In short, it should not be possible to speak, as one author did, of 'minor war crimes'.[69] Fundamentally, it is essential for the credibility of international criminal law to have a clear and exhaustive list of violations considered as war crimes. However, the list established by the Geneva Conventions and Additional Protocol I is not frozen once and for all. International criminal law must take into account societal evolution and the fact that some violations of customary international law which were not included in these treaties are nonetheless considered war crimes today.

Despite its many advances, the 1974–1977 Diplomatic Conference could not overcome one major obstacle — the recognition of the notion of war crimes in non-international armed conflicts. The main reason was similar to that used in 1949: A majority of states were reluctant to open the door to universal jurisdiction for the repression of crimes committed in such conflicts. They were afraid of what would be, in their minds, an unacceptable interference in their national sovereignty. This fear also appeared in the discussion about international armed conflict. Article 11 of Additional Protocol I, in particular, dealt with the protection not only of people who are in the power of the adverse party, but also of those who are deprived of liberty 'as a result of the situation' of international armed conflict. Deserters or traitors detained by their own government enter into this category. But paragraph 4 of Article 11 refers to war crimes as violations of this article with respect to 'any person who is in the power of a Party *other than the one on which he depends*'.[70] And this difference was effectively 'justified as being a protection of the

68 Official records, *supra* note 62, CDDH/I/SR.61, §§ 61, 62, 69 and 84 as well as CDDH/I/SR 64, § 10.

69 P. Boissier, 'La répression des petits crimes de guerre', *Revue internationale de droit pénal* (1948) 293–309.

70 Our emphasis.

national sovereignty'.[71] Another example of this attitude is provided by Article 75 of Additional Protocol I, which enumerates the fundamental guarantees for all persons 'who are in the Power of a Party to the conflict and who do not benefit of a more favorable treatment under the Conventions and under this Protocol ... in so far they are affected by a situation' of international armed conflict. Those who were in favour of including violations of this article in the list of grave breaches 'abandoned this idea in a spirit of compromise in the face of opposition from those who were afraid of extending the concept of grave breaches – subject to universal jurisdiction — to breaches committed by a Party to the conflict against its own nationals'.[72]

This reluctance may be curious as the notion of a crime against humanity was accepted as an international crime and covered crimes of a state against its own nationals. But a great difference between war crimes and crimes against humanity is that the latter have to be committed on a 'large scale'. Although this requirement was not specified in the Nuremberg Statute, reference is made to a policy of terror 'certainly carried out on a vast scale'.[73] This criterion can also be found in subsequent texts and is still present in the Rome Statute of the International Criminal Court. To be considered as crimes against humanity, the enumerated acts must be 'part of a widespread or systematic attack directed against any civilian population'.[74]

It was difficult after the horrors committed by the Germans under the Nazi regime against some of their own citizens to contest the existence of crimes against humanity, but to include individual crimes committed by a government against its own citizens as war crimes would have been a step further. There was, therefore, no logical contradiction in the mind of those who did accept the notion of crime against humanity but refused the extension of war crimes to non-international armed conflicts, as specified by a delegate to the 1974–1977 Diplomatic Conference, who explained that: '... crimes against another person than an enemy could only be crimes against humanity and that this type of crimes was not treated in the Protocols'.[75]

C. Further Developments

In 1995, the notion that serious violations of international humanitarian law constitute war crimes, whether committed during international or non-international armed conflicts, was finally accepted.[76] The basis for this shift

71 Official Records, *supra* note 62, CDDH/II/SR.99.

72 Y. Sandoz, S. Swinarski and B. Zimmermann, *Commentary on the Additional Protocols of 8 June 1977* (Geneva: ICRC and Nijhoff) 993, § 2469; Official Records, *supra* note 62, CDDH/I/SR 60, at 280 and §§ 9–11, at 283; CDDH/I/SR.61, § 86.

73 Judgment of 1 October 1946, 'International Military Tribunal Judgment and Sentence', 41 *AJIL* (1947) 172, at 254.

74 Art. 7 ICCSt.

75 Official Records, *supra* note 62, CDDH/II/SR.99.

76 See the definition of war crimes by the International Law Commission of the United Nations, Art. 20(f) UN Doc. A/51/10 (1996).

was compelling. That the same horrible crime committed in an armed conflict could be considered as a war crime or not depending on where the conflict was international or non-international in character was always difficult to accept. This abandonment of this arbitrary distinction can be attributed in large measure to the establishment of the ad hoc international criminal tribunals. Under Article 3 of the Statute of the International Criminal Tribunal for the former Yugoslavia, the Tribunal has the power to prosecute persons violating the laws and customs of war. This provision has been interpreted in the famous Appeals Chamber's decision in the *Tadić* case as including violations of Article 3 common to the four Geneva Conventions, Article 3 being said to be part of customary law and entailing criminal liability in case of serious violations of its provisions. As for the Statute of the International Criminal Tribunal for Rwanda, Article 4 specifically gives jurisdiction for violations of Additional Protocol II and common Article 3.

At the same time, the Rome Statute of the International Criminal Court also reflects this broad definition of war crimes.[77] In Article 8(2) it defines 'war crimes' as including a 'grave breach of the Geneva Convention of 12 August 1949', and then names those acts that are considered crimes against persons or property protected under the relevant Geneva Convention.[78] Article 8(2)(b) considers as war crimes other acts that are 'serious violations of the law and customs applicable in international armed conflict, within the established framework of international law.' Finally, 8(2)(c), (d) and (e) list those acts that are 'in the case of an armed conflict not of an international character, serious violations of Article 3 common to the four Geneva Conventions of August 12, 1949, namely, any of the following acts committed against persons taking no active part in the hostilities'.[79]

It is also noteworthy that the International Law Commission (ILC) establishes a broad definition of war crimes that takes into account the most recent developments in the repression of violations of international humanitarian law.[80] The definition of war crimes given by the ILC includes: Grave breaches of the four Geneva Conventions; grave breaches listed in Article 85 of Additional Protocol I; violations of Article 3 common to the Geneva Conventions and Article 4 of Additional Protocol II; violations of the laws and customs of war; and also violations of Articles 35 and 55 of Additional Protocol I.

77 See the Statute of the International Criminal Court, UN Doc. A/CONF.183/9 (17 July 1998). Also see M. Cherif Bassiouni (ed.), *Statute of the International Criminal Court: A Documentary History* (Ardsley, NY: Transnational Publishers Inc., 1999).

78 Art. 8(2)(a) ICCSt.

79 Art. 8(2)(c), (d) and (e) ICCSt. For a further in-depth discussion on the ICC definition of war crimes, see M. Cherif Bassiouni, 'The Normative Framework of International Humanitarian Law: Overlaps, Gaps and Ambiguities', 8 *Transnational Law and Contemporary Problems* (1998) 199 and Appendix II.

80 *Report of the International Law Commission on the work of its forty-eighth Session* (6 May to 26 July 1996), Supp. No. 10, UN Doc. A/51/10 (1996).

This prompts us to ask three questions. Are the war crimes listed in the Geneva Conventions and Additional Protocol I all covered by the Rome Statute? Are some violations not considered as grave breaches in the Conventions and Additional Protocol I defined as war crimes in the Rome Statute? And, have any acts previously considered to be war crimes been omitted from the Rome Statute? We shall briefly examine these three questions.

Not all states are parties to the additional protocols and although some provisions of Additional Protocol I are a confirmation of existing customary law, some are considered as a development. Another difficulty is that some provisions which were considered as a development when adopted have since entered into international customary law. Therefore, on one hand, the negotiators of the Rome Statute refused to integrate some innovations from Additional Protocol I but, on the other hand, they criminalized other acts that had not even been identified as war crimes in the Geneva Conventions or the Additional Protocol.

In comparison with Additional Protocol I, the Rome Statue contains many substantial differences. One important omission is the wilful and unjustifiable delay in the repatriation of prisoners of war and civilian internees. The Third Geneva Convention does not define this as a grave breach, whereas Additional Protocol I does, and this evolution was not considered as part of international customary law by the drafters of the Rome Statute. There are also quite a few differences between Additional Protocol I and the Rome Statute on provisions concerning the conduct of hostilities, in particular those concerning the attack of dangerous forces, the violation of the proportionality principle, and perfidy. The conclusion to be drawn from those differences is that some war crimes according to the Additional Protocol I are not war crimes according to the Rome Statute and international customary law, with the consequence that only those states that are party the Convention and linked to the perpetrator may enjoy universal jurisdiction over the crime.

The Rome Statute extends the concept of war crimes to crimes committed in non-international armed conflicts, the list of which it sets out in Article 8(2)(c) and (d) of the Statute. The Statute achieves this by introducing new war crimes in non-international armed conflicts, not by extending the grave breaches regime to non-international conflicts by analogy. In other words, the grave breaches regime remains segregated from other categories of war crimes.

Regarding international armed conflicts, the language of some crimes also seems to expand the list of grave breaches contained in the Geneva Conventions and Additional Protocol I. It is therefore useful to consider whether the change is purely semantic or if new breaches have indeed been added. Launching an attack with the knowledge that it 'will cause widespread, long-term and severe damage to the natural environment which would be clearly excessive in relation to the concrete and direct overall military advantage anticipated' is not defined as a war crime in Additional Protocol I. Its definition as such in the Rome Statute is a positive signal of the growing awareness of environmental problems, but it is no cause for jubilation. The rule, as set out in Additional Protocol I, is already vague and the Rome

Statute considers only as war crimes attacks that are 'clearly excessive in relation to the concrete and direct overall military advantage anticipated'. Therefore, if states appear to have demonstrated their concern for the protection of the natural environment, it is at very little cost. It would be very surprising if the International Criminal Court was able to indict anyone on this very vague basis in the coming years.

Another novelty is the specific reference, in Article 8(2)(b)(iv), of intentional attacks 'against personnel, installations, material, units or vehicles involved in a humanitarian assistance or peacekeeping mission in accordance with the Charter of the United Nations ...'. Without really defining a new war crime, this article nevertheless usefully emphasizes the important problem of the protection of such personnel and objects, especially for peacekeeping missions and for non-governmental organizations (NGOs). Neither of these groups were specifically covered by war crimes beforehand, although the same acts would have been covered by war crimes such as attacks on civilian objects.

Some crimes listed in the Rome Statute also develop provisions of the Geneva Conventions that were not modified by Additional Protocol I. For example, Article 8(2)(b)(xii) of the Rome Statute defines as a war crime 'destroying or seizing the enemy's property'. This is also considered a grave breach of Article 147 of the Fourth Geneva Convention, but is limited to 'extensive destructions and appropriation of property, not justified by military necessity and carried out unlawfully and wantonly', whereas in the Rome Statute the destruction or seizure of enemy property is considered a war crime 'unless such destruction or seizure be imperatively demanded by the necessities of war'.

Some crimes which were not even mentioned in the Geneva Conventions or Additional Protocol I are also included, such as Article 8(2)(b)(xxiv) of the Rome Statute, which makes it a war crime to declare 'abolished, suspended or inadmissible in a court of law the rights and actions of the nationals of the hostile party'. This provision is derived from Article 23(h) of the 1907 Hague Regulations.

Some provisions of the Rome Statute go into greater detail and clarify usefully the content of some crimes. Article 8(2)(b)(xxi) and (xxii), for instance, mention a number of acts — outrages upon personal dignity, in particular humiliating and degrading treatment, rape, sexual slavery, enforced prostitution, forced pregnancy, enforced sterilization — that were only covered by the generic mention of 'inhuman treatment' in the Geneva Conventions (common Articles 50, 51, 130 and 147). They underscore certain specific and particularly odious forms of behaviour and help to clarify the meaning of 'inhuman treatment'. It is the same for the starvation of the civilian populations, specifically forbidden by Article 54 of Additional Protocol I but not listed as a war crime in Article 85. Starvation could have been considered as covered by the 'inhuman treatment clause', but the specific mention of it at Article 8(2)(b)(xxv) of the Rome Statute put a very useful emphasis on this prohibition.

Under the generic heading of 'inhumane treatment', the Rome Statute goes even further than previous provisions in criminalizing the use of 'human shields'. It considers the mere fact of using civilians as human shields, with or without their consent, as a war crime in Article 8(2)(b)(xxiii). If such practice could be considered as covered as inhumane treatment for those who were forced to be human shields, it would have been difficult to invoke inhumane treatment for those doing it voluntarily. In this sense, the ICC definition of the crime is novel.

Another important evolution is Article 8(2)(b)(xxvi), which mentions 'conscripting or enlisting children under the age of fifteen years into the national armed forces or using them to participate actively in hostilities'. This was introduced as a violation by Article 77 of Additional Protocol I but not listed as a grave breach in Article 85.

Finally, the Rome Statute provides a measure of clarity in respect of forbidden weapons, stipulating, in Article 8(2)(b)(xxviii) and (xix), that it is a war crime to employ poison or poisoned weapons, asphyxiating, poisonous or other gases, and all analogous liquids, materials or devices, or bullets which expand or flatten easily in the human body, such as bullets with a hard envelope which do not entirely cover the core or that are pierced with incisions.

5. Final Remarks

There were never armies without rules of discipline and criminal sanctions for those who violate the rules — a system of rules and sanctions is inherent to the organization of any army, even groups of bandits have their own code. Of course, this system of rules was developed by states for their armies, but it has now transformed into a full system of international criminal justice for wartime crimes.

Although, to a certain extent, some rules of this nature were observed since the beginning of humanity,[81] they have been specially clarified and developed by scholars since the 17th century. The 'laws and usages' of war were more or less known and observed in the armies of sovereign states that developed in the Westphalian system. A hierarchy of these rules was quickly established, reflected at least initially in the penalties ascribed to various conduct. The death penalty was envisaged for the gravest violations whereas more minor offences were punished by a range of more minor sanctions. In this regard, a system of grave breaches is inherent to any penal system.

The transformation of those 'laws and usages' of war into international rules contained in multilateral treaties started only in the middle of the 19th century. And two factors were decisive for the concept of 'grave breaches' in this regard — the inclusion of rules on penal sanctions within treaties and an increasing willingness to define these rules with more and more specificity.

81 As Geoffrey Best mentioned, 'the idea of the control of war is as old as war itself'. But as he also wrote, no faith is to be placed in the strict observation of humanitarian rules: 'It is a common place that under the hammer of war the best of men can be driven to behave in the worst of ways' in idem, 'The Restraint of War in Historical Perspective' in A. Delissen and G. Tanya (eds), *Humanitarian Law or Armed Conflicts: Challenges Ahead, Essays in Honour of F. Kalshoven* (Dordrecht-Boston-London: Martinus Nijhoff, 1991) 3–27.

The language used to describe these offences was initially very timid, starting with a reminder to states to sanction violations of the international humanitarian rules through the use of domestic law. A call to coordinate their penal legislation was then mentioned within international treaties, before references to a more elaborate notions of international justice, international tribunals, and universal jurisdiction. As soon as international justice was envisaged, a hierarchy of norms was again necessary: those who were in charge of establishing a list of international war crimes after the First and Second World Wars had of course to focus on the gravest breaches. Moreover, in introducing the system of universal jurisdiction within the Geneva Conventions, the states responsible for negotiating the Geneva Conventions could not proceed without selecting the limited number of grave breaches that justified criminal punishment — international justice could not encumber itself with minor offences. The debate has and will continue to focus on the choice of grave breaches: this discussion will and has to remain open, depending on the evolution of the society. As for war crimes, the recurrent violence against women, the recruitment of child soldiers or the impact of war on our environment, should further influence the development of new norms. Likewise, we should not forget aggression and weapons of mass destruction, for which an exact reference and definition could not be finalized in the negotiations of the Rome Statue. On a more general level, we could ask ourselves if the emerging international justice is not focused more on the horrors committed in the 20th century — with the crime of genocide, crimes against humanity and war crimes — than on the challenges of 21st century, which will face new threats such as international networks of bandits involved in the trafficking of human beings, drugs and arms; failing states and high levels of corruption. Within this context, discussions of grave breaches have to be integrated into a broad debate on the role of justice in the search for peace and the establishment of a global international system adapted to the main global challenges of the 21st century.

[9]

The Universality Principle and War Crimes

Yoram Dinstein

I

ONE OF THE MOST FUNDAMENTAL TENETS of international law is that it determines the permissible limits of the jurisdiction of States.[1] While issues relating to the exercise of State jurisdiction may extend to every aspect of human conduct, the crux of the matter is criminal jurisdiction.[2] Criminal jurisdiction is vested in a given State only when there exists between that State and either the specific offense or the alleged offender a legitimate link, that is to say, a link which is legitimate in the eyes of international law. In the absence of such a legitimate link, the State is not entitled to assert criminal jurisdiction.

Five principles have emerged in international law as legitimate bases for the exercise of the criminal jurisdiction of States over alleged offenders.

- *Territoriality*, namely, the fact that the offense was committed within the territory of the State asserting jurisdiction (including ships and aircraft registered therein). Although this is ostensibly the simplest base of criminal jurisdiction, it must be appreciated that the question of whether an offense actually takes place within the territory is not always easily answered. Above all, it is difficult to determine when an act committed outside—yet having effects inside—the territory comes within the scope of legitimate criminal jurisdiction.[3]

• *Nationality of the alleged offender* (or "active personality"), namely, the fact that the person charged with the offense is a national of the State asserting jurisdiction. In most instances in which criminal jurisdiction is exercised by a State, the circumstances would satisfy both the territoriality and the active personality principles, inasmuch as the criminal act is perpetrated by a national within the geographic confines of the home country. Hence, the real need for invoking the active personality principle *per se* arises chiefly when the offense is committed by a national extraterritorially. The active personality principle usually also covers non-nationals serving the State in different capacities (such as members of the diplomatic service or of the armed forces), and at times it is even extended to permanent residents.

• *Nationality of the victim of the offense* (or "passive personality"), namely, the fact that—irrespective of the *situs* of the offense and the nationality of the perpetrator—the victim is a national, or conceivably even a permanent resident, of the State asserting jurisdiction. Strong opposition has often been expressed against the passive personality principle when standing alone, *viz.*, when a national of State A is prosecuted by State B for criminal activity affecting nationals of State B carried out within the boundaries of State A (or even State C).[4] All the same, in at least some settings the passive personality principle is too well entrenched in State practice today to be seriously contested.[5]

• *Protection of certain vital national interests of the State*, namely, authorizing a State to exercise criminal jurisdiction irrespective of location or nationality (even when the alleged offenders are foreigners and they acted extraterritorially). The "protective" principle is circumscribed to acts against the national security of a State; counterfeiting its currency, national emblems, seals or stamps; forgery, fraud or perjury committed in connection with official documents, especially passports and visa permits; and improper use of or insult to the national flag.[6]

• *Universality*, namely, "the authority of the State to punish certain crimes wherever and by whom[soever] committed."[7] This authority, which is vested in every State regardless of territory and nationality, is limited to the exercise of jurisdiction over *delicta juris gentium* (i.e., acts defined as crimes by international law). The view that the universality principle encompasses "common crimes such as murder," although shared by several scholars, is not in conformity with customary international law.[8] Had the universality principle been applicable to a broad range of ordinary crimes, there would be no *raison d'être* for the other bases of jurisdiction. After all, universal jurisdiction's "limitless scope renders all other forms of jurisdiction superfluous."[9] The universality principle must be looked upon as an exceptional measure granting the State special extraterritorial powers. It is limited to specific offenses defined by international law, and it must be exercised strictly in accordance with limitations imposed by that law.

Actually, the universality principle does not apply in an automatic fashion to all international offenses, although there seems to be a presumption today in favor of such application.[10] A prime example of an international treaty, which defines an international offense yet explicitly adheres to the territoriality—rather than the universality—principle, is that of Article 6 of the 1948 Convention on the Prevention and Punishment of the Crime of Genocide.[11]

II

The universality principle is strongly rooted in customary international criminal law. The incontrovertible "prototype"[12] is the age-old law for the suppression of piracy (currently codified in Article 105 of the 1982 United Nations Convention on the Law of the Sea).[13] Over the last few decades, universal criminal jurisdiction has been extended to numerous other offenses by conventional international law (see *infra*), and in at least some instances the extension has in all likelihood already crystallized into generally binding custom.

The proposition that belligerent States are accorded an international legal right to prosecute members of the enemy armed forces charged with war crimes has long been doctrinally recognized;[14] and was authoritatively restated in the early part of the twentieth century.[15] It was reaffirmed in connection with the horrendous war crimes of World War II, even prior to the postwar trials.[16] These trials have had a salutary impact on the progressive development of international law in general (e.g., insofar as the evolution of the separate concept of crimes against humanity is concerned).[17] One of their invaluable achievements is that the postwar trials removed any plausible doubt that might have lingered about the practice of States confronted with war crimes. The trials established, first and foremost, that all belligerents into whose hands war criminals have fallen can exercise concurrent jurisdiction.[18] The trials further demonstrated that belligerent States have jurisdiction over war crimes perpetrated by enemy civilians as much as by members of the enemy armed forces.[19] Additionally, the trials made it plain that a belligerent State is entitled to bring to justice not only enemy nationals but also nationals of allied or

The Universality Principle and War Crimes

neutral States,[20] and that it can even assume jurisdiction over war crimes committed before its own entry into the war.[21] The corollary is that neutral States can equally prosecute belligerent war criminals.[22]

In the *Eichmann* trial, the Israel Supreme Court—which unequivocally endorsed the application of the universality principle to war crimes[23]—arrived at the conclusion that "no importance attaches to the fact that the State of Israel did not exist when the offenses [including war crimes] were committed."[24] This position has been reinforced by the judgment of the United States Court of Appeals (Sixth Circuit) in the *Demjanjuk* case of 1985:

> Further, the fact that the State of Israel was not in existence when Demjanjuk allegedly committed the offenses is no bar to Israel's exercising jurisdiction under the universality principle. When proceeding on that jurisdictional premise, neither the nationality of the accused or the victim(s), nor the location of the crime is significant. The underlying assumption is that the crimes are offenses against the law of nations or against humanity and that the prosecuting nation is acting for all nations. This being so, Israel or any other nation, regardless of its status in 1942 or 1943, may undertake to vindicate the interest of all nations by seeking to punish the perpetrators of such crimes.[25]

The extension of the purview of jurisdiction over war crimes of all stripes is perfectly justifiable. The import of bringing the universality principle to bear upon war crimes is that all States without exception—rather than merely belligerent States—are possessed of the power to mete out justice to any war criminal and that they can ignore the geographic, temporal, or national dimensions of the offense.[26] While some scholars continue what may be called a rear-guard action against acceptance of the universality principle as appertaining to war crimes,[27] by now it must be abundantly clear that the issue has been settled in customary international law.[28] Patently, war crimes can be assimilated to piracy in the frame of reference of universality of jurisdiction.[29]

The four Geneva Conventions of 1949 for the Protection of War Victims include a common stipulation governing "grave breaches" of these instruments:

> Each High Contracting Party shall be under the obligation to search for persons alleged to have committed, or to have ordered to be committed, such grave breaches, and shall bring such persons, regardless of their nationality, before its courts. It may also, if it prefers, and in accordance with the provisions of its own legislation, hand such persons over for trial to another High Contracting Party concerned, provided such High Contracting Party has made out a *prima facie* case.[30]

Yoram Dinstein

In accordance with Article 85(5) of the 1977 Additional Protocol I to the Geneva Conventions, the grave breaches referred to (as well as those supplemented by the Protocol itself) "shall be regarded as war crimes."[31]

In the opinion of the present writer, the text of the common clause of the Geneva Conventions constitutes a pellucid expression of the universality principle. True, this is not unanimously avowed. One eminent scholar argues, "The view that the 1949 Geneva Conventions provide for universal jurisdiction, though sometimes asserted, is probably incorrect."[32] But surely, the correct interpretation of the Geneva text is the one offered by Hans-Heinrich Jeschek:

> According to the Geneva Conventions of 1949, signatory States are not only empowered to punish war crimes, but also are obliged to do so, unless the accused is extradited to another signatory State (*aut dedere aut punire*). The duty to punish attaches not only to the States to which the accused owes his allegiance or to the injured State, but to all the signatory States; this duty even extends to neutrals in an armed conflict, and it exists without regard to the nationality of the perpetrator or victim or to the place where the crime took place. Hence the Geneva Conventions provide universal jurisdiction for the punishment of war crimes coupled with a duty to prosecute, since the goal is the protection of common and universal interests.[33]

It is sometimes contended that only more serious war crimes (like the grave breaches of the Geneva Conventions)—rather than war crimes of a technical nature—activate the universality principle.[34] But this is a misconception. The correct view is that technical violations of the laws of war simply do not constitute war crimes.[35] Once violations of the laws of war qualify as war crimes, all come under the sway of the universality principle.

In 1996, the International Law Commission defined War Crimes in Article 20 of its Draft Code of Crimes against the Peace and Security of Mankind.[36] Although, in part, the definition may give rise to debate,[37] it mostly consists of grave breaches of the Geneva Conventions and Protocol.[38] Article 8 of the Draft Code[39] "establishes the principle of the concurrent jurisdiction of the national courts of all States parties to the present Code based on the principle of universal jurisdiction" for crimes set out in Article 20.[40]

III

The universality principle embraces solely offenses established and defined by international law, with a view to protecting the interests of the international community in its entirety. It must not be confused with the protective principle, which applies to the national interests of individual States. Both principles admittedly lead to a similar outcome: States may assert criminal jurisdiction over foreigners acting extraterritorially. Nevertheless, the two principles proceed from radically different points of departure. One principle is designed to protect the single State against those trying to subvert its vital interests. That single State, which is the only one affected, is exclusively allowed to take action—no other State can invoke jurisdiction on its behalf (although any State may act on the ground of territoriality or active personality where appropriate). The second principle is equally protective, but it lends its aegis to the collectivity of States (the "family of nations"). "It is founded upon the accused's attack upon the international order as a whole."[41] All States are supposed to have a stake in suppressing *delicta juris gentium*, and all are simultaneously endowed with the authority to exercise criminal jurisdiction. Consequently, as a rule, there cannot be a genuine overlap between the universality principle and the protective principle. The present writer disagrees with the reliance on the protective principle—as an auxiliary base of extraterritorial jurisdiction, side by side with the universality principle—by the District Court of Jerusalem (with the approval of the Israel Supreme Court), in the context of genocide, in the *Eichmann* trial.[42] However, even if mass-scale genocide directed at the entire Jewish people can be exceptionally construed as impinging upon the vital interests of the State of Israel (albeit perpetrated before the birth of the State), thereby triggering the protective principle, only the universality principle is apposite to war crimes.

There is no similar disconnection between the universality principle, on the one hand, and the territoriality, active personality, or passive personality principles, on the other. Universality postulates the irrelevance of either territory or nationality (of the victim as well as the offender). Still, if the territorial State or the State of nationality—when actually asserting criminal jurisdiction—prefers to act as such without invoking the universality principle, nothing prevents it from doing so. International law enables any State to turn a blind eye to the territorial or national link once universality is vouchsafed, but there is no compulsion to do so. When a State prosecutes members of its own armed forces who have committed war crimes, it benefits from an incontrovertible advantage if it acts in the name of the active personality principle rather than the universality principle. The trial can then be predicated solely on the domestic military penal code and need not take into account the limitations imposed on the State when availing itself of the special powers emanating from the universality principle.[43] By contrast, if the State wishes to prosecute enemy soldiers as war criminals, it has no alternative but to act within the framework of the universality principle (unless the victims are its own nationals or the crimes were committed on its territory).

IV

When the universality principle is applicable, the outcome is concurrent jurisdiction of all States. If all States acquire jurisdiction, all can exercise it. Evidently, "[c]oncurrent jurisdiction is no obstacle to the exercise of jurisdiction by any single-state."[44] Yet, when (as in the above-quoted text of the Geneva Conventions) the universality principle is couched in a binding language, amounting to a duty—rather than in a permissive manner simply creating a right—the potential competition engendered by the multiplicity of choices of forum must be addressed. Hence, the duty incurred under the Geneva Conventions and other instruments is generally represented in optional terms: either to render or to prosecute the accused.[45] Normally, the Latin formula is adduced: *aut dedere aut judicare*. The alleged offender can be rendered to another State (principally through the mechanism of extradition) for the exercise of foreign jurisdiction.[46] Still, when no such rendition takes place (because extradition is either not sought or denied, or for whatever other reason), there is a manifest duty to proceed with the exercise of local jurisdiction. The main thing is that one State or another will exercise its concurrent jurisdiction, so that an offender does not go scot-free.

All too often (perhaps especially where war crimes are concerned), there are problems with both alternatives, *judicare* and *dedere*. States may be reluctant or even unable to institute judicial proceedings themselves. In Theodor Meron's words:

> Universal jurisdiction over war crimes means that all states have the right under international law to exercise criminal jurisdiction over the offenders. Most states do not have the necessary resources or interest to prosecute offenders when the state itself was not involved in the situation in question. Many states also do not have national laws in place that allow them to prosecute offenders.[47]

At the same time, extradition—if sought—is frequently frustrated for technical or other reasons.[48]

As against the all-too-familiar factual situation where no country is overeager to prosecute war criminals, it is necessary to pose the reverse state of affairs (however rare) wherein several countries vie to lay hands on the accused, each desirous of exercising in practice its respective (concurrent) jurisdiction. The question is whether any particular State, by dint of being more closely linked to the case at hand, has a better claim and therefore priority.

No general rule regulating this matter has evolved in general international law. It is noteworthy, however, that no less than ten conventions pertaining to international criminal law have established a hierarchy formula in which a measure of priority is conferred on certain States (without negating the jurisdiction of others). The trail-blazing provision appears in Article 4 of the 1970 Hague Convention for the Suppression of Unlawful Seizure of Aircraft, which reads:

> 1. Each Contracting State shall take such measures as may be necessary to establish its jurisdiction over the offence and any other act of violence against passengers or crew committed by the alleged offender in connection with the offence, in the following cases:
>
> (a) when the offence is committed on board an aircraft registered in that State;
>
> (b) when the aircraft on board which the offence is committed lands in its territory with the alleged offender still on board;
>
> (c) when the offence is committed on board an aircraft leased without crew to a lessee who has his principal place of business or, if the lessee has no such place of business, his permanent residence, in that State.
>
> 2. Each Contracting State shall likewise take such measures as may be necessary to establish its jurisdiction over the offence in the case where the alleged offender is present in its territory and it does not extradite him pursuant to Article 8 to any of the States mentioned in paragraph 1 of this Article.
>
> 3. This Convention does not exclude any criminal jurisdiction exercised in accordance with national law.[49]

What is the correct interpretation of Article 4?[50] In effect, the drafters of the Convention set forth that every State has a right (and indeed a duty) to exercise jurisdiction over the offense of aircraft hijacking. All the same, a double-tiered structure of jurisdiction is constructed. There are three preferred States with primary jurisdiction: the State of registration of the aircraft, the State where the aircraft lands with the offender still on board, and the State of the operator of the aircraft when it is on lease.[51] The expectation is that in the natural order of things, one of the three preferred States will be able and willing to exercise jurisdiction over the offender. However, should this not come to pass owing to failure of extradition, whichever State has the hijacker in its hands is entitled and required to prosecute him, in keeping with the maxim *aut dedere aut judicare.*

The double-tiered structure of jurisdiction (with different lists of preferred States, as the subject matter dictates) is also adopted in the following conventions pertaining to international criminal law:

- Article 5 of the 1971 Montreal Convention for the Suppression of Unlawful Acts against the Safety of Civil Aviation.[52] Here there are four preferred States: the State of territoriality plus the three States enumerated in the Hague Convention.
- Article 3 of the 1973 Convention on the Prevention and Punishment of Crimes against Internationally Protected Persons, including Diplomatic Agents.[53] The three preferred States are the State of territoriality (explicitly including ships and aircraft registered therein), the State of nationality, and the State of passive personality (determined by virtue of function rather than strict nationality).
- Article 5 of the 1979 International Convention against the Taking of Hostages.[54] The four preferred States are the first two listed in the 1973 Convention (plus a discretionary jurisdiction over habitual residents who are stateless), the target State, and (where the State considers it appropriate) the passive personality State (based on the nationality of the victim).
- Article 8 of the 1980 Convention on the Physical Protection of Nuclear Material.[55] The two preferred States are the first two indicated in the 1973 Convention (without reference to stateless persons). There is also a specific reference in another paragraph to the State of export or import.
- Article 5 of the 1984 Convention against Torture and Other Cruel, Inhuman or Degrading Treatment or Punishment.[56] The three preferred States are again the first two catalogued in the 1973 Convention (without provision for stateless persons), and the last of the 1979 Convention.
- Article 6 of the 1988 Convention for the Suppression of Unlawful Acts against the Safety of Maritime Navigation.[57] The three preferred States are the flag State of a ship, the State of territoriality, and the State of nationality. Three other States are on a lesser standing, but still preferred in relation to the rest: the State of stateless habitual residents, the State of passive personality (based on nationality), and the target State. The interests of the flag State in case of several requests for extradition are particularly accentuated in Article 11(5).[58] The priority claim of the flag State to exercise jurisdiction is still not absolute, but it should have greater weight.[59]

• Article 4 of the 1988 United Nations Convention against Illicit Traffic in Narcotic Drugs and Psychotropic Substances.[60] The two preferred States are the State of territoriality and the State of the vessel flying its flag or the aircraft registered in it. A lesser status is bestowed on the State of nationality or habitual residence (irrespective of statelessness) and two additional special cases.

• Article 9 of the 1989 International Convention against the Recruitment, Use, Financing and Training of Mercenaries.[61] The two preferred States are the first two enumerated in the 1979 Convention.

• Article 10 of the 1994 Convention on the Safety of United Nations and Associated Personnel.[62] The two preferred States are the first two listed in the 1973 Convention. The 1988 Maritime Convention formula of three semi-preferred States is also repeated.

In all, notwithstanding inevitable variations in the multifarious instruments, the fundamental approach is the same. Whereas some preferred States are endowed with primary jurisdiction—with no mandatory priority—what emerges in the final analysis is universal jurisdiction.[63] It goes without saying that none of the conventions cited is germane to the issue of war crimes. Still, in future practice the nonbinding preference scheme may be looked upon with favor in that setting too. As for the choice of the States with a preferred status, judging by the trend highlighted in the conventions, it is probably safe to prognosticate that the three States to be generally deemed most closely connected to war crimes would be: the State of territoriality (including ships and aircraft registered therein), the State of active personality, and the State of passive personality.

V

Concurrent jurisdiction of all States over war criminals—in consequence of the universality principle—means not only that the judicial authorities of each State separately can sit in judgment over alleged offenders, but that any combination of States can set up an international penal tribunal with a view to carrying out the same mission on a multinational level. Thus, in the 1945 London Agreement for the Prosecution and Punishment of the Major War Criminals of the European Axis (initially adopted by the four big powers—the United States, the USSR, the United Kingdom and France—and later acceded to by many other Allied nations), an International Military Tribunal was established.[64] Pursuant to Article 6 of the Tribunal's Charter, it had jurisdiction over war crimes as well as crimes against peace and humanity.[65]

Yoram Dinstein

Following a celebrated trial conducted at Nuremberg, the 1946 Judgment proclaimed that in creating the International Military Tribunal the Contracting Parties to the London Agreement had "done together what any one of them might have done singly."[66] In other words, given the umbrella of the universality principle, either the United States or any other country could have prosecuted Nazi war criminals while acting alone. In joining forces, the Contracting Parties to the London Agreement merely pooled together their resources, avoided competition and conflict, and ensured that justice would be done.

This is also the best rationalization for the creation by the UN Security Council, in Resolution 827 (1993), of the International Criminal Tribunal for the Former Yugoslavia,[67] with subject-matter jurisdiction, *inter alia*, over grave breaches of the Geneva Conventions and violations of the laws and customs of war (Articles 2-3 of the Tribunal's Statute).[68] The legitimacy of the establishment of the Tribunal by fiat of the Security Council has been called into question by some commentators against the background of the UN Charter.[69] The Appeals Chamber of the Tribunal rejected at some length a challenge to its jurisdiction on that score.[70] Without getting into this complex issue, which is beyond the scope of the present paper, it must be perceived that irrespective of the range of powers allocated in the UN Charter, the establishment by the Security Council of an international penal tribunal with jurisdiction over war crimes is sanctioned by the universality principle. The Member States of the United Nations have done together what each of them might have done singly. No doubt, universal jurisdiction "is not synonymous with centralised jurisdiction," but the two are not mutually exclusive either.[71]

When an international penal tribunal is installed for the trial of war criminals, a problem that immediately comes to mind is whether the ordinary option of *aut dedere aut judicare* endures and whether the international tribunal has a status merely resembling that of an ordinary foreign court (with the same loose guidelines of preference in extradition discussed *supra*). Article 9 of the Statute of the Yugoslav Tribunal addresses the issue head on, and while confirming the concurrent jurisdiction of national courts, decrees that the Tribunal "shall have primacy over national courts" and that the Tribunal may formally request the latter to defer to its competence.[72]

The notion of primacy of an international tribunal over national courts was assailed by the defense in the *Tadič* case. The Appeals Chamber of the Yugoslav Tribunal held that when an international penal tribunal is created, "it *must* be endowed with primacy over national courts," for otherwise stratagems may be used to defeat the purpose of diligently prosecuting international offenders.[73] The Tribunal's explanation is conspicuously valid; indeed, perhaps the primacy concept should be construed within the ambit of that explanation. Intervention by an international penal tribunal in national proceedings (when a State wishes to exercise jurisdiction over a person in its custody) should not be undertaken unless there is reason to suspect that otherwise international justice is liable to be obstructed. In essence, this was also the opinion expressed by several Permanent Members of the Security Council in the course of its debates.[74]

This brings up a related issue. One of the most salient human rights recognized by contemporary international law is freedom from double jeopardy: no one can be retried for an offense for which he has already been finally convicted or acquitted by a competent court.[75] The pleas of *autrefois acquit* or *autrefois convict* are universally accepted as effectively barring further prosecution for the same offence.

Under Article 86 of Geneva Convention III, the principle of *non bis in idem* applies to prisoners of war, who may not "be punished more than once for the same act or on the same charge."[76] This provision, which covers the prosecution of war criminals, is applicable when double jeopardy is derived from the operation of judicial authorities in the territory of a single State. But what about transboundary retrials of war criminals (or other international offenders)? The matter seems to be unsettled in customary international law.[77] However, this writer believes that the concept of *non bis in idem* should apply in principle to attempts by courts of several States to prosecute the same person for the same offense—while invoking the universality principle—no less than it does to parallel attempts by courts of an individual State. There is in fact doctrinal support for the position that a State ought to have no criminal jurisdiction over persons who have already been prosecuted elsewhere for the same offense.[78]

A vexing issue arises, however, in the singular context of concurrent jurisdiction over war crimes (and other international offenses). There may be a disquieting apprehension that the judicial authorities of a particular State who view the acts of the alleged offender with leniency (owing to ethnic, political, ideological or religious motivations) would go through the motions of a sham trial and either acquit him or impose on him—after conviction—a nominal sentence, thereby thwarting the administration of justice. If justice is to be done (and especially appear to be done), this apprehension must be dispelled.

Article 10 of the Yugoslav Statute handles this matter with finesse.[79] In paragraph 1 it pronounces that no person shall be tried before a national court for criminal acts for which he has already been tried by the International Tribunal. Paragraph 2 provides:

> 2. A person who has been tried by a national court for acts constituting serious violations of international humanitarian law may be subsequently tried by the International Tribunal only if:
>
> (a) the act for which he or she was tried was characterized as an ordinary crime; or
>
> (b) the national court proceedings were not impartial or independent, were designed to shield the accused from international criminal responsibility, or the case was not diligently prosecuted.

Paragraph 3 adds that in imposing a penalty the International Tribunal shall take into account any sentence served by a convicted person as a result of an earlier national trial.

Attention should be drawn to the fact that apart from the scenario of spurious or biased national proceedings, the text of the Yugoslav Tribunal's Statute also permits retrial if the original prosecution related to ordinary crimes. This is quite sensible. As indicated by the International Law Commission, should an individual be tried by a national court for a "lesser crime" (that is, national rather than international), the prior decision of that court should not immunize him from subsequent international proceedings expected to "encompass the full extent of his criminal conduct."[80]

The *non bis in idem* formula—used in the Yugoslav Tribunal's Statute—was replicated in the 1994 Statute of the International Tribunal for Rwanda;[81] it was followed by the International Law Commission (the same year) in Article 42 of the Draft Statute for an International Criminal Court.[82] However, the formula does not come to grips with the prospect of a trial by a national court of State A subsequent to a trial for the same offense by a national court of State B. The International Law Commission, in Article 12 of its 1996 Draft Code of Crimes against the Peace and Security of Mankind, after reiterating the same formula in regard to international proceedings, goes on to specify that retrial by a national court of another State is allowed if that other State is the territorial State or was the main victim of the crime.[83] This is a most unsatisfactory solution to the dilemma, applying as it does even in the absence of any claim that the previous proceedings entailed a travesty of justice or that they were other than impartial. This writer is convinced that the same formula ought to

The Universality Principle and War Crimes

apply to retrial by the national courts of another State as by an international tribunal.

VI

There are three dimensions to the criminal jurisdiction of States under international law: jurisdiction to prescribe (i.e., to legislate), jurisdiction to adjudicate (i.e., to put on trial), and jurisdiction to enforce (i.e., to punish).[84] The need to distinguish between the three facets of jurisdiction becomes prominent when the principle of universality is invoked, as in the case of war crimes.

Jurisdiction to Prescribe. *Ex hypothesi,* once the universality principle applies, no State is vested with jurisdiction to prescribe in the full sense of the term. The major premise underlying the universality principle is that the forbidden acts are *delicta juris gentium*, meaning that they have been criminalized by international law. The State "must ensure that its legislation does not extend the definition of the offense beyond the limits of international law."[85] It must be fully appreciated that only acts branded as war crimes by international law are subject to universal jurisdiction. Therefore, the domestic legal system is not free to add its own versions of putative war crimes to the list prescribed (and proscribed) by international law. Should the domestic legal system label as "war crimes" acts not deemed war crimes by international law, the universality principle would not be in effect. Only war crimes *juris gentium* can sustain a claim to universal jurisdiction.

Jurisdiction to prescribe in the context of the universality principle has to be understood in a different sense. Every State has a right—and indeed a duty—to enact any enabling legislation required to lay the foundation for the domestic prosecution and punishment of international offenders. Such enabling legislation is ordained by each of the four Geneva Conventions of 1949: "The High Contracting Parties undertake to enact any legislation necessary to provide effective penal sanctions for persons committing, or ordering to be committed, any of the grave breaches of the present Convention defined in the following Article."[86]

Jurisdiction to Adjudicate. Jurisdiction to adjudicate in criminal matters means the prosecution and trial of offenders. Traditionally, jurisdiction to adjudicate has been treated as "ancillary to jurisdiction to prescribe."[87] However, in the case of the universality principle, every State is vested with jurisdiction to adjudicate notwithstanding the absence of jurisdiction to prescribe in the full sense of the term.

When a State exercises its universal criminal jurisdiction to adjudicate by sitting in trial over war criminals, it must of course comply with all the standards of due process of law, as demanded by international law.[88] The duty devolving on a State in the absence of *dedere* is consequently only one of *judicare* rather than *punire*. It is entirely possible that indictment of an alleged offender will end in acquittal.

The prosecutorial authorities in the State wherein the alleged offender happens to be present must have discretion in assessing the case at hand: much depends on where the witnesses and the rest of the evidence are. It is important not to prosecute hastily, lest there be acquittal and the principle *non bis in idem* apply. To be sure, the alleged offender may benefit from a potential gap in the system if the prosecutorial authorities in the State where he is present lack enough evidence to indict, yet another State (which does have enough evidence) fails to request extradition. Such a turn of events, characterized by neither *dedere* nor *judicare*, would produce a fiasco.

Can a State exercise criminal jurisdiction over war criminals *in absentia?* "[L]iterally hundreds of war crimes cases" were tried in France and Belgium after both world wars in the absence of the accused.[89] Article 12 of the Charter of the International Military Tribunal (sitting at Nuremberg) expressly allowed the Tribunal to take proceedings against a person in his absence.[90] Bormann, who was not in custody, was indicted accordingly, and the Tribunal issued a special Order making it possible to go on with his trial;[91] ultimately Bormann was convicted and sentenced to death.[92] A fictitious assertion of criminal jurisdiction over war crimes is apparently permissible. However, since Bormann has never been caught, his sentence only exposed the futility of *in absentia* proceedings. It is not clear what advantages are to be gained from such an academic exercise if the accused is not within grasp. In any event, the Nuremberg precedent was not followed in the case of the Yugoslav Tribunal, which does not possess jurisdiction to try persons *in absentia*.[93]

Jurisdiction to Enforce. Jurisdiction to enforce in the domain of war crimes means, primarily, punishment of persons convicted and sentenced by a competent court. Usually, trials of war criminals are held and sentences served within the boundaries of the same country. Yet, by agreement a State may keep in its prison facilities offenders convicted and sentenced by an international tribunal,[94] or even by a national court of a foreign country.[95]

The Universality Principle and War Crimes

Jurisdiction to enforce also relates to preventive and other coercive measures taken by a State with a view to the suppression of war crimes. Under the universality principle, every State is empowered to take these steps against international offenders. However, the empowerment is embedded in the assumption that the State is acting within its territory (including vessels and aircraft registered therein) or on the high seas. The universality principle does not authorize a State to take coercive action within the territory of another State without the latter's consent. Differently put, the police of one State are not allowed to enter the territory of another (absent consent) in order to arrest an individual, "not even to enforce law that is subject to universal jurisdiction."[96]

It is true that in egregious circumstances there have been occasions in which enforcement measures were carried out within the territory of another State without its consent. The abduction of Eichmann from Argentina for trial in Israel is a leading example. But it must be borne in mind that the crimes he perpetrated were staggering and that in realistic terms abduction "was the only means of obtaining physical jurisdiction over" him.[97] Security Council Resolution 138 (1960), which resolved the dispute over the abduction—and which declared (quite disingenuously) that "if repeated," the acts affecting the sovereignty of a Member State may endanger international peace and security—did not fail to note "the concern of people in all countries that Eichmann should be brought to appropriate justice for the crimes of which he is accused."[98] The Eichmann precedent must be considered overall as a rare exception rather than the rule: the rule of enforcement is and remains based on respect for the sovereignty of foreign States.

Notes

1. *See* 1(1) OPPENHEIM, INTERNATIONAL LAW 456 (Jennings & Watts eds., 9th ed. 1992).

2. As the Permanent Court of International Justice stated, "this might be the outcome of the close connection which for a long time existed between the conception of supreme criminal jurisdiction and that of the state, and also by the especial importance of criminal jurisdiction from the point of view of the individual." *S.S. Lotus* (1927), 2 WORLD COURT REPORTS 36 (Hudson ed., 1935).

3. The effects doctrine dominated the opinion of the majority of the Court in the *Lotus Case, id.* at 38–39.

4. *See, e.g.*, the dissenting opinion of Judge John Bassett Moore in the *Lotus Case, id.* at 82.

5. *See, e.g.*, Tokyo Convention on Offences and Certain Other Acts Committed on Board Aircraft, Sept. 14, 1963, art. 4(b), 20 U.S.T. 2941, T.I.A.S. No. 6763, 704 U.N.T.S. 219, 2 I.L.M. 1042, 1963 U.N. JURID. Y.B. 136, 137.

Yoram Dinstein

6. For a full discussion, see Dinstein, *The Extra-Territorial Jurisdiction of States: The Protective Principle*, 65(2) ANNUAIRE DE L'INSTITUT DE DROIT INTERNATIONAL 305–315 (1993).

7. Schachtei, *International Law in Theory and Practice. General Course in Public International Law*, 178 RECUEIL DES COURS 9, 262 (1982).

8. BROWNLIE, PRINCIPLES OF PUBLIC INTERNATIONAL LAW 304 (4th ed. 1990) (for quotation).

9. Gilbert, *Crimes Sans Frontières: Jurisdictional Problems in English Law*, 63 BRIT. Y.B. INT'L L. 415, 424 (1992).

10. *See* THE AMERICAN LAW INSTITUTE, 1 RESTATEMENT OF THE LAW, THE FOREIGN RELATIONS LAW OF THE UNITED STATES 257, §401 (3rd ed. 1987) [hereinafter RESTATEMENT].

11. Convention on the Prevention and Punishment of the Crime of Genocide, adopted by the U.N. General Assembly on Dec. 9, 1948, 78 U.N.T.S. 277, *reprinted in* THE LAWS OF ARMED CONFLICTS: A COLLECTION OF CONVENTIONS, RESOLUTIONS AND OTHER DOCUMENTS 231, 232–233 (Schindler & Toman eds., 3d ed. 1988).

12. *See* Schachter, *supra* note 7, at 262.

13. United Nations Convention on the Law of the Sea, 1982, Official Text 34 (1983), U.N. Doc. A/CONF.62/122.

14. *See* DE VATTEL, THE LAW OF NATIONS OR THE PRINCIPLES OF NATURAL LAW, bk. III, ch. VIII, §141; vol. 3, p. 280 (Fenwick trans., Classics of International Law ed., 1993).

15. *See* 2 OPPENHEIM, INTERNATIONAL LAW 309-310 (2d ed. 1912).

16. *See, e.g.*, Cowles, *Universality of Jurisdiction over War Crimes*, 33 CAL. L. REV. 177, 218 (1945).

17. *See* Dinstein, *Crimes against Humanity*, *in* THEORY OF INTERNATIONAL LAW AT THE THRESHOLD OF THE 21ST CENTURY, ESSAYS IN HONOUR OF K. SKUBISZEWSKI 891–908 (Makarczyk ed., 1996).

18. *See, e.g.*, Hostages Case (U.S. v. List *et al.*), 11 T.W.C. 1230, 1241 (U.S. Mil. Trib., 1948).

19. *See* Brand, *The War Crimes Trials and the Laws of War*, 26 BRIT. Y.B. INT'L L. 414, 414 (1949).

20. *See* MCDOUGAL & FELICIANO, THE INTERNATIONAL LAW OF WAR: TRANSNATIONAL COERCION AND WORLD PUBLIC ORDER 716–717 (1994).

21. *See* Akehurst, *Jurisdiction in International Law*, 46 BRIT. Y.B. INT'L L. 145, 160 n. 4 (1972–1973).

22. *See* Baxter, *The Municipal and International Law Basis of Jurisdiction over War Crimes*, 28 BRIT. Y.B. INT'L L. 382, 392 (1951).

23. Attorney-General v. Eichmann, 36 I.L.R. 277, 300–302 (Isr. S. Ct., 1962). *See also* Green, *The Maxim Nullum Crimen Sine Lege and the Eichmann Trial*, 38 BRIT. Y.B. INT'L L. 457 (1962).

24. *Id.* at 304.

25. Demjanjuk v. Petrovsky, 776 F.2d 571, 582–583 (6th Cir. 1985).

26. *See* MCDOUGAL & FELICIANO, *supra* note 20, at 718.

27. *See, e.g.*, Bowett, *Jurisdiction: Changing Patterns of Authority over Activities and Resources*, 53 BRIT. Y.B. INT'L L. 1, 12 (1982).

28. *See* Randall, *Universal Jurisdiction under International Law*, 66 TEX. L. REV. 785, 800–815 (1988).

The Universality Principle and War Crimes

29. Even those maintaining that universal jurisdiction is not as widespread as suggested in this paper do not challenge its current attachment to war crimes. Some scholars sum up the position as follows: "There are probably today only two clear-cut cases of universal jurisdiction, namely the crime of piracy *jure gentium*, and war crimes." STARKE, INTERNATIONAL LAW 212 (Shearer ed., 11th ed. 1994).

30. Geneva Convention I for the Amelioration of the Condition of the Wounded and Sick in Armed Forces in the Field, 1949, art. 49 (second para.), 75 U.N.T.S. 31, *reprinted in* THE LAWS OF ARMED CONFLICTS, *supra* note 11, at 373, 391; Geneva Convention II for the Amelioration of the Condition of Wounded, Sick and Shipwrecked Members of Armed Forces at Sea, 1949, art. 50 (second para.), 75 U.N.T.S. 85, *reprinted in id.* at 401, 418; Geneva Convention III Relative to the Treatment of Prisoners of War, 1949, art. 129 (second para.), 75 U.N.T.S. 135 *reprinted in id.* at 423, 476; Geneva Convention IV Relative to the Protection of Civilian Persons in Time of War, 1949, art. 146 (second para.), 75 U.N.T.S. 287, *reprinted in id.* at 495, 547.

31. Protocol I Additional to the Geneva Conventions of 12 August 1949, and Relating to the Protection of Victims of International Armed Conflicts (Protocol I), 1977, 76 I.L.M. 1391 (1977), *reprinted in* THE LAWS OF ARMED CONFLICTS, *supra* note 11, at 621, 672.

32. Bowett, *supra* note 27, at 12.

33. Jeschek, *War Crimes*, 4 ENCYCLOPEDIA OF PUBLIC INTERNATIONAL LAW 294, 297 (Bernhardt ed., 1982).

34. *See* Carnegie, *Jurisdiction over Violations of the Law and Customs of War*, 39 BRIT. Y.B. INT'L L. 402, 423 (1963).

35. *See* Dinstein, *The Distinctions between War Crimes and Crimes against Peace, in* WAR CRIMES IN INTERNATIONAL LAW 1, 3-4 (Dinstein & Tabory eds., 1996).

36. Report of the International Law Commission, 48th Session (1996), 110–112 (U.N. Doc. A/51/10, mimeographed) (Text).

37. *See* Rosenstock, *The Forty-Eighth Session of the International Law Commission*, 91 AM. J. INT'L L. 365, 370 (1997).

38. *See* Report of the International Law Commission, 48th Session, *supra* note 36, at 114-115 (Commentary).

39. *Id.* at 42 (Text).

40. *Id.* at 45 (Commentary).

41. Mann, *The Doctrine of Jurisdiction in International Law*, 111 RECUEIL DES COURS 9, 95 (1964).

42. Attorney-General v. Eichmann, *supra* note 23, at 18, 54 (D. Ct., 1961), 304 (S. Ct.).

43. Thus, charges by U.S. authorities against American personnel relating to the commission of war crimes in Vietnam "were actually brought not on the basis of international law but of the law of the United States and the Uniform Code of Military Justice." Green, *War Crimes, Crimes against Humanity, and Command Responsibility*, NAVAL WAR C. REV., Spring 1997, at 26, 40.

44. Shachor-Landau, *Extraterritorial Penal Jurisdiction and Extradition*, 29 INT'L & COMP. L.Q. 274, 285 (1980).

45. The option "either to surrender or to punish" a culprit first appears in GROTIUS, DE JURE BELLI AC PACIS, bk. II, ch. XXI, §IV; translation, vol. 2, at 528 (Kelsey trans., Classics of International Law ed., 1984).

46. On the distinctions between extradition and other procedures (deportation and exclusion), see SHEARER, EXTRADITION IN INTERNATIONAL LAW 76–93 (1971).

47. Meron, *International Criminalization of Internal Atrocities*, 89 AM. J. INT'L L. 554, 573-574 (1995).

Yoram Dinstein

48. *See* van den Wyngaert, *The Suppression of War Crimes under Additional Protocol I*, *in* HUMANITARIAN LAW OF ARMED CONFLICT: CHALLENGES AHEAD, ESSAYS IN HONOUR OF F. KALSHOVEN 197, 204–205 (Delissen & Tanja eds., 1991).

49. Convention for the Suppression of Unlawful Seizure of Aircraft, Dec. 16, 1970, 22 U.S.T. 1641, 10 I.L.M. 133 (1971), 1970 U.N. JURID. Y.B. 131.

50. For a full treatment of the subject, see Dinstein, *Criminal Jurisdiction over Aircraft Hijacking*, 7 ISR. L. REV. 195–206 (1972).

51. The choice of the three preferred States is debatable. *See id.* at 203–204.

52. Montreal Convention for the Suppression of Unlawful Acts against the Safety of Civil Aviation, Sept. 23, 1971, 24 U.S.T. 564, 10 I.L.M. 1151 (1971), 1971 U.N. JURID. Y.B. 143, 145.

53. Convention on the Prevention and Punishment of Crimes against Internationally Protected Persons, including Diplomatic Agents, adopted by the U.N. General Assembly, Dec. 14, 1973, T.I.A.S. No. 8532, 13 I.L.M. 41 (1977), 1973 U.N. JURID. Y.B. 75, 76.

54. International Convention against the Taking of Hostages, adopted by the U.N. General Assembly, Dec. 17, 1979, 18 I.L.M. 1456 (1979), 1979 U.N. JURID. Y.B. 124, 125.

55. Convention on the Physical Protection of Nuclear Material, 1980, *reprinted in* INTERNATIONAL CRIMINAL LAW, A COLLECTION OF INTERNATIONAL AND EUROPEAN INSTRUMENTS 55, 57–58 (van den Wyngaert & Stessens eds., 1996).

56. Convention against Torture and Other Cruel, Inhuman or Degrading Treatment or Punishment, adopted by the U.N. General Assembly, Dec. 10, 1984, 24 I.L.M. 535 (1985), 1984 U.N. JURID Y.B. 135, 136.

57. Convention for the Suppression of Unlawful Acts against the Safety of Maritime Navigation, 1988, 27 I.L.M. 672, 675–676 (1988).

58. *Id.* at 679.

59. *See* Halberstam, *Terrorism on the High Seas: The Achille Lauro, Piracy and the IMO Convention on Maritime Safety*, 82 AM. J. INT'L L. 269, 302–303 (1988) (on the priority claim of the flag State).

60. United Nations Convention against Illicit Traffic in Narcotic Drugs and Psychotropic Substances, 1988, 28 I.L.M. 497, 503–504 (1989).

61. International Convention against the Recruitment, Use, Financing and Training of Mercenaries, 1989, 29 I.L.M. 91, 94 (1990).

62. Convention on the Safety of United Nations and Associated Personnel, 1994, 34 I.L.M. 485, 488–489 (1995).

63. *See* LAMBERT, TERRORISM AND HOSTAGES IN INTERNATIONAL LAW—A COMMENTARY ON THE HOSTAGES CONVENTION 140–165 (1990).

64. London Agreement for the Prosecution and Punishment of the Major War Criminals of the European Axis, 1945, *reprinted in* THE LAWS OF ARMED CONFLICTS, *supra* note 11, at 911, 912.

65. *Id.* at 913, 914.

66. Judgment, 1 T.M.W.C. 171, 218 (Int'l Mil. Trib., 1946).

67. S.C. Res. 827 (1993), 32 I.L.M. 1203, 1204 (1993).

68. Secretary-General's Report on Aspects of Establishing an International Tribunal for the Prosecution of Persons Responsible for Serious Violations of International Humanitarian Law Committed in the Territory of the Former Yugoslavia (1993), *id.* at 1159, 1171–1172.

69. *See, e.g.*, Arangio-Ruiz, *The Establishment of the International Criminal Tribunal for the Former Territory of Yugoslavia and the Doctrine of Implied Powers of the United Nations*, *in* DAI TRIBUNALI PENALI INTERNAZIONALI AD HOC A UNA CORTE PERMANENTE 31–45 (1996).

The Universality Principle and War Crimes

70. International Tribunal for the Prosecution of Persons Responsible for Serious Violations of International Humanitarian Law Committed in the Territory of Former Yugoslavia since 1991, Appeals Chamber, The Prosecutor v. Tadič, Jurisdiction (Oct. 2, 1995) 8 (IT-94-1-AR72), 35 I.L.M. 32, 41–45 (1996).

71. *See* Fox, *The Objection to Transfer of Criminal Jurisdiction to the UN Tribunal*, 46 INT'L & COMP. L.Q. 434, 437 (1997) (for quotation).

72. Secretary-General's Report, *supra* note 68, at 1177.

73. The Prosecutor v. Tadič, *supra* note 70, at 52.

74. Shraga & Zacklin, *The International Criminal Tribunal for the Former Yugoslavia*, 5 EURO. J. INT'L L. 360, 371-372 (1994).

75. *See* Article 14(7) of the 1966 International Covenant on Civil and Political Rights, adopted by the U.N. General Assembly, Dec. 16, 1966, 999 U.N.T.S. 171, 6 I.L.M. 368 (1967), 1966 U.N. JURID. Y.B. 178, 183. As observed by the Trial Chamber of the Yugoslav Tribunal in the Tadič case, "this provision is generally applied so as to cover only a double prosecution within the same State." International Tribunal for the Prosecution of Persons Responsible for Serious Violations of International Humanitarian Law Committed in the Territory of Former Yugoslavia since 1991, Trial Chamber, The Prosecutor v. Tadič, Decision on the Defence Motion on the Principle of *non bis in idem* (Nov. 14, 1995) 8 (IT-94-1-T, mimeographed).

76. Geneva Convention III, *supra* note 30, at 460.

77. *See* Paust, *It's No Defense: Nullum Crimen, International Crime and the Gingerbread Man*, 60 ALB. L. REV. 657, 662 (1997).

78. *See* Boss, *The Extraterritorial Jurisdiction of States*, Revised Draft Resolution, Article 8(6), 65(1) ANNUAIRE DE L'INSTITUT DE DROIT INTERNATIONAL 148, 151 (1993).

79. Secretary-General's Report, *supra* note 68, at 1177.

80. Report of the International Law Commission, 48th Session, *supra* note 36, at 69.

81. The provisions of Articles 9 (concurrent jurisdiction) and 10 (*non bis in idem*) of the Yugoslav Tribunal's Statute are replicated in Articles 8 and 9 of the Statute of the International Tribunal for Rwanda, established by the Security Council in Resolution 955 (1994), 33 I.L.M. 1600, 1605–1606 (1994). The latter Statute does not deal, however, with war crimes.

82. Report of the International Law Commission, 46th Session, (1994) II(2) Y.B.I.L.C. 1, 57.

83. Report of the International Law Commission, 48th Session, *supra* note 36, at 66.

84. For the three categories of jurisdiction, see 1 RESTATEMENT, *supra* note 10, at 232 (§401).

85. Green, *The German Federal Republic and the Exercise of Criminal Jurisdiction*, 43 U. TORONTO L.J. 207, 212 (1993).

86. Geneva Convention I, art. 49 (first para.); Geneva Convention II, art. 50 (first para.); Geneva Convention III, art. 129 (first para.); Geneva Convention IV, art. 146 (first para.), *supra* note 30, at 391, 418, 475–476 & 546–547.

87. 1 RESTATEMENT, *supra* note 10, at 304.

88. Essential rules pertaining to judicial proceedings against persons charged with war crimes are incorporated in Article 99 of Geneva Convention III, *supra* note 30, at 463-464. For the application of these rules to prisoners of war accused of war crimes, see COMMENTARY, III GENEVA CONVENTION 415–416 (de Preux ed., 1960).

89. *See* LEVIE, TERRORISM IN WAR—THE LAW OF WAR CRIMES 35, 433 (1993).

90. London Agreement, *supra* note 64, at 915.

91. Order of the Tribunal regarding Notice to Defendant Bormann, 1 T.M.W.C. 102, 102 (Int'l Mil. Trib., 1945).

92. International Military Tribunal, Judgment, *supra* note 66, at 340–341, 367.

93. *See* Guillaume, *The Future of International Judicial Institutions*, 44 INT'L & COMP. L.Q. 848, 857 (1995).

94. *See* Article 27 of the Statute of the Yugoslav Tribunal, Secretary-General's Report, *supra* note 68, at 1188.

95. If a trial for war crimes is conducted by a Detaining Power holding a prisoner of war, his transfer to another Power will additionally be governed by Article 12 of Geneva Convention III, *supra* note 30, at 434–435.

96. Henkin, *International Law: Politics, Values and Functions. General Course on Public International Law*, 216 RECUEIL DES COURS 9, 313 (1989).

97. Silving, *In re Eichmann: A Dilemma of Law and Morality*, 55 AM. J. INT'L L. 307, 338 (1961).

98. S.C. Res. 138 (1960), 4 UNITED NATIONS RESOLUTIONS, SERIES II: RESOLUTIONS AND DECISIONS OF THE SECURITY COUNCIL 14, 14 (Djonovich ed., 1989).

[10]

THE LAW OF NATIONS AND THE PUNISHMENT OF WAR CRIMES[1]

By PROFESSOR H. LAUTERPACHT, M.A., LL.D.
Whewell Professor of International Law in the University of Cambridge

I

THE question whether the punishment of war crimes committed by the enemy is desirable, expedient and practicable is a problem of politics rather than of law. It includes such questions as the relative merits and disadvantages of providing a deterrent against criminal violations of the law of war; the prospective effectiveness of such deterrent; the taking into account of a widespread and not inherently reprehensible desire for retribution; the consequences of impunity upon national and international law and morality; the desirability, partly in the interest of the culprits, of containing a hitherto ruthlessly suppressed craving for revenge within the channels of a regularized legal procedure; and the effects of a policy of punishing war crimes upon the prospects of reconciliation or, at least, of a return to a minimum degree of normalcy in international relations. It is not proposed to discuss these questions in the present article.

There is, however, one series of considerations which lies in what may be described as the realm of legal policy, but which the international lawyer and those who have at heart the future of international law may find it difficult to leave on one side. War crimes are crimes against international law. Punishment of these crimes, however distasteful it may be in its concrete application, is a by no means belated measure of enforcement of international law. The maintenance of the authority of the law of nations is inconsistent with the view that it is a system of law whose means of enforcement are confined to pressure of public opinion or pecuniary compensation, and that as it is a law between, but not above sovereign States, the very idea of punishment is repugnant to its fundamental notions. International law must reject the idea that it is, in this matter, doubly impotent for two contradictory reasons usually adduced in support of this view: (1) because it is legally inadmissible to punish the State as such on the ground that the corporate entity of the State cannot properly be deemed to possess a criminal intent and be the object of criminal punishment in the persons of its organs; and (2) for the alleged reason that it is legally improper to visit punishment upon individuals on the ground that the precepts and the injunctions of international law are not addressed to individuals but to the corporate entity of the State.[2] These views have been given currency

[1] This article has grown out of a Memorandum submitted in July 1942 to the Committee concerned with Crimes against International Public Order (under the chairmanship of Sir Arnold D. McNair). The Committee was set up by the International Commission for Penal Reconstruction and Development established by the Department of Criminal Science in the University of Cambridge.

[2] For a recent advocacy of this point of view see Manners in *American Journal of International Law*, 37 (1943), pp. 407–435. But see Finch, *ibid.*, pp. 81–88; Cohn in *Transactions of Grotius Society*, 26 (1940), pp. 125–51; Schwarzenberger in *Czechoslovak Year Book of International Law*, 1942, pp. 67–88; and Hyde in *Proceedings of the American Society of International Law*, 1943, pp. 39–46.

with particular reference to the question of war crimes in disregard of the fact that the potentialities for irretrievable mischief inherent in the modern State call for an intensification rather than a relaxation of the repressive, deterrent and punitive consequences of criminal conduct.

Once we have dissociated ourselves from a trend of thought which is juridically unsound and retrogressive, we shall be justified in giving—and bound to give—full weight to any possible legal limitations upon the right of the victor to punish enemy nationals accused of war crimes and to any safeguards calculated to ensure the proper exercise of that right. For the cause of international law demands not only the punishment of persons guilty of war crimes. It requires that such punishment shall take place in accordance with international law. Circumstances accompanying the defeat of the enemy, the confusion surrounding the transfer of authority in territory which he had occupied, and the release of suppressed passions may result in acts of summary retribution which foresight and magnanimity may not be able to prevent. But in so far as the punishment of war crimes is intended to take place within the framework of a legal process, it will enhance both its effectiveness and the respect for international law if such limitations as the law of nations imposes are rigidly adhered to. Moreover, there must not only be in fact just punishment. That punishment must also appear to be just and in accordance with the law as the result of the effective provision of practicable measures of impartiality and mutuality.

In the existing state of international law it is probably unavoidable that the right of punishing war criminals should be unilaterally assumed by the victor. This is so in particular when, as may be the case at the close of the second World War, the victorious side represents the overwhelming majority of states and when there are few neutral states left capable of ensuring the impartial administration of justice. Circumstances such as these constitute an additional reason why the manner in which the punishment of war criminals takes place should be not a manifestation of victorious power but an act of international justice. Moreover, the very effectiveness of the attempt to punish war crimes depends to a large extent on the preservation of the essential requirements of fair and impartial judicial process inasmuch as their absence must influence the decision of neutral states to extradite or surrender persons accused of war crimes who have taken refuge in their territory. For these reasons it is proposed to examine in this article the following questions:

(1) What, if any, is the legal basis and justification of the demand, unaccompanied by a reciprocal offer, made upon the defeated State to surrender war criminals to the victor?

(2) What are the legal limitations upon the right to punish war crimes, in particular having regard to the absence or the varying degrees of criminal *mens rea* as the result:

(i) of obedience to superior orders;
(ii) of the uncertainties of rules of warfare;
(iii) of the operation of reprisals?

(3) What are, in this matter, the possible safeguards of impartiality and of a requisite measure of legal equality as between the victor and the vanquished?

(4) What are the basis and the extent of the legal duty, if any, of neutral States to extradite or to surrender war criminals who have taken refuge on their territory?

It is proposed to examine these questions in a general manner, though much of what follows necessarily refers, directly or by implication, to the question of the punishment by the United Nations of war crimes committed during the second World War by Germany and her allies.

II. *The Legal Basis of the Demand for Surrender of War Criminals*

In the course of the second World War, the Governments of most of the United Nations gave repeated expression to their intention to demand, as one of the terms of the armistice, the surrender, for trial and punishment, of nationals of their adversaries accused of war crimes.[1] What is the legal basis of such a demand? Is it the mere power of the victor to exact vindictive retribution from the defeated State and to challenge accepted notions of equality before the law by the underlying assumption that his—the victor's—forces or authorities have been free of any imputation of violating the law of war? Or is it a right, or the corollary of a right, which is firmly grounded in the principles and in the practice of international law?

There may be room for the view that the war crimes committed by Germany and her allies during the second World War were so unprecedented in their premeditation and ruthlessness as to warrant a departure from accepted forms and principles of international law. That view might be supported by the independent, and probably unimpeachable, argument that the armistice or the treaty of peace are not acts of application of international law. The law of these instruments is the will of the victor; there are, in theory, few limits to his power to change established law and precedent as between himself and the vanquished. However, the victor may justly

[1] These include: the Declaration of 13 January 1942, adopted by the Governments of Belgium, Czechoslovakia, Greece, Luxemburg, the Netherlands, Norway, Poland and Yugoslavia and by the Free French National Committee (Document issued by the Inter-Allied Information Committee, London, H.M. Stationery Office, 1942); the statement by Lord Simon, Lord Chancellor. on 7 October 1942 in the House of Lords, outlining the task of the proposed United Nations Commission for the Investigation of War Crimes (*Parl. Debates*, House of Lords, vol. 124, pp. 577 *et seq.*) and endorsed on the same day by the President of the United States; the Declaration on Atrocities adopted in October 1943 at Moscow by Great Britain, the United States, and Russia. The main part of the Declaration may conveniently be quoted:

"At the time of the granting of any armistice to any Government which may be set up in Germany, those German officers and men and members of the Nazi Party who have been responsible for or have taken a consenting part in the above atrocities, massacres and executions will be sent back to the countries in which their abominable deeds were done in order that they may be judged and punished according to the laws of these liberated countries and of the Free Governments which will be erected therein. Lists will be compiled in all possible detail from all these countries, having regard especially to the invaded parts of the Soviet Union, to Poland and Czechoslovakia, to Yugoslavia and Greece, including Crete and other islands, to Norway, Denmark, the Netherlands, Belgium, Luxemburg, France and Italy.

"Thus Germas who take part in wholesale shootings of Polish officers or in the execution of French, Dutch, Belgian or Norwegian hostages or of Cretan peasants, or who have shared in the slaughters inflicted on the people of Poland or in the territories of the Soviet Union which are now being swept clear of the enemy, will know that they will be brought back to the scene of their crimes and judged on the spot by the peoples whom they have outraged. Let those who have hitherto not imbrued their hands with innocent blood beware lest they join the ranks of the guilty, for most assuredly the three Allied Powers will pursue them to the uttermost ends of the earth and will deliver them to the accusers in order that justice may be done.

"The above declaration is without prejudice to the case of German criminals, whose offences have no particular geographical location and who will be punished by a joint decision of the Governments of the Allies."

consider it unwise to disdain the aid which existing law is in a position to offer. He may consider it unwise to do so at the close of a war the essential purpose of which is to vindicate the law of nations—a claim on the part of the United Nations which history is unlikely to stigmatize as sanctimonious and false. For a considerable period after the first World War German writers gave emphatic and repeated expression to the accusation that the provisions of the Treaty of Versailles for the surrender of German war criminals were in flagrant contradiction both with international law and with general principles of law. They were supported by writers in other countries.[1] It is possible that that view, somewhat uncritically accepted, was not without some effect on the eventual fate of these clauses of the Treaty. It is, accordingly, of importance to scrutinize the accuracy of any similar accusation in relation to the corresponding demand of the United Nations in the second World War.

The first relevant fact in the situation is that the practice and the doctrine of international law as well as the municipal law of a considerable number of states recognize that a belligerent is entitled to punish for war crimes those members of the armed forces of the opponent who fall into his hands. There is hardly a dissenting voice in the general approval of that rule. Neither is it a new doctrine in international law. Francisco de Vitoria, writing in 1532, stated the underlying principle in *De Jure Belli*: ". . . etiam parta victoria, recuperatis rebus, pace etiam securitate habita, licet vindicare injuriam ab hostibus acceptam, & animadvertere in hostes, & punire illos pro injuris illatis. . . ." He elaborated the wider reasons of the validity of this principle: ". . . nec pax, nec tranquillitas, quae est finis belli, aliter haberi potest, nisi hostes malis & damnis afficiantur, quibus deterreantur, ne iterum aliquid tale committant."[2] Grotius, while pleading for prisoners of war who have surrendered or desire to do so, says: "in order to warrant their execution it is necessary that a crime shall have been previously committed, such a crime, however, as a just judge would hold punishable by death."[3] Christian Wolff, the German philosopher and lawyer, writing in 1764, reproduces, almost literally, the same view.[4] Johann Jakob Moser, a leading German positivist writer of the same period, is even more emphatic: "Enemy combatants who act contrary to international law need not, when they fall into the hands of the belligerent, be treated as prisoners of war, but may be treated as robbers, murderers and so on."[5] The Institute of

[1] It may be of interest, as showing the strength of the feelings of German jurists on the subject, to quote a passage from the Opinion of Professor Meurer, a German Privy Councillor and an international lawyer of repute, delivered in the course of the work of the Commission on War Crimes appointed by the German *Reichstag* after the first World War. Referring to Articles 228–30 of the Treaty of Versailles, he said: "The Allies thus imposed upon Germany a breach of most elementary legal principles and a forced departure from entire German legal history. Already in 1356 the Golden Bull prohibited 'for all times' the delivery of Germans for punishment by a foreign State. It declared that this prohibition was merely a confirmation of an immemorial right and custom. . . . The German Government could not, it is true, prevent Articles 228–30 of the Treaty of Versailles from becoming law, but when it came to giving effect to their provisions, the torn German people rediscovered its unity and resisted like one man a demand which constituted a cultural outrage" (*Völkerrecht im Weltkrieg* (as to which see below, p. 84), vol. III (1), p. 57).

[2] V. Prop., 19.

[3] Book III, XVI. I.

[4] *Jus Gentium Methodo Scientifica Pertractatum*, § 798.

[5] *Grundsätze des Völkerrechtes in Kriegszeiten* (1752), § 18.

International Law expressed the same view in 1882.[1] Holland, writing in 1908, was very definite on the subject: "Individuals offending against the laws of war are liable to such punishment as is prescribed by the military code of the belligerent into whose hands they fall, or in default of such code, then to such punishment as may be ordered, in accordance with the laws and usages of war, by a military court. . . . When a whole corps systematically disregards the laws of war, e.g., by refusal of quarter, any individuals belonging to it who are taken prisoners may be treated as implicated in the offence."[2] It is unnecessary to amplify these citations of authorities.

As will be submitted presently, this generally acknowledged right of the belligerent to punish enemies guilty of war crimes, far from being irrelevant to the question of the legal propriety of demanding the handing over of criminals to the victorious belligerent, is closely related to it. In the meantime it is sufficient to note that the general recognition of that right supplies a conclusive answer to those who regard as legally abhorrent the idea of the belligerent, favoured by the accident of being able to possess himself of the person of the enemy, acting as judge in his own cause. In default of a reasonable prospect of war crimes being punished by the offender's own State,[3] and in the absence of conditions rendering possible a truly international tribunal, there may be justification, subject to practicable judicial safeguards, for risking the taint of partiality associated with the application of the law by the injured party.

However, the generally acknowledged right of the belligerent to penalize the infractions of the law of war committed by the forces of his opponent is grounded in legal considerations more persuasive than the mere fact of the general recognition of that right. What are these considerations? In so far as war crimes have been perpetrated in the territory of the belligerent claiming the right to inflict punishment, they may be deemed to be covered by the ordinary territorial principle of criminal law. A State is entitled to punish crimes committed on its territory.[4] The application of the territorial principle covers, in the first instance, all violations of international law in the territory under military occupation of the enemy—the main source of war crimes in the second World War. For it is fundamental that the territory

[1] *Annuaire*, V (1881–2), p. 174.

[2] *The Laws of War on Land*, §§ 117, 118.

[3] See below, p. 85.

[4] The issue has been occasionally obscured in reliance on the principle of immunity of armed forces on foreign soil. The ordinary rules of extraterritoriality, based on international comity and consent implied from the mutual respect for the rights of sovereignty in time of peace, do not obtain in time of war. They cover armed forces present on foreign soil *with the permission* of the lawful sovereign—a distinction clearly laid down by Hyde, *International Law*, § 247. In time of peace the operation of the principle of extraterritoriality of foreign armed forces stops short of an immunity for acts directed against the safety of the State. In time of war even forces of an ally are not necessarily immune from local criminal jurisdiction in respect of crimes committed by the members of these forces. See, e.g., the British-Czechoslovak Treaty of 25 October 1940. The conferment of such immunity upon the forces of the United States in Great Britain in 1942 was in the nature of a concession which was not granted without serious consideration of the problems involved. See United States of America (Visiting Forces) Act, 1942, and the Schedule thereto embodying notes exchanged on the subject between the British and American Governments. In any case, the very notion of punishment of war criminals implies an obvious exception to the principle, if any, of the jurisdictional immunity of foreign armed forces. On the contrary view, the belligerent would be entitled to punish war crimes committed by the forces of the adversary in the territory of the latter, but not in his own, occupied, territory.

occupied by the enemy remains under the sovereignty of the belligerent temporarily divested of his jurisdictional rights. For this reason, jurisdiction thus accruing under the territorial principle covers crimes committed not only against the nationals of the State whose territory is subject to belligerent occupation, but also against the nationals of other states, including those of the occupying power—as in the case of the Jewish nationals of Germany brought by her to occupied territories during the second World War in pursuance of a proclaimed policy of racial extermination—and against stateless persons. The same territorial principle includes crimes committed in and from the air over the territory of the State assuming jurisdiction. The question of the extent to which acts committed in the course of air warfare may properly come within the purview of punishment of war criminals is discussed below,[1] but there ought to be little doubt that, in so far as they have taken place over the territory of the State which is in a position to claim jurisdiction, they are covered by the territorial principle. This is so particularly in view of the almost universal acceptance of the principle of the sovereignty of the state in the superincumbent air. The same applies, finally, to acts committed on the high seas by naval or air forces of the enemy seeing that the effect of such acts takes place on the vessels of the belligerent claiming the right to punish war crimes. This extension of the territorial principle received the approval of the Permanent Court of International Justice in *The Lotus* case; even prior to that case it had substantial authority behind it.[2] Thus interpreted, the territorial principle would cover effectively any war crimes committed against vessels—and their passengers and crews—of the United Nations by enemy ships or enemy aircraft.

The territorial principle—the principle that a State is entitled to punish unlawful acts committed within its territory—supplies a substantial, though not the only and not the most important, explanation of the existing rule authorizing a belligerent to punish war crimes committed by the enemy. In the circumstances of the second World War, in the course of which the major part of the European continent was occupied by Germany, the territorial principle thus conceived would cover most of the war crimes with which Germany has been charged. With regard to acts committed in the territory of the adversary, like maltreatment of prisoners of war, the belligerent may, in applying his municipal law to war criminals, rely on the rule, which many states have adopted and which general international law has not stigmatized as illegal, that a State may punish criminal acts committed by foreigners abroad against its own safety or against its nationals.

It has been shown that there exists a broader basis, in addition to the fact of an uncontroverted custom of warfare, for the rule of international law which concedes to belligerents the right to punish such war criminals as may fall into his hands. That basis is the generally recognized right of the State to punish crimes committed within its territory as well as the right claimed by some states and not denied by international law to punish crimes wherever committed against the safety of the State and its nationals. However, this

[1] See below, p. 75. [2] See below, p. 88.

explanation of the established rule, although probably satisfactory in itself, lacks the persuasive force which is indicated in the circumstances unless we realize that the belligerent is, in essence, enforcing not only his municipal law, but also the law of nations. For acts committed by members of the armed forces of the belligerent in the course of hostilities can be treated by the municipal law of the adversary as criminal acts only if there is no justification for them in international law, that is to say, only if they are contrary to the law of war. Such taking of life as is in accordance with the law of war is not murder according to municipal law. Such taking of property as is in accordance with the law governing contributions and requisitions is not theft or robbery. War criminals are punished, fundamentally, for breaches of international law. They become criminals according to the municipal law of the belligerent only if their action finds no warrant in and is contrary to international law. When, therefore, we say that the belligerent inflicts punishment upon war criminals for the violation of his municipal law, we are making a statement which is correct only in the sense that the relevant rules of international law are being applied, by adoption or otherwise, as the municipal law of the belligerent. Intrinsically, punishment is inflicted for the violation of international law. When the British *Military Manual* authorises punishment for the violation of "recognized rules of warfare" it is referring to violations of international law, and not of English municipal law. The rules of warfare, like any other rules of international law, are binding not upon impersonal entities, but upon human beings. The rules of war are binding not upon an abstract notion of Germany, but upon members of the German Government, upon German individuals exercising governmental functions in occupied territory, upon German officers, upon German soldiers. When we say that a belligerent has the right to punish members of the enemy forces for violations of the Hague Conventions, we do not intend to assert that he has the right to punish them for the infraction of his municipal law. The Hague Conventions have not, in the case of most states, become part of their municipal law by any express act of incorporation.[1] In no other sphere does the view that international law is binding only upon States and not upon individuals lead to more paradoxical consequences and nowhere has it in practice been rejected more emphatically than in the domain of the laws of war. In the course of the second World War the Supreme Court of the United States, in a case involving spying and sabotage, affirmed emphatically the direct criminal liability of individuals for violations

[1] In Great Britain the Hague Conventions ratified by the Crown are probably binding upon courts independently of special legislation (see McNair, *The Law of Treaties* (1938), p. 17). In Germany, Convention No. IV was appended in 1911 as Annex II to the Army Regulations. This was only in a loose sense in accordance with Article I of the Convention which laid down that "the Contracting Powers shall issue instructions to their armed forces which shall be in conformity with the Regulations respecting the Laws and Customs of War on Land, annexed to the present Convention." In March 1914 the German military authorities issued regulations concerning collective punishment which the *Reichstag* Commission on War Crimes designated as clearly contrary to the Hague Regulations. When in 1901 Major Friederich was instructed to prepare for the use of the army a manual entitled "Customs of War on Land" (*Kriegsbrauch im Landkriege*), he did not refer to the Hague Regulations. He testified on oath before the Commission that he had no detailed knowledge of the Hague Regulations at that time (*Völkerrecht im Weltkrieg*, I, p. 27). The comprehensive Italian Code of the Laws of War and Neutrality of 8 July 1938 does not refer to the Hague Conventions.

of the laws of war.[1] The immediate subjection of individuals to the rules of warfare entails, in the very nature of things, a responsibility of a criminal character.

Some confusion has been caused, without good reason, by such provisions as Article 3 of Hague Convention No. IV, which lays down that "a belligerent party which violates the provisions of the Regulations shall be liable to pay compensation", and Article 24 of the unratified Hague Rules of Air Warfare, according to which a belligerent State is liable to pay compensation for injuries to persons or property caused by the violation by any of its officers or forces of the provisions relating to aerial warfare.[2] From these and similar rules the conclusion has occasionally been drawn that responsibility for the violation of rules of warfare is limited to pecuniary compensation. There ought to be no doubt that these provisions refer to the responsibility of the State as a whole, and that they were not intended to exclude the responsibility of individuals or the customary right of States to punish enemy individuals for the violation of rules of war.

There is a weighty additional reason why the Hague Conventions must be considered to be binding upon individuals irrespective of the question whether they have been expressly incorporated as part of municipal law. This is so for the reason that they formulate and are largely declaratory of the fundamental rules of warfare as dictated by generally recognized principles of humanity. The same applies to the main aspects of the provisions of the Geneva Conventions of 1929 on the treatment of prisoners of war and of sick and wounded, or of the London Naval Treaty of 1930 and of the London Protocol of 1936 in respect of the elementary duty of safeguarding the lives of civilians in submarine warfare. In their broad purpose, as distinguished from their specific regulations, these international conventions are expressive, in the words of the preamble to Hague Convention No. IV, "of the principles of the law of nations, derived from usages established among civilized peoples, from the laws of humanity, and from the dictates of public conscience". Similarly, the relevant provisions of the London Naval Treaty of 1930 are expressly prefaced by the significant statement: "The following are accepted as established rules of international law." When the German *Staatsgerichtshof*, on 16 July 1921, in the case of *The Llandovery Castle*, found the accused guilty of killing defenceless persons in lifeboats, it did so on the ground that they acted against a clear and uncontested principle of international law as against which even the plea of superior orders offered some but not an absolute defence.[3]

The above considerations supply also a corrective to any undue preoccupation with the question as to what law must be applied in connection with the prosecution and punishment of war criminals. That law is, and

[1] *Ex parte Quirin et al.* (1942) 317 U.S. 1. And see comment thereon, from this point of view, by Hyde in *American Journal of International Law*, 37 (1943), pp. 88–91. And see Brierly in *The Norseman*, vol. 2 (1944), pp. 166–172, for a lucid exposition of the view that war crimes are violations of international law as distinguished from the municipal law of the State against which they have been committed.

[2] The Commission which drafted the Rules decided not to include a provision for the punishment of persons guilty of breaches of the crucial articles of the Rules. But, it added, "its absence will not in any way prejudice the imposition of punishment on persons who are guilty of breaches of the laws of aerial warfare" (Cmd. 2201, p. 59).

[3] *Annual Digest of Public International Law Cases*, 1923–4, Case No. 235.

must be, primarily, the law of nations.[1] For, it must be repeated, it is only to the extent that the acts of the offenders are prohibited by international law, that they can at all be considered as crimes according to the law of the individual states. The fact that the law of nations may be regarded as forming part of the municipal law of the belligerent in question is an important

[1] With regard to the law applied by British military courts, a distinction must be made between the law applied by ordinary courts-martial in the narrower sense of the word and that applied by military courts under martial law. The first is the law mainly laid down in the Army Act, the Naval Discipline Act and the Air Force Act; it governs the conduct and the internal discipline of officers and men of the British armed forces in time of peace and war, both at home and abroad; it is administered by courts-martial—regimental, district, or general—established under these Acts. On the other hand, the law applied by military courts under martial law comes into operation: (*a*) in relation to the civilian population in connection with the suspension of the ordinary law in case of invasion, riots and insurrection, and (*b*) in connection with the application and enforcement of the laws and customs of war by the armed forces of the Crown in occupied enemy territory or in the theatre of war operations generally. We are here concerned with the latter courts only.

These courts, in addition to enforcing the laws and regulations laid down by the commanding general in charge of the occupied territory, apply the laws and customs of war as set forth in Chapter XIV of the *Manual of Military Law* (1929) (Amendment No. 12) notified by the Army Council in the Army Orders for January 1936. Although Chapter XIV of the *Military Manual* has not been given statutory force it is, in general, an exposition of the conventional and customary rules of international law as understood by Great Britain. The business of the military courts, in this particular sphere, is not to apply English criminal law either in its substantive or procedural sense. As said, they apply international law as well as the specific law prescribed by the commanding general in charge of the occupied territory. The discretion of the commanding officer and of the military courts established under his authority is circumscribed by the duty to follow the laws and usages of war. It is significant that in the 1936 edition of the *Military Manual* certain passages in the previous editions of the *Manual*, which emphasized the discretion of the occupying general, have been omitted. The law which these courts apply covers, accordingly, both civilians and members of the enemy armed forces. It is highly improbable that they are bound by the territorial principle of English criminal law. In fact, their primary purpose is to punish offences committed in occupied enemy territory or in the theatre of war operations generally.

At the same time it does not seem to be essential that military courts engaged in applying the laws and usages of war (including the prosecution of war crimes) should be established either within occupied territory or within the immediate vicinity of military operations. The view has been widely held that when Great Britain is at war any portion of its territory is, in relation to enemy aliens, within the "zone of operations". It would appear therefore that the operation of military courts in the wider sense (i.e. courts applying the laws and usages of war) is not necessarily confined to occupied territory or to the area of military operations. Similarly, courts-martial established under the Army Act (or the Naval Discipline Act or Air Force Act) may have conferred upon them by statute jurisdiction over persons, or in respect of acts, not otherwise subject to military law in the narrower sense. Thus in 1914 the Defence of the Realm Consolidation Act (5 Geo. V, c. 8) provided for punishment by courts-martial of certain categories of persons assisting the enemy as if they were subject to military law and had on active service committed an offence under the Army Act. The Treachery Act, 1940, which provided for the death penalty for acts "designed or likely to give assistance to the naval, military or air operations of the enemy, to impede such operations of His Majesty's Forces, or to endanger life", laid down that an alien enemy may be prosecuted for such offences before a court-martial as if he were at the time of the commission of the offence subject to military law. According to the Naval Discipline Act there are subject to the Act spies and persons on board H.M. ships endeavouring to seduce persons subject to the Naval Discipline Act from their duty of allegiance.

With regard to ordinary criminal courts, it is clear that they cannot, according to existing law, exercise jurisdiction with regard to offences committed abroad (except in the matter of offences committed on the high seas or from the air on the high seas and affecting persons on board a British ship). There is probably no serious legal difficulty which would make it impossible for Parliament to alter the existing law in regard to specified categories of war crimes committed abroad. The fact that, as mentioned above, ordinary courts-martial in Great Britain have, by virtue of special war legislation, had conferred upon them jurisdiction over civilians with regard to a number of offences, shows that there is no particular difficulty in the way of modifying established principles, in particular those of a jurisdictional character, in order to meet situations arising out of the war.

but in no way essential addition to the strength of the jurisdictional claim of the belligerent proceeding to punish persons guilty of war crimes. This being so, it is proper, in assuming jurisdiction over war criminals, to lay stress not on any exceptional or summary character of such jurisdiction, military or otherwise, but on its essential conformity with the law of nations. Once it is realized that the offenders are being prosecuted, in substance, for breaches of international law, then any doubts due to inadequacy of the municipal law of any given State determined to punish war crimes recede into the background. There is in this matter no question of any vindictive retroactivity arising out of the creation of crimes of which the accused could not possibly be cognizant. There is even no question of procedural retroactivity by subjecting him to a foreign jurisdiction in defiance of established law and principles. The law of Great Britain, of the United States, and of many other States, does not, as a rule, recognize the competence of national courts in respect of criminal acts committed by aliens abroad. But there would be no question of any retroactivity, contrary to justice and to established principles of law, if Great Britain were to alter her law so as to enable her tribunals, civil or military, whether functioning in Great Britain or abroad, to assume jurisdiction over German nationals who committed in Germany criminal offences against British prisoners of war or British civilians in circumstances not authorized by international law.

It would thus appear that there is no novelty about the principle that a belligerent is entitled to punish such perpetrators of war crimes as fall into his hands; that that principle, far from being a mere assertion of power, grudgingly assented to by international law, on the part of the fortunate belligerent is, in turn, grounded in the fact of recognition by international law of the jurisdiction of States based on the territorial and cognate principles as well as in the fact that in punishing war criminals the belligerent applies and enforces, in essence, the rules of the law of nations which are binding upon the individual members of the armed forces of all belligerents; and that there is no question of any retroactive application of the law from any material point of view.

However, granted that the belligerent is entitled to punish enemy war criminals who happen to fall into his hands, where is the warrant, apart from the undoubted right of the victor to lay down the conditions of the armistice, for the claim that the defeated State should hand over the accused to the victorious belligerent? The answer is that international law permits the punishment of war criminals by the opposing belligerent regardless of the manner in which they happen to fall into his power. The war criminal may fall into the hands of the enemy as a prisoner of war in the course of military operations. But this result may be achieved by other means. The belligerent may possess himself of the war criminals of the enemy as the result of the occupation—before or after the armistice or even after the peace treaty—of enemy territory. Such occupation may be actual or, in the case of the total defeat of the enemy, it may be constructive. After the enemy has been totally defeated, his adversary may proceed to the occupation of the entire enemy territory—a course which, with regard to German territory, was advocated by some at the end of the first World War. In that case he is legitimately in a position to lay his hands on the offenders. If, while abstaining voluntarily from occupying the territory of the defeated belligerent, he stipulates for the handing over of the criminals, what he is in fact doing is to exact from the authorities of the defeated State the performance of a task which he would be in a position to fulfil but for the self-denying decision to refrain from occupation. The entire territory of the defeated opponent is at the mercy and within the reach of the victor. The war criminals are, constructively, in his hands. The defeated and disarmed army of the opponent, as well as his government and administration, are, in a real sense, in the hands of the victorious belligerent. In the event of the second World War terminating with the occupation of the entire German (or Japanese) territory by the armed forces of the United Nations, the war criminals will be seized, either by the occupying Powers or by the German (or Japanese) authorities acting under their direction, and the conditions for the application of the established rule will be fully and literally realized. The situation is hardly different if for political reasons counselling restraint the victorious State refrains from actually occupying the territory of the defeated opponent. The rule of international law which authorises the belligerent to mete out punishment to war criminals who fall into his hands thus covers fully the case of his right to punish those who are, at his will, in his power. This is no mere juridical quibble. To quarrel with it is to quarrel with a rule which is well established as a matter of practice and which has behind it sound legal principle.

In this context it is necessary to consider the objection, on the ground of the absence of mutuality, to the exercise of the right of punishment, on the part of the victorious belligerent, of persons handed over by the enemy. For, clearly, no similar right is conceded to the defeated State.[1] It will be submitted presently[2] that ways may be found for securing a measure of mutuality. But, essentially, the position is not dissimilar to that which arises when the belligerent punishes a prisoner of war for a war crime committed prior to capture. He does so regardless of the ability of the adversary to exercise, effectively, the same right. The same applies to the situation in which war criminals fall, *en masse*, into the hands of the victorious belligerent as the result of an actual or what may be termed a constructive occupation of enemy territory. Undoubtedly, it may happen that the power, thus secured, to exercise the right of punishment may become the monopoly of the belligerent who, in the ultimate judgment of history, has identified himself with the cause of evil. The removal of such contingencies, resulting from the deficient organization of international society, must, like the eventual elimination of war itself, be regarded as a legitimate and desirable object of political endeavour. In the meantime, the victorious belligerent, while applying an inelegant and rough rule of law, must fortify himself by the conviction that in meting out justice he has conscientiously observed the canons of impartiality and the limitations which the existing law of war imposes upon the punishment of war crimes. These will now be considered.

[1] The word "objection" is not used here in a technical sense. In strict law, there is, as pointed out above, nothing to prevent the victorious belligerent from imposing his own conditions of the armistice.

[2] See below, p. 82.

III. *The Limits of Punishment of War Crimes*

The problem of confining the punishment of war crimes within the limits of international law can be conveniently examined under three heads:

(1) the plea of superior orders;

(2) the uncertainties of the law of war;

(3) the operation of reprisals.

(1) THE PLEA OF SUPERIOR ORDERS

The limitation connected with the so-called plea of superior orders constitutes what is from the practical point of view perhaps the most important problem incidental to the punishment of war crimes. It was widely discussed during the first World War. In its report presented to the Preliminary Peace Conference at Paris in 1919 the Commission on Responsibilities stated: "We desire to say that civil and military authorities cannot be relieved from responsibility by the mere fact that a higher authority might have been convicted of the same offence. It will be for the court to decide whether a plea of superior orders is sufficient to acquit the person charged with responsibility."[1] Although this reference to the plea of superior orders was, in its context, limited to one particular situation, the above statement was probably intended to give a general answer to the problem raised by the plea of superior orders. It appears from the statement as quoted: (*a*) that the Commission desired to dissociate itself from the view expressed, among others, in the British *Military Manual* (as well as in the United States *Rules of Land Warfare*) that "members of the armed forces who commit such violations of the recognized rules of warfare as are ordered by their Governments or by their commander are not war criminals and cannot therefore be punished by the enemy",[2] and (*b*) that the Commission did not consider it within its province—or within the reach of agreement among its members—to lay down detailed principles for the guidance of national courts in the matter.

[1] Printed in *American Journal of International Law*, 14 (1920), p. 117.

[2] Section 443, which continues as follows: "He may punish the officials or commanders responsible for such orders if they fall into his hands, but otherwise he may only resort to the other means of obtaining redress which are dealt with in this chapter." This principle appears for the first time in Chapter XIV, prepared in 1914 by Professor Oppenheim and Colonel Edmonds, under the title "The Laws and Usages of War on Land". Article 366 of the United States *Rules of Land Warfare* repeats, almost literally, the British rule. There is no trace of it in the Instructions, drafted by Lieber in 1863, for the Government of Armies of the United States in the Field (for these Instructions see Halleck, *International Law*, vol. II, pp. 40–55). Chapter XIV of the British Manual has no statutory force. However, published as it is by the War Office and under the authority of the Army Council, it may fairly be regarded as representing, at the time, an authoritative British view. It is probable that in any case its provisions must be interpreted by reference to other parts of the Manual, in particular to those which stress the duty of obedience to lawful orders only. The view of the law as expressed in § 443, though disapproved of by the Commission on Responsibilities, which included a British representative, set up by the Peace Conference of 1919, appears, unaltered, in the 1936 edition of the Military Manual. It is at variance with the corresponding principles of English criminal and constitutional law (see below, p. 71). It is not believed to represent a sound principle of the law of war, and it is in no sense binding upon Great Britain in the international sphere. But it is clear that, unless the scope of prosecutions for war crimes is to be drastically and unduly curtailed, any British enactment relating to the prosecution of war crimes by British courts, military and other, will have to free them, by means of an express provision from the shackles of the rule as at present formulated.

It is not surprising that the Commission found it necessary to dissociate itself from the view that superior orders are a sufficient justification. A rule of this nature, unless reduced to legitimate proportions, would in most cases result in almost automatic impunity in consequence of responsibility being shifted from one organ to another in the hierarchy of the State or its armed forces. If the rule as stated in the British and American military manuals actually represented the existing position in international law, the prospect of bringing to justice any substantial portion of offenders would indeed be slender.

The activity of the German *Reichsgericht* in the course of the Leipzig trials in 1921, in connection with the charges put forward by the Allied Powers against higher German officers, illustrates in an illuminating manner the true implications of an unqualified acceptance of the doctrine of superior orders. The person first on the British list of individuals whose prosecution for war crimes was demanded was Grand Admiral Tirpitz, Secretary of State of the German Navy between August 1914 and March 1916.[1] He was charged with having ordered unrestricted submarine warfare. The *Reichsgericht* quashed the proceedings on the ground that, in addition to the fact that unrestricted submarine warfare was not contrary to international law, the Grand Admiral was not responsible for the order in question. The *Reichsgericht* found also that that order was not given by Admiral von Capelle, who was Secretary of the Navy from March 1916 to July 1918; nor by Admiral Scheer, Commander of the Fleet from January 1916 to June 1918; nor by Admiral Hipper, Commander of the Fleet from August 1918 to November 1918; nor by Admiral Muller, Chief of the Naval Cabinet of the Emperor throughout the war—all of whom were on the list of accused persons. Who *did* give the order? The judgments of the *Reichsgericht* do not elucidate this point. But in the decision concerning Admiral von Hipper the *Reichsgericht* to some extent lifted the veil of discretion by stating that it was not the Chief of Fleet who was responsible for the order of unrestricted submarine warfare, but the Head of the Supreme Command of Naval Operations—presumably the Emperor himself. In view of this it is not surprising that the Supreme Court acquitted, as having acted under superior orders, individual naval commanders whom the British list charged "with sinking ships without warning in circumstances of unusual cruelty and inhumanity". If this interpretation of the plea of superior orders were to prevail, then it is clear that in many cases no one but the Head of the State, especially under a régime of absolutism or dictatorship, could be held responsible for decisions of major importance involving a breach of international law—a solution the futility of which is enhanced by the international irresponsibility, asserted by some, of the Head of the State.

The problem raised by the plea of superior orders is, by general admission, one of great complexity both in international and in municipal law. How intricate it is may be gauged from the fact that the solution adopted in the British and American military manuals with regard to war crimes is at variance with that in force in both countries in the domain of constitutional

[1] The list, with a summary of the decisions of the *Reichsgericht*, is compiled in *Völkerrecht im Weltkrieg* (a report of the Commission of Enquiry set up by the German National Assembly in 1919, as to which, see below, p. 85), vol. IV (1927), pp. 337 et seq.

and criminal law. Moreover, the law on the subject in these and other countries in the field of municipal law is not free of ambiguities and apparent inconsistencies. In Great Britain and in the United States a soldier cannot validly adduce superior orders as a circumstance relieving him of liability for an illegal act. This is a rule established by a long series of decisions in both countries. On the other hand, according to English law, the soldier is bound to obey lawful orders of his superiors, and he is liable to punishment by the summary process of a court-martial in case of disobedience—though, when an order which on the face of it is lawful turns out to have been illegal, the soldier who obeyed it is answerable before ordinary courts if obedience to the order involved a crime. The difficulties resulting from the possible conflict between the duty of the soldier to obey orders[1] and his subjection to the general law of the land are appreciated by judges and writers, and sympathy is occasionally expressed with the predicament of the soldier who is thus subject to two possibly conflicting jurisdictions. But the major rule, although qualified in some decisions and although mitigated by the admitted right of executive remedial action in the form of the right of pardon, has remained intact.

The fact is that the law—even military law—does not reduce the soldier to the status of a mere mechanism. While enjoining upon him obedience to orders, it adds the substantial qualification to the effect that obedience is due only to lawful orders. The law oscillates, with perhaps unavoidable hesitation, between the dictates of absolute discipline and efficiency in what is essentially an instrumentality of power and the equally inescapable subjection of that instrument of power to the authority of the law. The result is that in addition to the natural risks of his calling the soldier has, in theory, to face the dangers of a conflict between his duty of obedience to orders and his duty to obey the law. We say "in theory", for in fact the law does not ignore altogether the resulting difficulty. Numerous decisions of courts in the United States recognize that while, in principle, superior orders are not

[1] For, it will be noted, according to English military law the soldier is bound to obey lawful commands only. The wording of Section 9 of the Army Act is explicit on the matter. The law on the subject has undergone significant changes. The Military Code of 1715 provided that "any officer or soldier who should refuse to obey the military orders of his superior officer" shall be liable to capital punishment. The Code contained no qualifications as to the lawfulness of the command. But in 1749 the wording of the Military Act was changed so as to render criminal disobedience to any *lawful* command. Judicial decisions show the same tendency. In *Sutton* v. *Johnstone* (1786, 1 T.R. 493, 546) we still find Lord Mansfield saying: "A subordinate officer must not judge of the danger, propriety, expediency, or consequence of the order he receives: he must obey; nothing can excuse him but a physical impossibility." It will be noted that notwithstanding the apparent rigidity of this statement, there is no reference in this passage to the question of the *legality* of the order. In any case this pronouncement must now be read in the light of the express wording of statutory enactments like the Army Act and of subsequent decisions. Thus the case of *Warden* v. *Bailey* (1811, 4 Taunt. 67) is described in Chapter VIII of the Military Manual as discountenancing the duty of absolute obedience in a soldier enunciated in *Sutton* v. *Johnstone*. As pointed out, according to English military law the duty of obedience, far from being absolute, extends only to lawful orders. There is a significant passage on the subject in Stephen's *History of Criminal Law of England* (vol. I, pp. 205–6). He says: "The doctrine that a soldier is bound under all circumstances whatever to obey his superior officer would be fatal to military discipline itself, for it would justify the private in shooting the colonel by the orders of the captain, or in deserting to the enemy on the field of battle on the order of his immediate superior." It is probably accurate to say that no warrant can be found in British military law for the view that the existence of any duty of absolute obedience gives colour to an unqualified recognition of the plea of superior orders.

a valid defence, obedience to an order which is not on the face of it illegal and is within the scope of the superior officer, relieves the soldier of liability. Some State laws go even further in that direction. In England, where the courts have been loth to depart from the logical rigour of the established rule, it is generally recognized that the exercise of the right of pardon by the Executive is in such cases a proper remedy. As Dicey says: ". . . a soldier runs no substantial risk of punishment for obedience to orders which a man of common sense may honestly believe to involve no breach of law."[1] And there are judicial decisions to the effect that the soldier obeying orders which are not "necessarily or manifestly illegal" will be protected by the courts themselves.[2]

Conversely, many countries which, in the interest of the efficiency of their armed forces, have adopted the rule that obedience to superior orders excludes liability, make an exception in cases in which the orders are illegal. They, in turn, differ as to the necessary degree of the obviousness of the illegality. The German Code of Military Criminal Law, prior to the second World War, provided that the subordinate is liable to punishment as an accomplice if, when obeying an order, he knows that the act ordered involves a crime or misdemeanour.[3] According to the law of other states, the immunity of the soldier obeying orders ceases if he knows or *ought to have known* of the unlawful nature of the order.[4] There are indeed some states, in particular France, in which there is, apparently, no qualification to the rule that, in relation to the armed forces, superior orders are in all circumstances a valid excuse. Writers of authority, like Duguit, have defended that rule with vigour on the ground that it is indispensable to the cohesion and to the efficiency of the army.[5] But it has not been asserted that its effect is to relieve French nationals of responsibility when tried before foreign tribunals for violation of the municipal law of those countries or of international law even if the foreign country concerned has itself adopted an identical rule. For it is, by necessary implication, a rule applicable only to the State's own nationals and only in respect of its own municipal law. In fact, no country has more emphatically than France rejected the plea of superior orders when put forward by enemy soldiers and officers accused of war crimes.[6] It is an interesting gloss on the complexity of the problem that in Great Britain and in the United States the plea of superior orders is, on the whole, without

[1] *The Law of the Constitution*, 8th ed. (1927), p. 302.

[2] Mr. Justice Willes in *Keighley* v. *Bell* (1866), 4 F. & F. 763, at p. 790.

[3] S. 42 (2). [4] E.g., Article 3 of the Polish Military Penal Code of 1932.

[5] *Traité de droit constitutionnel* (2nd ed., 1923), vol. III, pp. 289, 290—while denying that superior orders offer a valid excuse in other spheres: *ibid.*, pp. 286–9.

[6] Mérignhac in *Revue générale de droit international public*, 24 (1917), p. 53. But see Nast, *ibid.*, 26 (1919), p. 123. The crucial *sedes materiae* in French law appears to be Article 64 of the Criminal Code according to which an act committed under duress (which, apparently, includes the case of a soldier bound to obey orders) is neither a crime nor a misdemeanour. Article 327 excludes liability in case of acts "ordonnés par la loi et commandés par l'autorité". So does Article 190. Articles 70 and 71 of the Belgian Penal Code reproduce substantially Articles 64 and 327 of the French Penal Code. Article 43 of the Dutch Criminal Code recognizes generally the defence of superior orders, while Article 40 lays down the general exception of duress. On the other hand, the Military Criminal Code of Czechoslovakia (which is in this respect based on the Austrian Military Penal Code of 1855) lays down, in Article 8, that, subject to the exceptions provided by the law, the order of a superior does not justify a crime or a misdemeanour. The exception is that of Article 158 relating to the duty to obey orders—unless such orders clearly aim at the commission of a crime or of a misdemeanour.

decisive effect in internal criminal or constitutional law, although it is apparently treated as a full justification in relation to war crimes, while in France, where the plea of superior orders is an absolute defence in the municipal sphere, it is disregarded in the matter of war crimes.

There is no international judicial authority on the subject, but writers on international law have almost universally rejected the doctrine of superior orders as an absolute justification of war crimes.[1]

In view of the substantial diversity, both apparent and real, in the judicial and legislative practice of various states, it is necessary to approach the subject of superior orders on the basis of general principles of criminal law, namely, as an element in ascertaining the existence of *mens rea* as a condition of accountability. In the first instance, there can be no liability, or there must be diminished liability, if the accused acted in the legitimate belief that he was proceeding in accordance with law, both municipal and international. In his estimate of the legal position, the circumstance that he has received orders to act in a certain way must be regarded, *prima facie*, as creating in the accused the conviction of the lawfulness of the action as ordered. By the same token, the clearly illegal nature of the order—illegal by reference to generally acknowledged principles of international law so identified with cogent dictates of humanity as to be obvious to any person of ordinary understanding—renders the fact of superior orders irrelevant.[2] Secondly, such a degree of compulsion as must be deemed to exist in the case of a soldier or officer exposing himself to immediate danger of death as the result of a refusal to obey an order excludes *pro tanto* the accountability of the accused—unless, indeed, we adopt the view, which cannot lightly be dismissed, that the person threatened with such summary punishment is not entitled to save his own life at the expense of the victim or, in particular, of many victims.[3] The result of the combination of these two principles will be, at the one end, that a person obeying an obviously unlawful order the refusal to obey which would not put him in immediate jeopardy, will not be able to shield himself behind the excuse of superior orders. At the other end, a person obeying, in an isolated case, an illegal order which is not on the face of it unlawful and disobedience to which would expose him to the full rigours of summary military discipline, may rely on the plea of superior orders. There will be a variety of intermediate situations between these two extremes.

There ought to be no doubt that should courts entrusted with the trial of war crimes disregard altogether the plea of superior orders, they would be adopting a course which could not be regarded as defensible. On the other hand, while the fact of superior orders sets a limit to the punishment of acts which might otherwise constitute war crimes, it need not warp the effectiveness of the law in a manner which may rightly be regarded as a perversion of justice. It will not cover crimes committed by superior authorities and officers acting under their own responsibility and initiative; it will not protect

[1] For the literature on the subject see Oppenheim, *International Law*, vol. II (6th ed., 1940), p. 454, n. 2. See also Sack in *Law Quarterly Review*, 60 (1944), pp 63–8.

[2] This was clearly recognized by the German Supreme Court in 1921 in *The Llandovery Castle*, though it treated the fact of superior orders as an extenuating circumstance: *Annual Digest*, 1923–4, Case No. 232.

[3] *R.* v. *Dudley* (1884), 14 Q.B. 273.

criminal acts committed by subordinates for purposes of private gain and lust; it will not shield acts committed in pursuance of orders so glaringly offending against fundamental conceptions of law and humanity as to remove them from the orbit of any possible justification, including that of immediate danger to the person charged with the execution of the orders; it will not excuse crimes committed in obedience to unlawful orders in circumstances in which the person executing the crime was not acting under the immediate impact of fear of drastic consequences of summary martial justice following upon a refusal to act (the latter being crimes perpetrated by the vast army of officials in the occupied territories). If these limits of the doctrine of superior orders are taken into consideration, then its judicious application, far from defeating the ends of justice, may testify in a significant manner to the determination of the victorious belligerent to abide by the limitations of international law.

(2) UNCERTAINTIES OF THE LAW OF WAR

Similar considerations apply to the second factor which must in some ways limit both the scope of prosecutions for war crimes and their punishment. That factor results from the controversial character of some of the most important aspects of modern war. There are acts of warfare which an impartial international tribunal would hold to be contrary to international law, but the lawfulness of which has been to a sufficient degree a subject of controversy or uncertainty to preclude them from properly being the subject of a criminal prosecution before the tribunals of the victorious belligerent. Thus, for instance, it appears probable that—apart, perhaps, from the doubtful operation of the law of reprisals—an international tribunal would hold that the methods adopted by Germany in both World Wars in the matter of mine-laying or general devastation were contrary to international law. Yet, because of the controversial state of international law on those matters, there may be lacking in respect of such acts that degree of *mens rea* which, in matters of this kind, constitutes an essential condition of criminality. Such acts as general devastation or indiscriminate mine-laying may supply ample reason for condemnation and protest; they may afford ground for retaliatory action of a most sweeping and comprehensive nature like the British Retaliatory Orders in Council of November 1939 and July 1940; they may, at the end of the war, justify the imposition of collective sanctions by way of compensation or otherwise as distinguished from individual penalties of a criminal nature. But criminal proceedings before the municipal courts of the victor may seem to many a questionable method of removing outstanding doubts and laying down authoritatively the existing law on subjects of controversy.

Total war has altered the complexion of many a rule. At a time when the scorched earth" policy, with regard to the belligerent's own territory, has become part of a widespread practice, general destruction of property ordered as an incident of broad military strategy will not properly form the subject-matter of a criminal indictment. Modern warfare has raised, and, in some respects, left unsolved the problem of reconciling the fundamental distinction between combatants and non-combatants with the advent of new weapons and with the increase of the numbers of both combatants and non-combatants engaged in work of vital importance for the war effort. This applies in particular to the question of aerial bombardment of centres of population. The ubiquity and indefiniteness, enhanced by elaborate camouflage and by the dangers of vastly improved methods of defence, of legitimate objectives; the difficulty of localizing the effects of bombardment; and bombing by way of retaliation—all these factors may make it difficult to answer the question of the legitimacy of aerial bombardment by way of criminal prosecutions against individuals. It is doubtful whether, in this and similar matters, tribunals entrusted with the task of punishing war criminals are a proper agency for solving controversial and difficult problems of the law of war. For this reason it is probable that retribution for much of the ravages of war, of loss of life, and of destruction of property perpetrated with a criminal intent may have to remain outside the scope of prosecution of individuals for war crimes before the courts of the former enemy. This does not mean that the guilty State will escape all the consequences of such actions committed on its behalf. There remains, in particular, the duty of compensation such as is envisaged in Article 3 of Hague Convention No. IV or in Article 25 of the so-called Hague Air Warfare Rules of 1923. Neither will any uncertainty of the law shield persons accused of clearly criminal acts unrelated to the major aspects of disputed rules, such as deliberate machine-gunning of civilian refugees or, possibly, such acts of mere terrorism and frightfulness as the bombardment of Rotterdam in April 1940.

Moreover, it does not appear that the difficulties arising out of any uncertainty as to the existing law have a direct bearing upon those violations of the rules of war which have provided the impetus for the almost universal insistence on the punishment of war crimes. Acts with regard to which prosecution of individuals for war crimes may appear improper owing to the disputed nature of the rules in question arise largely in connection with military, naval and air operations proper. No such reasonable degree of uncertainty exists as a rule in the matter of misdeeds committed in the course of military occupation of enemy territory. Here the unchallenged authority of a ruthless invader offers opportunities for crimes the heinousness of which is not attenuated by any possible appeal to military necessity, to the uncertainty of the law, or to the operation of reprisals.

The fact of the controversial character of some of the rules of war tends not only to impose a limitation upon the scope of offences which may properly be prosecuted as war crimes. It has a direct bearing on the question of the plea of superior orders. If it is true that, as pointed out above, the obviousness and the indisputability of the crime tend to eliminate one of the possible justifications of the plea of superior orders, then the controversial character of a particular rule of war adds weight to any appeal to superior orders. An international tribunal may find that the order was illegal. But any justifiable element of doubt, however ill-founded, preliminary to such a finding must weigh with particular force in the decision of the court to dismiss the plea of superior orders.

(3) THE EFFECT OF THE OPERATION OF REPRISALS

The same considerations apply, with even greater force, to the effect of the operation of reprisals—both in general and in relation to the plea of superior orders. In the first and in the second World War reprisals have been the legal cloak for the departure, some of which was unavoidable, from many of the accepted rules of warfare. In the sphere of maritime war the operation of reprisals in both World Wars has, in practice, replaced most of the traditional rules. In a sense, reprisals have often fulfilled the function which would normally have been left to agreement between States, namely, that of the adaptation of the law to the changed conditions of modern warfare. For this reason it is not always profitable to enquire whose original illegality opened wide the flood gates of retaliation. It is sufficient to note that the torrent swept away with devastating thoroughness many of the elaborate, though often controversial, rules.

A war crime does not necessarily cease to be such for the reason that it is committed under the guise of reprisals. But, as a rule, an act committed in pursuance of reprisals, as limited by international law, cannot properly be treated as a war crime. A tribunal confronted with the plea of reprisals as a justification of the offence will be faced with a task of considerable difficulty. International law regulates, in a necessarily rough and indeterminate manner, the occasions for and the use of reprisals both in peace and in war. It postulates the requirements of a prior attempt at redress by negotiation, of proportionality, of reasonableness, of compliance with fundamental principles of war such as respect for the lives of non-combatants, and of due consideration for the legitimate interests of neutrals. But the law on the subject is necessarily elastic.

The element of reprisals may have a significant and perplexing bearing upon the plea of superior orders. It has been shown that the strength of the plea of superior orders is conditioned by the degree of heinousness of the offence and its approximation to a common crime apparently divorced both from belligerent necessity and from elementary considerations of humanity. But the force of this latter consideration may become considerably impaired —though never totally eliminated—when the act has been ordered, or represented to the subordinate as having been ordered, in pursuance of reprisals against a similar or identical crime committed by the adversary. The subordinate may be expected, when confronted with an order utterly and palpably contemptuous of law and humanity alike, to assert, at the risk of his own life, his own standard of law and morality. This is an exacting though unavoidable test. But no such independence of conviction and action may invariably be expected in cases where the soldier or officer is confronted with a command ordering an act admittedly illegal and cruel but issued as a reprisal against the similarly reprehensible conduct of the adversary. We may attribute to the accused a rudimentary knowledge of the law and an elementary standard of morality, but it may be more difficult to expect him to be in possession of the necessary information to enable him to judge the lawfulness of the retaliatory measures in question in relation to the circumstances alleged to have given rise to them. An example will illustrate the position: No person can be allowed to plead that he was unaware of the prohibition of killing prisoners of war who have surrendered at discretion. No person can be permitted to assert that, while persuaded of the utter illegality of killing prisoners of war, he had no option but to obey an order. But the situation is more complicated when the accused pleads not only an order, but the fact that the order was represented as a reprisal for the killing by the adversary of the prisoners of his own State. When the German Supreme Court in the case of *The Dover Castle* acquitted in 1921 the accused who pleaded guilty of torpedoing a British hospital ship, the Court expressed the view that the accused were entitled to hold, on the information supplied to them by their superiors, that the sinking of enemy hospital ships was a legitimate reprisal against the abuse of hospital ships by the enemy in violation of Hague Convention No. X.[1] Moreover, there is room for the view that if the victorious belligerent has himself, in pursuance of reprisals, set aside international law in a particular sphere, he cannot properly make such acts on the part of his opponent the subject of prosecution for a war crime.

On the other hand, as in the matter of the uncertainty of the law of warfare, the impact of the operation of reprisals is not as considerable as would appear at first sight. In particular, it does not seriously affect that most potent source of war crimes which originates in the lawlessness and the brutality of the occupying State.

While it is imperative that we should bear in mind the limitations upon the prosecution and punishment of war criminals—limitations such as those following from the plea of superior orders, from the controversial character of some of the laws of war, and from the application of reprisals—it is of equal importance that we should not in this matter lose sight of the wood for the trees. These exceptions may make the work of the tribunals more intricate and more responsible, but there is no reason to assume that they will invariably affect the issue. Superior orders may be invoked, uncertainties of the law of war may be relied upon, and reprisals may be cited as an excuse—but that does not mean that when thus appealed to they will confound the ends of justice. They will be subjected to judicial scrutiny. They may be found sufficiently weighty to warrant acquittal; they may be considered in the light of and as having the effect of extenuating circumstances; or they may, upon careful investigation, be brushed aside as a flimsy device to cover the horrors of a war crime. At the same time, it is clear that all these three factors imply a limitation upon the punishment of war crimes which cannot be disregarded consistently with the determination to conduct the trials of war criminals within the limits which law and justice impose.

In addition to the limitations which the absence of *mens rea* imposes, in various degrees, upon the right of punishing war crimes there must be considered the question as to what can properly be regarded as a war crime such as to warrant the demand for extradition or surrender to and punishment by the victorious belligerent. In particular, does every violation of a rule of warfare constitute a war crime? It appears that, in this matter, textbook writers and, occasionally, military manuals and official pronouncements have erred on the side of comprehensiveness. They make no attempt to distinguish between violations of rules of warfare and war crimes. The Commission on Responsibilities set up by the Paris Conference in 1919 included under the list of charges of war crimes such acts as "usurpation of sovereignty during military occupation", "attempts to denationalize the

[1] *Annual Digest*, 1923–4, Case No. 231.

inhabitants of occupied territory", "confiscation of property", "exaction of illegitimate or exorbitant contributions and requisitions", "debasement of the currency and issue of spurious currency", "imposition of collective penalties", and "wanton destruction of religious, charitable, educational and historic buildings and monuments". In view of the comprehensiveness of this list it is in the nature of an anti-climax to note that the number of persons whose delivery the Allied States eventually demanded was inconsiderable.[1] It is possible that one of the reasons for the failure to give effect to the decision to prosecute war criminals after the first World War was the extent of the list of offences as adopted by the Conference and the absence of a distinction between violations of international law and war crimes in the more restricted sense of the term.

In drawing up, in an exhaustive fashion, the list of war crimes the Paris Commission followed the somewhat academic treatment of the subject found in some of the manuals of military law. Thus the British *Manual*[2] adopts a vague and somewhat tautologous definition of "war crimes" as "the technical expression for such an act of enemy soldiers and enemy civilians as may be visited by punishment or capture [*sic*] of the offenders".[3] These war crimes, according to the *Manual*, include, in particular, "violations of the recognized rules of warfare by members of the armed forces". Within that category the *Manual* enumerates the following as "the more important violations": making use of poisoned and otherwise forbidden arms and ammunition; killing of wounded; refusal of quarter; treacherous request of quarter; maltreatment of dead bodies on the battlefield; ill-treatment of prisoners of war; firing on undefended localities; abuse of the flag of truce; firing on the flag of truce; abuse of Red Cross flag and badge, and other violations of the Geneva Conventions; use of civilian clothing by troops to conceal their military character during battle; bombardment of hospitals and other privileged buildings; improper use of privileged buildings for military purposes; poisoning of wells and streams; pillage and purposeless destruction; ill-treatment of inhabitants of occupied territory.

The above enumeration is admittedly by way of example. In that order of thought, a more detailed list might include such violations of the rules of warfare as capturing enemy vessels employed in coast fisheries, or vessels charged with scientific or philanthropic missions; interference with mail boats or mailbags in breach of Hague Convention No. XI; unjustified destruction of enemy prizes; laying mines in breach of Hague Convention No. VIII; violation of such accepted rules of international law as exist in the matter of contraband and blockade; or the breach of any of the numerous and detailed provisions of the Geneva Convention of 1929 on the treatment of the sick and wounded and of prisoners of war.

It must be a matter for serious consideration to what extent an attempt to penalise by criminal prosecution at the hand of the victorious belligerent all and sundry breaches of the law of war may tend to blur the emphasis which must be placed on the punishment of war crimes proper in the limited

[1] The list comprised eight hundred and ninety-seven persons.

[2] Following closely the section on "Punishment of War Crimes" in Oppenheim's *International Law*, vol. II, §§ 251 and 252.

[3] Chapter XIV, s. 441.

sense of the term. These may be defined as such offences against the law of war as are criminal in the ordinary and accepted sense of fundamental rules of warfare and of general principles of criminal law by reason of their heinousness, their brutality, their ruthless disregard of the sanctity of human life and personality, or their wanton interference with rights of property unrelated to reasonably conceived requirements of military necessity. There is room for the view that the punishment of war crimes by the victorious belligerent ought to be limited to offences of this nature—offences which, on any reasonable assumption, must be regarded as condemned by the common conscience of mankind. Suggestions for some such limitation will occasionally be found in textbooks. Hall, in his weighty and precise manner, expressed an opinion to this effect. Referring to the right of the belligerent of "punishing persons who have violated the laws of war, if they afterwards fall into his hands", he points out that no objection can be felt to the exercise of this right "so long as the belligerent confines himself to punishing breaches of universally acknowledged laws".[1] More recently, an able Italian writer, in a careful examination of the question, has suggested some such limitation.[2]

The task of defining, from this point of view, the scope of violations of the laws of war which ought to fall within the purview of punishment by the victorious belligerent is one of considerable difficulty. A seemingly administrative act of a political nature, like deportation or segregation of large sections of the population of the occupied territory, may, in its effects upon human life and in the cruelty of its execution, be indistinguishable from the common crime of deliberate murder. But it is a task which ought to be attempted. The result of the differentiation thus established between the two categories of violations of the law of war would not necessarily be to render immune from punishment or from the duty of compensation the less heinous manifestations of lawlessness. But these would be governed by a different procedure; in particular they would not fall within the purview of any demand for surrender as part of the armistice stipulations. On the other hand, it is probably unprofitable to attempt a distinction between the acts of the defeated State as such and acts attributable directly to individuals. All acts of the State are attributable to individual persons. There are none which cannot be traced to a decision of an individual or of a plurality of individuals. Neither is it helpful to establish a rigid distinction between offences against life and limb and those against property. Pillage, plunder and arbitrary destruction of private and public property may, in their effects, be no less cruel and deserving of punishment than acts of personal violence. There may, in effect, be little difference between executing a person and condemning him to a slow death of starvation and exposure by depriving him of shelter and means of sustenance. Finally, no just or working differential test can be found in the possibility of establishing a direct connection between the criminal act and any individual victim or victims. The person who issues general orders for the killing of hostages is no less guilty than the person to whom we may be able to bring home a specific order for shooting a particular hostage or group of hostages. A commander who issues a general order calculated to prevent the saving of life after the sinking of merchant

[1] *International Law*, 3rd ed. (1883), s. 135.
[2] Balladore Pallieri, *La Guerra* (1935), p. 385.

vessels is no less guilty than an officer or soldier who is found to have committed on his own initiative a crime of this kind. Assuming that indiscriminate bombardment of towns for the purpose of terrorizing the civilian population and the deliberate machine-gunning of civilian refugees are to be treated as war crimes irrespective of the plea of superior orders, the mere fact that an individual formed part of a bombing squadron responsible for such acts may be sufficient to stamp him as a war criminal although it is impossible to prove a direct connection between his conduct and the death of any individual person. Some legal systems recognize that when a group of persons, such as a gang of robbers, commit a crime, each and every member of the group may be convicted without proving that any particular member committed the criminal act.

IV. *Safeguards of Impartiality and of Legal Equality in the Trial of War Criminals*

It is incumbent upon the victorious belligerent intent upon the maintenance and the restoration of international law, to make it abundantly clear by his actions that his claim to inflict punishment on war criminals is in accordance with established rules and principles of the law of nations and that it does not represent a vindictive measure of the victor resolved to apply retroactively to the defeated enemy the rigours of a newly created rule. The persuasive force of any such professions must be impaired unless it is accompanied by the provision of safeguards of impartiality and by a measure of equality in the application of the law. The preservation both of the substance and of the appearance of impartiality is of particular importance in view of the fact that, in the circumstances of the situation, there cannot be any question of formal equality by a concession to the defeated belligerent of the identical right to punish any war criminals of the victor. Under existing international law this is in no way a condition of the valid exercise of that right by the victorious belligerent. Even in this respect, there may be means for mitigating the inequality fully authorized by the existing law.[1]

However, the most important aspect of the problem is that of guarantees of impartiality in the punishment of war crimes. These guarantees may, in theory, be achieved in three ways: I. By means of an International Criminal Court; II. By way of appropriate modifications of the organization of the municipal courts of the victorious belligerents adjudicating upon war crimes; III. By a system of quasi-international courts conceived as municipal courts of the belligerent the composition of which is not confined to its own nationals.[2]

I. *The International Criminal Court.* The problem of an International Criminal Court, in particular with reference to the punishment of war crimes, has been an almost continuous subject of discussion since the first World War. Not all of the reasons which have been adduced against the establishment of a court of this nature can be described as sound. This applies in

[1] See below, p. 82.

[2] For a detailed discussion of the various types of court to try war criminals see Glueck in *Harvard Law Review*, 56 (1942–3), pp. 1059–89. See also the judicious suggestions by Professor Hyde in *Proceedings of the American Society of International Law*, 1943, pp. 43–6.

particular to the objection based on the difficulty of reaching an agreement as to the law to be applied by it. In principle, there appear to be compelling reasons for the establishment in the future of an International Criminal Court having jurisdiction to try the crime of war (i.e. resort to war in violation of international law[1]) as well as certain categories of war crimes arising out of the conduct of hostilities proper and not involving common crimes against life and property. The jurisdiction over the latter, especially when committed in occupied territory, would seem more properly to lie within the province of local tribunals suitably reinforced by an international and neutral element acting expeditiously and having direct access to available evidence. However, regardless of the feasibility of establishing an International Criminal Court in the future, weight must be given to the following considerations of a practical nature:

(i) The establishment of an international institution of a novel character and of the scope and significance of an International Criminal Court is not a task which can be accomplished within a short period. At the same time there are compelling reasons which make it undesirable and impracticable to postpone the punishment of war crimes for any prolonged period of years. It follows that, unless an International Criminal Court is already in existence at the time of the cessation of hostilities, those who link up the punishment of all war crimes with the establishment of such a court run the danger of sacrificing the substance of an urgent task for what may well prove to be the shadow of its intricate machinery.

(ii) In so far as the primary purpose of the establishment of an International Criminal Court is to secure an unimpeachable measure of impartiality, that purpose must be viewed in the light of the contingency, such as will arise at the termination of the second World War, that the world may be divided, with insignificant exceptions, into two opposing camps of belligerents. In such circumstances an International Criminal Court would hardly partake of the character of an impartial and detached judicial body. This is also a contingency which must be taken into consideration in connection with any war involving the great majority of states. No "international" court in any true sense of the word is possible in such cases.

(iii) For the same reasons no adequate solution can be found in the establishment of an international tribunal composed of neutral judges or, generally, in giving neutral States a major share in the proceedings. There may be only a very few neutral states left. Some of them may be only nominally neutral. They may have identified themselves for many purposes with the cause or the outlook of one side. In a general war in which the overwhelming majority of States is animated by the consciousness that their cause is one of vindication and of survival of law and civilization, there will be a tendency to view at least some of the remaining neutral States as having

[1] In this matter the position is now different from that which obtained in 1914 and which prompted the Commission on Responsibilities set up in 1919 by the Paris Conference to declare that "by reason of the purely optional character of the institutions at The Hague for the maintenance of peace (International Commissions of Enquiry, Mediation and Arbitration) a war of aggression may not be considered as an act directly contrary to positive law". The law of any international society worthy of the name must reject with reprobation the view that between nations there can be no aggression calling for punishment. It must consider the responsibility for the premeditated violation of the General Treaty for the Renunciation of War as lying within the sphere of criminal law.

shown themselves deficient in their sense of international solidarity at a supreme period of trial.

II. *Means for Securing Impartiality within the Framework of Municipal Tribunals.* If the establishment of an International Criminal Court is not an adequate instrument for securing the requisite degree of impartiality in the trial of war criminals, there arises the further question as to the possible safeguards on that behalf within the framework of the municipal courts of the victorious belligerent. The following are believed to deserve consideration:

(i) *Jurisdiction of Special Courts Composed of Professional Judges with the Participation of Military Assessors or Judges.* Some such composition of tribunals for the trial of war criminals, while not interfering seriously with their efficiency, would add to their authority and remove from them the reproach of a purely summary procedure. Exclusively military jurisdiction is fully justified during the actual hostilities. The justification is less obvious after the cessation of hostilities in respect of persons not captured in the course of military operations but surrendered by the enemy or neutral States after the conclusion of the armistice.

(ii) *The Expansion of Military Tribunals by the Inclusion of Lay Judges.* There is no compelling reason to assume that the result of some such expedient would be a serious impairment of the speed of the trials. There are weighty reasons for disposing of the trials of war criminals in the period between the armistice and the peace treaty, but it is doubtful whether this implies the necessity for anything in the nature of a summary procedure. The state of popular feeling in the period immediately following the armistice and the legal difficulties likely to be involved in some of the prosecutions may require that purely military courts should be reinforced by the inclusion of persons of judicial experience and possessing a wider knowledge of the law.

(iii) *Participation of Neutral Assessors.* Subject to what has been said above concerning the position of neutral States at the end of hostilities, there is a strong case for associating neutral assessors with the trial of war criminals. Neutral assessors might be given the right to participate actively in the trial by addressing questions to witnesses and to the accused, by being present at the deliberations of the court, and by being entitled to express concurrence with or dissent from its decision. It might be found possible to attach practical consequences to any dissent on their part, for instance, by way of granting to the accused a right of appeal in such cases.

(iv) *Participation of Enemy Assessors.* The attempt to secure not only the substance but also the forms of impartiality and of equality before the law need not stop at this point. There is force in the view that the defeated enemy should be given the opportunity, by providing assessors of his own, of participating in the work of the courts of his adversary engaged in trying war criminals. In particular, it must be considered whether, in the case of the participation of both neutral and enemy assessors, a judgment from which they have both dissented should not automatically be liable to review by a superior court regardless of any appeal by the accused.

III. *Quasi-international Courts of Appeal and Courts of First Instance.* Quasi-international tribunals are, in this connection, municipal tribunals of the victorious belligerent enlarged by the inclusion of judges from other countries, co-belligerent and neutral. This is a machinery particularly suitable for any appellate jurisdiction which may be set up. There may be obvious advantages from the point of view of justice and expediency in providing appellate courts which, while acting with all requisite expedition, would be in a position to bring to bear upon the cases before them a higher degree of detachment and a wider range of legal knowledge. Quasi-international courts thus set up might prove to a large extent a substitute for an International Criminal Court adjudicating upon war crimes. The presence of judges of foreign nationality, while not calculated decisively to influence the issue and while in no way derogating from the authority or reputation for impartiality of the national courts, would add to their proceedings the indispensable elements of publicity and detachment.

In considering these and similar safeguards it is necessary to bear in mind the fact that the due punishment of war criminals, unless it is accompanied by all practicable safeguards of impartiality and, to some extent, of mutuality, may be deficient both in effectiveness and in the part which it might otherwise play in the re-establishment of international law. Such proposals may be severely criticized by those who may see in them legalistic attempts to interfere with the just rigour of retribution; they may be adversely commented upon by others as not going far enough in preventing the punishment of war crimes from becoming a one-sided weapon of revenge wielded by the victors. In any case they must be studied in the light of the situation brought about by the victory of one of the belligerents able to impose upon the defeated enemy the surrender of war criminals. In a situation like this there can be no such degree of mutuality as alone would satisfy the purist, namely, the delivery to the defeated States of nationals of the victorious belligerents accused of having perpetrated war crimes. But even here there is room for a consideration of measures likely to ensure some approximation to equality. The victorious belligerent may openly proclaim his determination to investigate and to bring to trial any charges of violations of the law of war committed by his armed forces; he may give full publicity to the resulting judicial proceedings; he may offer to invite neutral or enemy participation in any procedure that may be adopted. Thus while taking steps towards ensuring an impartial trial of enemy nationals accused of war crimes, the victorious belligerents would at the same time do much to meet the reproach that justice has overtaken only the criminals among the defeated and not those among the victors. True statesmanship ought not to give any justifiable and avoidable excuse for any such reproach. Strengthened by the consciousness that he has gone to the extreme practicable limit of securing impartiality and equality before the law, the victorious belligerent will be in a position to disregard the charge that, amidst a sanctimonious claim to virtue, he has combined the rôles of party and judge. In addition, he will be entitled to insist that, as a matter both of probability and of experience, the impartiality of the courts of the defeated State cannot be assumed. This is so not because the courts of the victorious belligerent are intrinsically entitled to a higher claim to excellence and impartiality. The reason is that the courts of the defeated State must, in the circumstances, act under the impact of bitter national resentment and hostility unredeemed by such magnanimity and foresight as the victor may be able to afford.

This latter consideration merits special emphasis. It may be usefully illustrated by reference to the activity of German courts which, in 1923 and 1924, were called upon to conduct the trial of German nationals accused of war crimes. German writers have repeatedly asserted that the German Supreme Court which tried the accused persons displayed a high degree of conscientiousness and impartiality. It is doubtful in the extreme whether that claim can be substantiated. Of the 901 cases which came before the Supreme Court, only thirteen ended in the condemnation and conviction of the accused. In those few cases the Supreme Court found the accused guilty of such crimes as maltreatment of prisoners of war[1] and firing on the boats of survivors from hospital ships sunk by a submarine.[2] The Court inflicted relatively mild sentences of imprisonment. In 692 cases the Court came to the conclusion that there were no legal grounds justifying the continuation of proceedings. In a considerable number of cases relating to maltreatment of prisoners of war the Court found that the accused, far from having been guilty of the charges, had gone out of their way to treat the prisoners with special consideration. The doctrine of superior orders and the plea of military necessity were elevated to paramount legal principles—a line of conduct which the Supreme Court pursued in subsequent years in connection with the interpretation of the Hague Regulations[3] and with attempts to punish for high treason German nationals accused of denouncing to the Allied Powers the violations by Germany of her obligations in the matter of disarmament under the clauses of the Treaty of Versailles.[4]

Neither, in the light of experience, are we in a position to place reliance upon the findings of any special commission of investigation instituted by a legislative body of the defeated State, however democratically constituted. In August 1919 there was set up, as part of a general committee on war responsibilities appointed by the German *Reichstag*, a sub-committee to investigate the charges of violations of the laws of war committed by both Germany and her allies. The Commission, whose work was largely under the direction of Professor Schücking, a distinguished international lawyer and subsequently one of the Judges of the Permanent Court of International Justice, produced a series of reports published in 1927 in five volumes under the title *Völkerrecht im Weltkrieg*. A study of these volumes permits the conclusion that the Commission did not exhibit a degree of detachment higher than that displayed by the Supreme Court. It exonerated Germany from the major charges of lawlessness and levelled grave accusations against the Allied Powers.

In the matter of charges of ruthlessness and terrorism in the course of the occupation of Belgium, the Commission accepted as proven the fact that

[1] The *Muller* and *Neumann* cases, Cmd. 1422, pp. 26, 36.

[2] *The Llandovery Castle*, *ibid.*, p. 45.

[3] Thus in a case decided in November 1924, the German *Reichsgericht* held that the requisition by Germany of machines in occupied Belgium and their subsequent sale to private manufacturers was legitimate although contrary to the Hague Regulations. For these, in the view of the Court, left intact the principle that a State's right of self-preservation has precedence over international treaties (*Annual Digest*, 1923–4, Case No. 230).

[4] The *Reichsgericht* rejected the view that the conviction of the accused would violate the rule of international law which prescribes that treaties must be fulfilled in good faith. For that principle, in the view of the Court, binds only the contracting party and not individuals (March 14, 1930: *Annual Digest*, 1927–8, Case No. 5).

there was waged a popular war (*Volkskrieg*) against the German forces and that there existed, accordingly, full justification for the resulting acts of suppression. In this connection Professor Meurer, the principal *rapporteur* of the Commission, justified the indiscriminate killing of hostages. He said: "In war every one is a sacrificial lamb. What appears to be humane is, from a higher standpoint, often the most inhumane. Is it not the innocent soldier who falls victim to the war crime on the part of the inhabitant, and is not the killing of hostages meant to prevent this? . . . The commander who wishes to be humane may in fact prove very inhumane in relation to the soldiers entrusted to him and thus incur a grave responsibility."[1] The Commission had no difficulty in holding that the "dragging" (*Verschleppung*) by the French authorities of the inhabitants of the occupied parts of Alsace and Lorraine to France at the outbreak of war was contrary to international law.[2] But it expressed the considered view that the German decree of October 28, 1916, by virtue of which "unemployed Belgian workmen who, after they had refused to accept work offered to them in Germany and, as the result, had become a charge upon public resources, were compulsorily transported to Germany in order to be provided with employment, was in accordance with Article 43 of the Hague Regulations and with international law at a time where there was not sufficient employment in Belgium and when that measure seemed to be urgently required for the restoration and maintenance of public order and public life." The Commission had no doubt that these measures were not inconsistent with Articles 46 and 52 of the Hague Regulations which guarantee the rights of inhabitants, seeing that military requirements are paramount and that the maintenance of public order and public life are a military necessity.[3] The *Reichsgericht* had previously decided, in the course of criminal proceedings against Field-Marshal Hindenburg in respect of this charge, that his action was lawful.

With respect to the use of poison gas by the German armies, the Commission agreed that artillery projectiles containing such gases were first used by the German armies. But it declined to see in that practice a violation of the prohibition, contained in the Hague Declaration of 1899, "of the use of projectiles the sole object of which is the diffusion of asphyxiating and deleterious gases" on the ground that this was not the "sole object" of the explosives launched by the German artillery.[4] Neither, in the view of the Commission, was the use of these projectiles contrary to the prohibition, laid down in Article 23 (*a*) and (*e*) of the Hague Regulations, of the use of poison and poisoned weapons on the ground that these did not include poison gas. At the same time the Commission found that the French army was equipped with and first used weapons clearly prohibited by the Hague Declaration and the Hague Regulations, and that the subsequent use of the gas weapon by Germany was justified as a measure of reprisals. In the matter of air warfare, and in particular of air bombardment, the conclusion of the Commission was that the rules of international law on the subject had been violated not by Germany but by the Allied Powers.[5] The conduct of unrestricted submarine warfare by Germany was declared to have been in

[1] *Das Völkerrecht im Weltkrieg*, vol. II, p. 221.
[2] *Ibid.*, vol. I. pp. 167–85.
[3] *Ibid.*, vol. I, p. 193.
[4] *Ibid.*, vol. IV, pp. 7–9, 39–42.
[5] *Ibid.*, vol. IV, p. 53.

accordance with international law as a legitimate measure of reprisals against the unlawful blockade proclaimed by the Allies.[1]

Occasionally, it was only after a circuitous legal argument that the Commission arrived at a conclusion favourable to Germany. Thus with regard to Article 23 (*g*) of the Hague Regulations which prohibited "belligerents to destroy or seize enemy property unless such destruction or seizure be imperatively demanded by the necessities of the war", the Commission agreed that that article lent itself both to a restricted and to a wide interpretation. "Necessities of war" could mean either imperative military necessity directly connected with offensive or defensive action, or, generally, any military advantage accruing from devastation. The Commission expressed the view that the restricted interpretation was to be preferred. However, in a curious *non sequitur*, it proceeded to state that for the purposes of the investigation it was sufficient if it was satisfied that the military authorities in question considered in good faith military necessity to be involved: "The Commission could not safely undertake a technical review of military necessity." Having gone thus far, it had no difficulty in considering as legitimate the general devastation effected by the German army at the time of the retreat in 1917 to the so-called Siegfried line; the devastation during the retreat in 1918; and the destruction of the mines in Northern France and Belgium.[2] As a rule, however, the Commission avoided the appearance of undue restraint. With regard to the action of the Allied Powers in Greece it put on record its conclusion that "there was hardly a rule of neutrality which had not been flagrantly violated by the Entente".[3] The Commission entertained no doubts as to its own impartiality. It described its work as an "historic innovation, seeing that never before had a parliamentary organ undertaken the task of pronouncing, exclusively by reference to international law, legal judgment on events and measures".[4]

The above record of the German Supreme Court and of the Commission on Violations of the Laws of War throws light on the prospects of impartial application of international law by the courts and other agencies of a defeated State. It is a much-needed reminder of the fact that the cause of impartial justice may be served in ways other than a mechanical equality in procedure. It cannot in any way be interpreted as justifying the victorious belligerent in adopting methods summary in their nature and deficient in the essential safeguards of orderly judicial process and, within the limits dictated by circumstances, of a minimum measure of reciprocity.

V. *Surrender from Neutral States*

The provision of safeguards of impartiality and of other essential requirements of judicial procedure in the prosecution and trial of war criminals is directly relevant to the question of any duty of neutral States to refuse admission to or to surrender to the victorious belligerent persons accused of war crimes. For should the neutral State have reasonable ground to assume that a prosecution in respect of which surrender is requested is of a political character by virtue either of the nature of the alleged offence or of the

[1] *Ibid.*, vol. IV, p. 113.
[2] *Ibid.*, vol. I, pp. 61–4.
[3] *Ibid.*, vol. II, p. 16.
[4] *Ibid.*, vol. I, p. 6.

absence of normal judicial safeguards of fair trial,[1] then in granting asylum and in insisting on maintaining it it may, it is submitted, be deemed to rely on the established principle of asylum for political offences. That principle, whatever may be its legal nature or extent, cannot accurately be denied a place in existing international law. This is one of the reasons why the question of admission of war criminals to and their surrender from neutral states cannot be exhaustively answered by the proposition that such persons have no right to asylum.[2] The implications of that proposition seem to be of some difficulty and must be considered in relation to admission, to extradition and to other forms of surrender.

The statement that there is no individual right of asylum is probably unimpeachable when viewed as a matter of admission of persons to the territory in which they claim asylum. It requires further consideration when looked at from the point of view of extradition. In this respect we must distinguish between any right of the individual under municipal and under international law. In some countries, like Great Britain and the United States, a person, once admitted, may be said, in respect of extradition, to have an individual right of asylum in two senses: in the first instance, in the absence of an extradition treaty he cannot be extradited. It is a rule of the common law that the Executive cannot hand over a person to a foreign jurisdiction unless in pursuance of a statute.[3] In these countries, statutory law makes extradition dependent upon the existence of a treaty of extradition with the foreign Power concerned. Secondly, by statute, a fugitive who is charged with a political offence or whose extradition has in fact been requested with the intention of trying him for a political offence,[4] cannot be extradited. In other countries—like Sweden, Switzerland, and Turkey[5]—a person can be extradited regardless of the existence of an extradition treaty, but not in respect of political offences. In these countries the fugitive may still be said to possess, under municipal law, a right of asylum so far as political offences are concerned.

To what extent can it be said that there is a right of asylum under international law? It is difficult to reject with emphasis the view that there is such a right in respect of political offences—though, having regard to the procedural incapacity of the individual in the international sphere, it is even

[1] The close connection between non-extradition for political offences and the proper trial of the accused may be gauged from the fact that some States decline extradition if it is proved that it is intended to try the accused before an extraordinary tribunal: see, e.g., Article 9 of the Swiss Extradition Law.

[2] A proposition cogently expressed by Lord Simon, the Lord Chancellor, in his speech on 7 October 1942. He said: "There is not, as many people suppose, any private right, recognized in International Law, called the right of asylum. That is to say, the fugitive—the criminal—who manages to get over the border into some other country, is not thereby by International Law entitled to claim to stay there. . . . It is perfectly competent for the country which receives the criminal, whether there is an extradition treaty or not, if that country thinks that it will be fulfilling its duty to the world, or if its conception of public policy requires or justifies it, to hand the criminal over": *Parl. Debates*, House of Lords, vol. 124, p. 582. For a qualification of the latter statement see below, p. 88. See also Moore, *Digest of International Law*, vol. II, § 291, on the laxity in the use of the term "right of asylum". And see Resolution of the Swiss Federal Council of 23 March 1921 (cited by Schlesinger in *Columbia Law Review*, 43 (1943), p. 964): "L'étranger n'a pas droit à l'asile. L'Etat a simplement la faculté, en vertu de sa souveraineté, d'admettre sur son territoire un étranger, et il prononce en toute liberté."

[3] For an emphatic affirmation of this rule see *Valentine* v. *United States* (1936) 299 U.S. 5.

[4] See s. 3 (1) of the Extradition Act, 1870.

[5] See below, p. 89, n. 2.

more difficult to assert its existence. However, apart from the latter limitation, we are confronted with the impressive fact that in the legislation of modern states there are few principles so universally adopted as that of non-extradition of political offenders. This being so, can we not maintain that the principle has become one of those "general principles of law recognized by civilized states" which Article 38 of the Statute of the Permanent Court of International Justice has elevated to the authority of a source of international law?[1] The question may properly be raised although, in the context, it is largely theoretical for the reason that, as will be pointed out presently, war criminals are not, as a rule, political offenders.

Once we have reduced to its true proportions the question of the individual right to asylum, we may inquire into the legal grounds on which the victorious[2] belligerent can base his claim for the surrender of enemy war criminals who have taken refuge in neutral territory. That legal basis is provided, in the first instance, by the existing extradition treaties between the neutral State and the belligerent. These cover primarily, though not exclusively, offences committed in such parts of the territory of the requesting State as were occupied by the enemy. Thus, for instance, war crimes committed during the second World War in Russia by members of the German army of occupation and German officials who have taken refuge in Sweden will be covered by any extradition treaty in force between Russia and Sweden. Probably, if we take into account the locality of the causation (or of the origin) of the injurious action as distinguished from the locality of its effect, the treaty will cover orders issued in Germany and taking effect in Russia. There are impressive judicial authoritative pronouncements in the national and international sphere asserting some such extension of the territorial principle.[1] Thus, while the provisions of the extradition treaties in existence between neutral states and the belligerent must be studied in detail in relation to any concrete situation, it is clear that they are likely to cover most of the possible war crimes both *ratione loci* and *ratione materiae*. They will cover, *ratione loci*, acts committed in such parts of the territory of the requesting State as were under enemy occupation; acts in or from the air over the territory of the requesting State and having effect in its territory; acts, wherever committed, having effect on what is constructively State territory, namely, vessels flying the flag of the belligerent;[2] and, probably, acts ordered by persons present in enemy territory but having effect in the territory of the belligerent requesting extradition. They will include, *ratione*

[1] Suppose State A surrenders to State B a national of State C on a charge of having committed a political offence. The alleged offender clearly has no enforceable right under international law. But can his State complain that State A has violated an established principle of international law? Has the principle of non-extradition of political offenders crystallized into a customary rule of international law? In *Fiscal* v. *Samper*, decided in 1934, the Spanish Supreme Court held that "delinquents who take refuge in a foreign country relying on legislation which promises them protection have acquired a true right, disregard of which would tend to weaken the law of nations and to introduce lack of confidence into international relations": *Annual Digest*, 1938–40, Case No. 152.

[2] The problem, it will be noted, does not arise as between the defeated belligerent and neutral states. The former, even if it were not prevented from doing so by the terms of the peace treaty, will have no occasion for requesting the surrender of the war criminals of the victorious belligerent. These will not find it necessary to take refuge in neutral territory.

[1] See the authorities surveyed in the Dissenting Opinion of Judge Moore in *The Lotus* case, Permanent Court of International Justice, Series A, No. 10, pp. 73–83.

[2] See, for a clear statement of the underlying principle, Moore, *Extradition* (1891), § 104.

materiae, the common crimes usually enumerated in extradition treaties like murder, assassination, manslaughter, wilful assault resulting in death or permanent disablement, rape, false imprisonment, crimes against personal liberty, robbery, and so on. Most of the illegalities perpetrated in occupied territory can be reduced to crimes such as those enumerated above.

Moreover, the limitation of extraditable offences to those committed within the territory of the requesting State is not an invariable feature of extradition treaties.[1] It is therefore possible that the extradition treaty between the belligerent and the neutral may cover offences committed in the territory of the defeated belligerent.

Although it is only the existence of an extradition treaty which entitles the victorious belligerent to insist on extradition as a matter of strict legal right, the municipal law of most states permits the granting of extradition irrespective of treaty—usually on the assurance of reciprocity or, occasionally, as a matter of international solidarity in the suppression of crime.[2] In so far as it is permissible to speak of principles of international law in the matter of extradition, there is therefore no principle which requires the existence of a treaty as a condition of extradition or which prevents a State whose municipal law has hitherto been based on that requirement from abandoning it when necessary. If it attaches importance to its maintenance and if no valid extradition treaty exists between the neutral State and the victorious belligerent, it may still be open to and proper for the former to conclude an extradition treaty on traditional lines and subject to the accepted safeguards in the matter of political offences. A treaty so concluded and covering acts committed prior to its conclusion would in no way amount to an introduction of the reprehensible principle of retroactivity in the sphere

[1] For numerous examples of treaties in which this is not the case see *Harvard Research in International Law, Extradition* (1935), pp. 92, 93. See also *In re Amper*, decided by the Italian Court of Cassation, for an emphatic refusal to admit the relevance of "questions of territorial jurisdiction if its own jurisdiction is not involved": *Annual Digest*, 1933–4, Case No. 149.

[2] Article 1 of the Swiss Law on Extradition of 22 January 1892 provides for extradition "on the condition of reciprocity [not necessarily through an extradition treaty], or, as an exception, even without that condition." The same article lays down that extradition may be granted for an offence not envisaged in the treaty (*Harvard Research, Extradition*, p. 420). Similarly, the Swedish Extradition Law of 4 June 1913 provides, in Article I, that extradition may be granted in the absence of an extradition treaty if the requesting State promises reciprocity (*ibid.*, p. 414). The position in Turkey is similar (*ibid.*, p. 428). The German Extradition Law of 23 December 1929 merely requires reciprocity (*ibid.*, p. 385). So does the Argentinian Extradition Law of 25 August, 1885 (*ibid.*, p. 356). The French Extradition Law of 10 March 1927 is to the same effect: see *Decerf's Case, Annual Digest*, 1935–7, Case No. 164. In *In re Vilca* the Supreme Court of Chile decided, notwithstanding the absence of an extradition treaty, to ask for the extradition of the accused from Peru on the ground that the crime (homicide) with which he was charged was "in the nature of a serious crime against humanity" and that "these are circumstances in which extradition of fugitives is proper, according to rules of public international law uniformly accepted by both States": *ibid.*, 1931–2, Case No. 156. In *In re Fernando Benet* the Federal Court of Venezuela, while denying, in the absence of a treaty, extradition on the charge of embezzlement, admitted that "it was a generally admitted doctrine of Public International Law that crimes for which extradition must be granted [in the absence of a treaty] are crimes of a serious character and grave consequences constituting an equal danger to all nations": *ibid.*, 1925–6, Case No. 225. See also, to the same effect, *In re Diogenes Gonzalez, ibid.*, Case No. 226. For other examples of extradition notwithstanding the absence of a treaty see *In re Doelitzsch* (decision of the Italian Court of Cassation), *ibid.*, 1923–4, Case No. 156, and *In re Tsiaras* (a decision of the Roumanian Court of Cassation), *ibid.*, 1929–30, Case No. 173.

of criminal law. There is high authority in support of that view.[1] A treaty thus concluded would not convert into a crime acts which hitherto had been blameless. It would not constitute an abandonment of the principle of political asylum properly conceived. It would testify to the recognition on the part of the neutral State of its moral duty to co-operate in the maintenance of international law and in the international suppression of crime whether committed under the guise of war or otherwise.

Assuming that the offence is otherwise covered by a treaty of extradition or that extradition can be effected without an extradition treaty, to what extent does the principle of non-extradition of political offenders—a venerable principle of impressive universality—exclude the duty of surrender of persons accused of war crimes? This question is of paramount importance, for no demand for extradition from neutral states is likely—or ought—to succeed if it is contrary to the principle of non-extradition of political offenders. On the other hand, the very sanctity of that principle requires that it should not be abused for sheltering persons who, behind the screen of war, have been responsible for common crimes which have outraged civilized mankind.

The law of extradition as applied by municipal courts provides a useful and necessary corrective to the view that any act having a political complexion is a political act for the purposes of extradition. The conception of a political crime has a definite meaning in the law of extradition. A political crime is, in the first instance, one committed in the attempt to substitute one government for another or one form of government for another. Courts, including German courts, have attached decisive importance to that distinguishing feature of political crimes. Crimes committed by anarchists opposing all government;[2] crimes perpetrated as an act of political revenge;[3] crimes committed for motives of patriotism but unrelated to any attempt to change the government or the form thereof[4]—all these have been held by the highest municipal tribunals not to come within the category of political crimes protected from extradition. Municipal courts have long discarded the idea that the mere absence of a motive of personal gain is sufficient to impart to an offence the character of a political crime.[5] In the legislation of some countries, as, for instance, in the Belgian *attentat* clause, the predominance of particularly objectionable features of a common crime has sufficed to divest the offence of the otherwise clearly discernible complexion of a political offence.

[1] See, for instance, *United States* v. *Hecht*, decided in 1927 by the United States Circuit Court of Appeals, where the court held not only that extradition treaties cover offences committed prior to their conclusion, but also that there is nothing to prevent a contracting party from recognizing "somewhat belatedly . . . as criminal a well-known fact of commercial immorality": *Annual Digest*, 1927–8, Case No. 234. And see Hackworth, *Digest of Internationa] Law*, vol. IV (1942), p. 36. See also to the same effect the Swiss Law of Extradition ref erred to above, n. 2, page 89, and Articles 5 of the Japanese Extradition Law of 1895 (*Harvarp Research, Extradition*, p. 411).

[2] *In re Meunier* [1894] 2 Q.B. 415; *In re Kaphengst*, decided in 1930 by the Swiss Federal Court, *Annual Digest*, 1929–30, Case No. 189.

[3] *Pavan Case*, decided in 1928 by the Swiss Federal Court, *ibid.*, 1927–8, Case No. 239; *In re Richard Eckerman*, decided in 1929 by the Supreme Court of Guatemala, *ibid.*, Case No. 189.

[4] *Noblot Case*, decided in 1928 by the Swiss Federal Court, *ibid.*, Case No. 240.

[5] There is an interesting analogy between this development and the more recent practice of states which refuses to treat *animus furandi* as the decisive characteristic of piracy.

It is probable that the conception of a political crime as limited to acts aiming at a change in the government or in the form thereof, does not exhaust all possible connotations of a political offence—although this is the usual meaning of political crimes as interpreted by courts in connection with extradition treaties.[1] In particular, it is clear that political offences must be deemed to cover all acts of treason in its wider sense, including treason committed during war by joining or assisting the enemy.[2] In connection with war crimes it is submitted that the notion of a political offence must be deemed to cover, in particular, the following three categories: (1) persons upon whom the victorious belligerent intends to wreak his vengeance for the sole reason that they participated in a war waged against him; (2) persons accused of such violations of the law of war as do not on the face of it amount to a common crime against individuals or property; (3) persons accused of acts whose criminality is subject to legitimate dispute for the reason either of the controversial nature of the rules of war in question or of their having been committed by one or both sides in the course of reprisals. Thus, for instance, if extradition were asked for in respect of the crime of initiating the war in violation of the General Treaty for the Renunciation of War; if it were requested in connection with the charge of commencing the war in disregard of Hague Convention No. III providing for a declaration of war; if it were insisted on in respect of a decision on military policy in the conduct of war like the ordering of general devastation, or the abuse of a flag of truce; if it were demanded on account of requisitions and contributions contrary to the Hague Convention; or even, to adduce an extreme and controversial example, if extradition were requested of persons accused of sinking merchant vessels without warning—in all these cases there is room for asserting that they come within the general notion of political crime.

On the other hand, acts which *per se* constitute common crimes and which are contrary to rules of war cannot legitimately be assimilated to political offences. The fact that certain acts, otherwise criminal, like taking of life or causing bodily injury, are committed in pursuance of lawful warfare, deprives them of the stigma of criminality according to common law and renders them, in a certain sense, political. But once it has been established that such acts have been perpetrated in violation of the rules of lawful warfare, there vanishes the decisive factor which lifts them above the reprobation of common criminality.

Undoubtedly the border-line between lawful and unlawful acts of war is often a shadowy one, and to that extent the neutral State may deem itself entitled to considerable latitude in granting or refusing extradition. But the discretion wielded by the executive and judicial authorities of the neutral State must be exercised in good faith. Should the neutral State or its courts adopt a general policy of non-extradition in the matter of war crimes on the

[1] A person who, during war, has committed treason by having joined the enemy of his country is a political offender—although his act does not aim at a change in the government or of its form.

[2] The Supreme Federal Court of Brazil has described as political the offence of trading with the enemy: *In re Dr. Paulo Deleuze, Annual Digest*, 1919–22, Case No. 187. It will also be noted that the legislation of most States excludes from extradition purely military offences, (i.e. desertion and offences against discipline) as well as fiscal offences.

ground that they are political, the belligerent asking for extradition would, it is believed, be confronted *prima facie* with a breach of any existing extradition treaty. Should that happen, a remedy for the breach of the treaty might be found in some cases in any surviving obligation of compulsory judicial settlement. Thus, at the end of the second World War, as between Switzerland, for instance, and Poland, or Belgium, or Holland, the provisions of the Optional Clause might be found sufficient for the purpose. A decision of the Permanent Court of International Justice on the matter would, in substance, not be without effect as between states in whose relations the Optional Clause never was or has ceased to be operative, as, for instance, may be the case of Great Britain as the result of the British declaration of September 1939 suspending the operation of the Optional Clause with regard to disputes arising out of events occurring during the hostilities. A neutral State refusing to comply with its treaty obligations or to submit their disputed interpretation for international judicial decision would not only expose itself to a denunciation of the existing extradition treaties. The consequences of a breach of a treaty of this kind, in defiance of the public opinion of the world and in a misplaced insistence on the principle of asylum, may justifiably cover acts of reprisals and self-help appropriate to the occasion, especially if the neutral State can adduce no justifiable doubts as to the prospects of a fair and impartial trial.

It is now necessary to consider the question of surrender from neutral countries apart from the existence or the applicability of extradition treaties. What, in such cases, are the means by which neutral states may pursue a policy of abstaining from granting asylum to persons accused or likely to be accused of war crimes which cannot justifiably be treated as being of a political character? Assuming prudence and good faith on the part of the neutral State, the abuse of the right of asylum may be considerably reduced by its refusal to admit indiscriminately such persons to its territory. Their exclusion would be an administrative measure unlikely to raise problems of grave difficulty in the field of the municipal law of the neutral State. The belligerent may be in a position—and it will as a rule be wise for him to do so—to supply the neutral State with lists of persons accused of war crimes, with an indication of the nature and the circumstances of such crimes, so as to enable the neutral State to exercise discretion in the admission of enemy persons in case it does not wish to adopt a policy of general exclusion, a measure which it may deem incompatible with the principle of political asylum.

However, to consider this matter merely from the point of view of the admission of war criminals to neutral territory is to simplify the problem. The neutral State may not be able to prevent the illegal entry of such persons by land, by sea and, especially, by air. In that case, if it is unable or unwilling to surrender them to the *belligerent* owing to the absence or the inapplicability of an extradition treaty, it may still *deport* to their *home State* persons accused of war crimes who have entered its territory and with regard to whom no obvious considerations of political asylum prevent their deportation. The victorious belligerent will find means for bringing the deported individuals to justice in the same way as other enemy nationals accused of war crimes. Any previous warning by the neutral State against entering its territory will strengthen its position in the matter—just as any previous warning addressed by the belligerent to the neutral State[1] will put the latter on its guard against indiscriminate admission of fugitives fleeing from justice. Deportation is in most countries within the province of the executive authorities and although the law often limits their discretion in the matter, the antecedents of the persons concerned and the fact of their illegal entry are, generally, substantial factors in determining the discretion of the Executive. In proceeding to such measures of deportation, the neutral State will be legitimately guided by the respect due to the principle of political asylum conceived in the broad sense as indicated above. It will refrain, and legitimately and properly refrain, from a course of action which, in the natural course of events, might result in the delivery to the victorious belligerent of persons who, while having been guilty of violations of rules of warfare, are not accused of common crimes against life and, for reasons of private gain, against property. It will be entitled to take into consideration the prospects of a fair trial.

We may now examine the legal implications of the situation arising from any obstructive attitude of a neutral State which, in acting out of a misplaced attachment to the humanitarian principle of asylum or out of ideological affinity with the defeated State, insists on offering the shelter of impunity to persons accused of war crimes of a non-political character and on refusing to surrender them either by way of extradition or by way of deportation. If that attitude is in violation of a valid treaty of extradition, the legal position does not give rise to difficulty.[2] In strict law the position would also seem to be clear when there is no applicable extradition treaty; there is in such cases no legal duty to extradite or to surrender the fugitive. It is generally maintained that in such cases the duty, if any, is a moral one. However, this is a view which is too rigid to be fully acceptable. Undoubtedly, in any specific case a State is under no legal duty to extradite unless it is bound to do so by treaty. But if a State were to decide to refrain altogether from concluding extradition treaties and to open its doors to criminal fugitives to the detriment of the peace and safety of its neighbours, would its action be legally unobjectionable? Ought we not to distinguish between the refusal to conclude any particular extradition treaty and a general licence to fugitives from justice? Do extradition treaties merely prescribe the conditions on which States agree to limit their sovereign discretion or do they give expression to an underlying general duty of extradition? Moore, who speaks with authority in his own right and as the author of a leading treatise on extradition, says: "The right [to grant or to refuse asylum], therefore, is coupled with the duty, amply acknowledged by the multiplication of extradition treaties, to abstain from asserting the sovereign power for the purpose of shielding individuals charged with the crime from trial by competent judicial authorities. The right of sovereignty is conserved in determining the conditions and limitations under which the fugitive is to be delivered up."[3] On the other hand, Hall, in a weighty exposition, gives expression to

[1] Such as that addressed by Great Britain and the United States in July 1943 to Switzerland, Sweden, Spain, Portugal, Liechtenstein, Turkey, the Vatican City and Argentina.

[2] See above, p. 88.

[3] *Digest of International Law*, vol. III (1906), p. 757.

the predominant view in maintaining that "positive international law . . . does not recognize the duty of extradition".[1]

It is probable that a correct legal appreciation of the position must be sought by reference not to the limited subject of extradition but to the operation of the prohibition of an abuse of rights in relation to the territory of the State. The State's right of sovereignty over its territory, including its right to grant asylum to fugitives, is, in the absence of treaty obligations, exclusive and absolute. But if that right is used in a way prejudicial to the legitimate interests and claims of other States then it degenerates into an abuse of right which international law will not countenance. International law prohibits injurious use of territory not only in such matters as nuisance caused by uncontrolled emission of noxious fumes[2] or toleration of preparations for hostile expeditions into neighbouring territory.

The privilege and the moral duty of granting asylum to the persecuted ought not rashly to be interfered with. But the respect due to that privilege must, in turn, be conditioned by the manner in which it is exercised. The principle of asylum is put in jeopardy when it is used in a way amounting to a denial of justice to States which, in their collective capacity and in the persons of their citizens, deem themselves to have been victims of cruel and systematic crimes. An abuse of a right is not lightly to be presumed. The doctrine of abuse of rights is an innovation in international law. But, although an innovation, it has received endorsement by the Permanent Court of International Justice and, in obvious cases, it provides a legitimate starting point for remedial action.[3] The circumstance that extradition or surrender is refused in respect of crimes condemned by international law and international conventions to which the neutral State in question is a party, would be particularly relevant. The situation, in that case, would be totally different from that which arose as the result of the refusal of Holland to deliver William II of Hohenzollern whom the Allied and Associated Powers arraigned, in Article 227 of the Treaty of Versailles, "for a supreme offence against international morality and the sanctity of treaties". Neither the accusation of the Treaty of Versailles nor the request subsequently made in pursuance thereof was primarily based on law. As M. Clemenceau put it in his Note of January 11,1920, this "was not a case of a public accusation fundamentally of a legal character, but of an act of high international policy demanded by the conscience of mankind". The situation is different when the insistence on extradition or surrender is based on charges of violation of the law and when the victorious belligerent is in a position to assert that the crimes perpetrated by the enemy were unprecedented both in their extent and in their studied disregard of legal restraints. Any dogmatic and obstructive attitude of the neutral in defiance of the sentiment of the overwhelming majority of States and in disregard of the moral obligation to co-operate in the enforcement of international law may create a situation in which the belligerent concerned may, in the interests of justice, feel called upon to enforce the law by self-help and by acts of retaliation—not to

[1] *International Law*, § 13 (3rd ed., 1890, p. 61).

[2] See the Award in the *Trail Smelter Arbitration* (*United States* v. *Canada*), *Annual Digest*, 1938–40, Case No. 104.

[3] See Oppenheim, *International Law*, vol. 1 (5th ed., 1927), § 155*aa*.

mention such measures of retorsion as every State is entitled to adopt in face of an unneighbourly and unfriendly attitude. Such measures, when prompted by the righteous indignation of powerful and numerous States and their peoples resisting what they deem to be a parochial and short-sighted generosity displayed in aloof disregard of the outraged sentiment of the vast majority of mankind may, in their effect, be indistinguishable from many a drastic sanction normally reserved for glaring breaches of the law of nations.

Undoubtedly, neutral States are entitled to ask for an assurance that the intended prosecution for war crimes will not be used as an instrument of revenge. They are entitled to claim the right to refuse extradition or deportation in cases in which, in their view, the alleged offence partakes of the character of an offence against the rules of warfare in its wider sense rather than of a common law crime and in which they are prepared to submit that preliminary question to judicial determination. They may avail themselves of any offer, and insist on making it as effective as possible, to associate neutral assessors with the work of the courts charged with the trial of war criminals. But once such guarantees may be reasonably held to exist, any insistence by neutral states on sheltering war criminals constitutes not only an unfriendly act but also an assertion of formal rights of sovereignty in denial of that community of law which alone, in the long run, renders possible the normal observance of accepted rules of international law.

[11]

THE MUNICIPAL AND INTERNATIONAL LAW BASIS OF JURISDICTION OVER WAR CRIMES

Richard R. Baxter

THE International Law Commission of the United Nations has recently defined war crimes as all 'acts in violation of the laws or customs of war'.[1] In so far as the definition departs from the view that only 'grave breaches' of the law of war are war crimes,[2] the statement is meaningful, but the equating of war crimes with violations of the law of war otherwise merely restates the problem, which is essentially: What acts in warfare are violations of international law? There is a category of conduct which has often in the past been loosely referred to in terms of international law but which is actually not internationally criminal in the sense that a prescription of international law requires its punishment. There remain those acts, comprising for the most part cruel and inhuman treatment of prisoners of war, the sick and wounded, and civilian populations, which are universally recognized as war crimes in the proper sense of the word. An examination of the different theories under which states have prosecuted war crimes may thus not only assess the function of international law in dealing with violations of the law of war, but also serve as a basis for defining those violations themselves.

1. *International and municipal law applied to war crimes*

The great cleavage in the prosecution of war crimes has been between the practice of charging suspected war criminals with violation of international law and the process of prosecuting such persons under municipal law for offences defined by the ordinary criminal law. A common feature of charges presented before British military courts, convened in conformity with the Royal Warrant of 14 June 1945,[3] and United States military tribunals, other than those constituted pursuant to Control Council Law No. 10,[4] was a simple averment that the acts alleged to have been committed by the accused were in 'violation of the laws and usages [or customs] of war'.[5] Although it has some-

[1] Article 2 (11), Draft Code of Offences against the Peace and Security of Mankind, *Report of the International Law Commission Covering its Third Session*, 16 May–27 July 1951 (U.N.Doc. A/CN. 4/48, 30 July 1951), para. 59.

[2] But cf. Lauterpacht, 'The Law of Nations and the Punishment of War Crimes', in this *Year Book*, 21 (1944), pp. 78–79.

[3] Army Order 81/45; see *War Crimes Reports*, vol. i (1947), p. 105.

[4] 20 December 1945, *Official Gazette of the Control Council for Germany*, No. 22, p. 22.

[5] *In re Schonfeld et Al.* (1946), *War Crimes Reports*, vol. xi (1949), p. 64, and *In re Killinger et Al.* (1945), ibid., vol. iii (1948), p. 67, are representative of British practice; for charges presented to American tribunals see, for example, *United States* v. *Eisentrager et Al.* (1947), ibid., vol. xiv (1949), p. 8, *United States* v. *Sawada et Al.* (1946), ibid., vol. v (1948), p. 1.

times been said that American practice in this respect was the result of a transformation of international law into municipal law,[1] it does not appear that the courts of the United States have been so sophistical as to allege that they were applying international law while covertly invoking municipal law. The Supreme Court of the United States, while disclaiming any intention to 'make' international law, has plainly stated that it enforces it,[2] and statements concerning the role of statutes in making this possible have placed emphasis on the fact that the effect of Congressional enactments has been to bring violations of the laws and customs of war within the jurisdiction of certain designated courts.[3] The manner in which jurisdiction has been conferred on military courts of the Commonwealth, including the United Kingdom, Canada,[4] and Australia,[5] has given even less basis for the extreme claims of the dualists. Judges Advocate and Legal Members, with rare exceptions, scrupulously dispelled any illusions created by counsel that the accused were being tried for offences defined by the municipal law of the country concerned and made clear that distinctions like that between murder and manslaughter were not relevant.[6] Analogies offered by domestic law, however, often proved helpful in areas wherein no relevant principles of international criminal law had yet been developed.[7]

In striking contrast to Anglo-American practice was that generally prevailing in France and some other countries. Not long after the invasion of France in 1944, a French ordinance was promulgated providing for the punishment of acts which were not justified by the laws and customs of war and constituted violations of existing French law.[8] Certain provisions of the *Code Pénal* and of the *Code de Justice Militaire* were, by the terms of the Ordinance, interpreted in such a fashion as to apply to the war crimes to which they bore some resemblance. The forced labour of civilians, the improper employment of prisoners of war, and deportation were, for example, considered as *séquestration* within the meaning of Articles 341–4 of the *Code Pénal*.[9] The law acted on both a territorial and a protective[10] basis, for both crimes committed on French territory and crimes against French nationals and persons associated with French interests fell within the terms of the Ordinance. The effect of this legislation was to require two stages in the proof of a given offence, the first being a demonstration that the act was not lawful under international law and the second that the act was

[1] Schwarzenberger, 'The Problem of an International Criminal Law', in *Current Legal Problems*, 3 (1950), p. 270.

[2] 'We do not make the laws of war but we respect them so far as they do not conflict with the commands of Congress or the Constitution' (*In re Yamashita* (1946), 327 U.S. 1, 16; see also *Ex parte Quirin et Al.* (1942), 317 U.S. 1, 27).

[3] *Ex parte Quirin et Al.* (1942), 317 U.S. 1, 26, 35; *In re Yamashita* (1946), 327 U.S. 1, 7.

[4] Act respecting War Crimes (10 Geo. VI, c. 73): see *In re Meyer* (1945), *War Crimes Reports*, vol. iv (1948), p. 97, for a typical charge.

[5] War Crimes Act, 1945 (Act No. 48, 1945); Regulations under the War Crimes Act, 1945 (S.R. No. 164 of 1945 and S.R. No. 30 of 1946).

[6] *In re Eck et Al.* (1945), *War Crimes Reports*, vol. i (1947), p. 1; *In re Heyer et Al.* (1945), ibid., p. 88; cf. the Australian cases of *In re Kudo et Al.* (1946) and *In re Yamasaki* (1946), referred to in ibid., vol. xv (1949), p. 8.

[7] *In re Killinger et Al.* (British Military Court, Wuppertal, 1945), *War Crimes Reports*, vol. iii (1948), p. 67; *In re Heering* (British Military Court, Hanover, 1946), ibid. vol. xi (1949), p. 79; *United States* v. *Back* (1945), ibid., vol. iii (1948), p. 60.

[8] Ordonnance du 28 août relative à la répression des crimes de guerre, *Journal Officiel de la République Française*, 30 August 1944, p. 780.

[9] Article 2, paras. 5 and 6.

[10] In the sense of protection of the security of the state, as envisaged by Article 7, Draft Convention on Jurisdiction with Respect to Crime of the Harvard Research, in *American Journal of International Law*, 29 (1935), Supp., p. 439.

prohibited by the relevant provisions of the *Code Pénal* or the *Code de Justice Militaire*.[1] Crimes of the foregoing nature were tried before French Permanent Military Tribunals, while certain crimes not directed against French nationals or the other persons mentioned in the Ordinance of 1944 or taking place on French territory were tried by French occupation courts in Germany, acting in conformity with Control Council Law No. 10.[2] On the basis that international law was not operative in Norway until incorporated into municipal law by legislative action, that country similarly provided in its law relating to war crimes[3] that acts forbidden by the Norwegian criminal law which had been committed against Norwegian nationals or interests or in Norway and were in violation of the laws and customs of war could be tried according to Norwegian law. As originally applied, the Netherlands law, promulgated in the Extraordinary Penal Law Decree of 22 December 1943,[4] followed the continental pattern by providing for the punishment of war crimes under local law, as supplemented by two further articles of the Decree. However, in *Re Ahlbrecht*,[5] the Special Court of Cassation, in quashing on jurisdictional grounds the sentence imposed on a war criminal, held that jurisdiction attaches with respect to war crimes only to those individuals who had violated the laws and customs of war and that Dutch penal law could not be said to be applicable to all German soldiers who could not show that some positive rule of international law afforded justification for their acts. The Court also criticized the attempt which had been made in the Decree to squeeze war crimes into the categories of domestic penal law. As a result the Extraordinary Penal Law Decree was amended in 1947[6] to make punishable war crimes and crimes against humanity as defined by the Charter of the International Military Tribunal at Nuremberg, while requiring that the punishment imposed should not exceed that provided for the same or most closely analogous act under the law of the Netherlands.

The theory upon which war criminals were tried by France, Norway, and initially by the Netherlands for offences against municipal law was grounded on the assumption that enemy soldiers enjoy an immunity from the criminal law of the state against which

[1] Representative instances are: *In re Bommer et Al.* (1947), *War Crimes Reports*, vol. ix (1949), p. 62; *In re Baus* (1947), ibid., p. 68; *In re Szabados* (1946), ibid., p. 59; *In re Holstein et Al.* (1947), ibid., vol. viii (1949), p. 22. In *Re Wagner et Al.* (1946), ibid., vol. iii (1948), p. 23, one of the issues presented to the Court of Cassation was whether the failure to put to the military judges specific questions concerning the legality or illegality under international law of the acts charged had resulted in a failure to resolve an essential issue in the proceedings. The Court held that separate questions as to this matter were not necessary, as they were inherent in questions concerning the guilt of the accused. Apparently in *Re Lex* (1946), ibid., vol. vii (1948), p. 74, the accused, a German civilian charged with instigating the deportation of French families and the looting of their property, was convicted of the offence of 'atteinte à la sûreté extérieure de l'État' under Article 79 of the *Code Pénal* without reference to the 1944 Ordinance and thus presumably under the ordinary French municipal law alone.

[2] See *War Crimes Reports*, vol. iii (1948), p. 100. French Military Government Courts had jurisdiction over the offences defined in Control Council Law No. 10.

[3] Law of 13 December 1946 (No. 14) on the Punishment of Foreign War Criminals, *War Crimes Reports*, vol. iii (1948), p. 81.

[4] Ibid., vol. xi (1949), p. 86. In the Netherlands East Indies, however, war crimes were tried under a decree which set forth an exhaustive listing of war crimes under international law (ibid., p. 91).

[5] *Na-Oorlogsche Rechtspraak, Tribunalen in Nederland*, 3rd Year, No. 747; see *Grotius International Yearbook, 1940–1946* (1948), pp. 54–56. The Special Court of Cassation stated that international law should not be looked upon as a justification for the acts of a state which had itself disregarded international law in occupying the Netherlands. This view appears to bear out the thesis that the law of war is 'prohibitive law'.

[6] See *War Crimes Reports*, vol. xi (1949), p. 90.

they fight only so long as they comply with the international law of war.[1] The burden is accordingly placed on the prosecution to prove that there has been a violation of international law such as to destroy the immunity of the accused or on the accused to assert his immunity by demonstrating that his conduct had been sanctioned by some rule of the law of war. In limiting jurisdiction to those offences committed against either nationals or the interests of the state concerned or on the territory of the prosecuting nation, this view tended to emphasize the protection of that state rather than of the international community. As the states which embraced this view had had an experience of enemy occupation which both Great Britain and the United States lacked, it is perhaps not unnatural that recourse should have been had to the convenient instrument of local law rather than to the long arm of the law of nations. In any case, the fundamental assumption that the soldier is exempt from enemy jurisdiction if he complies with international law is not peculiar to continental jurisprudence[2] and should not be productive of any serious disagreement, although it is less clear on what theoretical basis it may be laid. It may be, as Professor Kelsen asserts, that the act of the soldier who conforms to the law of war and does not engage in private acts of warfare is an act of state depriving the enemy state of jurisdiction,[3] or it may be that the humanitarian intervention of international law, which makes the soldier falling into the hands of the enemy not a criminal but a prisoner of war, subject only to prosecution for acts in violation of the law of war, produces that result in time of war.

International instruments defining war crimes and providing procedures for their punishment provide something more of a problem concerning the nature of the law applied by the tribunals thereby established. Neither the Charter of the International Military Tribunal[4] nor that of the International Military Tribunal for the Far East[5] specifically alluded to trial under international or municipal law, although war crimes were first defined as 'violations of the laws or customs of war'.[6] The Judgment of the Nuremberg Tribunal has been variously interpreted. But the Tribunal, by its frequent references to international law, to the treaties governing the conduct of war, to the amenability of individuals to international law, and to the responsibility of individuals under that law,[7] seems rather to have indicated that the substantive law which it applied

[1] Merle, *Le Procès de Nuremberg et le châtiment des criminels de guerre* (1949), p. 145. A similar view is held by a number of American writers, e.g. Manner, 'The Legal Nature and Punishment of Criminal Acts of Violence Contrary to the Laws of War', in *American Journal of International Law*, 37 (1943), p. 407; Garner, 'Punishment of Offenders against the Laws and Customs of War', ibid. 14 (1920), p. 70. But cf. the interesting case of *In re Motosuke* (1948), *War Crimes Reports*, vol. xiii (1949), p. 126, in which a Netherlands East Indies court found a Japanese officer to have killed a member of the Japanese armed forces without sanction in Japanese military law and therefore to have been guilty of a common law offence against the laws of the Netherlands East Indies and not of a war crime.

[2] *Freeland* v. *Williams* (1889), 131 U.S. 405. *Coleman* v. *Tennessee* (1878), 97 U.S. 509, and *Dow* v. *Johnson* (1879), 100 U.S. 158, imply that a soldier of the occupying army is subject neither to the law nor to the jurisdiction of the courts of the occupied area, whether or not the soldier's act was in conformity with the law of war. See Glueck, *War Criminals, Their Prosecution and Punishment* (1944), p. 43, and cases cited therein, and Finch, 'Jurisdiction of Local Courts to try Enemy Persons for War Crimes', in *American Journal of International Law*, 14 (1920), p. 218.

[3] 'Will the Judgment in the Nuremberg Trial Constitute a Precedent in International Law?', in *International Law Quarterly*, 1 (1947), pp. 160–1; 'Collective and Individual Responsibility for Acts of State in International Law', in *Jewish Yearbook of International Law*, 1 (1948), pp. 230–1.

[4] Cmd. 6668.

[5] Special Proclamation of the Supreme Commander for the Allied Powers, 19 January 1946.

[6] Article 6 (*b*) of the Nuremberg Charter; Article 5 (*b*) of the Tokyo Charter.

[7] Judgment of the International Military Tribunal for the Trial of German Major War Criminals, Cmd. 6967 (1946), especially at pp. 38–42.

was international law and not a new internationally enacted system of municipal law. It pointed out that the Charter is 'the expression of international law existing at the time of its creation; and to that extent is itself a contribution to international law'.[1] In the so-called 'Nuremberg Subsequent Proceedings', the United States Military Tribunals established under Control Council Law No. 10 generally asserted that that law, which established their authority, was merely declaratory of customary international law,[2] although the Tribunal in the *Justice Trial*[3] found it necessary to add, perhaps unnecessarily, that in so far as Law No. 10 might go beyond established principles of international law, authority to enact it was to be found in the sovereign legislative power assumed after the unconditional surrender of Germany. The indictments against persons tried by these courts were drawn in comprehensive fashion and alleged violations of the laws and customs of war, of treaties governing war, of 'the general principles of criminal law as derived from the criminal laws of all civilised nations', and of the internal penal law of the countries where the offences were committed.[4] Despite the sweeping language of the indictments, the law applied by these tribunals was generally law which was, or purported to be, international law, and it was not necessary to allude to specific provisions of the criminal codes of the countries concerned.

In view of what appears to be the preponderant view in recent prosecutions of war criminals, i.e. that international law is directly applicable to such persons, the position adopted by some of the states represented at the Geneva Conference of 1949 was somewhat startling. Efforts to declare certain acts to be war crimes were strenuously resisted, not only by the delegates of European countries, as might be expected, but by those of the United States and Great Britain as well.[5] The insistence that what were finally referred to as 'grave breaches'[6] of the Conventions would not become crimes within the countries concerned until implementing legislation had been enacted is somewhat difficult to reconcile with the accepted Anglo-American view of the nature of war crimes, especially since most of the acts referred to as 'grave breaches' had been punished as war crimes under international law by Commonwealth and American

[1] Cmd. 6964, at p. 38.

[2] *United States* v. *Von Leeb et Al.* (1948), *Trials of War Criminals*, vol. xi (1950), p. 476; *War Crimes Reports*, vol. xii (1949), p. 61; *United States* v. *Krupp et Al.* (1948), *Trials of War Criminals*, vol. ix (1950), p. 1331, *War Crimes Reports*, vol. x (1949), p. 131; *United States* v. *Flick et Al.* (1947), ibid., vol. ix (1949), p. 16; see Lord Wright, 'War Crimes under International Law', in *Law Quarterly Review*, 62 (1946), p. 41.

[3] *United States* v. *Altstoetter et Al.* (1947), *Trials of War Criminals*, vol. iii (1951), p. 966, *War Crimes Reports*, vol. vi (1948), p. 34.

[4] A typical indictment stated: 'The said war crimes constitute violations of international conventions, particularly of Articles 4, 5, 6, 7, and 46 of the Hague Regulations, 1907, and of Articles 2, 3, and 4 of the Prisoner-of-War Convention (Geneva, 1929), the laws and customs of war, the general principles of criminal law as derived from the criminal laws of all civilized nations, the internal penal laws of the countries in which such crimes were committed, and of Article II of Control Council Law No. 10' (*United States* v. *Brandt et Al.* (1947), *Trials of War Criminals*, vol. i (1949), p. 15).

[5] *Diplomatic Conference of Geneva, Verbatim Report of the Twenty-first Plenary Meeting*, 30 July 1949 (CDG/PLEN/CR. 21), pp. 10, 11. The statement of a United States delegate that 'the term "crimes" is clearly inappropriate to express violations of this Convention, which will not be crimes until they are so made by domestic penal legislation' is particularly striking. This pronouncement echoes a similar view in the Memorandum of Reservations presented by the Representatives of the United States to the Report of the Commission on the Responsibility of the Authors of War and on Enforcement of Penalties of the Paris Peace Conference of 1919, in *American Journal of International Law*, 14 (1920), p. 127, at p. 141.

[6] Article 51, Wounded and Sick Convention; Article 130, Prisoners of War Convention; Article 147, Civilians Convention.

tribunals during the preceding four years. An opportunity to take a forthright stand on the primacy of international law was thus lost.

2. *War crimes and the part of international law*

It cannot be denied that on several practical grounds the trial of war criminals under national law has certain advantages. Provided the resemblance between the war crime and the ordinary crime under municipal law was close, courts were able to apply a law which was not only familiar but also possessed a high degree of certainty by contrast with the undeveloped state of the international law relating to war crimes. War criminals were, furthermore, tried under the same system of law as were so-called collaborationists, from whom they often differed only with respect to nationality and allegiance. It is true as well that municipal law also provided a *lex* to satisfy the demand of *nullum crimen sine lege*,[1] but the novel interpretations which were read into existing military and criminal codes by legislative or judicial action after the offence had taken place makes this claimed advantage more apparent than real. In contradistinction, existing international law antedated both the criminal acts committed by enemy personnel and the municipal legislation which provided sanctions against them.[2] Finally, it must be observed that, even in Anglo-American jurisprudence, municipal law relating to discipline within the armed forces will offer a sound basis for the punishment of war crimes committed by members of a belligerent's own forces.

However, if attention is paid to all the ramifications of trials under national law, the consequences of its employment are not conducive to optimism concerning the future course of the law of war. In the first place, the jurisdiction of war crimes tribunals is thereby normally confined to offences committed on the soil of the prosecuting state or against its nationals and residents. Special occupation courts therefore become necessary in order to deal with those war crimes which are within the jurisdiction of the prosecuting state only *qua* military occupant.[3] In the absence of these bases of jurisdiction, the state employing municipal law is powerless, by reason of self-imposed limitations, to deal with other offences committed even by the same accused, despite the fact that war criminals have often been guilty of a course of conduct which does violence to the nationals or interests of a number of states. Even the punishment of offences committed by allied forces who might be unwilling to enforce conformity with the law of war, or incapable of doing so, would be impossible in many circumstances. Secondly, on the ground of procedure, the theory of deprivation of immunity under international law followed by an establishment of the offence under municipal law creates a double problem of proof, leading to procedural complexity and perhaps even to acquittal of the guilty.[4] Thirdly, the trial of war criminals under local law leads to a diversity of substantive law such that an act may be punished as a war crime in one country but not in

[1] Malézieux, 'Le Statut international des criminels de guerre', in *Revue générale de droit international public*, 49 (1941–5), p. 173.

[2] Ibid., pp. 173–4; see the Netherlands case of *In re Rauter* (1949), *War Crimes Reports*, vol. xiv (1949), p. 89, in which Dutch municipal law was held not to be retroactive in effect, on the basis that it was only declaratory of international law.

[3] As authorized by Control Council Law No. 10. The jurisdiction of the French Permanent Military Tribunals was thus supplemented by that of Military Government Courts in the French Zone of Germany (*War Crimes Reports*, vol. iii (1948), p. 100).

[4] The accused Grüner in *Re Wagner et Al.* (1946), ibid., p. 23, was acquitted by a French Permanent Military Tribunal on the ground that the offence charged did not come within the Ordinance of 28 August 1944, it having been committed against an English prisoner in Germany.

another.[1] Besides these difficulties of legal administration, there are more fundamental objections to the use of municipal law. Of these, the fact that war crimes are of a basically different nature from crimes under national law is probably the most important, as has been indicated by the course of Netherlands jurisprudence in war crimes cases.[2] The war crimes of deportation and forced labour, for example, fit but awkwardly into the French municipal law concept of *séquestration*. Other violations of the international law of war, such as denationalization or interference with the religious rights of prisoners of war, probably have no counterparts in municipal law. Furthermore, during the Second World War war crimes were inspired by the state, were carried out on a widespread and systematic basis, and were actually seldom the private acts of individuals. Municipal law has hitherto not been called upon to deal with mass deportations and killings or with cruelty designed and executed by another state, nor can it offer much assistance to the court which is, for example, considering whether the accused committed a crime not in compelling prisoners to perform labour but in compelling them to perform a type of labour which the Geneva Prisoners of War Convention of 1929 forbids. Only to the extent that war crimes are tried under national law by transformation of the norms of international law into precepts of municipal law corresponding closely thereto are the difficulties inhering in the continental view rendered less troublesome. They still persist, however, in such forms as limitation of jurisdiction.

If, in those states in which war crimes are tried under municipal law, the function of international law is to furnish a justification for acts of warfare which are thereby recognized to be lawful, the law of war loses its reasonableness. The international law of war is 'prohibitive law' and its purpose is to place curbs upon the otherwise unrestrained violence of war. Belligerent acts in war are facts, not legal rights, and to set the law to justifying them, instead of keeping them within limits which comport with the dictates of humanity, leads to a law which places its emphasis on the rightness of war to the detriment of what is wrong in war. Any theory which relies on the law of nations as a defence for belligerent acts thus fails to accord with the true *raison d'être* of the law of war and with the many expressions of the intentions of those who have contributed to its development in recent years.

The argument concerning the relative virtues of municipal and international law in dealing with war crimes has been protracted and complex,[3] and it is not proposed to attempt its resolution here. If the Anglo-American and what appears to be the view of the two International Military Tribunals is accepted, the role of international law in the suppression of war crimes is obvious. But even if war crimes are to be tried under municipal law, their international significance is not altogether lost. Although a state may try war crimes committed against its interests or its nationals or on its territory or by its nationals under its own municipal law, whether or not to punish war crimes is not left to the unfettered discretion of the state. Both the Geneva Wounded and Sick Convention of 1929[4] and the Geneva Conventions of 1949[5] contain positive under-

[1] Merle, op. cit., p. 149; Glueck, op. cit., p. 44; see Notes to *In re Becker et Al.* (France, Permanent Military Tribunal at Lyon, 1947), *War Crimes Reports*, vol. vii (1948), p. 67.

[2] See p. 384, *supra*.

[3] There has, for example, been no agreement in France regarding the wisdom of French policy concerning the trial of war criminals (see Merle, op. cit.; de Vabres, 'Le Procès de Nuremberg devant les principes modernes du droit pénal international', in *Recueil des cours de l'Académie de droit international de la Haye*, 70 (1947), p. 477; Malézieux, loc. cit., p. 170; de la Pradelle, 'Le Procès des grands criminels de guerre et le développement du droit international', in *Revue de droit international privé*, 14 (1947), p. 16).

[4] Article 29.

[5] Article 49, Wounded and Sick Convention; Article 129, Prisoners of War Convention; Article 146, Civilians Convention.

takings to enact penal legislation necessary to punish violations of those treaties, and it would appear that a like requirement is imposed by the customary law of war.[1] Military commanders, it is clear, also have an obligation to prevent the commission of war crimes by their subordinates,[2] just as the state may be said to have with respect to its armed forces.

Further evidence of the interest of the international community in the suppression of war crimes of the atrocity type is furnished by the numerous instances in which the prosecution of war criminals has been the subject of international consideration or agreement. Provision was made in the Treaty of Versailles and other treaties of peace following both World Wars[3] for the punishment or surrender of persons who had committed 'acts in violation of the laws and customs of war' or 'war crimes'. While the Second World War was yet in progress, the punishment of war crimes was given active consideration by the United Nations.[4] The landmarks of this war-time planning—the Declaration of St. James's, the Moscow Declaration, and the London Agreement of 8 August 1945—recognize that war crimes possess not only an importance transcending national interests but also solemn undertakings, subscribed to even by those states which prosecuted war crimes under their own law, to participate and assist in the prosecution of such crimes. More recently, the International Law Commission of the United Nations has, at the behest of the General Assembly, formulated the Nuremberg Principles[5] and prepared a Draft Code of Offences against the Peace and Security of Mankind,[6] among which are included violations of the laws or customs of war. By contrast, in the documents which have been mentioned and in the Charters of the International Military Tribunals, in Control Council Law No. 10, and in the multifarious directives and laws defining war crimes and providing for their punishment, there are no references to the prosecution by the tribunals so constituted of the so-called 'war crimes' of espionage, illegal hostilities in arms, war treason, guerrilla warfare, and the like. The record of more than three decades affords striking evidence of international participation in the prevention of war crimes of the atrocity type and indicates by its silence with respect to unprivileged belligerency that conduct of that nature is not, in a positive sense, of substantial international concern.

Without attempting to enumerate the many ways in which international law may be violated in such a manner as to engage the criminal responsibility of the individual, it is still possible, on the basis of the foregoing considerations, to articulate a distinction of a general nature between 'war crimes' in their proper sense and hostilities conducted by persons not of the armed forces—a subject discussed elsewhere in this volume.[7] The tendency of international law and the particular emphasis of recent codification and

[1] See *Opinions of the Attorneys General of the United States*, 11 (1869), p. 307.

[2] *United States* v. *Yamashita* (1945), *War Crimes Reports*, vol. iv (1948), p. 1, habeas corpus denied, *In re Yamashita* (1946), 327 U.S. 1.

[3] Articles 228–30, Treaty of Versailles; Articles 173–6, Treaty of St. Germain; Articles 118–20, Treaty of Neuilly-sur-Seine; Articles 157–60, Treaty of Trianon; Article 45, Treaty of Peace with Italy, 1947; Article 5, Treaty of Peace with Bulgaria, 1947; Article 6, Treaty of Peace with Hungary, 1947; Article 6, Treaty of Peace with Roumania, 1947; Article 9, Treaty of Peace with Finland, 1947.

[4] For the history of this planning see *The United Nations War Crimes Commission and the Development of the Laws of War* (1948), pp. 87 ff.

[5] *Report of the International Law Commission covering its Second Session*, 5 June–29 July 1950, United Nations General Assembly, 5th Session, Official Records, Supp. No. 12 (U.N.Doc. A/1316), Part iii.

[6] *Report of the International Law Commission covering its Third Session*, 16 May–27 July 1951 (U.N.Doc. A/CN. 4/48, 30 July 1951), ch. iv.

[7] See above, pp. 324–45.

change in the law of war has been on the protection of categories of persons, the greater number of whom are persons who cannot, as a matter of fact, engage in hostilities. These protected classes are the wounded and sick, prisoners of war, civilians in the territory of a party to the conflict, and the populations of occupied areas.[1] In addition to these, members of the armed forces who are neither disabled nor in the hands of the enemy are, to a limited extent, also granted a protected status, for international law attempts to shelter them from unnecessary suffering and the unrestrained barbarities of war. Acts against any of these persons, by whomsoever committed, which are in violation of those fundamental principles of the law of war which forbid the infliction of unnecessary suffering and the creation of conditions which make impossible the restoration of peace therefore constitute war crimes. Hostile acts, however, which would if committed by members of the armed forces not be in violation of the law of war are not war crimes, since they do not prejudice the rights secured to protected categories of persons. It is the former category in which the international community has a substantial and continuing interest, made manifest by the number of occasions on which war crimes have been tried under international law or have been the subject of international agreements. This international concern in the protection of human rights and the restoration of peace can be vindicated only by the humanitarian intervention of international law and not merely by a denial of privileged status under the law of war. The resolution of those cases, notably those of ruses, which do not clearly fall into either the category of war crimes or that of unprivileged belligerency must therefore depend upon a determination whether the act complained of is of so perfidious or inhumane a character as to require the active intervention of the law of nations.

Stated in positive form, the trial of war criminals under international law permits the direct application of a uniform law of a specialized nature to acts which are distinguished from common law crimes by reason of their occurrence in time of war. International law also surmounts the jurisdictional barrier, as municipal law cannot, by recognizing the universality of jurisdiction enjoyed by war crimes tribunals. Recent prosecutions of conventional war crimes and crimes against humanity have afforded many significant instances in which the victims of crimes have included few or no nationals of the prosecuting state. In the *Zyklon B* case,[2] for example, those killed by poison gas supplied by the accused included Belgian, Dutch, French, Czech, and Polish nationals, and it was not alleged that any British subjects were among the victims. The Nuremberg Subsequent Proceedings conducted by the United States pursuant to Control Council Law No. 10 involved, in the great majority of cases, offences committed against other than United States citizens, whether they had been the victims of plundering by German industrialists,[3] members of occupied populations or prisoners of war for whose death or injury the German High Command was responsible,[4] or persons deprived of the

[1] The other means available to make effective the protection of these persons are of doubtful efficacy. The sanction of public opinion and protests to the offending belligerent through the protecting power or the International Committee of the Red Cross have not been sufficient to deter states bent upon a course of systematic violation of the law of war. To a considerable extent, the power to exact compliance with the law through the instrument of reprisals has been lost, for the Geneva Conventions of 1949 contain specific prohibitions of reprisals against prisoners of war (Article 13), including the wounded and sick, and civilians (Article 33), violence against whom has, in any case, been difficult to reconcile with the humanitarian purpose of the law of war.

[2] *In re Tesch et Al.* (British Military Court, Hamburg, 1946), *War Crimes Reports*, vol. i (1947), p. 93.

[3] *United States* v. *Krupp et Al.* (1948), *Trials of War Criminals*, vol. ix (1950), p. 1327, *War Crimes Reports*, vol. x (1949), p. 69.

[4] *United States* v. *Von Leeb et Al.* (1948), *Trials of War Criminals*, vol. xi (1950), p. 462, *War Crimes Reports*, vol. xii (1949), p. 1.

benefit of law by the defendants in the *Justice Trial*.[1] Consequently, not only did the *locus* of the particular offence become immaterial,[2] but the United States also prosecuted persons who had been responsible for war crimes before that country had become involved in war.[3] In addition to the many prosecutions of nationals of states at war with the United Nations, there are numerous instances of the trial of Allied nationals and even of nationals of neutral states who had taken part in such crimes.[4] Although the prosecution of these persons was rationalized on the basis that the individuals concerned had subjected themselves to the jurisdiction of Allied war crimes tribunals by associating themselves with the enemy, they nevertheless point to a tendency to universality in the prosecution of such acts. It must be conceded that true universality has not been attained by those countries which apply international law to enemy war criminals, for the victims of conventional war crimes were, almost without exception, nationals of states allied with the prosecuting state or of the prosecuting state itself and the accused were either enemy nationals or persons who had voluntarily associated themselves with the enemy forces or administration. Crimes against humanity have, it should be observed, gone beyond these confines since even the enemy's conduct with respect to its own population has been said to be cognizable by a tribunal to which has been presented a charge of a crime against humanity.[5]

It may fairly be objected at this point that, although a distinction of a theoretical nature may exist between the problems of the qualifications of belligerents and of war crimes, as properly defined, no practical consequences flow from this dichotomy. Whether the individual is prosecuted for a war crime or is considered not to be entitled to prisoner of war status, the maximum penalty of death can, and often will, be imposed, and it matters little to the individual facing execution that there were two different possible bases for his impending death. This objection, however, overlooks a number of collateral legal problems for which the distinction is significant and disregards the importance of sound theory for the future development of the law of war.

In the first place, the state on whose behalf secret warfare is conducted and the states allied with it have neither a responsibility to restrain that form of warfare nor an obligation to punish its conduct. By contrast, there exists a duty for states not only to deal with war crimes committed by its enemies but also to punish war criminals amongst its own nationals as well, including the regular armed forces, civilians, and unprivileged belligerents fighting on its behalf.

It would also appear that the obligations of neutral states—if that expression can be said to retain any significance—differ with respect to the war criminal and the unprivileged belligerent. The duty of the neutral with respect to the latter would seem to be

[1] *United States* v. *Altstoetter et Al.* (1947), *Trials of War Criminals*, vol. iii (1951), p. 954, *War Crimes Reports*, vol. vi (1948), p. 1.

[2] *In re Sandrock et Al.* (British Military Court, Almelo, 1945), ibid., vol. i (1947), p. 35; *United States* v. *Eisentrager et Al.* (1947), ibid., vol. xiv (1949), p. 8, habeas corpus denied, *Johnson* v. *Eisentrager* (1950), 339 U.S. 763; *United States* v. *Hisakasu et Al.* (1946), *War Crimes Reports*, vol. v (1948), p. 66; *United States* v. *Sawada et Al.* (1946), ibid., p. 1.

[3] *United States* v. *Remmele* (1947), ibid., vol. xv (1949), p. 44.

[4] *In re Kramer et Al.* (British Military Court, Luneburg, 1945), ibid., vol. ii (1947), p. 1 (Polish nationals); *In re Jepson et Al.* (British Military Court, Luneburg, 1946), ibid., vol. xv (1949), p. 46 (Danish national); *United States* v. *Espinosa* (1947), ibid., p. 46 (Spanish national); and other cases cited ibid., pp. 45–46; see Control Council Law No. 10, Article II, para. 2.

[5] *United States* v. *Altstoetter et Al.* (1947), *Trials of War Criminals*, vol. iii (1951), p. 982, *War Crimes Reports*, vol. vi (1948), p. 40; *United States* v. *Ohlendorf et Al.* (1948), *Trials of War Criminals*, vol. iv (1949), p. 499; *United States* v. *Milch et Al.* (1947), ibid., vol. ii (1949), p. 791, *War Crimes Reports*, vol. vii (1948), p. 40.

indicated by his combatant status and to entail the internment of the individual.[1] To turn such an individual over to the enemy thereafter would appear to be as much a violation of neutral obligations as would the rendition to the enemy of a member of the armed forces who had come into the territory of the neutral. However, there is no like obligation imposed by international law to prevent a neutral state from turning over to a belligerent for trial a person against whom a valid prima facie case of war criminality may be made out.[2] It is in accordance with the principle of universality in dealing with war crimes and with the international interest in the suppression of such offences, from which that jurisdiction is derived, that neutral states should not be in a position to thwart the prosecution of violators of international law without themselves becoming chargeable with an abuse of rights.[3] To the extent that the theory which applies municipal law to war crimes emphasizes the national interest in their punishment, the extradition of war criminals becomes correspondingly more difficult to justify on grounds of policy and of logic.

What is referred to as universality of jurisdiction over war crimes[4] falls considerably short of that goal as long as the jurisdiction is exercised by a belligerent only over persons associated with its enemies. There is reason to suppose, however, that one of the intermediate stages on the way to a true international penal jurisdiction[5] may be the recognition that any state, including a neutral, has jurisdiction to try war crimes. By what state prosecution of a particular offence will actually be undertaken would then be determined, as it is now between allied or associated belligerents, by the convenience of the forum.[6] If a neutral state should, by reason of the availability of the accused, witnesses, and evidence be the most convenient *locus* in which to try a war crime, there is no reason why that state should not perform that function. On the other hand, the penalizing of so-called 'unprivileged belligerency'[7] on the part of spies, saboteurs, and the like, is an aspect of belligerency rather than an exercise of international penal jurisdiction, and there is accordingly every reason for denying jurisdiction to any state other than the offended belligerent or a state allied or associated with it.

Jurisdiction over war crimes continues until the termination of war by a treaty of peace, unless the treaty itself extends its duration.[8] By contrast, both 'unprivileged belligerency', which partakes of the nature of a ruse, and the enemy's jurisdiction to penalize it should be said to terminate either by the return of the individual to his own army or by reason of a definite cessation of hostile activity. In all probability, the cessation of hostilities between belligerents should have a like effect on unprivileged belligerency, since the death penalty which may be imposed in such cases is juridically akin

[1] Partisans were so interned by Switzerland during the Second World War (*Report of the International Committee of the Red Cross on its Activities during the Second World War (September 1, 1939–June 30, 1947)* (1948), vol. ii, p. 304; see also the case of the two German secret agents interned in Ireland in 1944, referred to in Spaight, *Air Power and War Rights* (3rd ed., 1947), p. 317.

[2] See Neumann, 'Neutral States and the Extradition of War Criminals', in *American Journal of International Law*, 45 (1951), p. 495; Morgenstern, 'Asylum for War Criminals, Quislings, and Traitors', in this *Year Book*, 25 (1948), p. 382.

[3] Lauterpacht, 'The Law of Nations and the Punishment of War Crimes', in this *Year Book*, 21 (1944), p. 93.

[4] See Brand, 'The War Crimes Trials and the Laws of War', in this *Year Book*, 26 (1949), p. 416; Cowles, op. cit., pp. 177–218.

[5] See *Historical Survey of the Question of International Criminal Jurisdiction* (1949), U.N.Doc. A/CN. 4/7/Rev. 1.

[6] *In re Kramer et Al.* (British Military Court, Luneburg, 1945), *War Crimes Reports*, vol. ii (1947), p. 8.

[7] See above, pp. 324–45.

[8] *In re Yamashita* (1946), 327 U.S. 1, 12.

to death in battle. Jurisdiction over war crimes is thus observed to be of greater duration than that over spies, *francs-tireurs*, and guerrilla fighters.

A distinction between war crimes and unprivileged belligerency also indicates the several paths which must be taken in dealing with the punishment of these two types of acts. In the case of the former, the objective must be the creation of a mature system of criminal jurisprudence on a universal basis, possibly culminating in the establishment of permanent international tribunals. In the case of unprivileged belligerency, international law, it is submitted, should merely concern itself with assuring a fair determination of the individual's status by the belligerent in whose hands he is and, where appropriate, with the establishment of maximum punishments. The increasing meaninglessness of the uniform as determinative of rights may ultimately lead to a recognition of all belligerents, or of all armed belligerents, as 'lawful'.

The law of war to which reference has been made in this Note is, of course, the conventional law of war governing the hostilities of enemy states. It may be anticipated that in the future the law of war may become a body of law relating to hostilities conducted between forces under the aegis of the international community and those of a state which has violated international law in resorting to war.[1] While changes in the law of war may be expected to accompany this transformation, there is no basis for concluding that all the belligerents of the offending states will be regarded as criminal in an international sense or that the armed forces of an international police force will be subject to no legal restraints.[2]

R. R. B.

[1] Jessup, *A Modern Law of Nations* (1950), pp. 188 ff.

[2] See Oppenheim, *International Law*, vol. ii (7th ed. by Lauterpacht, 1952), § 61.

[12]

Superior Orders and the Reasonable Man

L. C. GREEN

RECENT ALLEGATIONS CONCERNING a "massacre" of Vietnamese by United States forces in the Song My area of Vietnam, together with disclosures of a similar event during British anti-guerrilla operations in Malaya, have drawn renewed attention to the problem of the behaviour of troops in war, and the extent to which they may be expected to obey the laws of war. This is not the place to examine the philosophical aspect of whether there are or can be any rules of war, particularly if one of the belligerents is waging an "illegal" or "criminal" war, or is not recognized as a state so that the operations do not technically qualify as a war in the traditional sense. The *Kawasaki* case[1] demonstrates that "war" may exist, even though neither the parties nor third states recognize the operations as such. It is also clear, at least since the Geneva Conventions of 1949[2], that laws regarding the humane treatment of wounded and sick, prisoners of war and civilians in occupied territory operate even in armed conflicts not of an international character[3], as well as those which only one party regards as a war, or if only one is party to the Conventions, or if territory is occupied and no resistance met.[4]

Since the laws of war apply to all such hostilities, members of the armed forces accused of breaking these laws are likely to be tried by court martial or a war crimes tribunal. In the case of members of one's own forces, there is no need to charge war crimes; every army

---

Professor of the University, University of Alberta.

---

1 *Kawasaki Kisen Kabushiki Kaisha of Kobe* v. *Bantham S.S. Co.* [1939] 2 K.B. 544.

2 I, 75 UNTS 31; II, *ibid.*, 85; III, *ibid.*, 135; IV, *ibid.*, 287.

3 Art. 3 of each Convention.

4 Art. 2 of each Convention.

is subject to its own system of law and normally has a penal code based on its ordinary municipal law. Troops are under the jurisdiction of their national command and there is no need to seek any extraordinary ground to establish jurisdiction over them. With members of another armed force, be it allied or enemy, this basis for jurisdiction does not exist and some special authority has to be found. This is provided by international law which permits those — including neutrals[5] — into whose hands offenders against the laws of war may fall to try them for the alleged breaches of the law, and the Oradour trial in France, when the trial for war crimes of French traitors was severed from that of their German colleagues, illustrates the type of problem that may well arise because of the conflict of jurisdictions.[6]

Invariably in these trials the accused contends that as a member of the armed forces he is obliged to obey the orders of his superiors, and he frequently seeks to evade personal responsibility on the ground that whatever act he is alleged to have committed was performed as the result of an order, so that, if criminal liability lies against anybody, it is against the authority who issued the order. In the trials that followed the Second World War, the order-issuing authority was frequently alleged to have been Hitler or some other of his senior dignitaries who were either dead or whose whereabouts were unknown; if the plea served to provide the factual actor with a defence, it would have been impossible to proceed against anyone. However, it must not be thought that the plea is to be found only in connection with offences committed by military personnel. Thus it is provided by the Norwegian Penal Code that "in cases where a superior cannot be punished for a misdemeanour committed by somebody in his service, the subordinate can always be held respon-

[5] Thus, the 1949 Conventions, at least where "grave breaches" are concerned, require each High Contracting Party to seek out those, regardless of nationality, alleged to have committed or ordered such breaches, and try them before local courts or transfer them for trial to another High Contracting Party "cornerned," provided the latter has made out a prima facie case (Art. 49, 50, 129, 146). See Canada's Geneva Conventions Act, 1964 (S.C. 1965, c. 44), s.3, and "Unit Guide to the Geneva Conventions," 1949, CFP 318(4), para. 702 (2), which states that "Canada, or any other nation bound by the Conventions including the enemy, may capture and try any person who commits or orders to be committed any of the acts defined as grave breaches of the Convention." See, also, Cowles, "Universality of Jurisdiction over War Crimes," 33 Calif. L. Rev. 177 (1945).

[6] *The Times* (London), Jan. 2, 13, 14, 16, 17, 19-21, 29-31, Feb. 4, 9-14, 19, 20 and 23, 1953.

sible, even if the penal provision, according to its wording alone, is directed against the superior."[7]

In civilian life the position of hierarchic authority that exists in the armed services is not frequently come across, but accused persons have been known to put forward the plea of obedience in an ordinary criminal process, and this was particularly true in the earlier days of colonial rule. They have also alleged that some other person exercised such coercion, compulsion or duress upon them that they were obliged to act as they did, but had not done so as free agents. Before examining the problem from the point of view of military or international law, it is useful to refer to the position in municipal criminal law, for members of the armed forces do not normally lose their liability under that law merely by virtue of having joined the forces; some of the Penal Codes make express reference to the problem.

According to the German Penal Code, "no act constitutes an offence if its perpetrator was compelled so to act by *irresistible force* or by a threat entailing an *immediate and otherwise not avertible danger* to his own or one of his family member's body or life."[8] The 1916 Criminal Code of Lagos, East and West Nigeria provides that "a person is not criminally responsible for an act or omission if he does or omits to do the act . . . (2) in obedience to the order of a competent authority which he is bound by law to obey, unless the order is *manifestly unlawful* . . . but this protection does not extend to an act or omission which would constitute an offence punishable with death, or an offence of which grievous harm to the person of another, or an intention to cause such harm, is an element. . . . *Whether* an order is or is not *manifestly unlawful is a question of law*."[9] The Colombian Penal Code recognizes the liability of both the actor and the superior ordering the action, but provides for mitigation of punishment: "An act is justified when committed pursuant to . . . an obligatory command of a competent authority. . . . [T]he person causing another to act shall be liable. . . . Anyone performing an act under [such] circumstances who *exceeds the limits imposed by law*, [or] by the authorities . . . shall be subject to a [reduced] punishment. In cases specially favorable for the accused, the sentence may be suspended."[10] The Turkish Criminal

[7] 1902/61, s.41 (Andenaes ed., 1961, at 28).

[8] 1871/1961, s.52 (Mueller ed., 1961, at 41, italics added).

[9] S.32 (Brett and McLean ed., 1963, at 482, italics added).

[10] 1936, ss.25,26,27 (Eder ed., 1967, at 21, italics added).

Code is in somewhat similar terms: "No punishment shall be imposed if the perpetrator acted (1) in order to execute ... an order given by a responsible authority, execution of which is the perpetrator's duty; ... *if the order* issued *is contrary to law*, the *punishment* for the felony resulting from the violation of the law, *shall be suffered by the person who has issued the order. Whoever* while performing [such] an act ..., *surpasses the limit prescribed either by law*, by competent authority, *or by necessity, shall be punished* in accordance with a specified scale of reduced penalties."[11]

The Canadian Criminal Code puts the issue of obedience in juxtaposition with that of coercion. By section 15, "[N]o person shall be convicted of an offence in respect of an act or omission in obedience to the laws for the time being made and enforced by persons in *de facto* possession of the sovereign power in and over the place where the act or omission occurs." It would appear from this wording that there could be no reproduction of the trials of the regicides in Canada[12], and the immunity extends to acts done in obedience to "public functionaries holding office thereunder"[13]. As to the problem of duress, section 17 provides that "[A] person who commits an offence under compulsion *by threats of immediate death or grievous bodily harm from a person who is present when the offence is committed* is *excused* for committing the offence *if he believes that the threats will be carried out* and if he is not a party to a conspiracy or association whereby he is subject to compulsion, but this section does not apply where the offence that is committed is treason, murder, piracy, attempted murder, assisting in rape, forcible abduction, robbery, causing bodily harm or arson." Thus in *Dunbar* v. *R.*[14] the appellant contended that he had been compelled by threats to his life to act as chauffeur for a robbery during which murder was committed; it was held that his choice to participate in the undertaking made him a party to the unlawful common undertaking, and that since murder had been committed the compulsion would not excuse him, even though he was not present at the actual killing. As to the defence of superior orders, this was put forward in *R.* v. *Laroche* when a municipal treasurer pleaded that she had paid moneys to the mayor on his instructions, in the honest belief

[11] 1926/64, ss.49,50 (Gürelli ed., 1965, at 28).

[12] See references to *Axtell* and *Cooke, infra* notes 33, 34.

[13] Constantineau on *De Facto Doctrine*, c. *Martin's Criminal Code*, 1955, at 55.

[14] [1936] 4 D.L.R. 737. See also *R.* v. *Farduto* (1913), 10 D.L.R. 669.

that he was entitled to receive them; the majority of the Supreme Court was of opinion "that there could be no honesty or honest opinion of right in these transactions."[15]

Broadly speaking, the position of a member of the Canadian armed forces is identical with that of a civilian under municipal law. By section 125 of the National Defence Act all civil defences are available to an accused serviceman appearing before a military tribunal, and by QR&O 103.03 the terms of section 17 of the Criminal Code on compulsion are spelled out. By QR&O, Chapter 19, "every officer and man shall obey the orders of officers and men who are senior to him . . . [but i]f an officer or man is given an order that he considers to be in conflict with the *National Defence Act*, QR&O, or general or particular orders binding on him, he shall point out the conflict orally, or in writing if the order does not require immediate obedience, to the superior by whom the order was given. If the superior still directs him to obey the order, he shall do so."[16] Queen's Regulations and Orders do not indicate what his position will be if he carries out the order and it transpires that it was in fact illegal. The only guidance that is given is to be found in section 74 of the National Defence Act which demands obedience to "lawful commands." QR&O 103.16(J) stipulates that the command must be lawful, and gives as an example that a man would be justified in refusing to sign a receipt for pay if he considered it incorrect, even though he were ordered to sign. Presumably, if it is not lawful for him to be ordered to sign such a receipt, it would not be lawful for him to be ordered to commit a war crime and, if he obeyed that order, then presumably he would be liable. Some evidence for this contention may be derived from *Fitch* v. *The Queen* in which Cameron J. pointed out that the order must "be one relating to a military duty. For example, a command given by an officer to a man to perform some domestic office not relating to military duty is not a command within the meaning of this section."[17] A man would be placed upon the horns of a dilemma if he were called upon to decide whether an order given him by an officer constituted a lawful requisition or unlawful looting.

The last Penal Code to which reference need be made is that of India. By section 76 there is no offence if the act were done "by a person who is, or who by reason of a mistake of fact and not by

[15] [1964] S.C.R. 667, 673.

[16] QR&O 19.015,19.02.

[17] (1954) 1 C.M.A.R. 249,251.

reason of a mistake of law in good faith believes himself to be bound by law to do it." Commenting on this, Ratanlal points out that nothing but fear of instant death would constitute a defence for a policeman who tortured anyone on the orders of his superior, and he cites two nineteenth century cases as illustrative of his argument.[18] In *Gurdit Singh* the court considered the case of a naik and two men who had fired on a mob that was threatening them, and held that "they must be taken to have known that the naik was wrong in law in firing upon the mob, and that they were not bound to obey his illegal order."[19] A year earlier, a police officer who committed a wrongful act under the order of his superior officer had been held liable "as his mistake of law in supposing himself authorised cannot be accepted as a good defence though it may be a ground for mitigation of punishment."[20]

There seems to be little doubt that the Indian Penal Code was based on the principles that had evolved in England since the early days of the common law, and which later were adopted by the United States. The present situation in these two countries is easily stated. According to Halsbury:

> . . . No duress . . . excuses the taking of an innocent life. . . . [E]vidence of threats and violence to the accused may rebut the presumption that the accused intended the probable consequences of his act, and, where the offence is proved by the proof of the doing of an act, it seems that a plea of duress may be set up, not to show that no offence has been committed but to excuse from punishment. . . . The mere fact that a person does a criminal act in *obedience to the order of a duly constituted superior does not excuse the person who does the act from criminal liability*, but the fact that a person does an act in obedience to a superior whom he is bound to obey, *may exclude the inference of malice or wrongful intention* which might otherwise follow from the act. . . . Soldiers and airmen are amenable to the criminal law to the same extent as other subjects. . . . *Obedience to superior orders is not in itself a defence to a criminal charge.*[21]

This is in accord with the earliest Mutiny Act of 1688 and is supported by Stephen and by Dicey. The former states:

> [Soldiers] are bound to execute any *lawful* order which they may receive from their military superior. . . . Probably . . . the order of a military superior would justify his inferiors in executing any orders for

18 *Law of Crimes*, 1966, at 138.

19 P.R. No. 16 of 1883.

20 *Nga Myat Tha* (1882) S.J.L.B. 164.

21 3rd (Simonds) ed., vol. 10, ss.539,541,1169 (italics added).

giving which they might *fairly suppose* their superior officer to have good reasons.... The doctrine that a soldier is bound under all circumstances whatever to obey his superior officer would be fatal to military discipline itself [for example, an order to shoot the Commanding Officer or to desert].... [I]t is not less *monstrous to suppose that superior orders would justify a soldier in the massacre* of unoffending civilians in time of peace, or in the exercise of inhuman cruelties, such as the slaughter of women and children, during a rebellion.... [A] soldier should be *protected by orders* for which *he might reasonably believe his officer to have good grounds.*[22]

This would appear to impose upon a soldier the virtually impossible task of having to decide, when faced with an order that might not be lawful, whether in his view the officer had good grounds for issuance. Dicey does not go so far:

When a soldier is put on trial on a charge of crime, *obedience to superior orders* is not of itself a defence.... A soldier is *bound to obey any lawful order* which he receives from his military superior. But *a soldier cannot any more than a civilian avoid responsibility* for breach of the law *by pleading* that he broke the law in *bona fide obedience to the orders*.... [His] position is in theory and may be in practice a difficult one. He may... be liable to be shot by a Court-martial if he disobeys an order, and to be hanged by a judge and jury if he obeys it. ... The hardship of a soldier's position resulting from this inconvenience is much diminished by the power of the Crown to nullify the effect of an unjust conviction by means of a pardon.[23] While, however, a soldier runs no substantial risk of punishment for obedience to *orders which a man of common sense may honestly believe to involve no breach of law,* he... cannot avoid liability on the ground of obedience to superior orders for any act *which a man of ordinary sense must have known to be a crime.*[24]

Dicey's rejection of superior orders not only applies to members of the armed forces, but reaches to the ministerial level: "The Minister or servant of the Crown who... takes part in giving expression to the Royal will is legally responsible for the act in which he is concerned, and he cannot get rid of his liability by pleading that he acted in obedience to royal orders. Now supposing that the act done is illegal, the Minister concerned in it becomes at once liable to criminal or civil proceedings in a Court of Law."[25]

The position in the United States is almost identical. According

[22] 1 *History of the Criminal Law* 204-06 (1883) (italics added).

[23] See *R.* v. *Thomas* (1816), 4 M. & S. 441 (MS Bayley J.). Dicey points out that the Attorney-General could enter a *nolle prosequi.*

[24] *The Law of the Constitution* 298-99, 302 (8th ed., 1915) (italics added).

[25] *Ibid.*, 322-23.

to the *Corpus Juris Secundum*[26] "except in the case of homicide, an act which would otherwise constitute a crime may be excused when committed under duress or compulsion which is present, imminent and impending and which produces a well grounded apprehension of death or serious bodily harm if the act is not done.... As a general rule, a person who, while acting under the authority or direction of a superior, performs a criminal act is responsible therefor," and this is true even if the actor is the officer of a corporation, an agent or a servant. "The rules of law as to the liability of a soldier for the execution of the orders of his superiors are the same in criminal as in civil cases; thus he is not criminally liable for the execution of a lawful order, or one which is *fair and lawful on its face*; *but an order illegal on its face is no justification* for the commission of a crime."[27] These statements are fully backed up in the doctrinal writings in words that reflect the same attitudes as do those of Stephen and Dicey. According to Wharton:

> [W]here a person relies on a command of legal authority as a defense, it is essential that the command be a lawful one, which he was required to obey.... An order which is illegal in itself, and not justified by the rules and usages of war [here applied as much to the operations of the National Guard or armed forces in the case of internal disturbance as to war in the international sense] or which is, in substance, *clearly illegal*, so that *a man of ordinary sense and understanding would know* as soon as he heard the order read or given *that it was illegal*, will afford no protection for a homicide.... Moreover, if it is not part of the soldier's military duty to kill the particular victim, his act in so doing is criminal as though he were a private citizen. When an act committed by a soldier is a crime, even when done pursuant to military orders, the fact that he was ordered to commit the crime by his military superior is not a defense.[28]

As to the possibility of conflicts between the two systems of jurisprudence, "Recognition of the peculiar necessity of discipline in the military service and of the position in which the subordinate may find himself through no fault of his own, in the event that commands of his superiors clash with the civil authority, has led courts in well-considered cases to regard obedience to a military order as a justification for conduct which would otherwise give rise to civil or criminal liability, unless the order is *so palpably unlawful that a*

26 Vol. 22, "Criminal Law," ss.43,39.

27 C.J.S., vol. 6, "Army and Navy," s.37 (2) (italics added).

28 1 *Criminal Law and Procedure* 257-58, s.118 (1957 ed.) (italics added).

reasonable man in the position of the person obeying it would perceive its unlawful quality."[29] Perhaps the most comprehensive doctrinal statement of the United States position, and one that has been adopted by the courts[30], is by Hare:

The question is . . . had the accused *reasonable cause for believing in the necessity* of the act which is impugned, and in determining this point a soldier or member of the *posse comitatus* may obviously take the orders of the person in command into view as proceeding from one who is better able to judge and well informed; and, if the circumstances are such that the command may be justifiable, he should not be held guilty for declining to decide that it is wrong with the responsibility incident to disobedience, *unless the case is so plain as not to admit of a reasonable doubt.* A soldier consequently runs little risk in obeying any order *which a man of common sense so placed would regard as warranted by the circumstances.*[31]

The quotations from Wharton and Hare raise the problem of what is meant by the "reasonable man" in this context. However, before considering this or the relevance of the defence of superior orders to war crimes *per se*, it may be useful to look at some of the judicial applications of the doctrine outlined above. Perhaps the earliest cases in the United Kingdom were those concerning the regicides after the Restoration, when it was held that obedience to the Commonwealth did not extend to an accused the protection of the Act of 1494,[32] whereby obedience to a king de facto who was not also de jure king did not after a restoration render his adherents liable for treason. In *Cooke*'s case the former Chief Justice of Ireland was tried for his part in the proceedings against the King in that he presented the indictment and demanded judgment against him; his plea that "they were not my words, but their words that commanded me" was rejected, for "you know by a printed authority, that where a settled court, a true court is, if that court meddle with that which is not in their cognizance, it is purely void; the minister that obeys them is punishable; if it be treasonable matter, it is treason; if murder, it is murder. . . . [If the Common Pleas sentence a man to death when it should be the King's Bench,] it is murder in the Executioner. . . . You speak of a court: 1 It was not a court: 2 No courts whatsoever could have any power over a

29 135 ALR Annot. 10,37 (italics added).

30 See, for example, *Commonwealth, ex rel. Wadsworth* v. *Shortall* (1903), 55 Atl.952,956.

31 Hare, *Constitutional Law* 920 (1889) (italics added).

32 11 Hen. VII, c.1.

king in a coercive way, as to his person. . . . [T]he acting by colour of that pretended authority was so far from any extenuation, that it was an aggravation of the thing."[33] In this case there was constant reference to the fact that the accused was learned in the law and would therefore know what the position really was. In *Axtell*[34] there was no such basis for argument, for the accused was merely the guard commander at the execution, who "justified that all he did was as a soldier, by the command of his superiour officer, whom he must obey or die. It was resolved that was no excuse, for his superiour was a traitor, and all that joyned him in that *act* were traitors, and did by that approve the treason; and where the command is traiterous, there the obedience to that command is also traiterous." The court took the line that even a common soldier must have known that it was an act of treason to participate in any way in the execution of one's king.

The reasoning in *Axtell* appears to have provided the basis of the argument by the Advocate General of India during one of the Indian National Army Trials. The defence had contended that the acts of the accused were legal within the terms of the "Indian National Army Act" and so excepted from the Indian Penal Code and the Indian Army Act, to be met by this argument:

> [A]n act of treason cannot give any sort of rights nor can it exempt a person from criminal responsibility for the subsequent acts. Even if an act is done under a command, where the command is traitorous, obedience to that command is also traitorous. It is submitted that the accused cannot in law seek to justify what they did as having been done under the authority of the I.N.A. Act. No authority purporting to be given under that Act can be recognised by this court or indeed any court of this country. The assumption of any such authority was illegal from the beginning. Any tribunal or authority purporting to be established under that Act would be in repudiation of the allegiance which is inherent in a court of the country. Those who instituted or took part in the proceedings were themselves liable to be punished for offences against the State. All orders under the I.N.A. Act or by any tribunal or authority purporting to be established by it are without sanction. They cannot protect the persons who made such orders or acted upon them.[35]

It has been said above that a servant cannot plead in his defence that he was acting under the orders of his master. Nevertheless, in

[33] (1660), 5 St.Tr. 1077,1113,1115. See also *War Crimes (Preventive Murder) (Germany) case* (1960), 32 I.L.R. 563.

[34] (1661) Kelyng 13, 84 E.R. 1060.

[35] See Green, "The Indian National Army Trials," 11 Mod. L.R. 47, 53-54 (1948). See also *Hindustan Times*, Nov. 6, 1945.

Kidd's Case, Ward L.C.B. pointed out "It is true, a servant is not bound to obey his master but in lawful things, which [three of the accused] say they thought this was, and that they knew not to the contrary, but that their masters acted according to the King's commission,"[36] and the jury found them not guilty of piracy. This decision should be compared with *R.* v. *James* in which workers were charged with having unlawfully stopped up the airway to a colliery neighbouring that of their master, having been ordered by him so to do. It was there held that:

If a master told his servant to shoot a man, *he would know that was an order he ought to disobey*.... If a man claims a right which he knows not to exist, and he tells his servants to exercise it, and they do so acting *bona fide*, I am of opinion that that is not a felony in them, even if in so doing they obstruct the airway of a mine [contrary to 7 & 8, Geo.IV, c.30].... If these men acted *bona fide* in obedience to the orders of a superior, conceiving that he had the right which he claimed, they are not within this Act of Parliament. But if either of these men *knew that it was a malicious act on the part of his master*, I think then that he would be guilty of the offence charged.[37]

Another case concerning non-military personnel in which superior orders were important is *R.* v. *Trainer* charging manslaughter against the driver and fireman of a railway train; Willes J. said there:

[H]e should hold that in a criminal case an inferior officer must be held justified in obeying the directions of a superior, *not obviously improper or contrary to law* — that is, if an inferior officer acted honestly upon what he might *not unreasonably* deem to be the effect of the orders of his superior, he would not be guilty of culpable negligence, those orders *not appearing to him*, at the time, improper or contrary to law.... [T]heir duty was to obey the special instructions issued to them as well as they could, presuming there was *no apparent illegality* in them....[38]

Other cases considered by the English courts have referred to orders issued to military personnel, and the guiding statement, which has also been adopted in the United States, is perhaps that by Lord Mansfield in *Wall* v. *M'Namara* concerning an allegation of false imprisonment by the Lieutenant-Governor of Gambia:

In trying the legality of acts done by military officers in the exercise of their duty, particularly beyond the seas, ... great latitude ought to be

36 (1701), 14 St. Tr. 147, 185.

37 (1837), 8 C. & P. 131, 132-33; 173 E.R. 429, 430 (italics added).

38 (1864), 4 F. & F. 105, 111-12, 113; 176 E.R. 488, 491, 492 (italics added).

allowed, and they ought not to suffer for a slip of form, if their intention appears by the evidence to have been upright; it is the same as when complaints are brought against civil magistrates, such as justices of the peace, for acts done by them in the exercise of their civil duty. There the principal inquiry to be made is, by a Court of Justice, how the heart stood? And if there appears to be nothing wrong there, great latitude will be allowed for misapprehension or mistake. But . . . if the heart is wrong, if cruelty, malice, and oppression, appear to have occasioned or aggravated the . . . injury complained of, they shall not cover themselves with the thin veil of legal forms, nor escape, under the cover of a justification the most technically regular. . . . [39]

Another case of unlawful arrest was decided by Willes J. who remarked "I should probably hold that the orders [to arrest another member of the military] are an absolute justification in time of actual war . . . unless the orders were such as could not legally be given. . . . [A]n officer or soldier, acting under the orders of his superior — *not being necessarily or manifestly illegal* — would be justified of his orders."[40] Here Willes J. is referring to such orders as may be lawfully given, and in another case in the same year he referred to this again: "[I]f the military should injure [civilians] in their persons or their property, not even the command of a superior officer will justify a soldier in what he does, unless the command should turn out to be legal, and to be within the limits of the protection given by the Mutiny Act and the Articles of War. It is only by reason of the 88th section [of the Act], . . . that a soldier acting *bona fide*, and in discharge of what he supposes to be his duty, could ever set up as against a citizen not a soldier, the justification of superior command."[41] If such a test were to be the controlling measure, it would be almost impossible for a soldier ever to plead the defence of superior orders, at least when the act has been committed against a civilian. Perhaps a more practical approach was adopted by Howard J. before whom a police officer pleaded guilty to attempting to pervert the course of justice. Acting on instructions the constable had enlarged a hole in a door that he knew was to be inspected by magistrates, and the learned judge ruled that "no order, even if it were given by any superior officer, to do what you attempted to do, can possibly excuse you trying to do it."[42]

[39] (1779), 1 Term Rep. 536; 99 E.R. 1239.

[40] *Keighley* v. *Bell* (1866), 4 F. & F. 763, 790; 176 E.R. 781, 793 (italics added).

[41] *Dawkes* v. *Lord Rokeby* (1866), 4 F. & F. 806, 831; 176 E.R. 800, 811.

[42] *The Times*, December 15, 1962.

The attitude of the United States courts seems to have been a little more realistic and therefore more lenient than that of the English courts. In so far as the acts of servants in compliance with the orders of their masters are concerned, the leading case is *Giugni* v. *U.S.*, in which a sea captain pleaded that he was obeying the orders of his government; Woodbury, Circuit Judge, held that "[i]t requires no citation of authorities to support the proposition that an employee is not immune from punishment for his criminal acts for the reason that those acts were done on his employer's orders."[43] The other cases to be mentioned all refer to acts of the military, and relate to both civil and criminal liability. As to his civil liability, one of the earliest cases is *Mitchell* v. *Harmony*, which was an action for trespass arising from seizure of property in Mexico; Chief Justice Taney held that "the order given was to do an illegal act; to commit a trespass upon the property of another; and can afford no justification to the person by whom it was executed. . . . And upon principle, . . . it can never be maintained that a military officer can justify himself for doing an unlawful act, by producing the order of his superior. *The order may palliate, but it cannot justify*."[44] In an action arising from the arrest of a suspected "night rider," Carroll J. recognized that "It may be and doubtless is true that, looking at the matter from a military standpoint, the order to act as Franks did was *not such an unreasonable command as that a soldier of common sense* would feel authorized to refuse to obey. But . . . conduct like this is such an intolerable invasion of private rights, . . . that we cannot consent that all military orders, however reasonable they may appear, will afford protection in the civil or criminal courts of the state."[45]

The divergence between the military and the civilian approach to the same issue was discussed by the Supreme Court in *U.S. ex rel. Toth* v. *Quarles*[46], which arose from the arrest in the United States of a member of the air force after he had been demobilized for a murder he was alleged to have committed while serving in Korea, to which in accordance with the Uniform Code of Military Justice[47] he had been returned to stand trial by court martial. The Court held this was an unconstitutional invasion of the rights of a civilian

[43] (1942), 127 F.2d 786, 791.

[44] (1851), 13 How. 115, 137 (italics added).

[45] *Franks* v. *Smith* (1911), 134 S.W. 484, 490-91 (italics added).

[46] (1955), 350 U.S. 11, 18.

[47] 1950, 64 Stat. 109.

even though it meant, in the absence of Congressional legislation conferring jurisdiction on the municipal courts in such circumstances, that the accused went free and untried. Speaking for the majority, Mr. Justice Black recognized that "It is true that military personnel because of their training and experience may be especially competent to try soldiers for infractions of military rules. Such training is no doubt particularly important where an offense charged against a soldier is purely military, such as disobedience of an order, leaving post, etc.", but civilians are entitled to trial by jury, and "juries may reach completely different conclusions than would be reached by specialists in any single field, including specialists in the military field." That the special military knowledge of officers may be important in judicial proceedings has been recognized by Canadian military law and its significance was construed in *Chenoweth* v. *R.*[48] and *Hryhoriw* v. *R.*[49] This fact is of importance, as will be seen below, in construing the significance of "reasonableness" in a military context.

Just as they have recognized the fact that special knowledge may be important in relation to military circumstances, so have the courts recognized the dilemma in which a serviceman may find himself when confronted with an order which may be unlawful. The law has been well set out in *McCall* v. *McDowell*:

> Except in a plain case of excess of authority, where at first blush it is *apparent and palpable to the commonest understanding* that the order is illegal, I cannot but think that the law should excuse the military subordinate when acting in obedience to the orders of his commander. Otherwise he is placed in the dangerous dilemma of being liable in damages to third persons for obedience to an order, or to the loss of his commission and disgrace for disobedience thereto. . . . True, cases can be imagined where the order is *so palpably atrocious as well as illegal that one can instinctively feel that it ought not to be obeyed*, by whomever given. . . . Between an order plainly legal and one palpably otherwise — particularly in time of war — there is a wide middle ground, where the ultimate legality and propriety of orders depends or may depend upon circumstances and conditions of which it cannot be expected that the inferior is informed or advised. In such cases, justice to the subordinate demands . . . that the order of the superior should protect the inferior; leaving the responsibility to rest where it properly belongs — upon the officer who gave the command.[50]

48 (1954) 1 C.M.A.R. 253.

49 *Ibid.*, 277.

50 (1887), 1 Abb. 212, 218 (italics added).

References to the duty of a soldier to obey orders and the limitations imposed by the criminal law upon the ordinary man have been referred to in other cases. Thus in *Riggs* v. *State* it was held that "an order illegal in itself, and not justifiable by the rules and usages of war, so that *a man of ordinary understanding* would know, when he heard it read or given, that the order was illegal, would afford the private no protection for a crime under such order; but an order given by an officer to his private which *does not expressly and clearly show on its face, or on the body thereof its own illegality*, the soldier would be bound to obey, and such order would be a protection to him."[51] Arising out of a soldier's supposed duty to prevent an escape and "in obedience to what he believed to be his duty," Brown J. said in *U.S. v. Clark*: "I have no doubt [as to the position of] acts of a subordinate officer performed in compliance with his supposed duty as a soldier; and unless the act were *manifestly beyond the scope of his authority, or* . . . were such *that a man of ordinary sense and understanding* would know that it was illegal, that it would be a protection to him, if he acted in good faith and without malice. As there is no reason in this case to suppose that Clark was not doing what he conceived to be his duty, and the act was *not so clearly illegal that a reasonable man* might not suppose it to be legal,"[52] and since there was no malice, Brown was discharged. Here is an attempt to apply what Lord Mansfield called the test of the heart, military duty, and the concept of ordinariness, and presumably if the order were "manifestly" beyond the authority of the officer giving it then "a man of ordinary sense and understanding would know it was illegal."

Two other cases involving homicide in response to orders are of interest. The accusation in *U.S.* v. *Carr* arose from the suppression of a mutiny, and the court held:

> [A] soldier is bound to obey only the lawful orders of his superiors. If he receives an order to do an unlawful act, he is bound neither by his duty nor his oath to do it. . . . [A]n order from an officer to shoot another for disrespectful words merely would, if obeyed, be murder both in the officer and soldier. . . . Place yourselves in the position of the prisoner at the time of the homicide. Inquire whether at the moment he fired . . . , with his surroundings at the time, *he had reasonable ground to believe, and did believe,* that the killing or serious wounding was necessary. . . . If he had reasonable ground so to believe then the

[51] 3 Cold. 85 (Tenn.), 91 Am. Dec. 272 (italics added).

[52] (1887), 31 Fed. 710, 717 (italics added).

killing was not unlawful. But if . . . the mutinous conduct . . . had ceased, and it so appeared to the prisoner, or if he could reasonably have suppressed the disorder without the resort to such violent means as the killing of the deceased, and it would *so have appeared to a reasonable man under the circumstances*, the killing was unlawful. But . . . the law will not require an officer charged with the order and discipline of a camp or fort to weigh with scrupulous nicety the amount of force necessary to suppress disorders. The exercise of *a reasonable* discretion is all that is necessary.[53]

The reasoning in *Carr* together with the quotation from Hare[54] were cited with approval in *Commonwealth, ex rel. Wadsworth* v. *Shortall* which concerned homicide by a member of the National Guard during a coal strike. He had received orders "to shoot, and shoot to kill" anyone approaching a particular house and not stopping when challenged. Mitchell J. said that in the instant case "there was no ground for doubt as to the legality of the order to shoot . . . he . . . acted only on his orders when the situation appeared to call for action under them."[55]

Before leaving the American municipal decisions, reference might be made to two recent cases in which orders were pleaded, although the courts held that the situations with which they were dealing were not really military in character. An army convoy was proceeding along the road with orders not to break convoy, under threat of prosecution. One of the trucks crossed the traffic lights and was involved in a collision. Qua J. recognized that "Failure of instant obedience leads to military punishment, which may be severe. . . . [However, a]n order to keep the convoy together even if that involved continuing in the face of a red light, although illegal, *cannot* . . . under circumstances not here in dispute, *be deemed palpably and obviously illegal* to a private soldier in the position of the plaintiff," but such an order would not excuse reckless or negligent driving.[56] The remaining case must be the most amazing in which the plea of superior orders has ever been put forward. In *State* v. *Roy* the appellant had been convicted of assault with intent to commit rape, and appealed on the ground that he was a private soldier obeying the orders of his sergeant. It is perhaps not surprising that Denny J. felt "The contention has no merit. The duty of a subordinate to obey a superior officer, while one is subject to mili-

53 (1872), 1 Woods 480 (italics added).

54 *Op. cit. supra* note 31.

55 (1903), 55 Atl. 952, 957.

56 *Neu* v. *McCarthy* (1941), 33 N.E. 2d 570, 573-74 (italics added).

tary law, has reference only to lawful commands of such superior officer, in matters relating to military duty. And there is certainly nothing on this record to indicate that either of these defendants were engaged in any activity relating to military duties on the night in question."[57]

It would appear that in the view of municipal courts in the United States, a soldier may plead superior orders as a justification for his actions, provided the order was lawful or he had reasonable ground to believe in the circumstances that it was so, unless the order was so "palpably" outrageous that "a reasonable man of ordinary understanding" would have been repelled at the idea of committing the act ordered.

Having considered the problem from the point of view of the civilian courts, it is now time to see what military law and the international law of crimes have to say where this defence is concerned. The earliest case on record appears to be the trial of Peter of Hagenbach in 1474.[58] Hagenbach had been appointed *Landvogt* (Governor) of the Upper Rhine by Charles, Duke of Burgundy, and had sought to secure the submission of the populace to his master by a policy of what would today probably be described as crimes against humanity. On his capture, the Archduke of Austria, on whose territory he had been seized, ordered his trial by a tribunal consisting of judges appoined by the Allied towns. For the Archduke it was contended that Hagenbach had "trampled under foot the laws of God and man," but his counsel contended that "Sir Peter von Hagenbach does not recognise any other judge and master but the Duke of Burgundy from whom he had received his commission and his orders. He had no right to question the orders which he was obliged to carry out, and it was his duty to obey. Is it not known that soldiers owe absolute obedience to their superiors? Does anyone believe that the Duke's *Landvogt* could have remonstrated with his master or have refused to carry out the Duke's orders? Had not the Duke by his presence subsequently confirmed and ratified all that had been done in his name?" The tribunal rejected the defence and Hagenbach was executed.

The next case which is important from the point of view of the development of the doctrine of superior orders in time of war is the

57 (1951), 64 S.E. 2d 840, 841.

58 See 2 Schwarzenberger, *International Law*, "The Law of Armed Conflict," ch. 39, at 462-66 (1968) (Schwarzenberger first discussed this case in *Manchester Guardian*, September 24, 1946).

Wirz Trial,[59] arising from the atrocities committed against Federal prisoners of war at Andersonville during the American Civil War. Since this was a military trial, there was no judgment delivered, but as the court found Wirz guilty of the charges against him it must be presumed that the judges accepted the views expressed by the Judge Advocate:

> With what detestation must civilized nations regard that government whose conduct has been such as characterized this pretended confederacy. *An ordinary comprehension of natural right, the faintest desire to act on principles of common justice*, would have dictated some humane action, would have extorted from some official a recognition of international rules of conduct. . . . [I]t was not . . . ignorance of the law; it was the *intrinsic wickedness* of a few desperate leaders, seconded by mercenary and *heartless monsters*, of whom the prisoner before you is a fair type. . . . It is urged that during all this time [the accused] was acting under General Winder's orders. . . . A superior officer cannot order a subordinate to do an illegal act, and if a subordinate obey such an order and disastrous consequences result, both the superior and the subordinate must answer for it. General Winder could no more command the prisoner to violate the laws of war than could the prisoner do so without orders. The conclusion is plain, that where such orders exist both are guilty. . . . Strongly as it may strike you that strict justice would require the punishment of the arch-conspirator himself . . . you cannot stop the course of justice or refuse to brand [the accused's] guilt as the law and evidence direct. . . . Nothing can ever separate them. . . . [The accused] executed the bloody work with an industry which was almost superhuman and with a merriment which would have shamed a demon. . . . There could be no collision where the subaltern was only anxious to surpass an incomparable superior. . . . If the accused still answer that, admitting the facts charged, he did these things in the exercise of authority lawfully conferred upon him, and that what he did was necessary to the discipline and safety of the prisoners, I answer him in the language of Lord Mansfield [in *Wall* v. *M'Namara*].[60]

The case which is nowadays normally cited as being the point of departure for any analysis of the defence of superior orders is the South African case of *Reg.* v. *Smith*; in delivering judgment, Solomon J. declared that "it is monstrous to suppose that a soldier would be protected where the order is *grossly* illegal. [But that he] is responsible if he obeys an order not strictly legal . . . is an extreme proposition which the Court cannot accept. . . . [E]specially in time

[59] H.R. Exec. Doc. No. 23, 40th Cong., 2d Sess., 764, 773, 774, 802 (italics added).

[60] (1779), 1 Term Rep. 536 (see *supra* note 39).

of war immediate obedience . . . is required. . . . I think it is a safe rule to lay down that if a soldier *honestly believes* he is doing his duty in obeying . . . and the orders are *not so manifestly illegal* that he . . . ought to have known they were unlawful, [he] will be protected by the orders. . . . "[61]

The problem became of major significance during the war crimes trials that followed the First World War. By Article 228 of the Treaty of Versailles Germany recognized the right of the Allied Powers to try alleged war criminals by military tribunals and undertook to hand over such persons to stand trial, while by Article 229 it was provided that trials would be held by the Power against whose nationals the crimes were alleged to have been committed. It was subsequently agreed, however, that the German *Reichsgericht* (Supreme Court of the Empire) at Leipzig should be the court before which such accused would appear. By section 47 (2) of the German Military Penal Code, 1882, while the subordinate is bound to obey the orders of his superior, he would be punishable as an accomplice to a criminal act if he knew that the order concerned an act which was criminal by either civil or military law — and this was still the German law at the end of the Second World War. The scope of section 47 was discussed at Leipzig in two cases involving the destruction of hospital ships. The *Dover Castle* was torpedoed and the commander of the U-boat involved pleaded that he had acted on Admiralty orders issued in the belief that hospital ships, contrary to the law of war, were being used for military purposes.[62] He was acquitted, since "it is a military principle that the subordinate is bound to obey the rules of his superiors. . . . When the execution of a service order involves an offence against the criminal law, the superior giving the order is alone responsible. . . . The Admiralty Staff was the highest service authority over the accused. He was in duty bound to obey their orders in service matters. So far as he did that, he was free from criminal responsibility." The tribunal was of opinion that in the circumstances of the case the accused was entitled to believe that the orders concerning foreign hospital ships were not contrary to international law, but were reprisals.

Only six weeks later, the *Reichsgericht* showed that the defence was not as extensive as might have appeared from the *Dover Castle*

[61] (1900), 17 S.C. 561 (Cape of Good Hope) (italics added). See also *R.* v. *Werner*, [1947] 2 S.A.L.R. 828.

[62] (1921) Cmd. 1450 at 42; 2 Ann. Dig. 429.

decision. The accused in the *Llandovery Castle*[63] were alleged to have opened fire on the survivors of the torpedoed hospital ship causing grave loss of life, and pleaded the orders of the U-boat commander. On this occasion, the court said:

> [N]o importance is to be attached to the statements put forward by the defence, that the enemies of Germany were making improper use of hospital ships for military purposes, and that they had repeatedly fired on German lifeboats and shipwrecked people. . . . Whether this belief was founded on fact or not, is of less importance as affecting the case before the court, than the established fact that the *Llandovery Castle* at the time was not carrying any cargo or troops prohibited [under the Hague Convention on Naval Warfare (Convention X). The killing of the survivors was homicide under the German Penal Code, and was also] an offence against the law of nations. . . . Any violation of the law of nations in warfare is . . . a punishable offence, so far as, in general, a penalty is attached to the deed. The killing of enemies in war is in accordance with the will of the State that makes war (whose laws as to the legality or illegality on the question of killing are decisive), only in so far as such killing is in accordance with the conditions and limitations imposed by the law of nations. The fact that his deed is a violation of International Law must be *well-known* to the doer. . . . The rule of International Law, which is here involved, is *simple and universally known*. No possible doubt can exist with regard to the question of its applicability. . . . [The] order does not free the accused from guilt. . . . [A]ccording to para. 47 of the Military Penal Code . . . the subordinate obeying [an] order [involving a violation of the law] is liable to punishment, if it was *known* to him that the order of the superior involved the infringement of civil or military law. . . . It is certainly to be urged in favour of the military subordinates that they are under no obligation to question the order of their superior officer, and they can count upon its legality. But no such confidence can be held to exist, if such an order is *universally known to everybody, including also the accused*, to be *without any doubt whatsoever* against the law. As naval officers by profession [the accused] were *well aware* . . . that one is not legally authorized to kill defenceless people. They well knew that this was the case here. . . . They should, therefore, have refused to obey. As they did not do so, they must be punished.

The court rejected the idea that the orders might have been enforced by violence, pointing out that in such circumstances the order would have been impossible of achievement, but recognized that to "have refused to obey the order . . . would have required a specially high degree of resolution. A refusal to obey the commander of a submarine would have been something so unusual that it is

[63] (1921) Cmd. 1450, at 45; 2 Ann. Dig. 436 (italics added). Both these decisions are reproduced in Cameron, *The Peleus Trial* (1948).

humanly possible to understand that the accused could not bring themselves to disobey. That certainly does not make them innocent. . . . They had acquired the habit of obedience to military authority and could not rid themselves of it. This justifies the recognition of mitigating circumstances in determining the punishment. . . . The killing of defenceless shipwrecked people is an act in the *highest degree contrary to ethical principles. . . .*"

In some war crimes trials the defence is put forward, only to be rejected on the ground that no such order was in fact given. In the *Crusius* case it was alleged that accused had been ordered to shoot prisoners of war; the Leipzig Court found that the alleged remark related only to wounded enemies suddenly resuming hostilities, and "Such an order, if it were issued, would not have been contrary to international principles, for the protection afforded by the regulations for land warfare does not extend to such wounded who take up arms again and renew the fight. Such men have by so doing forfeited the claim for mercy granted to them by the laws of warfare. On the other hand, an order of the nature maintained by the accused Crusius would have had *absolutely no* justification."[64]

Despite the decision in *Smith* and the *Llandovery Castle*, and the provision in the German Military Penal Code, the principle was not generally accepted that superior orders provided no defence to a charge of war crimes, merely serving to mitigate the punishment. The first edition of Oppenheim's *International Law* stated that "in case members of forces commit violations ordered by their commanders, the members cannot be punished, for the commanders alone are responsible, and the latter may, therefore, be punished as war criminals on their capture by the enemy."[65] A similar statement appears in the 1914 edition of the British *Manual of Military Law*,[66] but this is perhaps not surprising in view of the fact that Oppenheim was joint author of the section of the *Manual* on the "Law and Usages of Warfare on Land." The United States *Rules of Land Warfare* were based on the British *Manual*, and a similar provision is to be found in the 1940 edition.[67] The first edition of Oppenheim published after the First Word War appeared with the statement unchanged, although Roxburgh as editor added a note that "the contrary is sometimes asserted . . . [but] the law cannot require an

[64] (1921), 2 Ann. Dig. 438, note *b*.

[65] Vol. 2, S. 253 (1906).

[66] Para. 443 (the 1929 ed. is to the same effect).

[67] 1914, Art. 366; 1940, Art. 345.

individual to be punished for an act which he was compelled by law to commit,"[68] and even in the fourth edition McNair seems to consider the statement to be consistent with customary law.[69] The first mention that is made of the *Llandovery Castle* in Oppenheim is to be found in the first edition prepared by Lauterpacht.[70] There is a simple reference to the decision in a footnote, but it is not regarded as having had any effect on what the editor regards as the traditional rule.

A fundamental change is to be found in the editions of 1940 and 1944, both of which were prepared by Lauterpacht. The entire paragraph has been rewritten to read:

> The fact that a rule of warfare has been violated in pursuance of an order of the belligerent Government or of an individual belligerent commander does not deprive the act in question of its character as a war crime; neither does it, in principle, confer upon the perpetrator immunity from punishment by the injured belligerent. . . . Undoubtedly, a Court confronted with the plea of superior orders adduced in justification of a war crime is bound to take into consideration the fact that obedience to military orders *not obviously unlawful*, is the duty of every member of the armed forces and that the latter cannot, in conditions of war discipline, be expected to weigh scrupulously the legal merits of the order received. . . . However, . . . the question is governed by the major principle that members of the armed forces are bound to obey lawful orders only and that they cannot therefore escape liability if, in obedience to a command, they commit acts which both violate *unchallenged rules of warfare and outrage the general sentiment of humanity.*[71]

This statement of the law is supported by a reference to the decision in the *Llandovery Castle*. Lauterpacht appears to justify his departure from previous editions, including his own, by stating that "a different view has occasionally been adopted in military manuals and by writers, but it is difficult to regard it as expressing a sound legal principle."[72] In explanation of the reference to "writers," he comments: "n.2. See, e.g., § 253 of the previous editions of this volume. . . . However, the great majority of writers is in favour of the view advanced in the text."

[68] 1921, S. 253, at 342, n. 3.

[69] 1926, S. 253, at 410, n. 2.

[70] 1935, S. 253, at 452, n. 1.

[71] 1944, S. 253, at 452-53 (italics added), and 453, n. 2 (the same statement appears in the 7th ed., 1952, the last edited by Lauterpacht).

[72] *Ibid.*, 453.

It was not only the leading English textbook on international law that was amended in this way after the outbreak of the Second World War. The British *Manual* statement was also changed, and the wording that Lauterpacht had introduced into Oppenheim was adopted *expressis verbis*.[73] Seven months later a similar amendment was made to the United States Field Service Manual to the effect that "individuals and organizations who violate the *accepted laws and customs of war* may be punished therefor,"[74] but superior orders "may be taken into consideration in determining culpability, either by way of defense or in mitigation of punishment."

The French authorities, too, felt that a restatement of the law on this subject was necessary. During the First World War the writers differed as to the availability of the defence to Germans accused of war crimes, with the majority rejecting the defence, and "In every case where the plea of superior command was invoked the courts made short shrift of it and if the evidence established the guilt of the accused he was condemned, even when he produced conclusive proof that he acted under orders."[75] Article 327 of the *Code Pénal* provides that "no crime or delict is committed when the homicide ... was ordered by law or by legal authority," but the Ordinance concerning the Prosecution of War Criminals removes this defence regarding "Laws, decrees or regulations issued by the enemy authorities, orders or permits issued by these authorities ... which are or have been subordinated to them ..., but can only, in suitable cases, be pleaded as an extenuating or exculpating circumstance."[76]

Other Allied countries tended to introduce similar legislation, frequently after their liberation, in order to make it clear that in trials before their military courts no accused would be able to avoid responsibility on the plea that he was acting under orders, especially as it was so easy to cite as the superior responsible some officer who was either dead or untraceable.[77] The practice of the tribunals established after 1945 illustrates the way in which the defence has developed in modern times, and for our purpose it is only necessary

[73] Amendment 34, April 1944 (text reproduced in Cameron, *op. cit. supra* note 63, at 150).

[74] Change No. 1, November 15, 1944 (italics added — *ibid.*, 152).

[75] 2 Garner, *International Law and the World War* 487 (1920).

[76] 3 UN War Crimes Commission, *Law Reports of Trials of War Criminals* 93, 96.

[77] For some of these laws, see *ibid.*, vol. 5, at 20-23; for the Soviet position, see Greenspan, *The Modern Law of Land Warfare* 491 (1959).

to draw attention to a relatively small selection of the trials that took place.

There is a general tendency to assume that the Nuremberg Judgment[78] is the only one that needs citing in connection with war crimes, but there were already a number of decisions in which the defence of superior orders had been considered before that judgment was rendered. Of those in Europe perhaps the most important was the *Peleus* case (1945),[79] the first of the trials to be held. Apart from the fact that the vessel was a merchant ship, the facts were almost identical with those in the *Llandovery Castle*, and on this occasion one officer successfully refused to obey the order to fire on survivors, although he subsequently did so. As to the defence, the Judge Advocate said:

> [T]he duty to obey is limited to the observance of orders which are lawful. There can be no duty to obey that which is not a lawful order. . . . The fact that a rule of warfare has been violated in pursuance of an order of a belligerent government, or of an individual belligerent commander, does not deprive the act in question of its character as a war crime, neither does it confer upon the perpetrator immunity from punishment by the injured belligerent. Undoubtedly a Court confronted with a plea of superior orders adduced in justification of a war crime is bound to take into consideration the fact that obedience of military orders *not obviously unlawful* is a duty of every member of the Armed Forces, and that the latter cannot in conditions of war discipline be expected to weigh scrupulously the legal merits of the order received. The question, however, is governed by the major consideration that members of the Armed Forces are bound to obey *lawful orders only*, and that they cannot therefore escape liability if in obedience to a command they commit acts which both *violate unchallenged rules of warfare and outrage the general sentiment of humanity.* It is quite obvious that no sailor and no soldier can carry with him a library of International Law, or have immediate access to a professor in that subject who can tell him whether or not a particular command is a lawful one. . . . [I]s it not fairly obvious to you that if in fact the carrying out of [the] command involved the killing of these helpless survivors, it was not a lawful command, and that it must have been *obvious to the most rudimentary intelligence that it was not a lawful command*, and that those who did that shooting are not to be excused for doing it upon the ground of superior orders? . . .

Among the other trials held before the Nuremberg Judgment was delivered, that concerning the atrocities at Jaluit Atoll and known

[78] 1946, H.M.S.O., Cmd. 6964; 41 Am. J. Int'l L. 172 (1947).

[79] Cameron, *op. cit. supra* note 63, at 128-29 (for an abbreviated text, see 13 Ann. Dig. 248, *sub. nom. In re Eck* — italics added).

as the *Masuda* case[80] is of interest. One of the defence counsel was an officer in the Japanese Navy and drew attention to the absolute discipline and obedience expected in the Japanese forces, citing the Imperial Rescript which states that "Subordinates should have the idea that the orders from their superiors are nothing but the orders personally from His Majesty the Emperor," and he contended that it was impossible to apply "the liberal and individualistic ideas which rule usual societies unmodified to this totalistic and absolutistic military society." The accused were sentenced to death, the Judge Advocate having accepted the statement from an earlier [unnamed] case that "An order *illegal in itself* and *not justified by the rules and usages of war*, or in its substance *clearly illegal, so that a man of ordinary sense and understanding would know* as soon as he heard the order read or given that it was illegal, will afford no protection for a homicide, provided the act with which he may be charged has all the ingredients in it which may be necessary to constitute the same crime in law." A somewhat similar view was taken by the Canadian Military Court which tried *Holzer* at Aurich, Germany.[81] The accused was charged with killing a Canadian prisoner of war and the Judge Advocate quoted Lauterpacht's statement from Oppenheim, and asserted that the *Llandovery Castle* had clearly established that "The defence of superior orders would afford no defence if the act was *manifestly and indisputably contrary to international law* as for instance the killing of unarmed enemies." He also applied the common law test with regard to the validity of a defence based on coercion or duress.

The British court in the *Buck* case[82] recognized that certain basic facts had to be recognized. As the Judge Advocate said, "What did each of these accused know about the rights of a prisoner of war? . . . The Court may well think that the men are not lawyers: they may not have heard either of the Hague Convention or the Geneva Convention; they may not have seen any book of military law upon the subject; but the Court has to consider whether men who are serving either as soldiers or in proximity to soldiers know as a matter of the *general facts of military life* whether a prisoner of war has

80 (1945), 1 *Law Reports of Trials of War Criminals* 71, 74 (italics added). In fact, Rear Admiral Masuda committed suicide before the trial opened and a *nolle prosequi* was entered in his case.

81 (1946), 5 *ibid.*, 15 (italics added).

82 (1946), 13 Ann. Dig. 293-94 (italics added).

certain rights . . . [including], when captured [the right to] security for his person. . . . The position under international law is that it is contrary to rules of international law to murder a prisoner. . . . " He then cited Oppenheim with approval and expressed the view that a man would be guilty of a war crime in pursuance of an order if "the order was *obviously unlawful*, if the accused knew that the order was unlawful, or if he *ought to have known it to be unlawful* had he considered the circumstances in which it had been given." The same British Military Court held only a month later that no one had to obey an unlawful order, and that it was no defence to argue that German law would not consider an order to kill in the circumstances of the case as unlawful, provided, said the Judge Advocate, that the Court was satisfied that "the order was *one which could not have been tolerated in any place where a system of justice was used. . . .*"[83]

In so far as the Nuremberg Tribunal was concerned, it had no option but to reject the defence of superior orders, for this was clearly provided by its Charter of establishment. The Tribunal dealt with the defence somewhat shortly:

> [I]ndividuals have international duties which transcend the national obligations of obedience imposed by the individual State. He who violates the laws of war cannot obtain immunity while acting in pursuance of the authority of the State if the State in authorising action moves outside its competence under international law. . . . That a soldier was ordered to kill or torture in violation of the international law of war has never been recognised as a defence to such acts of brutality, though . . . the order may be urged in mitigation of the punishment. The true test, which is found in varying degrees in the criminal law of most nations is not the existence of the order, but whether *moral choice* was in fact possible. . . . Superior orders . . . cannot be considered in mitigation where *crimes as shocking* and extensive have been *committed consciously, ruthlessly and without military excuse or justification*. . . . Participation in such crimes as these has never been required of any soldier and he cannot now shield himself behind a mythical requirement of soldierly obedience at all costs as his excuse for commission of these crimes. . . . [In fact,] many of these men have made a mockery of the soldier's oath of obedience to military orders. When it suits their defence they say they had to obey; when confronted with Hitler's brutal crimes, which are shown to have been within their general knowledge, they say they disobeyed. The truth is they actively participated in all these crimes, or sat silent and acquiescent, witnessing the commission of

[83] *Rohde Case* (1946), 5 *Law Reports of Trials of War Criminals* 54, 58 (italics added).

crimes on a scale larger and more shocking than the world has ever had the misfortune to know.[84]

Of the trials that took place in the years immediately following Nuremberg perhaps those of the United States Military Tribunals sitting at Nuremberg are the most important, and many of them are more concerned with public knowledge and understanding than the International Military Tribunal's concept of "moral choice." Thus, in *Re Milch* the tribunal pointed out:

[V]ery soon [after the accused joined the Nazi Party in 1933] he must have realized that he had joined a band of villains whose programme contemplated every crime in the calendar. The Nazi code was not a secret. It was published and proclaimed by the Party leaders. . . . The *humblest citizens* of Germany *knew* that *the iniquitous doctrines* of the Party were *being implemented by ruthless acts of persecution and terrorism which occurred in public view*. . . . The defendant did not live in a vacuum. He was not blind or deaf. Long before 1939; long before his military loyalty was called into play; long before the door to withdrawal was closed, he could have seen the bloody handwriting on the wall, for murder and enslavement of his own countrymen was there written in blazing symbols. But he had taken on the crimson mantle of the Party. . . . Others with more courage and higher principles and with more loyalty to the ancient German ideals rebelled and withdrew. . . . The defendant had his opportunity to join those who refused to do the evil bidding of an evil master, but he cast it aside. . . . By accepting such attractive and lucrative posts under a head whose power they knew to be unlimited, they ratify in advance his every act, good or bad. They cannot say at the beginning, "The Führer's decisions are final; we will have no voice in them; it is not for us to reason why; his will is law", and then, when the Führer decrees . . . barbarous inhumanities . . . to attempt to exculpate themselves by saying, "Oh, we were never in favour of *those* things". . . . [85]

Field Marshal Milch's case is typical of those involving senior officers, as became clear in the *High Command Trial* itself; the Tribunal there rejected the plea, saying:

All of the defendants in this case held official positions in the armed forces of the Third Reich. Hitler from 1938 on was Commander-in-Chief of the Armed Forces and was the Supreme Civil and Military Authority in the Third Reich, whose personal decrees had the force and effect of law. Under such circumstances to recognise as a defence . . . that a defendant acted pursuant to the order of his government or of a

[84] *Op. cit supra* note 78, at 42, 83, 92, 118; 221, 271-72, 283, 316 resp. (italics added).

[85] (1947), 7 *Law Reports of Trials of War Criminals* 27, 41-42 (italics added).

superior would be in practical effect to say that all the guilt charged . . . was the guilt of Hitler alone because he alone possessed the law-making power of the State and the supreme authority to issue civil and military directives. To recognise such a contention would be to recognize an absurdity. . . . The rejection of the defence of superior orders . . . would follow of necessity from our holding that the acts . . . are criminal . . . because they then were crimes under International Common Law. International Common Law must be superior to and, where it conflicts with, take precedence over National Law or directives issued by any governmental authority. A directive to violate International Common Law is therefore void and can afford no protection to one who violates such law in reliance on such a directive. . . . The defendants . . . who received *obviously criminal orders* were placed in a difficult position but servile compliance with orders *clearly criminal* for fear of some disadvantage or punishment not immediately threatened cannot be recognised as a defence. To establish the defence of coercion or necessity in the face of danger there must be a showing of circumstances such that a *reasonable man* would apprehend that he was in such imminent physical peril as to deprive him of freedom to choose the right and refrain from the wrong. . . . [Moreover,] . . . an article by Goebbels . . . contained the following correct statement of the law: "It is not provided in any military law that a soldier in the case of a *despicable crime* is exempt from punishment because he passes the responsibility to his superior, especially if the orders of the latter are in *evident contradiction to all human morality and every international usage of warfare*." . . . Within certain limitations, [a soldier] has the right to assume that the orders of his superiors and the State which he serves and which are issued to him are in conformity with International Law. Many of the defendants here were field commanders. . . . Their legal facilities were limited. They were soldiers — not lawyers. Military commanders in the field with far reaching military responsibilities cannot be charged under International Law with criminal participation in issuing orders which are not obviously criminal or which they are not shown to have known to be criminal under International Law. Such a commander cannot be expected to draw fine distinctions as to legality in connection with orders issued by his superiors. He has the right to presume, in the absence of specific knowledge to the contrary, that the legality of such orders has been properly determined before their issuance. He cannot be held criminally responsible for a mere error of judgment as to disputable legal questions.[86] It is therefore considered that to find a field commander criminally responsible for the transmittal of such an order, he must have passed the order to the chain of command and the order must be one that is *criminal upon its face*, or one which he is shown to have known was criminal.[87]

In the *Hostages Trial* the issue was complicated by reason of the

[86] Cp. comments of Lord Mansfield in *Wall* v. *M'Namara*, *supra* note 39.

[87] *In re Von Leeb* (1948), 12 *ibid.*, 1, 71-74 (italics added).

fact that the defence made use of the earlier statements of Oppenheim and the military *Manuals*; according to the court:

[T]he rule that superior order is not a defence to a criminal act is a rule of fundamental criminal justice that has been adopted by civilized nations extensively.... [T]he municipal law of civilised nations generally sustained the principle at the time the alleged criminal acts were committed. This being true, it properly may be declared as an applicable rule of International Law.... Implicit obedience to orders of superior officers is almost indispensable to every military system. But this implies obedience to *lawful orders only*. If the act done pursuant to a superior's order be murder, the production of the order will not make it any less so. It *may mitigate but it cannot justify* the crime.... [I]f the illegality of the order was not known to the inferior and he could not *reasonably* have been expected to know of its illegality, no wrongful intent necessary to the commission of a crime exists and the inferior will be protected. But the general rule is that members of the armed forces are bound to obey only the *lawful orders* of their commanding officers and they cannot escape criminal liability by obeying a command which violates International Law and *outrages fundamental concepts of justice*.... The defence relies heavily upon the writings of Prof. L. Oppenheim to sustain their position. It is true that he advocated this principle throughout his writings. As a co-author of the *British Manual of Military Law*, he incorporated the principle there. It seems also to have found its way into the United States *Rules of Land Warfare* (1940). We think Professor Oppenheim espoused a decidedly minority view.... [His] statement completely overlooks the fact that an illegal order is in no sense of the word a valid law which one is obliged to obey. The fact that the British and American armies may have adopted it for the regulation of their own armies as a matter of policy, does not have the effect of enthroning it as a rule of International Law.... [A]rmy regulations are not a competent source of International Law. They are neither legislative nor judicial pronouncements. They are not competent for any purpose in determining whether a *fundamental principle of justice has been accepted by civilized nations generally*. It is possible, however, that such regulations, as they bear upon a question of custom and practice in the conduct of war, might have evidentiary value, particularly if the applicable portions had been put into general practice. It will be observed that the determination whether a custom or practice exists, is a question of fact. Whether a fundamental principle of justice has been accepted is a question of judicial or legislative declaration. In determining the former, military regulations may play an important role but, in the latter, they do not constitute an authoritative precedent. Those who hold to the view that superior order is a complete defence to an International Law crime, base it largely on a conflict in the articles of war promulgated by several leading nations. While we are of opinion that army regulations are not a competent source of International Law where a fundamental rule of justice is concerned, we submit that the conflict in any event does not sustain the position claimed for it. . . . If the Court finds that the army regulations of some members of the family of nations provide that superior orders is a complete defence and that the army regulations of other nations express a contrary view, the Court would be obliged to hold . . . that general acceptance or consent was lacking among the family of nations. Inasmuch as a substantial conflict exists among the nations whether superior order is a defence to a criminal charge, it could only result in a further finding that the basis does not exist for declaring superior order to be a defence to an International Law crime. But . . . army regulations are not a competent source of International Law when a fundamental rule of justice is concerned. This leaves the way clear for the Court to affirmatively declare that superior order is not a defence to an International Law crime if it finds that the principle involved is a fundamental rule of justice and for that reason has found general acceptance. International Law has never approved the defensive plea of superior order as a mandatory bar to the prosecution of war criminals. This defensive plea is not available to the defendants . . . , although . . . it may be considered in mitigation of punishment. . . . [88]

It is perhaps unfortunate that the tribunal did not take the opportunity to point out that by both English and American criminal law the defence was strictly limited and far more restrictive than would appear from the *Manuals*. Moreover, as is pointed out in the 1956 edition of the American *Army Field Manual — Law of Land Warfare*, "those provisions of the Manual which are neither statutes nor the text of treaties to which the United States is a party should not be considered binding upon courts and tribunals applying the law of war,"[89] for military *Manuals* are just like textbooks merely for guidance as to what the law is. If they are not in accordance with established law, tribunals will disregard them. If it is felt that such statements represent the law and are adopted, it is the acceptance by the court and not the statement in the *Manual* or the textbook which is declaratory of the law. Furthermore, while it may be generally true that *lex specialis derogat generali*, the World Court has shown[90] that this is not an inevitable principle, and where the *lex specialis* itself purports to apply the *lex generalis* as does Anglo-

[88] *In re List* (1948), 15 Ann. Dig. 632, 649-52 (italics added).

[89] FM27-10, para. 1. See also, Garner, *op. cit.*, n. 75 above, vol. 1, at 12; who describes such *Manuals* as "for the guidance of military and naval forces . . . [which] may, of course, be altered by the government which issues them, except in so far as the obligatory character of their rules is established by international law."

[90] *Rights of Minorities in Upper Silesia (Minority Schools)*, P.C.I.J. Ser. A, No. 15, at 31, 33 (1928); *Ambatielos case* (Prelim. Obj.), (1952) I.C.J. Rep. 28, 42.

American military law it is by no means improper that, when it is found that the *lex specialis* is incompatible with the *lex generalis*, the former is amended to bring it into line.

Of all the decisions of the American tribunals dealing with the defence, perhaps that in the *Einsatzgruppen Trial*[91] is the most comprehensive; there the tribunal said:

[T]he obedience of a soldier is not the obedience of an automaton. A soldier is a reasoning agent. He does not respond, and is not expected to respond, like a piece of machinery. It is a fallacy of widespread consumption that a soldier is required to do everything his superior officer orders him to do [e.g., shoot a superior]. . . . [A]n order to require obedience must relate to military duty.[92] . . . And what the superior officer may not militarily demand of his subordinate, the subordinate is not required to do. Even if the order refers to a military subject it must be one which the superior is authorised under the circumstances to give. The subordinate is bound to obey only the lawful orders of his superior and if he accepts a criminal order and executes it with a malice of his own, he may not plead Superior Orders in mitigation of his defense. If the nature of the ordered act is *manifestly beyond the scope* of the superior's authority, the subordinate may not plead ignorance of the criminality of the order. If one claims duress in the execution of an illegal order it must be shown that the harm caused by obeying the illegal order is not disproportionately greater than the harm which would result from not obeying the illegal order. It would not be an adequate excuse . . . if a subordinate, under orders, killed a person known to be innocent, because by not obeying it he himself would risk a few days of confinement. Nor if one acts under duress, may he, without culpability, commit the illegal act once the duress ceases. . . .

After citing the Nuremberg Judgment, the tribunal referred to German military codes going back to that of Prussia, 1845, which provided for punishment if the subordinate knew the order "related to an act which is *obviously aimed at a crime*" and finished its survey by referring to the German author Schwinge who wrote in 1940: "Hence, in military life, just as in other fields, the principle of absolute, i.e., blind obedience, does not exist." It then continued:

Yet, one of the most generally quoted statements on this subject is that a German soldier must obey orders though the heavens fall. The statement has become legendary. The facts prove that it is a myth. . . . To plead Superior Orders one must show an *excusable ignorance of their illegality*. . . . What S.S. man could say that he was unaware of the attitude of Hitler towards Jewry? . . . But it is stated that in military

91 *In re Ohlendorf* (1948), 15 Ann. Dig. 656, 665-68 (italics added).

92 Cp. *State* v. *Roy*, *supra* note 57.

law even if the subordinate realizes that the act he is called upon to perform is a crime, he may not refuse its execution without incurring serious consequences, and that this, therefore, constitutes duress.... [T]here is no law which requires that an innocent man must forfeit his life or suffer serious harm in order to avoid committing a crime which he condemns. The threat, however, must be *imminent, real and inevitable*.... The test to be applied is whether the subordinate acted under coercion or whether he himself approved of the principle involved in the order. If the second proposition be true, the plea of Superior Orders fails. The doer may not plead innocence to a criminal act ordered by his superior if he is in accord with the principle and intent of the superior. Where the will of the doer merges with the will of the superior in the execution of the illegal act, the doer may not plead duress under Superior Orders. If the mental and moral capacities of the superior and subordinate are pooled in the planning and execution of an illegal act, the subordinate may not subsequently protest that he was forced into the performance of an illegal undertaking. Superior means superior in capacity and power to force a certain act. It does not mean superiority only in rank.... If the cognizance of the doer has been such, prior to the receipt of the illegal order, that the order is *obviously but one further logical step in the development of a program which he knew to be illegal in its very inception*, he may not excuse himself from responsibility for an illegal act which could have been *foreseen by the application of the simple law of cause and effect*.... One who embarks on a criminal enterprise of *obvious magnitude* is *expected to anticipate* what the enterprise will logically lead to. In order successfully to plead the defense of Superior Orders the opposition of the doer must be constant. It is not enough that he mentally rebel at the time the order is received. If at any time after receiving the order he acquiesce in its illegal character, the defense of Superior Orders is closed to him.[93]

The American tribunals were not alone in their attitude. In *Müller's Case* the Belgian Court of Cassation agreed that the defence would not lie when the order " 'should be disobeyed in view of its *manifest violation of a superior principle of humanity*' ... [and its] '*flagrantly illegal character* ... *universally recognised* as being contrary to law'."[94]

Since the termination of war crimes trials by Allied tribunals, there had been little opportunity for comment upon the defence of superior orders other than from German and Israeli tribunals, until United States courts martial began hearings in Korea and Vietnam.

93 See, however, *Peleus Trial*, *supra* note 63, re accused Lenz, and debate initiated by Lord Cork and Orrery in House of Lords, April 25, 1950.

94 *Auditeur-Général près la Cour Militaire* v. *Müller* (1949), 16 Ann. Dig. 400, 402 (italics added).

The new Bundeswehr was founded in 1956 and a year later a new military criminal law — *Wehrstrafgesetz* — was introduced concerning the rights of a soldier in peacetime, and expressly recognizing his right to disobey an order he believes to be criminal. Under the new law, an order can be disobeyed when it would lead to the commission of a crime or misdemeanour; if the subordinate nevertheless carries out the order, he incurs no guilt if he does not know, and it is not *apparent* to him that a crime or misdemeanour is thereby committed.[95] This reminds one of the position in Canada, although there is no provision made for the manner in which the subordinate is to record his doubts and apparently compliance after indicating those doubts would not be considered sufficient to ground a defence.[96] As regards trials arising out of the war, German courts have been faced with the usual plea of compliance with orders. In the *Burmeister Case* the accused stated that he did not think about his orders, assuming that since it was wartime and they came from the highest quarters, they must have been alright. The Bonn Court rejected the plea of obedience to orders since the accused had supported the Nazi "death machine" and "had been *clearly aware* that the extermination of Jews was a crime."[97] In a later case the court took the line that the accused were entitled to the benefit of the doubt to an extent sufficient to reduce murder charges to manslaughter findings.[98] The verdict is not easy to accept, even though one might agree with the judge that there were "little fishes sitting in the dock, while the sharks swim around free"; it is difficult to see how nurses participating in the euthanasia programme who had injected fatal doses on instructions from doctors could possibly be unaware of the illegality of their actions or of their abuse of the patients' trust. A more dignified attitude was adopted by Alfred Rapp, a former S.S. commander of an extermination camp; he stated that "what has happened is so frightful that I neither can nor will ask for lenience" and declined to plead obedience to orders, although he maintained that it had been impossible for anyone to go against them.[99] This does not tally with evidence given at the S.S. cavalry trial at Frankfurt, at which Dr. H. G. Seraphim, a historian, stated that not one case was known of an S.S. man being

95 *The Times*, February 8, 1957.

96 See *supra* note 16.

97 *The Times*, December 12, 1962, April 1, 1963.

98 *Ibid.*, March 13, 1965.

99 *Ibid.*, March 19, 1965.

punished for refusing to take part in mass executions, although there were countless examples of refusal to obey such orders receiving little or no attention; he agreed, however, that it probably required more than a little courage to refuse to obey.[100]

One of the most famous war crimes trials of recent years was that of Adolf Eichmann,[101] who insisted that everything he did was in accordance with superior orders. The District Court pointed out that for the defence to succeed necessitated considering whether the orders were "*manifestly unlawful*" and held that whether this was in fact the case was a question of law to be decided by the court by objective tests. Their task was facilitated, however, by Eichmann's own statement "that I see in this murder, in the extermination of Jews, one of the gravest crimes in the history of humanity . . . I already realised at the time that this solution by the use of force was something unlawful, something terrible. . . . " The Supreme Court repeated that the orders were "*manifestly unlawful . . . contrary to the basic ideas of law and justice*," and pointed out that Eichmann "performed the order of extermination at all times *con amore*, with full zeal and devotion to the task." In fact, as the District Court made clear, its decision was in line with that of the Israeli District Military Court and Court of Appeal in *Chief Military Prosecutor* v. *Melinki*,[102] a trial of Israeli military personnel arising out of their actions at Kafr Kassem in 1956. In the District Court Judge Halevy, one of the members of the court trying Eichmann, said:

> [T]he distinguishing mark of a "manifestly unlawful order" should fly like a black flag above the order given, as a warning saying "Prohibited". Not formal unlawfulness, hidden or half-hidden, nor unlawfulness discernible only by the eyes of legal experts, is important here, but *a flagrant and manifest breach of the law, definite and necessary unlawfulness appearing on the face of the order itself, the clearly criminal character of the acts ordered to be done, unlawfulness piercing the eye and revolting the heart, be the eye not blind nor the heart stony and corrupt* — that is the measure of "manifest unlawfulness" required to release a soldier from the duty of obedience upon him and make him criminally responsible for his acts.

100 *Ibid.*, April 7, 1964. See also evidence of Dr. Adelaide Hurtval in *Dering* v. *Uris*, [1964] 2 W.L.R. 1298 for an example of a prisoner successfully refusing to take part in medical experiments (Hall and Williams, *Auschwitz in England*, 1965).

101 *A.G., Israel* v. *Eichmann* (1961/62), 36 I.L.R. 5 (District Court), 277 (Supreme Court), 257-58, 314-15, 318 (italics added).

102 (1958) cited *Eichmann, ibid.*, 256-57 (italics added).

The Court of Appeal put it in slightly less dramatic terms, "calling in aid the *feeling of lawfulness* which lies hidden deep *within the conscience of every human as such*, even if not conversant with the law books."

In view of the experience gained after the Second World War and as if determined to avoid being faced with similar contentions concerning superior orders again, including, as in the *Einsatzgruppen* case, allegations of *ex post* legislation, the British and American governments issued new military *Manuals* in which the references to superior orders are fully in accord with modern practice. According to the 1951 edition of the British *Manual of Military Law*,[103] physical force removes the stigma of criminality, as does, generally speaking, threats, "moral force," violence not amounting to physical compulsion, hunger or danger to life or property. As to superior orders, it provides that if an order is "manifestly illegal, [a person] is under a legal duty to refuse to carry out the order and if he does carry it out he will be criminally responsible for what he does in doing so." It goes on to say that even if the order relates to an act which is illegal, but not manifestly so, the subordinate actor will not be excused, although it may give rise to a defence on other grounds, such as reducing a charge of culpable negligence. That part of the *Manual* which deals with "The Law of War on Land"[104] clearly states that "obedience to the order of a government or of a superior, whether military or civil, or to a national law or regulation, affords no defence to a charge of committing a war crime but may be considered in mitigation of punishment." It also provides that no criminal responsibility lies in the face of physical compulsion against his will, or if his own life is in danger, unless the act involves the taking of innocent life. Otherwise threats are no defence, but may again mitigate punishment, as would compulsion arising from hunger or immediate danger to life or property. This latter does not concern itself with physical compulsion by a third party. The American *Field Manual* on "The Law of Land Warfare"[105] likewise makes no reference to manifest illegality, although it does say that armies are only obliged to obey "lawful orders." In so far as the law of war has been violated as the result of an order, the order does not "constitute a defense in the trial of an accused individual, unless he did not know and *could not reasonably have been expected to know*

103 Part I, ch. V, s. 23.

104 Part III, paras. 627-30.

105 FM27-10, 1956, para. 509.

that the act ordered was unlawful," but even then the order may result in punishment being mitigated.

It was probably not expected that the first test of the present American approach to superior orders would be experienced against American troops alleged to have committed crimes against an enemy in an undeclared war. But this is the situation as a result of the wars in Korea and Vietnam. The uproar in the public media concerning the Song My (My Lai) atrocities has implied that the United States authorities have been unaware of the methods of unlawful warfare engaged in by their forces or have sought to "hush up" any cases of which they may have learned. In fact, this is far from being the case and long before this *cause célèbre* became known, American courts martial in operation areas were trying United States personnel for what, if they had been committed by the enemy or an ally — although the tendency has been to leave the allied authorities to try their own if they so wish — would have been treated as war crimes. In 1966 an accused charged with the premeditated murder of a Vietnamese was sentenced to 35 years, and in the course of its judgment the tribunal said that "the issuance or execution of an order to kill under the circumstances of this case is unjustifiable under the laws of this nation, the principles of international law, or the laws of land warfare. Such an order would have been beyond the scope of authority for a superior to give and would have been *palpably unlawful*."[106] In an effort to define "palpable unlawfulness," reference might be made to Winthrop's *Military Law and Precedents*,[107] which indicates what is regarded as an illegal order in words that have been accepted by courts martial: "... but to justify an inferior in disobeying an order as illegal, the case must be an extreme one and the illegality not doubtful. The order must be clearly repugnant to some specific statute, to the law or usage of military service, or to the general law of the land. The unlawfulness of the command must thus be a fact, and, in view of the authority of military orders emanating from official superiors, the onus of establishing this fact will, in all cases — except where the order is palpably illegal upon its face — devolve upon the defense and clear and convincing evidence will be required to rebut the presumption."[108] This statement forms the basis for the relevant paragraph

[106] *U.S.* v. *Schultz* (1966, court martial; 1968 Review Board) 39 C.M.R. 133, 136 (italics added).

[107] 2d ed., 1920, at 575.

[108] See, for example, *U.S.* v. *Ciesielski* (1968), 39 C.M.R. 839, 850.

of the *Manual for Courts Martial* that, "to justify from a military point of view a military inferior in disobeying the order of a superior, the order must be one requiring something to be done which is palpably a breach of law and a crime or injury to a third person, or is of a serious character (not involving unimportant consequences only) and if done would not be susceptible of being righted. An order requiring the performance of a military duty or act can not be disobeyed with impunity unless it has one of these characteristics."[109] However, it must be borne in mind that "an order requiring the performance of a military duty or act is presumed to be lawful and is disobeyed at the peril of the subordinate."[110]

Many of the American cases refer to the allegedly unlawful killing of prisoners or suspected enemy sympathizers and the guiding rules are to be found in the *Manual for Courts Martial* which provides as follows:

> [A] homicide committed in the proper performance of a legal duty is justifiable. Thus . . . killing to prevent the escape of a prisoner if no other apparent means are adequate, killing an enemy in battle and killing to prevent the commission of an offense attempted by force or surprise . . . are cases of justifiable homicide. The general rule is that the acts of a subordinate, done in good faith in compliance with his supposed duty or orders, are justifiable. This justification does not exist, however, when those acts are manifestly beyond the scope of his authority, or the *order is such that a man of ordinary sense and understanding would know it to be illegal,* or the subordinate wilfully or through negligence does acts endangering the lives of innocent parties in the discharge of his duty to prevent escape or effect an arrest.[111]

The significance of these rules was examined in *U.S.* v. *Kinder*[112] arising from the killing of a Korean civilian, whom the evidence did not disclose as an enemy, ally, intended saboteur or thief, and who was in custody and not resisting, violent or attempting to escape or commit any offence. The order to shoot the prisoner was apparently given to scare other locals from entering the prohibited area in which he had been arrested and to boost the morale of the troops. After the killing the officer returned a false report of the circumstances, as did the accused on the instructions of the officer concerned. The accused was found guilty and sentenced to life imprisonment, which was reduced by the confirming officer to two

109 1951, para. 416.

110 *Ibid.*, para. 169B. See *U.S.* v. *Trani* (1952), 3 C.M.R. 27.

111 Para. 197 (italics added).

112 (1954), 14 C.M.R. 742, 763, 770, 773-75, 776, 781 (italics added).

years,[118] a sentence approved by the Board of Review. The accused testified that his officer had stated

> . . . that any orders that he gave were definitely not to be questioned in any way . . . and . . . he fully understood he was to obey the orders of Lieut. Schreiber no matter what they were. He knew it would have been wrong to shoot the Korean without an order. He thought Lieut. Schreiber had the authority to order the Korean shot. At the time he did not know the difference between a legal and an illegal order and thought that any order Lieut. Schreiber gave him was legal. He thought the order to shoot the Korean was legal. . . . He would not have thought an order to kill another American was illegal but he would not have obeyed it. . . . He did not know what Lieut. Schreiber would have done to him if he had not obeyed but he does not believe he would have had him shot. He had not heard of anyone being shot for an offense without getting a trial. . . .

The Board of Review found that "neither the laws of our nation, federal or military, nor the laws and usages of war as recognized by our nation and its allies, justify the issuance of an order by the accused's superior officer to kill the victim under the circumstances shown. . . . [T]he superior officer issuing the order was fully aware of its illegality . . . and maliciously and corruptly issued the unlawful order. . . ." The Board then examined a number of military and civil precedents, embracing most of the cases analyzed earlier in connection with the position under United States law, and concluded:

> [No justification will lie if the homicide is the result of an order] manifestly beyond the scope of the superior officer's authority and . . . *so obviously and palpably unlawful as to admit of no reasonable doubt on the part of a man of ordinary sense and understanding.* . . . [I]n the context of the evidence, the conclusion is inescapable that the accused was aware of the criminal nature of the order, not only from the palpably illegal nature of the order itself, but from the surreptitious circumstances under which it was necessary to execute it. . . . Of controlling significance . . . is the *manifest and unmistakable illegality* of the order. . . . Human life being regarded as sacred, moral, religious and civil law proscriptions against its taking existing throughout our society, we view the order as commanding an act so *obviously beyond the scope of authority* of the superior officer and *so palpably illegal on its face as to admit of no doubt of its unlawfulness to a man of ordinary sense and understanding*. The distance from the battle line and other

[118] In a Saigon (Vietnam) case in 1970, when the court discovered that the mandatory sentence for the crime of which the accused was found guilty was life imprisonment, it found him guilty of a different offence carrying a lesser penalty.

circumstances ... cannot be reasonably considered as furnishing any basis to *a man of ordinary sense and understanding* to assume that the laws and usages of war ... would justify the killing. In our view no rational being of the accused's age [20], formal education [grade 11], and military experience [two years] could have ... considered the order lawful. Where one obeys an order to kill ... for the apparent reason of making [the] death an example to others, the evidence must be strong indeed to raise a doubt that the slayer was not aware of the illegality of the order.... The inference of fact is compelling ... that the accused complied with the palpably unlawful order fully aware of its unlawful character.... [As to the contention] that the accused was mistaken in law as to the legality of the order of his superior officer, the defense fails for a prerequisite of such defense is that the mistake of law was an honest and reasonable one and ... the evidence ... justifies the inference that the accused was aware of the illegality of the order.

The Board rejected the argument that the accused mistakenly believed that all orders must be obeyed, and cited the *Einsatzgruppen Case*[114] to show

... that a soldier or airman is not an automaton but a "reasoning agent" who is under a duty to exercise judgment in obeying the orders of a superior officer to the extent, that where such orders are manifestly beyond the scope of the issuing officer's authority and are *so palpably illegal on their face that a man of ordinary sense and understanding would know them to be illegal*, then the fact of obedience to the order of a superior officer will not protect a soldier for acts committed pursuant to such illegal orders.... [Further,] where an airman is fully aware of the existence of a conspiracy between his superior officer and another to accomplish an unlawful purpose and in compliance with a palpably illegal order, the unlawful nature of which he is aware, commits an overt act to effect the object of the conspiracy, the necessary criminal intent is present and he has become a co-conspirator and cannot claim obedience to orders of a superior officer to prevent his conviction of conspiracy.... [115]

In *Kinder*, there was evidence to show that the superior officer had made it clear that all his orders were to be obeyed, but this did not avail the accused. In one of the Vietnam cases,[116] also involving a charge of unpremeditated murder in compliance with orders, there was evidence to show that the actions taken were "in line with training received from the Marine Corps," but the Board of Review

114 See *supra* note 91.

115 The Board agreed that if the order had been *lawful*, the accused could not have been found guilty of conspiracy: *U.S.* v. *Saglietto* (1941), 41 F. Supp. 21. For the trial of the officer issuing the order to Kinder, see *U.S.* v. *Schreiber* (1955), 18 C.M.R. 226, and see *supra* note 46.

116 *U.S.* v. *Keenan* (1969), 39 C.M.R. 108, 117 (italics added).

held, confirming the court martial's decision and Law Officer's summation, that "Marine Corps training" would not constitute a defence:

> [T]he acts of a Marine done in good faith and without malice, in compliance with the orders of a superior . . . [are] justifiable, unless such acts are manifestly beyond the scope of his authority and such that *a man of ordinary sense and understanding* would know them to be illegal. Therefore, if you find beyond a reasonable doubt that the accused under the circumstances of his age and military experience could not have honestly believed the order issued . . . "to be legal under the laws of war", then the killing of the alleged victim was without justification. A Marine is a reasoning agent, who is under a duty to exercise judgment in obeying orders to the extent that when such orders are manifestly beyond the scope of the authority of the one issuing the order, and were *palpably illegal upon their face*, then the act of obedience to such orders will not justify acts pursuant to such illegal orders.

The last case to which reference need be made here, and which expressly relied upon the *Kinder* decision, is *U.S.* v. *Griffen.*[117] Again a prisoner was shot on the orders of a superior officer; some time earlier all the members of the slayer's platoon had been killed or wounded in the same general area, and the slayer felt that the platoon's security might have been endangered if the prisoner were kept. The Review Board pointed out that "the killing of a docile prisoner taken during military operations is not justifiable homicide." It accepted as good law the view of the *Manual* that "the act of a subordinate, done in good faith in compliance with the supposed order of a superior, is not justifiable when the order is such that *a man of ordinary sense and understanding would know it to be illegal* . . . [and] it is difficult to conceive of a military situation in which the order of a superior would be more patently wrong. Accordingly, we view the order as commanding an act so obviously beyond the scope of authority of the superior officer and *so palpably illegal on its face as to admit of no doubt of its unlawfulness to a man of ordinary sense and understanding*."

It is clear from these cases that the courts have tended to measure "palpable illegality" by the "man of ordinary sense and understanding," although in both *Kinder* and *Keenan* reference was made to the understanding of the accused, given his age, education and military experience. This is similar to the Canadian stand[118] and the

[117] (1968), 3 C.M.R. 586.

[118] See *supra* notes 48 and 49.

decisions in *Cooke* and the *War Crimes (Preventive Murder) (Germany) case*,[119] in both of which the court paid attention to the fact that the accused were legally qualified. This raises the fundamental issue whether "the man of ordinary sense and understanding" is the proper agent for measuring the "palpable unlawfulness" of a military order. As was brought out in some of the United States courts martial, the circumstances may be such (for example, the act may be committed well behind the lines) that there is no real military necessity for it, and in such a situation the measure of the order may well be that of "the man on the Clapham omnibus." This would probably apply to most offences committed against prisoners of war once they had been removed from the scene of capture. It would also probably apply to the cases alleged to have occurred in Vietnam of prisoners being dropped from helicopters *pour encourager les autres*, a practice which was expressly condemned in *Kinder*.

But there are offences which are of such a kind and occur in circumstances so closely connected with operations that it is probably unfair to measure them by any standard other than that of the "reasonable soldier," and it may even be unfair to judge them by persons other than those possessed of military experience. It is true that there have been attempts made in the United States, as a result of the experience gained by a large civilian conscripted army, to bring the military within normal civil jurisdiction,[120] but the Supreme Court has shown its awareness of the possibility of a civilian tribunal reaching a decision very different from that of a tribunal made up of military specialists.[121] It may even be questioned whether a military code, manual or directions to courts martial drafted by lawyers, newly qualified or not, who carry military ranks merely because they serve in the Judge Advocate's or Defence Departments, but who have no idea of the realities of service life particularly in action, are the proper persons to be responsible for preparing these regulations and legislation. Likewise, it may be that permanent courts martial with permanent presidents who have achieved senior rank by long service are not the best judges of the actions of young soldiers whose experience of warlike conditions has been gained under conditions that were completely unknown when their judges were serving personnel.

119 See *supra* note 33.

120 See Johnson, "Unlawful Command Influence: A Question of Balance," 19 JAG Journal 1965, at 87.

121 *U.S. ex rel Toth* v. *Quarles*, *supra* note 46.

In deciding whether the order was one which a soldier "of ordinary sense and understanding would know to be illegal" on the face of it, justice may well demand that consideration be paid to the general conditions in which the accused found himself, the length of time he had been in action, the nature of the hostilities, the type of enemy confronting him and the methods of warfare employed against him. While some attention must be paid to the casualties born by the accused's comrades as a result of illegal methods of warfare, care must be taken, as was brought out in *Griffen*, not to allow resentment, hatred, anger or sorrow to overcome even a soldier's reasonable understanding of right and wrong. While one might expect a soldier to be more likely to fire and kill persons awaiting interrogation who appear to be making a break for freedom, as is alleged to have happened in North Malaya in 1948,[122] than might be the case with an escape from civil custody, there is little doubt that even a soldier "of ordinary sense and understanding" would appreciate the "palpable unlawfulness" of an order to enter a village in what is understood to be a "cleared area" and exterminate all life, regardless of age, sex or allegiance, as is alleged to have happened at Song My.

It may not only be necessary to change the concept of reasonableness in so far as superior orders addressed to a military subordinate are concerned. If justice is to be achieved, it may also be necessary to change the law with regard to prejudice in relation to military trials. In the case of Malaya, the British authorities announced that a commission had been set up to investigate the facts and recommend whether proceedings should be instituted. In the meantime, a complete news blackout was imposed. Where Song My is concerned, there has been a veritable trial by news media. The accused, their counsel, potential prosecution witnesses and the command have issued statements, as have those engaged in a Congressional enquiry. The danger now is that, even if there be adequate grounds for a trial, and even if the honour of the United States may demand that the matter be fully aired in a judicial fashion with the guilty being made to pay, there is a grave risk that no action can be taken because of prejudice, even though it is assumed that a military court may consist of persons sufficiently honest and aware of military reality to pay attention only to the facts, and to be as capable of closing their minds to extraneous and biased matter as it is presumed a jury is to an improper question.

[122] *The Times*, February 4, 1970.

From the discussion that has taken place about superior orders in both civil and military courts, whether in time of peace or armed conflict, it is clear that, while they may constitute ground for mitigating punishment, these orders cannot be accepted as justifying an illegal act — at least where the act ordered is of such a character that the order is "palpably unlawful." In deciding whether it is so palpable, which is a question of law for the court, it is submitted the standard of measurement cannot be universal, but must depend on whether the accused is a civilian or a serviceman and whether the offence is of a kind that can be considered as being civil in character though committed by a soldier. If the act is essentially military in character and has been committed in war conditions, then the palpability must be looked at from the point of view of the reasonable soldier, and decided by military personnel who are themselves likely to be aware of how the reasonable soldier thinks, reacts and does.

[13]

COMMAND RESPONSIBILITY FOR WAR CRIMES*

By Major William H. Parks **

An historical and comparative analysis of war crimes trials involving command responsibility in order to determine the standards of conduct required of a military commander in combat with regard to the prevention, investigation, reporting, and prosecution of war crimes. The author includes as part of his examination a view of the criminal responsibility of the combat commander, possible offenses, and the degree of intent required under both domestic and international law.

I. INTRODUCTION

The Vietnam conflict and the abberation which occurred in the subhamlet of My Lai (4) in Song My Village, Quang Nai Province, in the Republic of South Vietnam on March 16, 1968, reawakened questions concerning the responsibility of a military commander for the unlawful acts of his subordinates.[1] For some, it constituted an opportunity to re-assert theories of responsibility previously argued and rejected by courts of law;[2] others saw it

---

* This article is adapted from a thesis presented to The Judge Advocate General's School, U. S. Army, Charlottesville, Virginia, while the author was a member of the 21st Advanced Course. The opinions and conclusions presented herein are those of the author and do not necessarily represent the views of The Judge Advocate General's School or any other governmental agency.

** U. S. Marine Corps; Instructor, Criminal Law and International Law Divisions, TJAGSA. B.A. 1963, J.D. 1966, Baylor University. Member of the Bars of Washington and Texas, the U. S. Supreme Court, and the U. S. Court of Military Appeals.

1 *See, e.g., The Clamor Over Calley: Who Shares the Guilt?* TIME, April 12, 1971, at 14; *Who Else is Guilty?* NEWSWEEK, April 12, 1971, at 30; Sheehan, *Should We Have War Crimes Trials?*, Seattle Post-Intelligencer, April 11, 1971, at 17, col. 5. *See generally* T. TAYLOR, NUREMBURG AND VIETNAM: AN AMERICAN TRAGEDY (1970); S. HERSH, MY LAI 4 (1970) and R. HAMMER, ONE MORNING IN THE WAR (1970).

2 Telford Taylor, chief prosecutor in the *High Command Case*, discussed *infra* p. 38 *et seq.*, argued (unsuccessfully) for a theory of strict liability of a commander (XI TRIALS OF WAR CRIMINALS BEFORE THE NUERMBURG MILITARY TRIBUNALS UNDER CONTROL COUNCIL LAW NO. 10 [hereinafter "TWC"] 544 [1948]; the argument is renewed in *Nuremburg and Vietnam*,

as yet another way to indict the nation's leaders, and particularly the military, for the United States' involvement in Vietnam.[3] It is not the intent of this article to rebut these arguments, as this has already been done by others.[4] Rather it is intended to examine the standards of responsibility previously applied in order to ascertain the existing standards, municipal and international, and to determine if an identical municipal-international standard is feasible.

A. DEVELOPMENT OF THE CONCEPT—PRE-1945

The concept of command responsibility—and the commensurate duty of a commander to control his troops—was developed along two paths, not reaching fruition *per se* until delineated by the post-World War II tribunals. The first path dealt with the question of the general responsibility of command; the second, with the specific criminal responsibility of the commander. It is alternatively submitted that (a) the natural development of the former would lead to inevitable inclusion of the latter, and (b) there was in fact an intertwining of the development of the two from the outset. It is further submitted that the development of an international standard was incidental in nature, occurring only where states manifested such conduct as to make it apparent that no

---

supra note 1, at 180-181, and in an interview on the Dick Cavett Show on January 8, 1971, as reported by Neil Sheehan in the New York Times, January 9, 1971, at 3, col. 1. In that interview Professor Taylor opined that if one were to apply to Secretary of State Dean Rusk, Secretary of Defense Robert S. McNamara, Presidential advisors McGeorge Bundy and W. W. Rostow, President Lyndon B. Johnson, and General William C. Westmoreland the same standards of command responsibility as were applied in the trial of General Tomoyuki Yamashita in 1945, discussed *infra*, "there would be a strong possibility that they would come to the same end as he did." General Yamashita was found responsible for war crimes committed by his subordinates and hanged on February 23, 1946. A. Frank Reel, one of General Yamashita's defense counsel and author of a book relating the defense view of the case (THE CASE OF GENERAL YAMASHITA, 1949), has been similarly quoted, as noted in D. BERGAMINI, JAPAN'S IMPERIAL CONSPIRACY at 1112, n.5 (1972).

[3] *See, e.g.*, CRIMES OF WAR (R. Falk, G. Kolko, and R. Lifton, eds., 1971); and WAR CRIMES AND THE AMERICAN CONSCIENCE (E. Knoll and J. McFadden, eds., 1970).

[4] *See* Solf, *A Response to Telford Taylor's Nuremburg and Vietnam: An American Tragedy*, 5 AKRON L. REV. 43 (1972); DEPARTMENT OF THE ARMY, *Final Report of the Research Project: Conduct of the War in Vietnam* (1971); Paust, *My Lai and Vietnam: Norms, Myths, and Leader Responsibility*, 57 MIL. L. REV. 99 (1972); Hart, *Yamashita, Nuremburg and Vietnam: Command Responsibility Reappraised*, XXV NAVAL WAR COLLEGE REVIEW 19 (1972); and Paust, XXV NAVAL WAR COLLEGE REVIEW 103 (1973).

COMMAND RESPONSIBILITY

satisfactory municipal standard was to be applied, and the other parties to the conflict were in a position to impose what was considered to be an appropriate international standard on culpable commanders of the offending state.[5] When such an international tribunal was conducted, it generally followed the municipal standard of responsibility of the convening state.[6]

Sun Tzu, in what is considered to be the oldest military treatise in the world, wrote in 500 B.C.:

> When troops flee, are insubordinate, distressed, collapse in disorder, or are routed, it is the fault of the general. None of these disorders can be attributed to natural causes.[7]

---

[5] In a report issued October 28, 1953, the U.S. Army disclosed that in June, 1953, thirty-four war crimes cases arising out of the Korean conflict were ready for trial, but that the alleged perpetrators had to be released in the prisoner exchange following the armistice (July 27, 1953) in that conflict, GREENSPAN, THE MODERN LAW OF LAND WARFARE 30, n. 82 (1959). Thus even where a state may legally detain and try prisoners of war for war crimes (as is recognized by Articles 85, 115, and 119 of the Geneva Convention Relative to the Treatment of Prisoners of War, 1949), this right may be forfeited by the terms of armistice between the conflicting states. Only where there is a clear "winner" and "loser" is there likelihood of international war crimes trials. In the Korean and Vietnam wars, it was apparent that the Communist states had no intention of punishing those commanders responsible for the commission of war crimes; and by the terms of the respective peace agreements between the parties and the circumstances of execution of those agreements, their adversaries were incapable of imposing sanctions upon those commanders, even where they were within the control of the Free World states. In the India-Pakistan-Bangladesh conflict, where military success was more readily defined, Bangladesh was ultimately persuaded by India to postpone its plans to try 195 Pakistans accused of war crimes in the interest of "fulfilling a larger vision of harmony and peace in the (Indo-Pakistani) subcontinent." The Bangladesh insistence of trial of the 195 accused was considered the "most crucial point" in negotiations during the twenty months between cessation of hostilities and conclusion of the peace accord. Simons, *Bangladesh Divided Over Issue of War Crimes Trials*, Wash. Post, August 17, 1973, at p. A22, col. 1. Ratzin, *Pakistan, India Set Accord*, Wash. Post, August 29, 1973, at p. 1, col. 8; and *India to Release 90,000 Pakistans in Peace Accord*, N. Y. Times, August 29, 1973, at p. 1, cols. 7,8. This dilemma has been the rule more than the exception, and has been offered as explanation in part for the dearth of international war crimes trials prior to the unconditional surrender of World War II. Gross, *The Punishment of War Criminals, II* NETHERLANDS I. L. REV. 356 (1955) as cited in Paust, *My Lai and Vietnam: Norms, Myths, and Leader Responsibility*, 57 MIL. L. REV. 99 at 111, fn. 38 (1972).

[6] This was advocated by Polish legal scholar Manfred Lachs in 1945 in *War Crimes: An Attempt to Define the Issues*, and generally followed by all Tribunals, *e.g.*, the Soviet Union utilized exclusively the Soviet concept of criminal negligence in defining command responsibility. U.S. DEPARTMENT OF THE ARMY, *Prisoner of War Study* (Step Two: The Functioning of the Law [VIII National Attitudes and Legal Standards 22]), 1969 (hereinafter cited as the "Harbridge House Study").

[7] S. TZU, THE ART OF WAR 125 (S. Griffith transl. 1963).

Recognizing the responsibility of the commander, he also recognized the correlative duty of the commander to control his subordinates. Upon publication of his principles of war, Sun Tzu was summoned before a leading warrior king and asked to submit his theories to a test; Sun Tzu consented. Two companies of women, untrained in military matters, were formed up and each placed under the command of one of the king's favorite concubines. They were armed and given cursory instruction in the then-current manual of arms and close order drill. Then, to the sound of drums, Sun Tzu gave the order, "Right turn!" The only response of the "companies" was one of laughter. Sun Tzu remarked: "If the words of command are not clear and distinct, if orders are not thoroughly understood, then the general is to blame."

Again uttering the same command and receiving the same response, Sun Tzu then declared:

> If the words of command are not clear and distinct, if orders are not thoroughly understood, the general is to blame. But if his orders are clear, and the soldiers nevertheless disobey, then it is the fault of their officers.

So saying and much to the consternation of the warrior king, Sun Tzu ordered the two company commanders beheaded and replaced by a member of each company. The execution was viewed by all, the drum was again sounded for drill, and the companies thereafter executed all maneuvers with perfect accuracy and precision, never venturing to utter a sound.[8]

The concept of national—and criminal—responsibility was recorded at an early date, Grotius declaring ". . . a community, or its rulers, may be held responsible for the crime of a subject if they knew it and do not prevent it when they could and should prevent it." [9]

While Grotius' statement on its face limits itself to national responsibility rather than addressing the liability of the individual military commander, international recognition of the latter occurred as early as 1474 with the trial of Peter von Hagenbach. Brought to trial by the Archduke of Austria on charges of murder, rape, perjury and other crimes against "the laws of God and man," Hagenbach was tried by an international tribunal of twenty-eight judges from allied states of the Holy Roman Empire.

---

[8] S. Tzu, The Art of War 9 (L. Giles Transl. 1944).

[9] II Grotius, De Jure Belli Ac Pacis 523 (C.E.I.P. ed., Kelsy trans. 1925).

Despite a plea of superior orders, Hagenbach was convicted, deprived of his knighthood for crimes which he as a knight was deemed to have a *duty* to prevent, and executed. While an "international" trial, his trial in theory was not a "war crimes" trial as no state of war existed at the time of the commission of the offenses, the Swiss-Burgundian war not occurring until 1476.[10]

In 1621 King Gustavus Adolphus of Sweden promulgated his "Articles of Military Lawwes to be Observed in the Warres," Article 46 of which in part provided: "No Colonel or Captaine shall command his souldiers to do any unlawful thing; which who so does, shall be punished according to the discretion of the Judges . . ."

In 1689, after unsuccessful seige of Calvanist Londonderry, Count Rosen was sternly reprobated and relieved from all further military duties by the exiled James II—not for failure to accomplish his mission, but for his outrageous seige methods, which included the murder of innocent noncombatants.[11]

On April 5, 1775, the Provisional Congress of Massachusetts Bay adopted the Massachusetts Articles of War. The eleventh article provided:

> Every *Officer commanding*, in quarters, or on a march, *shall keep good order*, and to the *utmost of his power*, redress all such abuses or disorders which may be committed by any Officer or Soldier under his command; if upon complaint made to him of Officers or Soldiers beating or otherwise ill-treating any person, or committing any kind of riots to the disquieting of the inhabitants of this Continent, he, the said commander, who shall refuse or omit to see Justice done to this offender or offenders, and reparation made to the party or parties injured, as soon as the offender's wages shall enable him or them, upon due proof thereof, be punished, as ordered by General Court-Martial, in such manner as if he himself had committed the crimes or disorders complained of.[12]

Article XII of the American Articles of War, enacted June 30, 1775, contained the same language. The provision was re-enacted as section IX of the American Articles of War of 1776 on September 20, 1776. Thus from the very outset of this nation, there was imposed upon the military commander the duty and responsibility for control of the members of his command.

---

10 Solf, *supra* note 4 at 65, and Paust, *supra* note 4 at 57 MIL. L. REV. 112 (1972).

11 Hargreaves, *The Rule Book of Warfare*, MARINE CORPS GAZETTE, August 1970, at 44.

12 Emphasis supplied. Articles of War, Provisional Congress of Massachusetts Bay, April 5, 1775.

In promulgating the Articles of War of 1806, the provision was re-enacted, this time however authorizing specific punishment of the offending commander by cashiering, if deemed appropriate.[13] In addition, Article 33 provided:

> When any commissioned officer or soldier shall be accused of a capital crime, or of having used violence, or committed any offense against the person or property of any citizen of any of the United States, such as is punishable by the known laws of the land, the commanding officer and officers of every regiment, troop, or company to which the person or persons so accused shall belong, are hereby required, upon application duly made by, or in behalf of, the party or parties injured, to use their utmost endeavors to deliver over such accused person or persons to the civil magistrate, and likewise to be aiding and assisting to the officers of justice in apprehending and securing the person or persons so accused, in order to bring him or them to trial. If any commanding officer or officers shall willfully neglect, or shall refuse upon the application aforesaid, to deliver over such accused person or persons to the civil magistrates, or to be aiding and assisting to the officers of justice in apprehending such person or persons, the officer or officers so offending shall be cashiered.[14]

At approximately the same time, Napoleon I re-emphasized the responsibility of the commander in the briefest maxims: "There are no bad regiments; there are only bad colonels." [15]

During the War of 1812, American soldiers needlessly burned some buildings near their encampment in Upper Canada. Their commanding officer was summarily dismissed from the service. Another commander was brought before a United States military tribunal for a similar occurrence at Long Point.[16]

During the Black Hawk War of 1832, militia captain Abraham Lincoln was convicted by a court-martial for failure to control his men, some of whom had opened the officers' supply of whiskey and partaken freely thereof, while others were inclined to straggle on the march. Captain Lincoln was sentenced to carry a wooden sword for two days.[17]

In 1851 the United States Supreme Court affirmed a lower court's decision finding Colonel David D. Mitchell responsible for illegal acts which occurred during the Kearney campaign into Mexico in 1846. Colonel Mitchell had received illegal orders from his immediate superior which he had passed on to his subordinates

---

[13] Articles of War, Article 32 (1806).

[14] Articles of War, Article 33 (1806).

[15] R. Heinl, Dictionary of Military and Naval Quotations 56 (1966).

[16] Colby, *War Crimes*, 23 Mich. L. Rev. 482, 501-02 (1925), as cited in Paust, *supra* n. 10 at 113.

[17] C. Sandburg, Abraham Lincoln: The Prairie Years and The War Years 30 (1961).

and in some cases personally carried into execution. Although the case concerned civil rather than criminal penalties, the conclusions reached with regard to certain principles of responsibility—*viz.* the execution or passing on of a patently illegal order, and the defense of superior orders—were exactly those prescribed almost a century later in the *Hostage* and *High Command* cases.[18]

In 1863, the United States promulgated General Order No. 100, better known as the Lieber Code. Article 71 thereof provided for punishment of any commander ordering or encouraging the intentional wounding or killing of an already "wholly disabled enemy," whether that commander belonged to the "Army of United States, or is an enemy captured after having committed his misdeed." Two years later, Captain Henry Wirz, Swiss doctor and Commandant of the Confederate prisoner of war camp at Andersonville, Georgia, was convicted by military commission and hanged for violation of the Lieber Code, having ordered and permitted the torture, maltreatment, and death of Union prisoners of war in his custody.[19] Winthrop in his *Military Law and Precedents* makes reference to other post-Civil War investigations, concluding that the burning of Columbia, South Carolina, on February 17, 1865, ". . ., cannot fairly be fixed upon any *responsible* commander. . . ."[20] for lack of evidence and interceding factors.

In 1873 in the course of hostilities in Northern California six Modoc indians, including Captain Jack, the chief, were tried by military tribunal for the murder of Brigadier General Canby and Reverend E. Thomas, who as peace commissioners had entered the Modoc village under a flag of truce. All were convicted and sentenced to hang. The sentences of the principal perpetrators and Captain Jack were affirmed, the latter for ordering the murders. In affirming those sentences, the Attorney General of the United States observed:

> All the laws and customs of civilized warfare may not be applicable to an armed conflict with the Indian tribes upon our Western frontiers, but the circumstances attending the assassination of Canby and Thomas are such as to make their murder as much a violation

[18] *Mitchell v. Harmony*, 54 U.S. (13 How.) 420 (1851). The plaintiff received a judgment against Colonel Mitchell personally of $90,806.44 for seizure of plaintiff's goods not justified by military necessity. *See Infra*, text at footnotes 120 and 195.

[19] THE TRIAL OF CAPTAIN HENRY WIRZ, 8 AMERICAN STATE TRIALS 666 (1865), as cited in THE LAW OF WAR: A DOCUMENTARY HISTORY 783 (L. Friedman ed. 1972).

[20] Emphasis supplied. WINTHROP, MILITARY LAW AND PRECEDENTS 782 n. 46 (2nd ed. 1895).

> of the laws of savage as of civilized warfare, and the Indians concerned in it fully understood the baneness and treachery of their act.[21]

On June 22, 1874, the American Articles of War were repromulgated, Article 54 repeating the previous provisions concerning command responsibility. Winthrop in 1886 further defined the duty of the commander in armed conflict, providing some overlap between the responsibility of the military commander as stated in the Articles of War and the obligations of the laws of war:

> The observance of the rule protecting from violence the unarmed population is especially to be enforced by commanders in occupying or passing through towns or villages of the enemy's country.
>
> All officers or soldiers offending against the rule of immunity of non-combatants or private persons in war forfeit their right to be treated as belligerents, and together with civilians similarly offending, become liable to the severest penalties as violators of the laws of war.[22]

Elsewhere, he re-emphasized this point:

> It is indeed the chief duty of the commander of the army of occupation to maintain order and the public safety, as far as practicable without oppression of the population, and as if the district were a part of the domain of his own nation.[23]

With the deployment of United States forces to the Philippine Islands in 1901, United States forces met the question of the trial of foreign combatants for war crimes head on. By General Order No. 221, Headquarters, Division of the Philippines, August 17, 1901, insurrection First Lieutenant Natalio Valencia was tried, convicted, and sentenced to death for illegally ordering the execution of a non-combatant. By General Order No. 264 of that headquarters, September 9, 1901, Pedro A. Cruz, identified as a "leader" of guerrillas, was condemned to death for *permitting* the murder of two American Army prisoners of war in his custody.[24]

---

[21] 14 OPINS. ATT'Y GEN. 249 (1873), as cited in WINTHROP, *Id.* at 786, n. 78.

[22] WINTHROP, *supra* n. 20 at 779 (footnote omitted).

[23] *Id.* at 800, (footnote omitted.) citing Johnson v. McIntosh, 8 Wheaton 581 (1821) which provides at 589: "A conquered people are not to be '*wantonly* oppressed: . . ." [Emphasis supplied].

[24] Brief for the Respondents in Opposition, In the Matter of General Tomoyuki Yamashita for Writs of Habeas Corpus and Prohibition, pp. 33-34. United States Supreme Court, October Term 1945 No. 61, Misc; No. 672. *Also In re* General Tomoyuki Yamashita, 327 U.S. 1 at 16, n. 3 (1946). These two orders were cited by the majority in recognizing the existence of "an affirmative duty" on the part of a commander who is additionally the commander of an occupied territory "to take such measures as [are] within his power and appropriate in the circumstances to protect prisoners of war and the civilian population" of that occupied territory.

COMMAND RESPONSIBILITY

In April, 1902, Brigadier General Jacob H. Smith, United States Army, was tried and convicted by general court-martial for inciting, ordering and permitting subordinates to commit war crimes during counterinsurgency operations on the island of Samar. In approving the conviction and sentence of dismissal, President Theodore Roosevelt stated:

> The findings and sentence of the court are approved. I am well aware of the danger and great difficulty of the task our Army has had in the Philippine Islands and of the well-nigh intolerable provocations it has received from the cruelty, treachery, and total disregard of the rules and customs of civilized warfare on the part of its foes. I also heartily approve the employment of the sternest measures necessary to put a stop to such atrocities, and to bring this war to a close. It would be culpable to show weakness in dealing with such foes or to fail to use all legitimate and honorable methods to overcome them. But the very fact that warfare is of such character as to afford infinite provocation for the commission of acts of cruelty by junior officers and the enlisted men, must make the officers in high and responsible position peculiarly careful in their bearing and conduct so as to keep a moral check over any acts of an improper character by their subordinates. Almost universally the higher officers have so borne themselves as to supply this necessary check; and with but few exceptions the officers and soldiers of the Army have shown wonderful kindness and forbearance in dealing with their foes. But there have been exceptions; there have been instances of the use of torture and of improper heartlessness in warfare on the part of individuals or small detachments. In the recent campaign ordered by General Smith, the shooting of the native bearers by the orders of Major Waller was an act which sullied the American name and can be but partly excused because of Major Waller's mental condition at the time; this mental condition being due to the fearful hardship and suffering which he had undergone in his campaign. It is impossible to tell exactly how much influence language like that used by General Smith may have had in preparing the minds of thoses under him for the commission of the deeds which we regret. Loose and violent talk by an officer of high rank is always likely to excite to wrongdoing those among his subordinates whose wills are weak or whose passions are strong.[25]

---

[25] S. Doc. 213, 57th Cong. 2nd Session, p.5. After learning of the widespread commission of war crimes by the insurrectionists — including torture and murder of all prisoners of war, mutilation of their bodies, murder of noncombatants, use of poison, and refusal to respect flags of truce— General Smith issued the following order to Major of Marines Líttleton Waller Tazewell Waller, whose battalion had been deployed as part of General Smith's command:

> I want no prisoners. I wish you to burn and kill; the more you burn and kill, the better it will please me. The interior of Samar must be made into a howling wilderness.

General Smith further instructed Major Waller to kill all persons capable of bearing arms, designating the lower age limit as ten years of age. In the next sixty days, Major Waller and his Marine expeditionary force through constant contact virtually destroyed a numerically superior enemy force without resorting to the illegal methods urged by General Smith. In January

Major Edwin F. Glenn, United States Army, was tried and convicted for violation of paragraph 16 of the Lieber Code, torture of a prisoner, for ordering use of the "water cure" and other means of torture as interrogation methods of prisoners taken during the Samar campaign.[26] Another Army officer, Captain Cornelius M. Brownell, was accused of ordering and directing the "water cure" interrogation of one Father Augustine de la Pena, who died while being so interrogated; Brownell escaped prosecution, however, as he had been released from the Army prior to discovery of the offense by higher authorities—a jurisdictional refrain which, through lack of Congressional action, returned to haunt the nation at the time of discovery of the My Lai offenses.[27]

On October 18, 1907, the Fourth Hague Convention of 1907, respecting the laws and customs of war on land, was executed by forty-one nations. Article 1 of the Annex thereto laid down as a condition which an armed force must fulfill in order to be accorded

---

1902, however, the Marine force was beset by a number of problems, many of which were caused by the repeated treachery of that force's Filipino guides and bearers, who Major Waller discovered were plotting to massacre the entire Marine party. Feeling that his drastic situation called for drastic measures, Major Waller convened a drumhead court-martial of eleven Filipino bearers on January 20, 1902, of which he noted: "When I learned of the plot and heard everything, I sent [the bearers] out and had them shot." Major Waller maintained subsequently that the bearers were executed not only for their gross betrayal of the Marines, but in reprisal for the slaughter of Company C of the 9th Infantry at Balangiga, where Moro bolo-men had ripped open the entrails of butchered Army officers and poured in jam looted from the messhall.

General Chafee ordered Major Waller tried by general court-martial. Despite extreme command pressure, the court acquitted Major Waller. When General Chafee disapproved the acquittal, the Judge Advocate General of the Army disapproved the entire court-martial proceeding inasmuch as the Marine force had never been detached for service with the Army by Presidential order, as required by Sec. 1621, R.S. (1895) of the Articles of War. *See also* R. HEINL, SOLDIERS OF THE SEA 123-6 (1962); and J. SCHOTT, THE ORDEAL OF SAMAR (1964).

[26] S. Doc. 213, 57th Cong., 2nd Sess., pp. 20-28. The "water cure" method of interrogation consisted of the forcing of large quantities of water into the mouth and nose of the victim, which not only caused the victim to suffocate but served to severely distend the stomach; whereupon the interrogator(s) would strike the victim in the stomach or even jump on his abdomen.

[27] *Id.* at pp. 80-92. The offenses of Major Glenn and Captain Brownell were uncovered as the result of statements by former members of their respective commands—again a striking resemblance to My Lai. By letter of May 10, 1902, George B. Davis, Judge Advocate General of the Army, suggested to Senator H. Cabot Lodge that these jurisdictional defects be cured, a plea which has to this day gone unheeded. For a discussion of this point, *see* Paust, *After My Lai—The Case for War Crime Jurisdiction Over Civilians in Federal District Courts*, 50 TEX. L. REV. 6 (1971).

the rights of a lawful belligerent, that it must be "commanded by a person responsible for his subordinates." [28] Similarly Article 19 of the Tenth Hague Convention of 1907, relating to bombardment by naval vessels, provided that commanders of belligerent fleets must "see to the execution of the details of the preceding articles" in conformance with the general principles of that Convention.[29] Article 43 of the Annex to the Fourth Hague Convention of 1907 further requires that the commander of a force occupying enemy territory "shall take all measures in his power to restore, and ensure, as far as possible, public order and safety, while respecting, unless absolutely prevented, the laws in force in the country." [30] The latter principle was not unlike that advocated by Winthrop two decades previous; Hague Convention Four, it is submitted, is a manifestation and codification of that which was custom among the signatory nations, giving early recognition to the duties and responsibilities of the commander.

Article 54 of the 1916 Articles of War provided that a commander has a duty of insuring "to the utmost of his power, redress of all abuses and disorders which may be committed by an officer or soldier under his command." General John A. Lejeune, thirteenth Commandant of the Marine Corps, reiterated the general responsibility of a commander in the 1920 *Marine Corps Manual:*

> ...officers, especially commanding officers, are responsible for the physical, mental, and moral welfare, as well as the discipline and military training of the young men under their command.[31]

At the conclusion of World War I, an international "Commission on the Responsibility of the Authors of the War and on Enforcement of Penalties" met at Versailles. As part of their final report, delivered in March, 1919, the Commission recommended the establishment of an international tribunal "appropriate for the trial of these offenses (crimes relating to the war)." [32] Part III thereof concluded that:

> All persons belonging to enemy countries, however high their position may have been, without distinction of rank, including

[28] 36 Stat. 2277; Treaty Series No. 539; MALLOY TREATIES, VOL. II, 2269 (1910).

[29] 36 Stat. 2351 (1910).

[30] 36 Stat. 2277.

[31] Marine Corps Manual, U. S. Marine Corps, 1920.

[32] Committee on the Responsibility of the Authors of the War and on Enforcement of Penalties—Report Presented to the Preliminary Peace Conference, Versailles, March, 1919, Part IV.

> Chiefs of Staff, who have been guilty of offenses against the laws and customs of war or the laws of humanity, are liable to criminal prosecution.[33]

It is submitted that this resolution was predicated by two events unusual for the most part in the annals of warfare; (1) acts of war beyond normal public apprehension which shocked the conscience of the world, for example, the commencement of large-scale unrestricted submarine warfare, and (2) the virtually total defeat of Germany and her allies. This created a demand for retribution—perhaps to insure that this was indeed "the war to end all wars"—as well as the potential means for satisfying that demand in the form of the League of Nations.

Such was not to be, however, as some nations for individual reasons voiced reluctance for proceeding. The United States, through its representatives, Secretary of State Robert Lansing and international law scholar James Brown Scott, dissented from the proposed procedure of trial by international tribunal as it was without precedent; rather, any accused should be tried by military tribunals of the conquering nations which had "admitted competence" in the matter.[34] The Japanese delegation dissented from prosecuting

> . . . highly-placed enemies on the sole ground that they abstained from preventing, putting an end to, or repressing acts in violation of the laws and customs of war [feeling] some hesitation [in admitting] a criminal liability where the accused, with knowledge and with power to intervene, abstained from preventing or taking measures to prevent, putting an end to, or repressing acts in violation of the laws and customs of war.[35]

Sweeping these objections aside, Articles CCXXVII and CCXXVIII of the Versailles Treaty demanded the trial of the Kaiser by international tribunal and persons accused of violating the laws of war by international military tribunals.[36]

On February 3, 1920, the Allies submitted to the German government a list of 896 alleged war criminals they desired to try in accordance with Article CCXXVIII of the Versailles Treaty. The list including such high-ranking officers as the son of the Kaiser, Count Bismark (grandson of the Iron Chancellor), and Marshalls

---

[33] *Id.* as reported in 14 AM. J. INT. L. 95 (1920).

[34] *Id.* at Annex II.

[35] Greenspan, *supra* n.5 at 478, n.286.

[36] The accused was to be tried by a military tribunal of the nation which had jurisdiction over the offense(s) alleged; if more than one nation could claim jurisdiction, a multinational military tribunal was to be appointed.

COMMAND RESPONSIBILITY

Von Hindenburg and Ludendorff. The German Cabinet strenuously objected, warning the Allies that Army leaders would resume hostilities if the demand was pressed. The German government advised the Allies that the Supreme Court of the Reich at Leipzig would conduct the trials and apply international rather than municipal law in trying the cases. The Allies consented on February 13, 1920, tendering to the Germans a list of forty-five names. The Germans eventually tried twelve of the forty-five, acquitting six. Of those convicted, only one was convicted on the basis of command responsibility. Major Benno Crusius was found guilty of ordering the execution of wounded French prisoners of war and sentenced to two years confinement.[37] In the *"Llandovery Castle" Case,* the German Supreme Court of Leipzig noted in their opinion that under their own Military Penal Code,

> [I]f the execution of an order in the ordinary course of duty involves such a violation of the law as is punishable, the superior officer issuing such order is alone responsible.[38]

---

[37] The name of each accused ultimately tried, the charge, and the finding and sentence are as follows:

ACCUSED	CHARGE	FINDING	SENTENCE
Sgt. Karl Heymen	Mistreatment of POWs	Guilty	10 months
Capt. Emil Muller	Mistreatment of POWs	Guilty	6 months
Pvt. Robert Neumann	Mistreatment of POWs	Guilty	6 months
Lt. Capt. Karl Neumann	Torpedoing the hospital ship *Dover Castle*	Not Guilty	
1st Lt. Ludwig Dithmar	Firing on survivors in lifeboats of hospital ship *Llandovery Castle*	Guilty	4 years
1st Lt. John Boldt	Firing on survivors in lifeboats of hospital ship *Llandovery Castle*	Guilty	4 years
Max Ramdahr	Mistreatment of Belgian children	Not Guilty	
Major Benno Crusius	Ordering the Execution of POWs	Guilty	2 years
1st Lt. Adolph Laule	Murder of a POW	Not Guilty	
Lt. Gen. Hans von Schock	Mistreatment of POWs	Not Guilty	
Maj. Gen. Benno Kruska	Mistreatment of POWs	Not Guilty	
Lt. Gen. Karl Stenger	Ordering the execution of prisoners of war	Not Guilty	

U. S. DEP'T OF ARMY, PAMPHLET NO. 27-161-2, INTERNATIONAL LAW 221-222 (1962).

[38] Friedman, *supra* n. 19, 881.

The demands for international standards of responsibility by and large went unanswered and unheeded, as the world was to discover two decades later. The Red Cross Convention for the Amelioration of the Condition of the Wounded and Sick of Armies in the Field, promulgated in 1929, recognized in Article 26 that the commander had "the duty . . . to provide for the details of execution of the foregoing articles [of the Convention] as well as for the unforseen cases." [39] Thus the belligerent states entered World War II with a custom of command responsibility, codified in large part by the Hague Conventions of 1907 and the 1929 Red Cross Convention, and with somewhat of a warning based on the essentially unfilled demands of the Versailles Treaty that concepts of command responsibility would be implemented at the conclusion of any future conflict.[40]

Objections by the Allies to the leniency of the German trials at Leipzig, as well as the actions of Japan, such as their rape of Nanking in 1937, and German genocidal practices from the very outset and even prior to commencement of World War II, again shocked the conscience of the world, the two serving as catalyctic impetus virtually from the outset of hostilities for

[39] 47 Stat. 2074 (1932).

[40] The concept of command responsibility was well recognized prior to World War II, even by the so-called "Oriental mind," as Marine General A. A. Vandegrift indicates in his autobiography, ONCE A MARINE (at p. 75). In 1928, then-Major Vandegrift was stationed with the Marine expeditionary force in China. He relates the following:

> For a Christian general, Feng Yu-hsiang (the famous "Christian general" who baptized his troops en masse [with fire hoses] and had them sing hymns each night before retiring) proved an anomaly. As was the custom with Chinese forces, plainclothes agents preceded the main forces into the city. These men, generally cruel, plundered at will and treated the Chinese folk very harshly.
>
> Soon after Feng's advance [to Tientsin], I learned that some of his agents were persecuting the natives in a small village close to one of our defense areas. After confirming the report I hastened to Feng's headquarters . . . he received me most courteously, explained that such acts were contrary to his orders, and promised to deal with the offenders if General [Smedley D.] Butler would let troops transit our area. Butler gave permission by telephone and I accompanied a platoon to the trouble spot. We caught the looters redhanded. Before I could say anything the Chinese platoon leader lined six of them up and beheaded them, an example to anyone else so tempted. The rest of them he marched back to the Chinese city, lined them against a wall and had them shot.

Japanese General Tomoyuki Yamashita testified at his trial (discussed *infra* n. 64) that he recognized and acknowledged the concept as a valid one, and one to which he maintained he adhered. United States v. Gen. Tomoyuki Yamashita, Tr. 3650, 3652, 3653, 3674.

thoughts of the establishment of international tribunals for the conduct of war crimes trials once that conflict was concluded. Stories of the many atrocities committed by the German armies led representatives of many of the victimized states to issue the St. James Declaration in January, 1942, which promised to punish, "through the channels of organized justice," those responsible for war crimes.[41] On March 9, 1943, the United States issued "solemn warnings" to the Axis powers that all those responsible for war crimes, either directly or indirectly, would be held accountable.[42] In July, 1943, the United Nations War Crimes Commission was established to collect and collate evidence of war crimes. The Commission concerned itself primarily with such crimes as mistreatment of prisoners of war, atrocities against civilians, inhumane treatment of concentration camp inmates, execution of hostages, and other killing of noncombatants. On November 1, 1943, Great Britain, the United States, and the Soviet Union issued the Moscow Declaration on German Atrocities, which provided that those accused of war crimes would either be (a) "brought back to the scene of their crimes and judged on the spot by the peoples whom they have outraged," or (b) where offenses had no particular geographic localization, "punished by the joint decision of the Government of the Allies."

Formal protests to the Axis powers went unanswered; radio broadcast warnings went unheeded. On January 29, 1944, statements by United States Secretary of State Cordell Hull and British Foreign Secretary Anthony Eden were broadcast—and received by the Japanese—giving the details of the Bataan Death March. The United States also disclosed that the Japanese would not permit the United States Government to send food and supplies to United States and Filipino prisoners. Secretary Hull, in speaking of the treatment of prisoners of war in Japanese hands, stated:

> According to the reports of cruelty and inhumanity, it would be necessary to summon the representatives of all the demons available anywhere and combine their fiendishness with all that is bloody in order to describe the conduct of those unthinkable atrocities on the Americans and Filipinos.[43]

---

41 Friedman, *supra* n. 19, 778.

42 89 Cong. Rec. 1773 (daily ed. March 9, 1943).

43 Judgment of the International Japanese War Crimes Trial in the International-Military Tribunal for the Far East (hereinafter cited as "IMTFE") (1948), pp. 49, 748-750.

Secretary Eden in turn declared that the Japanese were violating not only international law but all human, decent civilized conduct. He warned the Japanese Government that in time to come the record of their military atrocities would not be forgotten. Secretary Hull closed his statement with the remark that the United States was assembling all possible facts concerning Japanese treatment of prisoners of war and that it intended to seek full punishment of the responsible Japanese authorities. Upon landing in the Philippines in October, 1944, General Douglas MacArthur issued warnings to the Japanese commanders that he would hold them immediately responsible for any failure to accord prisoners of war and civilians proper treatment. Like the Hull-Eden broadcast, General MacArthur's message was recorded in the Japanese Ministries.[44] On August 8, 1945, the Allies signed the London Agreement, establishing an International Military Tribunal for trial of war criminals whose offenses had no particular geographical location.[45] Jurisdiction for the trial of military commanders, as well as national leaders, was established in Article 6 of the Charter of the International Military Tribunal:

> Article 6. The Tribunal established by the Agreement referred to in Article 1 hereof for the trial and punishment of the major war criminals of the European Axis countries shall have the power to try and punish persons who, acting in the interests of the European Axis countries, whether as individuals or as members of organizations, committed any of the following crimes.
>
> The following acts, or any of them, are crimes coming within the jurisdiction of the Tribunal for which there shall be individual responsiblity:
>
> (b) WAR CRIMES: namely, violations of the laws or customs of war. Such violations shall include, but not be limited to, murder, ill-treatment or deportation to slave labor or for any other purpose of civilian population of or in occupied territory, murder or ill-treatment of prisoners of war or persons on the seas, killing of hostages, plunder of public or private property, wanton destruction

---

44 *Id.* at 749.

45 Until execution of the London Agreement, Great Britain was of the mind that the German leaders should be considered wanted outlaws to be shot on sight, even if they voluntarily surrendered. Friedman, *supra*, n.19, p. 777.

Despite these preliminary moves, some international legal sholars throughout the war doubted the practicality of international war crimes trials. A. Berriedale Keith, in his seventh edition of WHEATON'S INTERNATIONAL LAW (1944) declared "[t]he idea of war crimes trials by neutral tribunals . . . fantastic, rather than practicable" (p. 242); and that ". . . the probability of anything effective being devised . . . is negligible" (p. 587). He also questioned whether individuals committing war crimes under order of their governments could be held liable for their actions (p. 586).

> of cities, towns or villages, or devastation not justified by military necessity;
>
> Leaders, organizers, instigators, and accomplices participating in the formulation or execution of a common plan or conspiracy to commit any of the foregoing crimes are responsible for all acts performed by any persons in execution of such plan.[46]

Individual states, in establishing military tribunals for trial of lesser officials accused of committing war crimes, promulgated comparable rules relating to the criminal responsibility of lesser commanders.

The initial United States definition, although never incorporated into any promulgating order, dealt both with direct commission of an offense and

> . . . omission of a superior officer to prevent war crimes when he knows of, or is on notice as to their commission or contemplated commission and is in a position to prevent them.[47]

Subsequently, each American theater of operations promulgated its own regulations for trial of war criminals. The commanders of the Pacific and China theaters issued orders which defined both subject jurisdiction and jurisdiction of the person:

> 5. OVER OFFENSES — a. The military commissions established hereunder shall have jurisdiction over the following offenses: murder, torture or ill-treatment of prisoners of war or persons on the seas; killing or ill-treatment of hostages; murder, torture or ill-treatment, or deportation to slave labor or for any other illegal purpose, of civilians of, or in, occupied territory; plunder of public or private property; wanton destruction of cities, towns or villages; devastation, destruction or damage of public or private property not justified by military necessity; planning, preparation, initiation or waging of a war of aggression, or an invasion or war in violation of international law, treaties, agreements or assurances; murder, extermination, enslavement, deportation or other inhumane acts committed against any civilian population, or persecution on political, racial, national or religious grounds, in execution of or connection with any offense within the jurisdiction of the commission, whether or not in violation of the domestic law of the country where perpetrated; and all other offenses against the laws or customs of war; participation in a common plan or conspiracy to accomplish any of the foregoing. Leaders, organizers, instigators, accessories and accomplices participating in the formulation or execution of any such common plan or conspiracy will be held responsible for all acts performed by any person in execution of that plan or conspiracy.[48]

---

[46] Friedman, *supra* n. 19, 885.

[47] JCS Directive 1023/3, September 25, 1944, as cited in Douglass, *High Command Case: A Study in Staff and Command Responsibility*, INT'L LAWYER, 686, 687 (October 1972).

[48] United States Armed Forces, Pacific, *Regulations Governing the Trial of War Criminals* (24 September 1945); United States Armed Forces,

Article 3 of the Law of August 2, 1947, of the Grand Duchy of Luxemborg, on the Suppression of War Crimes, reads as follows:

> Without prejudice to the provisions of Articles 66 and 67 of the Code Penal, the following may be charged, according to the circumstances, as co-authors or as accomplices in the crimes and delicts set out in Article 1 of the present law: superiors in rank who have tolerated the criminal activities of their subordinates, and those who, without being the superiors in rank of the principal authors, have aided those crimes or delicts.[49]

A special provision was made in the Netherlands relating to the responsibility of a superior for war crimes committed by subordinates. Article 27(a)(3) of the Law of July, 1947, adds, *inter alia,* the following provision to the Extraordinary Penal Law Decree of December 22, 1943: "Any superior who deliberately permits a subordinate to be guilty of such a crime shall be punished with a similar punishment. . . ."[50]

Article 4 of the French Ordinance of August 28, 1944, "Concerning the Suppression of War Crimes," utilized for the trial of persons accused of war crimes within metropolitan France, Algeria, and the then-existing French colonies, provided:

> Where a subordinate is prosecuted as the actual perpetrator of a war crime, and his superiors cannot be indicted as being equally responsible, they shall be considered as accomplices in so far as they have tolerated the criminal acts of their subordinates.[51]

Trials within Germany were all subject to Law No. 10 of the Allied Control Council ("Punishment of Persons Guilty of War Crimes, Crimes Against Peace and Crimes Against Humanity"). Article II(2) provided:

> Any person without regard to nationality or the capacity in which he acted, is deemed to have committed a [war] crime, . . . if he was (a) a principal, or (b) was an accessory to the commission of any such crime or. ordered or abetted the same, or (c) he took a consenting part therein . . .[52]

Article IX of the Chinese Law of October 24, 1946, "Governing the Trial of War Criminals," states that:

China, Regulations (21 January 1946). The former were used in the trial of Generals Yamashita and Homma and in the *Jaluit Atoll Case, infra,* then superseded by the *Regulations Governing the Trials of Accused War Criminals* of December 5, 1945, for all subsequent trials.

[49] United Nations War Crimes Commission, IV LAW REPORTS OF TRIALS OF WAR CRIMINALS 87 (hereinafter cited as "—L.R.T.W.C.—") (1948).

[50] *Id.,* 88

[51] III L.R.T.W.C. 94.

[52] I TWC XVI.

> Persons who occupy a . . . commanding position in relation to war criminals and in their capacity as such have not fulfilled their duty to prevent crimes from being committed by their subordinates shall be treated as the accomplices of such war criminals.[53]

Article 8 (ii) of the British Royal Warrant relating to the trials of persons accused of the commission of war crimes provided:

> Where there is evidence that a war crime has been the result of concerted action upon the part of a unit or group of men, then evidence given upon any charge relating to that crime against any member of such unit or group may be received as *prima facie* evidence of the responsibility of each member of that unit or group for that crime . . .[54]

The Canadian rules expanded this point, incorporating British rule 8 (ii), then providing in their Rule 10:

> (4) Where there is evidence that more than one war crime has been committed by members of a formation, unit, body, or group while under the command of a single commander, the court may receive that evidence as *prima facie* evidence of the responsibility of the commander for those crimes.
> (5) Where there is evidence that a war crime has been committed by members of a formation, unit, body, or group and that an officer or non-commissioned officer was present at or immediately before the time when such offense was committed, the court may receive that evidence as *prima facie* evidence of the responsibility of such officer or non-commissioned officer, and of the commander of such formation, unit, body, or group, for that crime.[55]

B. SUMMARY

Command has always imposed responsibility; yet few instances are recorded prior to the end of World War II where that responsibility was either criminal or international in nature. The responsibility existed prior to that time, but there was not sufficient warrant or authorization to interfere in what was essentially an area of "state action." The frustrations with the Leipzig trials after World War I, the genocidal acts of the Axis, and the absolute cessation of any form of government in the defeated Axis states, gave the world both the cause and the means for demanding a day of reckoning.

---

53 IV L.R.T.W.C. 88.

54 I L.R.T.W.C. 108-9. Article 139 (b), UCMJ (10 U.S. Code § 939(b)), relating to redress of injuries to property similarly provides that where such injuries are committed by a unit and the individual perpetrators cannot be identified, damages may be assessed against all individual members of the command who are shown to have been present at the time the damages complained of were inflicted.

55 IV L.R.T.W.C. 128.

Based on the foregoing rules, the Allied nations entered the trials believing a commander to be responsible for the unlawful actions of his subordinates where (a) he personally ordered the illegal act charged, or (b) with knowledge that such actions were taking place, he failed in his duty as a commander to prevent such offenses, either intentionally (The Netherlands, France, and Luxemborg) or through neglect (United States, China, Great Britain and Canada).[56] It remained for the tribunals to apply those rules to the cases presented.

II. WORLD WAR II TRIALS

A. *"WAR CRIMES" DEFINED*

Before proceeding, the term "war crimes" as used generally and in this thesis warrants definition. The United States Army defines "war crimes" as "the technical expression for a violation of the law of war by any person or persons, military or civilian." [57] The present British definition is similarly imprecise.[58]

Field Manual 27-10 provides some delineation by including those acts defined by the Geneva Conventions of 1949 as "grave breaches," if committed against persons or property protected by those Conventions; [59] Paragraph 504 includes other acts as "representative" of war crimes, *viz.*:

---

[56] The requirement of knowledge presents itself by implication only in all but the United States JCS definition (*supra*, n. 47), which included knowledge or notice.

[57] U.S. DEP'T OF ARMY, FIELD MANUAL NO. 27-10, LAW OF LAND WARFARE, para. 499 (1956) [hereinafter cited as FM 27-10]).

[58] British War Office, III MANUAL OF MILITARY LAW (LAW OF WAR ON LAND, 1958), para. 624, defines "war crime" as "the technical expression for violations of the laws of warfare, whether committed by members of the armed forces or by civilians."

[59] Paragraph 502 provides:

502. Grave Breaches of the Geneva Conventions of 1949 as War Crimes.

The Geneva Conventions of 1949 define the following acts as "grave breaches," if committed against persons or property protected by the Conventions:

a. GWS and GWS Sea:

Grave breaches to which the preceding Article relates shall be those involving any of the following acts, if committed against persons or property protected by the Convention: Wilful killing, torture or inhuman treatment, including biological experiments, wilfully causing great suffering or serious injury to body or health, and extensive destruction and appropriation of property, not justified by military necessity and carried out unlawfully and wantonly. (GWS, art. 50; GWS Sea, art. 51.)

a. Making use of poisoned or otherwise forbidden arms or ammunition.
b. Treacherous request for quarter.
c. Maltreatment of dead bodies.
d. Firing on localities which are undefended and without military significance.
e. Abuse of or firing on the flag of truce.
f. Misuse of the Red Cross emblem.
g. Use of civilian clothing by troops to conceal their military character during battle.
h. Improper use of privileged buildings for military purposes.
i. Poisoning of wells or streams.
j. Pillage or purposeless destruction.
k. Compelling prisoners of war to perform prohibited labor.
l. Killing without trial spies or other persons who have committed hostile acts.
m. Compelling civilians to perform prohibited labor.
n. Violation of surrender terms.[60]

The United States Navy has defined war crimes

> . . . as those acts which violate the rules established by customary and conventional international law regulating the conduct of warfare. Acts constituting war crimes may be committed either by members of the armed forces of a belligerent or by individuals belonging to the civilian population.[61]

The Charter of the International Military Tribunal established by the Allied Powers at the conclusion of World War II for

---

b. GPW
Grave breaches to which the preceding Article relates shall be those involving any of the following acts, if committed against persons or property protected by the Convention: Wilful killing, torture or inhuman treatment, including biological experiments, wilfully causing great sufferings or serious injury to body or health, compelling a prisoner of war to serve in the forces of the hostile Power, or wilfully depriving a prisoner of war of the rights of fair and regular trial prescribed in this Convention. (GPW, art. 130.)
c. GC.
Grave breaches to which the preceding Article relates shall be those involving any of the following acts, if committed against persons or property protected by the present Convention: wilful killing, torture or inhuman treatment, including biological experiments, wilfully causing great suffering or serious injury to body or health, unlawful deportation or transfer or unlawful confinement of a protected person, compelling a protected person to serve in the forces of a hostile Power, or wilfully depriving a protected person of the rights of fair and regular trial prescribed in the present Convention, taking of hostages and extensive destruction and appropriation of property, not justified by military necessity and carried out unlawfully and wantonly. (GC art. 147.)

60 FM 27-10 para. 504 (1956).

61 U.S. Department of the Navy, Law of Naval Warfare, para. 320 (NWIP 10-2, 1955).

prosecution and punishment of the major war criminals of the European axis defined "war crimes" as:

> . . . namely, violations of the laws or customs of war. Such violations shall include, but not be limited to, murder, ill-treatment or deportation to slave labor or for any other purpose of civilian population of or in occupied territory, murder or ill-treatment of prisoners of war or persons on the seas, killing of hostages, plunder of public or private property, wanton destruction of cities, towns or villages, or devastation not justified by military necessity . . .[62]

The definition formulated by the United Nations in the Nuremburg Principles of 1946 is similar in language. France in contrast left the term undefined, feeling that any offenses to be punished were such infractions of French law as were not made justifiable by the laws and customs of war.[63] This is not unlike the Navy definition and the general definition, rather than specific definition, would seem to be preferred: a war crime is any act not justified by military necessity and otherwise prohibited by custom or international convention regulating the conduct of war.

B. THE TRIAL OF GENERAL TOMOYUKI YAMASHITA[64]

Of the trials which address the question of command responsibility, the trial of Japanese General Tomoyuki Yamashita by Military Commission remains the most controversial, primarily (a) because of an ill-worded opinion prepared sua sponte by the lay court; (b) because of a book written by one of General Yamashita's defense counsel; and (c) inasmuch as it was one of the first war crimes trials completed, it gained the benefit of judicial review by the United States Supreme Court.

General Tomoyuki Yamashita served as commanding general of the Fourteenth Army Group of the Imperial Japanese Army in the Philippine Islands from October 9, 1944, until his surrender on September 3, 1945.[65] As such, the evidence established conclusively that he was the commander of all Japanese forces in the

---

[62] CHAPTER II, CHARTER OF THE INTERNATIONAL MILITARY TRIBUNAL, Article VI (b).

[63] III L.R.T.W.C. 105.

[64] Unless otherwise noted, all facts recited herein or documents referred to are from the record of trial, *United States of America vs. Tomoyuki Yamashita*, a Military Commission appointed by Paragraph 24, Special Orders 110, Headquarters United States Army Forces, Western Pacific, dated 1 October 1945. [hereinafter referred to as Tr. ——].

[65] Stipulation, October 29, 1945, between the United States and Tomoyuki Yamashita.

Philippines.[66] He served concurrently as the military governor of the Philippines.[67]

On October 2, 1945, General Yamashita was served with the following Charge:

> Tomoyuki YAMASHITA, General Imperial Japanese Army, between 9 October 1944 and 2 September 1945, at Manila and at other places in the Philippine Islands, while commander of armed forces of Japan at war with the United States of America and its allies, unlawfully disregarded and failed to discharge his duty as commander to control the operations of the members of his command, permitting them to commit brutal atrocities and other high crimes against people of the United States and its allies and dependencies, particularly the Philippines; and he, General Tomoyuki YAMASHITA, thereby violated the law of war.[68]

On October 8, 1945, as a result of a motion made by the defense during arraignment of the accused,[69] the prosecution submitted

---

[66] By stipulation (*Id.*) General Yamashita agreed that in addition to his regular forces he commanded the Kempei Tai (military police). General Yamashita claimed that the naval troops in Manila were only under his tactical command and therefore not within his disciplinary command and control (Tr. 3622); his chief-of-staff, General Muto, testified that any officer having command of troops of another branch under him did have the authority and duty to restrain those men from committing wrongful acts (Tr. 3049, 4034). The Commission, in their findings, concluded " . . . [t]hat a series of atrocities and other high crimes have been committed by members of the Japanese armed forces *under your command.*" [Emphasis supplied]. If these naval forces were not under Yamashita's command and control, they had to be under the command and control of Admiral Soemu Toyoda, Commander-in-Chief of the Combined Fleet. Admiral Toyoda's case is discussed, *infra* page 69, charged with criminal responsibility for the war crimes committed by the naval troops in question in Manila, the tribunal before which he was tried, in acquitting Admiral Toyoda, concluded that command, control, and responsibility for these forces lay in General Yamashita, not Admiral Toyoda. (Toyoda transcript, page 5012). The Japanese air Forces in the Philippines came under General Yamashita's command and control on January 1, 1945 (Yamashita transcript, p. 3589). He was also commander of all Prisoner of War Camps in the Philippines (Tr. 2675, 3251, 3252.)

[67] *In re* Yamashita, 327 U.S. 1 at 16 (1946).

[68] Tr. 23. The government of Japan was bound by a number of conventions to observe the rules and customs of land warfare. It had been a signatory of the Hague Convention No. IV of 1907 (Respecting the Laws and Customs of War on Land) and the Red Cross Convention of 1929 (Convention for the Amelioration of the Condition of the Wounded and Sick of Armies in the Field), and at the outbreak of the war, had agreed to apply the Red Cross Convention of 1929 to civilian internees. Although it had not ratified the Geneva Convention of 1929 (Treatment of Prisoners of War), upon the outbreak of war Japan had agreed to apply the provisions of that Convention *mutatis mutandis* and to take into consideration the national and racial customs of prisoners.

[69] Tr. 34.

a Bill of Particulars containing sixty-four specifications, prefaced by the statement that

> Between 9 October 1944 and 2 September 1945, at Manila and other places in the Philippine Islands, members of Armed Forces of Japan under the command of the Accused committed the following: . . .[70]

Susequently, on October 29, 1945, a Supplemental Bill of Particulars was filed containing an additional fifty-nine specifications, prefaced by the allegation that

> . . . members of the armed forces of Japan, under the command of the Accused, were permitted to commit the following during the period from 9 October 1944 to 2 September 1945 at Manila and other places in the Philippine Island: . . . .[71]

Trial on the merits commenced on October 29, 1945, concluding December 7, 1945, after hearing 286 witnesses and receiving 423 documents in evidence.[72] The evidence substantially supported the crimes alleged in most of the 123 particulars; General Yamashita admitted neither the commission of the acts nor that they were violations of the laws of war.[73] Rather, he denied ordering the offenses alleged, and denied having any knowledge of their commission, the latter as a result of the extreme tactical situation in which he found himself from the very outset of assumption of command.[74] Had he known of or forseen these acts, he would have concentrated all of his efforts toward preventing them.[75] In concluding his testimony, General Yamashita specifically denied either receiving from superior authority or giving any order to massacre "all the Filipinos." [76]

[70] Tr. 37.
[71] Tr. 74.
[72] Tr. 4058.
[73] Tr. 3917 *et seq.;* United States v. Yamashita, 327 U.S. 1 at 14.
[74] Tr. 3537, 3654-6.
[75] Tr. 3656.
[76] Tr. 3656. David Bergamini, in JAPAN'S IMPERIAL CONSPIRACY (1972) indicates Japanese records are to the contrary. General Yamashita's subordinates received such a directive from Tokyo Imperial Headquarters and carried it out despite General Yamashita's efforts to prevent its execution. (pp. xxii, 1111-1112) If this is true, the *Yamashita* case factually resembles the situation presented in the war crimes trial of Generalfeldmarschall Wilhelm von Leeb. On receipt of The Commissar Order, General von Leeb called his subordinate commanders together, advised them that he considered that order to be in violation of international law, and advised them of his opposition to it. As the court stated in acquitting him of charges relating to its subsequent implementation, "If his subordinate commanders . . . permitted . . . enforcement, that is their responsibility and not his." U.S. v. Von Leeb, XI TWC 557-558, discussed *infra* p. 44 *et seq.* The so-called "Yam-

COMMAND RESPONSIBILITY

The evidence presented the Commission directly and circumstantially refuted the testimony of General Yamashita, the latter on five bases: (a) the number of acts of atrocity, (b) the number of victims, (c) the widespread occurrence of atrocities, (d) the striking similarity in the method of execution, and (e) the vast number of atrocities carried out under the supervision of an officer.

Of the 123 atrocities included within the Charge, evidence was adduced on ninety.[77] Forty-four occurred in Manila substantially during the two-week period from 6 to 20 February 1945, during which time over 8,000 men, women, and children, all unarmed noncombatant civilians, were killed and over 7,000 mistreated, maimed or wounded.[78] While General Yamashita had displaced his headquarters from Manila some two months previous, and while communications were generally precarious, his headquarters nevertheless possessed and utilized the capability of communication with Manila until June, 1945.[79] The war crimes which occurred in Manila were carried out pursuant to written orders[80] and under the supervision of officers of the army and navy.[81] Many advised their victims-to-be that they were acting pursuant to orders from higher authority.[82] A pattern of execution and an

---

ashita doctrine" of strict liability, as argued and asserted by chief prosecutor Telford Taylor, was specifically rejected by the Tribunal in the *von Leeb* case. XI TWC 534-44. One can only speculate as to what success General Yamashita may have had proffering this argument (assuming *arguendo* Bergamini is correct) rather than asserting the improbable denial of knowledge.

77 Annex to the Review of the Theater Judge Advocate, United States Army Forces, Pacific (December 26, 1945).

78 Tr. 212, 271, 348, 370, 412, 429, 445, 587, 606, 669, 717, 743, 778, 806, 871, 1147, 1159, 1197, 1200, 1222, 1262, 1270, 1299, 1370, 2211, 2223. Annex, *id.* items 3, 10, 13, 15, 15, 17, 20, 23, 24, 25, 27, 28, 29, 30, 32, 34, 35, 36, 41, 48, 50, 51, 52, 53, 60, 61, 62, 63, 64, 68, 77, 80, 88, 89, 93, 97, 98, 99, 101, 102, 104, 105.

79 Tr. 3524-3527, 3654-3656, 3123, 3387, 2674.

80 An order of the Kobayashi Heidan group dated 13 February 1945 directed that all people in or around Manila except Japanese and Special Construction Units (Filipino collaborators) be executed (Tr. 2905, 2906; Ex. 404). An operations order of the Manila Naval Defense Force and Southwestern Area Fleet, part of the landbased naval forces, directed that in executing Filipinos, consideration was to be given to conserving ammunition and manpower; and that because the disposal of bodies was "troublesome" they should be gathered into houses which were scheduled to be burned or destroyed (Tr. 2909).

81 Tr. 833, 2174.

82 During the Paco massacre in Manila on February 10, 1945, in which twelve unarmed noncombatant civilians were executed (Annex, *supra* n. 64, item 29), a Japanese officer informed his intended victims, "You very good

orderliness and dispatch emerged: assembly of the victims in a central location, usually a house or large building,[83] where the most "economical" means of execution were utilized in order to conserve the expenditure of ammunition.[84] In a number of instances extensive advance preparation of the site, for example, installing strings to set off explosives, cutting holes in the floor for bodies to fall through, digging mass graves, and staging gasoline for the burning of bodies and buildings, was made to facilitate executions.[85] The bodies were then disposed of by throwing in the river, burning with a house or building, or burying in mass graves.[86] Similar war crimes were documented throughout the Philippines, manifesting the same pattern of orderliness, planning, and direction for the most part during the same two-week period in February, 1945.[87] In addition, there was extensive evidence concerning the starvation, torture, lack of medical care for, and murder of American prisoners of war and civilian internees.[88] General Yamashita never inspected any of the prisoner of war camps, even though his headquarters was located within, adjacent to, or in the vicinity of two different camps where a substantial

---

man but you die," and "Order from higher officer, Kill you, all of you." (Tr. 833). At Dy Pac Lumber Yard in Manila on February 2, 1945, (Annex, *supra* n.64, items 16 and 93), before executing 117 noncombatant civilians, the Japanese captain in charge advised his victims that they were to die because of "an order from above" he had to follow. (Tr. 2174). Outside Manila, on April 10, 1945, during the murder of civilians near Sumayao, a Japanese soldier said "It was Yamashita's order to kill all civilians." (Tr. 2317). On Bataan Island, an American aviator was tortured, then buried alive. The commander of the execution party stated that the execution was carried out as a result of a direct order from General Yamashita that "American prisoners of war in the Philippine Islands will be killed." (Tr. 2609-12, 2616, 2621).

[83] Tr. 190, 410, 429, 450, 463, 587, 606, 715, 738, 767, 775, 797, 823, 2167; Ex. 131.

[84] Tr. 148, 192, 271, 283, 348, 405, 453, 587, 621, 717, 745, 779, 798, 833, 1134, 1197, 2151, 2168; Ex. 126.

[85] Tr. 445, 467, 477, 589, 669, 768, 778, 823, 2151, and 2268.

[86] 467, 607, 639, 768, 778, 806, 865, 1188, 1200, 1237, 2152; Ex. 91, 92, 93, 114, 124.

[87] Tr. 1491, 1506, 1515, 1524, 1533, 1546, 1556, 1621, 1628, 1647, 1652, 1655, 1661, 1671, 1707, 1710, 1714, 1736, 1737, 1739, 1764, 1775, 1783, 1790, 1813, 1839, 2182. On February 12, 1945, more than 2,500 men, women, and children of the town of Calamba on Luzon were executed by bayoneting or burning. (Tr. 1977. 1979. 1981. 1985. 1992, 1999, 2004, 2008. 2012.) On February 24, 1945, all male residents of San Pablo between the ages of 15 and 50 — some 6,000 to 8,000 in all — were executed (Tr. 2064, 2069, 2070, 2072, 2083, 2084, 2088).

[88] Annex, *supra* n. 64, items 2, 4, 6, 7, 9, 13, 69, 73, 76, 83, 86, 87, 89, 94, 95, 109, 122.

number of violations occurred.[89] After General Yamashita personally ordered the suppression of guerilla activities in December, 1945, two thousand Filipinos incarcerated in Manila as guerrilla suspects were given cursory trials, none of which lasted more than five minutes and none of which even conformed to Japanese legal requirements, transported to North Cemetery in trucks, and beheaded.[90] General Yamashita's staff judge advocate, Colonel Hideo Nishiharu, testified that he advised General Yamashita that these guerrilla suspects were in custody, that there was insufficient time to give them proper trials, and that the Kempei Tai "would punish those who were to be punished." [91] Knowing that this meant that these guerillas would be executed without trial, General Yamashita nodded in apparent approval.[92] General Yama-

[89] Tr. 3537, 3573. General Yamashita's headquarters were at Fort McKinley until December 23, 1944, where four hundred disabled American prisoners of war were held from October 31, 1944 until January 15, 1945. The prisoners were crowded into one building, furnished no beds or covers and kept within the inclosure of a fence extending thirty feet beyond each side of the building. Their two meals a day consisted of one canteen cup of boiled rice, mixed with greens; once a week the four hundred men were given twenty-five to thirty pounds of rotten meat, filled with maggots. Occasionally they would go a day or two without water and at times were reduced to eating grass and sticks they dug in the yard. (Tr. 2756-2758). These conditions existed within walking distance of General Yamashita's headquarters; yet, while recognizing a duty to prevent such occurrences, and despite his testimony that had he forseen or known of these conditions he would have "concentrated all [his] efforts toward preventing it," he never conducted nor directed the conduct of an inspection of the facilities. (Tr. 3654-3656). He transferred his headquarters to Baguio in 1945, where in one incident on April 18, 1945, eighty-three men, women, and children all noncombatants, were executed. (Tr. 2655-2661).

[90] Tr. 2253-2311.

[91] Tr. 3762-3763.

[92] Tr. 3762, 3763, 3814, 3815. Aware that Colonel Nishiharu's testimony directly connected General Yamashita to 2,000 deaths and generally weakened the defense argument of lack of knowledge, defense counsel A. Frank Reel did everything he could to discredit Colonel Nishiharu's testimony. Utilizing a little literary license and a pair of editing scissors, he met with greater success in his book *The Case of General Yamashita* (1949) than before the Commission. In his book, Reel asserts that the Commission, impatient with Colonel Nishiharu, conducted its own cross-examination, concluding:

> The Commission doubts that further exploration of the point would serve any useful purpose. . . . We have great doubt that lengthy cross-examination will be worth consideration of this court.

To which Reel then added:

> And that, I believe, disposed of Nishiharu.

A reading of the transcript lends itself to a different interpretation. A colloquy between the Commission and Reel indicates that any impatience of the Commission was with Reel and his line (and length) of cross-examination. After extensive cross-examination concerning Colonel Nishiharu's role in the decision-making process, particularly as it related to the execution of the 2,000 prisoners, the Commission interrupted:

shita subsequently issued a written order to the Kempei Tai unit responsible for the executions commending them for their "fine work." [93]

> The answers will probably be quite immaterial, anyway. No commander could possibly be in a position where the recommendations by a staff officer, if accepted, would place the responsibility upon the staff officer. In all armies, it is presumed to be a standard practice that staff officers make recommendations to commanders, which may or may not be accepted, but if they are accepted then it becomes the decision of the commander; the staff officer's responsibility is finished.

(Tr. 3792).

Reel maintained he was merely attacking Colonel Nishiharu's credibility, and resumed his line of examination. His attempts were interrupted for clarification purposes by both government counsel and the Commission. Once the point in question — approval by the Commanding General of death sentences — was clarified by the Commission's questions, the Commission then advised Captain Reel. "You may proceed, and the Commission doubts that further exploration of this point would serve any useful purpose. Do you propose to explore it further?" (Tr. 3799)

While answering initially in the negative, Reel's subsequent explanation indicated that he in fact did intend to renew the same line of question. The Commission then replied:

> Well, we have great doubt that lengthy cross examination will be worth consideration of the Court. It is entirely possible you may wish to explore into the details of the alleged execution of the one thousand or thereabouts Filipinos charged with being guerrillas, just before the headquarters was moved from Fort McKinley.
>
> I will ask you to consider very carefully the necessity of much more cross-examination of this witness.

(Tr. 3800)

Thereafter, rather than "disposing" of Colonel Nishiharu, Captain Reel continued his examination for another twenty-one pages.

The author's reading of the transcript is borne out by a conversation with the government counsel in the *Yamashita* trial, Major Robert M. Kerr, on November 23, 1972. Mr. Kerr thought the testimony of Colonel Nishiharu both significant and conclusive, believed the Commission accepted his testimony, and was in complete disagreement with Reel's conclusions concerning that testimony.

Colonel Nishiharu's testimony is supported by the testimony of Richard M. Sakakida (Tr. 2253-2302), a Nisei interpreter who worked in Colonel Nishiharu's office. Sakakida testified that during December 1944, trial of Filipino civilians consisted merely in the accused signing his name and giving his thumb-print, in reading the charge to him and in sentencing him. In the event a sentence of death was passed, the victim was not informed of this until arrival at the cemetery. In one week in December 1944, the cases of 2,000 Filipinos accused of being guerrillas were so handled by General Yamashita's headquarters. If Japanese soldiers were tried, however, they were accorded a full trial in accordance with Japanese procedures. No Japanese soldiers were tried after October 1944, however.

The testimony of Richard M. Sakakida was overlooked by Mr. Reel in *The Case of General Yamashita*.

[93] Tr. 905-906, 3763. The captured diary of a Japanese warrant officer assigned to a unit operating in the Manila area contained an entry

Two other witnesses appeared on behalf of the prosecution to directly link General Yamashita to the offenses alleged. While both were in the custody of United States forces as suspected collaborators, and while both previously had offered to exchange information as to Filipino and Japanese collaborators in return for their freedom, both testified that they had received no promise or reward for their testimony in the trial of General Yamashita.[94]

The first, Narciso Lapus, was private secretary from June 1942 to December 1944 to General Artenio Ricarte, a prominent member of the Japanese puppet government of the Philippines. Lapus was advised by Ricarte in October 1944 that Yamashita had informed him that:

> We take the Filipinos 100 percent as our enemies because all of them, directly or indirectly, are guerrillas or helping the guerrillas. In a war with the enemies [sic] we don't need to give quarter. The enemies should go.[95]

According to Lapus, General Yamashita then advised Ricarte that he planned to allow the Americans to enter Manila; he would then counter-attack, destroying Manila, the American forces, and the population of Manila. His plan of defense coincided with orders he had received to destroy Manila, particularly the populated and commercial areas of the city. General Yamashita further advised General Ricarte that he had ordered Japanese forces to wipe out any population area that gave any signs of pro-American movement or action; and that when Ricarte asked General Yamashita to rescind the order, General Yamashita refused.[96]

The second witness, Joaquin S. Galang, testified that he overheard a conversation between Generals Yamashita and Ricarte in December 1944 in which General Ricarte asked General Yamashita to rescind his order to kill all Filipinos. General Yamashita replied: "The order is my order. And because of that it should not be broken or disobeyed. It ought to be consumed, happen what may happen." [97]

The testimony of Galang was rebutted by the defense: Galang had testified that General Ricarte's 12-year-old grandson had served as an interpreter for the conversation overheard by Galang;

---

dated December 1, 1944: "Received orders, on the mopping up of guerrillas last night. Our object is to wound and kill the men, to get the information and to kill the women who run away." (Tr. 2882; Ex. 385).

[94] Tr. 913, 1059.

[95] Tr. 917.

[96] Tr. 917, 923, 939, 940, 947, 1023.

[97] Tr. 1063, 1068, 1069.

the defense produced the grandson, Bislumo Romero, who denied interpreting the conversation in question.[98]

The trial concluded on December 7, 1945. In reaching a finding of guilty, the Commission, none of whom were lawyers, saw fit to issue a written opinion, which states in part:

> The Prosecution presented evidence to show that the crimes were so extensive and wide-spread, both as to time and area, that they must have been wilfully permitted by the Accused, or secretly ordered by the Accused . . .
>
> The Accused is an officer of long years of experience, broad in its scope, who has had extensive command and staff duty in the Imperial Japanese Army in peace as well as war in Asia, Malaya, Europe, and the Japanese Home Islands. Clearly, assignment to command military troops is accompanied by broad authority and heavy responsibility. This has been true in all armies throughout recorded history. It is absurd, however, to consider a commander a murderer or rapist because one of his soldiers commits a murder or a rape. Nonetheless, where murder and rape and vicious, revengeful actions are widespread offenses, and there is no effective attempt by a commander to discover and control the criminal acts, such a commander may be held responsible, even criminally liable, for the lawless acts of his troops, depending upon their nature and the circumstances surrounding them. Should a commander issue orders which lead directly to lawless acts, the criminal responsibility is definite and has always been so understood. The Rules of Land Warfare, FM 27-10, United States Army, are clear on these points. It is for the purpose of maintaining discipline and control, among other reasons, that military commanders are given broad powers of administering military justice. The tactical situation, the character, training and capacity of staff officers and subordinate commanders as well as the traits of character, and training of his troops are other important factors in such cases. These matters have been the principle considerations of the Commission during its deliberations. . . .
>
> . . . The Commission concludes: (1) That a series of atrocities and other high crimes have been committed by members of the Japanese armed forces under your command against people of the United States, their allies and dependencies throughout the Philippine Islands; that they were not sporadic in nature but in many cases were methodically supervised by Japanese officers and noncommissioned officers; (2) that during the period in question you failed to provide effective control of your troops as was required by the circumstances.[99]

Review of the evidence presented, the record of trial, and the Commission's "opinion" indicates four theories of command responsibility upon which the Commission could have depended to reach their decision: (1) that General Yamashita ordered the offenses committed; (2) that, learning about the commission of the offenses, General Yamashita acquiesced in them; (3) that, learn-

[98] Tr. 2014, 2021.
[99] Tr. 4059-4063.

COMMAND RESPONSIBILITY

ing about the commission of the offenses, General Yamashita failed to take appropriate measures to prevent their reoccurrence or to halt them; (4) the offenses committed by the troops under General Yamashita were so widespread that under the circumstances he exhibited a personal neglect or abrogation of his duties and responsibilities as a commander amounting to wanton, immoral disregard of the action of his subordinates amounting to acquiescence.

The question of knowledge, an element of the first three theories, was the subject of re-examination during the trial of General Yamashita's Chief of Staff, Lieutenant General Akira Muto. Tried by the International Military Tribunal for the Far East, a tribunal composed of lawyer-judges from eleven nations, Muto was charged with the same offenses as Yamashita; much of the evidence received was taken directly from the Yamashita transcript. Muto's defense to these charges was the same: lack of knowledge owing to the extreme tactical situation. In addressing this defense, the Tribunal stated:

> . . . During his tenure of office as such Chief-of-Staff a campaign of massacre, torture and other atrocities was waged by the Japanese troops on the civilian population, and prisoners of war and civilian internees were starved, tortured and murdered. Muto shares responsibility for these gross breaches of the Laws of War. *We reject his defense that he knew nothing of these occurrences.* It is wholly incredible.[100]

General Yamashita's case received daily review during the progress of the trial by the staff judge advocate for the convening authority.[101] A daily summary of evidence was made and as a result the staff judge advocate's review of the case was completed on December 9, 1945. In conclusion, the staff judge advocate stated:

---

100 II Tokyo Judgment 1, 186 [Emphasis supplied.]; *Also see* Volume 203, Official Transcript of the International Japanese War Crimes Trial, In The International-Military Tribunal for the Far East, pages 49, 820-49, 821. The specific count of the indictment, Count 55, contained language similar to that with which Yamashita was charged:

> . . . being by virtue of (his) respective (office) responsible for securing the observance of the said Conventions and assurances and the Law and Customs of War . . . in respect of many thousands of prisoners of war and civilians then in the power of Japan belonging to the United States . . . (and) the Commonwealth of the Philippines . . . deliberately and recklessly disregarded (his) legal duty to take adequate steps to secure the observance and prevent breaches thereof, and thereby violated the laws of war.

(Count 55 of the Indictment, Annex No. A-6, Tokyo Judgment).

101 United States Army Forces, Western Pacific.

> The evidence affirmatively shows a complete indifference on the part of accused as commanding officer either to restrain those practices or to punish their authors. The evidence is convincing that the overall responsibility lay with the Army Commander, General Yamashita, who was the highest commander in the Philippines; that he was charged with the responsibility of defending the Philippines and that he issued a general order to wipe out the Philippines if possible and to destroy Manila; that subsequently he said he would not revoke the order.
>
> The pattern of rape, murder, mass execution and destruction of property is wide spread both in point of time and of area to the extent a reasonable person must logically conclude the program to have been the result of deliberate planning.
>
> From all the facts and circumstances of record, it is impossible to escape the conclusion that accused knew or had the means to know of the widespread commission of atrocities by members and units of his command; his failure to inform himself through official means available to him of what was common knowledge throughout his command and throughout the civilian population can only be considered as a criminal dereliction of duty on his part.[102]

Defense counsel for General Yamashita had previously filed a petition for writs of habeas corpus and prohibition with the United States Supreme Court on November 25, 1945;[103] a petition for writ of certiorari was subsequently filed on January 7, 1946.[104] In the interim, the military continued its review process. On December 26, 1945, the review of the theater staff judge advocate was completed. After extensive review of the evidence, the theater staff judge advocate stated:

> The only real question in the case concerns accused's responsibility for the atrocities shown to have been committed by members of his command. Upon this issue a careful reading of all the evidence impels the conclusion that it demonstrates this responsibility [reciting facts]. All this leads to the inevitable conclusion that the atrocities were not the sporadic acts of soldiers out of control but were carried out pursuant to a deliberate plan of mass extermination which must have emanated from higher authority or at least had its approval. From the widespread character of the atrocities as above outlined, the orderliness of their execution and the proof that they were done pursuant to orders, the conclusion is inevitable that the accused knew about them and either gave his tacit approval to them or at least failed to do anything either to prevent them or to punish their perpetrators. Accused himself admitted that he ordered the suppression or "mopping up" of guerrillas

[102] Review of the Staff Judge Advocate of the Record of Trial by Military Commission of Tomoyuki Yamashita, Headquarters, United States Army Forces, Western Pacific, December 9, 1945.

[103] In the Matter of the Application of General Tomoyuki Yamashita. United States Supreme Court, October Term. 1945, No. 61, Miscellaneous.

[104] General Tomoyuki Yamashita, Petitioner, v. Lieutenant General Wilhelm D. Styer, Commanding General, United States Army Forces, Western Pacific, United Supreme Court, October Term, 1945, No. 672.

> and that he took no steps to guard against any excesses in the execution of this order. One cannot be unmindful of the fact that accused, an experienced officer, in giving such an order must have been aware of the dangers involved when such instructions were communicated to troops the type of the Japanese. Accused stoutly insists that he knew nothing of any of the atrocities and assigns as the reason for his lack of knowledge the complete breakdown of communications incident to the swift and overpowering advance of the American forces and to his complete preoccupation with plans for the defense of the Philippines. He states that his troops were disorganized and out of control, leaving the inference that he could not have prevented the atrocities even had he known of them. With respect to Manila, he insists that he had only tactical command of naval troops operating in the city and although he had authority to restrain such troops committing disorders, he could not discipline them, the situation being thus complicated by dual control between himself and the Navy. Here in particular the defense witnesses testified to a breakdown of communications with the forces in Manila. While, however, it may be conceded that the accused was operating under some difficulty due to the rapidity of the advance of the Americans, there was substantial evidence in the record that the situation was not so bad as stated by the accused. General Yokoyama admitted that he had communication with troops in Manila until 20 February and with the accused until June and made frequent reports to him. Surely a matter so important as the massacre of 8,000 people by Japanese troops must necessarily have been reported. (Since accused had authority to control the operations of the naval troops he cannot absolve himself of responsibility by showing that others had the duty of punishing them for disorders.) There is no suggestion as to any breakdown in communications with Batangas where late in February some of the most widespread atrocities occurred, nor is there any substantial proof that communications with other points in the islands at which atrocities occurred were at all interrupted. It is also noteworthy that the mistreatment of prisoners of war at Ft. McKinley occurred while accused was present in his headquarters only a few hundred yards distant and some of the other atrocities transpired close to the proximity of Baguio where he had his headquarters after removal from Manila. Taken all together, the court was fully warranted in finding that accused failed to discharge his responsibility to control his troops thereby permitting the atrocities alleged and was thus guilty as charged.[105]

In re Yamashita was argued before the Supreme Court of the United States on January 7, 1945.

The substance of the Court's opinion [106] addressed three issues: (a) jurisdiction of a military commission over the accused; (b) failure to state an offense against the law of war, that is, jurisdiction over the offenses; and (c) entitlement to and denial of the ac-

105 Review of the Theater Staff Judge Advocate of the Record of Trial by Military Commission of Tomoyuki Yamashita, General Headquarters, United States Army Forces, Pacific, December 26, 1945.

106 *In re* Yamashita, 327 U.S. 1 (1945).

cused's fundamental right of a fair trial thereby divesting the Commission of jurisdiction to proceed.

This article limits its discussion to (b)—was there such a duty imposed upon a military commander that its disregard constituted a violation of the law of war? In determining that the acts alleged stated an offense against the law of war, the Court first addressed the question of command responsibility:

> . . . it is urged that the charge does not allege that petitioner has either committed or directed the commission of such acts, and consequently that no violation is charged against him. But this overlooks the fact that the gist of the charge is an unlawful breach of duty by petitioner as an army commander to control the operations of the members of his command by "permitting them to commit" the extensive and widespread atrocities specified. The question then is whether the law of war imposes on an army commander a duty to take such appropriate measures as are within his power to control the troops under his command for the prevention of the specified acts which are violations of the law of war and which are likely to attend the occupation of hostile territory by an uncontrolled soldiery, and whether he *may be charged with personal reponsibility for his failure* to take such measures when violations result. That this was the precise issue to be tried was made clear by the statement of the prosecution at the opening of the trial.
>
> It is evident that the conduct of military operations by troops whose excesses are unrestrained by the orders or efforts of their commander would almost certainly result in violations which it is the purpose of the law of war to prevent. Its purpose to protect the civilian population and prisoners of war from brutality would largely be defeated if the commander of an invading army could with impunity neglect to take reasonable measures for their protection. Hence the law of war presupposes that its violation is to be avoided through the control of the operations of war by commanders who are to some extent responsible for their subordinates.[107]

Citing the provisions relative to command of Articles 1 and 43 to the Annex of the Fourth Hague Convention of 1907, Article 19 of the Tenth Hague Convention, and Article 26 of the Geneva Red Cross Convention of 1929,[108] the Court stated:

> These provisions plainly imposed on petitioner . . . an affirmative duty to take such measures as were within his power and appropriate in the circumstances to protect prisoners of war and the civilian population.[109]

In concluding that the charge stated an offense against the law of war, the majority, in refusing to review the evidence before the Commission, nevertheless noted:

---

107 *In re* Yamashita, 327 U.S. 1, 14-15 (1945) [Emphasis supplied.].
108 *See* text at notes 28, 29, 30, 39 and 40, *supra*.
109 *In re* Yamashita, 327 U.S. 1, 16 (1945).

> There is no contention that the present charge, thus read, is without the support of evidence, or that the Commission held petitioner responsible for failing to take measures which were beyond his control or inappropriate for a commanding officer to take in the circumstances . . . It is plain that the charge on which petitioner was tried charged him with a breach of his duty to control the operations of the members of his command, by permitting them to commit the specified atrocities. This was enough to require the Commission to hear evidence tending to establish the culpable failure of petitioner to perform the duty imposed on him by the law of war and to pass upon its sufficiency to establish guilt.
>
> . . . we conclude that the allegations of the charge, tested by any reasonable standard, adequately allege a violation of the law of war and that the Commission had authority to try and decide the issue which it raised.[110]

The majority thus concluded (a) that a commander has a duty to control the conduct of his subordinates, insuring their compliance with the law of war, and (2) that where such a duty exists, a charge alleging less than personal participation in or ordering of an act in violation of the law of war states a violation of the law of war.

In a dissent laden with emotion, Justice Murphy charged:

> . . . He was not charged with personally participating in the acts of atrocity or with ordering or condoning their commission. Not even knowledge of these crimes was attributed to him. It was simply alleged that he unlawfully disregarded and failed to discharge his duty as commander to control the operations of the members of his command, permitting them to commit the acts of atrocity. The recorded annals of warfare and the established principles of international law afford not the slightest precedent for such a charge.[111]

However, Justice Murphy conceded that "inaction or negligence may give rise to liability, civil or criminal," [112] subsequently observing that "this is not to say that enemy commanders may escape punishment for clear and unlawful failures to prevent atrocities." [113] Justice Murphy's objection was not to the standard of responsibility, but to the seeming inconsistency in the facts between the picture painted, first, of a thoroughly defeated commander, retaining operational command but having lost tactical control, under constant attack by vastly superior forces and, second, a commander who was not exercising proper administrative control over his subordinate units. This is a factual determina-

---

110 *Id.* at 17, 18. *See also*, n. 4 at 327 U.S. 1, 16.

111 *Id.* at 28. *See also*, 327 U.S. 1, 47 (Justice Rutledge concurrence in this view).

112 *Id.* at 39.

113 *Id.* at 40.

tion balanced by the Commission and eventually determined adversely to the accused based on their professional opinion, as soldiers, that the accused failed to fulfill his duties as a commander as required by the circumstances.

It has been fairly speculated that the emotive dissents of Justices Rutledge and Murphy—manifested by the shaking voice and castigating looks of Justice Murphy in reading his dissent—came about as a result of the serious procedural questions raised by the case.[114] Unable to accept the majority's logic on these points, the dissenting justices accepted all arguments of counsel for the accused.[115] The respective petitions were denied, and the case was returned to the military for disposition on February 4, 1946, the date of the Court's decision.[116]

General Yamashita's fate lay in the hands of General Douglas MacArthur, Commanding General, United States Army Forces, Pacific. That decision came on February 7, 1946: General MacArthur approved the findings and sentence of the commission [117]

---

[114] KERR, *supra* n. 92.

[115] Justice Murphy's opinion embraced all defense arguments *in toto* and in most cases verbatim; his famous language concerning General Yamashita's purported lack of knowledge (327 U.S. 1 at 34) comes directly from the brief filed with the Supreme Court by the defense (pages 28-29).

An independent source confirms that the dissenting Justices — indeed, the entire Court — were in disagreement over procedural questions only; no reveiw of the merits was attempted. A. MASON, HARLAN FISKE STONE: PILLAR OF THE LAW (1956), 666-671.

[116] Denial of Motion for Leave to File Petition for Writ of Habeas Corpus and Prohibition, Supreme Court of the United States, October Term, 1945, No. 61, Miscellaneous; and Denial of Petition for Writ of Certiorari, No. 672.

[117] It is not easy for me to pass penal judgment upon a defeated adversary in a major military campaign. I have reviewed the proceedings in vain search for some mitigating circumstance on his behalf. I can find none. Rarely has so cruel and wanton a record been spread to public gaze.

> Revolting as this may be in itself, it pales before the sinister and far reaching implication thereby attached to the profession of arms. The soldier, be he friend or foe, is charged with the protection of the weak and unarmed. It is the very essence and reason for his being. When he violates this sacred trust he not only profanes his entire cult but threatens the very fabric of international society. The traditions of fighting men are long and honorable They are based upon the noblest of human traits—sacrifice. This officer, of proven field merit, entrusted with high command involving authority adequate to responsibility, has failed this irrevocable standard; has failed his duty to his troops, to his country, to his enemy, to mankind; has failed utterly his soldier faith. The transgressions resulting therefrom as revealed by the trial are a blot upon the military profession, a stain upon civilization and constitute a memory of shame and dishonor that can never be forgotten. Peculiarly callous and pur-

and on February 23, 1946, General Yamashita was hanged.[118]

The value of the study of the Yamashita trial lies not in its often misstated facts nor in the legal doctrine of strict liability it purportedly espoused (but did not), but in the legal conclusions it actually reached. *Yamashita* recognized the existence of an affirmative duty on the part of a commander to take such measures as are within his power and appropriate in the circumstances to wage war within the limitations of the laws of war, in particular exercising control over his subordinates; it established that the commander who disregards this duty has committed a violation of the law of war; and it affirmed the *summum jus* of subjecting an offending commander to trial by a properly constituted tribunal of a state other than his own. In the latter it became the foundation for all subsequent trials arising from World War II. In the former its value lies primarily in the general rather than the spe-

---

poseless was the sack of the ancient city of Manila, with its Christian population and its countless historic shrines and monuments of culture and civilization, which with campaign conditions reversed had previously been spared.

It is appropriate here to recall that the accused was fully forewarned as to the personal consequences of such atrocities. On October 24 — four days following the landing of our forces on Leyte — it was publicly proclaimed that I would "hold the Japanese Military authorities in the Philippines immediately liable for any harm which may result from failure to accord prisoners of war, civilian internees or civilian non-combatants the proper treatment and the protection to which they of right are entitled.

No new or retroactive principles of law, either national or international, are involved. The case is founded upon basic fundamentals and practice as immutable and as standardized as the most matured and irrefragable of social codes. The proceedings were guided by that primary rational of all judicial purpose — to ascertain the full truth unshackled by any artificialities of narrow method or technical arbitrariness. The results are beyond challenge.

I approve the findings and sentence of the Commission and direct the Commanding General, United States Army Forces, Western Pacific, to execute the judgment upon the defendant, stripped of uniform, decorations and other appurtenances signifying membership in the military profession.

(signed) Douglas MacArthur
(typed) DOUGLAS MacARTHUR,
General of the Army, United States
Army, Commander-in-chief

Action of the confirming authority, General Headquarters, United States Army Forces, Pacific, in the case of General Tomoyuki Yamashita, Imperial Japanese Army, February 7, 1946.

118 Notification of Death, Office of the Surgeon, Headquarters, Philippine Detention & Rehabilitation Center, February 23, 1946.

cific sense—while recognizing the duty of the commander and the violation of the law of war for failure to exercise that duty, the duty was all the more absolute in *Yamashita* because of General Yamashita's additional responsibilities as military governor of the Philippines. As military governor, all trust, care, and confidence of the population were reposed in him. This was in addition to his duties and responsibilities as a military commander, a point refined in the *High Command* and *Hostages* cases which follow.[119]

C. THE "HIGH COMMAND" CASE

Perhaps the most important of the war crimes trials involving the question of command responsibility was the Nuremburg trial of *United States v. Wilhelm von Leeb*,[120] also known as "The High Command Trial." The accused were thirteen of the higher ranking German officers in American custody;[121] all held important staff and/or command positions in the German military. The Tribunal hearing the case was composed of Presiding Judge John C. Young, former Chief Justice of the Supreme Court of Colorado; Associate Judge Justin W. Harding, formerly U.S. District Judge, First Division, District of Alaska; and Associate Judge Winfield B. Hale, a Justice on the Tennessee Court of Appeals on leave of absence.[122]

---

[119] The other major objection to the trial of General Yamashita — lack of due process — has generally been mooted by the provisions of the Geneva Conventions of 1949 which provide fundamental legal protections for those charged with violation of the Conventions or other laws and subjected to trial by a state other than their own.

[120] Vols. X and XI TWC.

[121] Generalfeldmarschall (General of the Army) Wilhelm von Leeb, Generalfeldmarschall (General of the Army) Hugo Sperrle, Generalfeldmarschall (General of the Army) Georg Karl Friedrich-Wilhelm von Kuechler, Generaloberst (General) Johannes Blaskowitz, Generaloberst (General) Hermann Hoth, Generaloberst (General) Hans Reinhardt, Generaloberst (General) Hans von Salmuth, Generaloberst (General) Karl Hollidt, Generaladmiral (Admiral) Otto Schniewind, General der Infanterie (Lieutenant General, Infantry) Karl von Roques, General der Intanterie (Lieutenant General, Infantry) Hermann Reinecke, General der Artillerie (Lieutenant General, Artillery) Walter Warlimont, General der Infanterie (Lieutenant General, Infantry) Otto Woehler, and Generaloberstabsrichter (Lieutenant General, Judge Advocate) Rudolf Lehmann.

General Johannes Blaskowitz committed suicide in prison on 5 February 1948, and thereby the case against him was terminated. XI TWC 462-463.

[122] XI TWC 462.

COMMAND RESPONSIBILITY

The indictment alleged four offenses: (1) Crimes Against Peace[123] (2) War Crimes[124] (3) Crimes Against Humanity[125] (4) Conspiracy to Commit the Crimes Charged in Counts

[123] None of the accused were found guilty of Count One, as none were considered to have been involved in the policy-making decisions alleged.

[124] Count Two — War Crimes — Count two of the indictment, paragraph 45, is as follows:

> 45. Between September 1939, and May 1945, all of the defendants herein . . . committed war crimes and crimes against humanity . . . in that they participated in the commission of atrocities and offenses against prisoners of war and members of armed forces of nations then at war with the Third Reich or under the belligerent control of or military occupation by Germany, including but not limited to murder, illtreatment, denial of status and rights, refusal of quarter, employment under inhumane conditions and at prohibited labor of prisoners of war and members of military forces, and other inhumane acts and violations of the laws and customs of war. The defendants committed war crimes and crimes against humanity in that they were principals in, accessories to, ordered, abetted, took a consenting part in, were connected with plans and enterprises involving, and were members of organizations and groups connected with, the commission of war crimes and crimes against humanity.

Then follows paragraph 46, which in general terms sets out the unlawful acts.

Paragraph 47 alleged issuance and execution of the "Commissar" Order, which provided for summary execution of Soviet political commissars; Counts 48 and 49, the issuance and execution, respectively, of the "Commando" Order, which directed that all allied troops on commando missions, even if in uniform, whether armed or disarmed, offering resistance or not, were "to be slaughtered to the last man." Counts 50 through 53 dealt with alleged use of prisoners of war for prohibited labor; while Counts 54 through 58 alleged murder and ill-treatment of prisoners of war. As part of these charges the accused allegedly implemented a number of illegal orders. The Barbarossa Jurisdiction Order was intended for application on the eastern front and concerned the military jurisdiction of military commanders over enemy civilians or inhabitants of that area. The Night and Fog Decree directed that non-German civilians be taken to Germany for handling by the Ministry of Justice in Germany. Other orders provided for the taking of hostages and the execution of reprisals.

[125] Count Three — Paragraph 59 of the indictment, is as follows:

> 59. Between September 1939, and May 1945, all of the defendants herein . . . committed war crimes and crimes against humanity... in that they participated in atrocities and offenses, including murder, extermination, ill-treatment, torture, conscription to forced labor, deportation to slave labor or for other purposes, imprisonment without cause, killing of hostages, persecutions on political, racial and religious grounds, plunder of public and private property, wanton destruction of cities, towns and villages, devastation not justified by military necessity, and other inhumane and criminal acts against German nationals and members of the civilian populations of countries and territories under the belligerent occupation of, or otherwise controlled by Germany.

The following paragraphs 60 to 82 set forth generally and particularly the unlawful acts, such as enslavement of the population, plunder of public

One, Two, and Three.[126] Before entering judgment as to the guilt or innocence of each of the accused, the Tribunal discussed the offenses at length. As in *Yamashita,* there was no question that the offenses occurred; the only questions to be resolved concerned the standard of responsibility and, based on that standard, the individual responsibility of each accused.

It was to the standard of responsibility that the Tribunal first addressed itself. Initially, the Tribunal stated:

> For a defendant to be held criminally responsible, there must be a breach of some moral obligation fixed by international law, a personal act voluntarily done with knowledge of its inherent criminality under international law.[127]

From the outset the prosecution urged a theory of strict liability of the commander, even where orders were not obviously criminal or where an order is routinely passed without review by a commander from a superior headquarters to a subordinate. The Tribunal rejected these arguments, stating that

> . . . to find a field commander criminally responsible for the transmittal of such an order, he must have passed the order to the chain of command and the order must be one that is criminal upon its face, or one which he is shown to have known was criminal.[128]

---

and private property, murder, etc., and participation of the defendants in the formulation, distribution and execution of these unlawful plans.

[126] Count Four was subsequently struck by the Tribunal on the basis of duplicity, inasmuch as it tendered no issue not contained in the preceding counts (XI TWC 483).

[127] XI TWC 510. It is submitted that the use of the word "moral" was a poor choice, as any obligation if "fixed by international law" is legal rather than moral. While a moral obligation through custom may have become a legal obligation, one does not normally risk criminal liability for violation of a purely moral obligation.

[128] The Tribunal continued, careful to distinguish between implementation and transmittal:

> Transmittal through the chain of command constitutes an implementation of an order. Such orders carry the authoritative weight of the superior who issues them and of the subordinate commanders who pass them on for compliance. The mere intermediate administrative function of transmitting an order directed by a superior authority to subordinate units, however, is not considered to amount to such implementation by the commander through whose headquarters such orders pass. Such transmittal is a routine function which in many instances would be handled by the staff of the command without being called to his attention. The commander is not in a position to screen orders so transmitted. His headquarters, as an implementing agency, has been bypassed by the superior command.
>
> Furthermore, a distinction must be drawn as to the nature of a criminal order itself. Orders are the basis upon which any army operates. It is basic to the discipline of an army that orders are

COMMAND RESPONSIBILITY

The Tribunal next addressed the problem of the commander's criminal responsibility for actions committed within his command pursuant to criminal orders passed down independent of his command.[129] The Tribunal stated the commander has four alternatives in such a situation: (1) he can issue an order countermanding the order; (2) he can resign his commission; (3) he can sabotage the enforcement of the order within a somewhat limited sphere; or (4) he can do nothing.

In discussing these alternatives under the pluralistic or dual command system which existed in Nazi Germany, the Tribunal found none of the alternatives viable, yet nevertheless concluded that the commanders concerned must be responsible.[130] Citing Control Council Law No. 10, Article II, paragraph 2,[131] the Tribunal concluded that "[a]ny participation in implementing such orders, tacit or otherwise, any silent acquiescence in their enforce-

---

> issued to be carried out. Its discipline is built upon this principle. Without it, no army can be effective and it is certainly not incumbent upon a soldier in a subordinate position to screen the orders of superiors for questionable points of legality. Without certain limitations, he has the right to assume that the orders of his superiors and the state which he serves and which are issued to him are in conformity with international law.
>
> Many of the defendants here were field commanders and were charged with heavy responsibilities in active combat. Their legal facilities were limited. They were soldiers—not lawyers. Military commanders in the field with far reaching military responsibilities cannot be charged under international law with criminal participation in issuing orders which are not obviously criminal or which they are not shown to have known to be criminal under international law. Such a commander cannot be expected to draw fine distinctions and conclusions as to legality in connection with orders issued by his superiors. He has the right to presume, in the absence of specific knowledge to the contrary, that the legality of such orders has been properly determined before their issuance. He cannot be held criminally responsible for a mere error in judgment as to disputable legal questions.

XI TWC 510-11.

[129] This situation while more likely to occur under the pluralistic system of command could occur under our bureaucratic system of command. See discussion *infra* at text to ns. 270-277.

[130] XI TWC 511-512.

[131] Control Council Law No. 10, Article II, paragraph 2, provides in pertinent part as follows:

> Any person without regard to nationality or the capacity in which he acted, is deemed to have committed a crime as defined in paragraph 1 of this article, if he * * * (b) was an accessory to the commission of any such crime or ordered or abetted the same or (c) *took a consenting part therein* or (d) *was connected with* plans or enterprises involving its commission * * *. [Emphasis supplied by Tribunal] XI TWC 512.

ment by his subordinates, constitutes a criminal act on his part." [132]

The Tribunal found the situation analogous to any other plea of superior orders; while no defense, it was a mitigating circumstance.[133]

In next considering the responsibility of commanders for orders issued by members of their staff, the Tribunal did not see fit, under ordinary circumstances, to vary the traditional military adage that while a commander may delegate authority, he may never delegate responsibility.[134]

After considering the legality of the various orders which the accused allegedly issued, the Tribunal again addressed the collective question of command responsibility and again rejected any concept of strict liability:

---

[132] *Supra* n. 130, at 512. It is submitted that the Tribunal found itself treading a very thin line in distinguishing implementation of orders, "tacit or otherwise," and "mere transmittal," discussed *supra* n. 114, the former requiring knowledge and intent, the latter being an uninformed ministerial act. The question of culpability would seem to turn on whether the command had a duty to know the contents of the order transmitted.

[133] *Id.* at 512. Both denial of the plea of superior orders as a defense and its consideration in mitigation were prescribed by Article II, § 4(b) of Control Council Law No. 10.

[134] *Id.* at 514. The accused found their positions in conflict, not only with each other but with themselves. Those on trial as commanders pointed out that there were certain functions which they of necessity left to their chiefs of staff and that at times they did not know of orders which might be issued under authority of their command. Staff officers on trial urged that a commander was solely responsible for what was done in his name. Several accused had served in both capacities, and hence were caught on the horns of the dilemma.

U.S. Army field manuals of that time and at present support the concept of the non-delegable responsibility of the commander. FM 100-5, OPERATIONS OF ARMY FORCES IN THE FIELD, provides at paragraph 3-1:

> The authority vested in an individual to direct, coordinate, and control military forces is termed "command." This authority, which derives from law and regulation, is accompanied by commensurate responsibility that cannot be delegated. The commander alone is responsible for the success or failure of his command under all circumstances.

U.S. DEP'T OF ARMY, FIELD MANUAL 101-5, STAFF OFFICERS FIELD MANUAL: STAFF ORGANIZATION AND PROCEDURE (1972), provides:

> *Paragraph 1-4*
>
> b. The commander alone is responsible for all that his unit does or fails to do. He cannot delegate this responsibility.

Paragraph 1-9 is applicable to the situation presently under consideration:

> b. When the commander authorizes staff officers to issue orders in his name, the commander retains responsibility for these orders.

For discussion of staff responsibility *see* Douglass, *High Command Case: A Study in Staff and Command Responsibility*, 6 INT. LAWYER 686 (October 1972).

COMMAND RESPONSIBILITY

> Military subordination is a comprehensive but not conclusive factor in fixing criminal responsibility. The authority, both administrative and military, of a commander and his criminal responsibility are related but by no means coextensive. Modern war such as the last war entails a large measure of decentralization. A high commander cannot keep completely informed of the details of military operations of subordinates and most assuredly not of every administrative measure. He has the right to assume that details entrusted to responsible subordinates will be legally executed. The President of the United States is Commander in Chief of its military forces. Criminal acts committed by those forces cannot in themselves be charged to him on the theory of subordination. The same is true of other high commanders in the chain of command. Criminality does not attach to every individual in this chain of command from that fact alone. There must be a personal dereliction. That can occur only where the act is directly traceable to him or where his failure to properly supervise his subordinates constitutes criminal negligence on his part. In the latter case, it must be a personal neglect amounting to a wanton, immoral disregard of the action of his subordinates amounting to acquiescence. Any other interpretation of international law would go far beyond the basic principles of criminal law as known to civilized nations.[135]

The Tribunal next addressed the duties and responsibilities of a military commander of an occupied territory whose authority has been limited by his own government or is not otherwise absolute:

> Concerning the responsibility of a field commander for crimes committed within the area of his command, particularly as against the civilian population, it is urged by the prosecution that under the Hague Convention, a military commander of an occupied territory is *per se* responsible within the area of his occupation, regardless of orders, regulations, and the laws of his superiors limiting his authority and regardless of the fact that the crimes committed therein were due to the action of the state or superior military authorities which he did not initiate or in which he did not participate. In this respect, however, it must be borne in mind that a military commander, whether it be of an occupied territory or otherwise, is subject both to the orders of his military superiors and the state itself as to his jurisdiction and functions. He is their agent and instrument for certain purposes in a position from which they can remove him at will.
>
> In this connection the *Yamashita* case has been cited. While not a decision binding upon this Tribunal, it is entitled to great respect because of the high court which rendered it. It is not, however, entirely applicable to the facts in this case for the reason that the authority of Yamashita in the field of his operations did not appear to have been restricted by either his military superiors or the state, and the crimes committed were by troops under his command, whereas in the case of the occupational commanders in these proceedings, the crimes charged were mainly committed at the instance of higher military and Reich authorities.

135 *Supra* note 130 at 543-544.

> It is the opinion of this Tribunal that a state can, as to certain matters, under international law limit the exercise of sovereign powers by a military commander in an occupied area, but we are also of the opinion that under international law and accepted usages of civilized nations that he has certain responsibilities which he cannot set aside or ignore by reason of activities of his own state within his area. He is the instrument by which the occupancy exists. It is his army which holds the area in subjection. It is his might which keeps an occupied territory from reoccupancy by the armies of the nation to which it inherently belongs. It cannot be said that he exercises the power by which a civilian population is subject to his invading army while at the same time the state which he represents may come into the area which he holds and subject the population to murder of its citizens and to other inhuman treatment. The situation is somewhat analogous to the accepted principle of international law that the army which captures the soldiers of its adversary has certain fixed responsibilities as to their care and treatment.
>
> We are of the opinion, however, as above pointed out in other aspects of this case, that the occupying commander must have knowledge of these offenses and acquiesce or participate or criminally neglect to interfere in their commission and that the offenses committed must be patently criminal.[136]

Where such authority has been allegedly removed from a commander, or where a commander has denied knowledge of illegal activities by other units, the Tribunal stated a court should examine both objective and subjective factors in considering the validity of any such defense.[137]

The Tribunal, in concluding, turned to the individual accused and their responsibility for the acts alleged.[138]

1. Wilhelm von Leeb: Von Leeb, a former General of the Army, was charged with offenses committed during the period in which he was commanding general of Army Group North.[139] These offenses dealt with: (a) The Commissar Order; (b) crimes against prisoners of war; (c) The Barbarossa Jurisdiction Order; (d)

---

136 *Id.* at 544-545.

137 *Id.* at 548-549. The accused were again confronted by the inconsistencies of their own arguments: they claimed they had been vested of executive authority for their territory by orders of the SD while denying knowledge of the duties and activities of the SD, which were established and defined by the same orders. For a discussion of the subjective criteria to be utilized in determining a commander's knowledge and responsibility, see *infra* text at notes 288-293.

138 Only the charges of those accused as commanders are discussed. For a discussion of the question of responsibility of the staff officer, see Douglass note 134 *supra.*

139 Von Leeb was Commander in Chief of Army Group North in the campaign against Russia until January 16, 1942, when he resigned primarily because of interference in technical matters by Hitler; he was then placed in reserve.

crimes against civilians; (e) pillage of public and private property; and (f) criminal conduct pertaining to the seige of Leningrad. The Tribunal considered each *seriatum*; in preface the Tribunal stated:

> The evidence establishes the criminal orders were executed by units subordinate to the defendant and criminal acts were carried out by agencies within his command. But it is not considered under the situation outlined that criminal responsibility attaches to him merely on the theory of subordination and over-all command. He must be shown both to have had knowledge and to have been connected to such criminal acts, either by way of participation or criminal acquiescence.[140]

a. The Commissar Order. The evidence showed that von Leeb recognized the Commissar Order to be in violation of international law from the outset, and voiced his opposition to those senior to him on a continuous basis. As a result of the resistance to the order by von Leeb and his fellow Russian front commanders, von Rundstedt and von Bock, the question of its application was resubmitted to Hitler on September 23, 1941, who refused to change the decree. In putting the order into effect, von Leeb's headquarters had no implementing authority; merely the administrative function of passing it to subordinate commanders. Yet the evidence showed that von Leeb not only advised his subordinate commanders of his opposition to the order, but advised them that he would fully implement the German high command's "maintenance of discipline" order, which provided for strict measures to be taken against any soldier committing war crimes. He continued to resist the order until his retirement in January, 1942. The Tribunal concluded:

> . . . we cannot find von Leeb guilty in this particular. He did not disseminate the order. He protested against it and opposed it in every way short of open and defiant refusal to obey it. If his subordinate commanders disseminated it and permitted its enforcement, that is their responsibility and not his.[141]

b. Crimes Against Prisoners of War. The Tribunal entered a finding of not guilty to this charge as the evidence failed to show von Leeb possessed either knowledge or a duty to know of crimes committed against prisoners of war. All responsibility for prisoners at that time was in the hands of the quartermaster general, who was responsible directly to the German High Command and Hitler rather than through the tactical chain of command. Subordinate units within General von Leeb's command responsible

[140] *Supra* n. 130 at 555.
[141] *Id.* at 557-558.

for the handling of prisoners of war were similarly responsible directly to the German High Command.[142] As General von Leeb was heavily engaged during this period with the initial phases of the seige of Leningrad, a matter he was desperately attempting to conclude before winter, he had neither the authority nor the means of ascertaining what treatment prisoners of war were receiving.[143] As the Tribunal stated:

> . . . [H]e . . . had the right to assume that the officers in command of those [subordinate] units [charged with responsibility] would properly perform the functions which had been entrusted to them by higher authorities, both as to the proper care of prisoners of war or the uses to which they might be put.[144]

c. The Barbarossa Jurisdiction Order. The evidence established that von Leeb, while expressing personal disapproval, implemented this order by passing it into the chain of command. The order was illegal in part; and, as his implementing order made no effort to clarify its instructions or prevent its illegal application, "having set this instrument in motion, he must assume a measure of responsibility for its illegal application." [145]

d. Crimes Against Civilians. This charge derived from the activities of a Nazi Security Police unit, which was assigned to and operated within General von Leeb's Army Group North area. While these activities included acts of mass murder—some by units subordinate to Army Group North but on order of the Security Police—and recruitment of slave labor, with one exception there was no evidence to establish that the orders for these illegal activities or reports thereof passed through or were received by Army Group North. In that one case, although reported to von Leeb as having been carried out by a local self-defense organization of Latvians, he immediately took action to prevent any reoccurrence. The Tribunal concluded that insufficient evidence existed to establish General von Leeb's knowledge of the acts alleged.[146]

e. Pillage of Public and Private Property. The evidence presented failed to establish that the acts committed were illegal under

---

[142] *Id.* at 558.

[143] *See generally* HART, HISTORY OF THE SECOND WORLD WAR (1971), p. 157 *et seq.* and SALISBURY, THE 900 DAYS (1969), p. 334 *et seq.*

[144] XI TWC 558. The author would qualify this statement with what may be the obvious, as follows: A commander has the right, *within reason,* to assume, etc. What is reasonable under the circumstances would depend on a number of criteria, all of which relate to putting a commander on notice. See discussion, *infra* text at ftnts. 288-293.

[145] *Id.* at 560-561.

[146] *Id.* at 561-562.

the circumstances, based on questions of military necessity.[147] Similar findings were made to charges concerning conduct pertaining to the seige of Leningrad.[148]

The Tribunal recognized several subjective matters in conclusion:

> We believe that there is much to be said for the defendant von Leeb by way of mitigation . . . . He was a soldier and engaged in a stupendous campaign with responsibility for hundreds of thousands of soldiers, and a large indigenous population spread over a vast area. It is not without significance that no criminal order has been introduced in evidence which bears his signature or the stamp of his approval.[149]

2. *Hugo Sperrle:* Former commanding general of the "Condor Legion" during the Spanish Civil War and the representative of the Luftwaffe in the High Command trial, Sperrle was acquitted of all charges, the Tribunal finding that Sperrle, rather than implementing the one order which formed the basis of the charge against him, on principle opposed it and sought to make it ineffective.[150]

3. *Georg Karl Friedrich-Wilhelm von Kuechler:* General von Kuechler served as a subordinate commander to General von Leeb, succeeding him as Commanding General of Army Group North in January 1942. He continued in this command until January 1944, when he was placed in the Reserves. The Tribunal addressed the list of charges in order.

a. The Commissar Order. Although von Kuechler testified concerning his opposition to the Commissar Order, the Tribunal found his testimony irreconcilable with an earlier affidavit in which he denied any knowledge of the order. There was no question that the order was transmitted to and through his headquarters, nor that it was enforced by subordinate units. Reports were made by these subordinate units to his headquarters that commissars were being executed by them. General von Kuechler denied knowledge of those reports, to which the Tribunal replied: "It was his business to know, and we cannot believe that the members of his staff would not have called these reports to his attention had he announced his opposition to the order." [151]

b. Neglect of Prisoners of War and Their Use in Prohibited Labor. Based on an order to subordinate units that General von

[147] *Id.* at 562-563.
[148] *Id.* at 563.
[149] *Id.* at 563.
[150] *Id.* at 565.
[151] *Id.* at 567.

Kuechler admitted must have passed through his headquarters, both civilians and prisoners of war were utilized for improper and dangerous work. The Tribunal concluded that the evidence supported a finding that General von Kuechler had knowledge of and approved such practice.

c. Illegal Execution of Russian Soldiers and Murder and Ill-treatment of Prisoners of War. While the evidence was extensive that Russian prisoners of war had been illegally executed and that they were executed pursuant to orders of the German High Command, the Tribunal did not feel that the evidence adequately established General von Kuechler's transmittal of them. The Tribunal did find that subordinate units submitted reports to his headquarters over a wide period of time, and noted: "These reports must be presumed in substance to have been brought to his attention." [152] His own testimony indicated he was aware of the reports, yet took no corrective action. The Tribunal concluded that he not only tolerated but approved the execution of these orders.[153] Nor was there any question, based on numerous reports received by his headquarters, the inordinately high death rate,[154] and by his own admission that he had personally visited every prisoner of war camp in his area, that he had knowledge of the extensive neglect and ill-treatment of prisoners of war in his area. The Tribunal held von Kuechler to be guilty of criminal neglect of prisoners of war within his jurisdiction.[155]

d. Deportation and Enslavement of the Civilian Population. The massive deportation program was carried out pursuant to orders executed by General von Kuechler, which the Tribunal found "establish beyond question the ruthless manner in which he contributed to this program and also the ruthless manner in which he evacuated hundreds of thousands of helpless people, contrary to the dictates of humanity and the laws of war." [156]

---

[152] *Id.* at 568.

[153] *Id.* at 568.

[154] On November 9, 1941, General von Kuechler's Chief of Staff received a report that "at present 100 men are dying daily." At another conference held at his headquarters on November 28, 1941, it was disclosed that all of the inmates in one camp were expected to die within six months because of ill-treatment and lack of adequate rations. XI TWC 569.

[155] General von Kuechler was convicted of ill-treatment offenses occurring while he was commander of 18th Army; he was acquitted of charges of neglect occurring after he relieved General von Leeb. XI TWC 569.

[156] XI TWC 576-577. The tribunal also found von Kuechler guilty of the use of the civilian population for work directly connected with the waging of war contrary to the rules of international law without discussion of the evidence in support thereof. XI TWC 577.

COMMAND RESPONSIBILITY

e. Murder, Ill-treatment, and Persecution of Civilian Population; and Enforcement of the Barbarossa Jurisdiction Order. Citing *Yamashita,* the prosecution again argued General von Kuechler's absolute liability as commanding general of the occupied territory for offenses committed by the Security Police.[157] While rejecting

[157] The Prosecution's theory as to the responsibility of a commanding general is revealed in the following paragraphs taken from the Memorandum on the responsibility of von Kuechler under Counts II and III:

> The annex to the 4th Hague Convention lays down as the first condition which an armed force must fulfil in order to be accorded the right of a lawful beligerent that "it must be commanded by a person responsible for his subordinates" (Annex to the 4th Hague Convention, Article I). Implicit in this rule is the point that in a formally organized army, the commander is at all times required to control his troops. He is responsible for the criminal acts committed by his subordinates as a result of his own inaction. As the Supreme Court of the United States held in *In re Yamashita:*
>
> > These provisions plainly imposed on petitioner, who at the time specified was military governor of the Philippines, as well as commander of the Japanese forces, an affirmative duty to take such measures as were within his power and appropriate in the circumstances to protect prisoners of war and the civilian population. This duty of a commanding officer has heretofore been recognized and its breach penalized by our own military tribunals. . . .
>
> Most extensive rights and corresponding responsibilities are conferred by positive provisions of international law upon the commanding general in occupied territory. The heading of Section III of the Hague Regulations mentions specifically the "military authority over the territory of the hostile State." Article 42 declares that "territory is considered occupied when it is actually placed under the authority of the hostile army." Article 43 imposes the duty on the occupant to restore and to ensure public order and safety and to respect the laws in force in the country,"the authority of the legitimate power having, in fact, passed into the hands of the occupant." In Article 57, it is expressly stated that no contribution shall be collected except under local order and on the responsibility of a C.-in-C.
>
> It follows that international law acknowledges no other bearer of executive power except the commander of the occupying army, and for this reason a unilateral delegation of this power to some agency other than the military commander is not recognized by international law, and is ineffective to relieve the military commander, *pro tanto,* of his duties and responsibilities.

Counsel for von Kuechler replied:

> The Prosecution attempts to explain these Rules of Land Warfare in such a way that it would appear that Field-Marshal von Kuechler, in his capacity of Commander-in-Chief, was territorially responsible for everything that happened at any time in the occupied enemy area.
>
> However, such a territorial responsibility exists neither in the practice nor in the theory of International Law. Even the Supreme Court in its judgment of Yamashita could not decide to recognize

this argument "for substantially the same reasons as given in the judgment concerning von Leeb," [158] the Tribunal found that both acts alleged were carried out pursuant to orders promulgated or disseminated by General von Kuechler by units under his command.[159] Initially manifesting knowledge of the illegal activities of the Security Police through a directive to his troops to avoid contact or interference with any such units, he subsequently distributed the anti-Semitic Reichenau Order on October 10, 1941, which the Tribunal set out in full in its opinion "because of its inhumanity." [160] Conviction on these counts, then, was based on his knowledge of, acquiescence in and, in some cases, direct order of the offenses alleged.

4. Hermann Hoth: General Hoth was also charged with offenses relating to commands held on the Russian front.

a. The Commissar Order. General Hoth was found to have passed to subordinate units an order which the Tribunal found was

---

such a responsibility. Such a responsibility—to use the words of the judgment of the jurists—would lead to the result:

> that the only thing for a Tribunal in a case would be to pronounce the declaration of guilty. . . .

The Yamashita Judgment, therefore, also takes the factual jurisdiction as a basis. Time and again it speaks of the armed forces under the orders of the Commander-in-Chief, of the soldiers who were bound to carry out his orders, of the units which he commanded.

The judgment against Field-Marshal List (Case 7, Military Tribunal V) cannot be interpreted in the meaning of territorial responsibility either, although there may be some items which point in this direction. The decisive factor is that the judgment always examines the factual jurisdiction. In this connection I want to refer to the expositions as on pages 10377 and 10419 of the German transcript. In the last-named case, the Tribunal investigated the relation of subordination of an SS Police leader and the Tribunal would have no need to undergo this work if it was to affirm unreservedly the maxim of territorial responsibility. It can be inferred herefrom that there will be a personal responsibility of a Commander-in-Chief only if:

> (1) An action took place in the territory which he controlled, or
>
> (2) If it was committed by somebody who was under his orders.

It is significant that the Hague Convention on Land Warfare only speaks of the "Occupying Power" and by this means the Occupying State. The counterpart of the indigenous civilian population, therefore, is not an individual person, but the occupying State. And that is only logical, because the war against the Soviet Union had been declared by the German Reich and not by some Commander-in-Chief, as, for instance, by Field-Marshal von Kuechler. As cited XII L.R.T.W.C. p. 108, n. 1.

158 *Supra* n. 130 at 578.

159 *Id.* at 577 (Barbarossa Jurisdiction Order); 578-583 (civilian population violations).

160 *Id.* at 578-580.

criminal on its face. The Tribunal concluded: "When those units committed the crimes enjoined by it, the superior commander must bear a criminal responsibility for such acts because he ordered their commission." [161]

After unsuccessfully pleading the defense of superior orders, Hoth offered the following in defense or mitigation (in the words of the Tribunal):

> . . . he simply passed it down without emphasizing it or attempting to mitigate it . . . he was certain that his subordinates were sufficiently radar-minded to pick up the rejection impulses that radiated from his well known high character and that he believed that they would have the courage he lacked to disobey the order.[162]

The Tribunal in rejecting his argument stated:

> . . . the mere unexpressed hope that a criminal order given to a subordinate will not be carried out is neither a defense nor a ground for the mitigation of punishment. That the character impulses were too weak or the minds of the subordinates were too insensitive to pick them up is shown by the documents.[163]

b. Prisoner mistreatment. Hoth was also charged with ill-treatment and improper use of prisoners of war, war crimes and crimes against humanity consisting of crimes against civilians, and cooperation with the Security Police in execution of their illegal programs. He was found guilty on all counts on the basis of orders issued by him and carried out by units of his command.[164]

5. Hans Reinhardt: General Reinhardt was charged with offenses that occurred while he was commander of Panzer Group 3, 3rd Panzer Army, and Commander in Chief of Army Group Center, all on the Russian Front.

a. The Commissar Order. General Reinhardt testified that in transmitting this order, he simultaneously issued verbal orders that it was not to be carried out. After an extensive listing of executions of Russian commissars by General Reinhardt's command, the Tribunal in rejecting this argument stated:

> If international law is to have any effectiveness, high commanding officers, when they are directed to violate it by committing murder, must have the courage to act, in definite and unmistakable terms, so as to indicate their repudiation of such an order. The proper report to have been made . . . when a request was made from the top level to report the number of commissars killed would have been that this unit does not murder enemy prisoners of war.[165]

---

161 *Id.* at 581-582.
162 *Id.* at 582.
163 *Id.* at 582.
164 *Id.* at 584-596.
165 *Id.* at 598.

In passing on this criminal order, the Tribunal found General Reinhardt bore the responsibility for its execution in his area.

b. The Commando Order: General Reinhardt was found guilty of passing this order, although the Tribunal noted:

> It may be stated as a matter somewhat in mitigation and as showing the personal attitude of . . . Reinhardt, that in November 1943, he issued an order that parachutists are lawful combatants and are to be treated as prisoners of war. That was at a time when the German Army was not so flushed with success and when it was a little more inclined to soften the treatment meted out to the Russians. The Tribunal has noted it as being a matter proper, at least for consideration, on the matter of mitigation. It should further be noted in this connection that it does not appear that Reinhardt, thought he received it, ever passed on literally or in substance the notorious Reichenau Order.[166]

c. Prohibited Labor of Prisoners of War, Murder, and Ill-Treatment of Prisoners of War, and Turning Over of Prisoners to the Security Police. The Tribunal found that Reinhardt had issued orders concerning the use of prisoners of war in prohibited labor and had received reports at his headquarters concerning all three illegal activities, in one instance manifesting his knowledge of these activities by opposing authorizing the Red Cross to make any search for prisoners missing in action for the following reason: "Overwhelmingly large number of POW's deceased without documentary deposition, and of civilians who disappeared due to brutal actions." [167]

Citing the opinion in *United States v. List*,[168] the Tribunal concluded that any reports made to General Reinhardt's headquarters were made for his benefit; therefore he was responsible for knowledge of their contents.[169]

d. Deportation and Enslavement of Civilians. The Tribunal found the evidence established that in the area of General Reinhardt's army, enforced labor by civilians was carried out as a policy and that it was implemented ruthlessly with General Reinhardt's knowledge and consent, and even pursuant to his orders;[170] forcible conscription for deportation was a fixed policy. In replying to Reinhardt's denial of such a policy, the Tribunal stated:

> . . . the orders and reports cited, and others to which we have not referred, show clearly that the deportation of civilian workers to the Reich was of such long continued and general practice, that

[166] *Id.* at 600.
[167] *Id.* at 602.
[168] XI TWC 759, discussed *infra* n. 195.
[169] *Supra* n. 130 at 603.
[170] *Id.* at 603-607.

even were there no orders signed by the defendant authorizing it, he must be held to have had knowledge of the practice and of its extent.[171]

e. Murder, Ill-Treatment, and Persecution of Civilian Populations; the Barbarossa Jurisdiction Order. Not only was it established that General Reinhardt passed on the Barbarossa Jurisdiction Order, but that he issued implementing instructions and received extensive reports concerning its execution. Addressing only the point of slave labor, the Tribunal stated "Slave hunting in his area was so general and long continued that without the direct evidence pointed out, knowledge would be imputed to him." [172]

6. *Hans von Salmuth:* General von Salmuth was charged with offenses which occurred while in command at the Corps and Army level on the Russian front.

a. The Commissar Order. Upon its receipt, General von Salmuth distributed the Order to his subordinate units, advising them that he rejected it and acquainting his division commanders with his objections. The Tribunal felt that the evidence tended to bear this out as the order was never carried out while General von Salmuth was in command, and acquitted him of this charge.[173]

b. The Commando Order. The Order was transmitted to subordinate units by General von Salmuth's Chief of Staff with directions that all copies be returned within twelve days. The Tribunal found General von Salmuth guilty of issuance of the Order despite his protestations that the chief of staff should not have signed the letter and was not authorized to do so, as he had done nothing to repudiate his subordinate's action nor did he reprimand him in any way. He subsequently requested clarifying instructions concerning the Order's application from higher headquarters, and through his Quartermaster issued further instructions to a subordinate command, both acts manifesting his knowledge of the order and its implementation within his command.[174]

c. Prohibited Labor of Prisoners of War; Murder and Ill-treatment of Prisoners of War; Deportation and Enslavement and Enslavement of Civilians; Illegal Reprisals. While the Tribunal could not conclude that General von Salmuth transmitted the Barbaroosa Jurisdiction Order, he did issue orders implementing the execution of the provisions of the order and remained actively in-

171 *Id.* at 614.
172 *Id.* at 616.
173 *Id.* at 616.
174 *Id.* at 616-625.

terested in their implementation.[175] In yet another basis for holding General von Salmuth criminally responsible, the Tribunal stated:

> Concerning the treatment of prisoners of war in the areas under the defendant, numerous reports from these areas show what must be considered an excessive number of deaths by shooting and otherwise among the prisoners of war. They imply a degree of negligence on the part of the defendant . . . . These reports show that prisoners of war were handed over to the SD, a police organization, and that thereafter the army exercised no supervision over them and apparently had no control or record as to what became of them.
>
> Whether or not they were liquidated, as many of them undoubtedly were, is not the question. The illegality consists in handing them over to an organization which certainly by this time [1941] the defendant knew was criminal in nature.
> . . . he must accept criminal responsibility for the illegal transfer of these prisoners to the SD. [176]

7. *Karl Hollidt:* General Hollidt was charged with offenses that occurred while he served as a division, corps, and army commander.

a. The Commissar Order. General Hollidt testified that on receipt of the Order he instructed his regimental commanders not to comply with it. The one isolated incident reported was described by the Tribunal as ambiguous. Furthermore, there was some question as to whether General Hollidt had actually assumed command of the unit at the time of the incident. Hence he was found not guilty of the offense.[177]

b. The Commando Order. General Hollidt acknowledged receipt of the Order but denied its transmittal. As there was no evidence that it was ever carried out by units under General Hollidt's command, the Tribunal found General Hollidt not guilty of this charge.[178]

c. Prohibited Labor of Prisoners of War. The evidence indicated that over a wide period of time prisoners of war were used by his subordinate units in the combat zone for construction of field fortifications. The Tribunal concluded this could only have been done with his knowledge and approval; thus, criminal responsibility attached.[179]

d. Murder and Ill-treatment of Prisoners of War. This charge constituted yet another refusal by the Tribunal to apply the strict

[175] *Id.* at 617.
[176] *Id.* at 617.
[177] *Id.* at 626.
[178] *Id.* at 627.
[179] *Id.* at 627.

liability theory urged by the prosecution. Concluding even if an assumption were made that certain executions were unjustified, the Tribunal concluded no criminal connection to General Hollidt was established.[180]

e. Deportation and Enslavement of Civilians. General Hollidt was found criminally responsible for the deportation and enslavement of civilians as orders were issued in the former case which also tended to show his knowledge and consent, if not preference, for use of labor forces locally for construction of field fortifications.[181]

8. Otto Schniewind: Admiral Schniewind was acquitted of those charges under Counts Two and Three inasmuch as there was no evidence showing implementation or enforcement by any of the units subordinate to him of the orders alleged, the Barbarossa Jurisdiction Order and the Commando Order. In discussing the Barbarossa Jurisdiction Order, the Tribunal refused to adopt the prosecution's argument that would have shifted the burden of proof to the defendant to show what he did to discourage or stop implementation of the order (which did not occur until after Admiral Schniewind's departure from the command), finding such argument "rather naive." [182]

9. Karl von Roques: Lieutenant General von Roques was charged with offenses committed while Commanding General of Rear Area of Army Group South (March 1941 to 15 June 1942) and Rear Area of Army Group A (July 1942 to December 1942). By his own testimony, General von Roques had executive power as the representative of the occupying power in his area. As such, he owed a duty to the civilians, he felt, because he needed their cooperation. The Tribunal noted despite this representation "neither his testimony nor his actions show that he appreciated the fact that he owed a duty as an occupying commander to protect the population and maintain order."[183] The Tribunal deemed it appropriate at this point to define executive power and the responsibility of a commander holding that power:

> General Halder in his testimony succinctly defines executive power as follows:
>
> > "The bearer of executive power of a certain area unites all the legal authorities of a territorial nature and legislative nature in his own person."

---

180 *Id.* at 628.
181 *Id.*
182 *Id.* at 629-630.
183 *Id.* at 631.

> The responsibility incident to the possession of executive power is well stated in the judgment [in the *List* case] as follows:
>
> " . . . This duty extends not only to the inhabitants of the occupied territory but to his own troops and auxiliaries as well. The commanding general of occupied territories having executive authority as well as military command will not be heard to say that a unit taking unlawful orders from someone other than himself was responsible for the crime and that he is thereby absolved from responsibility. It is here claimed, for example, that certain SS units under the direct command of Heinrich Himmler committed certain of the atrocities herein charged without the knowledge, consent, or approval of these defendants. But this cannot be a defense for the commanding general of occupied territory. The duty and responsibility for maintaining peace and order, and the prevention of crime rests upon the commanding general. He cannot ignore obvious facts and plead ignorance as a defense." [184]

After citing the duties of a commander of occupied territory as recited by the Supreme Court in *Yamashita,* the Tribunal concluded:

> We are of the opinion that command authority and executive power obligate the one who wields them to exercise them for the protection of prisoners of war and the civilians in his area; and that orders issued which indicate a repudiation of such duty and inaction with knowledge that others within his area violating this duty which he owes, constitute criminality.[185]

a. The Commissar Order. General von Roques denied issuing this order, a denial which the Tribunal found contrary to the facts but a factual differentiation unnecessary to resolve. The Tribunal found that whether or not the order was or was not passed on by him was immaterial; its implementation was so extensive in his territory as to require some action on his part to prevent the criminal action that was carried on by the units subordinate to his command and by agencies in his area. Commissars were regularly shot with his knowledge, and he did nothing about it. Furthermore, the Commissar Order which he received provided:

> II. *In the rear areas* — Commissars arrested in the rear area . . . are to be handed over to the 'Einsatzgruppe' or the 'Einsatzkommandos' of the SS Security Service (SD), respectively.[186]

During the periods in question, these security service units were subordinate to Lieutenant General von Roques. The evidence showed that in one instance he received a direct written report of 1,896 executions by an SS Brigade during one two-week operation; and that he continued to receive similar reports as well as

[184] *Id.* at 631-632.
[185] *Id.* at 632.
[186] *Id.* at 632.

issue orders directing the security police to participate in other operations. He also received and implemented an order which the Tribunal described as "so bestial as to be fit to be seen only by those to whom it was addressed" providing for extermination by security police elements of "unbearable elements." [187] The Tribunal concluded that General von Roques knew of the carrying out of the Commissar Order and therefore bore criminal responsibility for its implementation in his area.

b. Murder and Ill-treatment of Prisoners of War. The evidence was conclusive that General von Roques ordered the execution of paratroopers as guerrillas; that he had knowledge of and acquiesced in the execution of others; and through gross neglect of the sanitary conditions and lack of food in four prisoner of war camps permitted others to die at the rate of 100 per day, in three of those camps at rates in excess of 80 percent per year. The Tribunal concluded responsibility lay in General von Roques.[188]

c. The Barbarossa Jurisdiction Order. General von Roques was found criminally responsible for implementation of this order as he passed it down to his subordinates; personally issued other orders in the implementation of it or pursuant to it which the Tribunal found criminal; and that these subordinate units thereafter carried out these orders with his full knowledge, acquiescence and approval.[189]

d. Hostages and Reprisals. While General von Roques passed on an order directing that reprisals be taken against saboteurs, the Tribunal found themselves believing General von Roques' testimony that no such acts were actually carried out.[190]

e. Ill-treatment and Persecution of the Civilian Population. The evidence reflected the complete subservience of army units in General von Roques' area to the security police and their full cooperation with the security police program with "knowledge of its debased and criminal character." [191] While General von Roques issued orders directing his troops not to participate in the "arbitrary shooting" of Jews, he directed them to otherwise assist the security police in carrying out their orders.[192]

10. Otto Woehler: General Woehler was charged with offenses committed both as a commander and as a staff officer; concern here is only with the former.

[187] *Id.* at 636-637.
[188] *Id.* at 639-644.
[189] *Id.* at 645-647.
[190] *Id.* at 647.
[191] *Id.* at 648.
[192] *Id.* at 648.

a. Murder and Ill-treatment of Prisoners of War. One isolated incident involving the illegal execution of two Russian soldiers was reported by General Woehler to his next higher headquarters. While the evidence tended to show that he did nothing about this incident, the Tribunal refused to conclude that this established acquiescence and approval.[193]

b. Prohibited Labor of Prisoners of War. The Tribunal found that General Woehler had knowledge of and acquiesced in the use of prisoners of war by regiments of his command as illegal labor in forward combat areas. They rejected the *tu quoque* argument, stating "The fact that similar use was made of German prisoners by the enemy is only a factor in mitigation and not a defense." [194]

D. THE HOSTAGE CASE

The second significant joint trial at Nuremburg involving the question of command responsibility was the trial of *United States v. Wilhelm List,* also known as "The Hostage Case," tried between July 8, 1947 and February 19, 1948.[195] The accused, all high-ranking officers of the military,[196] were charged with being principals and accessories to the murder and deportation of thousands of persons from the civilian populations of Greece, Yugoslavia, Norway and Albania between September 1939 and May 1945 by troops under their command who were acting pursuant to orders issued, distributed and executed by the defendants.[197] Members of the

[193] *Id.* at 684-685.

[194] *Id.* at 685.

[195] Reported at XI TWC 759 to 1332.

[196] The accused were Generalfeldmarschall (General of the Army) Wilhelm List; Generalfeldmayschall Maximilian von Weichs; Generalaloberst (General) Lothar Rendulic; General der Pionere (Lieutenant General, Engineers) Walter Kuntze; General der Infantrie (Lieutenant General, Infantry) Hermann Foertsch; General der Gebirgstruppen (Lieutenant General, Mountain Troops) Franz Boehme; General der Flieger (Lieutenant General, Air Force) Helmuth Felmy; General der Gebirgotruppen Hubert Lanz; General der Infantrie Ernst Dehner; General der Infantrie Ernst von Leyser; General der Flieger Wilhelm Speidel; and Generalmajor (Brigadier General) Kurt von Geitner. Lieutenant General von Boehme committed suicide after indictment and prior to arraignment; General von Weichs became ill on October 6, 1947, and for medical reasons his case was subsequently severed from that of the remaining defendants.

[197] The charges against the defendants were:

COUNT ONE: Alleged the murder of "hundreds of thousands of persons from the civilian populations of Greece, Yugoslavia, and Albania. . ."

COUNT TWO: Alleged the "wanton destruction . . . and other acts of devastation not justified by military necessity, in the occupied territories of Norway, Greece, Yugoslavia, and Albania. . ."

Tribunal were two civilian jurists and an equally-distinguished civilian practitioner.[198]

The main precedental value of the *Hostage Case* is its examination of the law of reprisal; this concept will not be examined. Additionally, this review will concern itself only with those defendants charged with offenses allegedly committed while the defendants were holding positions of command.

In initially dealing with the question of command responsibility, the Tribunal found it necessary to address a factual dispute and its legal implications:

> We have been confronted repeatedly with contentions that reports and orders sent to the defendants did not come to their attention. Responsibility for acts charged as crimes have been denied because of absence from headquarters at the time of their commission. These absences generally consisted of visitations to points within the command area, vacation leaves and leaves induced by illness . . .
>
> We desire to point out that the German Wermacht was a well equipped, well trained, and well disciplined army. Its efficiency was demonstrated on repeated occasions throughout the war.
>
> The evidence shows . . . that they were led by competent commanders who had mail, telegraph, telephone, radio, and courier service for the handling of communications. Reports were made daily, sometimes morning and evening. Ten-day and monthly reports recapitulating past operations and stating future intentions were regularly made. They not only received their own information promptly but they appear to have secured that of the enemy as well. We are convinced that military information was received by these high ranking officers promptly, a conclusion prompted by the efficiency of the German armed forces.
>
> An army commander will not ordinarily be permitted to deny knowledge of reports received at his headquarters, they being sent there for his special benefit. Neither will he ordinarily be permitted to deny knowledge of happenings within the area of his command while he is present therein. It would strain the credulity

COUNT THREE: Alleged offenses committed against enemy troops and prisoners of war in Greece, Yugoslavia, and Italy, including refusal of quarter, denial of status as prisoners of war, and murder and ill-treatment of prisoners of war.

COUNT FOUR: Alleged the "murder, torture, and systematic terrorization, imprisonment in concentration camps, arbitrary forced labor on fortifications and entrenchments to be used by the enemy, and deportation to slave labor, of the civilian populations of Greece, Yugoslavia, and Albania . . ."
All offenses were alleged as "war crimes and crimes against humanity" committed "by troops of the German armed forces under the command and jurisdiction of, responsible to, and acting pursuant to orders issued, executed, and distributed by (the defendants)," listing specific acts.

198 The presiding judge was Charles F. Wennerstrum of the Supreme Court of Iowa; the members were Edward F. Carter of the Supreme Court of the State of Nebraska and George J. Burke, a member of the State Bar of Michigan.

> of the Tribunal to believe that a high ranking military commander would permit himself to get out of touch with current happenings in the area of his command during wartime. No doubt such occurrences result occasionally because of unexpected contingencies, but they are the unusual. With reference to statements that responsibility is lacking where temporary absence from headquarters for any cause is shown, the general rule to be applied is dual in character. As to events occurring in his absence resulting from orders, directions, or a general prescribed policy formulated by him, a military commander will be held responsible in the absence of special circumstances. As to events, emergent in nature and presenting matters for original decision, such commander will not ordinarily be held responsible unless he approved of the action taken when it came to his knowledge.[199]

Turning to acts committed by units not subordinated to a commander or by independent units subordinated to agencies other than the German Wermacht, the Tribunal stated:

> The matter of subordination of units as a basis of fixing criminal rsponsibility becomes important in the case of a military commander having solely a tactical command. But as to the commanding general of occupied territory who is charged with maintaining peace and order, punishing crime, and protecting lives and property, subordination are relatively unimportant. His responsibility is general and not limited to a control of units directly under his command. Subordinate commanders in occupied territory are similarly responsible to the extent that executive authority has been delegated to them.[200]

As in the *High Command* case, the Tribunal began its findings by rejecting the contentions that the accused were party to any overall conspiracy to decimate and exterminate the population. In determining questions of guilt or innocence, the Tribunal declared it would require proof

> . . . of a causative, overt act or omission from which a guilty intent can be inferred . . . . Unless this be true, a crime could not be said to have been committed unlawfully, willfully, and knowingly as charged in the indictment.[201]

The Tribunal, after brief historical review, turned itself to the individual defendants.

1. Wilhelm List: General List, fifth ranking field marshal in the German Army, was charged with offenses committed by units of his command while serving as Armed Forces Commander Southeast and as commander in chief of Army Group A on the Russian front. In the former position he was the supreme repre-

[199] XI TWC 1259-1260.
[200] *Id.* at 1260.
[201] *Id.* at 1261.

sentative of the armed forces in the Balkans, exercising executive authority in the territories occupied by German troops.

The evidence showed that General List both passed to subordinates illegal orders from the high command as well as issuing orders demanding "ruthless . . . measures" against the local population.[202] Of other orders, General List denied knowledge as he was away from his headquarters at the time the reports came in. The Tribunal reiterated its previous position regarding a commander's responsibility in such a case:

> A commanding general of occupied territory is charged with the duty of maintaining peace and order, punishing crime, and protecting lives and property within the area in his command. His responsibility is coextensive with his area of command. He is charged with notice of occurrences taking place within that territory. He may require adequate reports of all occurrences that come within the scope of his power and, if such reports are incomplete or otherwise inadequate, he is obliged to require supplementary reports to apprise him of all the pertient facts. If he fails to require and obtain complete information, the dereliction of duty rests upon him and he is in no position to plead his own dereliction as a defense. Absence from headquarters cannot and does not relieve one from responsibility for acts committed in accordance with a policy he instituted or in which he acquiesced. He may not, of course, be charged with acts committed on the order of someone else which is outside the basic orders which he has issued. If time permits he is required to rescind such illegal orders, otherwise he is required to take steps to prevent a recurrence of their issue.
>
> Want of knowledge of the contents of reports made to him is not a defense. Reports to commanding generals are made to their special benefit. Any failure to acquaint themselves with the contents of such reports, or a failure to require additional reports where inadequacy appears on their face, constitutes a dereliction of duty which he cannot use in his own behalf.
>
> The reports made to . . . List . . . charge him with notice of the unlawful killing of thousands of innocent people. . . . Not once did he condemn such acts as unlawful. Not once did he call to account those responsible for these inhumane and barbarous acts. His failure to terminate these unlawful killings and to take adequate steps to prevent their recurrence constitutes a serious breach of duty and imposes criminal responsibility.[203]

The Tribunal found General List guilty of counts one and three of the indictment.[204]

2. Walter Kuntze: General Kuntze was charged with offenses committed during his service as Armed Forces Commander Southwest. The Tribunal noted that General "Kuntze assumed command

202 *Id.* at 1263-64.
203 *Id.* at 1271-1272.
204 *Id.* at 1274.

on October 27, 1941, a month which exceeded all previous monthly records in killing innocent members of the population in reprisal for the criminal acts of unknown persons." [205] The Tribunal found it highly improbable that General Kuntz could assume command in the midst of the carrying out and reporting of these reprisal actions without gaining knowledge thereof and acquiescing in their execution. Other evidence indicated Kuntze personally ordered other reprisals and received confirming reports on their completion. The Tribunal found that he was advised of all such killings, and that he not only failed to take measures to prevent their recurrence but on several occasions urged more severe action to be taken by his subordinate commanders. The Tribunal ruled that his ordering of and acquiescence in these and other offenses made him criminally responsible for charges alleged under counts one, three, and four.[206]

3. Lothar Rendulic: General Rendulic was charged with offenses committed while he was serving as commander of 2nd Panzer Army, 20th Mountain Army, and Army Group North. All the charges related to offenses resulting from his orders or orders he passed on to subordinate units. He was found not guilty of issuing the Commando Order and was found justified by military necessity in his utilization of scorched earth tactics in a retreat under severe conditions and against overwhelming odds in Norway.[207]

4. Ernst Dehner: As commander of the LXIX Reserve Corps, Lieutenant General Dehner was charged with unlawful killing of hostages and reprisals taken against prisoners, and with wanton destruction of towns and villages, both in an effort to suppress guerrilla activities operating in his area of responsibility. Specifically, General Dehner was charged as one of the subordinate commanders of General Rendulic. The Tribunal noted:

> It appears to us from an examination of the evidence that the practice of killing hostages and reprisal [against] prisoners got completely out of hand, legality was ignored, and arbitrary action became the accepted policy. The defendant is criminally responsible for permitting or tolerating such conduct on the part of his subordinate commanders.[208]

5. The Remaining Commanders: The remaining commanders were found guilty of similar action or inaction. Lieutenant General von Leyser was found guilty of illegally conscripting indigen-

[205] *Id.* at 1276.
[206] *Id.* at 1281.
[207] *Id.* at 1295-1297.
[208] *Id.* at 1299.

ous persons for military service and compulsory labor service, as well as issuing the Commissar Order.[209] Lieutenant General Helmuth Felmy was found guilty of passing on illegal reprisal orders resulting in extensive unwarranted, excessive and illegal reprisals; in one instance, on receipt of reports concerning reprisals conducted well in excess of existing orders, General Felmy recommended the most lenient punishment of the regimental commander responsible without follow-up to determine what punishment, if any, was assessed.[210] Lieutenant General Hubert Lanz was convicted of failing to prevent illegal reprisals of which he had knowledge, and with ordering the unlawful execution of Italian officers and soldiers of the surrendered Italian army.[211] Finally, Lieutenant General Wilhelm Speidel was convicted of permitting illegal acts to occur of which he had knowledge.[212]

E. THE HIGH COMMAND AND HOSTAGE CASES—IN SUMMARY

In the *High Command* and *Hostage* cases, commanders at division, corps, and army level—men prominent in their profession—were tried by three-judge tribunals, also men of professional prominence. Each tribunal was presented a variety of situations involving the intricacies and complexities of command and control of a military force in combat; the considered responses of the tribunals offer some of the more definitive reasoning and logic in arriving at standards of responsibility for commanders.

As in *Yamashita,* there was seldom any question that the offenses occurred; the question left for resolution concerned the standard of responsibility and, given the determination of that standard, the individual responsibility of each accused. *Yamashita* had confirmed the existence of *duty* and *responsibility;* the *High Command* and *Hostage* tribunals sought to achieve some definitional value for each. *Yamashita* addressed the duty and responsibility of the commander with a broad brush; the *High Command* and *Hostage* cases provided much of the detail necessary to complete the picture. Significantly, both minimum and maximum lines were drawn, the latter in express rejection of any purported *Yamashita*-strict liability theory. That rejection was not merely

209 *Id.* at 1300-1305.
210 *Id.* at 1305-1309.
211 *Id.* at 1309-1313.
212 *Id.* at 1313-1317.

of the strict liability theory per se but of the proposition that *Yamashita* represents such a theory.

The *High Command* and *Hostage* cases are of greater value than *Yamashita* in that the respective opinions rendered therein are the product of judicial minds rather than of lay jurors, and prepared under less emotive circumstances; the blaze of war had died sufficiently to permit juristic scholarship providing necessary light for future interpretation rather than mere heat. The results of this careful examination have previously been analyzed.

F. THE TOKYO TRIALS

Of the war crimes trials conducted after World War II, the "International Japanese War Crimes Trial in the International-Military Tribunal for the Far East," otherwise known as and hereinafter called "The Tokyo Trial" was the longest, most complex, and perhaps least known.

Heard by distinguished jurists from eleven countries,[213] the Tokyo Trial brought before an international tribunal twenty-eight of the former leaders of Japan,[214] charged with crimes

---

[213] The Tribunal was composed of the following judges:

Australia:	Sir William Flood Webb, Chief Justice Supreme Court of Queenland; later Justice High Court of the Australian Commonwealth
Canada:	Stuart F. McDougall, Puisne Judge Quebec Court of King's Bench (Appeal Side)
China:	Mei, Juo-Ao, Acting Chairman, Foreign Affairs Committee, Legislative Yuan
France:	Judge Henri Bernard
Great Britain:	Lord Patrick, Senator, His Majesty's College of Justice in Scotland
India:	R. M. Pal, Judge, High Court of Calcutta
Netherlands:	Bernard V. A. Roling, Judge, Court of Utrecht
New Zealand:	Erima H. Northcraft, Justice, Supreme Court of New Zealand
Philippines:	Delfin Jaranilla, Justice, Supreme Court of the Philippines
Soviet Union:	J. M. Zaryanov, Major General of Justice, Military Collequim, Supreme Court of the Soviet Union
United States:	Myron H. Cramer, Major General, former Judge Advocate General of the United States Army.

[214] Those selected for indictment were former prime ministers Kaki Hirota, Kiichiro Hiranuma, Hideki Tojo and Kuniaki Koiso; foreign ministers Yosuke Matsuoka, Shigenori Togo, and Manoru Shigemitsu (a position which Hirota also held); war ministers Jiro Minami, Sadao Araki, Seishiro Itagaki, Shunroku Hata, and Tojo; navy ministers Osami Nagano and Shigetaro Shimada; finance minister Okinori Kaya; education ministers Koichi Kido and Araki; home ministers Hiranuma, Kido, and Tojo; overseas ministers Koiso and Togo; Presidents, Planning Board Naoki Hoshino and Teiichi Suzuki; Chiefs of Army General Staff Tojo and Yoshijiro Umezu; Ambassadors Hiroshi Oshima, Tashio Shiratori, Mamoru Shigemi-

against peace, murder and conspiracy to commit murder, and war crimes and crimes against humanity. Counts 54 and 55, part of the latter group of charges, accused certain of the defendants with having ordered, authorized and permitted conduct in violation of the Laws and Customs of War; and with violating the laws of war by deliberately and recklessly disregarding their legal duty to take adequate steps to secure observance of the Laws and Customs of War and to prevent their breach, respectively.[215] It is with these latter counts, 54 and 55, that this article is concerned.[216]

As in the *High Command* and *Hostage* cases, the Tribunal attempted to define the appropriate rules of law before examining the individual responsibility of each accused. In discussing the question of duties, responsibilities and responsibility under Counts 54 and 55, the Tribunal stated:

(b) RESPONSIBILITY FOR WAR CRIMES AGAINST PRISONERS

> Prisoners taken in war and civilian internees are in the power of the Government which captures them. For the last two centuries, this position has been recognized and the customary law to this effect was formally embodied in the Hague Convention No.IV in 1907 and repeated in the Geneva Prisoner of War Convention of 1929. Responsibility for the care of prisoners of war and of civilian internees (all of whom we will refer to as "prisoners") rest therefore with the Government having them in possession. This responsibility is not limited to the duty of mere maintenance but extends to the prevention of mistreatment. In particular, acts of inhumanity to prisoners which are forbidden by the customary law of nations as well as by conventions are to be prevented by the Government having responsibility for the prisoners.
>
> In the discharge of these duties to prisoners, governments must have resort to persons. In the multitude of duties and tasks involved in modern government there is of necessity an elaborate system of subdivision and delegation of duties.
>
> In general the responsibilty for prisoners held by Japan may be stated to have rested upon:
> (1) Members of the government;
> (2) Military or naval officers in command of formations having prisoners in their possession;

tou, and Togo; and military leaders Heitaro Kimura, Koiso, Itagaki, Kuriaki Koiso, Iwane Matsui, Minami, Akira Muto, and Takasmui Oka. Also indicted were Kingoro Hashimoto and Shume Okawa. Matsuoka and Nagano died during the course of the trial and the case against Okawa was not considered because of his mental condition.

[215] Annex A-6, Volume 2, TOKYO JUDGMENT; also Annex A-6, Volume 204, Official Transcript of the International Japanese War Crimes Trials in the International-Military Tribunal for the Far East.

[216] For an excellent analysis of the Tokyo Trials, see Horwitz, *The Tokyo Trial*, INTERNATIONAL CONCILIATION, No. 465, November 1950; *Cf.* MINEAR, VICTOR'S JUSTICE (1971).

(3) Officials in those departments which were concerned with the well-being of prisoner;

(4) Officials, whether civilian, military, or naval, having direct and immediate control of prisoners.

It is the duty of all those on whom responsibility rests to secure proper tereatment of prisoners and to prevent their ill treatment by establishing and securing the continuous and efficient working of a system appropriate for these purposes. Such persons fail in this duty and become responsible for ill treatment of prisoners if:

(1) They fail to establish such a system.

(2) If having established such a system, they fail to secure its continued and efficient working.

Each of such persons has a duty to ascertain that the system is working and if he neglects to do so he is responsible. He does not discharge his duty by merely instituting an appropriate system and thereafter neglecting to learn of its application.

Nevertheless, such persons are not responsible if a proper system and its continuous efficient functioning be provided for and conventional war crimes be committed unless:

(1) They had knowledge that such crimes were being committed, and having such knowledge they failed to take such steps as were within their power to prevent the commission of such crimes in the future, or

(2) They are at fault in having failed to acquire such knowledge.

If such a person had, or should, but for negligence or supineness, have had such knowledge he is not excused for inaction if his office required or permitted him to take any action to prevent such crimes. On the other hand it is not enough for the exculpation of a person, otherwise responsible, for him to show that he accepted assurances from others more directly associated with the control of the prisoners if having regard to the position of those others, to the frequency of reports of such crimes, or to any other circumstances he should have been put upon further enquiry as to whether those assurances were true or untrue. That crimes are notorious, numerous and widespread as to time and place are matters to be considered in imputing knowledge.

Army or Navy Commanders can, by order, secure proper treatment and prevent ill treatment of prisoners. If crimes are committed against prisoners under their control, of the likely occurrence of which they had, or should have had knowledge in advance, they are responsible for those crimes. If, for example, it be shown that within the units under his command conventional war crimes have been committed of which he knew or should have known, a commander who takes no adequate steps to prevent the occurrence of such crimes in the future will be responsible for such future crimes.[217]

Two points previously raised in the *Yamashita* trial were again raised by the military leaders in the Tokyo trial. The first was an objection to the theory of vicarious responsibility for acts committed by subordinates; this matter was dealt with in the Tribunal's general judgment previously discussed. Where a commander had the responsibility to act, while he could delegate the

[217] Volume 200, OFFICIAL TRANSCRIPT, pages 48,442 to 48,447.

authority, he could not delegate the responsibility; in the words of the Tribunal, "He does not discharge his duty by merely instituting an appropriate system and thereafter neglecting to learn of its application." [218]

The second defense went to the subjective standards in individual cases. Like General Yamashita, the defendants argued that their failure of compliance was based upon impossibility of performance; that the allied offensive had forced conditions to deteriorate not only in prisoner of war camps but overall, and that it was impossible for military commanders in the field to maintain communication and control of their troops because of the deteriorating conditions.[219] The Tribunal chose to consider this argument on an individual basis, although noting (1) that once Japanese forces had occupied territory and fighting had ceased, massacres were freely committed in subjecting the local population to the domination of the Japanese; [220] (2) that massacres of prisoners of war and civilian internees or conscripted laborers during the occupation were committed because they were no longer of any use or for other reasons had become a burden to the Japanese occupation force;[221] and (3) that other massacres were perpetrated in anticipation of a Japanese withdrawal or of an Allied attack.[222] The fact that these massacres occurred throughout the war tended to militate against this argument; rather, the Tribunal's detailed analysis of acts of murder, torture, mistreatment, vivisection, cannibalism, and neglect, often occurring as a result of direct orders from the Imperial Headquarters, often on a systematic basis throughout an occupied territory, led the Tribunal to conclude that such actions were carried out as a matter of policy by the Japanese Government or individual members thereof and by the leaders of the armed forces.[223]

In submitting specific findings as to each accused, the Tribunal first considered the case of General Konji Dohiharu. As commander of the 7th Area Army—an area which encompassed Malaya, Sumatra, Java, and for a time Borneo—from April 1944 until April 1945, he was responsible for the care of prisoners of war within his command. The evidence established prisoner

[218] Volume 200, OFFICIAL TRANSCRIPT, pages 48,444. *Also see*, I TOKYO JUDGMENT 30.

[219] Horwitz, *supra* n. 216 at 532.

[220] 202 OFFICIAL TRANSCRIPT, 49,634.

[221] *Id.* at 49,635.

[222] *Id.* at 49,636.

[223] *Id.* at 49,592.

deaths at an "appalling rate" due to starvation, malnutrition, and food deficiency diseases. General Dohiharu submitted such instances occurred due to the deterioration of Japan's war position and the severance of communications. The Tribunal, in noting that these conditions applied only to prisoners and not among their captors, concluded that food and medical supplies were available but withheld upon a policy for which Dohiharu bore responsibility.[224]

General Shunroko Hata was commander of forces in China which committed atrocities on a large scale over an extended period of time. In finding him guilty of a breach of duty under Count 55, the Tribunal concluded:

> Either Hata knew of these things and took no steps to prevent their occurrence, or he was indifferent and made no provision for learning whether orders for the humane treatment of prisoners of war and civilians were obeyed.[225]

Defense counsel for General Heitaro Kimura argued his innocence on the basis that he had issued orders to his troops to conduct themselves in a proper soldierly manner and to refrain from ill-treating prisoners. While doubting that such orders were even issued because of the extent of ill-treatment, the Tribunal found him at a minimum negligent in his duty to enforce the rules of war, stating:

> The duty of an army commander in such circumstances is not discharged by the mere issue of routine orders . . . . His duty is to take such steps and issue such orders as will prevent thereafter the commission of war crimes and to satisfy himself that such orders are being carried out. This he did not do. Thus he deliberately disregarded his legal duty to take adequate steps to prevent breaches of the laws of war.[226]

General Iwane Matsui was held criminally responsible for the infamous "Rape of Nanking." The Tribunal stated:

> . . . from his own observations and the reports of his staff he must have been aware of what was happening. . . . The Tribunal is satisfied that Matsui knew what was happening. He did nothing, or nothing effective to abate these horrors. He did issue orders before the capture of the city enjoining propriety of conduct upon his troops and later he issued further orders to the same purport. These orders were of no effect as is now known and as he must have known . . . . He had the power as he had the duty to control his

---

224 *Id.* at 49,779 to 49,780. The defense of "impossibility due to deteriorating war conditions" was also rejected in the case of General Seishiro Itagaki, at pages 49,789 to 49,800.

225 *Id.* at 49,784.

226 *Id.* at 49,809.

> troops and to protect the unfortunate citizens of Nanking. He must be held criminally responsible for his failure to discharge this duty.[227]

After finding that General Akira Muto shared criminal responsibility for the starvation, neglect, torture and murder of prisoners of war and civilian internees and the massacre of civilians by virtue of orders which he promulgated as Japanese military commander in Northern Sumatra, the Tribunal turned to a review of his activities as Chief-of-Staff to General Yamashita:

> Muto further demonstrated his disregard for the laws of war upon his transfer to become Chief-of-Staff under General Yamashita. . . . During his tenure . . . a campaign (of) massacre, torture, and other atrocities were waged by the troops under Yamashita and Muto on the civilian population of the Philippines, including the massacres in Batangau and massacres and other atrocities at Manila. These bore the same features and followed the pattern set eight years earlier at Nanking when Muto was a member of Matsui's staff. During this period prisoners of war and civilian internees were starved, tortured and murdered.[228]

Concluding, the Tribunal stated ". . . Muto shares responsibility for these gross breaches of the Laws of War. We reject his defense that he knew nothing of these occurrences. It is wholly incredible." [229]

G. THE TRIAL OF ADMIRAL TOYODA

Admiral Soemu Toyoda, former Commander-in-Chief of the Japanese Combined Fleet, the Combined Naval Forces, and the Naval Escort Command, occupying all three positions concurrently from May 3, 1944, to May 29, 1945, and Chief of the Naval General Staff from May 30, 1945 to September 2, 1945, was tried by military tribunal in Tokyo in a trial which commenced on October 29, 1948 and concluded in Admiral Toyoda's acquittal on September 6, 1949—one of the last, if not the last, of the major war crimes trials concluded. It is a case of some significance to the subject of this article.

Admiral Toyoda was charged with violating "the laws and customs of war," the Charge setting out five specifications:
(*Specification 1*) willfully and unlawfully disregarding and failing to discharge his duties by ordering, directing, inciting, causing, permitting, ratifying and failing to prevent Japanese Naval

[227] *Id.* at 49,815-816.
[228] *Id.* at 49,737.
[229] *Id.* at 49,821.

personnel of units and organizations under his command, control and supervision to abuse, mistreat, torture, rape, kill and commit other atrocities; (*Specification 2*) willfully permitting, etc. unlawful pillage, plunder and destruction; (*Specification 3*) unlawful use of non-military objects and places such as churches and hospitals as fortifications; (*Specification 4*) willful and unlawful disregard and failure to discharge his duties by ordering and permitting the unlawful interment, mistreatment, abuse, starvation, torture and killing of prisoners of war; (*Specification 5*) conspiracy to commit the above offenses.

The Bill of Particulars listed eighty-six separate offenses, approximately one-half of which originated in the *Yamashita* Bills of Particulars.

The seven-member military tribunal had as its president a Brigadier of the Australian Army. Three of its members were from the Air Force, three from the Army, including the law member of the Tribunal. It is suggested that in so composing the court—adding a member of a foreign service as the President and a law member—General MacArthur sought to avoid further criticism based on command influence, such as was alleged in the *Yamashita* trial, as well as to gain a more carefully-worded judgment in the event the Tribunal was disposed to writing one.[230]

The Tribunal was so disposed and contributed to the law of command responsibility in three ways:

(1) It resolved certain factual questions rising from the *Yamashita* judgment. Because many of the charges against Admiral Toyoda were the same or similar charges as those for which General Yamashita was tried, the Tribunal heard the same evidence and reviewed the record of that trial, as well as those of thirty-

[230] The correspondence file contained with the *Yamashita* record of trial, as well as the personal correspondence records of General MacArthur and his personal aide and confidant, BGen. Courtney Whitney, reveal an on-going flurry of correspondence over the concern over the *Yamashita* trial, which continued for some five years thereafter, spurred on initially by the dissenting opinions of Justices Murphy and Rutledge, then renewed by publication of Frank Reel's book in 1949 and General MacArthur's refusal to permit its publication in Japan. While these particular matters were not specifically addressed in any of the memordanda contained in these files, it is believed that they were viewed as reasonable improvements in the military tribnual system, particularly since Admiral Toyoda was an officer of even greater prominence, on trial in Tokyo rather than Manila, in a post-war Japan in which General MacArthur was making every effort to win the confidence and respect of the people. In the trial of General Yamashita, in contrast, General MacArthur's concern was for the Filippinos.

one other trials which the Tribunal deemed might have some relevance to or bearing on the trial of Admiral Toyoda.

The first point concerned command responsibility for the naval forces which perpetrated the "Rape of Manila." The defense in *Yamashita* maintained that while General Yamashita had operational control of those forces, administrative control flowed through a naval chain of command and it was through this latter chain of command that any responsibility should flow. The Tribunal, in addressing this point, declared:

> This Tribunal is convinced — as were the Commissions in the trials of Yamashita, Muta, and Yokoyama, with the conclusions of which this Tribunal can find no point of major issue — that these naval personnel were both legally and in fact commanded by the Japanese Army at the times and under the conditions here under consideration.[231]

After carefully documenting and delineating the joint army-navy agreements [232] which provided for this command arrangement, the Tribunal concluded:

> The Tribunal concludes that the so-called "Rape of Manila" was perpetrated by a force of 22,000 men, some 20,000 of whom were Navy personnel, under Rear Admiral Iwabuchi, the commander of the operation, who was under command of General Yokoyama, Commanding General of the Shimbu Shudan. The naval command channel . . . is not evident and the Tribunal cannot but conclude that it did not, in fact, exist. The much disputed definition of operational and administrative authority is not a point of issue here. The practicabilities of the situation, the obligations and duties of the immediate command, must be viewed with realism. The responsibility for discipline in the situation facing the battle commander cannot, in the view of practical military men, be placed in any hands other than his own. Whatever theoretical division of such responsibility may have been propounded, it is, in fact, impossible of delineation in the heat of "trial by fire." [233]

The second point of factual significance dealt with clarification of the issue of knowledge raised by the wording of the judgment of the commission in *Yamashita*. The Tribunal stated:

> It is not within the province of this Tribunal to comment on the action of the United States Supreme Court taken in the cases of General Yamashita and Lieutenant General Homma . . . . Their lives were not forfeited because their forces had been vanquished on the field of battle but because they did not attempt to prevent, even to the extent of issuing orders, the actions of their sub-

231 19 United States v. Soemu Toyoda 5011 [Official transcript of Record of trial].

232 *Id.* at 5011, 5013.

233 *Id.* at 5012.

orinates, of which actions the commanders must have had knowledge.[234]

(2) In addressing the question of command responsibility, the Tribunal determined, after review of the trials which had preceded it, what it considered the essential elements of command responsibility to be:

1. That offenses, commonly recognized as atrocities, were committed by troops of his command;
2. The ordering of such atrocities.

In the absence of proof beyond a reasonable doubt of the issuance of orders then the essential elements of command responsibility are:

1. As before, that atrocities were actually committed;
2. Notice of the commission thereof. This notice may be either:
   a. Actual, as in the case of an accused who sees their commission or who is informed thereof shortly thereafter; or
   b. Constructive. That is, the commission of such a great number of offenses within his command that a reasonable man could come to no other conclusion than that the accused must have known of the offenses or of the existence of an understood and acknowledged routine for their commission.
3. Power of command. That is, the accused must be proved to have had actual authority over the offenders to issue orders to them not to commit illegal acts, and to punish offenders.
4. Failure to take such appropriate measures as are within his power to control the troops under his command and to prevent acts which are violations of the laws of war.
5. Failure to punish offenders.

In the simplest language it may be said that this Tribunal believes the principle of command responsibility to be that, if this accused knew, or should by the exercise of ordinary diligence have learned, of the commission by his subordinates, immediate or otherwise, of the atrocities proved beyond a shadow of a doubt before this Tribunal or of the existence of a routine which would countenance such, and, by his failure to take any action to punish the perpetrators, permitted the atrocities to continue, he has failed in his performance of his duty as a commander and must be punished.[235]

(3) The Tribunal re-emphasized the practical limitations of command responsibility, reviewing those subjective factors which would determine whether a commander knew or had the means to know of the commission of offenses by units subordinate to him. By so doing, it refused to accept the vicarious responsibility or strict liability theory which *Yamashita* purportedly established:

In determining the guilt or innocence of an accused, charged with dereliction of his duty as a commander, consideration must be given to many factors. The theory is simple, its application is

[234] *Id.* at 5005.
[235] *Id.* at 5005-5006.

> not. One must not lose sight of the facts that even during the accused's period as Commander-in-Chief of Yokosuka Naval District, his nation had already begun to lose battles, its navy and, indeed, the war. The climax was being reached. His duty as a commander included his duty to control his troops, to take necessary steps to prevent commission by them of atrocities, and to punish offenders. His guilt cannot be determined by whether he had operational command, administrative command, or both. If he knew, or should have known, by use of reasonable diligence, of the commission by his troops of atrocities and if he did not do everything within his power and capacity under the existing circumstances to prevent their occurrence and punish the offenders, he was derelict in his duties. Only the degree of his guilt would remain.[236]

Admiral Toyoda was acquitted of all charges.

H. OTHER TRIALS

The trials of lesser commanders support the general body of law conceived by the preceding tribunals. General Anton Dostler, tried by United States military commission in Rome,[237] and Generals Mueller and Braver, tried by Greek court-martial in Athens,[238] were convicted of ordering subordinates to commit war crimes. General Kurt Meyer, tried before a Canadian military tribunal, was convicted of "inciting and counselling" troops under his command to execute prisoners of war.[239] In the *Essen Lynching* case, German Captain Erich Heyer gave instructions to a prisoner escort—before a crowd of angry townspeople—that the three Allied prisoners of war in his custody were to be taken to a Luftwaffe unit for interrogation. He ordered the escort not to interfere if the townspeople attempted to molest the prisoners, adding that the prisoners would or should be shot. The townspeople subsequently murdered the prisoners as the escort stood by. Heyer was sentenced to death for inciting the offenses.[240] An unidentified commander was reportedly found responsible for the murder of partisans, following his issuance of an order which read in part: "I will protect any commander who exceeds usual restraint in the choice and severity of the means he adopts while fighting partisans." [241]

Lieutenant General Harukei Isayama was convicted by a United States military commission in Shanghai of permitting,

---

236 *Id.* at 5006.
237 I L.R.T.W.C. 22.
238 XV L.R.T.W.C. 62.
239 IV L.R.T.W.C. 97.
240 I L.R.T.W.C. 88.
241 VIII L.R.T.W.C. 10.

authorizing, and directing an "illegal, unfair, unwarranted and false trial" before a Japanese court-martial of American prisoners of war.[242] Yuicki Sakamoto was convicted by a United States military commission in Yokohama for "permitting members of his command to commit cruel and brutal atrocities" against American prisoners of war.[243] Lieutenant General Yoshio Tachibana and Major Sueo Matoba of the Japanese Army and Vice-Admiral Kunizo Mori, Captain Shizuo Yoshii and Lieutenant Jisuro Sujeyoshi of the Japanese Navy were tried and convicted of like charges by a United States military commission at Guam,[244] as were General Hitoshi Imamura and Lieutenant General Masao Baba by Australian military courts sitting at Rabaul.[245] In a trial by British military court at Wuppertal, Germany, Major Karl Rauer was charged with neglect in the treatment of prisoners of war. Subordinates of Major Rauer were charged with and convicted of illegally executing British prisoners of war, then returning to report to Rauer the prisoner's death "while attempting to escape." Major Rauer was acquitted of the first charge, but convicted of the latter two, the court feeling that it was less reasonable for Rauer to believe after the second incident that the prisoners involved were shot while trying to escape, and that measures should have been taken to investigate and prevent repetition of the incident.[246]

The cases dealt with crimes committed in the commanding officer's absence. Major General Shigeru Sawada was tried by United States Military Commission in Shanghai for permitting the illegal trial and execution of three United States airmen. The trial occurred in General Sawada's absence; informed of the trial and its results, Sawada endorsed the record and forwarded it to the chain of command, making only verbal protest of the severity of the death sentences, which were subsequently carried out. The Court held General Sawada had ratified the illegal acts which occurred in his absence and therefore bore the responsibility for them.[247] General Tanaka Hisakasu was tried by similar Commission at Shanghai for the trial and execution of an American aviator, both of which occurred in his absence. Convicted by the Commission and sentenced to death, the findings and sentence were disapproved by the confirming authority on the basis of insuffi-

242 V L.R.T.W.C. 60.
243 IV L.R.T.W.C. 86.
244 IV L.R.T.W.C. 86.
245 IV L.R.T.W.C. 87.
246 IV L.R.T.W.C. 113.
247 V L.R.T.W.C. 1.

ciency of evidence of wrongful knowledge on his part.[248] Evidence of what action he took to punish his subordinates for this crime was apparently not raised or presented.

One case dealt with the question of responsibility for passing illegal orders. In the *Jaluit Atoll* case, a lieutenant in the Japanese Navy received an order from Rear Admiral Nisuke Masuda to execute three American aviators, an order which the lieutenant, the custodian of the prisoners, passed to three warrant officers who carried out the order. The warrant officers received death sentences; the lieutenant, ten years' imprisonment.[249]

Virtually simultaneous with the trial of General Yamashita occurred the trial of General Masaharu Homma, Japanese commander in the Philippines at the time of the Bataan Death March.[250] The evidence established that of 70,000 American and Filipino prisoners taken in the surrender of Bataan Peninsula on April 8-9, 1942, in excess of 10,000—2,000 American and 8,000 Filipino—were executed or perished from maltreatment during the 120-kilometer march from Mariveles to San Fernando.[251] Other charges alleged and proved included massacre of 400 Filipino soldiers on April 12, 1945; failure to provide adequate prisoner of war facilities, illegal prisoner of war labor, torture and execution of civilian internees, refusal to accept the surrender of enemy forces, bombing of hospitals, and bombing of an open city (Manila).[252] Tried in the Philippines by a United States military commission convened by General MacArthur, General Homma was found guilty of permitting members of his command to commit "brutal atrocities and other high crimes." [253] An appeal to the Supreme Court of the United States was unsuccessful.[254] In confirming the death sentence of General Homma, Gen-

---

248 V L.R.T.W.C. 66.

249 I L.R.T.W.C. 71. Admiral Masuda committed suicide prior to trial.

250 General Homma was arraigned on December 9, 1945; trial commenced on January 3, 1946, concluding February 11, 1946. He was acquitted of an additional charge which alleged that he refused to accept the surrender of United States forces on Corregidor and adjacent fortified islands on May 6, 1942.

251 Review of the Theater Staff Judge Advocate of the Record of Trial by Military Commission of Masaharu Homma, Lieutenant General, Imperial Japaneses Army, General Headquarters, Supreme Commander for the Allied Powers, March 5, 1946, pp. 2-3.

252 *Id.* at 6-13.

253 *Id.* at 1.

254 *In re* Homma, 327 U.S. 759 (1946). The majority filed no opinion in denying General Homma's appeal. Justices Murphy and Rutledge filed dissenting opinions attacking the haste with which the case was brought to trial. Both the Supreme Court and the military commission reached decision

eral MacArthur, a commander for forty-four years at that time, commented aptly in conclusion of this chapter:

> Soldiers of an army invariably reflect the attitude of their general. The leader is the essence. Isolated cases of rapine may well be exceptional but widespread and continuing abuse can only be a fixed responsibility of highest field authority. Resultant liability is commensurate with resultant crime. To hold otherwise would prevaricate the fundamental nature of the command function. This imposes no new hazard on a commander, no new limitation on his power. He has always, and properly, been subject to due process of law. Powerful as he may become in time of war, he still is not an autocratic or absolute, he still remains responsible before the bar of universal justice . . . .[255]

I. SUMMARY

The trials upon the conclusion of World War II gave international application on a major scale[256] to a custom first given sub-

---

on February 11, 1946, one week after the Supreme Court had rendered its decision in *Yamashita.*

[255] D. MACARTHUR, REMINISCENCES 298 (1964). BERGAMINI, *supra* n. 76 at p. 956-959 insists that General Homma was a scapegoat for Emperor Hirohito, who either ordered the Death March or permitted it. Says Bergamini (at p. 956): "knowledgeable former members of the Japanese General Staff place the entire responsibility for the Death March on these unwanted helpers: '[Colonel] Tsuji [Massanobu] and the China gang,' on 'staff officers from Imperial Headquarters,' on 'experts in Yen Hsi-shan operations'." General Homma was merely an automaton.

[256] Japanese figures indicate 4,000 suspects were tried by United States, British, Australian, and Chinese military tribunals. Eight hundred were acquitted, 2,400 were sentenced to three years or more imprisonment, and 809 were executed. BERGAMINI, *supra* n. 76, at 1109. Bergamini states the last figure includes 802 "minor" and seven "major" war criminals. He apparently considers only the seven defendants condemned by the Tokyo Tribunal (Dohiharu, Hirota. Itagaki, Kimura, Matsui, Muto, and Tojo) and not Generals Masaharu Homma and Tomoyuki Yamashita as "major" war criminals, even though General Akira Muto was General Yamashita's subordinate.

Between 1945 and March 1948 some 1,000 cases involving 3,500 persons were tried on the European continent before Allied courts. United States courts in Nuremburg from July 1945 to July 1949 tried 199 persons, of whom 38 were acquitted, 36 sentenced to death (18 were executed), 23 to sentences of life imprisonment, and 102 to shorter terms. American courts in Dachau sentenced 420 to death. Official German sources had recorded the following statistics through 1963:

American courts: 1,814 convicted; 450 given death sentence
British courts: 1,085 convicted; 240 given death sentence
French courts: 2,107 convicted; 104 given death sentence

German authorities estimate the Soviet Union convicted some 10,000 persons of war crimes. Germany itself through 1963 had arraigned 12,846 persons of whom 5,426 were convicted. E. DAVIDSON, THE TRIAL OF THE GERMANS 28-30 (1966).

These trials are continuing. On May 1, 1973, Hermine Braunsteiner Ryan, 53, an Austrian-born housewife from Queens, New York,

stantial recognition by its codification in Hague Convention IV of 1907. While that custom—an imposition of responsibility upon a commander for the illegal acts of his subordinates—existed prior to World War II, it was the action of commanders and national leaders during that conflict which so shocked the conscience of the world as to demand a strict accounting for the commencement and conduct of those hostilities. Seldom have judges been appointed to the bench with such a clear mandate of public opinion as were the judges of the World War II tribunals. The law of war, and as a part thereof the law of command responsibility, witnessed great progression through definition and delineation, perhaps reaching a high water mark as international jurists concentrated their efforts on the subject. In this sense the law of war is like all other parts of international law in its progression: "Its principles are expanded and liberalized by the spirit of the age . . . . Cases, as they arise under it, must be brought to the test of enlightened reason and of liberal principles. . . ." [257]

III. THE STANDARD DEFINED

Acceptance of command clearly imposes upon the commander a duty to supervise and control the conduct of his subordinates in accordance with existing principles of the law of war. Equally clear, a commander who orders or directs the commission of war crimes shares the guilt of the actual perpetrators of the offense. This is true whether the order originates with that commander or is an order patently illegal passed from a higher command through the accused commander to his subordinates. Only the *genre* of culpability may distinguish the commander from those members of his command accused of committing the war crimes for which he is charged.

A. INCITEMENT

No less clear is the responsibility of the commander who incites others to act, although there may be extremes in examples in such

was ordered extradited to West Germany to stand trial for war crimes (murder of more than 1,700 women and children) allegedly committed by her as the head female guard at Ravensbruck prison camp in Germany and Majdanek in Poland. Ross, *Extradition of Ex-Nazi Is Ordered*, Wash. Post, May 2, 1973, at A-13. *Also see In re* Extradition of Ryan, 360 F. Supp. 270 (E.D.N.Y. 1973), aff'd 478 F.2d 1397 (2d Cir. 1973).

[257] Bergman v. DeSieyes, 71 F. Supp. 334, 337 (S.D.N.Y. 1946).

a case. In the *Essen Lynching* case, by ordering his men before an angry crowd not to interfere if the crowd attempted to mistreat prisoners in their custody, Captain Heyer knowingly incited (a) an abandonment of responsibility by his subordinates and (b) perpetration of the main offense by persons not members of his command, resulting in the deaths of the prisoners. Would his incitement (and responsibility) be as clear had it been shown that (rather than the events occurring as they did) these same soldiers, while never receiving an order from Captain Heyer to neglect their responsibilities, nevertheless had heard him say that "the only good prisoner is a dead one," or refer to the enemy through racial epithets imputing to the enemy a less than human quality or status? *Black's Law Dictionary* defines "incite" as: "to arouse; urge; provoke; encourage; spur on; goad; stir up; instigate; *set in motion*." [258] *Webster's* defines "incite" as "*to move to a course of action;* stir up; spur on; urge on." [259] Certainly it would depend on the circumstances of the remark, the recipient, and whether the perpetrator of the offense charged to have occurred as a result of the alleged incitement was the intended recipient. The passing remark by the twenty-four year old company commander to his twenty-three year old executive officer over a drink certainly would not have the same effect as if that same company commander were briefing his troop for a combat assault—troops eighteen years old who have been trained to respect and obey every word uttered by their company commander. While the qualification, "unless illegal" should be added to the last sentence, this does not take into account the impressionability of the young soldier. Even where a commander's comments are in jest and intended as casual remarks for the ears of the executive officer or the company first sergeant, such remarks, particularly where repeated with some frequency, could lead to questions of incitement where overheard by the "casual private first class" who then carries them back to the barracks. Here the incitement abandons the normal image of an explosive, motivating harangue for the subtle suggestion of toleration of certain offenses. While it would be most difficult to attach criminal responsibility to such casual remarks overheard by the unintended eavesdropper, the impact on the subconscious of the young eavesdropper who subsequently finds himself in custody of a "mere ———" on a lonely trail cannot be under-

[258] BLACK'S LAW DICTIONARY 905 (4th ed. 1951) [Emphasis added].

[259] WEBSTER'S THIRD NEW INTERNATIONAL DICTIONARY 1142 (1966) [Emphasis added].

estimated. While it is most unlikely that criminal responsibility would attach for such a casual remark or remarks, it is nevertheless asserted — for moral and military mission reasons, if not legal[260] — that the commander's responsibility lies or should lie in affirmatively manifesting an intolerance for illegal acts under any and all circumstances; and that the dividing line between moral and legal responsibility as it relates to incitement of others to act is a fine one. This dividing line could move depending on the tactical situation of the commander and his command; the casual remarks of the commander of a maintenance unit in a conventional war would seem to have less impact than those of an infantry company commander in a counterinsurgency environment. Even when remarks which incite violate a legal responsibility, the degree of culpability may vary. Captain Heyer was found to be a principal for his remarks and as a result received a death sentence; while his remarks were not tantamount to orders, they were (a) given with the intent of inciting and (b) with full knowledge of the probable consequences. The single or even occasional cast-off remark would not normally indicate the same intent nor awareness of the possible circumstances, although it could amount to personal dereliction on the part of a commander if shown that he should have anticipated the probable consequences;[261] and, taken

260 The concept of intolerance of war crimes in order to accomplish the mission is simply one of not making unnecessary enemies (the civilian population) who will thus detract you through partisan warfare from your primary mission, or of giving the natural enemy cause to fight harder (the enemy soldier who believes he will die if taken prisoner will fight harder not to be taken prisoner). While the Vietnam "winning the hearts and minds of the people" program of civic action is the most recent example of this concept, Emporer Meiji of Japan, in his "Rescript to Soldiers and Sailors" of January 4, 1883, admonished:

> Those who appreciate true valor should in their daily intercourse set gentleness first and aim to win the love and esteem of others. If you affect valor and act with violence, the world will in the end detest you and look upon you as wild beasts. Of this you should take heed.

(HEINL, *supra* n. 15 at 172). Similarly, Sir Philip Sidney (1554-1586) declared: "Cruelty in war buyest conquest at the dearest price." (*Id.* at 20).

261 In this situation the dereliction may be one of the commander not knowing his troops. U.S. DEP'T OF ARMY, FIELD MANUAL 101-5, OPERATIONS OF ARMY FORCES IN THE FIELD, provides at paragraph 3-5:

> 3-5 THE HUMAN ELEMENT
> Despite advances in technology, man remains the most essential element on the battlefield. The commander must be acutely sensitive to the physical and mental condition of his troops, and his plans must take account of their strengths and weaknesses. He must make allowance for the stresses and strains the human mind and body are subjected to in combat. His actions must inspire and motivate his command with the will to succeed under the most adverse

alone, would only under the rarest circumstances be sufficient to find its speaker responsible, assuming a direct correlation between remark and act could be made. Thus, the degree of criminal responsibility may vary from the situation where the remarks of incitement are synonymous with orders as opposed to the situation where such remarks are unintended in the context received and erroneously perceived as a manifestation of acquiescence on the part of the speaker. The degree of responsibility is determinative of the degree of culpability, and is of particular significance where the misconduct charged is alleged to constitute a "grave breach" as that term is defined in the 1949 Geneva Conventions.[202]

B. ACQUIESCENCE

A commander who is shown to have knowledge of offenses which have occurred within his command may be found responsible to some degree for those offenses where he has manifested acquiescence in their commission. Responsibility may vary from that of a principal to dereliction of duty; the degree of culpability will be correlative to the degree of acquiescence, or better said, to the degree of manifestation of intent to join or assist the principals in perpetration of the primary offense. There is little difficulty with the situation where the commander takes no action, or where by his action he clearly manifests an intent to aid the commission of the offense after the fact; the difficulty lies in establishing a causal connection where acquiescence is due to dereliction of duty rather than a manifestation of specific intent. The commander is deemed to share responsibility where he has knowledge of an offense and fails to take reasonable corrective action. Assuming the principal offense and the commander's knowledge thereof are established, the commander would be responsible if (a) he took no action, either intentionally or through personal dereliction; or (b) the action taken is within the control of the commander and is patently disproportionate to the offense committed as to result in acquiescence therein.

conditions. He must assure his troops that hardship and sacrifice will not be needlessly imposed and that their well-being is of primary concern to him.

[262] Articles 146-148, Geneva Convention Relative to the Protection of Civilians: Articles 129-131, Geneva Convention Relative to the Treatment of Prisoners of War; Articles 49-51, Geneva Convention for the Amelioration of the Condition of the Wounded and Sick in Armed Forces in the Field; and Articles 50-52, Geneva Convention for the Amelioration of the Wounded, Sick and Shipwrecked Members of Armed Forces at Sea.

Thus a commander would not be responsible if an accused is referred to a general court-martial for murder of a noncombatant and is either acquitted or receives what on its surface appears to be a light sentence, unless there is established a pattern of such trials which would indicate that they have been no more than a sham or facade; but the commander who punishes the same accused through nonjudicial punishment (given circumstances indicating guilt of the offense charged) would be no less responsible than the one who awards no punishment. Any such acquiescence must be blatant in character rather than speculative "second guessing" after the fact.

Field Manual 27-10 fairly states the commander's duty relative to this point: "Commanding officers . . . must insure that war crimes committed by members of their forces . . . are *promptly* and *adequately* punished." [263]

While this represents a statement of the commander's *duty*, in seeking an answer to any question of a commander's *acquiescence* a reverse tack is required. Current British military law states this point by considering a commander to have acquiesced in an offense "if he fails to use the means at his disposal to insure compliance with the law of war;" [264] in comment it continues:

> The failure to do so raises the presumption — which for the sake of the effectiveness of the law cannot be regarded as easily rebuttable — of authorisation [sic], encouragement, connivance, acquiescense, or subsequent ratification of the criminal acts.[265]

Field Manual 27-10 similarly provides that a commander may be responsible under a theory of acquiescence "if he fails to take the necessary and reasonable steps to insure compliance with the law of war or to punish violations thereof." [266] Both the British "means at his disposal" test and the "necessary and reasonable" language of FM 27-10 suggest that, rather than estab-

---

[263] [Emphasis supplied.] Paragraph 507(b) strangely urges *prompt* and *adequate* punishment of war crimes committed against *enemy personnel* only; the admonishment applies regardless of the victim.

[264] *Supra* n. 58 at paragraph 631.

[265] *Id.* at n. 1. The note continues (after citing *Yamashita* as the principal case on acquiescence):

> The principle has also been recognized in the legislation regarding war crimes of some countries. However, it is probable that the responsibility of the commander goes beyond the duty as formulated above. He is also responsible if he fails, *negligently or deliberately*, to ensure by the means at his disposal that the guilty are brought to trial, deprived of their command or ordered out of the theater of war, as appropriate. [Emphasis supplied].

[266] Para. 501, FM 27-10 (1956).

lishing an absolute norm, the actions of the commander under the circumstances extant at the time of the discovery of the offense will determine whether he is deemed to have acquiesced in the offense.[267] To the commander whose forces are heavily engaged in an intense operation or pitched battle, no reasonable means may exist to secure prompt punishment of an offense prior to conclusion of that engagement; absent disengagement, there would come a point where some action must be taken against an alleged perpetrator of an offense regardless of the circumstances of the campaign, or where there has been sufficient disengagement from the campaign for the commander to turn his attention to matters other than tactics.[268] Put another way, the theory of prompt investigation, trial and punishment will be more stringently applied to a commander in a static tactical situation than one in a very fluid, fast-moving situation requiring complete devotion to accomplishment of the mission at hand.[269]

---

[267] The French and Luxemborg criteria of "tolerated" used immediately after World War II would seem to be in agreement with the British and United States views, while the Netherlands criteria of that period ("deliberately permitted") appears higher. *Cf.* the Netherlands proposed standard in n. 296 *infra*. The Republic of Zaire, in its Code of Military Justice of 1972, provides at Paragraph 502 that "(S)uperiors can . . . be considered accomplices to the crime to the extent that they organized or tolerated the (war) crimes of their subordinates." Article II of the Convention on the Nonapplicability of Statutory Limitations to War Crimes and Crimes Against Humanity (U. N. G. A. Res. 2391 [XXIII] December 9, 1968) provides that "(T)he provisions of this Convention shall apply to representatives of the state authority and private individuals who, as principals or accomplices, participate in or who directly incite others to the commission of any of those crimes, or who conspire to commit them, irrespective of the degree of completion, and to representatives of the state authority who tolerate their commission."

[268] This is particularly true today with the staff support which the commander receives. In proceeding against a member of his command accused of war crimes, there are few matters which require the personal attention or decision of the commander. With judge advocates assigned as special staff officers down to and including brigade or regimental level (the Marine Corps has non-lawyer legal officers at battalion level), and assuming adequate investigative services are available, it would seem that the tactical circumstances would most affect the company grade commander. Availability of staff assistance is perhaps most illustrative of the "means at his disposal" test.

[269] Care should be exercised in reading the preceding statement, as it addresses only the subjective standard to be utilized in weighing a commander's conformance with the laws of war; it in no way suggests that under any circumstances are those standards decreased.

Within individual units, the tactical situation may fluctuate rapidly and unexpectedly. Allied commanders on D-Day, June 6, 1944, were of necessity completely involved in mission accomplishment; thereafter their responsibility for prompt investigation, trial and punishment of any alleged offense became of more paramount concern. Initiation of the German Ardennes

COMMAND RESPONSIBILITY

C. Command and Control

The post-World War II tribunals concluded that responsibility for *control* of a unit existed with *command* of that unit, for example, the commander had the duty to control those troops and units subordinate to him in his command. These tribunals found that identification with and responsibility for certain units by particular commanders was not always clearly defined.

The tribunals in their examination of this point in *Yamashita*, *Von Leeb*, and *List* are in agreement that where a commander exercises executive power over occupied territory, he is responsible for acts committed within his area of responsibility regardless of whether a unit is subordinated to his command or not. As the commander bearing executive power, he is charged with responsibility for maintaining peace and order within the area over which his executive authority extends, and the duty of crime prevention rests upon him.[270]

In *List* the Tribunal deftly avoided the question of responsibility of the commander possessed solely of tactical command, noting in such case that the "matter of subordination of units as a basis for fixing criminal responsibility becomes important." [271] No difficulty in ascertaining responsibility exists where the tactical commander exercises both operational and administrative control; all authority and responsibility is vested in the single command. The question raised, but unanswered in *List*, addresses the splitting of operational and administrative control — tactical control reposed in one commander, with the authority to punish in another, as alleged in *Yamashita* regarding the atrocities committed by naval troops in Manila. Setting aside the responsibility of the tactical commander in whom executive autho-

Counteroffensive on December 16, 1944, affected the commander's ability to obtain prompt investigation, trial and punishment of an accused as well as his personal ability to concentrate his attention on disciplinary matters. A similar reasonable shifting of priorities would be exemplified by the United States Marine amphibious assault at Inchon, Korea, on September 15, 1950; the subsequent strategic withdrawal from the Chosin Reservoir, commencing December 1, 1950; as compared with the relatively stable six-month-period from October 1952 to March 1953 when Marine units formed a part of the United Nations Command line. The preoccupation of the commander with strictly tactical matters in the first two instances is much more significant than in the latter.

270 This responsibility is not exclusive but concurrent with that of unit commanders, whether tactically subordinate to the area commander or not, and under normal circumstances would be superior in authority to that of those unit commanders.

271 *Supra* n. 195 at 1260.

rity also was vested, to what degree can a commander be said to be responsible for the acts of subordinate units over which he exercises only operational control? The Supreme Court in *Yamashita* discussed responsibility for failure of a commander to take such measures as were within his *power* rather than his *authority*.[272] The Tribunal in *Toyoda*, all professional military officers, did not view any such division of authority as realistically giving rise to any control problems:

> The responsibility for discipline in the situation facing the battle commander cannot, in the view of practical military men, be placed in any hands other than his own. Whatever theoretical division of such responsibility may have been propounded, it is, in fact, impossible for delineation in the heat of "trial by fire." [273]

Thus, where a tactical commander has only operational control of a subordinate unit and not the authority to relieve or punish the subordinate commander, he will be expected to take such measures as are within his physical power under the circumstances to prevent or stop war crimes by that subordinate commander. It is the commander's responsibility to take all measures possible to prevent the commission of war crimes by subordinates; lack of administrative control and hence normal administrative remedies does not foreclose or preclude use of other measures.

For example, assume an infantry battalion is operating with an artillery battery attached. Because of operational exigencies, the battery is under operational control of the infantry battalion but under administrative control of its parent (artillery) battalion. The battery commander is authorized to fire only those missions requested by the supported unit. The battery commander receives a fire mission from another unit or from his parent artillery unit which is patently in violation of the rules of engagement or otherwise violates the laws of war, and the battery commander indicates he will fire the mission. On monitoring of that message in the supported infantry battalion's fire support coordination center by the infantry battalion commander or his representative, there is no question that he has the *duty*, the *authority*, and the *power* to prevent the perpetration of that offense. While certainly this example is more easily solved under our bureaucratic command system than the pluralistic system of the Third Reich, and less complex than that with which General

[272] *Supra* n. 107 at 15.
[273] *Supra* n. 231 at 5012.

Yamashita was confronted, it nevertheless seems to be the only reasonable result or conclusion which can be reached. It seems unconscionable in the example given that the infantry battalion commander could forego his responsibility by pleading a lack of administrative authority over the attached battery so long as he has the means of preventing perpetration of the offense.[274]

Other situations pose similarly perplexing problems. Assume a commander is assigned a tactical area of operation over which he exercises no executive authority. Other forces — whether allied forces from a third nation, forces of the host nation, or other United States forces — enter that area obviously bent on the commission of war crimes, for example, announcing openly the taking and execution of hostages. Certainly a duty exists to exercise those means within his control to prevent the intended acts, even if those means are limited to notification of his superiors in an effort of reaching a common commander with authority to prevent the offense, or to report those offenses if unsuccessful in their prevention; yet the degree of duty and commensurate liability for violation thereof, particularly where allied troops are involved, is not clearly defined. Article 1 of the Geneva Conventions of 1949 requires that all signatories thereto "respect" and "ensure respect" for the Conventions "in all circumstances." This language has been determined to be permissive rather than mandatory, however.[275] While Articles 13 and 16 of the Geneva Civilian Convention, taken together, require a signatory nation to assist, protect and respect, as far as military considerations allow, "persons exposed to grave danger," it has been said that Article 4 of the Convention emasculates any duty of the individual commander to intervene by suggesting that any intervention be conducted through normal diplomatic channels.[276] Insofar as that duty exists with regard to other American units, Field Manual 27-10 provides that:

---

[274] Responsibility in this case would not be exclusive. Where the requested fire mission comes from a separate unit, the artillery battalion commander has a two-fold responsibility (assuming he has knowledge before the mission is fired): (a) to use all means reasonably available to prevent the firing of the mission, and (b) to punish those responsible in the battery for commission of the offense.

[275] IV PICTET, COMMENTARY, GENEVA CONVENTION RELATIVE TO THE PROTECTION OF CIVILIAN PERSONS IN TIME OF WAR 16 (1958); PAUST, *supra* n. 4 at 57 MIL. L. REV. 157.

[276] PAUST, *supra* n. 4 at 57 MIL. L. REV. 158.

> The commander is . . . responsible if he has actual knowledge, or should have knowledge . . . that troops or other persons subject to his control are about to commit or have committed a war crime and he fails to take the necessary and reasonable steps to insure compliance with the law of war . . . .[277]

Combining this definition with the previously-cited British "means at his disposal" test, it would seem the commander with means of controlling the commission of war crimes has a duty to do so, not only within his own command but within his area of operations and command.

While not a commander, an adviser to an allied unit may be said to have a duty to prevent the commission of war crimes by the unit to which he is assigned because of his unique position within that unit. If, for example, an advisor should come upon a situation in which members of his advisee unit were about to commit a war crime, while lacking the authority to control the conduct of those forces, his means of otherwise preventing the commission of the offense are not entirely foreclosed. After protesting to the unit commander (assuming without success), he has the means to notify his next higher command by separate radio net — again in hopes of reaching a common senior headquarters that can prevent the offense. If the offense occurs, he has the limited means of preventing its reoccurrence by (a) reporting its occurrence and (b) seeking relief from his role as adviser to that unit, should the circumstances warrant. The latter suggestion not only follows the alternatives proposed in the *Tokyo* and *Von Leeb* trials, but would appear to be the practical solution where the rapport between the adviser and the advisee unit commander has been seriously jeopardized by their clash. The circumstances for relief as well as any question of acquiescence on the part of any adviser who remains with the unit would depend entirely on the circumstances and severity of the incident, however. The situation is not unlike that which the Tokyo Tribunal found in convicting Lieutenant General Akira Muto of war crimes perpetrated as General Yamashita's Chief of Staff: while not in the precise position in which the adviser finds himself, he was found criminally responsible inasmuch as he was deemed to have had the means to influence substantially command decisions; thus failure to utilize all means available to prevent the perpetration of war crimes may legitimately raise questions of criminal responsibility.

---

[277] *Supra* n. 57 at para. 501.

COMMAND RESPONSIBILITY

D. Knowledge

Given the established duty of a commander to control the conduct of his subordinates, responsibility for such conduct exists where the commander has or should have had knowledge of offenses and fails to act. Because of *Yamashita,* or what might be called the "popular" view of what *Yamashita* purportedly represents, this has been a point begging resolution. It is submitted that the difficulty lies not with *Yamashita* but in what a minority with vested interests claim *Yamashita* represents.

This so-called popular view, based on the writings of General Yamashita's defense counsel, Frank Reel, and the current writings of Telford Taylor, is that a commander may be convicted for the war crimes of a subordinate on the basis of *respondeat superior,* without any showing of knowledge. As previously noted, this theory was argued unsuccessfully by Telford Taylor at Nuremburg and was also rejected by the Tokyo Tribunal. The theory ignores the basic charge against General Yamashita that he

> . . . unlawfully disregarded and failed to discharge his duty to control the operation of the members of his command, *permitting* them to commit brutal atrocities and other high crimes . . .; and he thereby violated the laws of war.[278]

By definition, "permitting" implies knowledge of that which is permitted and acquiescence therein, which would suggest that the standard in *Yamashita* — of either knowledge or, possessing knowledge, of a failure to carry out the commander's duty to act — is no less nor more than that stated in the *High Command* case ". . . a personal neglect amounting to wanton, immoral disregard of the action of his subordinates amounting to acquiescence." [279]

A recent discussion of *Yamashita* can be found in Professor Arthur Rovine's writings on command responsibility in *The Air War in Indochina.*[280] In reviewing the Supreme Court's opinion in *Yamashita,* Professor Rovine stated:

> Our view is that the Yamashita decision does not carry the weight assigned to it by ardent supporters or critics. At no point did the military commission or the Supreme Court hold that knowledge was irrelevant. It is true that the original decision by the commission did not make a specific finding of knowledge, but it did quote from and apparently accept prosecution evidence "to

278 *Supra* n. 71.
279 XI TWC 543-44.
280 THE AIR WAR IN INDOCHINA (Rev. ed. R. Littauer and N. Uphoff, 1972).

show that the crimes were so extensive and widespread, both as to time and area, that they must either have been willfully permitted by the accused, or secretly ordered by the accused."

The Court refused to deal with the evidence on which General Yamashita was convicted, and did not deal with the question of knowledge one way or the other.

The Court did decide that the precise substantive question before it was whether the laws of war imposed on a military commander an obligation to take such appropriate measures as are within his power to control the troops under his command for the prevention of war crimes. The Court cited several provisions of conventional law to demonstrate the existence of an international legal obligation for the defendant amounting to an affirmative duty to take such measures as were within his power and appropriate in the circumstances to protect prisoners of war and the civilian population.

The proposition of law which General Yamashita was held to have violated was thus formulated in a rather elliptical manner that avoided the element of knowledge while leaving it as a variable for consideration by the court of first instance. Given the significance of the issue and the punishment of death, it is regrettable that the Supreme Court did not present a full-scale analysis of the legal significance of a commander's knowledge, or lack of knowledge, of war crimes committed by his troops. But the unsatisfactory nature of the Court's opinion in 1946 is certainly not to be taken as a clear statement that there is command responsibility for crimes of which a commander has *no* knowledge.[281]

After summarizing the *High Command* case, Professor Rovine concludes:

We think the *High Command Case* is far preferable to the Yamashita holding, because it deals clearly with a crucial issue—knowledge—rather than avoiding it, and because the doctrine it evokes appears to be more equitable and better law. Further, as an expression by an international tribunal rendering judgment in one of a large series of war-crimes trials, its legal weight is probably greater than a judgement (sic) even of the U.S. Supreme Court, at least in terms of formulating rules of international law. And, ironically, it is far more likely than the Supreme Court ruling to win acceptance in the United States, among lawyers, the public, and government and military decision-makers.[282]

Professor Rovine's comments lament the same point noted previously in this article — in rushing to try Generals Homma and Yamashita in order to placate his Filippino constituency, General MacArthur committed an equally great injustice to international law by failing to appoint a law member to those military tribunals. The resulting credence given the opinion of a lay jury is unprecedented and disproportionate in light of the number of

281 *Id.* at 140-1.
282 *Id.* at 141.

high-ranking officers tried by tribunals whose membership included members of the bar.

Obviously, all trials will not deal with the question of knowledge to the degree that *Yamashita* did. Where knowledge is obvious, given the failure to act, the commander will be deemed responsible. In other cases, knowledge may be reasonably imputed. Thus, in *List* the Tribunal imputed knowledge to a commander where reports were received by his headquarters, stating as to General List:

> Want of knowledge of the contents of reports made to him is not a defense. Reports to commanding generals are made for their special benefit. Any failure to acquaint themselves with the contents of such reports, or a failure to require additional reports where inadequacy appears on their face, constitutes a dereliction of duty which he cannot use in his own behalf.[283]

Similarly, of General von Kuechler in the *High Command* case the Tribunal stated "It was his business to know, and we cannot believe that the members of his staff would not have called these reports to his attention had he announced his opposition to the [Commissar Order]." [284]

These Tribunals, and it is submitted the Tokyo Tribunal in convicting General Muto and the Military Commission in convicting General Yamashita, further asserted that a commander may normally be presumed to have knowledge of offenses occurring within his area of responsibility while he is present therein. In addressing this point in the *Hostage* case, the Tribunal observed:

> It would strain the credulity of the Tribunal to believe that a high ranking military commander would permit himself to get out of touch with current happenings in the area of his command during wartime. No doubt such occurrences result occasionally because of unexpected contingencies, but they are unusual.[285]

The Canadian rule of 1945 reflects this.[286]

In discussing the responsibility of General von Roques for crimes committed within his area of responsibility, an area over

[283] *Supra* n. 203.
[284] *Supra* n. 151.
[285] *Supra* n. 199.
[286] *Supra* n. 55. Canadian rule 10(4) provides:
Where there is evidence that more than one war crime has been committed by members of a formation, unit, body, or group while under the command of a single commander, the court may receive that evidence as *prima facie* evidence of the responsibility of the commander for those crimes.

which he also had executive power, the Tribunal in *von Leeb* placed this in perspective, quoting from *List:* "[A commander] cannot ignore obvious facts and plead ignorance as a defense."[287]

This is not a presumption to be rebutted by the commander, but a subjective element which the court in its discretion may consider. Where the commander denies actual knowledge of the offenses alleged, it is an imputation of *constructive knowledge* where it is established that under the circumstances he *must have known.* Other subjective elements will weigh heavily on the value placed on this factor in considering whether the commander so accused has been derelict in the performance of his duties, for example, in obtaining knowledge, and under the circumstances to what degree he shares the guilt of the principal accused.

The standard to this point may be stated as follows: A commander may be liable for the actions of his subordinates if: (a) he has actual knowledge that an offense has occurred, and he fails to punish the perpetrators of the offense or take reasonable preventive measures within his power to prevent reoccurrence; or (b) he failed to exercise the means available to him to learn of the offense and, under the circumstances, he should have known and such failure to know constitutes criminal dereliction; or (c) there is sufficient evidence to impute knowledge.

E. SUBJECTIVE FACTORS

One author has suggested that (b) and (c) be ascertained by a "reasonable commander" standard.[288] The difficulty with this suggestion is just as there is no such thing as a "reasonable man," there is no such thing as a "reasonable commander"; and that the variable of the circumstances of command are too great to be considered in one "pat" test. Rather than attempt to define the elusive, it is asserted that a number of subjective criteria be recognized and considered in ascertaining and imputing knowledge and responsibility. Although these criteria may also be considered in determining any question of acquiescence, they are considered here only with regard to resolution of any question of knowledge. These criteria include:

(1) *The rank of the accused.* This may serve as a two-edged sword, for while rank is gained through experience it also serves

[287] *Supra* note 184.

[288] O'Brien, *The Law of War, Command Responsibility and Vietnam,* 60 GEO. L.J. 605, 629 (1972).

to isolate the commander from the everyday events of the battlefield.

(2) *Experience of the commander.* Ideally officers of equal rank are equal — in authority, responsibility, ability, and experience. Realistically nothing could be further from the truth. In the simplest of examples, a rifle company may be commanded by a captain with up to twelve years' commissioned service — experienced as a platoon leader, company executive officer, with additional professional schooling, and several years of experience as a company commander. The adjacent company may be commanded by another captain who by virtue of accelerated promotions in time of war may have only two years commissioned service, half of which was spent in training; or by a second lieutenant who joined the company, his first assignment, the day before as a platoon leader and who after a heavy assault finds he is the surviving officer in that company. Leadership comes not only from training but from experience; with it comes a sixth sense, an ability to anticipate problems before they arise as well as being cognizant of a greater variety of means or methods for dealing with or preventing them. Thus in the trial of General Yamashita the Commission specifically recognized the extensive and broad experience of the accused throughout the world in war and peace, in rejecting his plea of lack of knowledge.[289] Similar consideration would be given to the personal and professional qualities of the commander — his intelligence, his education, the amount of time spent in staff duties as opposed to command positions, or vice-versa, as well as the charisma of the commander. The last point is most important, however much a will-o'-the-wisp it may be; the commander whose troops will follow him to hell and back certainly has greater means of knowledge, as well as control, simply by virtue of the personal dedication to him by his subordinates than the commander who lacks the ability to lead his troops to the chow line. Thus given like facts in all other factors a court in one case may find a commander should have had knowledge simply because he was a better commander than his acquitted counterpart in another case.[290]

[289] *Supra* note 64 at 4060-1.

[290] The result of this conclusion is that it encourages mediocrity, an argument which the author is hard pressed to refute. The result in actuality, however, is that while a higher standard of *expected* performance of duty may be considered in the case of a superior commander, the high standard prescribed by precedent may never be lowered to accommodate the mediocre performance of a less capable commander. The same encouragement of

(3) *The duties of the commander by virtue of the command he held.* These considerations will extend not only to the type of command held by the commander but also to the operational commitments of that command. Thus it may be reasonable to conclude the commander of a stable support command should have had knowledge of an offense more readily than the infantry commander of a highly mobile and widely deployed unit. Similarly, the commander operating, for example, a battalion with supporting arms in general and even direct support is operating in a less complex environment than his counterpart operating with the same forces attached.

(4) *Mobility of the commander.* What the advent of the helicopter the commander has extended his means of knowledge. Yet a disparity exists from unit to unit. The commander of an air cavalry unit with a seeming overabundance of helicopters may be deemed to have a greater means of knowledge than his airborne counterpart who after initial deployment finds he is limited to the infantryman's traditional means of transportation — foot. While personal inspection of units certainly increases a commander's means of knowledge, the development of effective communications may have limited any argument of lack of mobility as a viable defense. It is nevertheless a point which deserves some consideration.

(5) *Isolation of the commander.* This concept goes hand-in-hand with its predecessor, the obvious example being the case of Admiral Toyoda, who was relegated to commanding a vast force covering the Pacific from a flagship anchored in home waters. In contrast commanders in Vietnam, if not actually on the ground with their command, hovered overhead in constant observation of the tactical situation. Isolation and mobility were usually capable of correction by a fifteen-minute helicopter flight. Yet that same commander could be virtually as isolated from his command as Admiral Toyoda by adverse weather conditions.

(6) *The "sliding probability ration" of unit/incident/command.* There certainly exists a sliding probability ratio, that is, the greater the size of the offense and/or the unit involved, the higher in the chain of command knowledge may be subjectively imputed. Obviously any one soldier can go out in a combat environment and murder an unarmed belligerent or noncombatant without

mediocracy exists under the "reasonable commander" rule, if not more so. Utilization of the subjective standards diminishes the likelihood of culpability turning on the one point.

anyone knowing otherwise. The introduction of each additional person, whether co-participant, observer, or victim, increases the likelihood of discovery of the offense; and the greater the number of participants or victims, the higher in the chain of command that information is likely to reach — or the more likely that a court will impute knowledge to the accused commander. It is conceivable that a small patrol could commit murder and the information not reach above the platoon leader; in such case, involving one or two deaths, it would be difficult to impute knowledge to the division commander absent a showing of offenses systematic in nature. Yet if that patrol walks into a village and executes fifty noncombatants, or if a platoon or company is witness to the murder of one noncombatant, or if a platoon or company murders fifty noncombatants, it would be reasonable for a court to conclude that a division commander and intermediate commanders between the platoon or company and the division knew or should have known of the offenses. Dereliction in failing to learn of the isolated offense may thus be imputed only to those commanders at lower levels in direct contact with the situation; but a commander's duties include as part of the exercise of command supervision of subordinates to insure that orders are carried out fully and properly. Hence the greater the severity of the offense or the frequency of offenses, the higher up the chain of command knowledge may be imputed because of the commander's failure to carry out his supervisory responsibilities.

(7) *Size of the Staff of the Commander*. While the size of the staff directly affects the commander's means of knowledge, and while a court may give this consideration in imputing knowledge, a commander may not "shrink" his staff to avoid learning about activities. He cannot avoid that which is his duty.

(8) *Comprehensiveness of the Duties of the Staff of the Commander*. Depending on circumstances, the duties of the staff may vary considerably in their comprehensiveness, thereby varying the means of gaining knowledge. Thus the commander and his staff engaged in a complex amphibious operation will have less opportunity for gaining knowledge than they would during a sustained land campaign. This does not permit a commander and his staff to operate in a vacuum, however, ignoring the obvious.

(9) *Communications Abilities*. While arguments were made in the *Hostage Case*, the *High Command Case*, *Yamashita*, and by General Muto before the Tokyo Tribunal that inadequate com-

munications were the cause of each accused's lack of knowledge, there was sufficient evidence to the contrary in each case for the court to reject this as a valid defense. Few commanders will permit their subordinates to lose contact with the command; and while communications (and hence the means of knowledge) may diminish, seldom will they cease. There is a disparity among units of equal level as well as units of different levels, however, and these variations in means should be taken into consideration by a court.

(10) *Training, Age and Experience of the Men Under His Command.* General Douglas MacArthur, in his *Annual Report of the Chief of Staff of the Army*, 1933, stated "In no other profession are the penalties for employing untrained personnel so appalling or so irrevocable as in the military." [291]

Even earlier, General W. T. Sherman had said of the value of experience:

> It was not until after Gettysburg and Vicksburg that the war professionally began. Then our men had learned in the dearest school on earth the simple lessons of war. Then we had brigades, divisions and corps which could be handled professionally, and it was then that we as professional soldiers could rightly be held to a just responsibility.[292]

Lack of training and experience is no excuse for the commission of war crimes, yet it may serve in the way of explanation should they occur and the commander argue his ignorance of their occurrence. This lack of training and experience may be deemed to put the commander on notice as to his additional responsibility of controlling untrained troops, for part of the identified responsibility of the commander is knowing his command, its capabilities and limitations.[293]

(11) *Composition of Forces Within the Command. Yamashita* emphasized one point: the joint or combined force is more difficult to control than the unified command, simply because of interservice or international rivalries. Things are done differently; hence just as a commander may be limited in his control of such an "allied" force, so may his means of knowledge be similarly limited in scope.

(12) *Combat Situation.* The extremes are obvious, one being the relatively stable combat environment as opposed to the fluid, rapid-moving situation. Consideration must be given to these

---

[291] HEINL, *supra* n. 15 at 329.
[292] *Id.* at 108-9.
[293] *See* n. 261, *supra.*

degrees of engagement as they have perhaps the greatest effect on the commander's ability to obtain knowledge and hence the ability to control his subordinates.

F. The Standard of Knowledge

Almost universally the post-World War II tribunals concluded that a commander is responsible for offenses committed within his command if the evidence establishes that he had *actual knowledge* or *should have had knowledge*, and thereafter failed to act. This remains the standard today. Field Manual 27-10 states that:

> The commander is . . . responsible, if he had *actual knowledge* or *should have had knowledge*, through reports received by him or through other means, that troops or other persons subject to his control are about to commit or have committed a war crime and he fails to use the means at his disposal to insure compliance with the law of war.[294]

Available information indicates the *knew or should have known* test was used by the Soviet Union in their war crimes trials after World War II and remains the Soviet standard of command responsibility.[295] The Netherlands has proposed that the *knew or should have known* test be codified as the international standard for responsibility.[296]

G. The Degree of Negligence: Enough, Too Much, or Too Little?

While there appears to be agreement on the general acceptability of the *knew or should have known* test, the difficulty lies in establishing the point at which criminal liability attaches. In the words of the *High Command Case,* at what point has a commander been guilty of "a personal neglect . . . amounting to acquiescence?" In the absence of an international definition, examination of municipal standards is required.

---

[294] *Supra* n. 57 at para. 501 (emphasis supplied).

[295] Harbridge House Study, *supra* n. 6 at 22.

[296] By CE/COM IV/45 the Netherlands recommended that the following paragraph he added to Draft Article 75 of International Committee of the Red Cross Draft Additional Protocol to the Four Geneva Conventions of August 12, 1949:

> 2. [The civilian and military authorities] shall be criminally liable for any failure on their part to take all those steps within their power to make an end to breaches of the laws of war which were, or ought to have been, within their knowledge.

In order to determine the degree of negligence required for culpability, a review of the possible offenses is in order. Under Article 130 of the 1949 Geneva Convention Relative to the Treatment of Prisoners of War grave breaches of the Convention are described as

> . . . *wilful* killing, torture or inhuman treatment, including biological experiments, *wilfully* causing great suffering or serious injury to body or health, compelling a prisoner of war to serve in the forces of the hostile Power, or *wilfully* depriving a prisoner of war of the rights of fair and regular trial prescribed in this Convention.[297]

Article 147 of the 1949 Geneva Convention Relative to the Protection of Civilian Persons in Time of War similarly defines grave breaches as

> . . . *wilful* killing, torture or inhuman treatment, including biological experiments, *wilfully* causing great suffering or serious injury to body or health, unlawful deportation or transfer or unlawful confinement of a protected person, compelling a protected person to serve in the forces of a hostile Power, or *wilfully* depriving a protected person of the rights of fair and regular trial prescribed in the present Convention, taking of hostages, and extensive destruction and appropriation of property, not justified by military necessity and carried out unlawfully and *wantonly*.[298]

Article 50 of the 1949 Geneva Convention for the Amelioration of the Condition of the Wounded and Sick in Armed Forces in the Field contains similar language to the preceding provisions. Such grave breaches are punishable by a sentence up to and including a sentence of death.

The 1949 Conventions thus codify the apparent degree of negligence used in the *High Command Case:* ". . . a personal neglect amounting to *wanton,* immoral disregard of the action of his subordinates amounting to acquiescence." [299]

Thus precedent and present Conventions appear to indicate that in order to hold a commander responsible for grave breaches of these Conventions or of war crimes tried before an international tribunal, absent actual knowledge there must be either (a) such serious personal dereliction on the part of the commander as to constitute wilful and wanton disregard of the possible consequences; or (b) an imputation of constructive knowledge, that is,

297 Treaties and Other International Acts Series 3364 (Emphasis supplied).

298 Treaties and Other International Acts Series 3365 (Emphasis supplied).

299 XI TWC 543-544 (Emphasis supplied).

that despite pleas to the contrary under the facts and circumstances of the case the commander must have known of the offenses charged and acquiesced therein.[300] The question remains, particularly in light of the severity of the penalty for commission of a grave breach, if the standard should be lower.

Under domestic law, there exist three degrees of negligence: (1) *Wanton:* This degree of negligence involves the doing of an inherently dangerous act or omission with a heedless disregard of the probable consequences.

(2) *Recklessness, Gross or Culpable Negligence:* Culpable negligence is a degree of carelessness greater than simple negligence.[301] It is a negligent act or omission accompanied by a culpable disregard for the forseeable (but not necessarily probable) consequences to others of that act or omission.

(3) *Simple Negligence:* Simple negligence is the absence of due care, that is, an act or omission of a person who is under a duty to use due care which exhibits a lack of that degree of care for the safety of others which a reasonably prudent man would have exercised under the same or similar circumstances.

It is submitted that only where there is a showing of *wanton* negligence has the commander manifested the *mens rea* to be held criminally responsible for the primary offense, that is, he has through his dereliction sufficiently aided and abetted the principals thereto as to make himself a principal or an accessory after the fact.

Article 77, Uniform Code of Military Justice, defines a "principal" as:

> Any person . . . who—
> (1) commits an offense . . ., or aids, abets, counsels, commands, or procures its commission; or
> (2) causes an act to be done which if directly performed by him would be punishable by this chapter; is a principal.[302]

300 Professor O'Brien, *supra* n. 288 at 649, utilizes an indirect/direct liability theory rather than the legal concept of imputed or constructive knowledge:

> . . . if . . . violations are such as to reveal demonstrable direct or implied negligence on the part of the relevant commanders. command responsibility dictates indirect liability for the crimes. If it can be shown that the commanders must have been aware that torture and mistreatment were regularly practiced, . . . they become participants with direct responsibility added to their indirect liability.

301 Para. 198b, MANUAL FOR COURTS-MARTIAL, 1969 (REV. ED.) [hereinafter cited as MCM, 1969 (Rev. ed.)].

302 10 U. S. C. § 877.

In discussing Article 77 the *Manual for Courts-Martial* states:

> To constitute one an aider and abettor under this article, and hence liable as a principal, mere presence at the scene is not enough nor is mere failure to prevent the commission of an offense; there must be an intent to aid or encourage the persons who commit the crime. *The aider and abettor must share the criminal intent or purpose of the perpetrator.*[303]

Article 78, UCMJ, Accessory after the Fact, states that

> Any person . . . who, knowing that an offense . . . has been committed, receives, comforts, or assists the offender in order to hinder or prevent his apprehension, trial, or punishment shall be punished as a court-martial may direct.[304]

In discussing Article 78, the *Manual* states that in addition to having actual knowledge that an offense has occurred "mere failure to report a known offense will not constitute one an accessory after the fact." [305]

Yet such failure to report will give rise to other liability, at least at the domestic level. Article 1139, Navy Regulations, states:

> *Obligation to Report Offenses.* Persons in the Department of the Navy shall report to the proper authority offenses committed by persons in the Department of the Navy which come under their observation.[306]

Likewise, Military Assistance Command, Vietnam, Directive 20-4 [307] required that any allegation of a war crime be reported not only to the next higher headquarters but directly to MACV headquarters in Saigon, bypassing the regular chain of command and communication channels.

Violation of either of these orders constitutes a violation of Article 92 of the Uniform Code of Military Justice, [308] either as a violation of a lawful general order or as an act which constitutes dereliction of duty. In the former charge, where there is a more substantial question of criminal intent, the maximum sentence is a dishonorable discharge (dismissal for officers) and confinement at hard labor for two years. In the latter case, where

[303] Para. 156, MCM, 1969 (Rev. ed.).

[304] 10 U. S. C. § 878.

[305] Para. 157, MCM, 1969 (Rev. ed.).

[306] United States Naval Regulations, 1973. These regulations apply to all members of the United States Navy and Marine Corps, active or reserve, and to Coast Guard units and personnel when attached to the Navy.

[307] MACV Directive 20-4 (20 April 1965). This requirement was in effect throughout the period of major United States' involvement in Vietnam, being republished in all subsequent editions of MACV Directive 20-4 (25 March 1966; 10 July 1970; and 2 March 1971).

[308] 10 U. S. C. § 892.

commission of the offense may occur through an act of simple negligence, the maximum punishment is three months' confinement.[309]

Where there exists the necessary *mens rea*, something more than a mere failure or refusal to disclose an act and some positive act of concealment, the person so acting is guilty of misprision of a felony, a violation of Article 134,[310] for which the maximum punishment is a dishonorable discharge (dismissal for officers) and confinement at hard labor for three years. Any greater degree of intent would place the individual charged within the realm of the previously-discussed area of principal or accessory after the fact. Thus the degree of negligence is in direct relation to the degree of liability, and under either domestic law, charging one as a principal or accessory after the fact to murder, or international law, charging one in essence as a principal or accessory after the fact to a war crime, there exists a requirement that the negligence of the commander be so great as to be tantamount to the possession of the necessary *mens rea* to so become such an active party to the offense. Only upon a showing of this degree of negligence can there be imposed the maximum penalty of death. Thus in the *Pohl* trial, SS Standartenfuehrer (Colonel) Erwin Tschentscher was charged with war crimes committed by members of his battalion in the first Russian campaign from the first of July until December 31, 1941. The court noted that there was some evidence that he had constructive knowledge of the participation of members of his command, but no evidence that he had actual knowledge of such facts. Rejecting any strict liability theory although quoting *Yamashita*, the court did not believe the participation was of sufficient magnitude or duration to constitute notice to Colonel Tschentscher, and thus to give him an opportunity to control the actions of his subordinates.[311] Had this been a court-martial, either of an individual normally subject to the Uniform Code of Military Justice or of a foreign officer being tried for war crimes pursuant to Article 18,[312] the

309 A commissioned officer additionally may be punished by punitive separation from the service, *i.e.* dismissal, when convicted by a general court-martial of any offense in violation of the Uniform Code of Military Justice. Para. 126*d*, MANUAL FOR COURTS-MARTIAL, UNITED STATES, 1969, (REV. ED.).

310 10 U. S. C. § 934.

311 V TWC 1010-12. Colonel Tschentscher was found guilty of other charges and sentenced to ten years' imprisonment.

312 10 U.S.C. 818. While a foreign officer would normally be charged with the commission of a war crime, Paragraph 12 Appendix 6a, Manual

prosecution could have proceeded under multiplicious charges and theories concerning the degree of negligence, absent actual knowledge and liability; as a minimum, given the Tribunal's judgment, Colonel Tschentscher would have been guilty of dereliction of duty. The standards of punishment parallel the standards of responsibility and proof under either domestic or international law; just as the Tribunal stated with regard to Colonel Tschentscher, proof of constructive knowledge under the Uniform Code of Military Justice does not constitute a showing of actual knowledge.[313]

Where domestic law exists, however, charges against United States personnel should normally be drawn under that law rather than under the general "war crime" offense.[314] No nation is going to charge its own citizen with the commission of a war crime for obvious political reasons. There certainly exist psychological reasons why such charges would be drawn alleging specific offenses rather than the commission of a war crime — a result of the heinous connotation of those words and, as a result, perhaps a greater reluctance by a court to convict an accused. A parallel to the *Tschenstcher* case would serve to illustrate this point.

The accused was a company commander in Vietnam. His company occupied a night defensive position with another company. During the night one of several enemy prisoners taken during the action of the preceding day was shot and killed. Although the offense occurred within his perimeter and within sixty feet of his position, the accused did not investigate; he did, however, receive a report that one of the prisoners had grabbed a weapon

for Courts-Martial, United States, 1969 (Revised edition), states that there is no jurisdictional error in the erroneous designation of a specification as a violation of an article of the Uniform Code of Military Justice.

313 United States v. Curtin, 9 USCMA 427, 26 CMR 207 (1958). There is no *per se* equation of the "should have known" test except through the previously-cited and discussed standards of negligence as applied to the individual case and its facts.

314 Paragraph 507b of FM 27-10 states:

> b. Persons Charges With War Crimes. The United States normally punishes war crimes as such only if they are committed by enemy nationals or by persons serving the interests of the enemy State. Violations of the law of war committed by persons subject to the military law of the United States will usually constitute violations of the Uniform Code of Military Justice and, if so, will be prosecuted under that Code. Violations of the law of war committed within the United States by other persons will usually constitute violations of federal or state criminal law and preferably will be prosecuted under such law (see paras. 505 and 506).

and shot the victim. He neither investigated the offense further nor did he report the offense in accordance with existing directives.[315] He was charged with and convicted of failure to obey a lawful general order and dereliction of duty, both offenses under Article 926.[316] While the evidence was sufficient to sustain a conviction under the charged domestic offenses,[317] it is arguable whether a conviction could have been obtained had the accused been charged with the commission of a war crime. As in *Tschentscher*, the appellate opinion declined to address the international *should have known* test, leaving to a commander some area in which he is permitted to exercise his personal judgment as to the necessity for further investigation; absent some serious personal dereliction manifesting some degree of *mens rea* the commander must be presumed to have acted in good faith, given all circumstances, unless the facts become so overbearing as to point an accusatory finger at him. These circumstances again require an examination and balancing of the subjective criteria previously discussed.

IV. SUMMARY

Out of the ashes of World War II there rose a desire to further define the responsibility of a commander for war crimes committed by his subordinates, a responsibility recognized by the earliest military scholars. Although the Tribunals after World War II sought to establish an international norm, there was of necessity much reliance on domestic standards in resolving questions of knowledge, responsibility, and negligence; and while the post-World War II trials from a legal point of view purportedly have no precedental value, the codification of many of the principals contained therein by the 1949 Geneva Convention would indicate that from a practical standpoint the standards formulated are recognized as international norms. All of the law of war is the formal expression of the principle of restraint; and it is to the commander, particularly the commander in the field, that the responsibility for exercise of restraint is most directed, inamuch as he has control of both the means of destruction

[315] USARV Reg 335-6 (24 June 1967), which served as an implementing instruction for all United States Army Forces in Vietnam for the previously-cited MACV Directive 20-4.

[316] 10 U. S. C. § 892.

[317] United States v. Golden, 43 C.M.R. 710 (ACMR 1970).

and the means of restraint. Thoughout the history of warfare the commander has received the glories of victory and the burden of defeat, whether deserved or not. [318] The role of the commander is a lonely one; its authority may be delegated, but never its responsibility. In accepting the position of commander, an officer accepts massive responsibility — responsibility to see that his troops are fed, clothed, and paid; responsibility for their welfare, morale, and discipline; responsibility for his unit's tactical training and proficiency; responsibility for close coordination and cooperation with adjacent and supported or supporting units; and responsibility for accomplishment of his mission. He is no less charged with the responsibility to accomplish that mission within the limitations of the laws of war, and to exercise due control over his subordinates to insure their compliance.

In order to find a commander responsible, the acts charged must have been committed by troops under his command. Normally this refers to troops of his unit or of another unit over which he has both operational and administrative control; but absent either he may still be responsible if he otherwise had a duty and the means to control those troops and failed to do so. If he has executive authority over a specified occupied territory, he is responsible for all illegal acts occurring within that territory, or at least for controlling or preventing their occurrence. While exclusion of any one of these factors may excuse him from liability under international standards, he may nonetheless be held responsible under domestic standards if he knows of an offense and, possessed of the duty to respond, fails to do everything within his power to prevent or report that offense.

In controlling his men, the commander has a *duty* to utilize all means available to him to know of and prevent the occurrence of war crimes within his command. In particular, he cannot shun or ignore the obvious and plead ignorance as a defense in an effort to escape liability.

The commander who directly orders the commission of a war crimes shares the guilt of the perpetrator of the offense. So, too, does the intermediate commander who receives an order patently illegal on its face who passes that order to subordinates for

---

[318] General Joseph Joffre, who led the French Army in repulsing the German offensive at the battle of the Marne in 1914, was once asked who had won that battle—he or his subordinate commander, Ferdinand Foch. General Joffre replied that he did not know who had won the battle, "but if it had been lost I know who would have lost it." A. VANDEGRIFT, ONCE A MARINE 9 (1964).

execution, although the plea of superior orders may be heard in mitigation. A commander may also be held responsible where he does not necessarily order certain illegal acts but is shown to have encouraged their perpetration or incited his men to act. Where he has neither ordered nor incited his men to carry out war crimes, he may be deemed responsible if by his acts he has acquiesced therein. Only the degree of culpability may distinguish the commander from the actual perpetrators in the instances cited above.

Essential to any allegation of command responsibility is the element of knowledge, either *actual knowledge* or the *means of knowledge* which the commander failed to exercise. Actual knowledge may be presumed in two instances: (a) where the commander has executive authority over occupied territory, and the offenses occur within that territory; and (b) where reports of offenses are made to his command, the presumption being that such reports are made for the benefit of the commander. These presumptions may be rebutted, for example, by a showing of absence from the command at the time of the offense or its report, or by illness; but this rebuttal is temporary in nature, extending only for the period of the absence or illness. Any inaction upon resumption of command raises a presumption of acquiescence, knowledge again being presumed.

No theory of absolute liability has found acceptance in either international or domestic law. No man, whether commander or the lowest private, is held responsible for the acts of another absent the establishment of some sharing of the *mens rea*. The absolute liability theory has been expressly rejected in every case in which it was argued. Only where there has been wanton, immoral disregard amounting to acquiescence in the offense has criminal responsibility attached. The conduct — a wanton disregard of the occurrence of offenses — must be such as to support a finding that the commander is an accomplice in the sense that he shared the criminal intent of his subordinates and that he encouraged their misconduct through a failure to discover and intervene where he had a duty to prevent their action. Absent actual knowledge there must be either (1) such serious personal dereliction on the part of the commander as to constitute wilful and wanton disregard of the possible consequences; or (2) an imputation of constructive knowledge, that is, despite pleas to the contrary the commander under the facts and circumstances of the particular case must have known of the offenses charged and acquiesced therein.

In determining whether the commander either should have known or must have known of the occurrence of the offenses charged, certain subjective criteria may be considered in an effort to determine his means of knowledge: (a) the rank of the commander; (b) the experience of the commander; (c) the training of the men under his command; (d) the age and experience of the men under his command; (e) the size of the staff of the commander; (f) the comprehensiveness of the duties of the staff of the commander; (g) the "sliding probability ratio" of unit-incident-command; (h) the duties and complexities of the commander by virtue of the command he held; (i) communications abilities; (j) mobility of the commander; (k) isolation of the commander; (l) composition of forces within the command; and (m) the combat situation.

In holding a commander responsible under international standards, the commander's acts of commission or omission must be tantamount to "wanton, immoral disregard" of the acts of his subordinates. This international standard is consistent with municipal standards for which the same maximum penalty of death may be imposed. Where lesser penalties may be exacted, such as for a negligent failure to discover or report an offense, lesser standards of negligence — either culpable or simple — are provided. There municipal standards are defined by the Uniform Code of Military Justice and by duties imposed by existing orders and regulations; international standards are defined by existing treaties and conventions, in particular the 1949 Geneva Conventions which require wilful and wanton conduct in order for there to be a grave breach of those Conventions. Any further definition must depend on the facts of the particular case and the previously-discussed subjective criteria rather than a precisely-defined international definition. The duty is well established, the responsibility well-defined.

A contemporary Marine Corps recruiting poster asserts the principle:

> Some men accept responsibility; others seek it.

Neither the principles of command nor the law of war can expect, nor accept, anything less.

[14]

Accountability for international crimes: From conjecture to reality

by
JELENA PEJIC

At a 1987 international colloquium devoted to the Nuremberg trials Professor Eric David posed a hypothetical question — could Augusto Pinochet be arrested and tried in Belgium for acts such as enforced disappearances, extra-judicial executions, torture and unlawful detention committed since his ascendance to power?[1] While Professor David answered in the affirmative,[2] at the time it was only academic conjecture that such a scenario could ever come to pass. And yet, just over a decade later, his hypothetical question proved to be prescient. Augusto Pinochet was arrested in the United Kingdom, whose highest court eventually ruled that he did not enjoy immunity from legal process for torture and conspiracy to commit torture perpetrated while he was in office.[3] It was a defining moment in the fight against impunity and perhaps the most important milestone in the struggle for international justice since the Nuremberg trials.

The proceedings against Pinochet did not, however, come out of the blue. Ever since the end of the Cold War and the resulting new impetus in international relations, the international community had been setting important markers in the fight against impunity. The trend only accelerated after the Pinochet case, allowing the full-fledged emergence of what can now be called a global movement

JELENA PEJIC is a Legal Adviser at the ICRC's Legal Division.

against impunity.[4] The purpose of this brief text is to outline some of the major developments along the way[5] and to mention some of the challenges that lie ahead. But, before that, tribute should be paid to the heroes of that endevour: the victims of crime and abuse of power worldwide, as well as their families, whose perseverance and fortitude have spurred governments to action and galvanized NGOs. They were and will continue to be at the very centre of the global fight against impunity.

International ad hoc tribunals

It is no exaggeration to say that the flurry of normative developments prompted by the horrifying legacy of the Second World War died down fairly quickly when it came to establishing mechanisms that would ensure individual accountability for crimes under international law. Early efforts to establish a permanent international

1 Eric David, "L'actualite juridique de Nuremberg", in *Le Procès de Nuremberg: Conséquences et actualisation*, Actes du Colloque international, Université Libre de Bruxelles, 27 March 1987, Editions Bruylant, Brussels, 1988, p. 168.

2 *Ibid.*, p. 171.

3 *Regina* v. *Bartle and the Commissioner of Police for the Metropolis and Others* Ex Parte *Pinochet*, (1999) 381 ILM 581 (UK House of Lords) [hereinafter *Pinochet Case*]; see Reed Brody and Michael Ratner (eds), *The Pinochet Papers: The Case of Augusto Pinochet in Spain and Britain*, Kluwer Law International, The Hague, 2000, p. 40 [hereinafter *Brody and Ratner*].

4 A very useful — and rare — definition of "impunity" reads as follows: "Impunity means the impossibility, *de jure* or *de facto*, of bringing the perpetrators of human rights violations to account — whether in criminal, civil, administrative or disciplinary proceedings — since they are not subject to any inquiry that might lead to their being accused, arrested, tried and, if found guilty, convicted, and to reparations being made to their victims": "The administration of justice and the human rights of detainees: Question of the Impunity of Perpetrators of Human Rights Violations (Civil and Political)", Final Report prepared by Mr Joinet Pursuant to Sub-Commission decision 1996/119, UN Doc. E/CN.4/Sub.2/1997/20, 26 June 1997, Annex II, pp. 13-14 [hereinafter Joinet Report]. The definitional section of the document also refers to genocide, war crimes and crimes against humanity as being "serious crimes under international law". *Ibid.*, p. 15.

5 Due to lack of space, this article will not cover truth commissions as a non-penal mechanism in the fight against impunity. For a comprehensive review of the issue, see Priscilla B. Hayner, *Unspeakable Truths: Confronting State Terror and Atrocity*, Routledge, London, 2001. See also Joinet Report, *op. cit.* (note 4), pp. 14-17.

RICR MARS **IRRC** MARCH 2002 VOL. 84 N° 845 **15**

criminal court[6] did not get very far owing to Cold War tensions. While international human rights law did develop quickly, its monitoring mechanisms at the international level remained primarily political or quasi-judicial at best. After several decades of hardly any progress, the breakthrough came in 1993 and 1994 respectively, with the establishment of the two ad hoc criminal tribunals for the former Yugoslavia (ICTY) and Rwanda (ICTR).

Even though the geographical focus of the two tribunals is different, they were created essentially because of the unwillingness or inability of the national authorities concerned to bring to justice the perpetrators of serious crimes under international law — genocide, war crimes and crimes against humanity. Regardless of how the totality of their jurisprudence and rules of procedure will be viewed in historical perspective, the precedential value of the ad hoc tribunals cannot be contested. Both tribunals were created by the Security Council which, treading on previously untested ground, drew on its Chapter VII powers to establish judicial organs with which all UN member States are legally obliged to cooperate. The tribunals, simply put, showed that international adjudicatory mechanisms were not only necessary but also possible, thus paving the way for the adoption, several years later, of a treaty for the world's first permanent International Criminal Court (ICC).[7]

In the almost nine years since its creation, the ICTY has clarified and developed key concepts of international humanitarian law and made an invaluable contribution to softening the distinction between the legal regimes applicable to international and non-international armed conflict. The way was paved fairly early on, with the well-known 1995 *Tadic Jurisdiction Decision*,[8] which essentially

6 See Report of the Committee on International Criminal Jurisdiction, 1-31 August 1951, UN Doc. A/2136 (1952); see generally Report of the 1953 Committee on International Criminal Jurisdiction, 27 July-20 August 1953, UN Doc. A/2645 (1954).

7 Rome Statute of the International Criminal Court, adopted by the United Nations Diplomatic Conference of Plenipotentiaries on the Establishment of an International Criminal Court on 17 July 1998, UN Doc. A/CONF.183/9, 17 July 1998 [hereinafter ICC or ICC Statute].

8 *The Prosecutor* v. *Dusko Tadic*, Case No. IT-94-AR72, Decision on the Defence Motion for Interlocutory Appeal on Jurisdiction, 2 October 1995 [hereinafter *Tadic Jurisdiction Decision*].

established that there is a common core of international humanitarian law rules applicable to armed conflicts *per se*, regardless of their character. In reaching that conclusion, the Tribunal relied on Article 3 of its Statute ("Violations of the laws or customs of war"), construing it as a residual basis of jurisdiction that may be invoked when more specific provisions of the Statute do not apply.[9] The *Tadic Jurisdiction Decision* was, moreover, "the first judgment rendered by an international tribunal confirming, in unequivocal terms, the criminal character of war crimes committed in [internal armed conflicts]".[10] The Decision also laid the groundwork for a number of later judgments in which the substantive content of the rules applicable to non-international armed conflict were developed.[11]

The ICTY's high point in practical terms has been the well-publicised transfer of former Yugoslav President Slobodan Milosevic to the Detention Unit at The Hague in June 2001. Milosevic, who is currently on trial, was initially indicted by the Tribunal — as the first ever serving head of State — for violations of the laws and customs of war and crimes against humanity committed against the Kosovo Albanian population in 1998-99. Since then he has also been separately indicted for grave breaches of the Geneva Conventions, violations of the laws or customs of war and crimes against humanity committed against the Croatian and other non-Serb populations in the Republic of Croatia and, in addition to those latter charges, for genocide and complicity in genocide during the war in

9 The more specific and related provisions would be Article 2 of the ICTY's Statute — Grave breaches of the Geneva Conventions of 1949 — which, according to the *Tadic Jurisdiction Decision*, *ibid.*, may be applied only to acts perpetrated in a conflict that has been established to be international.

10 Sonja Boelaert-Suominen, "The Yugoslavia Tribunal and the Common Core of Humanitarian Law Applicable to All Armed Conflicts", *Leiden Journal of International Law*, Vol. 13, Issue 3, 2000, pp. 630-631.

11 As Boelaert-Suominen points out, "this jurisprudence shows that war crimes charges based on grave breaches of the Geneva Conventions have a corollary in war crimes charges based on Article 3 common to the Geneva Conventions". Thus, for example, several ICTY Trial Chambers have ruled that there is no qualitative difference between the terms "wilful killing" as a grave breach and "murder" as used in common Article 3. Similarly, the grave breach of "inhuman treatment" corresponds to "cruel treatment" within the meaning of common Article 3. *Ibid.*, pp. 637-638.

RICR MARS **IRRC** MARCH 2002 VOL. 84 N° 845 **17**

Bosnia and Herzegovina.[12] In view of the factual and legal findings that the proceedings are expected to generate, as well as Milosevic's refusal to appoint defence counsel,[13] it may safely be said that his trial will be the most closely watched in the ICTY's history.

Milosevic's transfer to The Hague by the Serbian authorities was effected under huge international pressure and almost immediately caused the fall of the then federal Yugoslav government, one faction of which was opposed to his surrender. The difficulties in surrendering indictees and other forms of non-cooperation of national authorities remain one of the major obstacles to the fulfilment of the Tribunal's mandate.[14] Even though the Tribunal's Statute, as mentioned above, demands the cooperation of UN member States, there is no established enforcement mechanism on which the Prosecutor can rely to bring indictees in. It is, in fact, fortuitous that there is an international military presence in the former Yugoslavia and that contributing States can sometimes be persuaded by Tribunal representatives to arrest indictees. The situation would, presumably, be quite different if there were no such forces, a reality that the future ICC is likely to face far more frequently. The international community therefore still has to take the step from having established international accountability mechanisms to endowing them with enforcement capacity. It is to be hoped that this will be one of the next advances in the fight against impunity.

Internationalized tribunals

The establishment of the ad hoc Tribunals paved the way not only for negotiations on the ICC treaty, but also, at least indirectly, made it possible to pursue work on the creation of three other judicial bodies: the first dealing with crimes committed two and a half decades

12 See *Milosevic Case* (IT-01-51), Case Information Sheet (CIS), 26 November 2001, ‹http://www.un.org/icty/glance/milosevic.htm› as well as CIS of 9 and 29 October (IT 01-50 resp. 99 37 I).

13 For Milosevic's possible strategy in terms of legal assistance, see Mirko Klarin, "Analysis: Milosevic to put NATO on Trial", *IWPR's Tribunal Update*, No. 248, 10-15 December 2001, ‹http://www.iwpr.net›.

14 See Address to the United Nations Security Council by the Prosecutor of the International Criminal Tribunals for the former Yugoslavia and Rwanda, Mrs Carla Del Ponte, 27 November 2001, ‹http://www.ictr.org/ENGLISH/speeches/delponte271101sc.htm›.

ago in Cambodia; the second dealing with crimes committed in Sierra Leone not that long ago; and the third dealing with crimes committed before and after the UN-administered referendum on the independence of East Timor in 1999.

The "Khmer Rouge tribunal", as it is colloquially called, has been the object of lengthy and rather complicated negotiations between the Cambodian authorities and the United Nations for over two years. At the time of writing this text, the outcome of those discussions is still uncertain, although the tribunal's basic mandate and structure are known. It would be composed of both Cambodian and international judges (and prosecutors), organized in three extraordinary chambers within the domestic court system, with subject-matter jurisdiction over serious violations of Cambodian and international law committed by senior leaders and others during the period of Democratic Kampuchea (1975-1979).[15] Stumbling blocks in the negotiations between the Cambodian government and the UN have included the procedure for issuing indictments and reaching verdicts, amnesty provisions, rules on foreign defence counsel, rules of procedure and, most recently,[16] the official language to be used in court.[17] Needless to say, both international and Cambodian human rights activists believe that the Khmer Rouge tribunal, if properly established, would be "the beginning of the end of a culture of impunity"[18] in Cambodia.

15 Law on the Establishment of Extraordinary Chambers in the Courts of Cambodia for the Prosecution of Crimes Committed During the Period of Democratic Kampuchea, as adopted by the National Assembly on 2 January 2001, ‹http://www.phnompenh daily.com/06.01.01.htm›; see also Articles of Cooperation Between the United Nations and the Royal Government of Cambodia [in/Concerning] the Prosecution under Cambodian Law of Crimes Committed During the Period of Democratic Kampuchea, *Phnom Penh Post*, Issue 9/22, 27 October–9 November 2000, ‹http://www.phnompenh post.com› (both texts on file with the author).

16 See Colum Lynch, "UN Warns Cambodia on War Crimes Tribunal", *The Washington Post*, 3 February 2001, p. A22; see also Human Rights Watch Press Release, "Core Issues in the Khmer Rouge Tribunal Unresolved", 21 January 2001, ‹http://www.hrw.org/press/2000/01/cambo0121.htm›.

17 See "Khmer Rouge Trial Stalled Over Language", Reuters, Phnom Penh, 26 November 2001 (on file with the author).

18 Youk Chang, Director of Documentation Center of Cambodia, quoted in Amy Kazmin and Carola Hoyos, "Cambodia Moves Towards Tribunal of Khmer Rouge", *Financial Times*, 23 August 2001, ‹http://www.globalarchive.ft.com/globalarchive/›.

RICR MARS IRRC MARCH 2002 VOL. 84 N° 845 19

Moves to establish a special court for Sierra Leone were initiated by the government of that country in August 2000.[19] The UN Security Council responded in a matter of days, authorising the UN Secretary-General to negotiate an agreement with the Sierra Leonean government on the creation of an independent special court and requesting him to submit a report on ways of meeting the government's request.[20] According to the ensuing Secretary-General's report, this "treaty-based *sui generis* court of mixed jurisdiction and composition"[21] would have the power to prosecute persons "most responsible" for serious violations of "international humanitarian law and Sierra Leonean law committed in the territory" of that country since November 1996. The judges would be both Sierra Leonean and foreign; the Prosecutor would be appointed by the UN Secretary-General upon consultation with the government, while the Deputy Prosecutor would be Sierra Leonean. The special court would have concurrent jurisdiction with domestic courts, similar to the ad hoc tribunal model. Issues which generated further exchanges between the Security Council and the UN Secretary-General included the special court's jurisdiction over children[22] and how widely the net should be cast in terms of other aspects of the court's personal jurisdiction, as well as the future court's funding.[23] Despite the fact that not all the funding pledged had come in from UN member States, in January 2002 the United Nations and the government of Sierra Leone signed

19 See Letter dated 9 August 2000 from the Permanent Representative of Sierra Leone to the United Nations addressed to the President of the Security Council, UN Doc. S/2000/786, 10 August 2000.

20 UN Doc. S/RES/1315 (2000), paras 1 and 6, 14 August 2000.

21 Report of the Secretary-General on the Establishment of a Special Court for Sierra Leone, UN Doc. S/2000/915, para. 9. The Report, in its Annex, includes a draft Agreement between the United Nations and the Government of Sierra Leone on the Establishment of a Special Court for Sierra Leone, and, in Enclosure, a draft Statute of the Special Court for Sierra Leone.

22 See Letter dated 22 December 2000 from the President of the Security Council addressed to the Secretary-General, UN Doc. S/2000/ 1234, 22 December 2000; see also Letter dated 12 January 2001 from the Secretary-General addressed to the President of the Security Council, UN Doc. S/2001/40, 12 January 2001.

23 Letter dated 12 January 2001 from the Secretary-General addressed to the President of the Security Council, *op. cit.* (note 22).

an agreement setting up the Special Court to prosecute persons bearing "the greatest reponsibility" for crimes committed in that country.[24]

For most of last year, an internationalized domestic tribunal established by the United Nations Transitional Administration in East Timor (UNTAET) has been trying persons suspected of having committed crimes in that region in 1999. The tribunal is composed of Special Panels — made up of one East Timorese judge and two judges of other nationalities — which are part of the District Court of Dili. The Special Panels are authorised to hear cases of genocide, crimes against humanity, war crimes, torture and specific violations of the Indonesian Penal Code. The first judgment, against ten militiamen, was rendered in a crimes against humanity case in December 2001. While this internationalized domestic tribunal presents a model that could potentially be of benefit in other situations as well, researchers have pointed out that the tribunal's main failings have been its link to a very weak domestic criminal justice system and lack of adequate resources and funding for the Special Panels.

International Criminal Court

The issue of resources and funding might also plague the permanent International Criminal Court given that it will essentially operate on the voluntary contributions of States Parties unless its proceedings are initiated by a Security Council referral.[25] This, it is submitted, is a regrettable development, because it hampers the ability of international mechanisms engaged in the fight against impunity to properly carry out their mandate.

The ICC will come into operation once the 1998 Rome Treaty has been ratified by 60 States.[26] At the time of writing this text, the treaty has garnered 50 ratifications[27] and the expectation is that the requisite number will be achieved "well before the summer of

24 See "Sierra Leone: UN Government sign historic accord to set up special war crimes court", UN NewsCenter, 16 January 2002, ‹http://www.un.org./apps/news/story.asp?NewsID=2639&Cr=Sierra&Crl=court›.

25 ICC Statute, Article 115.

26 *Ibid.*, Article 126(1).

27 For up-to-date ratification status, see Rome Statute Signature and Ratification Chart, ‹http://www.iccnow.org/rome/html/ratify.html›.

RICR MARS **IRRC** MARCH 2002 VOL. 84 N° 845 **21**

2002".[28] The Court will be situated in the capital of the Netherlands, the government of which is already well advanced in its preparations for hosting this new international judicial body.[29] While the ICC has yet to start functioning, the adoption of the Rome Treaty can only be characterized as a momentous event in the struggle for international justice, one that would have been simply unthinkable just a decade ago. Apart from the already mentioned political climate that facilitated negotiations on the ICC Statute, the Court's creation is based on the recognition that national authorities have far too often proven unable or unwilling to deal with the perpetrators of serious crimes under international law. The ICC will not supplant national criminal jurisdictions but will, in accordance with the principle of complementarity,[30] be available to step in when domestic prosecutions and trials prove unfeasible.

Of the many achievements of the Rome Statute, two deserve special mention in a review of developments related to the fight against impunity: the first is the ICC's subject-matter jurisdiction over war crimes committed in internal armed conflict and over crimes against humanity,[31] and the second is the Statute's approach to victims. The expansion of war crimes to include acts committed in non-international armed conflict was by no means a foregone conclusion when the treaty negotiations began. Even though Article 3 common to the 1949 Geneva Conventions and Additional Protocol II of 1977 prohibit certain acts in internal armed conflict, not all governments were happy to see some of them defined as war crimes entailing individual criminal responsibility. Partly as a result of the jurisprudence of the ad hoc tribunals and partly due to the obvious prevalence of internal conflicts globally, those objections were overcome. The ICC Statute is thus the first international treaty to explicitly provide for individual criminal responsibility for "serious" violations of common Article 3 and for

28 See Statement by the Minister of Foreign Affairs of the Kingdom of the Netherlands, Jozias J. Van Aartsen, during the Eighth Session of the Preparatory Commission for the International Criminal Court, New York, 25 September 2001, <http://www.iccnow.org/html/Netherland speechPrepCom8.html>.

29 *Ibid.*

30 ICC Statute, Article 1. See also ICC Statute, Articles 17-19.

31 The ICC will have jurisdiction over genocide, war crimes, crimes against humanity and the crime of aggression (once the latter is defined). See ICC Statute, Article 5.

twelve other "serious violations of the laws and customs" applicable in non-international armed conflict, including intentional attacks against civilians, crimes of sexual and gender violence, and forced displacement.[32] There is no doubt that the list should have been more expansive, but at least the Rome Statute will, as a matter of law, put a stop to claims that crimes perpetrated in internal armed conflict are a matter of solely domestic jurisdiction.

The ICC Statute's definition of crimes against humanity (Article 7) is just as important. Arriving at a definition was no easy task given that there was no accepted definition or list of such crimes as a matter of treaty law. Previous definitions, such as those included in the Nuremberg and Tokyo Charters, Allied Control Council Law No. 10 and the Statutes of the ad hoc Tribunals differ in both their elements and in the enumeration of acts considered to constitute crimes against humanity. The ICC Statute definition is groundbreaking in that, for a start, it omits a nexus to armed conflict, thus clarifying that crimes against humanity may be committed in peacetime as well as in war. The Article 7 *chapeau* also provides that crimes against humanity may be committed either as part of a "widespread" or "systematic" attack against a civilian population, thus eliminating the need to prove a cumulation of these two elements. Lastly, the definition does not provide that persecution must be a motive for any of the acts listed as crimes against humanity; instead, persecution is included in that list as a separate crime.[33] It should also be noted that the Statute defines the crimes of torture and enforced disappearance[34] more expansively than the relevant human rights instruments[35] by dissociating them from the requirement of the perpetrator's official capacity.

Largely due to NGO lobbying and the responsiveness of several key governments, the ICC Statute did not circumvent the interests of victims. It mandates *inter alia* the creation, within the future

32 ICC Statute, Article 8(2)(c)(e)(i), (vi) and (viii).

33 ICC Statute, Article 7(1)(h).

34 ICC Statute, Article 7(2)(f) and (i).

35 See Convention against Torture and Other Cruel, Inhuman or Degrading Treatment or Punishment, 10 December 1984, Article 1 [hereinafter Convention Against Torture], and Declaration on the Protection of All Persons from Enforced Disappearance, GA Res. 47/133, 18 December 1992, preambular para. 3.

Court's Registry, of a Victims and Witnesses Unit charged with providing protective measures, security arrangements, counselling and other appropriate assistance for witnesses, victims who appear before the Court and others who may be at risk on account of testimony.[36] In a groundbreaking development, the treaty also includes provisions on reparations to victims and their families.[37] The Court may, either upon request or on its own motion (in exceptional circumstances), determine the scope and extent of any damage, loss and injury to, or in respect of, victims. It is authorised to order that a convicted person make reparations to the victims or their families, which may include restitution, compensation and rehabilitation. The Statute further provides for the establishment of a Trust Fund from which victims may be compensated[38] and permits the Court to order the seizure of property or assets of the convicted person or of the property used to commit the crime.[39] States Parties are obliged to implement a Court decision to that effect. The Statute's provisions on reparations have been further outlined in the ICC's Rules of Procedure and Evidence.[40]

Universal jurisdiction

As already mentioned, the ICC was created to offset the lack of willingness or ability of national authorities to mount domestic prosecutions and trials of perpetrators of serious crimes under international law. As a few high-profile cases have recently demonstrated, another avenue may in such circumstances be used to ensure justice — the exercise of universal jurisdiction by third States.[41] The most

36 ICC Statute, Article 43(6).

37 ICC Statute, Article 75.

38 ICC Statute, Article 79.

39 ICC Statute, Article 93(1)(k).

40 See Finalised Draft Text of the Rules of Procedure and Evidence, PCNICC/2000/1/Add.1, 2 November 2000, Sub-Section 4, Rules 94 to 99, ‹http://www.un.org/law/ icc/statute/rules/rulefra.htm›.

41 "Under the principle of universal jurisdiction, a state is entitled, or even required to bring proceedings in respect of certain serious crimes, irrespective of the location of the crime, and irrespective of the nationality of the perpetrator or the victim. The only connection between the crime and the prosecuting state that may be required is the physical presence of the alleged offender within the jurisdiction of that state": International Law Association, *Final Report on the Exercise of Universal Jurisdiction in Respect of Gross Human Rights Offences*, Committee on International Human Rights Law and Practice, London Conference, 2000, p. 2 (on file with the author) [hereinafter ILA Report].

celebrated example is the 1998-1999 *Pinochet Case*, based both on passive personality and universal jurisdiction. It should be noted, however, that courts in Europe had initiated and successfully concluded proceedings based on universal jurisdiction against alleged offenders from the former Yugoslavia and Rwanda prior to Pinochet's arrest in England.[42] Since then other cases have been brought as well.[43] It is submitted that the gradual, but steady expansion of the exercise of universal jurisdiction is likely to be a permanent trend in the struggle for international justice.

It was the Spanish *Audiencia Nacional*'s ruling that "Spain could investigate crimes committed in Chile and that the court could exercise universal jurisdiction over crimes committed by and against non-nationals outside of Spanish territory"[44] that provided the basis for the formal request for Pinochet's extradition issued in Spain in November 1998. The Spanish request was followed by extradition requests from Switzerland, France and Belgium, respectively.[45] Leaving aside other seminal aspects of the Pinochet case,[46] the proceedings in the UK affirmed that States Parties have an obligation under the 1984 Convention against Torture[47] to take measures that would enable them to assert jurisdiction over an offender present in their territory and to

42 *Ibid.*, Annex. The Annex contains a review of various cases brought under the principle of universal jurisdiction — before Pinochet's arrest — in Austria, Denmark, France, Germany and the Netherlands.

43 France most recently declared admissible a complaint filed by six victims against Tunisian officials, alleging acts of torture, regardless of lack of presence of the alleged perpetrators in French territory. See Comité pour le respect des libertés et des droits de l'homme en Tunisie, *Une brèche importante dans la lutte contre l'impunité: la plainte déposée en France contre des tortionnaires tunisiens est jugée recevable*, Paris, 28 November 1998 (text on file with the author).

44 See Mary Griffin, "Ending the Impunity of Perpetrators of Human Rights Atrocities: A Major Challenge for International Law in the 21st Century", *International Review of the Red Cross*, No. 838, June 2000, p. 382.

45 *Ibid.* It should be noted in this context that a Belgian *juge d'instruction* ruled in Pinochet-related proceedings that a person suspected of having committed crimes against humanity could be brought to justice in Belgium on the basis of customary international law. See Juge d'instruction à Bruxelles, ordonnance, 6 November 1998 (on file with the author), reprinted in *Revue de Droit Pénal et de Criminologie*, 1999, pp. 278-300.

46 For a review of the Pinochet case, see Brody and Ratner, *op. cit.* (note 3). See also *Crimes Against Humanity: Pinochet Faces Justice*, International Commission of Jurists, July 1999.

47 Convention Against Torture, Articles 4, 5 and 7.

either prosecute or extradite such a person. They also confirmed that a former head of State cannot invoke immunity from extradition and prosecution for torture and conspiracy to torture. Britain's highest court did, however, conclude that a serving head of State would *ratione personae* have enjoyed immunity for the acts alleged,[48] a finding which, it is submitted, contradicts both the letter of the Nuremberg Charter and Judgment and their normative legacy.[49] It should be noted that the UK proceedings also had an effect in Chile itself — upon his return from Britain, Pinochet's parliamentary immunity and his senator-for-life position were lifted, enabling the initiation of domestic proceedings.[50]

Less than a year after the Law Lords' ruling in the *Pinochet Case*, in February 2000 a Senegalese court indicted former Chadian President Hissene Habre on torture charges and placed him under house arrest.[51] This action by the Dakar Regional Court, initiated by Chadian victims as well as by Chadian and international human rights groups, is believed to have been the first exercise of universal jurisdiction for human rights offences in an African country.[52] In July 2000, the Court of Appeals dismissed the charges against Habre, ruling that Senegal had not enacted legislation to implement the Convention Against Torture and therefore had no jurisdiction to pursue the charges because the crimes were not committed in Senegal, and in March 2001 Senegal's highest court essentially confirmed that ruling.[53] If there is one lesson to be learned from the Habre case, it is the

48 See Brody and Ratner, *op. cit.* (note 3), p. 44.

49 For a good review of the principles on immunity as enunciated in the Nuremburg Judgment and the normative follow-up, see Amnesty International, *The Case of General Pinochet: Universal Jurisdiction and the Absence of Immunity for Crimes against Humanity*, EUR 45/21/98, October 1998.

50 See Federico Andreu-Guzman, "L'affaire Pinochet: historique des événements et exposé des incriminations, L'arrêt de la Cour suprême de justice du Chili et perspective du combat judiciaire contre l'impunité", Paper presented at the Journée d'études: L'immunité penale des gouvernants, FIDH — CEDIN, Assemblée nationale de France, 30 September 2000 (on file with the author).

51 See Frederic Kirgis, "The Indictment in Senegal of the Former Chad head of State", *ASIL Insights*, February 2000, <http://www.asil.org/insights/insigh41.htm>.

52 ILA Report, *op. cit.* (note 41), p. 27.

53 République Du Senegal, Cour d'Appel de Dakar, Chambre d'Accusation, Arrêt No. 135, 4 July 2000; see Human Rights Watch, "The Case against Hissene Habre", <http://www.hrw.org/justice/habre/intro_web2.htm>.

importance of States adopting implementing legislation (if required under domestic law) to give effect to the Convention's universal jurisdiction provisions. While non-implementation of the Convention Against Torture in Senegalese law ultimately defeated the proceedings, the Habre case did generate further developments well worth noting. It prompted the initiation of criminal proceedings against members of the political police that operated during Hissene Habre's regime by Chadian victims before Chadian courts. It also led the victims to request the UN Committee against Torture to apply interim measures of protection to prevent the former President from leaving Senegal except pursuant to an extradition demand, which the Committee granted.[54] Victims also filed a complaint against Habre in Belgium, under its law on universal jurisdiction mentioned below, seeking his extradition from Senegal.[55]

The purpose of universal jurisdiction is to deny safe haven to persons suspected of having committed egregious crimes which are an affront to the international community as a whole. Among them are genocide, war crimes, crimes against humanity, torture, slavery and piracy, and, some would argue, enforced disappearances as well. It should be remembered that the 1949 Geneva Conventions and their Additional Protocol I of 1977,[56] as well as the Convention Against Torture,[57] provide for mandatory universal jurisdiction by States Parties to those treaties. In practice, however, several conditions have to be met before proceedings in a third State can actually take place. To begin with, domestic implementing legislation will most often be required given that national judges will be hesitant to assert jurisdiction unless authorised to do so by domestic statute (Habre case). Unfortunately, fairly few States have so far taken that step.[58] A notable

54 Human Rights Watch, "The Case against Hissene Habre", *op. cit.* (note 53).

55 See Linda Keller, "Belgian Jury to Decide Case Concerning Rwandan Genocide", *ASIL Insights*, May 2001, <http://www.asil.org/insights/insigh72.htm> [hereinafter *ASIL Insights*].

56 See First Geneva Convention, Article 49(2); Second Geneva Convention, Article 50(2); Third Geneva Convention, Article 129(2); Fourth Geneva Convention, Article 146(2); Protocol Additional to the Geneva Conventions of 12 August 1949, and Relating to the Protection of Victims of International Armed Conflicts (Protocol I), 8 June 1977, Article 86(1).

57 Convention Against Torture, Article 5.

58 See ILA Report, *op. cit.* (note 41), p. 12.

exception is Belgium, whose 1993 universal jurisdiction law,[59] as amended in 1999,[60] permits the exercise of universal jurisdiction by Belgian courts for genocide, war crimes (committed in both international and non-international armed conflict) and crimes against humanity even when the suspect is not present in Belgian territory. The law does not allow the invocation of official immunity to prevent application of its provisions.

The first full trial completed under the Belgian law was the recent, well-publicized, case of four Rwandan defendants — including two nuns — who were convicted in 2001 by a Belgian jury for complicity in the 1994 Rwandan genocide.[61] Complaints by victims have also been filed against a number of former and current high-ranking politicians from all quarters of the globe, including Israeli Prime Minister Ariel Sharon and Palestinian leader Yasser Arafat.[62] The law's "success" has produced a backlash in Belgium, whose political authorities are worried that it has turned their country into a "magnet for the world's human rights cases",[63] and who point to the diplomatic difficulties caused. Belgium's Foreign Minister and other officials have called for amendments to the law that would effectively restrict its application by mandating political oversight over the judicial process.[64] Human rights groups have responded by emphasizing that the solution lies in getting more States to also adopt universal jurisdiction laws, rather than in Belgium limiting its own.[65] It should be noted that the ICC ratification process and the implementing legislation required of States for compliance with that treaty provide a good opportunity for

59 Loi relative à la répression des infractions graves aux Conventions internationales de Genève du 12 aout 1949 et aux Protocoles I et II du 8 juin 1977, additionels à ces Conventions, 16 June 1993, *Moniteur Belge*, 5 August 1993.

60 Loi relative à la répression des violations graves de droit international humanitaire, 10 February 1999, *Moniteur Belge*, 23 March 1999.

61 See *ASIL Insights*, *op. cit.* (note 55).

62 See "Rights Groups Support Belgian Law on Genocide", Agence France-Presse, Brussels, 26 November 2001. See also "Suit Against Sharon Defended", *International Herald Tribune*, 29 November 2001, p. 5.

63 See Press Release by Human Rights Watch, the International Commission of Jurists and the International Federation of Human Rights Leagues (FIDH), Brussels, 26 November 2001 (on file with the author) [hereinafter Joint Press Release].

64 See "Un sénateur veut restreindre la loi belge sur la compétence universelle", Agence France-Presse, Brussels, 20 June 2001.

65 See Joint Press Release, *op. cit.* (note 63).

appropriate amendments to domestic law that would allow the exercise of universal jurisdiction.

Amnesties

Apart from lack of implementing legislation, other obstacles to the exercise of universal jurisdiction include the possible official capacity — and therefore immunity from process — of the alleged perpetrator, lack of skills and resources in the third country, evidentiary problems and the effect of domestic amnesties.[66] Due to lack of space and to the fact that the issue of amnesties arises not only in proceedings based on universal jurisdiction in third countries, but also before national and international courts, it will be examined separately, albeit briefly, below.

The granting of amnesties to suspected perpetrators of serious crimes under international law violates the duty of States, under treaty-based and customary law, to bring to justice and punish suspected offenders.[67] If, over a decade ago, there might have been some doubt about the validity of this claim, a multitude of developments at both the national and international levels should have served to dispel it.[68] It is submitted that this trend is likely to not only continue, but accelerate.

At the international level, the incompatibility of amnesty laws with State obligations to investigate and punish serious crimes was indirectly recognized in the Vienna Declaration and Programme

66 See ILA Report, *op. cit.* (note 41), pp. 10-19.

67 International Covenant on Civil and Political Rights (Article 2), Convention Against Torture (Articles 4, 5 and 7), American Convention on Human Rights (Article 1), Inter-American Convention on Forced Disappearance of Persons (Article 1), Inter-American Convention to Prevent and Punish Torture (Article 1). See also non-treaty human rights standards such as the Declaration on the Protection of All Persons from Enforced Disappearance, GA Res. 47/133, 18 December 1992, and the Principles for the Effective Prevention and Investigation of Extra-Legal, Arbitrary and Summary Executions, ECOSOC Res. 1989/65, 24 May 1989.

68 For an excellent review of the current state of the law on impunity and the effect of amnesties, see "Argentina: Amicus Curiae Brief on the Incompatibility with International Law of the Full Stop and Due Obedience Laws", presented by the International Commission of Jurists, Amnesty International and Human Rights Watch before the National Chamber for Federal Criminal and Correctional Matters of the Republic of Argentina (June 2001), *International Commission of Jurists Occasional Papers*, 2001, p. 23 [hereinafter ICJ Amicus Brief].

of Action adopted at the 1993 World Conference on Human Rights which called on States "to abrogate legislation leading to impunity for those responsible for grave violations of human rights such as torture and prosecute such violations, thereby providing a firm basis for the rule of law".[69] The UN Human Rights Committee dealt with the issue as early as 1978 in relation to Chile's amnesty law and has since made similar observations in regard to amnesty laws passed by Lebanon, El Salvador, Haiti, Peru, Uruguay, France, Yemen, Croatia and Argentina.[70] In its General Comment on Article 7 of the International Covenant on Civil and Political Rights prohibiting torture, the Committee stated that "amnesties are generally incompatible with the duty of States to investigate such acts; to guarantee freedom from such acts within their jurisdiction; and to ensure that they do not occur in the future. States may not deprive individuals of the right to an effective remedy, including compensation and such full rehabilitation as may be possible".[71] Non-treaty standards such as the already cited Joinet Principles have also dealt with the issue of amnesties, determining that the perpetrators of serious crimes may not be included in amnesties unless the victims have been able to obtain justice by means of an effective remedy.[72]

In July 1999 the UN Secretary-General affirmed the notion that domestic amnesties for crimes under international law are not legally binding at the international level by instructing his Special Representative to sign the Sierra Leone peace agreement "with the explicit proviso that the United Nations holds the understanding that the amnesty and pardon in Article IX of the agreement shall not apply to international crimes of genocide, crimes against humanity, war crimes and other serious violations of international humanitarian

69 See the Vienna Declaration and Programme of Action, adopted by the World Conference on Human Rights, Vienna, 14-25 June 1993, A/CONF.157/24 (Part I), Chapter III, Section II, para. 60.

70 See ICJ Amicus Brief, *op. cit.* (note 68), pp. 30-32 and pp. 36-38.

71 See Human Rights Committee General Comment No. 20 on Article 7, Forty-fourth Session, 1992, para. 15.

72 Joinet Report, *op. cit.* (note 4), Principle 28(a).

law".[73] This understanding was reaffirmed in the Security Council's resolution calling on the Secretary-General to draw up a Statute for the Special Court[74] and a no-amnesty provision was included in the Court's Statute.[75] As already mentioned, differences over how to deal with a domestic amnesty have been a sticking point in the creation of the Khmer Rouge tribunal, the outcome of which is still uncertain.

Given that the obligations of States to repress grave breaches of the 1949 Geneva Conventions and of their Additional Protocol I of 1977 are well known, and that war crimes clearly fall within the designation of serious crimes under international law, there is no doubt that what has been said about amnesties thus far applies to these offences as well. What has sometimes generated controversy is the amnesty provision of Additional Protocol II of 1977 which allows, upon the cessation of hostilities in non-international armed conflict, for a broad amnesty to be granted to "persons who have participated in the armed conflict, or those deprived of their liberty for reasons related to the armed conflict, whether they are interned or detained".[76] It should be emphasized that this provision essentially seeks to encourage the release of individuals who might be, or are subject to, criminal or other proceedings under domestic law for the fact of having taken part in hostilities. It should in no way be read as supporting amnesties for war crimes or other international offences committed in internal armed conflict.[77]

Innovative regional jurisprudence on the incompatibility of amnesties with the American Convention on Human Rights

73 Seventh Report of the Secretary-General on the United Nations Mission in Sierra Leone, UN Doc. S/1999/836, 30 July 1999, para. 7.

74 UN Doc. S/RES/1315 (2000), preambular para. 5.

75 Statute of the Special Court for Sierra Leone, Article 10, reads: "An amnesty granted to any person falling within the jurisdiction of the Special Court in respect of the crimes referred to in articles 2 to 4 of the present Statute shall not be a bar to prosecution".

76 Protocol Additional to the Geneva Conventions of 12 August 1949, and Relating to the Protection of Victims of Non-International Armed Conflicts (Protocol II), 8 June 1977, Article 6(5).

77 Letter of the ICRC Legal Division to the ICTY Prosecutor of 24 November 1975 and to the Department of Law at the University of California of 15 April 1997 (referring to CDDH, Official Records, 1977, Vol. IX, p. 319)(on file with the author).

has also been handed down by the Inter-American Court and Commission.[78]

Finally, it should be noted that the carefully crafted edifice of amnesties has started to crumble at the domestic level as well. In a historic ruling rendered in March 2001, Argentine federal judge Gabriel Cavallo declared unconstitutional and null the main provisions of the "Full Stop" and "Due Obedience" laws that had enabled impunity for human rights violations during military rule in that country between 1976 and 1983.[79] His decision was confirmed in November 2001 by the National Chamber for Federal and Criminal Matters of Argentina.[80]

Conclusion

It seems fitting to close this review with the briefest possible mention of two challenges that henceforth should not escape attention. The first is the role of national criminal justice systems and the other is fair trial rights.

If the preceding review failed to focus on the role of domestic courts in the fight against impunity for serious crimes, it did so because there is, unfortunately, not so much to report. The international and third-State mechanisms outlined above came into being precisely because States fail to fulfil what is their primary duty — to bring to justice the perpetrators of serious crimes. While some countries can indeed plead lack of skills and resources, far too often the problem clearly lies elsewhere, in the lack of political will by national authorities to tackle current or past offences. Unless and until that will is created, international mechanisms of one sort or another, both penal and non-penal, will be necessary. The challenge for the global

78 See generally, ICJ Amicus Brief, *op. cit.* (note 68). See also Douglas Cassel, "Lessons from the Americas: Guidelines for International Response to Amnesties for Atrocities", *Law and Contemporary Problems*, Vol. 59, School of Law Duke University, No. 4, Autumn 1996, pp. 197-230.

79 See "Argentine Judge Annuls Immunity Laws", The Associated Press, Buenos Aires, 6 March 2001 (on file with the author). For a background to the case see ICJ Amicus Brief, *op. cit.* (note 68), pp. 5-9.

80 See "La Camara Federal Confirma: Las leyes de Punto Final y Obediencia Debida son invalidas e inconstitucionales", *Centro de estudos legales y sociales*, Archivos de HOY, <http://www.cels.org.ar/background/archivos/info2001/info_45_20011115.htm>.

movement against impunity is therefore to concentrate more on the local level and to ensure that domestic courts and other bodies are able and willing to perform their tasks in the fight for justice.[81]

Justice, it should not be forgotten, means not only doing good by individual victims or segments of society affected by crime, but also ensuring that the fair trial rights of suspects and accused in criminal proceedings are fully respected. Once again, national criminal justice systems often fail to implement even a modicum of internationally prescribed standards aimed at safeguarding the life, health and dignity of alleged offenders. Justice cannot be done, nor can it be seen to be done, unless persons presumed to have committed international or other crimes are treated with full due process. The challenges ahead for the global movement against impunuty in this context, too, are enormous. The recent resurgence of the debate on the "balance" between State security and human rights after the events of 11 September 2001 is a troubling case in point.

[15]

Law and Military Interventions: Preserving Humanitarian Values in 21st Conflicts

Prepared for the
Humanitarian Challenges in Military Intervention Conference
Carr Center for Human Rights Policy
Kennedy School of Government, Harvard University
Washington, D.C., November 29, 2001

by

Colonel Charles J. Dunlap, Jr., USAF*

Introduction

Is lawfare turning warfare into unfair? In other words, is international law undercutting the ability of the U.S. to conduct effective military interventions? Is it becoming a vehicle to exploit American values in ways that actually increase risks to civilians? In short, is law becoming more of the problem in modern war instead of part of the solution?

Some experts seem to think so. In his Foreign Affairs review of General Wesley Clark's fascinating book on the Balkan war, Professor Richard K. Betts laments the role law and lawyers played in that campaign as well as military interventions generally.[1] He asserts that the "hyperlegalism applied to NATO's campaign made the conflict reminiscent of the quaint norms of premodern war." Further, he alleges that lawyers "constrained even the preparations for decisive combat" and declares:

> One of the most striking features of the Kosovo campaign, in fact, was the remarkably direct role lawyers played in managing combat operations – to a degree unprecedented in previous wars.... The role played by lawyers in this war should also be sobering – indeed alarming – for devotees of power politics who denigrate the impact of law on international conflict....NATO's lawyers...became in effect, its tactical commanders.[2]

International lawyers David Riviken and Lee Casey express a somewhat different but darker view in a recent issue of The National Interest.[3] They contend that a "new" kind of international law is emerging that is "profoundly undemocratic at its core" and "has the potential to undermine American leadership in the post-Cold War global system." With respect to armed interventions, Riviken and Casey insist that the "American military is particularly vulnerable" because of the "unrealistic norms" – especially in relation to collateral damage - propounded by the advocates of this new international law. "If the trends of international law are allowed to mature into binding rules," they say, "international law may become one of the most potent weapons ever deployed against the United States."

Professor Betts, and perhaps to a lesser extent Messers Riviken and Casey, might find comfort in my conclusion about Operation Allied Force.[4] I believe the air campaign against Kosovo and Serbia may represent something of a high-water mark of

---

* ***The views and opinions expressed are those of the author alone, and do not necessarily represent those of the U.S. Government or any of its components.***

the influence of international law in military interventions, at least in the near term. The aftermath of that conflict, along with the repercussions of the terrible events of September 11th, seem to have set in motion forces that will diminish the role of law (if not lawyers themselves) much beyond the hyperlegalisms to which Betts objects. Explaining why I make this prediction is a prime purpose of the following discussion.

Initially, the essay will briefly examine the rise of law as a prime feature of modern military interventions. Next, it will contend that "lawfare," that is, the use of law as a weapon of war, is the newest feature of 21st century combat.[5] The paper will then outline how law and lawyers are integrated into the planning and execution of air operations conducted by the United States. The essay will survey legal issues that typically arise in air campaigns, as well as those that could flow from trends already in place. Following that discussion, the paper will provide a uniformed lawyer's perspective on the operational impact of selected international agreements. It concludes by making some observations about the future of law and war in the new millennium.

Although academic fashion favors the term "international humanitarian law" (IHL), this paper will not adopt it. There is really no universally accepted definition of the phrase, and in practice it too often appears to embrace not just treaties with specific obligations and accepted norms of customary international law, but also a collage of other (often amorphous) agreements, non-binding resolutions, unilateral declarations, and political statements. Instead of IHL, the paper will rely upon the descriptor "law of armed conflict" (LOAC). While many of the same objections might be raised about it as with IHL, far greater consensus exists as to its scope - if not its interpretation - in specific situations.

This essay will offer several broad themes for consideration: 1) law is not – and can never be – the vehicle to ameliorate the horror of war to the extent its advocates hope and, indeed, seem to expect; 2) although not yet fully institutionalized, the role of law and lawyers in American military interventions is surprisingly pervasive for practical, warfighting reasons as much as altruistic, human rights-oriented ones; 3) issues of international law that affect armed conflict are often ill-informed by the realities of military strategy and technologies; and 4) there is disturbing evidence that the rule of law is being hijacked into just another way of fighting (lawfare), to the detriment of humanitarian values as well as the law itself.

The Rise of International Law

How did international law become so important in military interventions? Actually, a number of rather disparate factors coalesce to give it the prominence it enjoys today. Basic to them is the long-standing desire of the world community (and especially the West[6]) to use law to prevent conflict altogether or, failing that, to make the conduct of war as humane as possible. The appalling experience of World War II gave new impetus to the latter idea, resulting in the Geneva Conventions of 1949 that today form LOAC's nucleus.[7]

A principle focus of that effort – and one that is very prominent today – was to spare noncombatants the adverse effects of war. Parenthetically, however, the record shows that the ratio of civilians to military personnel killed in armed conflicts has, in fact, *increased* since the Conventions of 1949.[8] It is a mistake, of course, to conclude that the Conventions themselves are to blame (the remorseless civil wars and internal conflicts of the postwar period are likely the cause). Still, it does make a melancholy point as to the limits of law as a mitigator of the suffering intrinsic to war.

More recently, LOAC indirectly benefited from a much larger international phenomenon: globalization. Globalization heightened the status of law generally if for no other reason than the need for certainty in international commercial transactions. Likewise, worldwide trade requires international administrative and judicial forums to resolve contract, claims, intellectual property, and similar disputes. Where law is absent, so are investors and others needed for economic development. Even otherwise repressive societies recognize that they must embrace law in their relations with other countries if they hope to gain the benefits of modernity.

The effect of globalization is especially felt in Europe where, coincidentally, many LOAC initiatives originate. In order to obtain the economies of scale needed to succeed in an extremely competitive business environment, Europeans progressively abandoned elements of their sovereignty in ways unthinkable to Americans. They are acculturated to binding themselves in their everyday life (as Americans have *not* consciously done) to a multitude of rules and regulations imposed from without.

Herein, perhaps, lies the genesis of some of the division we see in LOAC interpretations with our European colleagues. Europeans are comfortable, for example, with obeying the dictates of the European Parliament, essentially a foreign legislature vis-à-vis the citizens of any individual country; Americans fought a revolution so as never to do so. For this and other reasons the respective mindsets are different, and this is reflected in contrasting approaches to international law.[9]

One result is an acceptance of international law and nongovernmental organizations (NGOs) on the Continent far exceeding that on this side of the Atlantic. In particular, NGOs often enjoy more influence in LOAC matters in Europe than in the U.S. Many NGOs are wonderful, philanthropic groups who do selfless, difficult work in dangerous places. However, Americans are inclined to be wary those NGOs who purport to speak – literally – for the "world" on political issues, to include LOAC ones. Too often NGO positions look like political agendas. With respect to LOAC issues, it must always be kept in mind that NGOs are not political entities equivalent to a sovereign nation; rather, they are no more than self-selected, idiosyncratic *interest groups* who are not accountable to any ballot box. In my opinion these facts get lost at times - to the detriment of LOAC development and interpretation.

The pacifist and leftist leanings of a lot of NGOs, along with organizational practices that unabashedly discriminate on the basis of national origin, do not popularize the groups in the United States.[10] Along this line we also must frankly acknowledge there is an undeniable element of anti-Americanism in international law as it is developing today. Riviken and Casey argue quite persuasively that "the impetus in international law today stems from both our allies and our adversaries, who have chosen to use it as a means to check, or at least harness, American power."[11] This may be the real reason for the incessant criticism of U.S. positions that marks so much of the debate in the international legal community.

Another factor influential to the rise of LOAC is the Information Revolution. It spawned high-tech global news organizations that rapidly deliver information – to include graphic images of war - to publics everywhere. This is particularly important when considered in conjunction with another attribute of the information age: the spread of democracy.[12] Shaped by raw news footage, public perceptions of how conflicts are being fought significantly affect military interventions. Professors W. Michael Reisman and Chris T. Antoniou insist:

> In modern popular democracies, even a limited armed conflict requires a substantial base of public support. That support can erode or even reverse itself rapidly, no matter how worthy the political objective, if people *believe* that the war is being conducted in an unfair, inhumane, or iniquitous way.[13]

The velocity of today's communications' capabilities presents real challenges to democracies as well as those governments that if not democratic in a Western sense, nevertheless depend upon support from constituencies having access to globalized information sources.[14] When television airs unfiltered, near real-time film of what appears to be LOAC violations, complications result.[15]

General Clark found during the Kosovo operation that "[t]he new technologies impacted powerfully at the political levels. The instantaneous flow of news and especially imagery could overwhelm the ability of governments to explain, investigate, coordinate, and confirm." What is essential to understand is that increasingly foes of the United States see this development as a *vulnerability* to be exploited. No longer able to seriously confront - let alone defeat - America militarily, they resort to a strategy that can be labeled "lawfare."

Lawfare

Lawfare describes a method of warfare where law is used as a means of realizing a military objective.[16] Though at first blush one might assume lawfare would result in less suffering in war (and sometimes it does[17]), in practice it too often produces behaviors that jeopardize the protection of the truly innocent. There are many dimensions to lawfare, but the one ever more frequently embraced by U.S. opponents is a cynical manipulation of the rule of law and the humanitarian values it represents. Rather seeking battlefield victories, *per se*, challengers try to destroy the *will* to fight by undermining the public support that is indispensable when democracies like the U.S. conduct military interventions. A principle way of bringing about that end is to make it appear that the U.S. is waging war in violation of the letter or spirit of LOAC.

In this sense lawfare has a firm basis in Clausewitzean analysis. Carl von Clausewitz, the great military theorist, spoke of a "remarkable trinity" of the people, the government, and the military whose combined energies produce victory in war.[18] Belligerents attempt to impose the converse on their adversaries, that is, the deconstruction of Clausewitz's trinity. The traditional U.S. approach to accomplishing that – and the one LOAC endorses – focuses on the *military* element and seeks to diminish the enemy's armed strength. America's challengers focus on the *people* element and seek to diminish the strength of their support for the military effort.

Evidence shows this technique can work. The Vietnam War – where U.S. forces never suffered a true *military* defeat - is the archetype that today's adversaries repeatedly try to replicate. Of course, they hope to use the vastly accelerated news cycle to achieve success far more rapidly and at much less cost than did the

Vietnamese. If they can make the American electorate *believe*, as Reisman and Antoniou put it, that the "war is being conducted in an unfair, inhumane, or iniquitous way" necessary public backing might collapse. Even if U.S. public opinion is unwavering – as it appears to be with respect to the current war on terrorism[19] – the cooperation of coalition governments nevertheless might weaken if their people become disenchanted with the way armed force is being used.[20] This is especially problematic for the Air Force if it results in the denial of vital basing and overflight rights.[21]

As Reisman and Antoniou indicate, the mere *perception* of LOAC violations can significantly impact operations. The Gulf War provides two examples of situations where LOAC was not violated yet the perception that it may have been had clear military consequences. The first concerned the attack on the Al Firdos bunker in Baghdad that was believed by the allies to be a command and control node. Some experts concluded that the post-attack pictures of the bodies of family members of high Iraqi officials (who evidently used the bunker as a bomb shelter) being excavated from the wreckage achieved politically what the Iraqi air defenses could not do militarily: rendering downtown Baghdad immune from attack.[22]

Worried coalition leaders put the city virtually off-limits to avoid a repetition of like scenes reaching their peoples. Similarly, fears about the impact on coalition constituencies of the images of hundreds of burnt out vehicles along the so-called "Highway of Death" following an air attack on retreating Iraqi forces was a significant factor in the early termination of hostilities.[23] That result left the Republican Guard intact to slaughter Kurds and to help keep Saddam Hussein in power to this day.

America's enemies, who study such cases, may draw from them a lesson to emulate, that is, to callously capitalize on collateral damage incidents. As already suggested, their goal is to gain political leverage by portraying U.S. forces as insensitive to LOAC and human rights. To be candid, I personally think that by overselling precision weapons and other high-tech capabilities, the U.S. Air Force unwittingly made itself vulnerable to this very strategy. Unfortunately, opponents unconstrained by humanitarian ethics now take the strategy to the next level, that of *orchestrating* situations that deliberately endanger noncombatants.

One technique is to use civilians as involuntary (and sometimes voluntary[24]) human shields. In addition, adversaries collocate military assets with noncombatant facilities such as religious structures and NGO compounds in the hopes of either deterring attacks, or if attacks do take place, producing collateral damage media events that serve their cause. The Taliban, according to media reports, employed this tactic. Specifically, U.S. News & World Report says, "[h]eavy weaponry is being sheltered in several mosques to deter attacks. The Taliban has even placed a tank and two large antiaircraft guns under trees in front of the office of CARE International...."[25]

The use of NGO facilities to deter legitimate air attacks creates the potential for tension between the organizations and the armed forces. If an NGO area is surreptitiously employed to hide military equipment, should we expect that it would be reported immediately? If the NGOs fail to do so, do they become culpable as aiders and abettors of perfidious conduct, itself a war crime?

In any event, I have found that most senior U.S. military leaders, and certainly those in the Air Force, accept that the fact or perception of LOAC violations can frustrate mission accomplishment. They are also aware of the rising number of post-conflict investigations – both formal ones like the International Criminal Tribunal for the Former Yugoslavia's (ICTY) examination of the Kosovo operation,[26] as well as those conducted by NGOs, academics, and others. Consequently, savvy American commanders seldom go to war without their attorneys. Unsurprisingly, therefore, a significant number of military lawyers and paralegals deployed for Operation Enduring Freedom[27] to supplement those already serving in the region.[28]

Michael Ignatieff, who has written extensively about the role of law and lawyers in the Balkan conflict, provides real insight into the thinking of many senior officers. He maintains: "[Lawyers] provide harried decision-makers with a critical guarantee of legal coverage, turning complex issues of morality into technical issues of legality, so that whatever moral or operational doubts a commander may have, he can at least be sure he will not face legal consequences."[29] In short, the predominance of law and lawyers in U.S. military interventions is as much a concession to the verities of modern war as it is an altruistic commitment to human rights.

Integrating LOAC into Military Interventions: An Air Force Perspective

Until Operation Just Cause, the successful 1989 intervention that dethroned Panamanian strongman Manual Noriega, compliance with international law wholly depended upon the knowledge and disposition of commanders and their planners. Military lawyers taught LOAC classes – which rarely progressed much beyond the basics – and prosecuted those who violated it,[30] but were rarely found advising commanders on the legal aspects of combat operations.

Beginning with Just Cause, however, that changed - perhaps in recognition that after-the-fact prosecutions would not undo the political damage LOAC violations could inflict. During the Gulf War judge advocates (JAGs) vetted targets, worked rules of engagement (ROE) matters, and advised on other warfighting issues, all to favorable comment from senior military leaders.[31] Since then military lawyers regularly have made their way into command posts and planning cells in an effort to avoid the kind of incidents that could derail a military operation.

In U.S. operations the requirement for legal advice is embedded in specific military instructions. For example, the Chairman of the Joint Chiefs of Staff directs that "all operation plans...concept plans, rules of engagement, execute orders, deployment orders, policies, and directives are [to be] reviewed by the command legal advisor to ensure compliance with domestic and international law."[32] This provides the formal authority for JAGs to insert themselves into the planning and execution processes of combat operations. In practice this is done in a rather *ad hoc* fashion with the precise methodology much dependent upon the individual personalities involved.

Although this system has worked reasonably well over the years, the Air Force is now engaged in developing specific doctrine to institutionalize and standardize the role of lawyers[33] in the air operations center (AOC) - the nerve center for the application of airpower in military interventions.[34] This effort builds upon the lessons learned since 1989, the most critical being the importance of involving JAGs in each stage of the air tasking order (ATO) cycle that produces the master air attack plan (MAAP). Knowing exactly when and how to most productively provide legal advice is essential to a JAG's success in an AOC.

For example, raising legal objections after the MAAP is built is problematic because it is very difficult to re-target or re-weaponeer a particular sortie at that late stage.[35] If the legal objection is serious enough, the sortie may be lost entirely. To avoid such situations, JAGs in the AOC work around the clock with action officers as they develop strategy and select targets, weapons, and employment tactics, all of which can play into the overall legal assessment. Military lawyers also help write the ROE chapter of the Special Instructions (or SPINS in Air Force parlance) that become the aircrews' operational 'bible.'

Pre-planned targets in the MAAP ordinarily have a "BE" number that reflects its designation in what is called the "bomb encyclopedia." JAGs review the target folders associated with each BE. They evaluate the imagery and other intelligence products that show the target's military purpose as well as its potential for collateral damage. The quality and quantity of the intelligence can vary, but usually there is enough to make an informed judgment. The folder's data is used to apply what is known as a "tiered" analysis technique that results in an assessment of the collateral damage risk. The technical process takes into account specific weapons' characteristics to include their precision capabilities and fragmentation patterns. The analysis for certain targets – especially in cities - may include elaborate evaluations of the blast effects on the kind of buildings found near the weapon's estimated impact point. The results are interpolated with known population distributions to make casualty projections.

Computerized decision-support systems exist to help make collateral damage assessments.[36] While useful tools, they cannot (and should not) substitute for the considered judgment of lawyers or, for that matter, commanders. Warfighting remains an art, not a science reducible to the sterile algorithms of electronic data processing. Military history is littered with examples – Doolittle's Raid on Tokyo, McArthur's landing at Inchon, and, indeed, the American Revolution itself – for which no computer would predict success.

However, when applied to collateral damage forecasts, automated assessments produce what might be considered "evidence." In other words, if a commander chooses to pursue an attack in a way a machine tabulates as possibly causing unnecessary noncombatant losses, he or she may some day be called to account. Commanders are wise, therefore, to make some sort of contemporaneous record of the thinking that led to their decisions. Admittedly, it could be difficult to articulate the rationale (especially if the reason is mainly the commander's instinct honed by years of experience) but increasingly it may be necessary to try – and the JAG can assist in that process.

Computerized systems notwithstanding, much of the intellectual heavy lifting remains subjective and fact-specific. In my experience, JAGs very rarely are presented with issues that have straightforward answers in the law. The targeteers and planners are too well trained anymore to even think about proposing obviously illegal options. More often JAGs are dealing with 'gray' areas, just like the commanders they serve. How certain is the intelligence? Exactly how many civilians do we think might be hurt? How critical is the target? Do we have the right weapons available? These are the questions that are hashed out during the long hours of ATO development.

Some of the thorniest issues entail dual-use targets, that is, those involving assets – mainly infrastructure elements - that both civilians and military forces draw upon.[37] Dual-use targets can be contentious for two reasons:

First, determining the extent that they make a "concrete and direct military contribution"[38] to the enemy's war effort as required by LOAC is sometimes difficult and controversial. This is another area where U.S. practice is not always coterminous with that of coalition partners. Americans tend to take a more holistic approach to an enemy's war-making capability than do many other countries. The U.S. view readily appreciates that seemingly disparate parts of the civilian infrastructure collectively form indispensable components to the ability to conduct modern, high-tech war.

Second, assuming the proposed target does make the direct contribution LOAC requires, it still must be demonstrated that the anticipated military gain from the bombing outweighs the expected collateral damage.[39] Complicating the calculations is the fact that often there are few *immediate* casualties from an attack on a dual-use target. The adverse effect on civilians of infrastructure loss may only manifest itself over time.[40]

Electrical grids are an oft-cited example of a dual-use target. Contemporary societies, especially in urbanized settings, are as much - or more - dependent upon supplies of electricity as are their militaries. An Air Force study shows that because of the availability of alternate electricity sources for military sites, the utility of attacking the grid itself is often less than many airmen assume.[41] The issue is very fact-specific, and can vary widely from operation to operation. Nevertheless, interrupting the electrical flow despite the existence of backup systems can still yield significant military benefits. Doing so injects friction into the adversary's military machine as he frantically tries to switch, at a critical moment, to temporary power sources that themselves may be of uncertain reliability. When possible the Air Force employs means that disrupt electrical supplies (and other dual-use assets) without permanently destroying infrastructure.

An ancillary problem arises when the inherent ambiguity of dual-use targets is combined with the need to protect intelligence sources and methods. Although not an Air Force operation, the 1998 cruise missile attack on a Sudanese pharmaceutical factory illustrates the hazards. This facility was alleged to have been involved in the manufacture of compounds intended for terrorists' chemical weapons. Initially, there was a reluctance to disclose the intelligence information supporting the strike.[42] Unfortunately, this led to a questioning of the attack's legitimacy by many nations, including some of America's strongest allies. The lesson is that the U.S. must be prepared to prove its case in the 'court of world opinion' in addition to more conventional forums.[43] Thus, if the intelligence information is so sensitive that it cannot be disclosed, decisionmakers must carefully consider whether the target should be struck at all, especially if the purpose is mainly a psychological one.

Psychological or "message" targets sometimes present perplexing challenges. These are strikes aimed at bona fide military objectives but whose intended effect is primarily psychological. Legally, they are subject to the same analysis as any other target; nevertheless, they raise some interesting issues. For example, following the Gulf War, Air Force lawyers were criticized (unfairly in my view) for questioning the propriety of a proposal to strike a statue of Saddam Hussein.[44] That case aside, the real sticking point in these situations is whether or not enough objective data exists to conclude that the desired psychological effect will result. The evaluation becomes skewed when an

American bias is applied to the psychology of another culture. General Charles Horner, the air commander during the Gulf War, discussed this problem in the context of the bombing of the Baath Party headquarters:

> In terms of bombing the Baath Party headquarters, we looked at Saddam Hussein and the Baath Party as one. We wanted to show weakness in the Baath Party and thus weakness in Saddam Hussein. We wanted to embarrass him in front of his people as well as limit the loss of life. But what we didn't realize was that it doesn't matter what the people think. In the final analysis, we looked at it through American eyes, which was wrong.[45]

Somewhat ironically, JAGs spend a great deal of time not, as one might expect, trying to prevent LOAC violations, but rather explaining to targeteers, planners, and even commanders that the law is not the warfighting impediment they tend to think it is. In some instances this is the result of an incomplete understanding of LOAC. For example, during Desert Fox's 1998 strikes against Iraq,[46] a young targeteer expressed concern that bombing a Republican Guard barracks at night (when it presumably would be occupied) somehow violated the concept of proportionality.[47] Of course, proportionality in a LOAC sense seeks to weigh the military advantage against potential *noncombatant* casualties, *not* combatants like the Republican Guard. Indeed, killing them was the military basis for the strike in the first place.

A related issue engages the whole notion of collateral damage. Some military people believe that a prediction of high collateral damage *ipso facto* makes an attack unlawful. This is simply wrong. Anticipating high collateral damage merely means that the military value of the target must be great enough to justify the unintended losses. Savvy political reasoning might counsel against hitting a particular target solely out of fear of high civilian casualties, but that is altogether different from saying the *law* prohibits the attack.

A more debatable proposition relates to the status of *voluntary* human shields such as those Serb civilians who deliberately occupied bridges in Belgrade during the Balkan war. They hoped to deter NATO attacks by presenting a vexing quandary for military planners: how to attack the bridges without killing the "noncombatant" protesters. This issue is politically complex, but not - in my view - legally difficult. In attempting to defend an otherwise legitimate target from attack – albeit by creating a psychological conundrum for NATO – the bridge occupiers lost their noncombatant immunity. In essence, they made themselves part of the bridges' defense system. As such, they were subject to attack to the same degree as any other combatant so long as they remained on the spans.

As convoluted as these issues may appear, "time critical targeting" (TCT) presents a markedly more difficult challenge. This process relates to targets of opportunity (usually mobile ones). In certain cases this can require re-directing ("reflowing") a sortie from a preplanned target to an unplanned one. Because of growing pressure to minimize the sensor-to-shooter time,[48] TCT is the part of the air operations' process that probably is most vulnerable to incurring unintended collateral damage. By its very nature, the TCT dynamics do not allow for the studied examination of target folders that the preplanned process permits. This is yet another reason JAGs must be physically present in the AOC at all times to be available to work with the controllers when these "opportunities" arise.

TCT sometimes allows the JAG only a split-second to formulate advice involving life and death. He or she may be obliged to do so based on much less than perfect data. Mistakes can happen, both in terms of unexpected collateral damage as well as – conversely - missed opportunities to damage the enemy. Indeed, TCT issues in Enduring Freedom generated media reports critical of JAGs.[49] It is impossible at this time to verify the accuracy of those stories,[50] but they do highlight an important issue applicable to all operations. What, exactly, is the JAG's authority? Does the JAG sit as some kind of legal satrap with ultimate power over a commander's actions?

The short answer is "no." A good JAG asks the hard questions, plays devil's advocate, and demands the best of the intelligence assets and operational processes. In the end, however, the decision to attack belongs to the commander. If the commander directs what appears to be a LOAC violation despite clear legal advice – something, incidentally, I have never seen – the JAG is obliged to report the incident to a superior command who, in turn, must conduct an inquiry.[51] If that avenue is unavailable or inappropriate under the circumstances, by law a JAG can bypass the chain of command and communicate directly with any supervising JAG to include The Judge Advocate General of the Air Force.[52] In short, there are multiple ways of ensuring that an alleged LOAC violation is surfaced and investigated.

Concluding that a command action amounts to a breach of LOAC responsibilities is an extremely serious matter, and very different from merely disagreeing with the wisdom of a particular decision. It is important, therefore, that the JAG carefully and explicitly distinguish between an opinion as to prudent warfighting, and his or her formal, *legal* judgment on a LOAC matter, that is, one to be followed under pain of otherwise being considered (and reported as) a war criminal. Along this line, legal assessments of particular targets are generally the province of the JAGs in the AOC, not that of military or civilian lawyers at higher levels. In the usual course, lawyers in the upper chain of command do review the overall operations plan, rules of engagement, broad target categories, and even certain highly sensitive sites. However, those attorneys would not ordinarily provide real-time advice about targets of opportunity.

That said, Information Age capabilities present challenges for everyone involved in air operations, the legal function being only one of those affected. The technology now exists for persons far from the area of operations to receive much of the same data as is available in the AOC. This may suggest to some that the viewpoint of those distant from the battlefield is equally valid – especially in air operations – as those deployed forward. In my judgment this is a mistake. As I argued previously, warfighting is an art, and one that still very much depends upon human interaction. Even the most advanced communications systems do not replicate the intangible value of direct human interface. Person-to-person contact injects an important element of humanity into what can easily become an impersonal and potentially inhumane enterprise.

Serving in command centers does require the assigned JAG to acquire and maintain technical proficiency with the AOC's specialized communications and computer systems. Most AOCs employ the Theater Battle Management Core Systems (TBMCS). JAGs - like everyone else working in the AOC - must complete a specified course of study in order to master it. JAGs also receive focused instruction in operations law, and many have advanced (post-law school) degrees in international law from the nation's premier civilian institutions.

Equally important is the lawyer's knowledge of purely military matters. Access to decisionmakers is ephemeral and can be instantly forfeited if credibility is lost for any reason. For the JAG this means he or she must maintain an in-depth understanding of military history, equipment, strategy, and more. Senior Air Force leaders have high expectations in this regard, as General Hal M. Hornburg, a veteran of many combat operations and currently the Commander of Air Combat Command, noted in a June 2001 address:

> [JAGs] need to understand the big picture. I was in the CAOC during Desert Fox. Who do you think was standing right behind me? It was my JAG. That person needs to know the law and the rules of engagement, but he or she also needs to understand things bigger than just the law. They've got to understand combat.[53]

To ensure they do "understand combat' JAGs selected to work in AOCs are all uniformed officers who, by and large, are graduates of exactly the same staff schools and war colleges as any other officer. In fact, JAGs are routinely top graduates of professional military education (PME) institutions, and they are known to garner a disproportionate share of the academic prizes.

In my experience, the U.S. practice of deploying military lawyers as advisors for combat operations is not widely shared by coalition partners. Except for a smattering of British, Canadian, and Australian JAGs, non-U.S. lawyers of any kind are rarely found in command centers. In their absence, some contingents simply accept the legal interpretations given by American JAGs. Of course, this can present problems – to include ethical ones – where, for example, the U.S. is not a party to a LOAC-related treaty that a coalition partner has ratified.

When a coalition partner does deploy a JAG to work with his or her American counterparts, productive synergies can result. During Bright Star 99/00, a multinational exercise that took place in Egypt in 1999, the AOC legal cadre included a British JAG. Working together from the desert command post, the coalition JAG team used legal research software and U.S. communications capabilities to obtain the actual text of British law related to anti-personnel landmines.[54] Properly interpreted, this allowed U.K. forces to play a tangential but useful role in an operation involving American air-delivered munitions that contained anti-personnel mines.

Unhappily, such productive exchanges are all too uncommon. Many contingents look for legal guidance from civilian lawyers in their ministries of defense hundreds or thousands of miles away. (Protocol I of the Geneva Conventions does require legal advisors to be available at all levels of command,[55] although it does not specify what "available" means in physical terms.) This creates practical problems in terms of delays, as well as more substantive ones. The inability to communicate directly with legal advisor counterparts makes it extremely difficult to insure that all the facts and circumstances so critical to legal assessments are properly conveyed. In my judgment, more nations need to develop a trained cadre of *military* lawyers to support combat operations in the field. The emphasis on "military" is purposeful and is based on two key factors:

First, in addition to attendance at PME described above, it takes years of full-time immersion in the military environment at the tactical level to have the necessary familiarity with the weapons and their delivery systems to properly advise the commander-client. Successful lawyering in the AOC requires the ability to offer operational alternatives when LOAC issues arise, and few civilian lawyers have the right background to do that. In addition, legal issues should be couched whenever possible in operational terms that are meaningful to the military commander, and this requires first-hand military experience. In my opinion, professional warrior-lawyers working side-by-side with fellow officers are the best means to ensure legal considerations are taken into account during military interventions.

Second, there is an aspect to dealing with military leaders that is subtle but very real. Specifically, it is unlikely that *any* civilian lawyer (and especially one distant from the area of operation), can really penetrate the culture of the armed forces, however well trained and knowledgeable he or she may be. In my view, to have the necessary access, credibility, and trust the lawyer *must* be part of the officer corps. It is a mistake, as historian John Keegan observes, to assume a connection between a civilian and a military occupation (in this instance lawyering) equates to "identity or even similarity" with members of the military caste.[56] Frankly, it is difficult enough for a commissioned officer who is a member of a profession as unpopular as law to gain the acceptance and confidence of the operators; it would be near impossible for a civilian to do so.

<u>Informing International Law with the Military Perspective</u>

The differing military and civilian outlooks enlighten recent trends in international law. Too often it seems that initiatives suffer from an insufficient understanding of the direct military impact and a lack of adequate analysis of the *unintended* military consequences. This produces situations that do not make common sense to many in uniform, and serve to make the law an object of disdain. Consider the desire among international law activists to eliminate or control the emerging technologies of war. Many military people view technological change as inevitable and, regardless of efforts to limit or ban it, believe it will eventually appear on the battlefield.

U.S. military thinking is keenly aware of the axiom that "technology has permitted the division of mankind into ruler and ruled."[57] Indeed, the American way of war is *characterized* by technology. The U.S. is always looking for ways to substitute machines for manpower – and has enjoyed great success in doing so.[58] As Harry Truman once remarked, "we have won the battle of the laboratories."[59] Importantly, compared to allied populaces, U.S. taxpayers have borne more than their share of the cost of the development of expensive technology (e.g., precision weapons) that reduces casualties on both sides.[60] Accordingly, no one should be surprised that Americans and their armed forces are reluctant to welcome proposals that seem to limit the development and use of technology in warfighting.

Focusing LOAC efforts on technology seems more than a little ironic given the history of recent conflicts. Most people consider the machete-based slaughters in Rwanda, the deliberate amputation of the limbs of children in Sierra Leone, as well as the horrific genocide and rape that took place in the Balkans, as examples of the worst atrocities of late twentieth-century conflicts.[61] Each case employed decidedly low-tech means; in fact, it is generally the intervention of high-tech forces of the U.S. and the

West that finally brought a halt to such appalling behavior. Technology-empowered militaries are the ones more often than not that are trying to impose some measure of accountability for the inhumane crimes. Why take steps that that could compromise their effectiveness?

Nevertheless, well-funded efforts to limit or ban altogether certain technologies persist, and they often catch the fancy of international celebrities. The classic illustration is the campaign to ban antipersonnel landmines. The tragic death of Britain's Princess Diana, one of the movement's most enthusiastic supporters, served to propel the adoption of what is known as the Ottawa Convention.[62] Virtually every major nation has ratified the Convention, the U.S. being one of the conspicuous exceptions. It is true that landmines caused death and injury to thousands of innocent persons. It is equally true, however, that landmines *used as they should have been* under *pre-existing* agreements have *not* caused many casualties. Nor were many innocent people victimized by any of the new generation of self-neutralizing devices now available.

The Ottawa Convention illustrates two nagging issues in international law: 1) What is to be gained by expanding the scope of prohibitions when there is every expectation that existing bans are – and will be - ignored by those most responsible for the problem the new agreement is supposed to remedy?; and 2) What are the unintended consequences of trying to limit high-tech implements of war in an era when rapid technological change creates uses that were not (and could not be) envisioned or accounted for when the agreement was drafted?

Regarding the first concern, one must reject out of hand the argument that because some break the law there is no point to law in the first place. Nonetheless, very often – as in the case of landmines – the key causes of noncombatant suffering are already prohibited. For example, Protocol II to the 1980 Conventional Weapons Treaty (the U.S. and most other nations are parties to the relevant provisions)[63] bans the indiscriminate use of mines, and requires the marking of minefields and their post-hostilities removal so as to limit noncombatant casualties. If a party were disposed to ignore the requirements of the 1980 agreement, how would the Ottawa Convention deter them? Moreover, by prohibiting the production of advanced self-neutralizing mines, those fixated upon using the weapons – and they do and *will* exist - must resort to crude varieties instead of ones that render themselves harmless over time.

With respect to the second issue, is it possible the ban could produce unintended consequences that result in more, not less, human suffering? Is there a legitimate – and humane - military use today? I believe so. For example, I have never seen any consideration of the ban in the context of the complicated military problem occasioned by weapons-of-mass-destruction (WMD) facilities. How do you attack a WMD site? Do you use a high explosive that might scatter pollutants into the atmosphere? Must you resort to a weapon infinitely more ferocious than any landmine but that can achieve the extremely high temperatures needed to destroy certain contagions? In my opinion the objective of neutralizing a WMD capability might be more safely undertaken simply by dousing the installation with hundreds if not thousands of highly sophisticated landmines. Rendering it unusable until it can be brought under control by friendly forces would seem to be in keeping with humanitarian values.

Another similarly practical use of mines is against infrastructure targets. Consider airfields. From the military perspective, all that is often needed is to block the enemy from using the site, sometimes only temporarily. One way is to blow up the aircraft, tower, runway, support buildings, and so forth. Another way would be to shower the runway with a variety of landmines that make it impossible for aircraft to land or takeoff.[64] The advantage of the latter course is that once you enter the post-conflict stage, instead of a hopelessly destroyed asset you have recoverable infrastructure upon which to build the necessary postwar economy. This is the kind of real world problem that military and civilian decisionmakers face today.

Some organizations[65] want to apply the landmine ban to cluster munitions.[66] Although not designed as landmines, the failure rate of a cluster bomb's submunitions can leave some unexploded ordinance in enemy territory. Unwary noncombatants are in peril (in the same way as they are when treading upon any site where combat has taken place) if they come in contact with the devices. However, this relatively rare situation does not explain the weapon's humanitarian *virtues*. Specifically, because each bomblet contains only a small amount of explosive, they are not as destructive as other weapons, and this can save lives. For example, where an enemy places military equipment such as an anti-aircraft system on something like a dam, cluster munitions can attack the site without risking the catastrophic destruction of the dam itself.

It is easy to conjure up similar examples. Furthermore, banning cluster munitions invites adversaries to wage lawfare by placing military objects on or near facilities whose destruction by *other* weapons (e.g., high-explosives) puts civilians and their property at risk. This is especially a problem with the European Union's proposal to prohibit the use in what it defines as urban areas.[67] The EU policy could suggest to adversaries that they should locate themselves in urban areas to escape the weapon. Experience shows that fighting in cities inevitably causes far more adverse effects on more civilians than any cluster bomb submunition. Furthermore, the law should not be indifferent to the specific context of - and rationale for – the weapon's proposed use. Deputy Secretary of Defense Paul Wolfowitz responded to criticisms of cluster bomb use in Enduring Freedom by pointing out that the U.S. had lost thousands of civilians in a single day, and would "use the weapons we need to win this war."[68]

What makes bans on technology so problematic is the sheer unpredictability of future applications. Weapons expert and retired Army colonel John B. Alexander makes this point quite forcefully in the summer 2001 issue of the Harvard International Review.[69] Alexander contends that nonlethal technologies have great potential to minimize combatant and noncombatant casualties alike, but their development is blocked by what he charges are "emotionally based and broadly worded treaties."[70] Essentially, he contends that the agreements were established at a time when no one envisioned that various chemical and biological agents "could actually be used to reduce casualties."[71] Although he overstates his case somewhat (nonlethal riot control agents were *consciously* banned as a method of warfare in the 1993 Chemical Weapons Convention[72]) his essential point is correct: "Technologies do not cause bad behavior. It is people who use technologies for evil purposes that demonstrate bad behavior."[73]

Even the most horrific weapons can have humanitarian value depending upon how they are (or, perhaps more properly, are *not*) used. Nuclear weapons – probably the subject of more intense international negotiation than any other weapons' technology in the history of man – have a remarkable record that supports Alexander's thesis. Military historian Martin Van Creveld makes the interesting observation that "in every region where [nuclear weapons] have been introduced, large-scale interstate war has as good as disappeared."[74] The idea is not to advocate the spread of nuclear weaponry, but just to point out that limiting the technologies of war is not an unqualified virtue.

In any event, it is true that the development of nonlethal or low-lethality technologies is impeded by chemical, biological, and other weapons conventions.[75] While the limitations law places on nonlethal technologies are troubling to military professionals, real frustration arises when international lawyers assert as irrefutable truths principles that are unmistakably wrong. A good example is one of the most controversial air attacks of the Kosovo conflict. On 23 April 1999, Radio Television Serbia - or RTS, - the state-run media station in central Belgrade, was bombed by coalition aircraft. As a result of this attack, 16 people were killed, and another 16 injured. International lawyers, news organizations, and NGOs criticized the attack.[76] Typical of the rationale for the complaints is the Human Rights Watch report that asserted that RTS made "no direct contribution to the military effort" and that the "risks involved...grossly outweigh any perceived military benefit."[77]

Apparently relying on evidence that indicates the broadcasts whipped up ethnic hatreds for years,[78] Air Commodore David Wilby, a NATO spokesman, insisted, "Serb radio and TV is an instrument of propaganda and repression.... It is...a legitimate target in this campaign."[79] His statement, as a matter of fact, is consistent with U.S. legal thinking.[80] The RTS strike was subsequently the subject of a review by the ICTY[81] (and a lawsuit before the European Court of Human Rights[82]). Although the ICTY accepted the NATO's later explanation that the facility was being used for military communications, it made it clear that but for that circumstance, strikes against the broadcasting stations were likely unlawful. Specifically, the ICTY contended:

> While stopping such propaganda may serve to demoralize the Yugoslav population and undermine the government's political support, it is unlikely that either of these purposes would offer the "concrete and direct" military advantage necessary to make them a legitimate military objective.[83]

This is a rather startling statement in a military sense because even a passing familiarity with Clausewitz and other strategists - not to mention America's own experience in Vietnam - make it plain that "undermin[ing] the government's political support" *does* offer a *very* "direct and concrete" military advantage especially in today's world.[84] As already discussed, the people's support is clearly a "center of gravity"[85] in contemporary military interventions, and information age technologies like radio and television are instrumental in shaping that support. It appears that international lawyers fail to appreciate that even repressive regimes with powerful internal security mechanisms will fall if political support turns against them.

No less an authority than Pulitzer Prize winning historian and Librarian of Congress Emeritus Daniel Boorstin makes that case. Noting the almost bloodless collapse of the Soviet Union, he contends, "history proves that ruthless rulers can be removed by popular will."[86] In fact, a recent RAND study confirms that concerns about Serb popular will were a key reason Milosevic decided to settle when he did.[87] When interpretations of LOAC look as if they are disconnected to humanitarian values, support for the law inevitably wanes. To military professionals it is absurd – and even duplicitous – to contend, as the ICTY report seems to do, that it is somehow preferable to slaughter masses of enemy troops to achieve victory - in lieu of merely destroying a propaganda organ propping up a perverse regime (at the price of small, albeit regrettable, numbers of civilian casualties).

Another interesting "values" issue is raised by the international campaign against blinding lasers as a means of warfare.[88] No one would debate seriously the proposition that blindness is a gravely debilitating affliction. It is still difficult to understand why it is a more unfortunate condition than traumatic amputation, paralysis, or any other similar injury that occurs in war. Assuming a laser is used under circumstances where one could lawfully kill an opponent, it seems indisputably more humane to blind him than slay him. In advocating the ban, however, the International Committee of the Red Cross (ICRC) appears to draw a different conclusion.[89] The ICRC, evidently unaware of the philosophical implications of what it was saying, in essence argued that adversaries would just use other weapons to finish off blinded combatants. Again, this is the illogical argument that presumes that since a belligerent will break existing law (i.e., kill wounded *hors de combat*) enacting more law will somehow improve the situation.

The other part of the ICRC argument is rather profound, and illustrates the contrast between the European view of humanitarian values and that of the U.S. According to the ICRC, "blinding renders a person virtually unable to work or to function independently [resulting in] severe psychological depression." This simply is not true; millions of visually handicapped persons live happy, independent, and productive lives. Moreover, the obvious question remains: is blindness worse than being killed by "approved" weapons? I can only conclude that in Europe, where assisted-suicide and euthanasia have taken root, death is preferable to life with a disability. Regardless, the ICRC position hardly represents a universal value and its thinking should not be the rationale for banning a technology, especially one that by its very nature does not kill its targets.

Looking ahead, it will be interesting to see how the international legal community approaches the issue of unmanned and other robotic combat systems. These technologies are rapidly gaining acceptance in high-tech militaries like that of the U.S.[90] There are issues, however, as to how they should be employed. As one analyst notes, "[p]eople are generally more comfortable with somebody being in the loop when things are being shot and decisions are being made."[91] Nevertheless, as these weapons are considered, the focus should not be on *how* they achieve their effect, but rather the degree to which that effect honors LOAC and human rights. A more difficult and problematic issue is presented by the military challenges occasioned by Operation Enduring Freedom. The safest and most effective means, for example, of rooting enemy fighters out of caves may be to employ flamethrowers. This controversial weapon is not currently in the U.S. inventory, but press reports are now discussing its possible use.[92]

Operation Enduring Freedom raised other legal issues that may themselves stimulate technological development that, in turn, will generate debate in international law circles. Specifically, the U.S. was obliged to engage in extensive negotiation and diplomatic strategies to obtain legal rights for the basing and overflight of military aircraft. The difficulty in accomplishing that task, as well as the threat that lawfare will make obtaining like commitments even more troublesome in the future, militates towards permanent solutions. In my view one of these could be a greater militarization – indeed *weaponization* - of space.[93] Among other things, orbiting armed space systems would obviate the need for foreign basing or overflight permissions.[94] This would provide the U.S. with greater flexibility for unilateral military intervention if required. Of course, the weaponization of space will produce a host of legal and policy issues.[95] Nevertheless, as the leading spacepower the U.S. has the technological potential to bypass those adversaries who might pressure area nations to deny basing and overflight rights, as well as those who might be tempted to extract concessions in exchange for them in some future contingency.

Many of the emerging LOAC issues involve, as I have mentioned before, the American preference to use technology to avoid casualties.[96] This raises another apparent difference between the U.S. and European view: the relative perspectives on the profession of arms.[97] Despite the existence of an all-volunteer force, Americans in and out of uniform generally do not consider those who serve as anything other than citizens of equal or more value as any enemy combatant or noncombatant. Europeans, however, have a history of populating their militaries with long-term professionals and legions of hired foreigners.[98] This seems to create a certain sense that the armed forces are more tools of the state than citizenry in uniform. To me, this produces a collective societal ethic that gives the impression that military personnel are expendable assets. Of course, nowhere in LOAC is there an explicit assertion that the life of a soldier is of lesser value than any other. This may be another situation where a view acceptable in Europe is nevertheless insufficiently universal to make it a bona fide basis for initiatives in international law.

The affection of Americans towards those of its citizens who serve in the armed forces in large measure explains why resistance to proposals like the International Criminal Court (ICC)[99] continues to grow.[100] The spurious allegations of LOAC violations after the Balkan War all but guaranteed that the U.S. would not ratify the ICC treaty any time soon.[101] Concerns had already surfaced about the notion of trying American troops before a forum that fails to meet the minimum standards of an American court-martial.[102] The concerns are good ones: It is unwise, in my opinion, for a democracy obliged to maintain a large military establishment to suggest that those who defend it are somehow unworthy of the rights they serve to protect.

I do not see any inconsistency, incidentally, with opposing the ICC yet endorsing the President's recent order permitting military commissions (which bear no relationship to the U.S. court-martial system) for the trial of foreign terrorists.[103] In my opinion, because the ICC involves the possible trial of U.S. citizens it is understandably determined by domestic, civil-military relations' considerations. The military commissions are best analyzed from an international law perspective because they would only apply to foreign nationals. I believe the proposed commissions are fully consonant with international law.

As the widespread support for the ICC outside the U.S. proves, most nations are quite happy to have their nationals subject to a court that does not afford the rights that a U.S. court-martial or civilian proceeding provides. Foreign nationals would be subject to a process that meets or exceeds *international* standards; the point is that international standards are not necessarily the same as the domestic ones Americans want for their fellow citizens. Of course, it is somewhat ironic that European nations, who frequently badgered the U.S. about its refusal to ratify the ICC treaty, are now resisting the extradition of terrorists because they may be subject to trial before a military commission,[104] despite the striking similarities between that forum and the ICC.

Concluding Observations

As I offered earlier, I believe that the events of September 11th will have a profound effect on the role of law in military interventions. The psychological impact of savage attacks on the American homeland, along with fears raised by the anthrax incidents, radically diminishes the public's desire for what Professor Betts might describe as hyperlegalistic processes. Recognizing the dimensions of the new threat, Americans supported legislation giving law enforcement authorities vastly greater powers at the expense of what heretofore were accepted individual rights.[105] Considering Americans' willingness to sacrifice their own legal protections, they are unlikely to be overly demanding about the supposed legal rights of foreign belligerents.

Americans are much more concerned about finding and stopping the perpetrators of violence than they are about the niceties of international law. Despite the President's statements to the contrary, many pundits called for the outright killing of those responsible, and derided the notion of trying to bring the perpetrators to justice in a criminal court.[106] Unlike international law devotees, many Americans are exasperated with the law, especially when traditional applications of it proved to be an inadequate guarantor of basic security on September 11th. Stewart Baker, the former general counsel of the National Security Agency, concludes "[w]e have judicialized more aspects of human behavior than any civilization in history, and we may have come to the limit of that."[107] Consequently, in security matters contemporary American discourse is pervaded by the notion that "[t]he time for legal maneuverings, extraditions and trials is past."[108]

All of this affects Americans' perceptions of LOAC. While reports of civilian casualties in Enduring Freedom cause disturbances among allied populaces, the support of the U.S. electorate for the military intervention remains strong.[109] This is not a sign of callous indifference, but rather a growing acceptance among the body politic that war inevitably causes unintended tragedies. Additionally, the public is becoming better educated as to how adversaries are manipulating civilian casualties to wage lawfare. I believe they are much less prone to assume from media reports that U.S. forces are waging war "in an unfair, inhumane, or iniquitous way."[110] I also sense that the continued public support is an expression of the people's conviction that the U.S. military – which for years has topped the polls as the institution in which Americans have the most confidence[111] - is doing everything it can to minimize the impact on noncombatants.

Along these lines, I think the persistent criticisms of some international lawyers,[112] NGOs,[113] academics, and others regarding U.S. and coalition air operations in Iraq,[114] the Balkans, and Afghanistan have been extremely counter-productive in terms of enhancing the acceptance of LOAC in the minds of military people. In too many instances the criticisms appear alternately uninformed or patently politicized. Following Operation Allied Force the allegations that the altitudes flown during combat sorties caused unnecessary civilian casualties were especially infuriating to airmen.[115] The accusations did not seem to appreciate that the armed forces of democracies at war are properly guided by and subordinate to policies set by elected leaders, not the desires of those in uniform. That is the way the rule of law is supposed to work in free countries. Furthermore, some reports were wildly inaccurate - even Human Rights Watch could point to only one instance where high-altitude attacks *might* have caused unnecessary civilian injuries.[116]

Actually, it is impossible to find examples in human history where so much combat power was applied as discreetly as in the aforementioned air operations.[117] With respect to Operation Enduring Freedom, White House spokesman Ari Fleischer observed – quite accurately in my opinion – that "I don't think you'll ever witness a nation that has worked so hard to avoid civilian casualties as the Untied States has."[118] That is exactly what military leaders at every level believe. They are convinced that they are doing everything they can to comply with LOAC.

While one would always hope for perfection in any human endeavor, in real terms I cannot see how the adherence to LOAC and the humanitarian values it represents can significantly improve in future military interventions. It should be kept in mind that the recent conflicts took place under circumstances where U.S. forces were not *in extremis*. This allowed time for comparatively extensive and systematic evaluations of targets and strategies. We may not have that relative "luxury" in rapidly evolving future conflicts, and the warfighters know it.

By demeaning the sincere efforts of those tasked to use armed force in pursuit of national objectives, the critics put respect for the law itself in jeopardy. They unnecessarily alienate the very audience LOAC most needs to prosper in the proverbial 'real world.' I do not mean to imply that the armed forces are disposed to act in an illegal or immoral fashion, but rather to suggest that the seeming impossibility to satisfy the self-styled legal authorities encourages military leaders to pursue a more politically-oriented approach that searches for legal loopholes and technical compliance as opposed to a more expansive philosophical commitment. Put concisely, subjective measures of public tolerance might tend to replace reliance upon rigorous readings of LOAC as the principal guide. As much as popular support is critical to a democracy's ability to fight, the transient and often emotionally charged politics of a nation at war do not always reflect the enduring human rights principles that underlay LOAC. All too easily, this approach can devolve into *Kriegsraison* writ large.[119]

Will international law, and specifically LOAC, become – as Riviken and Casey predict, "one of the most potent weapons ever deployed against the United States?" Perhaps their hyperbole goes too far, but the point is an important one. It is not in the interest of anyone concerned with humanitarian values to *unnecessarily* handcuff the United States - or any democracy – when force is required to restore and safeguard human rights generally. We must remind ourselves that our opponents are more than ready to exploit our values to defeat us, and they will do so without any concern about LOAC. Consider this disquieting statement from Chinese military leaders: "War has rules, but those rules are set by the West...if you use those rules, then weak countries have no chance...We are a weak country, so do we need to fight according to your rules? No."[120]

We should expect to see unscrupulous antagonists engage in ever more sophisticated versions of lawfare. In Colombia, insurgents use sensitivity to human rights abuses to attempt to decapitate the nation's military leadership, thus jeopardizing South America's oldest democracy. The Wall Street Journal reports that "by intimidation and bribery" rebels force peasants to use the "courts to press false charges – anonymously – against the most capable military leaders."[121] At the same time the guerrillas are blaming others for human rights abuses, they commit them themselves. Even Human Rights Watch is disillusioned: "We've come to the conclusion that they're using international humanitarian law as just part of a P.R. campaign."[122] It is vital for the preservation of human rights to be concerned about developments such as this. If international law is to remain a viable force for good in military interventions, lawfare practitioners cannot be permitted to commandeer it for malevolent purposes.

This essay critiques aspects of LOAC as currently practiced, but it is not meant to denigrate its fundamental importance. Americans would not be Americans if they waged war unconstrained by the ethical values LOAC represents.[123] Rather, this paper is intended as a reminder that those interested in promoting law as an ameliorator of the misery of war are obliged to ensure it does not become bogged down with interpretations that are at odds with legitimate military concerns. LOAC must remain receptive to new developments, especially technological ones that can save lives – even if that means breaking old paradigms.[124]

We also must have a better linkage between those knowledgeable of military affairs and those civilian specialists expert in LOAC. Only productive cooperation can achieve the critical mass necessary to sustain international law as a guiding element in military interventions. We should encourage other nations to develop a robust cadre of uniformed lawyers ready to provide insightful advice to commanders in the field. Finally, we must not allow thoughtless, ill-informed, and politically motivated accusations to trivialize LOAC's fundamental principles. If it does, LOAC will lose its credibility with the very people – and the very nation - it most needs to make certain it is observed and, more importantly, preserved.

Notes

[1] Richard K. Betts, *Compromised Command*, Foreign Affairs, July/August 2001, at 126, (review of Wesley Clark's, Waging Modern War: Bosnia, Kosovo, and the Future of Combat).
[2] *Id.* At 129, 130.
[3] David B. Rivkin, Jr. & Lee A Casey, *The Rocky Shoals of International Law*, The National Interest, Winter 2000/01, at 35.
[4] For information about Operation Allied Force, *see* Dep't of Defense, *Operation Allied Force*, June 21, 1999 *accessible at* http://www.defenselink.mil/specials/kosovo/ (last visited 23 November 2001).
[5] The term "lawfare" seems to have first appeared in a manuscript by John Carlson and Neville Yeomans entitled *Whither Goeth the Law - Humanity or Barbarity, in* The Way Out - Radical Alternatives in Australia (M. Smith & D. Crossley, eds., 1975), *accessible at* http://www.laceweb.org.au/whi.htm (last visited 24 November 2001). Although their thesis is not entirely clear, they do assert that "lawfare replaces warfare and the duel is with words rather than swords" and this capture a key theme of lawfare as used in this essay.
[6] But see note 120, *supra*, and accompanying text.
[7] There were four main agreements concluded in 1949: the *Geneva Convention for the Amelioration of the Condition of the Wounded and Sick in Armed Forces in the Field*, 12 August 1949; the *Geneva Convention for the Amelioration of the Condition of the Wounded and Sick and Shipwrecked Members of Armed Forces at Sea*, 12 August 1949; the *Geneva Convention Relative to the Treatment of Prisoners of War*, 12 August 1949; and the *Geneva Convention Relative to the Protection of Civilians in Time of War*, 12 August 1949. *See* Department of the Army Pamphlet 27-1, *Treaties Governing Land Warfare* (7 December 1956). Texts of the treaties are accessible at http://www.icrc.org/ihl.nsf/WebCONVPRES?OpenView (last visited 20 November 2001).
[8] Geoffrey Parker, Cambridge Illustrated History of Warfare (Cambridge University Press, 1995), p. 369 ("the majority of the approximately fifty million people killed in war [since 1945] have been civilians").
[9] *See generally*, Roger Cohen, *To European Eyes, It's America the Ugly*, New York Times, May 7, 2001, at 1 (discussing European reaction to the U.S. position on various international agreements and policies) and Jessica T. Mathews, *Estranged Partners*, Foreign Policy, November/December 2001, at 48.
[10] *See e.g.*, Statutes of the International Committee of the Red Cross, 24 June 1998, art. 7 *accessible at* http://www.icrc.org/eng/icrc (last visited 20 November 2001) (limiting membership to Swiss citizens).
[11] Rivkin and Casey, note 3, *supra*.
[12] *See* Mark Malloch Brown, *Democracy and the Information Revolution*, Choices Magazine, September 2001 *accessible at* http://www.undp.org/dpa/choices/2001/september/commentary.pdf (last visited 25 November 2001).
[13] W. Michael Reisman and Chris T. Antoniou, The Laws of War xxiv (1994) (emphasis added).
[14] "The free flow of broadcast information in open societies has always had an impact on public opinion and the formulation of foreign policy. But now the flow has increased in volume and shortened news cycles have reduced the time for deliberation." Joseph Nye, *Redefining the National Interest,* Foreign Affairs, July/August 1999, at 22, 26.
[15] "Real-time television [puts] pressure on officials to respond rapidly." Toni Marshall, *Media Don't Make Foreign Policy*, Washington Times, June 9, 1997, at 16 (quoting Walter Strobel).
[16] *See* note 5, *supra*.
[17] For example, the U.S. used law to deny hostile uses of commercial satellite imagery. *See* Michael R. Gordon, *Pentagon Corners Output of Special Afghan Images*, New York Times, October 19, 2001 *reprinted in* Dep't of Defense, Current News Early Bird, 19 October 2001 (discussing the U.S. strategy of "buying all the rights to picture of Afghanistan taken by the world's best commercial satellites").

[18] Carl von Clausewitz, *On War* (Michael Howard and Peter Paret, ed., and trans. 1976) (1832), at 89.
[19] *See* The Gallup Organization, *No Wavering in Public Support for War Effort,* November 9, 2001 *accessible at* http://www.gallup.com/poll/releases/pr011109.asp (last visited 20 November 2001).
[20] *See e.g.,* Kevin Sullivan, *War Support Falls Worldwide*, Washington Post, November 7, 2001, at A1.
[21] *See* note 93 *supra* and accompanying text.
[22] *See* Michael Gordon and Bernard E, Trainor, The Generals' War (1995), at 324-326.
[23] *Id.*, at 476-477. *See also* Colin Powell, My American Journey (Random House, 1995), at 520 ("The television coverage... was starting to make it look as if we were engaged in slaughter for slaughter's sake.").
[24] *See, Libyans to Form Shield at Suspected Arms Plant*, Baltimore Sun, May 17, 1996, at 14 (reporting a Libyan threat to surround a suspected chemical weapons plant with a human shield composed of millions of Muslims).
[25] *See e.g.,* Mark Mazzetti and Kevin Whitelaw, *Into the Thick of Things*, U.S. News & World Report, November 5, 2001, at 24. Additionally, the Washington Post reports:

> By shifting soldiers and military equipment into civilian neighborhoods and taking refuge in mosques, archeological sites and other nonmilitary facilities, Taliban forces are confronting U.S. authorities with the choice of risking civilian casualties and destruction of treasured Afghan assets or forgoing attacks.

Bradley Graham and Vernon Loeb, *Taliban Dispersal Slows U.S.,* Washington Post, November 6, 2001, at 1.
[26] *See e.g.*, International Criminal Tribunal for the Former Yugoslavia, Final Report to the Prosecutor by the Committee Established to Review the NATO Bombing Campaign Against the Federal Republic of Yugoslavia (13 June 2000) *accessible at* http://www.un.org/icty/pressreal/nato061300.htm (last accessed 12 June 2001).
[27] For general information on the Air Force's role in Operation Enduring Freedom *see* Air Force Link, *Enduring Freedom*, *accessible at* http://www.af.mil/news/efreedom/index.shtml (last accessed 12 November 2001).
[28] *See* Vanessa Blum, *JAG Goes to War,* Legal Times, November 15, 2001 *at* http://www.law.com (last visited 23 November 2001).
[29] Michael Ignatieff, Virtual War (Metropolitan Books, 2000), at 199.
[30] The most famous case involves the My Lai massacre. *See* United States v. Calley, 48 C.M.R. 19 (C.M.A. 1973). However, there were many other trials of American troops that though charged as traditional offenses (e.g., murder) they amounted to what would likely be considered "war crimes." *See e.g.,* Gary D. Solis, Song Thang: An American War Crime (1997).
[31] *See* Lt Col Terrie M. Gent, *The Role of Judge Advocates in a Joint Air Operations Center*, Airpower Journal, September 1999, at 40-55 *accessible at* http://www.airpower.maxwell.af.mil/airchronicles/apj/apj99/spr99/gent.html (last accessed 27 October 2001).
[32] Chairman, Joint Chiefs of Staff Instr. (CJCSI) 5810.01A, *Implementation of the DoD Law of War Program*, para. 6(c)(5) (27 August 1999)
[33] The draft doctrine is Air Force Doctrine Document 2-4.5 *Doctrine for Legal Support of Aerospace Operations* (draft). This effort is underway at the Air Force Doctrine Center *see* http://www.doctrine.af.mil/.
[34] For a general discussion of the role of air operations centers and the doctrinal architecture for the application of airpower, *see* Dep't of the Air Force, Air Force Doctrine Document 2, *Organization and Employment of Aerospace Power*, 17 February 2000 *accessible at* http://www.doctrine.af.mil/.
[35] A "sortie" is "an operational flight by a single military aircraft." *See* The Oxford Essential Dictionary of the U.S. Military (Elizabeth J. Jewell, *et al.*, eds., 2001), at 405.

[36] Such systems even exist for nuclear targeting. See Charles J. Dunlap, Jr., *Taming Shiva: Applying International Law to Nuclear Operations*, 47 A.F. L. Rev. 157, 162 (1997) (describing U.S. Strategic Command's Strategic War Planning System (SWPS)).
[37] For example, 90% of the U.S. military's communications flow through civilian systems. John T. Correll, *Warfare in the Information Age*, Air Force Magazine, December 1996, at 3.
[38] *Protocol Additional to the Geneva Conventions of 12 August 1949, and Relating to the Protection of Victims of International Armed Conflicts* [Protocol I], art. art. 51.5(b). The U.S. is not, however, a Party to Protocol I but accepts this portion as reflecting customary international law.
[39] The principle of "proportionality" requires that the "collateral damage" to noncombatants or their property not be disproportionate in relation to the "concrete and direct military advantage anticipated." The concept was codified in arts. 51.5(b) and 57.2(iii) of Protocol I, note 38, *supra*. While the U.S. has not ratified Additional Protocol I, this portion is considered part of customary international law.
[40] *See* Commander James W. Crawford, *The Law of Noncombatant Immunity and the Targeting of National Electrical Power Systems*, 21 Fletcher Forum of World Affairs 101 (Summer/Fall 1997) (discussing secondary and reverberating effects).
[41] Major Thomas E. Griffith, Jr., USAF, *Strategic Attack of National Electrical Systems*, U.S. Air Force's School for Advanced Aerospace Studies, Air University, Maxwell Air Force Base, AL (October 1994).
[42] The Department of Defense would only say that there was "high confidence" that the factory was used to make a precursor compound for a chemical agent. *See* Dep't of Defense, Background Briefing, *Terrorist Camp Strikes*, 20 August 1998 *accessible at* http://www.defenselink.mil/news/Aug1998/x08201998_x820bomb.html (last visited 20 November 2001).
[43] The attack is the subject of on-going litigation in U.S. courts by the plant's owners. See Otis Bilodeau, When Bombs Miss their Mark, Legal Times, November 28, 2001 *at* http://www.law.com (last visited 28 November 2001).
[44] *See e.g.*, Williamson Murray, Air War in the Persian Gulf (1995), at 224-226 (criticizing the alleged role of Air Force lawyers with respect to a proposed bombing of a statue of Saddam Hussein). Murray's version of events is disputed by Colonel Scott L. Silliman, USAF (Ret.), the former Staff Judge Advocate of what was then known as Tactical Air Command (TAC) (Murray contends that TAC legal advice that the statue was a protected cultural monument "was simply wrong."). Silliman contends that no lawyer ever concluded that bombing the statue was illegal; lawyers only recommended that the target be carefully screened for conformance with existing legal standards. He believes the statue was removed from the target lists for unrelated reasons. E-mail from Scott L. Silliman to Colonel Charles Dunlap, Staff Judge Advocate, U.S. Strategic Command (19 Feb. 1998) (on file with author).
[45] Interview, General Charles Horner, Washingtonpost.com (1998), *accessible at* http://www.washingtonpost.com/wp-srv/inatl/longterm/fogofwar/hornertext.htm (lasted visited 1 May 2001).
[46] For information about Operation Desert Fox, *see generally*, Dep't of Defense, *Operation Desert Fox*, *accessible at* http://www.defenselink.mil/specials/desert_fox/ (last visited 20 November 2001).
[47] *See* note 39, *supra.*
[48] *See e.g.,* Elaine M. Grossman, *Air Force Chief Launches Major Effort To Improve Targeting Speed*, Inside the Pentagon, November 8, 2001, at 3.
[49] The media reports allege that opportunities to attack purported terrorists were lost due to overly cautious advice from a JAG. *See* Seymour M. Hersh, *King's Ransom*, The New Yorker, October 22, 2001 *accessible at* http://www.newyorker.com/FACT/?011022fa_FACT1 (last accessed 12 November 2001) and Thomas E. Ricks, *Target Approval Delays Irk Air Force Officers,* Washington Post, November 18, 2001, at A01.
[50] Both the Secretary of Defense and the Deputy Secretary of Defense refuted aspects of the Washington Post story, but neither specifically addressed the JAG issue. *See* Dep't of Defense, *News Briefing – Secretary Rumsfeld* (19 November 2001) *accessible at*

http://www.defenselink.mil/news/Nov2001/t11192001_t1119sd.html (last visited 19 November 2001); and Dep't of Defense, *Deputy Secretary Wolfowitz Interview with CBS Face the Nation* (transcript of 18 November 2001) *accessible at* http://www.defenselink.mil/news/Nov2001/t11182001_t1118wol.html (last accessed 19 November 2001).

[51] Dep't of the Air Force Policy Directive 51-4, 26 April 1993 (describing the reporting and investigation of any apparent violation of LOAC).

[52] *See e.g.,* 10 U.S.C § 806(b)

[53] General Hal M. Hornburg, *The Importance of Legal Professionals in the Air Force*, (June 27, 2001), *available at* http://www.aetc.randolph.af.mil/pa/Library/speeches/cc06.htm (last accessed 22 October 2001).

[54] *Cf.* note 62 and 63, *supra*, and accompanying discussion.

[55] Protocol I, note 38, *supra,* at art. 82.

[56] John Keegan, A History of Warfare (1993), at xvi.

[57] Ronald Haycock and Keith Neilson, Men, Machines, and War (1988) at xii.

[58] This success continues in the current war on terrorism. *See e.g.,* Paul Richter, *Despite Grim Predictions, U.S. Battle Toll Still Zero*, Los Angeles Times, November 24, 2001, *accessible at* http://www.latimes.com/news/nationworld/nation/la-112401nodead.story, (last visited 24 November 2001) *reprinted sub nom, In a Strange Kind of War, U.S. Casualties Are Few*, San Antonio Express-News, November 24 2001, at 17A ("The casualty rate reported by the Pentagon attests to the continuing technological advances that the U.S. military has made in developing an arm's-length, precision style of attack.").

[59] *As quoted by* Matthew Cooper *in Making the World Safer*, Time, November 26, 2001, at 83.

[60] The relative weight of the defense burden is yet another area where U.S. and European approaches diverge. *See e.g.,* Jeffrey Gedmin, *A Yawning Gap on Defense*, Washington Times, December 8, 1999, at 15. ("The United States currently spends 3.2 percent of its GDP on defense. The European allies in average 2.1%."). *See also* John Keegan, *The U.S. Is Not Amused By Our Redundant Military Gestures*, London Daily Telegraph, December 6, 1999 *reprinted in* Dep't of Defense, Current News Early Bird, 6 December 1999 ("The United States] has...continued to devote a larger proportion of its budgetary spending on defense - particularly defense research – than any European government ever has, to the great benefit of all its allies.").

[61] For a relatively dispassionate and comprehensive examination of war crimes in the modern context *see* Crimes of War Project *accessible at* http://www.crimesofwar.org/ (last visited 20 November 2001).

[62] The technical title of the Ottawa Convention is *The Convention on the Prohibition of the Use, Stockpiling, Production and Transfer of Anti-personnel Mines and on their Destruction*, 18 September 1997, *accessible at* http://www.icrc.org/ihl (last visited 20 November 2001).

[63] *Convention on Prohibitions or Restrictions of the Use of Certain Conventional Weapons Which May be Deemed to be Excessively Injurious or to Have Indiscriminate Effects*, October 10, 1980; *Protocol on Prohibitions or Restrictions on the Use of Mines, Booby-Traps and Other Devices* (hereinafter CCW Protocol II). Geneva, 10 October 1980, *accessible at* http://www.icrc.org/ihl (last visited 20 November 2001).

[64] One such munition in the U.S. inventory is the CBU 89, "Gator" mine system. For a description of it, see Federation of American Scientists, *CBU 89 Gator Mine, accessible at* http://www.fas.org/man/dod-101/sys/dumb/cbu-89.htm (last visited 23 November 2001).

[65] *See e.g.*, Brooks Tigner, *EU United on Restricting Cluster Bombs' Use*, Defense News, July 22, 2001, at 18; and Human Rights Watch, *Cluster Bombs in Afghanistan*, (October 2001), *accessible at* http://www.hrw.org/backgrounder/arms/cluster-bck1031.htm (last visited 23 November 2001).

[66] For a description of a cluster munition *see* Federation of American Scientists, *CBU-87/B Combined Effects Munitions (CEM), accessible at* http://www.fas.org/man/dod-101/sys/dumb/cbu-87.htm (last visited 23 November 2001).

[67] *See* Tigner, note 65 *supra.*

[68] *See* Dep't of Defense, News Transcript, *Deputy Secretary Wolfowitz Interview with the London Sunday Telegraph*, October 26, 2001 *accessible at*

http://www.defenselink.mil/news/Oct2001/t10282001_t1026dsd.html (last visited 23 November 2001).

[69] John B. Alexander, *Optional Lethality: Evolving Attitudes Toward Nonlethal Weaponry*, Harvard International Review, Summer 2001, at 64.

[70] *Id.*, at 69. Presumably, Alexander is referring to such widely-accepted agreements as the *Convention on the Prohibition of the Development, Production and Stockpiling of Bacteriological (Biological) and Toxin Weapons and on Their Destruction*, April 10, 1972, 26 U.S.T. 583, and the *Protocol for the Prohibition of the Use in War of Asphyxiating, Poisonous, or Other Gases, and of Bacteriological Methods of Warfare*, June 17, 1925, 26 U.S.T. 571. *See also* note 72 *supra*.

[71] Alexander, *Id.*, at 69.

[72] *Convention on the Prohibition of the Development, Production, Stockpiling and Use of Chemical Weapons and on their Destruction*, Paris, 13 January 1993, *accessible at* http://www.icrc.org/ihl (last visited 20 November 2001).

[73] Alexander, note 69, *supra*.

[74] Martin Van Creveld, *Technology and War (II), in* The Oxford Illustrated History of Modern War (Charles Townsend, ed., 1997), at 304 (emphasis in original).

[75] For example, rubber ball and paintball munitions were found to violate the antipersonnel landmine provision of CCW Protocol II. *See* Memorandum, Dep't of the Army, Office of the Judge Advocate General, to AMSTA-AR-CC, Picatinny Arsenal, New Jersey, subject: Bounding Non-Lethal Munition (BNLM) Legal Review (7 January 2000).

[76] *See* Walter J. Rockler, *War Crimes Law Applies to the U.S. Too*, Chicago Tribune, May 23, 1999 accessed 25 May 1999 at http://ebird.dtic.mil/May1999/e19990525warcrimes.htm.

[77] Human Rights Watch, *Civilian Deaths in the NATO Air Campaign*, Vol. 12, No. 1, (February 2000) *accessible at* http://www.hrw.org/reports/2000/nato/index.htm#TopOfPage (last accessed 25 November 2001).

[78] *See e.g.,* Jamie F. Metzl, *Information Intervention*, Foreign Affairs, November/December 1997, at 15.

[79] *As quoted by* William M. Arkin in *Changing the Channel in Belgrade,* Washington Post (online edition) May 25, 1990 *accessible at* http://www.washingtonpost.com/wp-srv/national/dotmil/arkin052499.htm (last visited 6 September 1999).

[80] According to the DoD General Counsel, "[w]hen it is determined that civilian media broadcasts are directly interfering with the accomplishment of the military force's mission, there is no law of war objection to using minimum force to shut it down." *See* Dep't of Defense, Office of General Counsel, *An Assessment of International Legal Issues in Information Operations*, May 1999, at 9.

[81] *See* note 26, *supra*, at para IV, B. iii.

[82] *Bankovic and others v. 17 NATO States*, Application No. 52207/99, European Court of Human Rights, *Pending Cases Before a Grand Chamber*, *accessible at* http://www.echr.coe.int/BilingualDocuments/PendCase.htm (last visited 25 November 2001) (The U.S. is not a party to this lawsuit.).

[83] *Id.*

[84] *See* note 18, *supra*, and accompanying text.

[85] Centers of gravity are "[t]hose characteristics, capabilities, or localities from which military forces derive freedom of action, physical strength, or will to fight." *See* Chairman of the Joint Chiefs of Staff, Joint Publication (Joint Pub) 1-02, *DoD Dictionary of Military and Associated Terms* 23 March 1994 as amended 29 June 1999 accessed 6 September 1999 at http://www.dtic.mil/doctrine/jel/doddict/data/c/01075.html.

[86] Daniel J. Boorstin, *Myths of Popular Innocence*, U.S. News & World Report, March 4, 1991, at 41.

[87] *See* Stephen T. Hosmer, *Why Milosevic Decided to Settle When He Did* (Rand, 2001).

[88] *Protocol on Blinding Laser Weapons*, 13 October 1995, CCW Protocol IV *see* note 63 *supra*. The U.S. is not a party to this Protocol.

[89] International Committee of the Red Cross, *Blinding Laser Weapons: Questions and Answers*, 16 November 1994, *accessible at* http://www.icrc.org/icrceng.nsf/5cacfdf48ca698b641256242003b3295/f0e784905f16867841256200004c5ae1?OpenDocument (last visited 23 November 2001).

[90] *See e.g.,* Thomas E. Ricks, *U.S. Arms Unmanned Aircraft*, Washington Post, October 18, 2001, at 1.
[91] *See* Gail Kaufman, *Attack Robots 'Kind of Frightening'*, Defense News, June 4-10, 2001, at 10.
[92] *See* Vince Crawley, *Flamethrowers: A Necessary Evil?*, Air Force Times, November 26, 2001, at 16.
[93] *See generally,* Donald G. Rumsfeld, et al., *Report of the Commission to Assess United States National Security Space Management and Organization*, January 11, 2001 *accessible at* https://www.space.gov/ (last visited 25 November 2001) (advocating greater U.S. military involvement in space)
[94] For a thorough discussion of LOAC in the space environment *see generally* Major Robert A. Ramey, USAF, *Armed Conflict on the Final Frontier: The Law of War in Space*, 48 A.F. L. Rev. 1 (2000).
[95] *Id. See also* Vernon Loeb, *Air Force's Chief Backs Space Weapons*, Washington Post, August 2, 2001, at 17 (discussing the Air Force Chief of Staffs support for space weapons but acknowledging that the policy decision to weaponize space has not yet been made).
[96] *See* notes 57 to 59, *supra*, and accompanying text.
[97] *See* note 115 and accompanying text.
[98] *See e.g.,* Embassy of France, The French Foreign Legion, *accessible at* http://www.info-france-usa.org/america/embassy/legion/legion.htm (last visited 24 November 2001); Ministry of Defense, British Army, *Brigade of Gurkhas, accessible at* http://www.army.mod.uk/army/organise/infan/gurkha/ (last visited 24 November 2001); Holy See, *Swiss Guard, accessible at* http://www.vatican.va/roman_curia/swiss_guard/ (last visited 24 November 2001).
[99] For information about the ICC *see* United Nations, *Rome Statute of the International Criminal Court,* (updated 5 November 2001) *accessible at* http://www.un.org/law/icc/index.html (last visited 24 November 2001).
[100] *See e.g.,* Dan Morgan, *Lawmakers Accept Provision Against World Court*, Washington Post, November 9, 2001, at 24.
[101] *See e.g.,* Steven Lee Meyers, *Kosovo Inquiry Confirms U.S. Fears of War Crimes Court*, New York Times, January 3, 2000, *reprinted in* Dep't of Defense, Current News Early Bird, 3 January 2001. .
[102] Helle Bering, *International Criminal Circus*, Washington Times, April 5, 2000 (discussing the "American Servicemembers Protection Act of 2000) *reprinted in* Dep't of Defense, Current News Early Bird, 5 April 2001.
[103] *See* White House, *Military Order: Detention, Treatment, and Trial of Certain Non-Citizens in the War Against Terrorism*, November 13, 2001 *accessible at* http://www.whitehouse.gov/news/releases/2001/11/20011113-27.html (last visited 24 November 2001).
[104] *See e.g.,* Sam Dillion with Donald McNeill, *Spain Sets Hurdle for Extraditions*, The New York Times, November 24, 2001, at A1, *accessible at* http://www.nytimes.com/2001/11/24/international/europe/24SPAI.html (last visited 24 November 2001).
[105] *See e.g.,* Uniting and Strengthening America by Providing Appropriate Tools Required to Intercept and Obstruct Terrorism (USA PATRIOT ACT) Act of 2001, Pub. L. No.__ (October 26, 2001) *accessible at* http://www.ins.gov/graphics/lawsregs/patriot.pdf (last visited 23 November 2001).
[106] *See e.g.,* Charles Krauthammer, *To War, Not to Court*, Washington Post, September 12, 2001, at 29 ("An open act of war demands a military response, not a judicial one")
[107] *As quoted by* John Lancaster and Susan Schmidt *in U.S. Rethinks Strategy for Coping with Terrorists*, Washington Post, September 14, 2001, at 9.
[108] Wayde Minami, *Attack is an Act of War; Treat it as such with quick Overwhelming Revenge*, Air Force Times, September 24, 2001, at 78.
[109] *See* note 19, *supra.*
[110] *See* note 13, *supra.*

[111] *See* The Gallup Organization, *Military Retains Top Position in Americans' Confidence Ratings,* June 25, 2001 *accessible at* http://www.gallup.com/poll/releases/pr010625.asp (last visited 20 November 2001).

[112] *See e.g.,* Ramsey Clark, et al., *War Crimes: A Report on United States Crimes Against Iraq to the Commission of Inquiry for the International War Crimes Tribunal,* 1992, *accessible at* http://www.deoxy.org/wc/ (last visited 24 November 2001).

[113] *See e.g.,* Amnesty International, *NATO/Federal Republic of Yugoslavia "Collateral Damage" or Unlawful Killings: Violations of the Laws of War by NATO During Operation Allied Force*, June 2000 *accessible at* http://www.amnesty.org/ (last visited 23 November 2001), and International Action Center, *Independent Commission of Inquiry: Hearing to Investigate U.S./NATO War Crimes Against the People of Yugoslavia,* June 2000, *accessible at* http://www.iacenter.org/warcrime/html (last visited 24 November 2001).

[114] *See e.g.,* Joseph Fitchett, *Bombing of Iraq 'Illegal' Paris Says*, International Herald Tribune, February 20, 2001, at 1.

[115] The author has previously discussed this issue in some detail. *See* Charles J. Dunlap, Jr. *Kosovo, Casualty Aversion, and the American Military Ethos: A Perspective*, J. of Legal Studies, Vol. 10, 1999/2000, at 95.

[116] *See* note 77, *supra.*

[117] *See e.g.,* Dep't of Defense, *Report to Congress: Kosovo/Allied Force After-Action Report*, 31 January 2000, at xvii, *available at* http://www.defenselink.mil/pubs/kaar02072000.pdf (last visited March 15, 2000) (noting that over 38,000 sorties were flown in the Balkan air operation).

[118] *As quoted by* Rowan Scarborough in *Change of Target Saved Hundreds of Taliban Soldiers*, Washington Times, November 21, 2001, at 10.

[119] *Kriegsraison is a* 19th Century German doctrine that asserts that military necessity could justify any measures – even violations of the laws of war – when the necessities of the situation purportedly justified it. It is rejected as a principle of international law. *See* Dep't of the Air Force Pamphlet 110-31, *International Law – The Conduct of Armed Conflict and Air Operations* (19 November 1976) at paragraph 1-3a(1).

[120] Col Wang Xiangsui, Chinese Air Force, *as quoted by* John Pomfret in *China Ponders New Rules Of 'Unrestricted War,* Washington Post, 9 Aug 1999, at 1, *accessible at* http://www.infowar.com/class_3/99/class3_081699a_j.shtml (last visited 23 November 2001). *See also* Qiao Liang and Wang Xiangsui, Unrestricted Warfare (1999) *accessible at* http://www.terrorism.com/documents/unrestricted.pdf (last visited 23 November 2001)

[121] Mary Anastasia O'Grady, *What About Colombia's Terrorists?*, Wall Street Journal, October 5, 2001, *reprinted in* Dep't of Defense, Current News Early Bird, 5 October 2001.

[122] Jose Miguel Vivanco, *as quoted by* Juan Forero in *Rights Group Lists Abuses By Guerrillas in Colombia*, New York Times, July 10, 2001, *reprinted in* Dep't of Defense, Current News Early Bird, 10 July 2001.

[123] *See* Geoffrey Best, Law and War Since 1945, at 289 (1994) ("[I]t must never be forgotten that the law of war, wherever it began at all, began mainly as a matter of religion and ethics...It began in ethics and it has kept one foot in ethics ever since").

[124] Although beyond the scope of this paper, one such paradigm needing re-thinking may be the whole notion of noncombatancy with respect to the sentient, adult population of democratic and quasi-democratic states. *See* Charles J. Dunlap, Jr., *End of Innocence: Re-Thinking Noncombatancy in the Post-Kosovo Era*, Strategic Review, Summer 2000, at 9.

Name Index

For Product Safety Concerns and Information please contact our EU
representative GPSR@taylorandfrancis.com
Taylor & Francis Verlag GmbH, Kaufingerstraße 24, 80331 München, Germany

www.ingramcontent.com/pod-product-compliance
Ingram Content Group UK Ltd.
Pitfield, Milton Keynes, MK11 3LW, UK
UKHW050234200926
475702UK00020B/3020

* 9 7 8 1 1 3 8 3 7 8 6 5 0 *